WOMEN LEADERS IN AMERICAN POLITICS

WOMEN LEADERS IN AMERICAN POLITICS

Edited by

James David Barber
Duke University

Barbara Kellerman
Fairleigh Dickinson University

Vivian Kallen

PRENTICE-HALL, INC., ENGLEWOOD CLIFFS, NEW JERSEY 07632

Library of Congress Cataloging in Publication Data
Main entry under title:

Women leaders in American politics.

Bibliography: p. 399
1. Women in politics—United States—History—Addresses, essays, lectures. 2. Women's rights—United States—History—Addresses, essays, lectures. 3. Feminism—United States—History—Addresses, essays, lectures. I. Barber, James David. II. Kellerman, Barbara.
HQ1236.5.U6W665 1986 305.4'2'0973 85-9424
ISBN 0-13-962267-5

Editorial/production supervision
and interior design: Virginia L. McCarthy
Cover design: Joseph Curcio
Cover photos: Stan Wakefield; Donna Ruscavage, Catholics for a Free Choice; UPI/Bettmann Archive; Library of Congress; U.S. Dept. of Transportation; Stan Wakefield
Manufacturing buyer: Barbara Kelly Kittle

Printed in the United States of America

10 9 8 7 6 5 4 3 2 1

ISBN 0-13-962267-5 01

Prentice-Hall International (UK) Limited, *London*
Prentice-Hall of Australia Pty. Limited, *Sydney*
Prentice-Hall Canada Inc., *Toronto*
Prentice-Hall Hispanoamericana, S.A., *Mexico*
Prentice-Hall of India Private Limited, *New Delhi*
Prentice-Hall of Japan, Inc., *Tokyo*
Prentice-Hall of Southeast Asia Pte. Ltd., *Singapore*
Editora Prentice-Hall do Brasil, Ltda., *Rio de Janeiro*
Whitehall Books Limited, *Wellington, New Zealand*

CONTENTS

INTRODUCTION

American women won, after generations of effort, the right to vote. But for a very long time that meant mainly the right to vote for men. Today, a second major step is in progress: the emergence, throughout the American political system, of women in official leadership positions. In the great agitations of the past that built new opportunity in America, women played their part. Women leaders were there, it turns out, in the Puritan wilderness, in the struggle to create a United States, in the battle against slavery and then for civil rights—despite all, women would be heard on those issues. But they had to be heard from the outside. They had to be heard through gates of prejudice and power firmly closed against their entry to office.

This is changing now. No one can tell how fast the change will proceed. But when the female half of humanity learns its disadvantage and sees its opportunity, it will get to power. The beginnings are there to see: women mayors, governors, Representatives, Senators, the first Supreme Court Justice and first Vice Presidential candidate, as well as the first co-anchor of network news.

Students of American government—male and female—need a chance to see and understand this fundamental advance. That is why this book is published: to set before a new generation the best examples we can find to illustrate the roots and the contemporary thrust of the graduation of women from outsiders to insiders in the political system. How, in fact, does that happen? What, in theory, does it mean? The best way to explore these questions, we believe, is to present striking cases of actual women who led themselves and others to influence and achievement, through key passages from their own writings and essays that display the political context.

The two of us have collaborated on every phase of this book's production. Kellerman took the lead in locating and editing materials. Barber took the lead in drafting the introductions and organizing the sequence of readings.

We are grateful for the superb assistance of Isabel Brachfeld, who helped in the search for many of the book's selections, Kathryn Christie, who identified material for Chapter 12, and especially Rosalind Kaplan, who diligently and expertly prepared the manuscript and coordinated our joint decision-making at a distance. Bruce Fulton did a remarkably thorough and accurate job of copy editing.

A major mystery remains: As women gain political power will they change American politics? If so, how? The women leaders portrayed in the chapters to follow may cast light on those critical questions of modern political science.

J.D.B.
B.K.

WOMEN LEADERS IN AMERICAN POLITICS

1

COLONIAL BEGINNINGS

Forty-one Englishmen signed the Mayflower Compact on November 11, 1620, binding themselves "togeather into a civill body politick." That first winter killed more than half of them; the surviving "freemen" constituted the governing body of the colony. Women had no share of political authority, though they shared the desperate dangers of frontier life in those colonial days. When Anne Hutchinson arrived in Boston from England in 1634, the Massachusetts "body politick" was in a precarious condition. The authorities, fearing anarchy, struggled to establish a stable social order in the wilderness. Mrs. Hutchinson, daughter of a minister who had been silenced for fifteen years for insisting on "able clergy," gathered worried women in her home. There she ministered to their illnesses and taught them that they too were children of God, not bearers of Eve's sinful seduction. Her liberal doctrines challenged the dominant powers, seemed to them to propose a liberty of conscience sure to undermine the unity essential to survival and salvation. Governor John Winthrop brought her to trial. She stood alone before her accusers, a grandmother in her midforties who had borne a dozen children. At that critical moment, she stood for the essence of what freedom would come to mean in the New World.

Anne Hutchinson Speaks Out

by Selma R. Williams

Alone Anne certainly was—but in the limelight. On center stage, every eye and ear riveted on her, she confronted her forty-nine inquisitors, possessing among themselves the highest concentration of wealth, power, and brains in the entire colony. Altogether there were nine magistrates and thirty-one deputies—in effect exercising

---

From Selma R. Williams, *Divine Rebel: The Life of Anne Marbury Hutchinson* (New York: Holt, Rinehart & Winston, 1981), pp. 147–53, 159–71.

the executive, legislative, and judicial functions of government—as well as eight ministers and one church elder. In addition, large numbers of the public had squeezed themselves into every bit of empty space in the barnlike, square-shaped meeting house (each side measuring just under forty feet).

Forced to remain standing, Anne faced her inquisitors seated in long rows of backless wooden benches—except for John Winthrop who, as governor, chief judge, and prosecutor, was accorded a separate desk, his own chair complete with cushion, and some extra breathing space. The longer Anne stood, always in strong focus, the more her judges seemed to dissolve into a blur of black hats perched on layer after layer of heavy clothing, topped by a greatcoat and thick gloves. The additional clothes were worn in a largely vain attempt to ward off the frigid winds blowing through the cracks in the mud-plaster walls of the flimsily constructed building. Wood-burning stoves and fireplaces for public buildings were a luxury for the distant future, and so there was absolutely no heat and very little light in the cavernous church-meetinghouse.

Even wearing heavy, asexual outer clothing, the lonely defendant was instantly recognizable as a woman. Whereas her inquisitors all had beards, ranging from scrubby to elegant, and shoulder-length hair falling beneath their hats, Anne's long hair was completely hidden under her bonnet, an occasional strand escaping onto her forehead in moments of head-shaking excitement. ("If a woman have long hair, it is a glory to her . . . ," the Bible decreed, I Corinthians 11:15. So be it, Western society agreed, but commanded that woman's hair, so seductive to man, so tempting to the Devil, be covered completely at all times, day, evening, and night.)[1]

Whenever the court finally decided to call the hearing to an end, Anne faced the loss of personal freedom through prison and banishment. But these proceedings were set up as a legislative hearing, with the ministers sitting in to act as advisors and chief witnesses for the prosecution. Therefore, she was allowed no lawyer to help in her defense. Nor would her husband of twenty-five years, William Hutchinson, to whom she was devoted—and vice versa—be allowed to testify in her behalf.[2]

Quite inadvertently, the colonial fathers, aiming to silence Anne then and there, instead promoted her to immortality by letting her address posterity in her own words. Governor Winthrop recorded his personal account of the hearing, as did a mysteriously anonymous scribe who, moderately sympathetic to Anne, narrated everything as she herself might have set it down.

Without greeting or smile—they were, after all, neighbors who had lived across the street from each other for almost three years—Governor Winthrop opened the hearing, letting loose against Anne all his pent-up grievances, accusations, and emotions:

Mrs. Hutchinson, you are called here as one of those that have troubled the peace of the commonwealth and the churches here; you are known to be a woman that hath had a great share in the promoting and divulging of those opinions that are causes of this trouble, and to be nearly joined not only in affinity and affections with some of those the court had taken notice of and passed censure upon, but you have spoken divers things as we have been informed very prejudicial to the honour of the churches and ministers thereof, and you have maintained a meeting and an assembly in your house that hath been condemned by the general assembly as a thing not tolerable nor comely in the sight of God nor fitting for your sex, and notwithstanding that was cried down you have continued the same. Therefore, we have thought good to send for you to understand how things are, that if you be in an erroneous way we may reduce you so you may become a profitable member here among us; otherwise if you be obstinate in your course that then the court may take such course that you may trouble us no further.

Hardly pausing to catch his breath, the governor—fully aware that as a woman Anne was not allowed to sign the Wheelwright petition—interjected a hypothesis he hoped would serve to prove her criminal involvement: "I would entreat you to express whether you do not assent and hold in practice to those opinions and factions that have been handled in court already, that is to say, whether you do not justify Mr. Wheelwright's sermon and the petition."

Anne was incensed by the governor's denunciation of her behavior as "nor fitting for your sex" and his threat that "we may reduce you so that you may become a profitable member here among us." If ever she agreed to abide by the governor's highly favored Covenant of Works, she was certain that, as a woman, she would—in the governor's own discouragingly apt phrase—be "reduced" to consummate outsider, completely subject to an all-male church and state, which would constantly interfere with the private dialogue between her conscience and God. Only under the Covenant of Grace could she expect to function as a worthy, individual, human being.

Refusing to dignify the governor's charges with any show of respect, she retorted defiantly: "I am called here to answer before you, but I hear no things laid to my charge."

For the next few minutes, spectators were treated to an angry exchange between the highest officer of their colony and the woman he had hauled into court:

Gov. I have told you some already and more I can tell you.
Mrs. H. Name one, sir.
Gov. Have I not named some already?
Mrs. H. What have I said or done?
Gov. Why for your doings, this you did harbour and countenance those that are parties to this faction that you have heard of.
Mrs. H. That's matter of conscience, sir.

The governor dropped this argument; Anne Hutchinson had fought him to a draw.

Still, he felt himself under political obligation and personal pressure to vanquish this woman. Certainly, she was the single worst threat to the continued existence of the colony to which he had single-mindedly devoted his life, family, and fortune for the better part of a decade.

The problem was that their points of view and aims were diametrically opposed and neither saw any way of making these compatible. As far as the governor was concerned, he agreed absolutely with the legendary Aesop who more than two thousand years before had made the pronouncement that in unity there is strength. In direct contrast, Anne was inspired by the still-uncompleted Renaissance to insist that in individualism lies the only hope for progress—and she emphasized her belief that individualism was androgynous. Unfortunately for Anne, the governor was in total charge and backed by the power of the entire Colonial Establishment. Anne, forced to be on the defensive, had recourse only to the power of her own words and intellect.

Under the circumstances, and with the colony sinking into chaos and endangered on all sides—by the King, native Americans, and the French and Spanish, all of whom were threatening imminent takeover—the governor was thoroughly convinced that this was the worst possible time for testing the feasibility of a middle ground. Besides, he had his own private reasons for displaying intense hostility toward Anne. The three elections he had lost for governor, in 1634, 1635, and 1636, were to opponents who had called him too lenient and wrongheaded. Returned to the highest office only in 1637, with the indispensable support of the clergy, he had an excellent opportunity to use the case before him to display his newfound toughness and superior leadership.

Consequently, the governor decided to bring forth another accusation. Anne Hutchinson had broken a pivotal law, he charged. This was the Fifth Commandment, "Honor thy father and mother," which the Puritans had deftly translated into a command to obey the rulers (fathers only) of the colony—"fathers of the commonwealth," John Winthrop called them. (In this era of no separation between church and state, on all questions of public concern, the Bible was the colonial code of laws. Religion was used to mold public opinion and the church enforced political decisions.)

But Anne defused the governor's arguments one after another until he brought this part of the dialogue to an end, snapping scornfully: "We do not mean to discourse with those of your sex but only this; you do endeavor to set forward this faction and so you do dishonor us."

Next, the governor reverted to the sensitive subject of Anne's twice-weekly meetings, insisting that she had no right to preach, even in the confines of her own home.

Here Anne decided to respond in kind. As far as she was concerned, the governor and his fellow Puritans had bent the Fifth Commandment for their own purposes. Very well, she would do the same. She returned to her perennially reconstructed paraphrase from the Bible: "I conceive there lies a clear rule in Titus, that the elder women should instruct the younger, and then I must have a time wherein I must do it."

Unmoved, the governor responded: "Suppose a man should come and say, 'Mrs. Hutchinson, I hear that you are a woman that God hath given his grace unto and you have knowledge in the word of God. I pray, instruct me a little.' Ought you not to instruct this man?"

Triumphantly, Anne taunted the governor: "I think I may. Do you think it not lawful for me to teach men and why do you call me to teach the court?"

The governor retorted: "We do not call you to teach the court but to lay open yourself."

Certain that female participation of the kind proposed by Anne would destroy social and political stability, the governor elaborated, "You have a plain rule against it: I permit not a woman to teach." For his cohorts, all thoroughly schooled in the Bible, the governor's New Testament paraphrase proved his point completely, casting Anne as a spoiler, sacrilegiously defying the Scriptures. From Anne's point of view, however, the full passage was a painful example of why she rejected strict, "legalist" reading of the Bible:

> But I suffer not a woman to teach,
> nor to usurp authority over the man,
> but to be in silence.
> For Adam was first formed, then Eve.
> And Adam was not deceived,
> but the woman being deceived
> was in the transgression.
>
> [*I Timothy* 2:*12–14*]

So far, not one of the other forty-eight inquisitors had spoken a single word. Not the two Anne counted on for support, Boston deputies William Coddington and William Colburn, her husband William's business colleagues and her own good friends. Not her old hero, the Reverend John Cotton, who over the past few months had sometimes come to her aid, and had sometimes sided with her opposition. And certainly not any of the members of the governor's huge clique of magistrates, deputies, and ministers. Anne and the governor continued their deadly duel, each aiming for public burial of the other's ideas:

Mrs. H. I desire that you would then set me down a rule by which I may put them away that come unto me and so have peace in so doing.

Gov. You must show your rule to receive them.
Mrs. H. I have done it.
Gov. I deny it because I have brought more arguments than you have.

[The session adjourned for the night. The next morning Governor Winthrop resumed the proceedings.]

So far, Anne had been an unyielding, unexpectedly effective adversary. Deciding that conciliation might be the best tactic, the governor allowed her to call her own witnesses. First came John Coggeshall, already rebuffed once, but willing to try again. "I dare say she did not say all that which they lay against her," he asserted.

"How dare you look into the court to say such a word," exclaimed Rev. Hugh Peter of Salem, taking it on himself to put the witness in his place.

"Mr. Peter takes upon him to forbid me, I shall be silent," Anne's first witness murmured, losing courage.

John Coggeshall was not heard from again at this fateful hearing.

Another witness, Thomas Leverett, a ruling elder of the church in new Boston and John Cotton's protector and disciple in the church at old Boston, said almost nothing, but said it wordily. No one reacted either way.

At this point, in a show of symbolic, though silent, support, the third defense witness, John Cotton himself, "came and sat down by Mrs. Hutchinson." When John Winthrop asked him to recall everything he could remember about the December conference between the ministers and Anne Hutchinson, he first blurted out a disclaimer: "I did not think I should be called to bear witness in this cause and therefore did not labor to call to remembrance what was done." Then he stammered out a long answer, expressing regret that rumor had spread throughout the colony "that she had spoken some condemning words of the ministry, and . . . sorry I was that any comparison should be between me and my brethren, and uncomfortable it was." He concluded: "If you put me in mind of anything I shall speak it."

Gently, John Winthrop prodded: "You say you do not remember, but can you say she did not speak so." Before the minister could respond, Rev. Hugh Peter jumped in, trying to draw an admission that Anne Hutchinson had indeed said that all ministers except John Cotton preached a Covenant of Works. But Cotton refused to nudge his memory.

Getting nowhere, John Winthrop, "weary of the clamor and so that all mouths be stopped," partially consented to Anne's demand and allowed three, who volunteered, to take an oath. Two ministers from Roxbury, Thomas Weld and John Eliot, volunteered to be officially sworn, as did Dorchester Assistant Israel Stoughton, leader of the 160 men Massachusetts had sent to fight the recent Pequot War.

Anne now made a long speech, riveting the courtroom with her story of the time "the Lord did reveal himself to me, sitting upon a throne of justice, and all the world appearing before him, and though I must come to New England, yet I must not fear nor be dismayed." Buttressing her words with a quote from Isaiah, she elaborated these divine directions: "The Lord spake this to me with a strong hand, and instructed me that I should not walk in the way of this people."

Desperate to subdue this woman who claimed leadership on the basis of direct communication with God, John Winthrop "demanded how she did know it was God that did reveal these things to her, and not Satan."

Her answer: "How did Abraham know that it was the voice of God when he commanded him to sacrifice his son, being a breach of the Sixth Commandment." ("Thou shalt not kill.") Anne here drew on personal feelings as mother of twelve living children, including six sons.

Clumsily, Deputy Governor Thomas Dudley, trying to come to the governor's aid, played into Anne's hands, responding that Abraham knew "by an immediate voice" that he was being commanded by God to sacrifice Isaac.

Triumphantly, Anne echoed: "So to me by an immediate revelation."

Then, furious that her judges continually took it upon themselves to behave in ways out of bounds to her because she was a woman—for example, throughout his political career in New England, John Winthrop reminded his constituents that his power in office was authorized directly by God—Anne felt called on to warn the court:

> You have no power over my body, neither can you do me any harm. . . . No further do I esteem of any mortal man. . . . I fear none but the great Jehovah, which hath foretold me of these things, and I do verily believe that he will deliver me out of your hands. . . . Therefore, take heed how you proceed against me; for I know that for this you go about to do to me, God will ruin you and your posterity, and this whole state.

Needing intellectual reinforcement, John Winthrop appealed to John Cotton "to deliver his judgment about Mistress Hutchinson, her revelations."

John Cotton was on the spot. But still he remained on Anne's side—and by his words in public court gave a good inkling as to how he must have acted and spoken to Anne in both old and New England:

> Though the word revelation be rare in common speech and we make it uncouth in our ordinary expressions, yet notwithstanding, being understood in the scripture sense I think they are not only lawful but such as Christians may receive and God bear witness to it in his word. . . .
>
> *That she may have some special providence of God to help her is a thing that I cannot bear witness against.* [Emphasis added.]

New Englanders revered John Cotton. For a long time there was even a rumor that they had named their leading town Boston in order to entice him to immigrate, and once here, to feel completely at home. But they feared Anne Hutchinson even more than they adored their most eminent minister. The strong majority here at the meetinghouse were certain, beyond any doubt, that they had to condemn Anne—but first they had somehow to bring John Cotton into line. Deputy Governor Dudley began badgering John Cotton, relentlessly asking the same question over and over again in different words: "I desire Mr. Cotton to tell us whether you do approve of Mrs. Hutchinson's revelations as she hath laid them down." And again: "Do you believe that her revelations are true?" And again: "Good Sir, I do ask whether this revelation be of God or not."

Unperturbed, and with more sympathy and understanding than anyone had shown Anne Hutchinson up to this point, Cotton at length responded with a question of his own: "I should desire to know whether the sentence of the court will bring her to any calamity, and then I would know of her whether she expects to be delivered from that calamity by a miracle or a providence of God."

Anne answered directly: "By a providence of God, I say I expect to be delivered from some calamity that shall come to me."

For the court, John Winthrop's response was to rely on this same "providence of God"—and at the same time, to proclaim victory: "The case is altered and will not stand with us now, but I see a marvellous providence of God to bring things to this pass that they are. . . . Now the mercy of God by a providence hath answered our desires and made her to lay open herself and the ground of all these disturbances to be by revelations."

Amid the chorus of agreement from the judges, and silence from Anne and her supporters, the unrelieved pressure on Cotton to join the majority continued:

Mr. Endecott: I speak in reference to Mr. Cotton. I am tender of you, Sir. . . . Mrs. Hutchinson hath spoken of her revelations as you have heard. . . . Do you witness for her or against her?

Mr. Cotton: This is that I said, Sir, and my answer is plain. If she doth look for deliverance from the hand of God by his providence, and the revelation be in a word or according to a word, that I cannot deny.

At this, John Endecott, always easily swayed by the last man to have spoken to him averred: "You give me satisfaction."

But Deputy Governor Dudley roared: "No, no, he gives me none at all." And when Cotton tried to save himself by equivocation, Dudley expostulated: "Sir, you weary me and do not satisfy me," adding irritably, "I . . . am sorry that Mr. Cotton should stand to justify her."

Fanatic Hugh Peter who, along with his fellow minister Thomas Weld of Roxbury, had been one of the most active promoters of Anne Hutchinson's prosecution, concurred: "I can say the same . . . and I think that is very disputable which our brother Cotton hath spoken."

John Cotton remained firm.

Obviously, the Devil was at work. Several members of the court decided that some good old-fashioned scare tactics were in order, the kind the Puritans had seen firsthand while they were growing up in England. Forty-three-year-old Increase Nowell of Charlestown, an assistant since the founding of the colony in 1630, and currently serving as secretary for Massachusetts, had previously proclaimed Anne's revelations "a devilish delusion." Deputy Governor Dudley now had a similar thought: "I am fully persuaded that Mrs. Hutchinson is deluded by the Devil, because the spirit of God speaks the truth in all his servants."

John Cotton refused to change his position, leading John Winthrop to turn full attention back to Anne Hutchinson, declaring: "Mr. Cotton is not called to answer to anything but we are to deal with the party now standing before us." The governor seemed on the verge of pronouncing censure, when Anne Hutchinson's friend William Coddington interrupted with the futuristic complaint that the court was allowing no freedom of speech or due process of law:

Sir, another thing you lay to her charge is her speech to the [ministers]. Now I do not see any clear witness against her, and you know it is a rule of the court that no man may be a judge and an accuser too. . . . I do not for my own part see any equity in the court in all your proceedings. Here is no law of God that she hath broken nor any law of the country that she broke and therefore deserves no censure.

Changing the subject completely, the aristocratic twenty-six-year-old Roger Harlaakenden spoke out for the first time, commenting that if only Anne had behaved herself as women are supposed to, she would not be facing her present difficulties, and could even hold small meetings if she chose.

So many serious subjects were swirling around the courtroom that a creature complaint roused absolutely no reaction. "We shall all be sick with fasting," whined the highly disciplined sixty-one-year-old deputy governor, cold, hungry, and restless after hours on a hard bench in the crude meetinghouse.

Without even a pause for acknowledgment, the hearing went right on. Coddington continued to demand civil liberties. Several of the ministers took out their personal pique at being compared adversely with John Cotton. And Cotton, chastened, remained silent. John Winthrop had been quiet for a long time, but in his private record of the proceedings let posterity in on the thoughts rushing through his mind as he prepared to pronounce judgment on Anne Hutchinson—in his dual role as her chief prosecutor and judge: "See the impudent boldness of a proud dame, that Attila-like makes havoc of all that stand in the way of her ambitious spirit; she had boasted before that her opinions must prevail, neither could she endure a stop in her way. . . . The Court did clearly discern where the fountain was of all our distempers."

At this point in his personal record, John Winthrop labeled the activities of Anne and her disciples a terrifying replica of the Anabaptist uprising at Munster, 1534–36—exactly one hundred years before Anne, in his view, embarked on her Massachusetts mission of anarchy, chaos, and destruction. He warned: "The tragedy of Munster . . . gave just occasion to fear the danger we were in . . . so as the like hath not been known in former ages that ever so many wise, sober, and well-grounded Christians should so suddenly be seduced by the means of a woman, to stick so fast to her, even in some things wherein the whole current of Scripture goeth against her."

Unfortunately for Anne, she would hear the Anabaptist "tragedy of Munster" used over and over as justification for silencing her and all Hutchinsonians. The Anabaptists were the left wing of the early-sixteenth-century Reformation, who practiced adult rebaptism of true believers, rejected the idea that infants were born in Original Sin, insisted on separation of the church (the community of the redeemed) and the state (the instrument used to punish sinners), and refused to take up arms, even for a "just war." (The refusal of Anne's Boston followers to rally to the support of the Pequot War was, of course, considered an ominous similarity by the governor and his colleagues.) They considered women believers the equals of men. Striving to attain the good life for good men and women, they forced civil and religious officials to renounce all claim to control of individuals who were true believers. Unhappily, hostile reports of these idealistic, anarchistic Anabaptists—virtually the only information available to John Winthrop and his cohorts—portrayed the Munster rebels as monsters intent mainly on institutionalizing polygamy, easy divorce, and sexual promiscuity.

In 1534, Protestants and Catholics had dropped their usual hostility to each other to join in strong measures against Anabaptists rebelling at Munster. In response, radical Anabaptists took over completely, forcing opponents to flee, so that the population dwindled to about 1700 men, 6800 women, and several thousand children. Following a year of terrorism and turmoil, the Roman bishop formerly in control regained power in Munster, and by 1536 put all Anabaptist leaders to death, burning the men and burying the women alive. Due to the population ratio then obtaining at Munster, the majority of these martyrs were female.

Among other things, this was a strong object lesson to New England Puritan authorities of the seventeenth century that women must be kept out of the political-religious arena completely.

Roger Clap, who arrived in 1630 with the Winthrop fleet and who witnessed the trials of Anne Hutchinson, wrote an account for his four surviving sons and two surviving daughters to warn them: "Dear Children, beware of false teachers, though they come unto you in sheep's clothing as some of the Anabaptists do. . . . One of them says . . . 'that the miseries and death that came by Adam's fall extendeth not unto all eternity.'" Under these circumstances, Anne probably should have been grateful that she was neither tortured nor directly put to death.

About to pronounce sentence on Anne Hutchinson, Governor Winthrop allowed

Rev. Hugh Peter of Salem and Assistant Israel Stoughton of Dorchester to make final statements:

Mr. Peter: I profess I thought Mr. Cotton would never have taken her part.

Mr. Stoughton: I say now this testimony doth convince me in the thing, and I am fully satisfied the words were pernicious, and the frame of her spirit doth hold forth the same.

With the stage thus set, Governor Winthrop summed up the proceedings and asked for a vote:

The court hath already declared themselves satisfied . . . concerning the troublesomeness of her spirit and the danger of her course amongst us, which is not to be suffered. Therefore, if it be the mind of the court that Mrs. Hutchinson for these things that appear before us is unfit for our society, and if it be the mind of the court that she shall be banished out of our liberties and imprisoned till she be sent away let them hold up their hands.

Only William Coddington and William Colburn of Boston voted against the sentence of banishment and imprisonment. Deputy William Jennison of Watertown announced that he had decided not to vote one way or the other. And John Cotton, lacking the stomach to be a minority of one among his fellow ministers, abandoned Anne to her fate and voted with the majority.

Isolated and abandoned though she was, Anne fought spiritedly to the very end. The governor, exhilarated by his successful struggle to save the colony, lost his usual self-control. Emulating the despotic English kings whom everyone in court had fled, he now intoned: "Mrs. Hutchinson, the sentence of the court you hear is that you are banished from out of our jurisdiction as being a woman not fit for our society, and are to be imprisoned till the court shall send you away."

Anne protested: "I desire to know wherefore I am banished."

The governor thundered: "Say no more, the court knows wherefore and is satisfied."

Significantly, the sentence, as officially recorded, is carefully detailed (except for the omission of Anne's own first name):

Mrs. _______ Hutchinson (the wife of Mr. William Hutchinson), being convented for traducing the ministers and their ministry in this country, she declared voluntarily her revelations for her ground, and that she should be delivered and the court ruined, with their posterity, and thereupon was banished, and the meanwhile was committed to Mr. Joseph Weld until the Court shall dispose of her.

Following Anne's hearing that Wednesday, November 8, 1637, the famous Pequot War soldier Captain John Underhill was stripped of all office and disfranchised for signing the Wheelwright petition. He was a married man whose sensationally reported dalliances with much younger girls gave proof for those who were digging for such evidence that Anne's followers were a bunch of libertines.

But beating the anti-Hutchinsonians at what they did best—reading the Bible "legalistically"—he wrote very tenderly and respectfully of his wife in his own memoir, *Newes from America*, and told the reader "instance Abraham" (Sarah, the barren wife of the patriarch Abraham, suggested that he conceive a child by her maid Hagar, Genesis 16). In an era when women produced children every eighteen to twenty-four months, Helena Underhill gave birth to only two children, born six years apart: Elizabeth, baptized February 14, 1636, and John, Jr., baptized April 24, 1642.

In any case, following the punishment and disfranchisement of Captain Underhill, the court finally adjourned—until the following Wednesday, when Anne's activities produced an unusual sequel: the placing of the college, which the General Court had already voted to establish, in Newtown (renamed Cambridge as of May 2, 1638) rather than in Boston. "The college is ordered to be at Newtown," read the official record, and in his memoirs Rev. Thomas Shepard of Newtown explained:

> The Lord having delivered the country from war with Indians and Familists (who arose and fell together), he was pleased to direct the heart of the magistrates (then keeping Court ordinarily in our town, because of these stirs at Boston) to think of erecting a school or college, and that speedily, to be a nursery of knowledge in these deserts, and supply for posterity. And because this town, then called Newtown, was, through God's great care and goodness, kept spotless from the contagion of the opinions, therefore, at the desire of some of our town, the deputies of the Court, . . . for that and sundry other reasons, determined to erect the college here. . . . The Lord put it into the heart of one Mr. Harvard, who died worth £1600, to give half his estate to the erecting of the School.

Reinforcing the contention that the heresies of Anne Hutchinson and her followers prompted the establishment of Harvard at Cambridge rather than at Boston, Edward Johnson, New England's early eyewitness historian—the very title of his book reflected unbridled ebullience: *The Wonder-Working Providence of Sions Savior in New England*—wrote a long, convoluted poem around the idea that the inhabitants of Newtown-Cambridge, "they no antinomians are."[3]

Twelve days after sentencing Anne Hutchinson, the General Court carried out a virtual coup d'état against the Hutchinsonians, ordering them, on Monday, November 20, to surrender their guns, powder, and ammunition at the house of Captain Robert Keayne (a wealthy Boston merchant who nonetheless had kept himself free of the taint of Hutchinsonianism, perhaps because his wife, Anne, was the sister of Elizabeth Wilson, wife of Anne Hutchinson's *bête noire*, pastor John Wilson). The order, prepared in the dark, hidden rooms of secrecy and issued precipitately, with no warning, again made ominous reference to the rebellion at Munster a hundred years before:

> Whereas the opinions and revelations of Mr. Wheelwright and Mrs. Hutchinson have seduced and led into dangerous errors many of the people here in New England, insomuch as there is just cause of suspicion that they, as others in Germany, in former times, may, upon some revelation, make some sudden eruption upon those that differ from them in judgment, for prevention whereof it is ordered that all those whose names are underwritten shall (upon warning given or left at their dwelling houses) before the 30th day of this month of November, deliver in at Mr. Keayne's house at Boston, all such guns, pistols, swords, powder, shot, and match as they shall be owners of, or have in their custody, upon pain of ten pound for every default to be made thereof; which arms are to be kept by Mr. Keayne till this Court shall take further order therein. Also, it is ordered, upon like penalty of ten pound, that no man who is to render his arms by this order shall buy or borrow any guns, swords, pistols, powder, shot, or match, until this Court shall take further order therein.

The list of fifty-eight men disarmed in Boston was headed by the rakish soldier Captain John Underhill. William Hutchinson was third on the list, following the surgeon Thomas Oliver, perhaps "tainted" by working professionally with Anne Hutchinson in crisis cases. Mentioned by name in the court order but, of course, not on the list herself, Anne was nevertheless represented (in addition to husband William) by her son Richard, brother-in-law Edward, and her sons-in-law John Sanford and Thomas Savage. Interestingly, among friends and neighbors on the list was the Charlestown-Boston ferryman and entrepreneur Thomas Marshall, whose job was turned over to an employee chosen by the colony and required, by law, to give all revenue to the newly established college at Cambridge.

In addition to the fifty-eight Boston men disarmed, there were seventeen from other towns: five from Salem, three from Newbury, five from Roxbury, two from Ipswich, and two from Charlestown—giving substance to Rev. Thomas Weld's complaint that Anne Hutchinson had a colony-wide following, her "tainted" supporters spreading what he was pleased to call "the infection."

Fearful that insurrection might follow these harsh measures, the General Court, at this same session of November 20, further "ordered that the powder and ammunition of the countries now at Boston should be delivered half to Newtown and half to Roxbury, to be appointed by Mr. Dudley and Mr. Harlaakenden."

Almost at once, thirty of the seventy-five men who were ordered disarmed decided that recantation was the better part of valor and had their gun-toting privileges restored, as did another group of five who denied supporting the trouble-causing Wheelwright petition, insisting that their names had been added without their consent or knowledge. The remaining forty stalwarts protested loudly, agitated furiously, "but at last, when they saw no remedy, they obeyed."

Following this veritable coup d'état, a large number of the Boston church attempted retaliation against Governor Winthrop. But the church elders would have none of it. John Winthrop succeeded in calming the situation with a speech declaring that always he had only the public interest in mind and had thus carried out all his obligations under the official oath of office to which he had solemnly sworn. "For his part, he was persuaded," he said, that the sentencing of Anne and her followers was "most for the glory of God and the public good." Like Anne—whose words the governor had seized on at her hearing as proving the case against her—the governor was determined to make himself heard and his words accepted. Therefore, again like Anne, he revealed that he had acted in partnership with God, on the basis of direct communication.

In a burst of compassion for Anne Hutchinson, the General Court had decided that the snow-filled winter season was unsuitable for banishing a woman.[4] They would wait till spring. Furthermore, the court granted her enough time to return to Boston, there to make provision for care of her seven children still at home: Francis, seventeen; Samuel, thirteen; Anne, ten; Mary, nine; Katherine, seven; William, six; Susanna, four; and Zuriel, one. Expenses for detaining her at the Roxbury home of Joseph Weld, brother of Rev. Thomas Weld, were ordered "to be defrayed by her husband." (It was customary for the prisoner or the prisoner's family to pay all expenses of food and shelter.)

Ruggedly wild Roxbury was a hard two-mile journey over scrawny Boston Neck, a long, ridiculously narrow isthmus running between the Charles River and the Atlantic Ocean and connecting the settlement at Boston with the land to the south. Here, members of the General Court congratulated themselves, Anne Hutchinson should be relatively inaccessible to her family, friends, and supporters; the clamor of her society-shaking ideas muffled if not silenced completely.

At the same time, the brothers Weld—Joseph, the jailer, and Thomas, the minister—could, between them, keep an eye on her day and night.

NOTES

1. Jewelry, which might have helped set Anne apart as a woman, was frowned upon by Puritans, who forbade even the wearing of a wedding ring.

2. For elaboration of seventeenth-century refusal to allow testimony by husband or wife, whether in favor

of or in opposition to a spouse, see the classic *Law of Evidence* by John H. Wigmore, Sec. 103.

3. For some mysterious reason, at the actual time of the controversy surrounding her, Anne Hutchinson and her followers were denounced as "Familists," but by the following decade, in retrospect, were labeled "Antinomians," a pejorative sixteenth-century epithet taken from the Greek, *anti* (against) and *nomos* (law), i.e., contemptuous of the law on which society depends.

4. Anne Hutchinson was in exclusive company when she was banished from Massachusetts in this controversy. Only three were so punished: her brother-in-law, Rev. John Wheelwright; William Aspinwall, accused of writing the Wheelwright petition; and Anne herself.

2

THE AMERICAN REVOLUTION

War erodes the walls between the sexes: sometimes men nurse the wounded and sometimes women produce weapons. In the American Revolution, women struggled to find a service they could contribute. The culture of the day had women locked into domesticity. But even that could be turned to wartime advantage. Women bought the household goods, so when the time came to boycott British products, women stepped forth to organize the ban. Women made flags and sewed and cooked—and wrote endlessly and informatively of the events they witnessed. The "Republican Mother" was a celebrated figure—worth educating so she could train her sons in soldierly virtue. Still, it took a giant leap of energy and imagination for the eighteenth-century middle-class American woman to engage in anything as raucous and masculine as politics. There were those who did it anyway.

Women and the War for Independence

by Linda Kerber

That women served the patriot war effort is clear. What these women thought of their actions and of wartime politics is not. It is difficult to find women activists who justify their patriotism in political terms; for example, the pamphlet with the promising title *Women Invited to War* by "A Daughter of America" is in fact a religious homily.[1]

From Linda Kerber, *Women of the Republic: Intellect and Ideology in Revolutionary America* (Chapel Hill: University of North Carolina Press, 1980), pp. 73–85, 99–105.

Any attempt to assess women's political consciousness must take into account the deep skepticism toward political behavior shared by the entire culture. Even those men who built successful political careers and displayed what by any measure would have to be called extraordinary ambition rarely acknowledged what they were doing, even to close friends; often they did not acknowledge their political drive to themselves.[2] As Hannah Griffitts wrote of Benjamin Franklin:

> To Covet Political fame,
> In Him, was degrading ambition
> A Spark, that from Lucifer Came,
> And kindled the flame of sedition.[3]

If coveting political fame was degrading even to the class of people who had always been seeking it, why should women be encouraged to take up this unsavory practice?

Participation in the national military forces during the war seems to have served as a bonding experience for many future political leaders since it widened men's allegiance from their colony to the nation. It is by no means clear that shared hospital service performed a similar politicizing function for army nurses and matrons. Most of the women who furthered the patriots' military purposes did not do so in an institutional context; as cooks, washerwomen, laundresses, private nurses, and renters of houses or of rooms, they served as individuals, sometimes along with their husbands and children. They did not change their domestic identity (though they put it to a broader service), and they did not seriously challenge the traditional definition of the woman's domestic domain.

The career of one army nurse, for whom we have unusual anecdotal evidence, suggests the dual elements of the wartime experience. We see Mary Waters only through the eyes of Benjamin Rush, who scribbled notes for her biography in 1791. Was the nurse's life an appropriate subject? "Why not?" Rush asked rhetorically. "Her occupation was a noble one—and her example may be interesting to thousands—Only a few men can be Kings—& yet Biography for a while had few other subjects." Rush respected Mary Waters as a professional, and it is clear from his comments that she saw herself that way. She was bored by simple cases: the sicker the patient, the more she welcomed the challenge. "She dislikes nursing *lying in women*—as well as all sick persons as *are not very ill*. Nothing but great danger rouses her into great activity and humanity." His account also verifies that she was regarded as a medical professional by the staffs of the military hospitals where she served. But this professionalism had little postwar significance. What Rush most admired in her service following the war was that despite all her experience, she remained deferential to doctors, and she did not steal patients. "She was once sent for to prescribe for a lady in a consumption, for her skill was known to many people. Before She went, She found Out whose patient this lady was, and upon being complimented by her when she entered the room She said 'Indeed madam I know nothing but what I learned from Dr. ______ (mentioning the name of the physician who attended her) in the military hospitals.' This at once . . . renewed [the lady's] confidence in her physician." Rush implied that Mary Waters, at least, did not use her wartime experience to increase her independence and her professional autonomy, and he thought this to her credit.[4]

The notion that politics was somehow not part of the woman's domain persisted throughout the war, expressed even by women whose own lives were in fact directly dependent on political developments and who had a sophisticated understanding of political maneuver. . . . Anne Hooper and her friends paid obeisance to this tradition of female passivity before demanding that the North Carolina government refrain from harassing tory wives.

Grace Growden Galloway also reveals this cluster of contradictory traits and is worth considering at some length. She was a formidable woman, and not surprisingly her biographers tend to describe her as "imperious." She was the daughter of one of the wealthiest and most powerful men in colonial Pennsylvania, and she married another, Joseph Galloway, Speaker of the Pennsylvania Assembly for the decade before war broke out and refugee behind British lines after it began. He returned temporarily when the British occupied Philadelphia, but left again, taking the Galloways' only daughter with him when the American troops returned in June 1778. His wife grimly stayed on in occupied Philadelphia, hoping by her presence to maintain her claim to the property she stood to inherit from her father. She began a diary when her husband and daughter left with the British. It is a marvelously opinionated document in which she registered her emotions as well as the weather and the names of her visitors. Despite her open scorn for the patriot cause, which she did not trouble to conceal, she did not expect to be evicted from the Galloways' confiscated house, and she was highly indignant when Charles Willson Peale came to evict her. Mrs. Galloway refused to leave voluntarily.

> I told them Nothing but force shou'd get me out of My house Smith said they knew how to Manage that & that they wou'd throw my cloaths in the street. . . . I told [Peale] . . . I was at home & in My own House & nothing but force shou'd drive me out of it he said it was not the first time he had taken a Lady by the Hand. . . . [I] said pray take Notice I do not leave my house of My own accord or with my own inclination but by force & Nothing but force shou'd have Made Me give up possession Peel said with a sneer very well Madam & when he led me down the step I said now Mr. Peel let go My Arm I want not your Assistance.[5]

As litigation to recover her property continued, her scorn for whigs was as vigorous and emphatic as any patriot castigation of the loyalists. "Nothing reigns here but interess," she wrote of Philadelphia. But despite her pride and her assertiveness, she continued to define herself in private terms. "I . . . laughed at the whole wig party," she wrote in her diary on April 20, 1779. "I told them I was the happiest woman in town for I had been striped and Turn'd out of Doors yet I was still the same and must be Joseph Galloways Wife and Lawrence Growdens daughter and that it was not in their power to humble Me."[6]

Grace Galloway was a resentful woman to the end. The war seemed an intrusion into a private—and luxurious—world in which she had expected to enjoy her inheritance safely. She did not particularly love her husband, but she proudly claimed his identity. Though she made no secret of her hostility to the patriots or her admiration for the crown, she failed to comprehend why she—a woman—should be expected to account for her views or why her views had any more public significance than a preference for silver over pewter. She was not a stupid woman, but she failed to recognize that her political gestures went beyond merely private behavior, and she never came to terms with the invasion of the political world into her private life.

Philadelphia Quaker women varied greatly in the extent to which they understood that their private choices had political dimensions. Sarah Logan Fisher, for example, vigorously supported the refusal of Quakers to accept Continental currency, but professed herself shocked at the subsequent exile of Quaker leaders. Congressmen were, she said, "the ravenous wolves and lions that prowl about for prey, seeking to devour those harmless innocents that don't go hand in-hand with them in their cruelty and rapine."[7]

The patriot circles also held politically conscious women. Among them were Sarah

Livingston Jay and Catharine Livingston, who, as daughters of the wartime governor of New Jersey, had been raised in political households and ultimately married strongly political men. Sarah Jay felt herself deeply committed to independence. In forsaking her child Peter in order to accompany John Jay on his ministry to Spain, weathering a transatlantic voyage that threatened shipwreck, and suffering the death of a newborn infant once on the Continent, Sarah Jay clearly had earned the right to claim that she had made the deepest of personal sacrifices for the patriot cause. Observing Spanish society, she was moved to an increased appreciation of her own and to vigorous support of the war. "Where is the country (Switzerland excepted)," she wrote in 1780, "where Justice is so impartially administered, industry encouraged, health and Smiling plenty so bounteous to all as in our much favored Country? And are not those blessings each of them resulting from, or matured by freedom, worth contending for?" But that came close to a call to arms, and she stopped herself short. "But whither, my pen, are you hurrying me? What have I to do with politicks? Am I not myself a woman, and writing to Ladies? Come then, the fashions to my assistance!"[8] She did not say that moving from politics to fashion was to move from the sublime to the ridiculous, but she certainly implied that sentiment in the cynical tone of her transition.

Sarah Jay sent home confidential and detailed disapproving reports of her brother Henry Brockholst Livingston's political behavior. She also directed criticism beyond her family circle to people to whom she was not related, especially those she saw as self-serving adventurers in federal service. Occasionally she felt she needed to mumble an apology: "I've transgress'd the line that I proposed to observe in my correspondence by dipping into politicks, but my country and my friends possess so entirely my thoughts that you must not wonder if my pen runs beyond the dictates of prudence."[9]

Sarah's younger sister Catharine, who was perhaps even more consciously political, could also admit to a sense of inadequacy when dealing with politics. After a long letter to her future husband, Matthew Ridley, in which she delineated in some detail an attack on financier Robert Morris and the campaign to censure him, she concluded, "I should fancy I hear'd you exclaiming what a rage this girl has for politics. I wish she would not so mistake her province and talents—but still I will give her credit for the wish she evinces of informing me of what I appear to her to have an interest in." The terms of her apologia are carefully chosen; she has spoken politically out of a desire to please Ridley by speaking of his interests, not because she had her own "rage for politics." She admitted that she might be mistaking "her province." She might have had in mind a letter Ridley had sent her the year before: "Politics I have done with, were they ever proper to entertain you with."[10]

Though Catharine Livingston was careful to set her comments in a deferential context, her letters are usually full of political news and often of shrewd political criticism. For many years she maintained a correspondence with Gouverneur Morris and with her brother-in-law John Jay, and the news they exchanged was not limited to family gossip. "I know your bent for Politics," her brother Henry Brockholst Livingston wrote to her from Spain in 1781, "and how little you value a Letter in which a few pages are not taken up with news."[11] She was very friendly with the daughters of Samuel Vaughan, who were similarly sensitive to political nuance. Sarah Vaughan, for example, perceived with real annoyance that the French Minister François Barbé-Marbois always happened to pay her a visit when dispatches from Europe were expected. "Neither am I disposed to have my brains picked for news," she wrote with displeasure.[12] Kitty Livingston and her circle were scornful of the marriage market, and they liked having Congress meet in Philadelphia because that body provided interesting conversational companions, not romantic ones. "Every body is bewailing the loss of Congress," Rebecca Vaughan wrote to Kitty late in 1784. "The only cry you hear is what are we to do for Beaux we [her own family] are not so much distressed about it; Beaux are not so necessary to our happiness."[13] Others were distraught: "Mr. Chew is in despair he said the other day before a great many people he knew not what he should do with his daughters now Congress were gone he believed he must *sell* them how very indelicate even the thought and much worse publishing it."[14]

Examples of this awkward juxtaposition of the political and the domestic can be easily multiplied. Ann Gwinnett, the widow of the president of Georgia, wrote to warn the Continental Congress that the rank and file of the Georgia troops were loyal but that the officer corps was riddled with tory sympathizers. But she was careful to conclude her intensely political comment on a humble note: "These things (tho from a Woman, & it is not our sphere, yet I cannot help it) are all true."[15] When the wife of an exiled tory tried to get Governor Alexander Martin's special permission for her husband to return to North Carolina, she argued theories of citizenship at some length and with great precision, maintaining that because her husband had never been a citizen of the state, he had never owed it any obedience. But first she placed herself on familiar grounds: "It is not for me, unacquainted as I am with politics and the laws, to say with what propriety this was done."[16] "You know I am nothing of a Politician," Catherine Read wrote on the eve of the Quasi-War with France. In some detail she went on to decry the prowar spirit: "For us Southern people to rejoice at a war is a species of madness." She insisted that she did not "always think it necessary" to think as her husband did.[17] Shortly after the Revolution, Abigail Adams's niece Elizabeth Palmer wrote to an English relative about the need for "a good commercial treaty"; then she explained self-consciously, "I verily believe this is the first Sentence of Politicks that ever Crep[d] into a letter of mine—whether 'tis *orthodox* or not I dare not determine—for I'm very ignorant of these matters."[18]

In the absence of an established tradition of female public political behavior, many women may have found it difficult to explain precisely their actions outside their private circles. Perhaps the formulaic, ritualized apologies with which they prefaced their political comments were their way of acknowledging that they were doing something unusual. A very few women did begin to develop a structured rationale for their actions, however, and the most interesting of these theorists is Mercy Otis Warren, the dramatist and historian. Her comments on female politicization were enriched as her experience changed.

Like Grace Galloway, Mercy Otis Warren was the daughter of one prominent man and the wife of another. She lived her entire life in intensely political circles. Her brother was the ardent patriot James Otis, who argued the Writs of Assistance case in 1761; her husband was the Massachusetts legislator James Warren. For many years her closest female friend was Abigail Adams. Their letters to each other are often highly political: when John Adams complained about the famous teasing reminder to "remember the ladies" in drawing up the laws of the Confederation, it was Mercy Otis Warren to whom Abigail Adams turned for a sympathetic ear. Both women admired Catharine Macaulay immensely. Mercy Warren was inspired by Mrs. Macaulay's accomplishments, and after the war wrote at least one political pamphlet and her own multivolume history of the American Revolution.

In their letters to each other, Mercy Otis Warren and Abigail Adams were obviously comfortable with their shared political sensibility. They discussed politics without apology. When the crown asserted the right to make direct appointment of the Massachusetts Council in 1774, Warren wrote, "I think the appointment of the new counsel is the last comic scene we shall see Exhibite'd in the state Farce which has for several years been playing off. I fear the Tragic part of the Drama will hastely Ensue, and that Nothing but the Blood of the Virtuous Citizens Can repurchase the Rights of Nature, unjustly torn from us by the united arms of treachery and Violence." Abigail Adams wrote Warren in February 1775, "I would not have my Friend immagine that with all my fears and apprehension, I would give up one Iota of our rights and privileges. . . . we cannot be happy without being free, . . . we cannot be free without being secure in our property, . . . we cannot be secure in our property if without our consent others may as by right take it away.—We know too well the blessings of freedom, to tamely resign it."[19]

John Adams relied explicitly on his wife for local political news, and he expected her to keep his political fences mended. "What a politician you have made me," she wrote on July 5, 1780. She was easily able to conceive of the possibility of voting and came close enough to the political process to assist at the polls. "If I cannot be a voter upon this occasion, I will be a writer of votes. I can do some thing in that way."[20]

The barrier between the male political world and the women's domestic domain eroded in the years of the war and its aftermath. Mercy Otis Warren did not seriously apologize for writing her postwar history. When John Adams was president, Abigail Adams handled some of his correspondence openly. When Elbridge Gerry was appointed to negotiate with France in 1797, she wrote the new ambassador: "The president knowing how sincere an interest I had taken in the result of your deliberations, communicated to me your Letter this morning received, and I do assure you, Sir, that it gave me great pleasure. I had anticipated many of your reasons, and arguments of a publick nature, and I did flatter myself that you would not decline so important an Embassy." By the War of 1812, Abigail Adams could not only report, she could openly criticize political events: "It seems as if every Naval victory was to be balanced, by some disgracefull defeat upon the Land. . . . I know not how to express my grief and chagrin at these repeated and stupid enterprises so unskillfully conducted."[21]

Abigail Adams and Mercy Otis Warren could not help knowing that they were unusual among their contemporaries, especially in the years before the war. One of Mercy Warren's friends, Hannah Lincoln, evidently wrote to her on the question of whether it was appropriate for women to address themselves to politics, implying that her own husband disapproved. Hannah Lincoln invited guidance.

The terms of Mercy Warren's reply, in the tense spring of 1774, are instructive. She was aware that women were vulnerable to criticism if they addressed themselves to politics, and in response she began to construct a rationale for women's interest in politics that was justified in terms of their right to free speech and self-expression. "I know not why any gentlemen of your acquaintance should caution you not to enter any particular subject when we meet," she wrote guardedly to Hannah Lincoln. "I should have a very ill opinion of myself, if any variation of sentiment with regard to political matters, should lessen my esteem for the disinterested, undesigning and upright heart; and it would argue great want of candour to think that there was not many such (more especially among our own sex) who yet judge very differently with regard to the calamities of our unhappy country . . . though every mind of the least sensibility must be greatly affected with the present distress; and even a female pen might be excused for touching on the important subject; yet I will not undertake to give a full answer to the queries proposed by my friend; for as the wisest among the other sex are much divided in opinion, it might justly be deemed impertinent or rather sanguine for me to decide." She would not get into an argument with Benjamin Lincoln. She did admit that politics was "a subject . . . much out of the road of female attention," but she began to construct a rationale that would permit women to attend to political matters without abandoning their domestic responsibilities, as men did. "But as every domestic enjoyment depends on the decision of the mighty contest, who can be an unconcerned and silent spectator? Not surely the fond mother, or the affectionate wife who trembles lest her dearest connections should fall victims of lawless power, or at least pour out the warm blood as a libation at the shrine of liberty."[22]

Mercy Warren argued that women's hearts and minds responded as accurately and as sensitively to public challenge as did men's, that women's duty to their own families required them to sort out public information accurately and to take a political position. Their political position—which they were to arrive at by informed discussion with men and women outside their families—could ultimately be expressed within the family and justified in terms of service to and protection of husbands and sons. Thus she counseled Hannah Lincoln to resist her husband's constraints on her political conversation, and at the same time assured her that a politically minded woman was not necessarily a threat to family politics. By 1797, when the Quasi-War threatened, Warren had no hesitancy in thinking of herself as a politician. She wrote to her son, "I dread it as a Woman, I fear it, as a friend to my country; yet think (as a politician) I see it pending over this land."[23]

For the most part, women confined their politics to their portfolios and their diaries. "July 4, Anniversary of Independance, 19 years," Elizabeth Drinker wrote in her diary in 1795. "General Orders in News-paper this forenoon, for a fuss and to do. I think, orders for peace and quietness, would be more commendable and consistant, in a well regulated Government or State." Hannah Griffitts wrote private poetry:

> The glorious fourth—again appears
> A Day of Days—and year of years,
>   The sum of sad disasters,
> Where all the mighty gains we see
> With all their Boasted liberty,
>   Is only Change of Masters . . .[24]

Abigail Adams wrote to her friends and her husband, not for publication. Kitty Livingston and Sarah Jay wrote within the broad Livingston political network, but did not venture outside it. They brought public perceptions to their private world.

It has been common for historians to regard this evidence of hesitancy as evidence of a sort of false consciousness.[25] The implication is that these women ought to have been openly, frankly political. Because they were not, they are accused of mincing and simpering, of stupidly not seeing what was before their very eyes or of seeing the realm of politics but denying its existence. But these women deserve more than this contemptuous dismissal. Their culture had pointedly established that politics was not a female province. The daily lives of women in a preindustrial society *were* largely spent in a domestic circle, a confinement impossible to ignore. But politics did intrude into the women's world during the trauma of the war and the Confederation, and as it did women acknowledged its presence and responded to it. The North Carolina women would not let their neighbors be deported without contest; Kitty Livingston would not refrain from scrutinizing the politicians she met. To ask what they might have done had they lived instead in a world that allowed political concerns to be women's concerns is to ask an unanswerable question. To criticize them for not acting as if they lived in such a world is pointless. . . .

The best-known organized political action by American women is the campaign of the female patriots of Philadelphia to collect funds for Washington's troops. Organized and led by Esther De Berdt Reed (in her role as wife of the president of Pennsylvania) and Benjamin Franklin's daughter, Sarah Franklin Bache, the campaign gained much publicity because its leadership included "the best ladies" of the patriot side. "Instead of waiting for the Donations being sent the ladys of each Ward go from dore to dore and collect them I am one of those, Honourd with this business. Yesterday we began our tour of duty and had the Satisfaction of being very Successfull," wrote Mary Morris. Collecting contributions door-to-door implied confrontation: "Of all absurdities," the loyalist Anna Rawle wrote to Rebecca Rawle Shoemaker, "the ladies going about for money exceeded everything; they were so extremely importunate that people were obliged to give them something to get rid of them."[26]

By July 4, 1779, Esther Reed was writing to George Washington that "the subscription set on foot by the ladies of this City for the use of soldiery" had resulted in some three hundred thousand paper dollars. When Washington suggested that the funds be directly deposited in the Bank of the United States, and in that way be united "with the gentlemen," Esther Reed replied coolly that it had not been the women's intention to give the soldiers "an article to which they are entitled from the public," but rather some special item that obviously came from an unusual source. The women wished to change the paper into hard specie and to give each soldier two dollars "to be entirely at his own disposal." Washington turned that down, claiming "a taste of hard money may be productive of much discontent, as we have none but depreciated paper for their pay." He also feared that the men would use specie to buy liquor. In the end the money was used to buy linen for making shirts. When Esther Reed died in the fall of 1780, the organization was taken over by Benjamin Franklin's daughter, Sarah Franklin Bache. In December, Sarah Bache sent Washington 2,200 shirts, with the wish that they "be worn with as much pleasure as they were made." If the women did not get their wish to provide each soldier with hard cash, they had at least managed to supply something distinctly from the ladies of Philadelphia; they had not merged their money into the common fund.[27]

Attempting to duplicate this project, New Jersey women organized a similar fund-raising drive. Wives of prominent politicians were given charge of soliciting contributions in each county, though the center seems to have been Trenton. Eventually Mary Dagworthy transmitted $15,488—without the Philadelphians' skepticism—directly to George Washington, to be used as he thought proper; wartime inflation was so bad that he found it provided only 380 pairs of stockings for New Jersey troops.[28] A smaller donation came from the women of Maryland, sent by Mary Lee, the wife of the governor; this money was used to buy shirts and stockings for the men of the southern army. Martha Washington seems to have suggested that the Philadelphia women's project could be imitated, and on her suggestion Martha Jefferson contacted the wife of the president of the College of William and Mary. "Justified by the sanction of her [Martha Washington's] letter in handing forward the scheme," Martha Jefferson wrote to Sarah Tate Madison, "I undertake with chearfulness the duty of furnishing to my countrywomen an opportunity of proving that they also participate of those virtuous feelings which gave birth to it." But Martha Jefferson was no activist and felt she could only promote the proposed drive "by inclosing to . . . [Mrs. Madison] some of the papers to be disposed of." Following this vague commitment, the scheme seems to have petered out.[29]

Many historians of women in the Revolution have admired the Philadelphia project excessively. "A noble Example!" cried Ezra Stiles. Benjamin Rush, whose wife was an enthusiastic participant in the campaign, wrote, "The women of America have at last become principals in the glorious American controversy."[30] But they were not principals, of course, they were fund raisers, and only for a brief time and in a single city. Nor were the female patriots principals in the controversy to the extent that being a principal implies emergence from the women's private domain, and they were not above teasing and flirting to get contributions, reminding those who were unenthusiastic that it was rude to refuse anything to pretty women.

Yet we ought to hesitate before dismissing this effort as short-lived philanthropy. Broadsides that accompanied the drives provided an ideological justification for women's intrusion into politics that would become the standard model throughout the years of the early Republic. The Philadelphia manifesto was entitled *The Sentiments of an American Woman*; the one circulated in New Jersey was called *The Sentiments of a Lady in New Jersey*. The two are differently phrased, but share many of the same themes.[31]

The Philadelphia version first stated that American women were "born for liberty, disdaining to bear the irons of a tyrannic Government" and claimed that "if the weakness of our Constitution, if opinion and manners did not forbid us to march to glory by the same paths as the Men," women would be found at least equal, and perhaps stronger, in their convictions and their loyalty to the Republic.

The broadside then presented a list of historical role models, examples of politically active women: Deborah, Judith, Esther. "Rome saved from the fury of a victorious enemy by the efforts of Volumnia. . . . famous sieges where the Women have been seen . . . building new walls, digging trenches." Some of their choices of "Sovereigns . . . who have held with so much splendour the scepter of the greatest States" revealed only their lack of historical information; they claimed to admire "the Elizabeths, the Maries, the Catherines, who have extended the empire of liberty." But they also remembered "the Maid of Orleans who drove from the kingdom of France the ancestors of those same British, whose odious yoke we have just shaken off, and whom it is necessary that we drive from this Continent."[32] The New Jersey variant eschewed classical role models and substituted contemporary female martyrs: "[The British have] even waged war against our sex. Who that has heard . . . of the tragical death of Miss M'Crea, torn from her house, murdered and scalped by a band of savages hired and set on by British emissaries, of the melancholy fate of Mrs. Caldwell, put to death in her own house . . . but would wish to avert from themselves, their kindred, their property, and their country in general, so heavy misfortunes."

NOTES

1. [Hannah Adams], *Women Invited to War, or a Friendly Address to the Honourable Women of the United States. By A Daughter of America* (Boston, 1787).

2. Americans' skepticism toward political ambition has been subtly evaluated in Douglass Adair, *Fame and the Founding Fathers: Essays by Douglass Adair*, ed. Trevor Colbourn (New York, 1974), and in Charles S. Sydnor, *Gentlemen Freeholders: Political Practices in*

Washington's Virginia (Chapel Hill, N.C., 1952). For John Adams's explanation of his ambition as an attempt to deserve posthumous fame, see Peter Shaw, *The Character of John Adams* (Chapel Hill, N.C., 1976). When Alexander Hamilton said the same, he was considered ambitious.

3. Nov. 1776, Hannah Griffitts Papers, Box 7422, Lib. Co. Phila.

4. Benjamin Rush Papers, n.d., 1791, Lib. Co. Phila. Elizabeth Drinker noted Waters's death: "Heard today of the death of Nurse Mary Waters who has been gone for some weeks past" (Diary of Elizabeth Drinker, Jan. 8, 1800, Hist. Soc. Pa.).

5. Raymond C. Werner, ed., "Diary of Grace Growden Galloway, Kept at Philadelphia . . . ," *PMHB*, LV (1931), 51–52.

6. *Ibid.*, 75–76, 88. In the late summer of 1779 she was in a despairing mood: "I am wrapped in impenetrable Darkeness; . . . Can it ever be removed & shall I once More belong to somebody. . . . Now I am like a pelican in the Desert." (Werner, ed., "Diary of Galloway," *PMHB*, LVIII[1934], 164)

7. Diary of Sarah Logan Fisher, Sept. 21, 1977, Hist. Soc. Pa., Philadelphia. See also *ibid.*, Jan. 4, Sept. 4, 1777.

8. Sarah Jay to Catharine Livingston, Mar. 1780, Richard B. Morris, ed., *John Jay: The Making of a Revolutionary* (New York, 1975), 692.

9. Complaints about Brockholst appear in Sarah Jay to William Livingston, June 24, 1781, John Jay Papers, Rare Book and Manuscript Library, Columbia University, New York. For her apology, see Sarah Jay to Catharine Livingston, July 16, 1783, *ibid.* Her aunt Margaret commented that though she acknowledged that exiling the loyalists was probably a wartime necessity, it was "a heart-hardening Subject, too much so, for women to deal with" (Margaret Livingston to Susan Livingston, July 1788, Ridley Papers, Mass. Hist. Soc.).

10. Catharine Livingston to Matthew Ridley [May 1785], Ridley Papers; Matthew Ridley to Catharine Livingston, n.d., 1784, *ibid.*

11. Henry Brockholst Livingston to Catharine Livingston, May 19, 1781, *ibid.*

12. Sarah Vaughan to Catharine Livingston, Mar. 28–31, 1785, *ibid.*

13. Rebecca Vaughan to Catharine Livingston, Dec. 1784, *ibid.*

14. Rebecca Vaughan to Catharine Livingston, Jan. 18, 1785, *ibid.*

15. Ann Gwinnett to John Hancock and the "other Members of the Grand Continental Congress" [Aug. 1777?], Papers Cont. Cong. (M-247), Roll 87, Item 73: 135, Natl. Archives.

16. Mrs. McLean to Alexander Martin, Dec. 11, 1783, Governor's Letterbook, V, 612, State Department of Archives and History, Division of Archives and History, Raleigh, N.C.

17. Catherine Read to Betsey Read Ludlow, July 15 [1798], Read Papers, S. Caroliniana Lib., Univ. S.C., Columbia.

18. Elizabeth Palmer to John Cranch, Oct. 12, 1784, Boston Public Library.

19. Mercy Otis Warren to Abigail Adams, Aug. 9, 1774, *Adams Family Correspondence*, I, 138; Abigail Adams to Mercy Otis Warren, Feb. 3[?], 1775, *ibid.*, 184.

20. Abigail Adams to John Adams, July 5, 1780, L. H. Butterfield *et al.*, eds., *The Book of Abigail and John: Selected Letters of the Adams Family, 1762–1784* (Cambridge, Mass., 1975), 264.

21. Abigail Adams to Elbridge Gerry, July 14, 1797, and Abigail Adams to William S. Smith, Feb. 18, 1813, Boston Pub. Lib.

22. Mercy Otis Warren to Hannah Lincoln, Sept. 3, 1774, Mercy Otis Warren Letterbook, Warren Papers, Mass. Hist. Soc., Boston.

23. Mercy Otis Warren to James Warren, Jr., June 4, 1797, *ibid.*, 232.

24. Diary of Elizabeth Drinker, July 4, 1795; Hannah Griffitts Papers, 1785.

25. See, for example, Lawrence J. Friedman, *Inventors of the Promised Land* (New York, 1975), 148–155, and Lawrence J. Friedman and Arthur H. Schaffer, "Mercy Otis Warren and the Politics of Historical Nationalism," *New England Quarterly*, XLVIII (1975), 194–215.

26. Mary Morris to Catharine Livingston, June 10, [1780], Ridley Papers; Anna Rawle to Rebecca Rawle Shoemaker, June 30, 1780, William Brooke Rawle, "Laurel Hill and Some Colonial Dames Who Once Lived There," *PMHB*, XXXV (1911), 398.

27. William B. Reed, *Life and Correspondence of Joseph Reed*, II (Philadelphia, 1847), 264, 265, 270, 429–449.

28. Mary Dagworthy to George Washington, July 17, 1780, Fitzpatrick, ed., *Writings of Washington*, XIX, 72. See also *ibid.*, XXI, 77.

29. George Washington to Mary Lee, Oct. 11, 1780, *ibid.*, XX, 158; Martha Jefferson to Mrs. James Madison, Aug. 8, 1780, Private Collection #634.1, State Dept. Archives and Hist., Raleigh, N.C. Benjamin Franklin's sister, Jane Mecom, was briefly tempted to spread the effort to Rhode Island: "I have, as you sopose heard of yr Ladies Noble and generous Subscription for the Army and honour them for it," she wrote to Sarah Franklin Bache, "and if a harty good will in me would Effect it we would follow your Example but I fear what my Influence would procure would be so Deminuitive we should be ashamed to offer it, I live in an obscure place have but Little Acquaintance and those not very Rich, but you may [say?] a mite has been Accepted and may be again but that

was a time when there was more Relidgon and less Pride" ([Fall, 1779?], Carl Van Doren, ed., *The Letters of Benjamin Franklin and Jane Mecom* [Princeton, N.J., 1950], 202).

30. July 5, 1780, Dexter, ed., *Literary Diary of Ezra Stiles*, II, 442; Benjamin Rush to John Adams, July 13, 1780, L. H. Butterfield, ed., *The Letters of Benjamin Rush*, I (Princeton, N.J., 1951), 253.

31. *The Sentiments of an American Woman* (Broadside), Philadelphia, June 10, 1780. The broadside of the Ladies of Trenton appeared in the *N.-J. Gaz.* (Trenton), July 12, 1780; a portion is reprinted in Gerlach, ed., *N.J. in the Revolution*, 348–349.

32. *Sentiments of an American Woman*. The analogy between French resistance to the English in the 15th century and the American resistance to the English in the 18th had been made forcefully by Thomas Paine in the first Crisis paper, which referred specifically to Joan of Arc and added the wish "that heaven might inspire some Jersey maid to spirit up her countrymen, and save her fair fellow sufferers from ravage and ravishment!" (*The American Crisis* [Dec. 23, 1776], in Philip S. Foner, ed., *The Complete Writings of Thomas Paine*, I [New York, 1945], 51) In John Daly Burk's play *Female Patriotism* (New York, 1798), act 4, sc. 1, Joan of Arc repeatedly expresses a vision of the Republic: " 'Tis not to crown the Dauphin prince alone/ That hath impell'd my spirit to the wars,/For that were petty circumstance indeed;/But on the head of every man in France/To place a crown, and thus at once create/A new and mighty order of nobility/To make all free and equal, *all men kings*/Subject to justice and the laws alone."

3

MAKING THE CONSTITUTION WORK

No woman served as delegate to the famous Constitutional Convention in Philadelphia, but in the political generation charged with turning the words of that great charter into the working machinery of free government, a woman had her say. Abigail Adams, a prodigious letter writer, was not her husband John's "sovereign," as one critic averred, but clearly a close adviser and avid partisan of the second president. As Adams and then Jefferson struggled to translate constitutional theory into practice and precedent, Mrs. Adams counseled both of them. At one point, she broke with Jefferson over his opposition to her John. But on May 20, 1804, after three and a half years of silence, she wrote to Jefferson at Monticello. She wrote because Jefferson's beloved daughter Mary had died at age twenty-five; he was shattered, felt he had "lost even the half of all I had." Abigail let "the powerfull feelings of my heart . . . burst through the restraint." Jefferson replied, and the correspondence continued for half a year.

Three basic constitutional issues are reflected in these letters. The contention between Jefferson and Adams was sparked by Federalist Adams's appointing numerous Federalists to office the night before he handed over the presidency to Republican Jefferson. The argument wound up in the Supreme Court. Chief Justice John Marshall seized on the issue to make a very significant point. The Court decided that it did not have the authority, despite the Judiciary Act of 1789, to enforce the appointments, but that it *did* have the authority to declare that act—and thus acts of Congress on other topics—unconstitutional. Thus was born judicial review.

The references to James Callender show how tenuously established the liberty of the press was in those early days. Adams, encouraged a good deal by Abigail, had got through sweeping legislation to suppress sedition—defaming the government. Callender went to jail for defaming Adams; Jefferson let him out and remitted his fine. (Callender, the ingrate, subsequently took to defaming Jefferson.) Abigail was bitter. The issue went far beyond their immediate dispute, to the fundamentals of free expression.

Finally, Abigail Adams's indignation over Jefferson's removal of her son John Quincy Adams from his government post reaches the broader question of patronage: how the criteria used in appointments—especially talent versus party loyalty—should be composed. It seems that possibly Jefferson, very busy with larger concerns, simply did not know that John Quincy was removed. Or perhaps he did know, and meant to replace him with a Republican. From then on, through Lincoln's patronage headaches and up to the present day, the tension persisted. In modern times it has been complicated by the belief that categories of citizens—including women—should be fairly represented in appointments.

As the correspondence begins, Mrs. Adams, not a person given to sentimentality, takes the initiative. The correspondence ends with her husband's footnote, declaring her independence.

Abigail Adams Counsels Thomas Jefferson

edited by Lester J. Capon

Abigail Adams to Jefferson

Quincy May 20th 1804

SIR

Had you been no other than the private inhabitant of Monticello, I should e'er this time have addrest you, with that sympathy, which a recent event has awakend in my Bosom. But reasons of various kinds withheld my pen, untill the powerfull feelings of my heart, have burst through the restraint, and called upon me to shed the tear of sorrow over the departed remains, of your beloved and deserving daughter,[1] an event which I most sincerely mourn.

The attachment which I formed for her, when you committed her to my care: upon her arrival in a foreign Land: has remained with me to this hour, and the recent account of her death, which I read in a late paper, brought fresh to my remembrance the strong sensibility she discovered, tho but a child of nine years of age at having been seperated from her Friends, and country, and brought, as she expressed it, "to a strange land amongst strangers." The tender scene of her seperation from me, rose to my recollection, when she clung around my neck and wet my Bosom with her tears, saying, "O! now I have learnt to Love you, why will they tear me from you"[2]

It has been some time since that I conceived of any event in this Life, which could call forth, feelings of mutual sympathy. But I know how closely entwined around a parents heart, are those chords which bind the filial to the parental Bosom, and when snaped assunder, how agonizing the pangs of seperation.[3]

I have tasted the bitter cup, and bow with reverence, and humility before the great dispenser of it, without whose permission, and over ruling providence, not a sparrow falls to the ground. That you may derive comfort and consolation in this day of your sorrow and affliction, from that only source calculated to heal the wounded heart—a firm belief in the Being: perfections and attributes of God, is the sincere and ardent wish of her, who once took pleasure in subscribing Herself your Friend

ABIGAIL ADAMS

From Lester J. Cappon, ed., *The Adams-Jefferson Letters*, Vol. I (Chapel Hill: University of North Carolina Press, 1959), pp. 268–82.

Jefferson to Abigail Adams

Washington June 13.04.

Dear Madam

The affectionate sentiments which you have had the goodness to express in your letter of May 20. towards my dear departed daughter, have awakened in me sensibilities natural to the occasion, and recalled your kindnesses to her which I shall ever remember with gratitude and friendship. I can assure you with truth they had made an indelible impression on her mind, and that, to the last, on our meetings after long separations, whether I had heard lately of you, and how you did, were among the earliest of her enquiries. In giving you this assurance I perform a sacred duty for her, and at the same time am thankful for the occasion furnished me of expressing my regret that circumstances should have arisen which have seemed to draw a line of separation between us. The friendship with which you honoured me has ever been valued, and fully reciprocated; and altho' events have been passing which might be trying to some minds, I never believed yours to be of that kind, nor felt that my own was. Neither my estimate of your character, nor the esteem founded in that, have ever been lessened for a single moment, although doubts whether it would be acceptable may have forbidden manifestations of it. Mr. Adams's friendship and mine began at an earlier date. It accompanied us thro' long and important scenes. The different conclusions we had drawn from our political reading and reflections were not permitted to lessen mutual esteem, each party being conscious they were the result of an honest conviction in the other. Like differences of opinion existing among our fellow citizens attached them to the one or the other of us, and produced a rivalship in their minds which did not exist in ours. We never stood in one another's way: for if either had been withdrawn at any time, his favorers would not have gone over to the other, but would have sought for some one of homogeneous opinions. This consideration was sufficient to keep down all jealousy between us, and to guard our friendship from any disturbance by sentiments of rivalship: and I can say with truth that one act of Mr. Adams's life, and one only, ever gave me a moment's personal displeasure. I did consider his last appointments to office as personally unkind.[4] They were from among my most ardent political enemies, from whom no faithful cooperation could ever be expected, and laid me under the embarrassment of acting thro' men whose views were to defeat mine; or to encounter the odium of putting others in their places. It seemed but common justice to leave a successor free to act by instruments of his own choice. If my respect for him did not permit me to ascribe the whole blame to the influence of others, it left something for friendship to forgive, and after brooding over it for some little time, and not always resisting the expression of it, I forgave it cordially, and returned to the same state of esteem and respect for him which had so long subsisted. Having come into life a little later than Mr. Adams, his career has preceded mine, as mine is followed by some other, and it will probably be closed at the same distance after him which time originally placed between us. I maintain for him, and shall carry into private life an uniform and high measure of respect and good will, and for yourself a sincere attachment. I have thus, my dear Madam, opened myself to you without reserve, which I have long wished an opportunity of doing; and, without knowing how it will be recieved, I feel relief from being unbosomed. And I have now only to entreat your forgiveness for this transition from a subject of domestic affliction to one which seems of a different aspect. But tho connected with political events, it has been viewed by me most strongly in it's unfortunate bearings on my private friendships. The injury these have sustained has been a heavy price for what has never given me equal pleasure. That you may both be favored with health, tranquility and long life, is the prayer of one who tenders you the assurances of his highest consideration and esteem.

TH: JEFFERSON

Abigail Adams to Jefferson

Quincy July 1st 1804

SIR

Your Letter of June 13th came duly to hand; if it had contained no other sentiments and opinions than those which my Letter of condolence could have excited, and which are expressed in the first page of your reply, our correspondence would have terminated here: but you have been pleased to enter upon some subjects which call for a reply: and as you observe that you have wished for an opportunity to express your sentiments, I have given to them every weight they claim.

"One act of Mr. Adams's Life, and *one* only, you repeat, ever gave me a moments personal displeasure. I did think his last appointments to office personally unkind. They were from among my most ardent political enemies."

As this act I am certain was not intended to give any personal pain or offence, I think it a duty to explain it so far as I then knew his views and designs. The constitution empowers the president to fill up offices as they become vacant. It was in the exercise of this power that appointments were made, and Characters selected whom Mr. Adams considerd, as men faithfull to the constitution and where he personally knew them, such as were capable of fullfilling their duty to their country. This was done by president Washington equally, in the last days of his administration so that not an office remained vacant for his successor to fill upon his comeing into the office. No offence was given by it, and no personal unkindness thought of. But the different political opinions which have so unhappily divided our Country, must have given rise to the Idea, that personal unkindness was intended. You will please to recollect Sir, that at the time these appointments were made, there was not any certainty that the presidency would devolve upon you,[5] which is an other circumstance to prove that personal unkindness was not meant. No person was ever selected by him from such a motive—and so far was Mr. Adams from indulging such a sentiment, that he had no Idea of the intollerance of party spirit at that time, and I know it was his opinion that if the presidency devolved upon you, except in the appointment of Secretaries, no material Changes would be made. I perfectly agree with you in opinion that those should be Gentlemen in whom the president can repose confidence, possessing opinions, and sentiments corresponding with his own, or if differing from him, that they ought rather to resign their office, than cabal against measures which he may think essential to the honour safety and peace of the Country. Much less should they unite, with any bold, and dareingly ambitious Character, to over rule the Cabinet, or betray the Secrets of it to Friends or foes. The two Gentlemen who held the offices of secretaries,[6] when you became president were not of this Character. They were appointed by your predecessor nearly two years previous to his retirement. They were Gentlemen who had cordially co-operated with him, and enjoyed the public confidence. Possessing however different political sentiments from those which you were known to have embraced, it was expected that they would, as they did, resign.

I have never felt any enmity towards you Sir for being elected president of the United States. But the instruments made use of, and the means which were practised to effect a change, have my utter abhorrence and detestation, for they were the blackest calumny, and foulest falshoods. I had witnessed enough of the anxiety, and solicitude, the envy jealousy and reproach attendant upon the office as well as the high responsibility of the Station, to be perfectly willing to see a transfer of it. And I can truly say, that at the time of Election, I considerd your pretentions much superior to his [Mr. Burr's], to whom an equal vote was given. Your experience I venture to affirm has convinced you that it is not a station to be envy'd. If you feel yourself a free man, and can act in all cases, according to your own sentiments, opinions and judgment, you can do more than either of your predecessors could, and are awfully responsible to God and your Country for the measures of your Administration. I rely upon the Friendship you still profess for me, and (I am conscious I have done nothing to forfeit it), to excuse the freedom of this discussion to which you have led with an unreserve, which has taken off the Shackles I should otherways have found myself embarrassed with.—And now Sir I will freely disclose to you what has severed the bonds of former Friendship, and placed you in a light very different from what I once viewd you in.

One of the first acts of your administration was to liberate a wretch[7] who was suffering the just punishment of the Law due to his crimes for writing and publishing the basest libel, the lowest and vilest Slander, which malice could invent, or calumny exhibit against the Character and reputation of your predecessor, of him for whom you profest the highest esteem and Friendship, and whom you certainly knew incapable of such complicated baseness. The remission of Callenders fine was a public approbation of his conduct. Is not the last restraint of vice, a sense of shame, renderd abortive, if abandoned Characters do not excite abhorrence.[8] If the chief Majestrate of a Nation, whose elevated Station places him in a conspicuous light, and renders his every action a concern of general importance, permits his public conduct to be influenced by private resentment, and so far forgets what is due to his Character as to give countanance to a base Calumniater, is he not answerable for the influence which his example has upon the manners and morals of the community?

Untill I read Callenders seventh Letter containing your compliment to him as a writer and your reward of 50 dollars, I could not be made to believe, that such measures could have been resorted to: to stab the fair fame and upright intentions of one, who to use your own Language "was acting from an honest conviction in his own mind that he was right." This Sir I considerd as a personal injury. This was the Sword that cut assunder the Gordian knot, which could not be untied by all the efforts of party Spirit, by rivalship by Jealousy or any other malignant fiend.

The serpent you cherished and warmed, bit the hand that nourished him,[9] and gave you sufficient Specimens of his talents, his gratitude his justice, and his truth. When such vipers are let lose upon Society, all distinction between virtue and vice are levelled, all respect for Character is lost in the overwhelming deluge of calumny—that respect which is a necessary bond in the social union, which gives efficacy to laws, and teaches the subject to obey the Majestrate, and the child to submit to the parent.

There is one other act of your administration which I considerd as personally unkind, and which your own mind will readily suggest to you, but as it neither affected character, or reputation, I forbear to state it.

This Letter is written in confidence—no eye but my own has seen what has passed. Faithfull are the wounds of a Friend. Often have I wished to have seen a different course pursued by you. I bear no malice I cherish no enmity. I would not retaliate if I could—nay more in the true spirit of christian Charity, I would forgive, as I hope to be forgiven. And with that disposition of mind and heart, I subscribe the Name of

ABIGAIL ADAMS

Jefferson to Abigail Adams

Washington July 22.04.

DEAR MADAM

Your favor of the 1st inst. was duly recieved, and I would not again have intruded on you but to rectify certain facts which seem not to have been presented to you under their true aspect. My charities to Callendar are considered as rewards for his calumnies. As early, I think, as 1796, I was told in Philadelphia that Callendar, the author of the Political progress of Britain, was in that city, a fugitive from persecution for having written that book, and in distress.[10] I had read and approved the book: I considered him as a man of genius, unjustly persecuted. I knew nothing of his private character, and immediately expressed my readiness to contribute to his relief, and to serve him. It was a considerable time after, that, on application from a person who thought of him as I did, I contributed to his relief, and afterwards repeated the contribution. Himself I did not see till long after, nor ever more than two or three times. When he first began to write he told some useful truths in his coarse way; but no body sooner disapproved of his writings than I did, or wished more that he would be silent. My charities to him were no more meant as encouragements to his scurrilities than those I give to the beggar at my door are meant as rewards for the vices of his life, and to make them chargeable to myself. In truth they would have been greater to him had he never written a word after the work for which he fled from Britain. With respect to the calumnies and falsehoods which writers and printers at large published against Mr. Adams, I was as far from stooping to any concern or approbation of them as Mr. Adams was respecting those of Porcupine,[11] Fenno, or Russell, who published volumes against me for every sentence vended by their opponents against Mr. Adams. But I never supposed Mr. Adams had any participation in the atrocities of these editors or their writers. I knew myself incapable of that base warfare, and believed him to be so. On the contrary, whatever I may have thought of the acts of the administration of that day, I have ever borne testimony to Mr. Adams's personal worth, nor was it ever impeached in my presence without a just vindication of it on my part. I never supposed that any person who knew either of us could believe that either meddled in that dirty work.

But another fact is that I 'liberated a wretch who was suffering for a libel against Mr. Adams.' I do not know who was the particular wretch alluded to: but I discharged every person under punishment or prosecution under the Sedition law, because I considered and now consider that law to be a nullity as absolute and as palpable as if Congress had ordered us to fall down and worship a golden image; and that it was as much my duty to arrest it's execution in every stage, as it would have been to have rescued from the fiery furnace those who should have been cast into it for refusing to worship their image. It was accordingly done in every instance, without asking what the offenders had done, or against whom they had offended, but whether the pains they were suffering were inflicted under the pretended Sedition law. It was certainly possible that my motives for contributing to the relief of Callender and liberating sufferers under the Sedition law, might have been to protect, encourage and reward slander: but they may also have been those which inspire ordinary charities to objects of distress, meritorious or not, or the obligations of an oath to protect the constitution, violated by an unauthorized act of Congress. Which of these were my motives must be decided by a regard to the general tenor of my life. On this I am not afraid to appeal to the nation at large, to posterity, and still less to that being who sees himself our motives, who will judge us from his own knolege of them, and not on the testimony of a Porcupine or Fenno.

You observe there has been one other act of my administration personally unkind, and suppose it will readily suggest itself to me. I declare on my honor, Madam, I have not the least conception what act is alluded to. I never did a single one with an unkind intention.

My sole object in this letter being to place before your attention that the acts imputed to me are either such as are falsely imputed, or as might flow from good as well as bad motives, I shall make no other addition than the assurances of my continued wishes for the health and happiness of yourself and Mr. Adams.

TH: JEFFERSON

Abigail Adams to Jefferson

Quincy August 18th 1804

SIR

Your Letter of July 22d was by some mistake in the post office at Boston sent back as far as New York, so that it did not reach me untill the eleventh of this Month. Candour requires of me a reply. Your statement respecting Callender, (who was the wretch referd to) and your motives for liberating him, wear a different aspect as explaind by you, from the impression which they had made, not only upon my mind, but upon the minds of all those, whom I ever heard speak upon the subject. With regard to the act under which he was punished, different persons entertain different opinions respecting it. It lies not with me to decide upon its validity. That I presume devolved upon the supreem Judges of the Nation: but I have understood that the power which makes a Law, is along competent to the repeal. If a Chief Majestrate can by his will annul a Law, where is the difference between a republican, and a despotic Government? That some restraint should be laid upon the asassin, who stabs reputation, all civilized Nations have assented to. In no Country has calumny falshood, and revileing stalked abroad more licentiously, than in this. No political Character has been secure from its attacks, no reputation so fair, as not to be wounded by it, untill truth and falshood lie in one undistinguished heap. If there are no checks to be resorted to in the Laws of the Land, and no reperation to be made to the injured, will not Man become the judge and avenger of his own wrongs, and as in a late instance, the sword and pistol decide the contest?[12] All the Christian and social virtues will be banished the Land. All that makes Life desirable, and softens the ferocious passions of Man will assume a savage deportment, and like Cain of old, every Mans hand will be against his Neighbour. Party spirit is blind malevolent uncandid, ungenerous, unjust and unforgiving. It is equally so under federal as under democratic Banners, yet upon both sides are Characters, who possess honest views, and act from honorable motives, who disdain to be led blindfold, and who tho entertaining different opinions, have for their object the public welfare and happiness. These are the Characters, who abhor calumny and evil speaking, and who will never descend to News paper revileing. And you have done Mr. Adams justice in believing him, incapable of such conduct. He has never written a line in any News paper to which his Name has not been affixed, since he was first elected president of the united States. The writers in the public papers, and their employers are alltogether unknown to him.

I have seen and known that much of the conduct of a public ruler, is liable to be misunderstood, and misrepresented. Party hatred by its deadly poison blinds the Eyes and envenoms the heart. It is fatal to the integrity of the moral Character. It sees not that wisdom dwells with moderation, and that firmness of conduct is seldom united with outrageous voilence [i.e., violence] of sentiment. Thus blame is too often liberally bestowed upon actions, which if fully understood, and candidly judged would merit praise instead of censure. It is only by the general issue of measures producing banefull or benificial effects that they ought to be tested.

You exculpate yourself from any intentional act of unkindness towards any one. I will freely state that which I referd to in my former Letter, and which I could not avoid considering as personal resentment. Soon after my eldest son's return from Europe, he was appointed by the district Judge to an office into which no political concerns enterd, personally known to you, and possessing all the qualifications, you yourself being Judge, which you had designated for office. As soon as congress gave the appointments to the president you removed him.[13] This looked so particularly pointed, that some of your best Friends in Boston, at that time exprest their regret that you had done so. I must do him the Justice to say, that I never heard an expression from him of censure or disrespect towards you in concequence of it. With pleasure I say that he is not a blind follower of any party.

I have written to you with the freedom and unreserve of former Friendship to which I would gladly return could all causes but mere difference of opinion be removed. I wish to lead a tranquil and retired Life under the administration of the Government, disposed to heal the wounds of contention, to cool the rageing fury of party animosity: to soften the Rugged Spirit of resentment, and desirious of seeing my Children and Grand Children, Heirs to that freedom and independance which you and your predesessor, united your efforts to obtain. With these sentiments I reciprocate my sincere wishes for your Health and happiness.

ABIGAIL ADAMS

Jefferson to Abigail Adams

Monticello. Sep 11.04.

Your letter, Madam, of the 18th. of Aug. has been some days recieved, but a press of business has prevented the acknolegement of it. Perhaps indeed I may have already trespassed too far on your attention. With those who wish to think amiss of me, I have learnt to be perfectly indifferent: but where I know a mind to be ingenuous, and to need only truth to set it to rights, I cannot be as passive.

The act of personal unkindness alluded to in your former letter is said in your last to have been the removal of your eldest son from some office to which the judges had appointed him. I conclude then he must have been a Commissioner of bankruptcy, but I declare to you on my honor that this is the first knolege I have ever had that he was so. It may be thought perhaps that I ought to have enquired who were such, before I appointed others, but it is to be observed that the former law permitted the judges to name Commissioners occasionally only for every case as it arose, and not to make them permanent officers. Nobody therefore being in office there could be no removal. The judges you well know have been considered as highly federal; and it was noted that they confined their nominations exclusively to federalists. The legislature, dissatisfied with this, transferred the nomination to the President, and made the offices permanent. The very object in passing the law was that he should correct, not confirm, what was deemed the partiality of the judges. I thought it therefore proper to enquire, not whom they had employed, but whom I ought to appoint to fulfil the intentions of the law. In making these appointments I put in a proportion of federalists equal I believe to the proportion they bear in numbers through the union generally. Had I known that your son had acted, it would have been a real pleasure to me to have preferred him to some who were named in Boston in what were deemed the same line of politics. To this I should have been led by my knolege of his integrity as well as my sincere dispositions towards yourself and Mr. Adams.

You seem to think it devolved on the judges to decide on the validity of the sedition law. But nothing in the constitution has given them a right to decide for the executive, more than to the Executive to decide for them. Both magistracies are equally independant in the sphere of action assigned to them. The judges, believing the law constitutional, had a right to pass a sentence of fine and imprisonment, because that power was placed in their hands by the constitution. But the Executive, believing the law to be unconstitutional, was bound to remit the execution of it; because that power has been confided to him by the constitution. That instrument meant that it's co-ordinate branches should be checks on each other. But the opinion which gives to the judges the right to decide what laws are constitutional, and what not, not only for themselves in their own sphere of action, but for the legislature and executive also in their spheres, would make the judiciary a despotic branch.

Nor does the opinion of the unconstitutionality and consequent nullity of that law remove all restraint from the overwhelming torrent of slander which is confounding all vice and virtue, all truth and falsehood in the US. The power to do that is fully possessed by the several state legislatures. It was reserved to them, and was denied to the general government, by the constitution according to our construction of it. While we deny that Congress have a right to controul the freedom of the press, we have ever asserted the right of the states, and their exclusive right, to do so. They have accordingly, all of them, made provisions for punishing slander, which those who have time and inclination resort to for the vindication of their characters. In general the state laws appear to have made the presses responsible for slander as far as is consistent with their useful freedom. In those states where they do not admit even the truth of allegations to protect the printer, they have gone too far.

The candour manifested in your letter, and which I ever believed you to possess, has alone inspired the desire of calling your attention once more to those circumstances of fact and motive by which I claim to be judged. I hope you will see these intrusions on your time to be, what they really are, proofs of my great respect for you. I tolerate with the utmost latitude the right of others to differ from me in opinion without imputing to them criminality. I know too well the weakness and uncertainty of human reason to wonder at it's different results. Both of our political parties, at least the honest portion of them, agree conscientiously in the same object, the public good: but they differ essentially in what they deem the means of promoting that good. One side believes it best done by one composition of the governing powers, the other by a different one. One fears most the ignorance of the people: the other the selfishness of rulers independant of them. Which is right, time and experience will prove. We think that one side of this experiment has been long enough tried, and proved not to promote the good of the many; and that the other has not been fairly and sufficiently tried. Our opponents think the reverse. With whichever opinion the body of the nation concurs, that must prevail. My anxieties on the subject will never carry me beyond the use of fair and honorable means, of truth and reason: nor have they ever lessened my esteem for moral worth; nor alienated my affections from a single friend who did not first withdraw himself. Wherever this has happened I confess I have not been insensible to it: yet have ever kept myself open to a return of their justice.

I conclude with sincere prayers for your health and happiness that yourself and Mr. Adams may long enjoy the tranquility you desire and merit, and see, in the prosperity of your family, what is the consummation of the last and warmest of human wishes.

TH: JEFFERSON

Abigail Adams to Jefferson

Quincy October 25 1804

SIR

Sickness for three weeks past, has prevented my acknowledging the receipt of your Letter of Sepbr the 11th. When I first addrest you, I little thought of entering into a correspondence with you upon political topicks. I will not however regret it, since it has led to some elucidations and brought on some explanations, which place in a more favourable light occurrences which had wounded me.

Having once entertained for you a respect and esteem, founded upon the Character of an affectionate parent, a kind Master, a candid and benevolent Friend, I could not suffer different political opinions to obliterate them from my mind, and I felt the truth of the observation, that the Heart is long, very long in receiving the conviction that is forced upon it by reason. Affection still lingers in the Bosom, even after esteem has taken its flight. It was not untill after circumstances concured to place you in the light of a rewarder and encourager of a Libeller whom you could not but detest and despise, that I withdrew the esteem I had long entertaind for you. Nor can you wonder Sir that I should consider as personal unkindnesses the instances I have mentiond. I am pleased to find that, which respected my son, all together unfounded. He was as you conjecture appointed a commissioner of Bankrupcy together with Judge Daws, and continued to serve in it, with perfect satisfaction to all parties. At least I never heard the contrary, untill superseded by a new appointment. The Idea sugested, that no one was in office, merely because it was not perminent, and concequently no removal could take place, I cannot consider in any other light, than what the Gentlemen of the Law would term a quible—as such I pass it. Judge Daws was continued, or reappointed which placed Mr. Adams, in a more conspicuous light, as the object of personal resentment. Nor could I upon this occasion refrain calling to mind the last visit you made me at Washington, when in the course of conversation you assured me, that if it should lay in your power to serve me or my family, nothing would give you more pleasure. I will do you the justice to say at this hour: that I believe what you then said, you then meant. With respect to the office it was a small object but the disposition of the remover was considered by me as the barbed arrow. This however by your declaration, is withdrawn from my mind. With the public it will remain, and here Sir may I be permitted to pause, and ask you whether in your ardent zeal, and desire to rectify the mistakes and abuses as you may consider them, of the former administrations, you are not led into measures still more fatal to the constitution, and more derogatory to your honour, and independence of Character? Pardon me Sir if I say, that I fear you are.

I know from the observations which I have made that there is not a more difficult part devolves upon a chief Majestrate, nor one which subjects him to more reproach, and censure than the appointments to office, and all the patronage which this enviable power gives him, is but a poor compensation for the responsibility to which it subjects him. It would be well however to weigh and consider Characters as it respects their Moral worth and integrity. He who is not true to himself, nor just to others, seeks an office for the benifit of himself, unmindfull of that of his Country.

I cannot agree, in opinion, that the constitution ever meant to withhold from the National Government the power of self defence, or that it could be considered an infringment of the Liberty of the press, to punish the licentiousness of it.[14]

Time Sir must determine, and posterity will judge with more candour, and impartiality, I hope than the conflicting parties of our day, what measures have best promoted the happiness of the people: what raised them from a state of depression and degradation to wealth, honor, and reputation; what has made them affluent at home, and respected abroad, and to whom ever the tribute is due to them may it be given.

I will not Sir any further intrude upon your time, but close this correspondence, by my sincere wishes, that you may be directed to that path which may terminate in the prosperity and happiness of the people over whom you are placed, by administring the Government with a just and impartial hand. Be assured Sir that no one will more rejoice in your success than

ABIGAIL ADAMS

Quincy Nov. 19. 1804. The whole of this Correspondence was begun and conducted without my Knowledge or Suspicion. Last Evening and this Morning at the desire of Mrs. Adams I read the whole. I have no remarks to make upon it at this time and in this place.

J. ADAMS[15]

NOTES

1. Mary Jefferson Eppes (Mrs. John Wayles Eppes, *d.* April 17, 1804). Malone, *Jefferson*, I, 434.

2. See AA to TJ, July 6 and 10, 1787 [Cappon, ed., *The Adams-Jefferson Letters*], 183–84, 185.

3. Her son, Charles Adams, had died on Nov. 30, 1800.

4. The Judiciary Act, passed Feb. 13, 1801, reduced the membership of the Supreme Court to five, increased the number of district judges, and relieved the Supreme Court justices from traveling the circuit. President Adams appointed Federalists to these new positions, to the discomfiture of his successor. The act was repealed by the Republican Congress of 1802. If the act was partisan in origin, it did provide some needed reforms. Max Farrand, "The Judiciary Act of 1801," *Amer. Hist. Rev.*, 5 (1899–1900), 682–86.

5. Since the electoral vote in 1800 was a tie, 73–73, between TJ and Aaron Burr, the election was thrown into the House of Representatives, where on Feb. 17, 1801, on the thirty-sixth ballot TJ was elected president. Cunningham, *Jeffersonian Republicans*, 239, 244. Since JA's appointments were not made until the beginning of March, AA's chronology is in error; therefore her defense of JA fails in part.

6. Benjamin Stoddert, secretary of the navy, 1798–1801; Samuel Dexter, secretary of war, 1800, secretary of the treasury, 1801–2.

7. James Thomson Callender, Scottish immigrant and pamphleteer, began his rabid attacks on the Federalist administration in 1797. After a stint in Philadelphia he moved to Virginia and wrote for the Richmond *Examiner*, a Republican paper. In 1800 Callender published *The Prospect before Us*, attacking the Federalist leaders. For his remarks about JA he was tried under the Sedition Law, fined $200, and sentenced to nine months' imprisonment by Justice Samuel Chase in June 1800. President Jefferson pardoned him in 1801 and remitted his fine. James Morton Smith, *Freedom's Fetters: The Alien and Sedition Laws and American Civil Liberties* (Ithaca, 1956), Chap. XV; Dumas Malone, "Callender, James Thomson," *DAB*, III, 425–26.

8. [See] Charles A. Jellison, "That Scoundrel Callender," *Va. Mag. of Hist. and Biog.*, 67 (1959), 295–306.

9. Callender soon turned against TJ, attacked the Republican administration with his vitriolic pen, and propagated scandal concerning TJ's private life. He died in 1803. *DAB*, III, 425–26.

10. Callender's pamphlet, criticizing the British government, had led to his indictment for sedition in Jan. 1793. He did not answer the court summons and so became a fugitive from justice and fled to the United States. *Ibid.*

11. *Porcupine's Gazette* was a Federalist newspaper published in Philadelphia, 1797–99, by William Cobbett.

12. Referring, no doubt, to the duel between Hamilton and Burr, fought on July 11, 1804, in which Hamilton was killed.

13. In his letter of Sept. 11, 1804, to AA, TJ provided a correct and satisfying answer to her complaint. See Bemis, *John Quincy Adams*, 112.

14. AA expressed the Federalist argument that freedom of speech and of the press could be defined only by the English common law, and that the First Amendment had not deprived Congress of the power to pass a sedition law. The Republicans argued that the First Amendment "not only rejected the English common law concept of libels against the government but also prohibited Congress from adding any restraint, either by previous restrictions, by subsequent punishment, or by an alteration of jurisdiction or mode of trial." Smith, *Freedom's Fetters*, 136, 140.

15. This note, in JA's hand, appears at the end of the letter-book copy in the Adams Papers.

4

CHANGING THE CONSTITUTION

The Constitution was not meant to be easy to change. Historically, it has been altered far more often by interpretation than by amendment. Summoning up the political energies to plow through the complex process of proposal and ratification has proved to be beyond the capacity of the great majority of reformers.

It was reasonable to think the Equal Rights Amendment would prove an exception to the rule. A simple, straightforward statement that "equality of rights under the law shall not be denied or abridged by the United States or by any state on account of sex," the ERA enjoyed massive initial support, both inside and outside government. The time seemed to have come to place the other half of the American people—the female half—under the explicit protections of our fundamental law. The courts would have to decide just what that change would mean, but at least they would have before them a plainspoken constitutional principle to refer to.

Why has the Equal Rights Amendment not passed into the Constitution? Does the failure of the most recent attempt reflect a sea change in public attitude away from support for women's rights? This chapter bears on the dual probability that ERA is likely to prove hard to pass and harder yet to dismiss from American politics.

The Equal Rights Amendment

BUILDING SUPPORT FOR THE EQUAL RIGHTS AMENDMENT

by Janet K. Boles

A case can be made that non-ratification of the Equal Rights Amendment (ERA) is a classic example of "snatching defeat from the jaws of victory." After all, the ERA had received overwhelming support in both houses of Congress, passing by a vote of 354 to 23 in the House and 84 to 8 in the Senate. Both major political parties had repeatedly supported the ERA in their national party platforms; not until 1980 did one party (the Republican) adopt a stance of neutrality. Every President from Truman to Carter had endorsed the amendment. And, by the end of the campaign for state ratification, more than 450 organizations with a total membership of over 50 million were on record in support of the ERA. While the amendment was before Congress in 1970–72, lobbying for the ERA was heavy and well-organized, and no countervailing forces were ever mobilized in any effective way. In view of this broad base of political and public support for the amendment, and little visible opposition, a reasonable prognosis in 1972 was that it would be ratified by the required 38 states long before the original deadline of March 22, 1979, set by Congress.

However, the ratification process was far more complex than either political observers or amendment supporters recognized initially. Although an intensive lobbying effort had been waged to push the amendment through Congress, supporters naively believed that it would be quickly ratified in the absence of pre-existing state groups poised to press for passage and without major allocation of national organizations' resources. The appearance of a politically formidable opposition movement forced supporters to recognize this miscalculation. Further, factors related to the constitutional amendment process, the symbolic issues raised by the ERA itself and the dynamics of policy making in America made the supporters' task even more difficult.

Group Coalitions for the ERA

In the early months of 1973, ERA supporters were admittedly caught by surprise by the emergence of effective ad hoc organizations in opposition. Proponent groups became aware of the need to develop a ratification strategy and to invest major financial and political resources in its implementation.[1]

One factor in the success of an interest group is the extent to which it forms ties and alliances with other groups. Nearly all governmental decision makers are hesitant to disregard the demands of a strong coalition of groups.[2] Cooperation among groups is believed to increase the power, access and tactical advantage of the groups, while decreasing the financial and political risks for each of the groups individually.

In the 10 years that the ERA was before the states, there was always a formal national coalition of proponent groups, ostensibly committed to coordinating the

---

From Janet K. Boles, "Building Support for the ERA: A Case of 'Too Much, Too Late,'" *PS* (Fall 1982), pp. 572–77.

campaign for ratification. The first, the ERA Ratification Council, was composed of approximately 30 groups. During its brief existence, 1972–1975, it had neither the staff and financial resources nor, some charged, the will to play a major role in national ratification efforts. Its successor, ERAmerica, opened an office in Washington, D.C., in January 1976. As originally conceived, it too was supposed to spearhead a nationwide campaign. Although ERAmerica sponsored several successful fund-raising events and engaged in ongoing direct mail appeals for money, it also lacked the resources to play the central role in ratification. Instead, it served primarily as a clearinghouse for information on the amendment, a coordinator of proponents' Washington press conferences and an occasional partner in events organized by other pro-ERA groups.

Despite these coalitions' limitations, their existence encouraged the formation of group alliances on the state level. In general, the experience in the states in organizing pro-ERA coalitions paralleled that on the national level. At the close of the 1973 legislative sessions, very few active state ERA coalitions existed. But by mid-1974, virtually all of the unratified states had developed impressive, formal pro-ERA coalitions containing up to 100 groups. Several had a permanent headquarters with full-time salaried staff and WATS lines. At the same time, by virtue of these coalitions' looseness, individual groups, like those on the national level, were free to use separate tactics in working for ratification.

Although allowing member groups to have different strategies and tactics can strengthen a coalition, in the case of the ERA this also was the source of internal conflicts. The strategies favored by activist women's rights groups, such as the National Organization for Women (NOW), differed from those of the League of Women Voters and the National Federation of Business and Professional Women's Clubs. A further barrier to coordination was that while the ERA was only one of several priority issues for these three very active member-groups, each wanted to be perceived as the leader in the push for ratification.

Shifts in Ratification Strategy

Phase I. There were three clearly demarcated phases in the campaign for state ratification. Phase I, which covered 1972–1977, was marked by a close adherence to the established techniques of legislative lobbying: presentation of research, testimony at hearings, contacts by constituents, letter and telegram campaigns, public education and election activities, such as contributing time or money to a pro-ERA candidate's campaign. The three most active proponent groups (NOW, the League and the National Federation of Business and Professional Women's Clubs) participated on a roughly equal basis during these years.

The state groups, however, engaged in full-scale lobbying only after the amendment encountered opposition in their particular state's legislature. Their strategies often were not fully implemented until after the legislature had failed to ratify in more than one session. In addition, many of the tactics used by proponents were ones often considered counterproductive because they violate the political "rules of the game" or are viewed as illegitimate. Although a majority of resources was devoted to more conventional methods of lobbying, tactics such as mass rallies and symbolic gifts of home-baked food also appeared during this period. Even so, in the use of the normal interest group tactics, proponents demonstrated superiority. And in elections in unratified states from 1974 [to] 1978, there was clear evidence of the power of women's groups to target and defeat legislators who opposed the amendment.

Yet after 1973, only five states ratified the ERA; the amendment ultimately fell three states short of ratification. Some legislators who had received campaign help from proponents on the basis of expressed support for the ERA were even voting against the amendment. "Doing *more* of the *same* things, but *better*" had proved to be an inadequate strategy.

Phase II. By January, 1977, 70 percent of Americans were living in ratified states. Attempts were made to encourage ERA supporters in these states to "adopt" one of the unratified states by providing financial and tactical assistance. However, few participated in that effort. Much more successful were two national campaigns begun that year by the National Organization for Women and which marked the ascendancy of NOW as the leading proponent of the ERA.

First, in an effort to achieve ratification before March 22, 1979, and to demonstrate political clout, NOW called for an economic boycott of unratified states. (By March, 1980, when the right of NOW to wage a boycott was upheld by the Eighth U.S. Circuit Court of Appeals, over 350 organizations had voted to hold their conventions only in ratified states.[3])

Second, NOW led the fight to ensure that the ERA would not be allowed to die if not ratified by three-fourths of the states by March of 1979. On October 20, 1977, as a hedge against failure to achieve ratification by the original deadline, Rep. Elizabeth Holtzman (D–N.Y.) introduced a resolution which would have extended the deadline for ratification to March 22, 1986. This precedent-setting strategy had first been suggested by two California law students, who were members of NOW. After an 18-month intensive lobbying campaign, including a rally which attracted over 100,000 people to Washington, D.C., Congress approved a 39-month extension (to June 30, 1982).

In 1979, NOW made explicit its shift in focus to a national campaign instead of one centered on the legislatures in unratified states. Eleanor Smeal, NOW President, explained: "A national campaign [is necessary] because this is an unratified country. We communicate as a nation, through national television, wire services, magazines and other media. Our political parties are nationally organized. Our states are economically interdependent. Our opposition is national."[4]

Phase III. Although NOW's strategy change had been announced much earlier, it was not until late 1980 that a genuine commitment was made to full implementation. The national conference of NOW, meeting in October, pledged a total mobilization for the ERA and agreed to increase the size, diversity and range of its ratification campaign.[5] One measure of NOW's success is the dramatic increase in the funds raised by its ERA Walkathons, held in August since 1977. The receipts progressively increased from $150,000 in 1977 to $200,000 in 1980. In 1981, the figure approached $1 million.[6] Speaking to the 1980 conference, Smeal declared, "We must have a peak performance so that on July 1, 1982, not one of us can say, 'if only we had done . . .' for we will know that we have done all things possible."[7]

During this final period, almost all conceivable tactics *were* utilized by groups supporting the ERA. Conventional lobbying techniques through state coalitions were not abandoned. Several national groups formed political action committees to raise money to elect pro-ERA candidates to state legislatures. The League of Women Voters in 1980 formed the National Business Council for ERA, composed of 155 corporate leaders who personally lobbied and spoke for the ERA in unratified states. Proponents provided new research on the anticipated impact of a federal ERA and that of the 16 state ERAs.

In addition, new strategies were devised: mass gatherings in all states which often brought together supporters from all over the country, campus tours to urge students to take a leave of absence to work for the ERA, door-to-door canvassing by NOW "ERA missionaries" in unratified states, and an increasing reliance on personal appearances by pro-ERA entertainers to capture media and public attention. The League, NOW and the National Federation of Business and Professional Women's Clubs each sponsored media projects. Though most ads ran primarily in unratified states, NOW aired a series of commercials on national television.

Beginning in 1980, nonviolent protest was increasingly used. Women chained themselves to a Mormon Temple in the state of Washington and to the Republican Party headquarters in Washington, D.C. A hunger strike by several women was begun in Illinois with less than two months remaining for ratification.

Finally, several tactics were borrowed from opponents of the amendment. Members of NOW's ERA Message Brigade sent thousands of postcards to legislators in the unratified states. Religious services and symbolism assumed greater prominence in the activities of ERA supporters. Attempts to make the Moral Majority and corporate greed scapegoats for the defeat of the ERA closely resembled the earlier very effective linkage of the term "the Women's Liberation Movement," widely considered to have negative connotations, with the ERA.

Why These Strategies Were Used and Failed

As the time for ratification expired, the National Women's Political Caucus released a roster of 12 state legislators who were either procedurally or politically blocking the decade-long drive for ratification.[8] If only a small number of legislators were preventing ratification, why was an expensive national media and mass mobilization campaign pursued rather than a narrowly focused state-by-state effort?

By 1977, the obstacles to ratification may have been insurmountable. The opposition movement had developed a strong organization, impressive funding and a sophisticated electoral strategy.[9] It is generally conceded that the side working for the adoption of any new policy is at a great disadvantage in American politics; the more controversial the issue and the higher the level of interest group conflict, the greater the likelihood that the status quo will be retained.[10] Also, ratification of a constitutional amendment is not easily achieved. Opponents needed only to maintain a one-vote plurality in one house of 13 state legislatures.

Furthermore, ERA supporters were championing their amendment during a period of conservative resurgence. Thus, coalition support from moderate and conservative groups was badly needed. Yet, the group that emerged as the leading proponent, NOW, was poorly situated—given its liberal to radical image—to form such alliances. Had they been formed, ratification still would not have been assured. The absence of strong state organizations to push for ratification in 1972 and 1973, before the opposition mobilized, may have been the key strategic error of the entire campaign. In forming such coalitions *after* the amendment had been redefined and distorted and *after* a pattern of defeat had been established, proponents were essentially fighting a rearguard action.

In retrospect, observers can criticize the strategies followed by ERA's supporters (particularly, NOW) after 1977. There is an extraordinarily weak linkage between a commercial run on national television during prime time and the vote of a Florida legislator. But if indeed the ERA was, in pragmatic terms, dead by 1977, the direction of the ERA campaign from then until 1982 was rational from an organizational perspective.

The issue of the ERA transformed the

National Organization for Women into a group with an impressive political capacity: 750 telephone banks, 300 full-time staff members, 6700 full-time volunteers and an ability to raise $1 million per month.[11] Since 1977, the organization's annual budget has gone from $700,000 to $8.5 million while its membership has gone from 55,000 to 210,000. Membership doubled between 1980 and 1982.[12]

The shift in NOW's ratification strategy in 1977 may reflect a transformation of organization goals. As an organization grows older, its officers often tend to place a greater emphasis on insuring its continued growth and survival and less emphasis on its purported goals.[13] Nor is it unusual for organizations to adopt new or modified goals when its original purposes are achieved, become irrelevant or, I would add, are thwarted.[14]

In the case of NOW, the phenomenon of "goal displacement" may have occurred, whereby the means-end relationship is reversed.[15] That is, the goal of the national campaign may have been organization-building and maintenance, *not* ERA ratification. And, as the most visible and widely acceptable single issue identified with feminism, the amendment may have become a means of goal attainment. However, it is not clear to what degree NOW's leaders were conscious that organization building had become their primary goal.

Although many supporters knew little about the potential impact of the amendment, the ERA continued to attract diverse and uniformly high levels of support during its ratification history.[16] Tactics such as the Message Brigade, missionary work and mass rallies could be successful and provide both solidarity and purposive rewards for participants. This was particularly true in the mid-70s when surveys indicated that feminist ideology was steadily diffusing through society. There was some speculation that the anti-feminist movement had actually consolidated support for the women's movement, which previously had been tentative and soft.[17]

In essence, the avenues for ERA ratification were largely shut off by the mid-70s. Although there were several hundred national groups that formally supported the amendment, few were actively involved in the drive for ratification. Even here, the ERA was only one of several priority issues for these groups. As chances for ratification became more remote, the National Organization for Women was able to capture the issue for its own purposes of building a strong network of political activists.

PUBLIC OPINION AND THE EQUAL RIGHTS AMENDMENT

by Mark R. Daniels, Robert Darcy, and Joseph W. Westphal

. . . During the years immediately following congressional approval of the ERA in 1972, the American public strongly favored the amendment (see Table 1). In 1974, three Americans favored the ERA for every one who opposed it. Support for the ERA continued at a ratio of about two to one throughout the early ratification years. Support was widespread among all demographic groups. In 1975–76, the Gallup Poll found that even within groups where opposition to the ERA was strongest a majority supported ratification. Specifically, persons with low incomes favored it 53 per-

From Mark R. Daniels, Robert Darcy, and Joseph W. Westphal, "The ERA Won—At Least in the Opinion Polls," *PS* (Fall 1982), pp. 578–84.

Table 1 Support and Opposition to the ERA by American Public

YEAR	FAVOR (%)	OPPOSE (%)	DON'T KNOW (%)	TOTAL %	TOTAL N
1974	73.6	21.1	5.2	100	(2822)
1975	58.3	23.7	18.0	100	(2762)
1976	56.7	24.5	18.8	100	(2798)
1977	65.5	26.5	8.0	100	(1000)
1978	58.0	31.0	11.0	100	(1010)
1980	52.3	28.3	19.4	100	(2780)
1981	55.5	28.1	16.4	100	(2740)
1982	61.5	23.4	15.1	100	(1506)

SOURCE: Gallup Polls: October 1974; March 1975; March 1976; July 1980; July 1981; Yankelovich Poll, March 1977; Gallup Opinion Index, July 16, 1978, p. 23; National Opinion Research Center General Social Survey, July 1982.

cent to 31 percent and those living in small towns supported it 54 percent to 29 percent.[18]

Only in 1980—eight years after the ERA was submitted to the states for ratification—did support dip down to its lowest level. This represented a second phase for the ERA—the 1980 presidential campaign—during which the amendment was transformed by candidate Ronald Reagan into a partisan issue and removed from the Republican platform. The withdrawing of support for the ERA by a popular political elite, in this case the leadership of the Republican Party, may have led many Americans to conclude that something was wrong with the ERA.[19] But even at its lowest level of support, the ERA continued to be favored by a majority of Americans. By 1982 the ERA had passed this partisan stage and once again enjoyed a two-to-one margin of support.

The pace of ERA ratification in its first calendar year, during which 22 states approved the ERA, was ahead of that achieved by 8 of the 11 amendments ratified in this century. At the end of the second year, the ERA's 30-state ratification total was still ahead of the pace of two successful amendments: the Twenty-second, which limited the tenure of presidents, and the Sixteenth, which permitted an income tax. By the end of the third year (1974), the ERA was still outpacing those two amendments. Even in its fourth year, the ERA had been ratified by 89 percent of the necessary states (34), whereas the Twenty-second Amendment had been only ratified by 66 percent after a comparable period of time. It was not until 1976, then, that the ERA appeared to be in serious trouble, having fallen behind the pace of all amendments which had succeeded.

What happened? The ERA had had momentum, prestigious support and little opposition; it was widely favored by all sectors of society. Why was it not ratified? Most explanations involve public opposition. The explanations examined here are: that it was killed by opposition from housewives and others committed to traditional roles; that it was killed by conservatives and religious fundamentalists; and that it was killed because popular opposition was centered in a minority of states, whose legislatures were able to block the ratification process.

Opposition of Housewives

Andrew Hacker argues that the ERA was originally viewed as an innocuous formal granting to women of rights previously guaranteed to religious minorities and blacks.[20]

Early in its course, the ERA lost its innocent status. In fact, this change occurred during the nine months after the amendment had left Congress and while it was winning quick approval from the necessary states. Stirred by their success, women who had worked for the ERA began to talk as if, quite literally, it signaled a new era. What began as a request for equal rights merged into the more militant cause of women's liberation. Guarantees purposely left vague in the wording of the amendment were now being discussed in concrete terms.[21]

The changes predicted by feminists aroused anxieties in housewives and other women committed to traditional roles. These women, according to Hacker, mobilized themselves to right the threat seemingly posed them by the ERA.

If the amendment's supporters erred, it was in ignoring the sensibilities of women not avid for careers or for whom that option appears to come too late. Women opposed the ERA because it jeopardized a way of life they had entered in good faith. And their legislators listened.[22]

But Hacker's argument has its weaknesses. While those lobbying legislators against ERA did their best to appear to be housewives, and may in fact have been housewives,[23] they were not representative of housewives and women committed to traditional roles. Surveys consistently found that more housewives favored the ERA than opposed it. . . . Only in 1980, when the ERA became a presidential campaign issue, did the proportion of housewives opposing the ERA come anywhere near the proportion supporting it. Thus, while the opposition to the ERA had been organized to appear to be a groundswell of housewives, only a minority of them actually opposed the amendment. David Brady and Kent Tedin,[24] Janet Boles,[25] and Kathleen Beatty[26] show that those who demonstrated against the ERA in Texas, Colorado and elsewhere were not typical housewives lacking previous political experience. Instead, they were members of the radical and religious Right characterized by previous political activism. Because opponents resembled housewives does not mean they *were* housewives nor does it mean they represented the views of most housewives.

Conservative and Religious Fundamentalist Opposition

The most vocal and visible opposition to the ERA came from conservative groups, such as the DAR, the John Birch Society, the American Independent Party and a number of *ad hoc* groups with conservative roots.[27] The identity of rank-and-file anti-ERA activists has been scrutinized by several political scientists. Kathleen Beatty in 1980 examined women who had petitioned to have ERA rescission included on the Colorado ballot in 1976.[28] She found ERA opponents typical of the radical and religious Right in their emphasis on salvation, their anti-egalitarian stance on the roles of men and women and strong religious connections. Brady and Tedin investigated women who lobbied the Texas legislature for rescission of ERA ratification in 1975.[29] Their findings, too, were that these women had beliefs and affiliations typical of the radical and religious Right, including fear of domestic communism and socialism and the feeling that the federal government was taking away individuals' freedom. Further, they found that "fundamentalist religion was a principal source of the political attitudes of the anti-ERA women. Their political beliefs may be viewed as extensions of their religious beliefs."[30] Further, these women were by no means political novices or alienated politically. "These women are participators: they vote, talk politics, give money and wear campaign buttons . . . their trip to Austin is only one facet of their overall high participation."[31]

Thus, the second explanation for the failure of the ERA can be constructed. Conservatives and fundamentalists opposed the Equal Rights Amendment. This opposition was effective in conservative states and not effective elsewhere. Even though most states supported the ERA, there were enough conservative states to prevent ratification.

This argument appears plausible at first since unratified states such as Utah, Georgia, Mississippi and Alabama are known to have strong conservative orientations. Conservative and fundamentalist groups and organizations have credibility and influence in these states that they may not have elsewhere.[32]

Yet, this argument also has its weaknesses. In the crucial ratification years of 1976 and 1977, when the ERA was losing momentum, a majority of conservatives favored the ERA. . . . Further, the approval margin was about two to one. Again, it was only in 1980, during the ERA's 1980 election phase, that slightly more conservatives opposed the ERA than supported it. This was likely a response to Republican candidate Reagan making the issue salient to conservatives. By 1981, however, a majority of conservatives sampled were once again favoring the ERA. Thus, while the ERA's opposition did come from conservatives, it was supported by a majority of conservatives during most of the ratification process.

Religious fundamentalists, too, have generally supported the ERA[33] . . . . In 1976, religious fundamentalists favored the amendment by more than three to one. Even though this support had dropped considerably by 1980, a plurality of religious fundamentalists continued to favor the amendment. While many anti-ERA activists were religious fundamentalists, most religious fundamentalists did not oppose the ERA.

The Unratified States

The constitutional ratification process guarantees that the opinion of a minority of the states be respected. It is possible that what opposition there was to the ERA may have primarily been confined to a few states, which were able to block the ERA. However, in 1974, public opinion in the unratified states favored the ERA three to one[34]. . . . By 1980, when there were fewer unratified states and the ERA became a presidential campaign issue, this margin had declined. Nevertheless, public opinion in the unratified states still favored the amendment.[35] Despite a gradual drop in the ERA's margin of support it was consistently supported by at least a plurality of people living in unratified states.

While it is true that the unratified states tend to be significantly more conservative both religiously and politically,[36] that does not mean the people of those states oppose the ERA. Boles cites polls taken in the unratified states of Missouri (1973), Mississippi (1974) and Illinois (1974) that all found large pro-ERA majorities.[37] Deborah Bokowski cites polls taken in the unratified states of Missouri (1975, 1976 and 1979) and Virginia (1978) which also uncovered large pro-ERA majorities.[38] Strong support existed for the ERA before the 1980 election in a number of unratified states.

On the other hand, ERA support was not necessarily uniform among the unratified states, nor was opinion necessarily stable over time. In polls taken in Oklahoma from 1978 to 1982, neither ERA's supporters nor its opponents were generally able to master a majority. And while the opponents were somewhat stronger over time, both sides had a plurality on more than one occasion. It was only *after* the final ratification failure in 1982 that a significant majority of Oklahomans opposed the amendment.

Conclusion

In the first years the ERA was before the states, it was supported by a large majority nationwide, a large majority of the people in the unratified states, a large majority of housewives, a large majority of conservatives and a large majority of religious fundamentalists. It was only after the amendment had been before the states six or eight years that opposition to the ERA within several of these groups began to approach the level of ERA support within them. After being used as an issue in the 1980 presidential campaign, the ERA regained much of its previous strength. Its national majority assumed its pre-1980 proportions. And its supporters included at least a plurality of people living in unratified states, housewives, conservatives and fundamentalists. Thus, the failure of the ERA cannot be attributed to public opposition. Instead, the amendment's failure must be attributed to systemic factors in the political processes of non-ratifying states which thwarted ratification[39] and produced legislator indifference to popular sentiment.[40]

NOTES

1. For a more extensive discussion of proponent strategies from 1972 to 1977 see Janet K. Boles, *The Politics of the Equal Rights Amendment* (New York: Longman, 1979).

2. See Lester Milbrath, *The Washington Lobbyists* (Chicago: Rand McNally, 1963), and Donald R. Hall, *Cooperative Lobbying—The Power of Pressure* (Tucson: University of Arizona Press, 1969).

3. "Organizations Supporting the Equal Rights Amendment," *National NOW Times*, 13 May 1980, 14–15.

4. "NOW National ERA Campaign Launched," *National NOW Times*, 11 February 1979, 1.

5. "Total ERA Mobilization Voted," *National NOW Times*, October/November 1980, 1.

6. Judy Goldsmith, "ERA Walks Raise $1 Million," *National NOW Times*, 14 September 1981, 1.

7. "Total ERA Mobilization Voted."

8. Demetra Lambros, "Caucus Indicts Twelve Who Roadblocked ERA," *Women's Political Times*, 7 July 1982, 1.

9. There is some evidence, for example, that anti-ERA groups were more effective in the use of campaign contributions. See Judson H. Jones, "The Effect of Pro- and Anti-ERA Campaign Contributions on the ERA Voting Behavior of the 80th Illinois House of Representatives," *Women & Politics* 2 (Spring/Summer 1982): 71–86.

10. See James S. Coleman, *Community Conflict* (New York: Free Press, 1957), and Robert L. Crain et al., *The Politics of Community Conflict* (Indianapolis: Bobbs-Merrill, 1969).

11. Paul Taylor, "NOW Seeking $3 Million War Chest to Oust ERA Foes, Fight New Right," *Washington Post*, 27 August 1982, A2.

12. Barbara Salsini, "Wisconsin Fan Seeks Top NOW Post," *Milwaukee Journal*, 2 September 1982, 8.

13. See Anthony Downs, *Inside Bureaucracy* (Boston: Little, Brown, 1967), 19.

14. Peter Blau refers to this as "succession of goals." See Blau, *The Dynamics of Bureaucracy* (Chicago: University of Chicago Press, 1955), 193–198.

15. See James G. March and Herbert Simon, *Organizations* (New York: John Wiley, 1958), 38.

16. See Debrah Bokowski and Aage R. Clausen, "Federalism, Representation and the Amendment Process: The Case of the Equal Rights Amendment" (Paper delivered at Annual Meeting of the Midwest Political Science Association, Chicago, 1979). Using University of Michigan Survey Research Center data, they found that despite an approval rating of 70 percent for the ERA, only 21 percent of the national sample had a position on the issue and knew the action taken on it by their own state legislature.

17. Keith T. Poole and L. Harmon Zeigler, "The Diffusion of Feminist Ideology," *Political Behavior* 3 (3 1981): 229–256.

18. *Gallup Opinion Index No. 128* (March 1976): 18.

19. *Politics of the ERA*, 17.

20. Andrew Hacker, "ERA–RIP," *Harper's Monthly*, September 1980, 10.

21. Ibid, [pp. 10–11].

22. Ibid, [p. 14].

23. Theodore S. Arrington and Patricia A. Kyle, "Equal Rights Amendment Activists in North Carolina" (Paper delivered at the Annual Meeting of the American Political Science Association, San Francisco, 1975).

24. David W. Brady and Kent L. Tedin, "Ladies in Pink: Religion and Political Ideology in the Anti-ERA Movement," *Social Science Quarterly* 56 (March 1976): 564–575.

25. Boles, *Politics of the ERA*.

26. Kathleen Beatty, "Values, Religion and Sex-Based Issue Positioning" (Paper delivered at the Annual Meeting of the Western Social Science Association, San Diego, 1981).

27. Boles, *Politics of the ERA*, 79.

28. Beatty, "Values."

29. Brady and Tedin, "Ladies in Pink."

30. Ibid., 574.

31. Ibid., 572.

32. Boles, *Politics of the ERA*, 136.

33. "Fundamentalists" are defined as Baptists and a number of other categories of Protestants. For an operational definition, see the University of Michigan Survey Research Center's *Election Study* for 1976 or 1980.

34. For a discussion of the disaggregation of national survey, see Charles Prysby, "A Note on Regional Subsamples from National Surveys," *Public Opinion Quarterly* 46 (Fall 1982): 422–424.

35. The University of Michigan Survey Research Center found in 1980 that public opinion in Illinois was evenly divided on the ERA and, thus, was not skewing the results for unratified states toward support of the amendment.

36. Ernest Wohlenberg, "Correlates of the Equal Rights Amendment Ratification," *Social Science Quarterly* 60 (March 1980): 676–684.

37. Boles, *Politics of the ERA*, 101–102.

38. Debrah Bokowski, "State Legislator Perceptions of Public Debate on the ERA" (Paper delivered at the Annual Meeting of the Political Science Association, Denver, 1982).

39. See Mark R. Daniels, Robert Darcy and Joseph Westphal, "State Innovativeness and the ERA: A Case of Arrested Diffusion" (Paper delivered at the Annual Meeting of the Midwest Political Science Association, Milwaukee, 1982), and Janet K. Boles, "Systemic Factors Underlying Legislative Responses to Woman Suffrage and the Equal Rights Amendment," *Women & Politics* 2 (Spring/Summer 1982): 5–22.

40. Bokowski, "State Legislator Perceptions."

5

THE FEDERAL SYSTEM AND THE STATES

American constitutional federalism split up legal powers as no other system had managed to do. But if power is at the root of our federalism, money is its branch. Each state has its own tax system. Some of them are very peculiar. More important, today states depend significantly on Washington for large chunks of revenue, which arrive with numerous strings attached. For every governor, the struggle with money—how to get it, how to spend it, how to save some for the next generation—is a top-priority political problem.

In Connecticut, "the Constitution State," the 1970's brought financial crisis. Connecticut had no state income tax. Republican governor Thomas Meskill, as well as Democratic governor John Dempsey, struggled to meet demands for government spending without crossing the line to an income tax. In 1974 a new governor, Ella Grasso, confronted the same crisis. The child of Italian immigrants, Grasso had been brought along politically by John Bailey, the classic party boss of the state, who helped her achieve election as Connecticut secretary of state and then gain two terms in the U.S. House of Representatives. Her election to the governorship constituted a victory for the ailing Bailey, but especially for Ella Grasso, the first woman in America to become governor of a state on her own, without succeeding her husband. Despite those who chided her as "Governess" Grasso, she set out to make a responsible record. But almost at once, the harsh realities of state finances hit her in the eye.

Governor Ella Grasso of Connecticut

by Susan Bysiewicz

The headlines from her huge victory ended quickly. At a private meeting held the day after the election, the governor told the governor-elect that his administration would be leaving a seventy million dollar debt. Ella found the news particularly

---

From Susan Bysiewicz, *Ella: A Biography* (Old Saybrook, Conn.: Peregrine Press, 1984), pp. 81–94.

shocking because in the past months Meskill had been promising he would end his term with a balanced budget. It appeared that the Republican governor, who himself had inherited Dempsey's two hundred and forty-four million dollar deficit, was returning the favor to the Democrats. Soon after Meskill's announcement, a cursory investigation revealed several months of unpaid medical bills in the welfare department as well as other unaccounted expenses which brought the projected deficit to more than two hundred million dollars.

At the meeting with Meskill the day after her election, Ella Grasso saw her political world begin to tumble down around her. Without abundant financial resources she could not provide the new social services she had promised. She could not amass political capital by wooing interest groups because she would have to spend more time and resources on the less popular task of balancing the budget. And she would face inevitable challenges to her reputation as a "caring" and "compassionate" advocate for the disadvantaged—a reputation upon which her previous political and electoral success had been built. Unremedied, the crisis threatened her immense personal popularity.

Though the severe revenue shortfall would soon change not only her program and strategy, but also her style and image, Ella Grasso responded in the interim period with her traditional tactics. Her immediate, and by now almost instinctive reaction to the news of the deficit came in the form of her characteristic displays of frugality. Lacking the power to do much in the way of substantial policy, the governor-elect took several symbolic steps to diminish the state's debt. She told the press that she would not order new stationery for the governor's office until all of Meskill's supply had been used and announced her intention to cross out his name and add her own. After the release, a Hartford printer who felt that even given the hard times Mrs. Grasso was taking things too far, personally donated new gubernatorial letterhead. Still, the public applauded her effort. Later that month, Ella announced that she would forego the use of the luxurious gubernatorial limousine and use her 1971 economy car or a state police cruiser instead.

On the more substantive side of the financial crisis, Ella coped with the situation in the interim period by calling into service a friend and colleague from her days in the Bailey braintrust, George Conkling. She asked Conkling, a former finance and transportation commissioner under Dempsey and then in semi-retirement, to represent her at conferences on the budget with the Meskill administration. Ella put him to work planning a program to remedy the state's financial ills.

Despite his rapidly failing health, John Bailey participated actively in the formation of the Grasso government after the election. Ella visited him at his home or in the hospital almost every day because she needed and wanted his advice on the hundreds of appointments she was called upon to make. There were even rumors manufactured by the press that Bailey left the hospital one day to hand out patronage at the Capitol. During the weeks before her inauguration, the governor-elect and the ailing party leader naturally focused their efforts on the selection of a finance commissioner because of the public concern over the state's fiscal condition. Mrs. Grasso sent the strongest candidates to Hartford Hospital to be interviewed by Mr. Bailey. When Jay Tepper answered "Yes" to the question of whether he could manage the state's finances without an income tax, Grasso and Bailey took the former Ohio finance commissioner on board the Connecticut ship.

Both Bailey and Grasso had been impressed with Tepper's credentials; he had studied economics and had a degree from the Wharton School of Finance. Like Tepper, the other people Ella chose as her close advisors were also young, bright, highly educated and devoted to her. The small circle of aides she brought together resembled the braintrust Bailey formed during his heyday at the Capitol. And almost all of Ella's "palace guard" had been well schooled in Bailey politics.

Nancy Lewinsohn, whom Ella chose as her executive aide, had gone to work as a special assistant for Senator Abe Ribicoff after earning a bachelor's degree from Smith and a master's and a doctorate degree from Harvard. She then had run Ella's congressional office for four years and had helped Bailey direct her second congressional and gubernatorial campaigns. Over the years, Ella had come to value Nancy's abilities and to trust her judgment. Lewinsohn would be the "undisputed boss of the staff" and Ella would rely on her heavily in all policy and personal matters.

Second in command would [be] Aaron Ment, the governor's legal counsel and legislative liaison. Ment, who was forty-one and a graduate of the University of Connecticut and of Boston University Law School, spent six years as an alderman in the big-city Democratic machine in Bridgeport. Since 1967, Ment acted as counsel to a succession of Party speakers and minority leaders in the General Assembly. During his years at the Legislature, he became friends with and gave legal advice to John Bailey.

Ella also signed on Jeff Daniels, a young and experienced journalist, to serve as a special assistant for policy and programs. Daniels would work on broad issue areas such as energy and utility regulation. As a reporter for the *Hartford Times* and several other newspapers, as well as a press aide in Grasso's campaign, Daniels had come to understand the dynamics of Bailey politics. Other key staff members Ella selected were Press Secretary Larrye deBear, a longtime Connecticut journalist and political analyst; Executive aide John Dempsey, Jr., son of the former governor, who had worked in her Congressional office and on her campaigns; and administrative assistant Charles McCollam, who was a Bailey-trained expert in local politics. With her braintrust assembled and major staff appointments considered, Ella was ready to take command.

Early on the morning of January 8, 1975, Ella Grasso, the governor-elect, went to worship with "her people" at St. Mary's Church in Windsor Locks. Friends, neighbors, and well-wishers joined Father Bollea to celebrate Ella's inauguration which would be held in Hartford later that day. One observer noted that the gathering at the Church looked like the crowded "Sunday-at-eight" service. After the mass ended, Ella met more townspeople at a reception held in her honor at the familiar Knights of Columbus Hall. She greeted by name nearly all of the three hundred who had gathered there. For the occasion, Ella wore a blue satin dress made for her by Bice Clemow, a male newspaper editor from West Hartford. Clemow, afraid that Ella would wear something unfashionable for the historic event, insisted on making her inauguration outfit. Ella radiated in the frock despite its rather unflattering color and uneven hemline. When the breakfast was over, Ella led her family and the entourage of press and security people to the town train station where they would catch the 9:50 A.M. train for Hartford. Her widely publicized ride was intended to dramatize the need for a consolidated and improved public transit system.

On the way to the station, Ella chatted in Italian and cautioned reporters not to walk in the streets. As the large group passed by the Doughnut Kettle, a "working-man's diner" in front of the water locks, she waved at the many patrons cheering: "Ella! Ella! Windsor Locks! Windsor Locks!" As they boarded the cars, Ella joked that years ago the conductor never waited for her when she had to catch the morning train to Chaffee. The crowd waved and cheered again. She was still holding a single red rose given to her at the mass earlier in the day. In the midst of this scene with Ella, the homely child of immigrant parents clad in homemade clothes and leaving for the big city, the myth created by the media appeared to mesh with reality for a warm moment.

Mrs. Grasso's virtuoso performance prior to her inaugural speech suggested that of an ethnic machine-style politician, but her address reflected that of a tough-minded fiscal manager. Though she did not appear to wholly abandon the political style she had developed in the Bailey years, the tone of her inaugural did not coincide with previous speeches given in the Party's big-spending heyday. She omitted the rhetoric which one journalist called "Kennedyish" and replaced it with the straight talk Hugh Carey had adopted in response to his state's failing finances. In her first words as governor, Ella recalled the beginning of her political career and spoke fondly of Windsor Locks. She indulged in this recollection only briefly, turning immediately and abruptly to Connecticut's unfavorable economic position:

> The situation is serious. The long-range prospects are not encouraging. Our course is clear.

With this introduction, she stated her goal of "efficient, compassionate, and humane" government and outlined her plan to overcome the projected two hundred million dollar deficit.

"Efficiency" meant restructuring. As chief executive, Ella, the ardent advocate of government reorganization, finally had not only compelling reason but also authority to initiate such a program. The Mount Holyoke economics scholar promised that under her administration every agency would be evaluated to ensure that every tax dollar met the "test of maximum effective use." Two departments—public works and welfare—she noted needed major overhauling. In order to maximize her ability to solve fiscal problems and to revitalize the state's economy, Mrs. Grasso announced her intention to bring the state's Council of Economic Advisors closer to the governor's office.

More importantly, efficiency meant major cuts in capital investment and in social programs. The "belt-tightening" she referred to would occur in the human service areas she had lobbied so strenuously for in her many years at the Capitol.

The governor struck an uncomfortable balance between the "efficient" and the "compassionate" and "humane." In her half-hour address, she did not mention the plight of the cities. The revenue-sharing which she had promised to earmark for urban aid would obviously now be used to pay the state's creditors. In the area of transportation, she spoke only of "consolidation" and "unification" rather than of expansion and development. And on the subject of education, her comments were vague—she pledged to "work to develop the means to better our children's world." Ella, the "compassionate" candidate that "cared," had little to say on behalf of the disadvantaged. Though she promised she would not forget the elderly, the handicapped, the ill and the veterans, she could offer almost nothing in the way of programs. To complete her seemingly sweeping dismissal of the groups that had strongly supported her, she did not even mention her vision for women or minorities.

Lack of money to expand and initiate social programs forced Ella to make reform the centerpiece of her first-year plan. She reiterated her commitment to open government. "Right-to-know" laws would be rewritten and strengthened. She announced that she would require all of her top level appointees to disclose their income and assets and asked all of her other state officers and Assembly members to do the same. She promised that public hearings would be held before serious budgetary and tax decisions were made. The governor called for changes in the state's leasing, bonding, and judicial selection practices, all of which had come under increasing scrutiny during Meskill's administration. Although Ella did not promise to refund utility consumers for overcharges, she did voice her support for the creation of a Public Utilities Control Authority to replace the ineffective Public Utilities Commission.

Even though Ella did not propose many new programs and ignored large segments in her constituency, she received hearty applause, more than twenty-seven times during her short speech. Indeed, many of her colleagues who had joined the new governor in the Hall of the House that day not only believed in her strategies to balance the budget, but also shared her moderate position on a number of substantive issues. This was most obviously reflected in the single standing ovation she got when she vowed that she would bring the state's finances in the black without "recourse to a personal income tax." The Party's commitment to maintaining the status quo was further evidenced in one of the votes taken later in the day immediately after the inaugural address. The large Democratic majority easily defeated a measure which would have made the process of judicial selection more open and less influenced by partisan considerations. It would have ended secret votes on confirmation of judges.

Ella was not the only Democrat to triumph in a virtuoso performance that day. While she led a parade of people in a march to the inaugural ceremonies from Hartford's Union Station, Mr. Bailey prepared to emerge from his hospital room for the day's festivities. The dying Democratic Chairman could not be kept away from the celebration of the sixth and last gubernatorial victory of his career. Wan and pale, but happy, the Boss gallantly presided at the Party's events. One political writer called his presence "bittersweet"—the Democratic family was briefly re-united, yet they knew it would not be long before they would lose their father. Their mother expressed her appreciation to the press: "I'm honored and proud that my good friend and political mentor was able to share this day with me."

Just ten days after the huge Democratic majority in the House voted to defeat a measure to open up the judicial process, the Party appeared to break another of its major campaign platform promises. Ella announced at a meeting of the state's mayors that she would no longer be able to make good on her pledge to increase the amount of federal revenue sharing funds given to cities from six million dollars to twenty-five million dollars for property tax relief. She even went so far as to suggest that "harsh realities" might prevent her from sending the six million dollars in earmarked funds to the municipalities. Some of the mayors offered to help sell an increase in the already burdensome sales tax to diminish the deficit. Ella, however, refused, not because she opposed the regressiveness of the tax, but because she felt she could not afford to do so politically. Her withdrawal of her commitment to urban aid fanned the flames of criticism from the party's liberal wing led by Nick Carbone and from her Republican opponents.

Ella Grasso did intend to make good on her promise to put the state on sound fiscal footing without resorting to a personal income tax. The governor's commissioners, journalists speculated, reflected Ella's strong desire to avoid the tax. Her small staff comprised of young, bright, energetic individuals contrasted sharply with her agency directors who were comparatively older and less creative. Her critics argued that she deliberately chose "mediocre" bureaucrats as department heads rather than "bright activists" who would spend their time creating new and costly programs she did not have the resources to implement.

The budget she submitted in February also made clear her commitment to avoid a progressive income tax. In it she proposed a long list of new taxes and increases in existing taxes. These hefty increases which totaled over two hundred million dollars in projected revenues included a request to raise the state's regressive sales tax by one percent to the burdensome level of seven percent. As she had previously announced, the governor did not earmark federal revenue sharing funds for the municipalities. Her budget address further horrified public and special interest groups with her proposals for major cuts in some human services and for maintenance of last year's funding in others. State workers, too, were shocked by her suggestion that automatic pay increases for civil service employees be eliminated.

True to her promise of open government, Ella held a series of public hearings after she submitted her first budget. Many "underfunded" and "overheated" individuals took full advantage of the opportunity to berate the governor for her broken campaign promises and for her lack of compassion. Those in education and advocates for the handicapped and the mentally retarded lamented the loss of a leader who had been their conduit to the General Assembly during the Ribicoff and Dempsey administrations. State workers also reacted angrily when they learned that their paychecks would be leaner, not fatter, as she had promised during her campaign.

Others pointed out her hypocrisy on the subject of the state income tax. At an energy conference she attended earlier that year, Ella argued that the burden of President Ford's proposed tax on imported oil would fall most heavily on those least able to pay. Ten days later, she promised she would make the burden of her new taxes as "easy as possible" and pledged to spread the levies as "broadly and equitably" as possible. Yet the increased sales tax which would go into effect in April certainly did not spread the burden broadly or equitably; the poor would still bear the brunt of this regressive tax.

Ella faced the intense public criticism alone. Her mentor and closest advisor lay deathly ill in the hospital. Though she continued to consult with Bailey on major appointments, the governor could not and would not involve him in the day-to-day operation of the state. On April 10, four days after she had sent two candidates for state police commissioner to be interviewed by the Chairman, Governor Grasso announced Bailey's death at a crowded press conference. While John Dempsey, Bob Killian, Gloria Schaffer, and other Democrats struggled to keep back the tears and steady their voices, only Ella remained composed. At that moment, the press and the politicians looked to the Party's matriarch. Ella took sole command. Staring straight ahead, with dry eyes, and in a strong voice, she delivered the first eulogy.

The protest to the governor's program did not subside—opposition to Ella's new tax schedule and spending plan culminated almost a month after Bailey's death. On May 7, several hundred state workers, educators, and people in anti-poverty programs descended on the Capitol to voice their protest. They stationed themselves outside the Hall of the House shouting: "Defeat the budget! Defeat the budget!" completely drowning out the floor debate. Welfare lobbyists surrounded the entrance to the governor's office chanting: "We want Ella! Where's Ella?" The ugly scene reminded many of a day a few years before when welfare mothers stormed up to the steps of the Capitol demanding to know where "Tough Tommy" was hiding.

During the tumultuous legislative session, no one missed John Bailey more than Ella Grasso. Not only did she face increasingly unhappy constituencies but she also confronted an undisciplined General Assembly. Even though the Democrats outnumbered the Republicans by 118 to 33 in the House and 29 to 2 in the Senate, the governor's captains in the Legislature could not easily put together a majority to pass her budget. The legislators, many of whom had been elected to their first term in the wave of opposition to Watergate, were leery of Party orders and were unwilling to slash programs that served their constituents. The freshmen lawmakers' refusals to follow Party orders angered Ella, a product of the school of strict Democratic discipline. Her response to their lack of cooperation was a studied aloofness. After much huffing and puffing, however, the Legislators adopted a tax and spending plan close to the one the governor had brought before them a few months before.

The end of the legislative session did not end Ella's troubles. A devout Catholic who opposed abortion on what she said were moral not religious grounds, Ella enraged feminists by endorsing the Social Services Department's decision not to pay for welfare recipients' abortions. Feminists, many of whom had criticized the governor for naming only two women to head major state departments, protested her position. Ella's friend and colleague from her days in Congress, Bella Abzug, chided Ella for her "outrageous" stand on the issue, chastising the governor for "imposing her own beliefs on the public."

Weary of the constant public criticism and from the long hours she had worked in the first nine months of her term, Ella decided to take a vacation with her husband at the end of September. Convinced by close friends and family to travel to Italy, the couple planned to visit the towns in the northern part of the country where their parents had been born. After little more than a week, Ella Grasso cut the trip short because she learned from Nancy Lewinsohn, her chief aide, that heavy rainstorms threatened to cause severe flooding. Anxious to avoid Meskill's fatal mistake of being away from Connecticut during a crisis, Ella rushed home to survey the damage in the state. Though severe flooding never occurred, Mrs. Grasso made it clear to people in the state that their governor was at the Capitol ready to take strong action if necessary. She would not be enjoying a pleasant holiday while her people braved hardships.

Talk of the 1976 Democratic presidential primaries that fall also helped to improve the governor's image. Rule changes for the selection of state delegates to the national convention ordered by the Democratic National Committee led to frequent mention of the potential presidential candidacy of Mrs. Grasso. New procedures for delegate selection called for a primary in all 169 towns. Any candidate that received at least fifteen percent of the Democratic votes would be entitled to national delegates. The Democratic Party organization, which could no longer choose its state delegates at a convention, did get some leeway in that they were granted a category of "uncommitted" delegates. That meant the party organization's leaders could support an uncommitted slate of delegates against the well-known presidential aspirants. Given this wide-open system based on proportional representation and the fact that many in the Connecticut organization were not ready to support any of the already announced candidates—Mo Udall, Scoop Jackson, and Jimmy Carter—the possibility of getting Mrs. Grasso into the political contest began to be widely discussed.

Her candidacy would offer many benefits to the state Party. It would rally the organization behind a single candidate, "a woman who could become the first serious contender for a presidential nomination." It would focus national attention on Connecticut during the peak of state presidential primaries. It would also give the state leaders increased bargaining power and authority at the national convention.

Outside Connecticut, Ella received some support for the 1976 race. Late in September, a committee of New York Democrats announced their efforts to draft her for the vice presidential nomination. The group led by Arthur J. Paone, "an average Brooklyn Democrat," hoped to enter a slate of delegates committed to Mrs. Grasso in several New York Congressional districts.

Though frequently mentioned as a "favorite daughter" during that fall, Ella remained publicly removed, as was her custom, from the presidential scurry in the state. She did not permit her name to be put forward in Connecticut as a candidate for the vice presidential or presidential nomination. Although aware of her national stature as the only female governor, Mrs. Grasso knew she would have difficulty drawing a substantial following in her home state especially after the passage of her first budget which had alienated large segments of her strong supporters. She appeared to be having difficulty in distinguishing her austerity administration from that of her predecessor, Thomas Meskill. As one journalist noted, she had introduced little progressive legislation to prove her "presidential timber." The governor, plagued by fiscal problems, apparently did not want to risk a statewide test of her popularity by entering the primary race.

The state's financial situation did not promise her greater popularity. Fiscal year 1975 ended with a deficit of over seventy million dollars. Ella's advisors predicted that even with the additional taxes adopted by the General Assembly that year, the state would be approximately eighty million dollars in debt by the close of fiscal 1976. Bent on balancing the books, the governor called the Legislature into special session in an attempt to put Connecticut in the black.

The revenue raising plan Governor Grasso put before the General Assembly in December probably represented one of the worst political mistakes of her quarter century career. Her program attacked two of the most powerful and organized groups in the state—civil servants and veterans. It included a proposal to increase the work week for state employees from thirty-five to forty hours per week without a pay increase and a provision to transfer thirty million dollars from the Soldiers, Sailors, and Marines fund to augment the General Fund. Both of these points in her budget-balancing plan created an uproar among constituents and created a stalemate in the General Assembly. State legislators, stymied by the strong veterans' and state employees' lobbies, adjourned without action on the governor's program. The lawmakers' refusal to pass the gubernatorial program or to come up with an alternative solution to the budget crisis caused Mrs. Grasso's popularity to plunge further. Forced to follow through with her threat to temporarily lay off state workers, she fired five hundred employees a few days before Christmas. This edict enraged state employees and their families, angered labor groups and provoked heavy criticism in the press.

Ella's proposals and the alternatives she finally chose at the end of the session stood in clear opposition to Bailey politics for they easily alienated two large segments of the electorate. Bailey probably would have advised his pupil to bet on the deficit being reduced by other measures, while keeping her good standing with the civil service employees.

Mrs. Grasso's action relating to the special session did not reflect a wholesale abandonment of the Chairman's principles. Rather, it merely reflected an instance, like the fight for the peace plank at the 1968 convention, when she felt she could risk her political property to gain greater political capital. She no doubt believed that the image of the lazy state worker and the general desire for austerity would rally the public behind her proposal to increase the work week. Yet unlike her brash demand for an end to the Vietnam war, her call for balancing the budget on the backs of veterans and state employees liquidated large amounts of the political capital she had worked hard to accumulate.

By the end of her first year in office, Governor Grasso had gathered some new political property. The state's unsound fiscal footing had not hampered reform because reform did not cost much money. She moved to restore confidence in government with her landmark freedom of information legislation which she had long championed. It won unanimous support in both houses. New Public Utilities Control Authority legislation, though not as strong as she had promised, would provide an independent consumer council with a full-time commissioner who had expertise to guard against automatic fuel adjustment charges. She could demonstrate her commitment to bettering the condition of elderly citizens by pointing to the creation of the new professional Department on Aging. These victories, however, did not balance favorably with the losses.

By the end of her first year in office, Governor Grasso had fulfilled few of her campaign promises; the rest were clearly broken or remained unaddressed. She had not provided corporate tax incentives which would improve employment prospects in the state. She had not provided aid to transportation and her commitment to education had fallen by the wayside in the wake of the budget crisis. Most of these losses, indeed, could be attributed to Connecticut's bare cupboard. She could not build programs on a financially unsound foundation.

Still, the people of the state remained disturbed and disappointed that Ella Grasso had gone back on her commitment to provide efficient, compassionate and humane government. Laying off hundreds of workers did not save a significant amount—someone forgot to remember that worker's compensation would necessarily be doled out to those fired from their jobs. Firing five hundred workers saved the state only about five hundred thousand dollars. This drastic measure hardly seemed "efficient." Firing five hundred workers before Christmas was not "compassionate" either. Eliminating paying for abortions for women on welfare was not "humane."

Ella's popularity plunged not merely because she did not make good on her campaign promises as a consequence of the state's fiscal condition. It also plunged because labor, women, and minorities began to realize that their champion was not as "liberal" as they had believed her to be. As governor of a troubled state, she could no longer conceal her stands on issues as she had been able to do in Congress, nor could she rally only behind popular causes as she had the opportunity to do as Secretary of State. As governor in a state with a large debt, she had to make hard decisions and demand unpopular solutions—solutions which sometimes alienated her strongest supporters. As chief executive in Connecticut, she could no longer concentrate all her energies on amassing political capital. She struggled to maintain the property she had once earlier held so easily.

6

THE FEDERAL SYSTEM AND CITY GOVERNMENTS

By all rights, big cities should have been the last refuge for the old-fashioned cigar-chomping, backslapping, deal-making male who was a professional politician. Certainly Chicago, poet Carl Sandburg's "hog butcher of the world" and long the domain of Richard Daley, the last of the big-time bosses, could be counted on as a man's town to the end. Until, that is, a woman named Jane Byrne took over. Mayor Byrne hit that fast track running. But nearly a year into her mayorship, when the following assessment appeared, Byrne's stumbles were famous and her hopes had not yet materialized.

Mayor Byrne was but one of a surprising, and quite varied, squad of new, female big-city mayors. In Houston, of all places, Mayor Kathy Whitmire shaped up the ways in which the city managed money, jobs, and space. In San Francisco, Mayor Dianne Feinstein adroitly held together the city's diverse factions and transformed a $127-million deficit into a $150-million surplus.

Femaleness is no protection from the tough challenges big-city politics throws at a mayor. As Jane Byrne found out, cities, like states, are plugged into a fast-changing federation of credit raters, unions, grant givers (and withholders), and candidates for president of the United States.

Mayor Jane Byrne of Chicago

by Eugene Kennedy

Last year, the same kind of killer winter that drove Napoleon out of Russia swept petite, blond, mostly unsmiling Jane M. Byrne into office as the Mayor of Chicago. A record seven and a half feet of snow not only contributed to more than 100 deaths but also created an avalanche of opposition to incumbent Mayor Michael A. Bilandic,

From Eugene Kennedy, "Hard Times in Chicago," *New York Times Magazine*, March 9, 1980, pp. 20 ff.

successor to the late Mayor Richard J. Daley. Jane Byrne, the commissioner of consumer sales whom Bilandic had fired after she accused him of having "greased" the way for a taxi-fare increase, challenged the almost exclusively male-Democratic organization and the man she branded "the abominable snowman." After she defeated Bilandic in the primary, her victory in the general election over Republican investment banker Wallace D. Johnson was a foregone conclusion.

"It's all mine, Jay," the new Mayor was heard to say to her grinning husband, real-estate reporter Jay McMullen, shortly after her inauguration last April.

"What," asked McMullen, whom the Mayor subsequently appointed as her $1-a-year press secretary, "are you going to do with it, babe?"

Chicago has been finding out ever since, as it tries to ride out the shocks of unaccustomed events, including a series of bloodlettings in the City Hall bureaucracy managed in the fashion of public floggings; a brief bus and subway strike the week before Christmas; a teachers' walkout and subsequent strike; and the first walkout by firemen in the city's history, just before dawn on Valentine's Day. Added to these have been other unprecedented crises. In September, for instance, Standard & Poor's Corporation, the bond-rating service, dropped the city's credit rating after years in which Chicago's fiscal well-being was never questioned. In November, the Board of Education, a separate entity from the city government, found that it could not market its bonds and began to collapse like a family business that had kept secret for years its bungling mismanagement.

The more than three million citizens of Chicago are rankled by jibes in the national media about the city by Lake Michigan that once took pride in its freedom from the political discord, fiscal distress and labor disruptions that have long plagued other aging urban areas. They shudder at comparisons to New York and Cleveland, and worry whether their city, despite its symphony orchestra, its Art Institute and its lakeside splendor, is still, as many Easterners always suspected, little more than a crossroads town, its evening clothes borrowed and its gleaming jewels due back in the pawn shop before dawn.

Chicagoans are not the only people whom events during Jane Byrne's mayoralty have unsettled. In October, President Carter came to town for a fund-raising dinner for the Mayor and thought he heard her endorse his renomination in front of the $100,000 paddle-wheel steamboat she had erected to make the Southerner feel at home. If the convention were held that very night, she told 12,000 guests at the largest political fund-raising dinner in Chicago's history, "I tell you that I would vote in our party caucus without hesitancy to renominate our present leader for another four years." The next day, the President told reporters that the Mayor's endorsement had been "perfect."

Two weeks later, however, and just a week before Iranian students seized the American Embassy in Teheran, Jane Byrne announced her support for Senator Edward M. Kennedy. Carter was a lost cause, she implied, saying, "I know if I were he and knew what it was like in Chicago and Illinois, I might consider not running."

But today, with the Illinois primary only nine days away, President Carter is still very much in the running, and Jane Byrne's ability to deliver Cook County to Ted Kennedy is in question. Critics are also questioning her ability to govern the proud city by Lake Michigan. Observers of the local political scene, accustomed to the Daley years, which were characterized by compromise and conciliation, are stunned by the style of confrontation that Jane Byrne has persistently employed. "She's able to create issues," observes liberal Alderman Martin J. Oberman, "where none should exist." He wrinkles his brow in thought as he searches for an explanation. "Ordinarily," he continues, "the leader's personality is not the issue, but it has become that here in Chicago." Meanwhile, 45-year-old Jane Margaret Burke Byrne stares down her detractors with the serenity of a mother superior certain that her vision has been granted by God.

The drama of Mayor Byrne's administration probably cannot be understood without some appreciation of Irish Catholicism and its relation to political life in Northern American cities like Chicago. Jane Byrne grew up in Sauganash, a prosperous community on the northern edge of Chicago, during the years when Catholics were striving for full citizenship in American society. Like hundreds of thousands of others, she attended the Catholic schools built by immigrant forebears to educate their dependents and at the same time to protect their religious faith. By 1955, when she graduated from Barat College in Lake Forest, Ill., American Catholics had begun to challenge their cultural isolation, but they had not yet elected a President nor glimpsed the twinkling smile of Pope John XXIII. Catholics were patriots, supporters of Eisenhower because he took a strong stand against Communism, and willing volunteers for service in such agencies as the F.B.I. and the C.I.A. Such a sense of calling was common among American Catholics at that time, and the aims of democracy and religious development seemed to overlap considerably.

One can detect in Chicago's Mayor the hint of a long-ago sadness whose angry edge can be felt to this day. Its origin may have been the sudden death of her young Marine Corps officer husband. Killed in a fiery plane crash in 1960, he left her, at the age of 25, with a 15-month-old daughter. Even today, when she recalls the moments immediately after she received the news, feeling invades the usually flat and controlled timbre of her voice. "I thought of how she would never know her father," she says, "of how she would never know his heritage. I thought of the children at school when I was growing up, the ones who had lost their fathers and seemed marked and different because of it."

It was the next year, while living in Chicago with her parents, that Jane Byrne heard Presidential hopeful John F. Kennedy speak about the servicemen who gave their lives during peacetime, saying that such men died for their country just as surely as those who lost their lives during a shooting war. This comment and the man who uttered it struck her forcibly, shedding some light on her loss, and turning her "in that moment," as she recalls it, toward politics. Following her sister's lead, she volunteered to work at the downtown Chicago headquarters of the Kennedy campaign.

One can appreciate the significance, as Irish as mournful songs in the night, of Jane Byrne's memories of John F. Kennedy. He is still a presence to her, and a large portrait of him hangs behind her in her City Hall office. A framed copy of his inaugural address and a photograph of Robert F. Kennedy, a gift from Ethel, stand on the console against the wall. The vision of Camelot that has faded in many places remains fresh in this office and offers a partial understanding of this woman who is emotionally linked to the Kennedy legend, to a family shield which, like her own, is splattered with blood. There is in her an Irish rage at the death of the young, at a world that can be so unfair—and all Chicago has felt it.

Jane Byrne speaks of a meeting with Mayor Daley, to whom, on the St. Patrick's Day after President Kennedy was killed, she had sent a telegram: "Hail to the day that gave saints and scholars and to the man and the day that gave us the first Irish Catholic President." She says that the Mayor asked her what she had expected to get out of working in the Kennedy campaign. The Irish rose in both of them as she threatened to stalk out of his office, declaring he was not "her kind" if he could ask such a question, and adding, "I thought that what I got out of it was the first Catholic President of the United States. With all your political clout, I thought, down deep inside of your heart, that was what you wanted."

It was no accident that at Jane Byrne's marriage to Jay McMullen on St. Patrick's Day, 1978, when the possibility of her becoming Mayor was considered extremely remote, themes from *Camelot* were playing in the background.

After working, at Mayor Daley's urging, at the neighborhood level of Chicago politics, Jane Byrne served as an antipoverty administrator until 1968, when the Mayor appointed her commissioner of consumer sales—the city's consumer-affairs advocate. He subsequently made her co-chairman (with himself) of the Cook County Democratic Central Committee. The move represented an effort by the Mayor to put a woman in a prominent place in the party, though he retained all the effective power. Mayor Daley enjoyed her spirited involvement, smiling when she took on critics of the political machine with an Irish flair for battle that he seldom publicly permitted himself.

On November 21, 1977, she was unceremoniously fired by Mayor Bilandic after she implicated him in an underhanded deal to raise cab fares. Both accuser and accused passed polygraph tests and, after a lengthy investigation, a grand jury found no evidence of wrongdoing on Mayor Bilandic's part. Jane Byrne moved out of City Hall vowing to challenge Mayor Bilandic in the next election. Her chances seemed minimal, though a political observer said at the time, "It may be impossible to beat a woman scorned with a name that lends itself so well to the headlines."

Mayor Bilandic revealed, in the judgment of many voters, an insensitivity to what the ordinary people endured as the wind and cold hardened Chicago's snows into stonelike mountains. Indeed, in one pronouncement prepared for delivery during the worst of the winter, Bilandic scratched out "suffering and hardship" and substituted "inconveniences." Anger had been bubbling for a long time beneath Jane Byrne's poker-faced determination, and people identified with that anger. They wanted something new, and they thought that she displayed the spark of leadership that might usher in a fresh spring for them and their city.

Moreover, at the outset of her campaign, when her chances seemed slim, Jane Byrne made promises designed to win her liberal support: she would eliminate evil influences in the party and strike down patronage as the cornerstone of municipal government. The elimination of patronage, which survives in Chicago with a vigor it possesses nowhere else, has long been the battle cry of perennially hardy but always discouraged liberals. Their hopes blossomed afresh with Jane Byrne's candidacy, and so did those of the minority groups, particularly the browns and blacks, who saw her challenge to the establishment as a long-deferred trumpet call to rise and claim their rights. As the snow finally disappeared and Jane Byrne took office, she enjoyed massive public support. She had slain Goliath, and a sense of admiring expectation filled the thawed-out city.

Mayor Byrne, however, had not been co-chairman of the Cook County Democratic Central Committee for nothing. If she had found inspiration in the romantic figure of the young John F. Kennedy, she had also received fatherly support as well as a first-hand course in the exercise of political power from Mayor Daley. "You must remember," a local editor observes, "that Jane was always of the machine, by the machine, and for the machine. She hasn't forgotten any of what she learned on the inside of it." She understood that successful party politics in Chicago rested on the ability to control patronage. As Mayor, she quickly showed that she had no intention of dismantling the machine but, rather, planned to dominate it for her own purposes—and this despite the precedent-setting Shakman decision, a recent Federal court ruling that prohibits hiring or firing municipal employees for political reasons. The liberals, blacks and Hispanics who had supported Mayor Byrne's election wailed in disbelief as the Mayor they had helped elect started acting less like Joan of Arc and more like Indira Gandhi. As one alderman said recently, "She's some tough broad. Put a cigar in her mouth and you couldn't tell her from the rest of us."

One of the issues Jane Byrne raised during the campaign involved "the cabal of evil men" who, in her judgment, enjoyed excessive—and highly profitable—influence in city affairs. But into the void of power that resulted from Jane Byrne's smashing populist victory moved not the reformers who had helped bring it about, but some of the very men she had vowed to throw out. Men like Aldermen Edward M. Burke and Edward R. Vrdolyak, and successful entrepreneur and Chicago Housing Authority head Charles R. Swibel became key allies. Leaders of Chicago's First Ward, who had long bridled at frequent accusations in the press of connections with organized crime, gained easy access to the Mayor's office. The Republican state's attorney, Bernard Carey, has publicly charged that some men are now frequenting City Hall who would not ordinarily appear there unless they had been subpoenaed.

The lines of power were given yet another twist in November after dark-browed Richard M. Daley, the late Mayor's eldest son, announced he would seek the Democratic Party's endorsement for the state's attorney race. Determined to eliminate the political threat of a crown prince with a magic name, Jane Byrne finally settled on none other than Edward Burke as her candidate for the post, provoking the young Daley to run against the regular Democratic organization. "It's better Himself is dead," an old Irishman observed, referring to the late Mayor, "than he'd live to see the great Daley name rejected by the machine."

Meanwhile, the rounds of firings in City Hall continued, to the bewilderment of career bureaucrats who could not understand the departure of nationally recognized and apolitical, first-quality administrators of the sort Mayor Daley had always insisted on in top governmental positions. While Daley, who fired very few people in his first years in office, might send off an employee by giving him a luncheon and a scroll of sentimental remembrance, Jane Byrne has frequently turned out even eminent staffers by announcing the fact to reporters as one might proclaim the enemy casualties of the day.

After accepting the resignation of the holdover police commissioner, she ran through two more men in the position before appointing a permanent chief. Louis Masotti, a professor of political science at Northwestern University who headed Jane Byrne's transition team, says that her decisions about appointments were characterized by impulse and improvisation. "She was like a chess player who concentrates on the move she's making and not on its consequences. Then, if she does something that doesn't work out, she can convince herself she never did it in the first place."

Mayor Byrne's main interest is not in administration, that devouring animal of bureaucratic dullness. In this she probably bears some resemblance to New York City Mayor Koch. She aspires, instead, to dramatic leadership and sucks nourishment from the excitement of battle. She does not approach power in the manner of Mayor Daley, who mastered each detail in the civic and political structure with a thoroughness that invested the slightest gesture of his restrained and taciturn style with unambiguous authority. Instead, she has attacked power as though it were a prize to be wrested from the forces that had occupied the great castle of City Hall before she arrived. Her critics charge that she has picked off dozens of precinct captains in wards controlled by suspected rivals, such as the patronage-rich 11th Ward that is young Daley's political base. "We've only fired 60 out of a ward of over 1,500 jobs," Mayor Byrne says in her defense, suggesting that the time has come for other neighborhoods of Chicago to receive a larger share of patronage jobs, that the wheel has turned in the chance-laden game of politics and regrets are out of order.

Speaking of her housecleaning at City Hall, Mayor Byrne notes, "It's been a real bastion of male chauvinism for years, one of the worst places in the country for it. It was filled with this big macho stuff and I had to take it on right from the start." She moves her coffee mug, inscribed "The Lucky Irish Shamrock," and pauses for a moment. "I learned it with these men when I first came to work here in 1968. They wanted me to be a good little girl. They could accept me that way. I understood that, so I wore a bow in my hair for six months. I played the demure part until I got established."

When she took over City Hall, Jane Byrne says in cool tones, "this place needed a real ventilating. People acted as if there were no protocol, as though they had a right to stay on even if I wanted to put new people in. If I hadn't won, the arrogance of those who had been in office would have been unbearable for the city in four years."

Many observers feel that Jane Byrne is not lacking in arrogance herself, and they worry that the new Mayor does not appreciate the need for keeping certain civic problems muted so that they can be contained while solutions are sought. If Richard Daley exaggerated Chicago as a garden of delights, hardly a day has gone by when the new Mayor has not criticized the city for its previous failures or its present problems. Although her almost daily firings of workers she calls "loafers" and her sarcastic criticisms of various programs as "puff pieces" may be effective street politics, she does not balance this, as Mayor Koch, for instance, does, by effusively boosting the city. An old-time Chicago politician warns, "One of a mayor's most important jobs is to make the city look good, to build it up, not to tear it down all the time."

"The mystique of the idea that Chicago was the city that worked was an invaluable asset," says Mayor Byrne's former budget director, Donald H. Haider, shaking his head as he describes Chicago's financial difficulties. "You can't put a price on it. There had never been a question of the financial stability of the city. The financial community knew that Chicago could always pull the banks, business and labor together. They knew Chicago was well managed." Haider sighs. "To blow that mystique, to shed that image, would do irreparable damage, from which the city might never recover."

Haider talks in the tones of someone who feels that if only you could rerun the film once more, you might still be able to head off the disaster building in the sequence of frames. "Here is what one of the bond rating services wrote just before it dropped the city's rating last fall. The antecedent is Mayor Byrne's steady public criticism of Chicago. It reads: We cannot ignore statements of chief executive officers of a city, even if they are untrue. We rank not simply the economic and financial viability of a city, but also the quality of its management. Quite frankly, we don't encounter a situation like this very often.' "

When she assumed power, Mayor Byrne charged that the previous administration had left a huge deficit because of some vague but sinister doctoring of the budget, and she vowed to establish honest and open fiscal policies. She used varying figures for the alleged deficit, some days claiming it was $100 million, and, on others, citing figures as high as $180 million. "She was using mirrors to get those numbers," says transition chief Masotti.

"There was absolutely no evidence of previous financial mismanagement," says Haider, a former assistant to the Office of Management and Budget in Washington whose appointment by Mayor Byrne was hailed by the media. Indeed, it was Mayor Daley's superb financial and political management that enabled Chicago to withstand the effects of inflation, unemployment and urban blight to which so many other cities succumbed. Chicago has been called "the city that works," and if it has ever merited this designation, it is because Mayor Daley was powerful enough and adroit enough to preserve a delicate balance between business, labor, banks and the other interests on whose cooperation the city's prosperity was built. The Mayor coached a team of football players who, although they may not have liked each other very much, were making too much money to let that interfere with their performance.

According to Haider, the deficits the new Mayor confronted were not the inevitable culmination of decades of decay, but short-term problems dating back only to 1974 and Mayor Daley's recuperation after suffering minor strokes and undergoing surgery. "The control he had always exercised—and he understood budgets very well—was missing. That period of hesitation and uncertainty, and the fact that Daley, even after his return, took a while getting things in order again, explains why these things began to happen." Daley's death at the end of 1976 expanded the period of hesitation because Bilandic, who could, in the judgment of many, curl up with a budget the way other people might with a detective story, felt that he had not won a four-year mandate on his own and therefore lacked the mandate to cut services and jobs while raising taxes in order to put the city back on a firm financial basis.

You simply can't compare Chicago to New York or Cleveland, says Haider, who has been involved in assessing and working out financial crises in both these cities, where the economic difficulties, he believes, are more deeply seated. "It was clear to me that we could turn the finances around quickly, so that Mayor Byrne could have the latitude to do what she wanted during her first four years. The worst would be over in terms of cuts and taxes."

Haider gives the new Mayor high marks for the diligence with which she worked on developing her own budget during the fall. "She did a marvelous job. She gave all her energies to that job and went carefully through every step of the process. She had to make cuts and she was very good about it. She delivered the budget message on Nov. 15 and it was only up 1 percent over the year before."

What, then, went wrong? "She couldn't live with the budget," Haider answers. "She couldn't carry through on the things she had to do to cut expenditures." When Haider sought to eliminate patronage jobs, he says, "everybody's rabbi was in, pleading with us to save this job and that."

It proved equally difficult dealing with the municipal unions, which had long enjoyed prevailing rate agreements with the city. This practice, part of the "handshake agreements" that began long before Daley became Mayor, was one of the signs of how long and how thoroughly Chicago had been a union town. The unions had no contracts and, in view of the benefits they were able to gain without them, they never wanted them. The prevailing rate allows a union to present the city with a contract currently in force elsewhere—a highly advantageous one, of course—and the city meets its requirements. This enormously expensive custom was the price Chicago paid for union peace, and, although its critics were many, others felt that in the long run it was far cheaper for the city to deal with this than with the recurrent labor strife that has racked cities like New York, whose mayors have often treated unions as opponents rather than partners.

Mayor Byrne and Haider felt that trimming the city's commitment to the prevailing rate agreements was a forthright way of dealing with Chicago's financial difficulties. Haider describes a strident meeting during which the 110-pound Jane Byrne dressed down the burly labor chiefs about the performance of many workers during the previous winter's snow emergency and threatened to break the prevailing rate for wages and benefits. "You do that," Teamsters' chief Louis Pleck fumed, "and you'll have labor war in Chicago."

Haider acknowledges that fatigue and a heavy schedule made him less willing to stroke the union leaders than he should have been as he proposed modifications in the city's agreements with them. "That's when the freeze-out with the Mayor began," Haider says. "I lost access to the Mayor at a critical time." It was at this point that Chicagoans were stunned by the news that the City Council had unwittingly passed an ordinance necessary for levying taxes that contained a $29 million error. The Mayor promptly fired her budget director, blaming him for the mistake and promising that it would shortly be rectified. Haider claims that the error was simply an excuse, and that he had already submitted his resignation because one of the conditions of his service to the city, ready access to the Mayor, had been denied.

"A colossal blunder," read an editorial in the *Chicago Sun-Times* decrying Haider's dismissal. A storm of negative reaction crested in the city and, for the first time, large numbers of ordinary citizens began to lose faith in the Mayor's works—a disillusionment that only accelerated when the Mayor, at the urging of her new financial adviser, Edwin H. Yeo 3d, announced that she wanted the $29 million mistake to stand in order to allow, in Yeo's phrase, for "budget enrichment" and, indirectly, to impress the bond-rating agencies with the city's determination to get its finances under control. Standard & Poor's promptly lowered the city's rating again, and Moody's Investors Service Inc. dropped it a notch, too.

With the almost unearthly calm that is characteristic of her at pressured times, Jane Byrne accepts her plummeting popular approval and explains it as an inevitable result of the massive problems she has had to identify and deal with. Indeed, Chicago's Mayor has demonstrated a knack that Houdini might have envied for stepping out of tightening nooses and other traps which, half the time, she seems to have set for herself.

When the Chicago Transit Authority went on strike in December, many observers felt that her handling of the negotiations had precipitated it. But by dramatizing the benefits and salaries that many bus drivers and motormen received—some in the $25,000 to $30,000 range—the Mayor was able to rally the deeply angered people to her side and to emerge, after riding one of the first strike-breaking trains operated by supervisory personnel, as a citizens' champion who had, by an almost flaunting display of willpower and her own anger, ended the strike by forcing it back to mediation.

Then, after weathering a teachers' walkout and subsequent week-long strike while she negotiated a financial package with Illinois Republican Gov. James Thompson that a Byrne aide described as "peace at any price," the Mayor was ready to face the walkout of firefighters on Feb. 14. She had promised the city's firemen a contract during her campaign when she badly needed their support. Firefighter's Union President Frank J. Muscare was anxious to obtain a contract because, observers say, he expected it would give him greater power in the union and his union greater power in the city. Only the previous year, Michael Bilandic had resisted negotiations for anything more than the traditional "handshake agreement" so smoothly that Muscare had not even been able to get his members to authorize him to call a strike.

Some observers suggest that Mayor Byrne drew Muscare out so that he would commit himself to a strike that she felt would give her huge popular support, such as that she had during the transit strike, to defeat the firemen and put an end to even the possibility of further contract negotiation. Others say Muscare felt that, with the safety of the city at stake, Jane Byrne would back away from a confrontation. If so, he was wrong.

Tension mounted swiftly as Chicagoans held their breath, jumping at the flare of a match while television, in a macabre footnote, screened *The Towering Inferno* over the weekend. The Mayor began hiring new recruits for the Fire Department, vowing that firemen who remained out "would never work in the city of Chicago again." In tones of finality that left no doubt about her self-confidence or her firmness, she said that she would never again speak to Muscare, whom she blamed personally for the breakdown in negotiations. No sooner was an agreement reached than it collapsed, and Muscare was jailed by the circuit judge who had been serving as mediator.

As the walkout entered its third week, the public remained on a fine edge between resentment at the firemen for striking and mounting irritation with the Mayor, who seemed to sit calmly and queenlike in the midst of the turmoil, waiting for the banners of unconditional surrender to be laid at her feet.

Jane Byrne has not missed many battles in her 11 months as Mayor. In the midst of the contorted struggle of the firemen's strike, she arrested the attention of the city, confused her opponents, and irritated many of those who supported her and wished her well. At the same time, she has retained a measure of respect, of grudging admiration, a thin sliver of regard for her forthright style even when it seems marred by distortions and inconsistencies, by the fierce blend of the Mayor's dominant personal characteristics, impulsiveness and steadfastness.

Jane Byrne speaks quietly but not demurely of the serial crises that her shake-up of official and political Chicago has caused. She pauses to light a cigarette. "I'm not even feisty, the way everybody writes of me, but I'm not a compromiser, and they're looking at me all the time to find some weakness. We'll get beyond all this and on to positive programs, things we haven't been able to announce. The days of Chicago as the center of the railroads, the hog butcher, all that Carl Sandburg stuff, that's over with. We're going to build a new Chicago, a truly international city. Chicago as a Midwestern city is a thing of the past. We have big plans, but we have to get through these problems. I've got them out in the open. I haven't gone along with covering them up or explaining them away. Once we've settled the firemen's strike, we'll get on to these other things."

And then she returns to the Kennedys, the heroes of her political dedication, the focus of emotion concealed from most and shared, one suspects, with hardly anyone else. "The quote that I often use is from Bobby Kennedy: 'When one man stands up for a principle or an idea, he will be joined by people all over the globe.' "

"That's what I've had to do. I had to say to myself about the previous administration, 'Something going on there is wrong.' Mayor Daley never asked me to compromise my principles, but those people did over the cabs and I wouldn't, and it worked out fine. I think moral courage is at the root of it. I never needed to get into politics. But I believe in standing up. That's exactly the same thing that happened when I went for Teddy. I couldn't be afraid of what an incumbent President could do or try to do to me. Did I want to shrink back? I'd only be a shadow of myself if I had."

Jane Byrne says that President Carter was aware of the coolness regular Chicago Democrats had long felt toward him when he came to the city in mid-October, hoping to receive the endorsement of the Mayor and the Democratic organization that for generations has been a significant prize for every Democratic Presidential hopeful. But the President did not know that the Mayor received that very day a telegram from Ted Kennedy that read: "I have known you and loved you and Chicago longer." Jane Byrne did, however, bring up the subject of the Justice Department's allegation of insufficient integration programs in Chicago's schools. President Carter assured her, as did his aide, Jack Watson, that they were "watching" the Federal case against the Chicago school system closely.

Jane Byrne's declaration for Ted Kennedy two weeks later was received with growls from fellow Democrats, who thought that she had committed herself and her power prematurely. It also exacerbated the widespread uneasiness among Chicagoans that Jane Byrne does not understand an essential corollary of politics. Politics works, so the veterans say, only because at some level you keep your word. That is the glue that makes government possible. Mayor Daley said little and kept the words he gave. Jane Byrne says a lot, but her critics feel that she does not keep her word or changes it so often, or denies what she has said even when reporters have preserved it on tape, that they wonder if she has any idea of what she is doing.

The Carter administration's reaction to Jane Byrne's turnabout was an angry threat of punitive measures. Transportation Secretary Neil E. Goldschmidt said that he would review the granting of Federal highway funds to Chicago because he had "lost confidence" in the Mayor. But Jane Byrne has remained coldly resolute, as though the opposition confirmed to her that she had done something as noble in conscience as Thomas More had in defying King Henry VIII. . . .

Jane Byrne's life has been the product of the interplay of fate and chance, of taking all-or-nothing risks like a gambler on an improbable lucky streak. She has seen the Irish rise and fall—not only the Kennedy family, but also her own priest uncle, Msgr. Edward M. Burke, who, having left his all-powerful position as chancellor of the archdiocese of Chicago, died lonely and forgotten in the exile of a North Side parish. Once he had taken his nieces and nephews to Europe, stopping at Monte Carlo and giving each of them, including the future Mayor of Chicago, $10 to spend on the casino games. The teen-age Jane Byrne promptly bet all her money on one turn of the wheel, lost it, and looked around impatiently for the next diversion.

By betting on long shots and doing everything her way, Jane Byrne has risked everything. People speak of voting for Richard M. Daley in the forthcoming primary race for state's attorney as their way of protesting the bewildering character of her administration. Posters of her circled into a dart board are selling well throughout the city.

But nobody is rash enough to underestimate Chicago's Mayor as she waits through the last days of a relatively snowless winter, long days during which the specter of a potentially terrifying fire has haunted the city. Jane Byrne is still taking on the world, ready to face the darkness the Irish expect to find in the world. That is the hatred, she says, "that you saw in Jack Kennedy's campaign, the same in Bobby's. It was strong enough one-on-one to kill both of them. And it's in Teddy's campaign, too. But they call it Chappaquiddick."

Jane Byrne looks toward the draped windows of her fifth-floor office and does not seem displeased with herself. "With the Irish, you know, only the strongest survive."

7

FREEDOM OF SPEECH

Perhaps the greatest of all political discoveries was that when you let people say what they want to say, the sky does not fall. For ages past, rulers assumed the opposite: words were sparks that, if uncontrolled, might rage into the fire of revolution. Only after eons of repression did the habit of tolerance replace the fear of chaos. Even in our age, however, freedom of speech is intermittently assaulted and eroded, continually in question, perpetually in need of stout defense.

For women to speak out politically, as Anne Hutchinson and Abigail Adams did, took great courage. For a woman to violate the law against telling her sisters how to avoid having too many babies, as Margaret Sanger did, was shocking in the extreme. But Margaret Sanger had seen too much of the suffering and despair women endured before birth control became common. She had reached a moral conclusion and had made up her mind to pursue the consequences. At every stage of her story, the barriers between free thinking and free speaking had to be overcome. Here Margaret Sanger tells what it was like to set forth on a lifetime of saying what had to be said.

Margaret Sanger Informs American Women

by Margaret Sanger

The *New York* was a nice ship and it was not too wintry to walk about on deck. After the children were safely in bed I paced round and round and absorbed into my being that quiet which comes to you at sea. That it was New Year's Eve added to the poignancy of my emotions but did not obscure the faith within.

From Margaret Sanger, *Margaret Sanger* (New York: Norton, 1938), pp. 106–120.

I knew something must be done to rescue those women who were voiceless; someone had to express with white hot intensity the conviction that they must be empowered to decide for themselves when they should fulfill the supreme function of motherhood. They had to be made aware of how they were being shackled, and roused to mutiny. To this end I conceived the idea of a magazine to be called the *Woman Rebel*, dedicated to the interests of working women.

Often I had thought of Vashti as the first woman rebel in history. Once when her husband, King Ahasuerus, had been showing off to his people his fine linens, his pillars of marble, his beds of gold and silver, and all his riches, he had commanded that his beautiful Queen Vashti also be put on view. But she had declined to be exhibited as a possession or chattel. Because of her disobedience, which might set a very bad example to other wives, she had been cast aside and Ahasuerus had chosen a new bride, the meek and gentle Esther.

I wanted each woman to be a rebellious Vashti, not an Esther; was she to be merely a washboard with only one song, one song? Surely, she should be allowed to develop all her potentialities. Feminists were trying to free her from the new economic ideology but were doing nothing to free her from her biological subservience to man, which was the true cause of her enslavement.

Before gathering friends around me for that help which I must have in stirring women to sedition, before asking them to believe, I had to chart my own course. Should I bring the cause to the attention of the people by headlines and front pages? Should I follow my own compulsion regardless of extreme consequences?

I fully recognized I must refrain from acts which I could not carry through. So many movements had been issuing defiances without any ultimate goal, shooting off a popgun here, a popgun there, and finally shooting themselves to death. They had been too greatly resembling froth—too noisy with the screech of tin horns and other cheap instruments instead of the deeper sounds of an outraged, angry, serious people.

With as crystal a view as that which had come to me after the death of Mrs. Sachs when I had renounced nursing forever, I saw the path ahead in its civic, national, and even international direction—a panorama of things to be. Fired with this vision, I went into the lounge and wrote and wrote page after page until the hours of daylight.

Having settled the principles, I left the details to work themselves out. I realized that a price must be paid for honest thinking—a price for everything. Though I did not know exactly how I was to prepare myself, what turn events might take, or what I might be called upon to do, the future in its larger aspects has actually developed as I saw it that night.

The same thoughts kept repeating themselves over and over during the remainder of the otherwise uneventful voyage. As soon as possible after reaching New York, I rented an inexpensive little flat on Post Avenue near Dyckman Street, so far out on the upper end of Manhattan that even the Broadway subway trains managed to burrow their way into sunlight and fresh air. My dining room was my office, the table my desk.

A new movement was starting, and the baby had to have a name. It did not belong to Socialism nor was it in the labor field, and it had much more to it than just the prevention of conception. As a few companions were sitting with me one evening we debated in turn voluntary parenthood, voluntary motherhood, the new motherhood, constructive generation, and new generation. The terms already in use—Neo-Malthusianism, Family Limitation, and Conscious Generation—seemed stuffy and lacked popular appeal.

The word control was good, but I did

not like limitation—that was too limiting. I was not advocating a one-child or two-child system as in France, nor did I wholeheartedly agree with the English Neo-Malthusians whose concern was almost entirely with limitation for economic reasons. My idea of control was bigger and freer. I wanted family in it, yet family control did not sound right. We tried population control, race control, and birth rate control. Then someone suggested, "Drop the rate." Birth control was the answer; we knew we had it. Our work for that day was done and everybody picked up his hat and went home. The baby was named.

When I first announced that I was going to publish a magazine, "Where are you going to get the money?" was volleyed at me from all sides. I did not know, but I was certain of its coming somehow. Equally important was moral support. Those same young friends and I founded a little society, grandly titled the National Birth Control League, sought aid from enthusiasts for other causes, turning first to the Feminists because they seemed our natural allies. Armed with leaflets we went to Cooper Union to tell them that in the *Woman Rebel* they would have an opportunity to express their sentiments.

Charlotte Perkins Gilman, the Feminist leader, was trying to inspire women in this country to have a deeper meaning in their lives, which to her signified more than getting the vote. Nevertheless, at that time I struck no responsive chord from her or from such intelligent co-workers as Crystal Eastman, Marie Howe, or Henrietta Rodman. It seemed unbelievable they could be serious in occupying themselves with what I regarded as trivialities when mothers within a stone's throw of their meetings were dying shocking deaths.

Who cared whether a woman kept her Christian name—Mary Smith instead of Mrs. John Jones? Who cared whether she wore her wedding ring? Who cared about her demand for the right to work? Hundreds of thousands of laundresses, cloakmakers, scrub women, servants, telephone girls, shop workers would gladly have changed places with the Feminists in return for the right to have leisure, to be lazy a little now and then. When I suggested that the basis of Feminism might be the right to be a mother regardless of church or state, their inherited prejudices were instantly aroused. They were still subject to the age-old, masculine atmosphere compounded of protection and dominance.

Disappointed in that quarter I turned to the Socialists and trade unionists, trusting they would appreciate the importance of family limitation in the kind of civilization towards which they were stumbling. Notices were sent to *The Masses*, *Mother Earth*, *The Call*, *The Arm and Hammer*, *The Liberator*, all names echoing the spirit which had quickened them.

Shortly I had several hundred subscriptions to the *Woman Rebel*, paid up in advance at the rate of a dollar a year, the period for which I had made my plans. Proceeds were to go into a separate revolving account, scrupulously kept. Unlike so many ephemeral periodicals, mine was not to flare up and spark out before it had functioned, leaving its subscribers with only a few issues when they were entitled to more. Eventually we had a mailing list of about two thousand, but five, ten, even fifty copies often went in a bundle to be distributed without charge to some labor organization.

I was solely responsible for the magazine financially, legally, and morally; I was editor, manager, circulation department, bookkeeper, and I paid the printer's bill. But any cause that has not helpers is losing out. So many men and women secretaries, stenographers, clerks, used to come in of an evening that I could not find room for all. Some typed, some addressed envelopes, some went to libraries and looked up things for us to use, some wrote articles, though seldom signing their own names. Not one penny ever had to go for salaries, because service was given freely.

In March, 1914, appeared the first issue

of the *Woman Rebel*, eight pages on cheap paper, copied from the French style, mailed first class in the city and expressed outside. My initial declaration of the right of the individual was the slogan "No Gods, No Masters." Gods, not God. I wanted that word to go beyond religion and also stop turning idols, heroes, leaders into gods.

I defined a woman's duty, "To look the world in the face with a go-to-hell look in the eyes; to have an idea; to speak and act in defiance of convention." It was a marvelous time to say what we wished. All America was a Hyde Park corner as far as criticism and challenging thought were concerned. We advocated direct action and took up the burning questions of the day. With a fine sense of irony we put anti-capitalist soapbox oratory in print. I do not know whether the financiers we denounced would have been tolerant or resentful of our onslaughts had they read them, or as full of passion for their cause as we for ours. Perhaps they too will have forgotten that emotion now.

My daily routine always started with looking over the pile of mail, and one morning my attention was caught by an unstamped official envelope from the New York Post Office. I tore it open.

> Dear Madam, You are hereby notified that the Solicitor of the Post Office Department has decided that the *Woman Rebel* for March, 1914, is unmailable under Section 489, Postal Laws and Regulations.
>
> E. M. Morgan, Postmaster.

I reread the letter. It was so unexpected that at first the significance did not sink in. I had given no contraceptive information; I had merely announced that I intended to do so. Then I began to realize that no mention was made of any special article or articles. I wrote Mr. Morgan and asked him to state what specifically had offended, thereby assisting me in my future course. His reply simply repeated that the March issue was unmailable.

I had anticipated objections from religious bodies, but believed with father, "Anything you want can be accomplished by putting a little piece of paper into the ballot box." Therefore, to have our insignificant magazine stopped by the big, strong United States Government seemed so ludicrous as almost to make us feel important.

To the newspaper world this was news, but not one of the dailies picked it out as an infringement of a free press. The *Sun* carried a headline, "'WOMAN REBEL' BARRED FROM MAILS." And underneath the comment, "Too bad. The case should be reversed. They should be barred from her and spelled differently."

Many times I studied Section 211 of the Federal Statutes, under which the Post Office was acting. This penal clause of the Comstock Law had been left hanging in Washington like the dried shell of a tortoise. Its grip had even been tightened on the moral side; in case the word obscene should prove too vague, its definition had been enlarged to include the prevention of conception and the causing of abortion under one and the same heading. To me it was outrageous that information regarding motherhood, which was so generally called sacred, should be classed with pornography.

Nevertheless, I had not broken the law, because it did not prohibit discussion of contraception—merely giving advice. I harbored a burning desire to undermine that law. But if I continued publication I was making myself liable to a Federal indictment and a possible prison term of five years plus a fine of five thousand dollars. I had to choose between abandoning the *Woman Rebel*, changing its tone, or continuing as I had begun. Though I had no wish to become a martyr, with no hesitation I followed the last-named course.

I gathered our little group together. At first we assumed Comstock had stopped the entire issue before delivery, but apparently he had not, because only the A to M's which had been mailed in the local post office had been confiscated. We took a fresh lot downtown, slipped three into one chute, four in another, walked miles around the city so that no single box contained more than a few copies.

The same procedure had to be pursued in succeeding months. Sometimes daylight caught me, with one or more assistants, still tramping from the printer's and dropping the copies, piece by piece, into various boxes and chutes. I felt the Government was absurd and tyrannical to make us do this for no good purpose. I could not get used to its methods then. I have not yet, and probably never shall.

The *Woman Rebel* produced extraordinary results, striking vibrations that brought contacts, messages, inquiries, pamphlets, books, even some money. I corresponded with the leading Feminists of Europe—Ellen Key, then at the height of her fame, Olive Schreiner, Mrs. Pankhurst, Rosa Luxemburg, Adele Schreiber, Clara Zetkin, Roszika Schwimmer, Frau Maria Stritt. But I also heard from sources and groups I had hardly known existed—Theosophist, New Thought, Rosicrucian, Spiritualist, Mental Scientist. It was not alone from New York, but from the highways and byways of north, south, east, and west that inspiration came.

After the second number the focus had been birth control. Within six months we had received over ten thousand letters, arriving in accelerating volume. Most of them read, "Will your magazine give accurate and reliable information to prevent conception?" This I could not print. Realizing by now it was going to be a fairly big fight, I was careful not to break the law on such a trivial point. It would have been ridiculous to have a single letter reach the wrong destination; therefore, I sent no contraceptive facts through the mails.

However, I had no intention of giving up this primary purpose. I began sorting and arranging the material I had brought back from France, complete with formulas and drawings, to be issued in a pamphlet where I could treat the subject with more delicacy than in a magazine, writing it for women of extremely circumscribed vocabularies. A few hundred dollars were needed to finance publication of *Family Limitation*, as I named it, and I approached Theodore Schroeder, a lawyer of standing and an ardent advocate of free speech. He had been left a fund by a certain Dr. Foote who had produced a book on *Borning Better Babies*, and I thought my pamphlet might qualify as a beneficiary.

Dr. Abraham Brill was just then bringing out a translation of Freud, in whom Schroeder was much interested. He asked whether I had been psychoanalyzed.

"What is psychoanalysis?"

He looked at me critically as from a great height. "You ought to be analyzed as to your motives. If, after six weeks, you still wish to publish this pamphlet, I'll pay for ten thousand copies."

"Well, do you think I won't want to go on?"

"I don't only think so. I'm quite sure of it."

"Then I won't be analyzed."

I took the manuscript to a printer well known for his liberal tendencies and courage. He read the contents page by page and said, "You'll never get this set up in any shop in New York. It's a Sing Sing job."

Every one of the twenty printers whom I tried to persuade was afraid to touch it. It was impossible ever, it seemed, to get into print the contents of that pamphlet.

Meanwhile, following the March issue the May and July numbers of the *Woman Rebel* had also been banned. In reply to each of the formal notices I inquired which particular article or articles had incurred disapproval, but could obtain no answer.

At that time I visualized the birth control movement as part of the fight for freedom of speech. How much would the postal authorities suppress? What were they really after? I was determined to prod and goad until some definite knowledge was obtained as to what was "obscene, lewd, and lascivious."

Theodore Schroeder and I used to meet once in a while at the Liberal Club, and he gave much sound advice—I could not go on with the *Woman Rebel* forever. Eventually the Post Office would wear me down by stopping the issues as fast as I printed them. He warned, "They won't do so and so unless you do thus and thus. If you do such and such, then you'll have to take the consequences." He was a good lawyer and an authority on the Constitution.

When my family learned that I might be getting in deep water a council was called just as when I had been a child. A verdict of nervous breakdown was openly decreed, but back in the minds of all was the unspoken dread that I must have become mentally unbalanced. They insisted father come to New York, where he had not been for forty years, to persuade me to go to a sanitarium.

For several days father and I talked over the contents of the *Woman Rebel*. In his fine, flowing language he expressed his hatred of it. He despised talk about revolution, and despaired of anyone who could discuss sex, blaming this on my nursing training, which, he intimated, had put me in possession of all the known secrets of the human body. He was not quite sure what birth control was, and my reasoning, which retraced the pattern of our old arguments, made no impression upon him.

Father would have nothing to do with the "queer people" who came to the house—people of whom no one had ever heard—turning up with articles on every possible subject and defying me to publish them in the name of free speech. I printed everything. For the August issue I accepted a philosophical essay on the theory of assassination, largely derived from Richard Carlile. It was vague, inane, and innocuous, and had no bearing on my policy except to taunt the Government to take action, because assassination also was included under Section 211.

Only a few weeks earlier, the war which Victor Dave had predicted had started its headlong progress. The very moment when most people were busy with geographies and atlases, trying to find out just where Sarajevo might be, the United States chose to sever diplomatic relations with me.

One morning I was startled by the peremptory, imperious, and incessant ringing of my bell. When I opened the door, I was confronted by two gentlemen.

"Will you come in?"

They followed me into my living room, scrutinized with amazement the velocipede and wagon, the woolly animals and toys stacked in the corner. One of them asked, "Are you the editor and publisher of a magazine entitled the *Woman Rebel*?"

When I confessed to it, he thrust a legal document into my hands. I tried to read it, threading my way slowly through the jungle of legal terminology. Perhaps the words became a bit blurred because of the slight trembling of my hands, but I managed to disentangle the crucial point of the message. I had been indicted—indicted on no less than nine counts—for alleged violation of the Federal Statutes. If found guilty on all, I might be liable to forty-five years in the penitentiary.

I looked at the two agents of the Department of Justice. They seemed nice and sensible. I invited them to sit down and started in to explain birth control. For three hours I presented to their imaginations some of the tragic stories of conscript motherhood. I forget now what I said, but at the end they agreed that such a law should not be on the statute books. Yet it was, and there was nothing to do about it but bring my case to court.

When the officers had gone, father came through the door of the adjoining room where he had been reading the paper. He put both arms around me and said, "Your mother would have been alive today if we had known all this then." He had applied my recital directly to his own life. "You will win this case. Everything is with you—logic, common sense, and progress. I never saw the truth until this instant."

Old-fashioned phraseology, but father was at last convinced. He went home quite proud, thinking I was not so crazy after all, and began sending me clippings to help prove the case for birth control—women who had drowned themselves or their children and the brutalities of parents, because even mother love might turn cruel if too hard pressed.

My faith was still childlike. I trusted that, like father, a judge representing our Government would be convinced. All I had to do was explain to those in power what I was doing and everything would come right.

August twenty-fifth I was arraigned in the old Post Office way downtown. Judge Hazel, himself a father of eight or nine children, was kindly, and I suspected the two Federal agents who had summoned me had spoken a good word on my behalf. But Assistant District Attorney Harold A. Content seemed a ferocious young fellow. When the Judge asked, "What sort of things is Mrs. Sanger doing to violate the law?" he answered, "She's printing articles advocating bomb throwing and assassination."

"Mrs. Sanger doesn't look like a bomb thrower or an assassin."

Mr. Content murmured something about not all being gold that glittered; I was doing a great deal of harm. He intimated he knew of my attempts to get *Family Limitation* in print when he said, "She is not satisfied merely to violate the law, but is planning to do it on a very large scale."

Judge Hazel, apparently believing the charges much exaggerated, put the case over until the fall term, which gave me six weeks to prepare my answer, and Mr. Content concurred, saying that if this were not enough time, I could have more.

The press also was inclined to be friendly. Reporters came up to Post Avenue, looked over the various articles. They agreed, "We think the Government absolutely wrong. We don't see how it has any case." Unfortunately, while we were talking, Peggy, who had never seen a derby before, took possession of their hats and sticks, and in the hall a little parade of children formed, marching up and down in front of the door. One of the gentlemen was so furious that I hid Peggy in the kitchen away from his wrath. As he went out he remarked, "You should have birth controlled them before they were born. Why don't you stay home and spend some thought on disciplining your own family?"

I had many things to do which could not be postponed, the most important among them being to provide for the children's future. This occupied much of my time for the next few weeks. Temporarily, I sent the younger two to the Catskills and Stuart to a camp in Maine, arranging for school in the fall on Long Island.

Defense funds were always being raised when radicals got into trouble to pay pseudo-radical lawyers to fight the cases on technicalities. I was not going to have any lawyer get me out of this. Since my indictment had not stopped my publishing the *Woman Rebel*, through the columns of the September issue I told my subscribers I did not want pennies or dollars, but appealed to them to combine forces and protest on their own behalf against government invasion of their rights. That issue and the October one were both suppressed.

During what might be called my sleepwalking stage it was as though I were heading towards a precipice and nothing could awaken me. I had no ear for the objections of family or the criticism of friends. People were around me, I knew, but I could not see them clearly; I was deaf to their warnings and blind to their signs.

When I review the situation through the eyes of those who gave me circumspect advice, I can understand their attitude. I was considered a conservative, even a bourgeoise by the radicals. I was digging into an illegal subject, was not a trained writer or speaker or experienced in the arts of the propagandist, had no money with which to start a rousing campaign, and possessed neither social position nor influence.

In the opinion of nearly all my acquaintances I would have to spend at least a year in jail, and they began to condole with me. None offered to do anything about it, just suggested how I could get through. One kind woman whom I had never seen before called late one evening and volunteered to give me dancing lessons. In a small six-by-four cabin she had developed a system which she claimed was equally applicable to a prison cell and would keep me in good health. She even wrote out careful directions for combining proper exercises with the rhythm of the dance.

But I myself had no intention of going to jail; it was not in *my* program.

One other thing I had to do before my trial. *Family Limitation* simply must be published. I had at last found the right person—Bill Shatoff, Russian-born, big and burly, at that time a linotype operator on a foreign paper. So that nobody would see him he did the job after hours when his shop was supposed to be closed.

At first I had thought only of an edition of ten thousand. However, when I learned that union leaders in the silk, woolen, and copper industries were eager to have many more copies to distribute, I enlarged my plan. I would have liked to print a million but, owing to lack of funds, could not manage more than a hundred thousand.

Addressing the envelopes took a lot of work. Night after night the faithful band labored in a storage room, wrapping, weighing, stamping. Bundles went to the mills in the East, to the mines of the West—to Chicago, San Francisco, and Pittsburgh, to Butte, Lawrence, and Paterson. All who had requested copies were to receive them simultaneously; I did not want any to be circulated until I was ready, and refused to have one in my own house. I was a tyrant about this, as firm as a general about leaving no rough edges.

In October my case came up. I had had no notice and, without a lawyer to keep me posted, did not even know it had been called until the District Attorney's office telephoned. Since Mr. Content had promised me plenty of time, I thought this was merely a formality and all I had to do was put in an appearance.

The next morning I presented myself at court. As I sat in the crowded room I felt crushed and oppressed by an intuitive sense of the tremendous, impersonal power of my opponents. Popular interest was now focused on Europe; my little defiance was no longer important. When I was brought out of my reverie by the voice of the clerk trumpeting forth in the harshly mechanical tones of a train announcer something about *The People v. Margaret Sanger*, there flashed into my mind a huge map of the United States, coming to life as a massive, vari-colored animal, against which I, so insignificant and small, must in some way defend myself. It was a terrific feeling.

But courage did not entirely desert me. Elsie Clapp, whose ample Grecian figure made her seem a tower of strength, marched up the aisle with me as though she, too, were to be tried. I said to Judge Hazel that I was not prepared, and asked for a month's adjournment. Mr. Content astonished me by objecting. "Mrs. Sanger's had plenty of time and I see no reason, Your Honor, why we should have a further postponement. Every day's delay means that her violations are increased. I ask that the case continue this afternoon."

A change in Judge Hazel's attitude had taken place since August. Instead of listening to my request, he advised me to get an attorney at once—my trial would go on after the noon recess.

I was so amazed that I could only believe his refusal was due to my lack of technical knowledge, and supposed that at this point

I really had to have a lawyer. I knew Simon H. Pollock, who had represented labor during the Paterson strike, and I went to see him. He agreed with me that a lawyer's plea would not be rejected and that afternoon confidently asked for a month's stay. It was denied. He reduced it to two weeks. Again it was denied. At ten the following morning the case was to be tried without fail.

From the Post Office Department I received roundabout word that my conviction had already been decided upon. When I told this to Mr. Pollock he said, "There isn't a thing I can do. You'd better plead guilty and let us get you out as fast as we can. We might even be able to make some deal with the D.A. so you'd only have to pay a fine."

I indignantly refused to plead guilty under any circumstances. What was the sense of bringing about my indictment in order to test the law, and then admit that I had done wrong? I was trying to prove the law was wrong, not I. Giving Mr. Pollock no directions how to act, I merely said I would call him up.

It was now four o'clock and I sought refuge at home to think through my mental turmoil and distress. But home was crowded with too many associations and emotions pulling me this way and that. When my thoughts would not come clear and straight I packed a suitcase, went back downtown, and took a room in a hotel, the most impersonal place in the world.

There was no doubt in my mind that if I faced the hostile court the next morning, unprepared as I was, I would be convicted of publishing an obscene paper. Such a verdict would be an injustice. If I were to convince a court of the rightness of my cause, I must have my facts well marshaled, and that could not be done in eighteen hours.

Then there was the question of the children's welfare. Had I the right to leave them the heritage of a mother who had been imprisoned for some offensive literature of which no one knew the details?

What was I to do? Should I get another lawyer, one with personal influence who could secure a postponement, and should we then go into court together and fight it out? I had no money for such a luxury. Should I follow the inevitable suggestion of the "I-told-you-so's" and take my medicine? Yes, but what medicine? I would not swallow a dosage for the wrong disease.

I was not afraid of the penitentiary; I was not afraid of anything except being misunderstood. Nevertheless, in the circumstances, my going there could help nobody. I had seen so many people do foolish things valiantly, such as wave a red flag, shout inflammatory words, lead a parade, just for the excitement of doing what the crowd expected of them. Then they went to jail for six months, a year perhaps, and what happened? Something had been killed in them; they were never heard of again. I had seen braver and hardier souls than I vanquished in spirit and body by prison terms, and I was not going to be lost and broken for an issue which was not the real one, such as the entirely unimportant *Woman Rebel* articles. Had I been able to print *Family Limitation* earlier, and to swing the indictment around that, going to jail might have had some significance.

Going away was much more difficult than remaining. But if I were to sail for Europe I could prepare my case adequately and return then to win or lose in the courts. There was a train for Canada within a few hours. Could I take it? Should I take it? Could I ever make those who had advised me against this work and these activities understand? Could I ever make anyone understand? How could I separate myself from the children without seeing them once more? Peggy's leg was swollen from vaccination. This kept worrying me, made me hesitate, anxious. It was so hard to decide what to do.

Perfectly still, my watch on the table, I marked the minutes fly. There could be no retreat once I boarded that train. The torture of uncertainty, the agony of making a decision only to reverse it! The hour grew later and later. This was like both birth and death—you had to meet them alone.

About thirty minutes before train time I knew that I must go. I wrote two letters, one to Judge Hazel, one to Mr. Content, to be received at the desk the next day, informing them of my action. I had asked for a month and it had been refused. This denial of right and freedom compelled me to leave my home and my three children until I made ready my case, which dealt with society rather than an individual. I would notify them when I came back. Whether this were in a month or a year depended on what I found it necessary to do. Finally, as though to say, "Make the most of it," I enclosed to each a copy of *Family Limitation*.

Parting from all that I held dear in life, I left New York at midnight, without a passport, not knowing whether I could ever return.

8

FREE SPEECH AND "SUBVERSION"

In July 1968, Angela Davis paid dues of fifty cents and became a member of the Communist Party, U.S.A. She thus took on a label that in the minds of many Americans linked her with one of history's vilest movements, one responsible for establishing throwback, freedom-hating, totalitarian governments from China to Cuba. A young philosophy instructor, Davis soon found her career and even her life in serious danger, from fellow citizens as well as from the police paid to protect her and everyone else. Her story dramatizes the point that civil liberty is tested most severely when advocates urge causes the great majority find most obnoxious. When the advocate is black and female, reaction escalates. If the case of Margaret Sanger sounds antique, the case of Angela Davis happened only yesterday and no doubt another like it will appear tomorrow. Angela Davis tells it her way.

Angela Davis's Challenge to Power

by Angela Davis

I did not discover until I returned to the coast that an FBI agent had published an article in the campus newspaper about a Communist who had recently been hired by the Philosophy Department. William Divale revealed in his article that he had been instructed by the FBI to infiltrate the Communist Party. Undoubtedly he had also been instructed to publish the article about my membership in the Party.

From Angela Davis, *Angela Davis: An Autobiography* (New York: Random House, 1974), pp. 216–40.

Another article had appeared in the *San Francisco Examiner*, under the by-line of Ed Montgomery, one of the most reactionary reporters in the state. According to him, I was not only a member of the Communist Party, U.S.A., but (despite the contradiction) I was a Maoist as well. The article alleged that I also belonged to the Students for a Democratic Society and the Black Panther Party. Moreover, he said he had information that I was a gun runner for the Black Panther Party, and that he knew for a fact that I had been under surveillance for some time by the San Diego Police Department.

When I read this nonsense, I laughed. But at the same time, I sensed that I was in the midst of a serious situation. My suspicions were confirmed when I learned that the governing body of the university—under the leadership of Governor Ronald Reagan—had instructed the chancellor of the Los Angeles campus to formally ask me whether I was a member of the Communist Party.

I was somewhat shocked, I admit, by this march of events. Not that I had expected the issue of my membership in the Communist Party to be totally ignored. What shocked me was the ceremonious character of the confrontation and what seemed the beginning of an inquisition à la McCarthy.

When I accepted the job at UCLA, I was unaware of the regulation in the Regents' handbook—dating back to 1949—prohibiting the hiring of Communists. This clearly unconstitutional statute was pulled out of the closet, and invoked by Ronald Reagan and company in order to prevent me from teaching at UCLA.

As this whole affair was brewing, I realized that the personal goals I had set for myself were about to collide head-on with the political requirements of my life. Originally I had not intended to begin working that year. I had not yet completed my Ph.D. dissertation and wanted to get that out of the way before I went out job-seeking. Later I had decided to accept the position at UCLA because its light teaching load would leave me the time and flexibility I needed to finish writing the thesis. I wanted desperately to get that part of my academic life behind me. But now, I had been challenged. To accept the challenge meant that I would have to abandon the idea of receiving my degree before the end of that school year.

My comrades in the Che-Lumumba Club immediately committed themselves to building a campaign within the Black community in Los Angeles around my right to teach at UCLA. White comrades were active as well. On the campus, the Black Student Union and the Black Professors' organization took up the banner. Large numbers of students and professors began to understand the need to fight the Regents' political encroachments on the autonomy of the university.

The unanimous position of the Philosophy Department was to condemn the Regents for interrogating me about my political beliefs and affiliations. None of them had been asked, as a condition of their employment, whether they were members of the Democratic, Republican, or any other party. The chairman of the Philosophy Department, Donald Kalish, had assumed a principled, unyielding position from the outset. It was largely because of his work, and the efforts of the few Black professors, that the movement to support my right to teach expanded throughout the faculty.

The stage was set for the battle. The first step was to answer the chancellor's letter asking me whether I was a member of the Communist Party. Only my lawyer—John McTernan—and a few close friends and comrades were aware of the way I was going to reply to the question. Most people assumed that I would invoke the Fifth Amendment to the Constitution, declining to answer on the grounds that I might incriminate myself. During the McCarthy era, this had been the strategy of most Communists, for at that time, if it could be established that a person was a Communist, he or she could be sentenced, under the Smith Act, to many years in prison. Gus Hall and Henry Winston, the General Secretary and the Chairman of our Party, had spent almost ten years of their lives behind walls.

Since there was going to be a fight in any event, I preferred to pick the combat area, and to determine myself the terms of the struggle. The Regents had moved in with an attack on me. Now I would assume the offensive and would move in with an attack on them.

I answered the chancellor's letter with an unequivocal affirmation of my membership in the Communist Party. I strongly protested the posing of the question in the first place, but made it clear to them that I was prepared to fight openly, as a communist.

My reply caught the Regents unawares, and some of them considered my announcement of my membership in the Communist Party a personal affront. I am sure that they had taken for granted that I would call upon the Fifth Amendment. Their strategy, in turn, would have been to publicly ransack my immediate past in order to prove that I was in fact a Communist.

They countered my move with an impetuous, angry response: they announced their intention to fire me.

The racists and anti-Communists throughout the state responded with furor. Threatening calls and letters poured into the Philosophy Department and into the offices of the Communist Party. A man broke into the Philosophy Department offices and physically attacked Don Kalish. A special telephone line had to be installed in my office, so that all my calls could be screened before they reached me. The campus police had to be placed on alert at all times. Several times they had to check out my car because of bomb threats I had received.

For security purposes, a brother was assigned by my comrades in Che-Lumumba to stay with me at all times, and I had to change many of my personal habits and remold them for the requirements of security. Things which I had taken for granted for so long were now completely out of the question. If, for instance, I got bogged down on some work I was doing, I could no longer go out alone for a walk or a drive at two o'clock in the morning. If I needed cigarettes at an hour when most people were sleeping, I would have to wake Josef and ask him to go with me.

It was difficult for me to accept the necessity of someone's being with me practically all the time, and I was constantly criticized by members of the Che-Lumumba Club for taking security so lightly. Kendra and Franklin Alexander kept reminding me that if anything ever happened to me they would be the ones to be blamed. Whenever I made light of the need for security, they reminded me of all the incidents that had already occurred. There had been the time when I was pursued by the police while driving home alone at night. They had followed me for some distance and as I slowed down to turn into my driveway, the cops aimed their spotlight into the car and kept it trained on me until I reached the door. I had assumed that this was just one more of their attempts to harass me, so I ignored them. But afterward, a comrade remarked I underestimated them—they could have been setting me up for an assassination.

It wasn't just a question of police either. The comrades would often remind me that out of the thousands of threats that had been made on my life, there might be one person crazy enough to actually try to kill me. Just one person, one crazy person.

After our first victory in court—an injunction prohibiting the Regents from firing me for political reasons—the hate letters and threats multiplied in number and ferocity. Bomb threats were so frequent that after a while the campus police stopped checking under the hood of my car for explosives. Of necessity, I had to learn the procedure myself. One afternoon, a Black plainclothesman interrupted my class to tell me that serious threats had been received and that the campus police had instructed him to guard me until I was ready to go home. That day several calls had been received at various points on the campus warning that I would not get off the grounds alive. Apparently the same person had made calls all over Los Angeles, to friends and acquaintances of mine and people involved in the movement. When I walked out of the classroom, Franklin, Gregory and several other comrades from Che-Lumumba were waiting to take me home, their long coats not quite concealing the shotguns and rifles they had brought along. We all remembered that barely a year ago John Huggins and Bunchy Carter, two members of the Black Panther Party, had been shot to death on that campus—not far from where I was holding my class.

If the need for constant security made life unwieldy for me, it was only one facet of the larger problem of getting used to the fact that I had been transformed into a public figure overnight. I hated being the center of such excessive attention. The snooping, often parasitic news reporters jarred my nerves. And I loathed being stared at like a curiosity object. I had never aspired to be a "public revolutionary"; my concept of my revolutionary vocation had been vastly different. Still, I had accepted the challenge which the state initiated and if that meant I had to become a public personality, then I would have to be that personality—despite my own discomfort.

But there were the enormously moving moments which more than compensated for the unpleasant aspects of my public life. Once I was grocery shopping in the supermarket near my house. I could tell that the middle-aged Black woman behind a nearby cart thought she recognized me. When our eyes met, hers lit up. She rushed over and asked, "Are you Angela Davis?" When I smiled and said yes, tears came into her eyes. I wanted to hug her, but she was faster than I. With a firm, warm embrace, she told me in a motherly way, "Don't worry, child. We're behind you. We're not going to let them take your job. Just keep on fighting."

If this one moment had been the only fruit of the many seasons I had devoted to the movement, it would have made all the sacrifices worthwhile.

There was never a doubt in my mind that my mother and father, in their own gentle way, would stand with me. I knew they would not bend under the terrible pressures to denounce their "Communist daughter." At the same time I realized that the more strongly they defended me, the more their own safety would be placed in jeopardy; I worried a great deal about them.

As I thought of their being exposed to the most virulent Southern racism and anti-communism, my apprehension mingled with fears I had experienced during my childhood in Birmingham. I remembered how terrified I had felt when I heard the bombs explode, ripping to pieces the houses across the street. I remembered how my father's weapons had always been waiting in his top drawer in anticipation of an attack. I thought about the time when the slightest sound was enough to send my father or my brothers searching for a hidden explosive device outside. One night after the publicity broke, I spoke to my youngest brother, Reginald, who was attending college in Ohio. He, too, was very much afraid that our parents might come under attack and he wanted to go back to Birmingham to protect them.

Whenever I talked to our mother and father, they assured me that things were going well. Perhaps there had been no physical assault, but I could detect in their voices that they were being hurt in other ways. Maybe someone who was supposed to be a friend had been frightened away because he did not want to be associated with the parents of a Communist.

The psychological impact of anti-communism on ordinary people in this country runs very deep. There is something about the word "communism" that, for the unenlightened, evokes not only the enemy, but also something immoral, something dirty.

Among the many reasons for my decision to publicly talk about my membership in the Communist Party, was my belief that I could help explode some of the myths on which anti-communism thrives. If only oppressed people could see that Communists are profoundly concerned about them, they would be forced to reevaluate their irrational fear of "the Communist Conspiracy."

I soon discovered that in the ghetto, among poor and working-class Black people, anti-Communist reactions were often not deeply ingrained. To relate only one example: A brother who lived across the street from me came over one day and asked me what communism was. "There must be something good about it," he said, "because the man is always trying to convince us that it's bad."

But in Birmingham, the image most people had of me was doubtlessly abstract and irrational. Many people who had known me as a child, people who still wanted to love me, probably assumed very simply that I had been captured, led astray and brainwashed by the Communists. I could imagine them using every euphemism they could think of in order to avoid calling me such a dirty name as Communist.

While I was home during the Christmas break, my mother admitted that people who had counted themselves among her friends had broken down under the pressure. Some, she said, had abruptly stopped calling or coming around to visit. Some of my father's customers at the service station had suddenly disappeared.

Yet at the same time, she insisted, many of her friends had taken forthright positions in my defense. If someone even implied that I had been innocently lured into the Communist Party, they would firmly declare that I had made up my own mind about my political affiliations.

My mother and father had always encouraged my sister, my brothers and me to be independent. From the time we were very small, they repeatedly counseled us to forget about what other people said and to do what we felt was right. I was proud that both my parents were determined to defend my right to seek an independent, revolutionary answer to the oppression of our people.

I kept in close touch with my brother Ben, who is a football player with the Cleveland Browns. If there were any repercussions on his job because I was a Communist, I wanted to be prepared to defend him immediately. Although nothing overt happened at that time—the problems were still to come—he was very much conscious of the conspicuous silence which surrounded him. No one had even asked him whether he was with me or against me.

My sister, Fania, was living only a hundred miles away in the San Diego area at the time. She and her husband, Sam, were attending the University of California in San Diego. There was a greater than average concern about the UCLA affair there because I had attended the university for two years and was officially still a philosophy graduate student, studying for my doctorate under Professor Herbert Marcuse.

I had kept my little apartment near the university in Cardiff-by-the-Sea, thinking that it would be a perfect refuge when I wanted to get away from the hectic pace of Los Angeles. Since the rent was forty dollars a month and my place in Los Angeles was only eighty dollars, I had decided I could afford to keep the two places. Fania and Sam had stayed there before they moved into a place of their own. Afterward, they continued to use it whenever they felt like it.

After the Regents fired me, and my membership in the Communist Party was thoroughly publicized and attacked in the press throughout the state, I could not help worrying about Fania and Sam. The San Diego area was home territory for the Minutemen, Southern California's version of the Ku Klux Klan. The police were not much better. With recent memories of being followed by the police for being in the leadership of the Black Student Council at UCSD, I warned them to be on their guard.

My fears were not unfounded. One morning in the fall the telephone beside my bed rang so early that I knew something was wrong. My heart was beating fast when I said hello.

"Angela," whispered a voice which I immediately recognized as my sister's, "Sam's been shot." She sounded like she was talking in her sleep. Her words were so unreal.

"What do you mean?" I asked unbelievingly.

"The pigs shot Sam," was all she said. She didn't say whether he was still alive, and fearing the worst, I didn't want to ask. Instead, trying to sound calm, I asked her to tell me exactly what had happened.

Two sheriff's deputies had broken into their house and fired on Sam, hitting him in the shoulder. He had grabbed the shotgun they kept in the house, fired back and run them out of the house. When she said that he was in the hospital, I felt tremendous relief; now I could ask her how he was doing.

The bullet had lodged a mere quarter of an inch from his spine. But it had already been removed, and she thought he was going to be all right. The biggest problem at that moment was that they had placed him under arrest. As soon as he was released from the hospital, they were going to put him in jail.

She said she was calling from Evelyn and Barry's—the upstairs section of the house in Cardiff where my apartment was. I told her to hold on, and that I'd drive down as soon as I could.

After I woke Josef and told him, I called Kendra and Franklin to have them alert the other comrades. Kendra said she was going with me. Franklin volunteered to go to Riverside, where I was scheduled to speak at the university that day. After apologizing for my absence and delivering a speech himself, he said he would head for San Diego.

When we arrived in Cardiff, we found Evelyn and Barry in a state of panic. Shortly after Fania called me, several sheriff's cars had pulled up in front of the house. With their weapons drawn, they had rushed in announcing that they had a warrant for the arrest of Fania Davis Jordon. They had handcuffed her and led her away to a patrol car. Some police had ransacked both my apartment and Evelyn and Barry's place upstairs. Evelyn was in a state of rage because one of the cops had aimed his rifle at her baby. Hearing the infant squirming in his bed behind a closed door, the cop had broken into the room, pointing his weapon at the bed.

Both Fania and Sam were subsequently charged with "attempted murder of a peace officer." It took two days to raise the money for their bail—and it would have taken much longer were it not for the fact that Herbert and Inge Marcuse contributed a substantial sum.

The story of their arrest was splashed across newspapers up and down the state. ANGELA DAVIS KIN ARRESTED FOR ATTEMPTED MURDER was a typical headline. In all the papers I saw, with the exception of the *People's World* and a few underground weeklies, the fact most emphasized was that Fania and Sam Jordon were the sister and brother-in-law of the "self-avowed Communist," Angela Davis.

Later Fania told us that the cops and matrons had continually called her "Angela" and had tried to rile her with their vulgar, anti-Communist remarks.

I publicly accused the San Diego Sheriff's Department of collaborating, in the basest way, with the most reactionary forces of the state. In particular, I charged them with carrying Ronald Reagan's racist, anti-

Communist policies to the extremes of premeditated murder. In the scuffle in their house, Sam would certainly have been killed if Fania had not been as bold as she was. After the cop had fired on Sam and hit him once, she grabbed his gun arm, deflecting the rest of the bullets into a nearby wall.

Fania and Sam were indicted twice by the Grand Jury. Both times, the judge assigned to the case realized how futile it was to try to prosecute them and dropped the charges. But their case dragged on for well over a year.

At the turn of the year, with one academic quarter behind me, my job was temporarily secure. The courts had declared unconstitutional the rule prohibiting the hiring of Communists. Everyone knew that although the Regents had been immobilized for the time being, they were seeking other ways of eliminating me before the beginning of the next school year. They had devised a system of provocation and espionage carried out by people posing as students in my classes; I was struggling with them daily.

As time went by, it became clear that the assault on my job was only a tiny part of a systematic plan to disarm and destroy the Black Liberation struggle and the entire radical movement. The fight for my job had to be interwoven with a larger fight for the survival of the movement.

Repression was on the rise throughout the country. The worst victims of judicial frame-ups and police violence were members of the Black Panther Party. Bobby Seale and Ericka Huggins had been indicted in New Haven. Fred Hampton and Mark Clark were murdered by Chicago policemen as they slept in their beds. And in Los Angeles, the Black Panther Party headquarters was raided by the Los Angeles Police Department and their special tactical squad, with the National Guard and the Army on alert.

I witnessed this raid firsthand and, along with my comrades, helped to organize resistance within the Black community. Our success in pulling together a grass-roots challenge to this repression put the city and state government on the defensive for a short time. It also doubtlessly increased their desire to eliminate all of us.

Early one morning—toward five A.M.—I received a telephone call about an emergency situation at the Panther headquarters on Central Avenue. The police had tried to break into the office, but the sisters and brothers inside had held them off and were still fighting back, guns in hand. I woke Josef and told him to get dressed as quickly as he could—I would explain the rest in the car.

The area surrounding the office had been cordoned off; each station of the blockade was at least three blocks away from the shooting. Circling the area, we caught sight of a figure spread out against a wall, being frisked by a policeman. When I looked more closely I saw it was Franklin. Kendra and a few other comrades were standing some twenty-five yards down the street. We jumped out of the car to ask them what was going on.

They said they had been trying to get as close as possible to the scene of the battle when a policeman had come up and aimed his shotgun at Franklin, ordering him up against the wall. Kendra, Taboo and the others had been told that if they didn't get out of the way their heads would be blown off. It was Franklin who interested them. When they found a piece of Party literature on him, they said something like "You dirty Communist" and led him away to a patrol car.

All the while gunshots could be heard in the background. As we walked down Central Avenue toward the police cordon, dawn was just beginning to break. In the new day's light, armed figures, dressed in black jumpsuits, were creeping snakelike along the ground or hiding behind telephone poles and cars parked along the avenue. From time to time, they discharged their weapons.

More black-clad figures were stationed on roofs along the entire block where the office was located. A helicopter hovered overhead. A bomb had just been dropped on the roof of the Panther office. Regular Los Angeles patrolmen were swarming throughout the entire area.

None of these cops were talking to one another. Their concentration on the attack had a hypnotic, even insane quality about it. They were like robots. The assault was too efficient to have been spontaneous. It appeared to have been planned well in advance, perhaps even down to the position of each cop.

The silence was almost total, broken only by the sound of gunshots. If shots were still being fired from the office, this was the only evidence that at least some of the Panthers were still alive.

A few people were standing around in the area. One woman looked extremely pained each time she heard a burst of shots. Her daughter, I learned, was inside. From our observation point—through the binoculars we had secured—the situation looked dismal. Between the guns and the dynamite, the office had been practically destroyed. The woman said nothing. No words could have expressed the terrible anguish that stood so clearly in her eyes.

I walked over to her and, as gently as possible, told her not to worry. I told her about the chains of telephone calls that had been started, carrying the message to people throughout the city to rush down to the Panther office immediately. There would soon be hundreds of people out in the streets. Their presence alone would force the police to retreat. Her daughter Tommie was going to be all right.

By seven A.M. people from the neighborhood and from throughout the city had crowded into the area. But the cordon had been extended. Only those of us who had come down early were close enough to see what was happening. We found ourselves inside the cordon.

Kendra and I and the other members of our club were extremely worried about Franklin. We were torn between the need to stand vigilance over the battle and our desire to find out what the police had done with him. I volunteered to try to get out of the cordon, survey the situation outside, determine whether Franklin was around and try to return. Josef was going with me.

We discovered an alley which we thought would take us safely through the cordon, but just as we thought we were on the other side, we caught sight of some policemen and had to turn around. Looking for another alley, we noticed a group of children from the neighborhood. Realizing that they probably knew the area better than anyone, we asked them whether they could get us through the blockade. They eagerly agreed and proceeded to lead us through labyrinthine walkways, backyards and alleys which could not be seen from the streets. If someone sighted the police, a sign was given, and we quickly retreated and tried another route.

Finally we made it to the other side. There were crowds of people with anger written all over their faces. As we searched the area for Franklin, we met scores of movement sisters and brothers we knew. We reached the block where Jefferson High School is located. The police motorcycle corps was parading in front of the school, trying to pull off a grand show of force. Over a hundred cops, all trying to look tough, and managing only to look racist, were speeding through the streets. They gunned the motors of their cycles, thinking the roar was the sound of their own power. At that moment, I saw in this scene historical traces of Hitler's troops trying to terrorize the Jews into submission.

One young sister, moved by righteous indignation, picked up a bottle and threw it into the procession. The motorcycle parade came to a halt. There was an extraordinary moment of tension. Many of us were certain that a full-scale confrontation was about to explode. But this peacock parade of force was only for show. The cops had not been ordered to go into combat. The procession started up again and the pigs continued to flaunt their presence through the ghetto.

Rumors were sprouting in the crowd and spreading at full speed. Peaches was dead, someone said. Bunchy and Yvonne Carter's baby was in the office, according to someone else, and had been killed by the pigs. The crowd's anger was mounting. Its size was greater than the visible police force. The students from Jefferson High School were angry. People who lived in the community were angry.

One woman who had just gotten off work was telling a small group that she couldn't even get to her own house because the police had blocked off that area. "These pigs think they can come into our community and take over." Some wanted to fight. Others counseled caution for the moment, because those inside the Panther office were still in danger.

Josef and I continued to search for Franklin. Finally, we saw him walking in our direction on the other side of the street. We were about to run over to him when we noticed him subtly motioning us away. He returned shortly, telling us that he had thought he was being followed and didn't want to jeopardize us.

He had been working with the students at Jefferson High School, helping them to prepare the conditions for a community rally inside the school. Totally absorbed by the immediate problems of the rally, he had almost forgotten the incident of earlier that morning. The police had locked him in the patrol car and had parked it close to the Panther headquarters. He had literally been able to see the bullets flying. After an hour or so, they had driven him off and had pushed him out of the car some ten blocks away in a typical act of police harassment.

The location of the LAPD Command Post had been discovered, so Franklin told us. Someone returned to Central Avenue to get Kendra and the other comrades while we headed for the house which the chief of police had taken over as his headquarters. It was surrounded by cops, and reporters were swarming all over the place. Some of them recognized me and immediately wanted to know whether I had come to act as an "intermediary" between the police and the Panthers. I told them in so many words that I had nothing but contempt for the LAPD. My loyalties were with the sisters and brothers under attack.

The woman who lived across from the house which had been commandeered by the LAPD was indignant about the police invasion of the community. She offered us—sisters and brothers from the Panthers, the Black Student Alliance and Che-Lumumba—the use of her house as headquarters for the resistance. A call went through to the Panther office. The sisters and brothers inside were all still alive, although most of them had been shot up and hurt in the explosion.

They said they were prepared to leave the building, but only if community people and the press could observe them coming out. They realized that if they had not defended themselves from the beginning, they might have all been shot down in cold blood. They had tried to hold out until we could gather enough people to witness the aggression, as well as to stand watch as they lay down their weapons and left the building.

A piece of white fabric was thrown out of the window. Everyone was silent. When the sisters and brothers walked out, eleven of them altogether, they were all standing strong. They were bleeding, their clothes were torn, and they were dirty from the debris of the explosion. But they were still standing strong. I found out later that Peaches had been shot in both legs. Yet she had marched proudly out of the building.

When the last of the eleven had come out, a huge roar of applause and cheers surged up from the crowd. Slogans were triumphantly shouted: "Power to the People." "No more pigs in our community." This was indeed a victory. The police had crept into the community in the early hours of the morning and launched a murderous attack on the Panthers. Without a doubt, they had planned to kill as many as they could and capture the rest, thus destroying the Panther chapter in Los Angeles. But with the support of the people outside, the Panthers had emerged victorious.

With the sisters and brothers out of the building, the crowd grew bolder. One sister actually jumped out and hit one of the cops from behind. Before he realized what had hit him, she was back under the cover of the crowd.

The students Franklin had talked to earlier had made preparations for a rally. They had informed their administration that they were going to use the gym for a community meeting to protest the unwarranted police raid on the Panther headquarters. The word was passed in the crowd to move over to Jefferson for the rally.

Emotions were high. The speeches were passionate. All carried the theme of the need to protect and defend the Panthers and the need to protect and defend the community. Some of the students gave speeches, as did a brother from the Black Student Alliance, Franklin and myself. By the time the rally was over, the students had called for a walkout so that they could spread the news of the attack throughout the Los Angeles Black community. They committed themselves to help mobilize the community for the coming fight, and we all walked out of the hall singing, "I want to be a Mau Mau. Just like Malcolm X. I want to be a Mau Mau. Just like Martin Luther King."

In order to organize the resistance, a coalition was established between the Black Panther Party, the Black Student Alliance and our Che-Lumumba Club. On the basis of this coalition of the Black Left, we felt we could call for a broad united resistance emanating from all sectors of the Black community.

That night we sponsored a meeting, attended by delegates from Black organizations throughout the city. This body approved a call for a general strike two days later in the Black community. On that day, we would hold a massive protest rally on the steps of City Hall. We had about thirty-six hours to put the rally together. It was no time at all, but the quicker the community reacted in an organized way, the more effective our protest would be.

That very night, thousands of leaflets were printed. The next morning, teams saturated the community with literature about the attack and the need to resist. The local Black radio station and an underground FM station gave us free time to issue the strike call and to publicize the rally. Others announced the rally as a part of the news.

I personally recorded spot announcements and held press conferences, since my name was known in the community. Yet I also felt the need to involve myself on a grass-roots level. I needed to acquire a sense of the mood of the community—and that could not be done from behind a microphone.

A team was on its way to Jordon Down Projects in Watts to distribute leaflets. I decided to go along. In all my experience of door-to-door community work, never had I seen such unanimous acceptance of our appeal. Literally no one was abrupt, no one tried to shut us out, and all agreed that we had to resist the attack on the Panthers. Many of the people recognized me, and I was surprised that they also volunteered their support for me in the fight for my job. Virtually every person with whom I spoke made a firm promise to observe the general strike and to attend the rally the next morning.

There were problems back at the Panther office. The woman who lived in the house behind the office had reported that early in the morning the police had returned and shot teargas cartridges into the office. The fumes were stronger now than shortly after the attack had halted. It was impossible to remain inside for any length of time without becoming sick.

It was decided, as a result, to hold a vigil in front of the office at all times. Participants in the vigil would form themselves into shifts in order to clean out all the debris. When the sun went down, there were still more than a hundred people taking part in the vigil. The tear-gas fumes had not abated and most of the group was clustered at the end of the block so no one would be overcome by the gas. The plans were to keep the vigil going throughout the night. Franklin led the group in freedom songs.

While the singers were warming up, I noticed some strange movements in the area: police cars creeping by—unmarked, but unmistakably police cars with agents peering out at us. I assumed that this was the normal surveillance. It seemed unlikely that they would try anything on a group which included not only the usual young movement people, but ministers, professors, politicians as well.

The singing broke into full blast. Perhaps the police felt affronted by the words of "Freedom Is a Constant Struggle" and "I Woke Up This Morning with My Mind Staid On Freedom" because they abruptly interrupted with a voice projected through a loudspeaker. "The Los Angeles Police Department has declared this an illegal assembly. If you do not move out, you will be subject to arrest. You have exactly three minutes to disperse."

Even if we had tried, we could not have dispersed in three minutes. We decided immediately not to disperse, but rather to form ourselves into a moving picket line. As long as we kept moving, we would not be an "assembly" and would theoretically have the right to remain. Senator Mervyn Dymally, a Black state senator, decided that he was going to speak to the policeman in charge, thinking he could calm them down.

The line stretched from the corner where the group had been singing, well past the office, which was near the next corner.

I moved toward the end nearest the Panther office. It was dark and difficult to determine exactly what was happening at the other corner. Suddenly there was a dash of the crowd. Thinking that this had been precipitated by nothing more serious than a show of force at the other end, I turned to calm everybody and tell them not to run. But at that moment, I saw a swarm of the black-suited cops who had executed the attack on the office the day before. They were already beating people further down, and some of them were about to converge on us.

I had been facing the crowd. I turned quickly, but before I could break into a run, I was knocked to the ground. I hit my head on the pavement and was momentarily stunned. During those seconds of semiconsciousness, I felt feet trampling on my head and body and it flashed through my mind that this was a terrible way to die.

A brother screamed, "Hey, that's Angela down there." Immediately, hands were pulling me up. I could see the billy clubs smashing into these brothers' heads. Someone told me later that as soon as the police realized who I was, they had come after me with their sticks.

Once on my feet, I ran as fast as I could. This was insane. Clearly, the police had no intention of arresting us. They only wanted to beat us. Even Senator Dymally hadn't been immune. After his futile conversation with the chief of police, I learned later, he had been the first to be hit.

We raced through the neighborhood, across lawns, through alleys, wherever it seemed we could find temporary refuge. As I ran across a front yard with some sisters and brothers I didn't even know, I heard a voice coming from the dark porch, telling us to come in. We ran into the house, lay down on the floor and tried to catch our breath. It was a middle-aged Black woman who had opened her doors to us. When I tried to thank her, she said that after what had happened the day before, this was the very least she could do.

We were on a side street, off Central Avenue. I looked through the draperies in the front room and could see nothing except a police car cruising by. Then I noticed some of our people on a porch across the street and decided I would try to get over to that house.

In all the excitement, I hadn't noticed how badly I had been bruised by the fall. Blood was streaming down my leg and my knee was throbbing with pain. But there was no time to think about that now. I thanked the woman, said good-bye and ran toward the house across the street as fast as I could.

The family who lived there had allowed a comrade from our Party to organize a first-aid station in the house. People with blood all over their faces were already waiting to be tended, and a squad had gone out searching for others who were wounded. Apparently, people throughout the neighborhood had opened their doors. Their spontaneous show of solidarity had saved us from a real massacre.

I was worried about Kendra, Franklin, Tamu, Taboo and the rest of my Che-Lumumba comrades whom I had not yet seen. The Panther leaders not under arrest as a result of the original assault were also missing, as were key members of the Black Student Alliance. A brother from the BSA said he would accompany me around the neighborhood in order to determine what had happened to our friends. People were crowded in the storefronts along Central Avenue. By hiding in the shadows along the way, we were able to reach one of the storefronts without incident. The people we were worried about were among the crowds in the storefronts. One person had been arrested.

On Central Avenue, a squadron of cops in black jumpsuits was marching in formation. When they saw one of our people in the street, several of them would jump out of line, swing at the person with their billy clubs and then calmly fall back into the march. It appeared they were determined to hold us prisoner indefinitely in these houses and storefronts.

Later, we learned that the police in the black jumpsuits were members of the Los Angeles Police Department's counterinsurgency force—the Special Weapons and Tactical Squad. Subsequent research determined that the SWAT Squad was composed primarily of Vietnam veterans. For over a year, they had been in training, learning how to wage counterurban guerrilla warfare, learning how to "quell" riots, and obviously also how to provoke them. They had made their public debut with the attack on the Panther office. Their offensive against our vigil was their second official appearance.

The attack on us had begun around six o'clock in the evening. It wasn't until ten-thirty or eleven that it appeared we might be able to leave the houses and storefronts. Around that time, one of Senator Dymally's aides got word to us that the police were prepared to retreat if we all left the area immediately. Whether or not this guarantee was good was a matter for speculation.

Even in this moment of crisis, our most important concern was making the rally a success. Most of the organizers and speakers for the meeting were down on Central Avenue. There was only one logical explanation for this ruthless siege: the police were trying to sabotage our rally. We had to take the chance of trying to get people out of the area so that we could go on with preparations for the mass meeting.

The exit took place without incident. After almost everyone had left, Kendra and I, together with other comrades, headed for a house to hold an emergency Che-Lumumba meeting. Everyone was cautioned to shake off all police tails before arriving.

There we discussed a proposal we were going to present to other members of the coalition the next morning: a march, at the conclusion of the rally, to the county jail where the Panthers were being held. The march would culminate in a demonstration raising the demand for their immediate freedom.

In the middle of our discussions, the brother on security out front rushed into the room to tell us that the police were cruising by in unusual numbers. They had discovered our meeting place, and we had no idea what they would try to do. Our uncertainty, our firm belief based on previous experience that the Los Angeles Police would stop at nothing to crush their adversaries meant that we would have to prepare for the worst.

Weapons were checked out, loaded and distributed. In the formidable silence, in the tension-laden room, we waited in readiness. Fortunately, the attack did not materialize. Despite the excitement and the threat of an assault looming over us, we managed to get through our meeting early enough to catch a few hours' sleep before the rally. Everyone else was going home. But it was too dangerous to go to my house on Raymond Street. I had to resign myself to sleeping on Kendra and Franklin's floor.

I woke up the next morning with a terrible feeling of apprehension that only a few hundred people might show up. If the rally were poorly attended, then L.A. ruling circles, particularly the LAPD, might take it as a sign that the Black community was accepting the repression without resisting it. The police could therefore claim a mandate to escalate their aggression. They would attempt to totally obliterate the Black Panther Party and would move on to other militant Black organizations. The arbitrary police violence in the ghetto would mount.

With these fears digging at my stomach, I drove down to City Hall with Kendra, Franklin and other members of the club. It was about an hour and a half before the meeting was scheduled to begin. We arrived early to see that equipment was set up and raise the question of the march with the others.

What we saw when we arrived made us all feel euphoric. At least a thousand people were already on the steps—and four-fifths of them were Black. People were still steadily streaming into the area.

By the time the first speaker took the microphone, the crowd had swelled to eight or ten thousand strong. It was a magnificent multitude, studded with signs and banners demanding an end to police repression, demanding a halt to the offensive against the Panthers, demanding immediate release of the captured Panthers.

The speeches were powerful. As we had previously agreed, the theme of the rally—the theme of all the speeches—was genocide. The aggression against the Panthers embodied the racist policy of the U.S. government toward Black People. Carried to its logical conclusion, this policy was a policy of genocide.

The Panthers had been charged with conspiracy to assault police officers. In my speech, I turned the idea of conspiracy around and charged Ed Davis, the Chief of Police, and Sam Yorty, the mayor of L.A., with conspiring with U.S. Attorney General John Mitchell and J. Edgar Hoover to decimate and destroy the Black Panther Party.

Months later, the existence of just such a plan was revealed to the public. The government had decided to wipe out the BPP throughout the entire country. J. Edgar Hoover had called the Panthers "the greatest threat to the internal security of the country," and police forces in most of the major cities had moved on local Panther chapters.

As I emphasized in my speech, our defense of the Panthers had to be a defense of ourselves as well. If the government could carry out its racist aggression against them without fearing resistance, then it would soon be directed against other organizations and would finally engulf the entire community.

We needed more than a one-day stand. Papers circulated in the crowd to be signed by those who wanted to play an active role in organizing the mass movement we needed. By the time the speeches were over, the people were in a fighting mood. Franklin took the microphone and called for the march and demonstration. It was instantly approved with unanimous and roaring applause. We set out for the jail.

When we reached the County Courthouse where the jail was located, the collective anger was so great that the people could not be contained. Defiant throngs pressed forward through the doors of the building. So great was their rage that they began to destroy everything in sight. As they attacked the coin machines in the lobby, they were probably fantasizing about ripping down the iron bars of the jail upstairs.

There were only two ways out of the lobby—one exit on each side. If the police decided to attack, it would be a bloodbath, without a doubt. They only had to lock off the exits and we would be bottled in the building, with no place to run, no room for maneuvering.

But the crowd was ungovernable. I tried to get their attention. But my voice does not carry well without the aid of a microphone and it was drowned out in the clamor. It was Franklin who eventually assumed the role he always seems to excel in: he stood at the top of the lobby steps and with his voice blasting forth like a trumpet, he elicited complete silence from the raging demonstrators. He explained our immediate tactical disadvantages. The police had already sealed off one of the entrances. They were stationed throughout the area and could fall upon us in just a matter of minutes.

It was not enough to explain the dangers of the moment. What had to be emphasized was that the Panther prisoners would be freed by the actions of a *mass movement*. The militant protests of a movement of masses, the determined thrust of thousands of people, could force our enemy to release the sisters and brothers upstairs. Rather than waste our energies giving vent to our frustrations, we should be trying to organize ourselves into a permanent movement to defend our fighters and to defend ourselves.

The people left the courthouse and the demonstration continued outside in full force and with unabated enthusiasm. Thousands marched around the jailhouse chanting slogans of resistance.

Later, the street in front of the Panther office was overflowing with people who came down to assist in the ongoing work of this movement. In all respects, this had been an extraordinarily triumphant day. The rally had more than served its purpose. But in order to realize the potential of what we had just witnessed, much day-to-day organizing was needed. Sisters and brothers would have to commit themselves to work that might not be as visible or dramatic as what we had just done, but which, in the final analysis, would be infinitely more effective.

In the aftermath of the rally, its immediate effects could already be seen. For a while, at least, there was a noticeable let-up of police violence in the community. If you were stopped, you could see that the L.A. police were not as self-confident and certainly not as arrogant as they had been before. By the same token, the collective confidence, pride and courage of the community was definitely on the rise. I felt deeply gratified each time someone in the community expressed his satisfaction to me that something was finally being done about the brutality and insanity of the police.

9

EQUALITY OF RIGHTS

The roots of the civil-rights movement run way back—to the Puritans' belief in equality before God as well as to the prayers of the first miserable slaves dragged from their homelands to the American shore. The Declaration of Independence set an ideal violated every time a human being was sold to another human being, every time the law compelled racist behavior. The first giant step in overcoming these wrongs was to confront them. For until the nation could see beyond its complacency to the horror of slavery, nothing would be done.

Of the many women, nameless and known, who lent force to the long march to freedom, a white housewife and mother named Harriet Beecher Stowe probably did the most to change the national vision of slavery. She did it with a book, *Uncle Tom's Cabin*, which broke the abolitionist cause out of the sermons and philosophic analyses and made it into a stunning human story. Mrs. Stowe's long-term prescription for the problem may be dubious and her portrayal exaggerated. But she opened the eyes of a generation to the most massive social malady in American life.

Harriet remembered the home she grew up in as a wonderful, happy place, filled with intellectual energy. By age sixteen she was teaching school, a shy, thin girl. At twenty-four she married; within seven years she had borne five children. She read to them endlessly, especially from the novels of Sir Walter Scott. She wrote stories of her own. And she read the news reports of the torture and degradation slaveholders committed. She and her husband once helped a girl escape the clutches of the slave catchers. Her brothers, Edward and Henry Ward, railed against the Fugitive Slave Act from their pulpits in Boston and Brooklyn.

One day, as she took communion, a vivid vision of the death of a slave flashed through her mind. She went home and wrote her book.

Harriet Beecher Stowe and the Challenge to Slavery

by John Anthony Scott

When the Constitution was drawn up in 1787 it guaranteed to slaveholders the right to have returned to them runaways who fled their plantations and took refuge in the North. What this meant in practice was spelled out by the Fugitive Slave Act which Congress passed in 1793. Slaveholders, under this law, were authorized to "seize and arrest" runaways. They were then supposed to apply to a magistrate for a piece of paper authorizing them to take the fugitive back South from whatever state he had been arrested in. But most slaveholders did not bother with this formality. They just crossed the Ohio River or the Pennsylvania line, seized their runaways and dragged them home. For years fugitive black people were taken back to the land of slavery as casually as if they had been lost children or stray animals.

The first Fugitive Slave Act of 1793 made possible terrible abuses, and a profitable business grew up in kidnapping free black people who lived in the northern states and had never run away at all. Slave catchers simply seized these people, dragged them south under the pretense that they were "runaways," and sold them to slave traders.

This was a shame and a scandal, and antislavery people loudly denounced so wicked an abuse of the law. To cope with the situation, therefore, state after state in the North passed measures to protect the rights of free black people and to prevent them from being whisked off in the dead of night. These "liberty laws," as they were called, guaranteed *all* black people charged with being fugitives a court hearing, a jury trial, counsel for their defense, and the right to produce witnesses on their own behalf—all the rights, in fact, guaranteed to white people charged with having committed a crime.

By the 1830s then, it was becoming a serious offense in most northern states to seize a black person and to remove him or her from the state without first having gone through the procedure prescribed by state law. The Liberty Laws certainly protected free black people from kidnapping; but they also made it much harder for slaveholders to catch runaways. The fact is that as antislavery sentiment grew in the North white people who saw blacks being seized and dragged back to slavery got mad. They rescued runaways from jail and even threatened the slave catchers with violence. And, of course, even if there were no actions of this type, court procedure was in itself slow and time-consuming. It now made it much more expensive than before to retrieve a runaway.

In 1842 the slaveholders' dismay over this situation turned to glee. In January of that year the United States Supreme Court handed down a decision—*Prigg v. Pennsylvania*—that declared all the Liberty Laws to be unconstitutional. With a wave of the hand, as it were, the Court swept them all away. A slaveholder's right to seize a runaway, said the Court, was guaranteed in the Constitution. It was a *national* right, which the federal government had the duty to protect and to enforce. No state had the power to defeat or nullify this right by laws that placed obstacles in the way of its realization.

After this it should, theoretically, have been easier than before to catch runaways. But the Prigg decision had exactly the opposite effect. "The job of catching slaves

---

From John Anthony Scott, *Women Against Slavery: The Story of Harriet Beecher Stowe* (New York: Thomas Y. Crowell, 1978), pp. 97–108, 118–23.

and seeing that they are returned is a *federal* duty," said the states; "very well! Let the federal government do it all: we want no part of it." State after state now passed new Liberty Laws telling all their people—private citizens, jailers, police officers, and judges—not to cooperate in any way at all with slaveholders seeking to recapture runaways.

Thus by 1850 the northern states had moved into open defiance of the Fugitive Slave Act of 1793 and of any kind of slave-catching at all that might take place on northern soil. Such now was the feeling throughout the North concerning the immorality of permitting slaves to be hunted upon free soil that slave-catching in many states had come almost to a halt.

In September 1850, when Charles Edward Stowe was barely two months old, a second Fugitive Slave Act was passed by Congress as part of the Compromise of 1850. This law, which aroused antislavery leaders like Henry Ward and Edward Beecher to a new pitch of fury, spelled out the ways in which the federal government itself would be authorized to go into the business of catching runaways and returning them to their owners. It is easy to see why such a law would be welcome to the slave masters. It provided massive federal aid, in men and money, to anybody seeking the capture of fugitives. And, of course, the taxpayer footed the bill.

Under this new Fugitive Slave Law of 1850 special federal commissioners were appointed to hear cases involving runaways and to issue the proper papers to owners seeking to take black people back to the South. If hostile crowds threatened the slave catchers, the commissioners were empowered to "employ so many persons as they may deem necessary to overcome such force." In plain language, the government might call out the army, the navy, and the marines to protect slaveholders and to prevent the liberation of runaway slaves.

But this wasn't all. Suppose a runaway had hidden himself in a hayrick and his owner was loudly demanding that he be dragged out? Federal officials in such a situation were entitled to ask anybody standing by to help them. If you refused to help catch a fugitive when you were ordered to do so, it was a federal crime; you could be punished by fine or imprisonment in a federal jail. "This law," as Ralph Waldo Emerson put it, "makes slave catchers of us all."

Opposition to the Fugitive Slave Law of 1850 was instant, violent, and continuous. A series of acts of defiance electrified the nation. In 1850 a black man named Shadrach was tracked to Boston, arrested, and jailed; but before the federal commissioner could arrange to have him sent back South, a mob broke open the jail and set him free. In April 1851 Tom Sims, a fugitive from Georgia, was seized in Boston and sent back South; but it took an escort of three hundred armed men to "protect" Sims from the crowd that would otherwise have liberated him as he was marched through the streets and placed on board a steamer. And this was moderate compared with what was to come. When in 1854 Anthony Burns was arrested in Boston and sent back to Virginia on the order of the federal commissioner, it took an army of one thousand men to march Burns to the dock.

In the fall of 1850, when all Boston was seething over the case of Shadrach, Isabel Beecher, Edward's wife, wrote to Harriet and urged her to speak out against the Fugitive Slave Act. "If I could use a pen as you can," wrote Isabel, "I would write something that would make this whole nation feel what an accursed thing slavery is." Harriet wrote back promising that she would do what her sister-in-law asked. "As long as the baby sleeps with me nights," she wrote, "I can't do much of anything, but I will do it at last."

Where would she publish the sketch or sketches of slavery that she was now planning? Harriet's first step was to write to

Dr. Gamaliel Bailey, whom she had known in Cincinnati as editor of *The Philanthropist*. Bailey was now editor of *The National Era*, an antislavery weekly newspaper published in Washington, D.C. She sent him a couple of short stories and asked if he would be interested in publishing them. Bailey's response was encouraging. He accepted the stories and sent a check for $100 in payment.

But still Harriet hesitated. She wanted, more than anything, to take up her pen and to write about slavery, but she was terrified at the thought of it. It was one thing, in those days, for women to write novels or short stories; to enter the field of politics and to write an attack upon slavery—that was something almost unheard of.

Early in January 1851 Henry Ward Beecher came to Boston to deliver a lecture; and then he took the train to Brunswick to visit his sister. Late in the evening, when the children were in bed and the snow lay thick outside, Harriet confided in her now-famous brother. She told him what she had in mind; was it right for a woman, she asked him, to write about slavery? Henry Ward's answer was both enthusiastic and emphatic. "Do it, Hattie!" he said.

Harriet's time to begin writing about slavery had now come. One Sunday in February 1851 she took the children to church. "My heart," as she told her son Charles Edward years later, "was bursting with anguish excited by the cruelty and injustice our nation was showing the slave, and praying to God to let me do a little and cause my cry to be heard." As she sat in the pew with her children around her, Harriet began to daydream. The church, the service, the children, all were forgotten. There came before her eyes, as real as life, the scene that Sarah Grimké had told about years before in Theodore Weld's *American Slavery as It Is*. It was a black man being brutally beaten and dying under the lash because he would not deny the existence of his true master, Jesus Christ.

That afternoon Harriet went to her room and wrote down what she had seen. In creating this episode, in turning it into a dramatic picture and putting it down on paper, Harriet had taken the crucial first step that is so familiar to creative writers. She had as yet not the faintest idea of the size and scope of the project that she was now embarking upon. But she had broken through a psychological barrier, a fear of her own inadequacy to handle the theme which she was tackling. She had made the all-important beginning in which, as literary artist, she saw also the possibility of carrying it through to the end.

Rapidly now the story that she planned to weave around Uncle Tom and his tragic death began to take shape. Early in March Harriet wrote to Dr. Bailey once again. Would he, she asked, be interested in publishing a story about slavery in serial form? "Up to this year," she told her old friend, "I have always felt that I had no particular call to meddle with this subject. . . . But I feel now that the time has come when even a woman or a child who can speak a word for freedom and humanity is bound to speak. . . . Such peril and shame as now hangs over this country is worse than Roman slavery, and I hope every woman who can write will not be silent."

Gamaliel Bailey wrote accepting Harriet's proposal, and he also sent her a check for $300 as payment in advance for her story. No more than Harriet did Bailey at that time have the faintest conception of the undertaking to which he was committing himself. He certainly did not conceive Harriet's "story" as anything more than a series of sketches showing the evils of slavery in five or six installments.

Harriet was now fairly launched upon her writing, and there was no stopping. She performed the endless household chores, but she would not allow them to distract her from the central task. In one letter she talked of having been interrupted "at least a dozen times; once for the fishman, to buy a codfish; once to see a man who had brought me some barrels of apples; . . . then to Mrs. Uphams to see about a drawing I promised to make for her; then to nurse the baby; then into the kitchen to make a chowder for dinner"; and always she returned to her desk. "Now I am at it again," she wrote, "for nothing but deadly determination enables me ever to write; it is rowing against wind and tide."

As Harriet wrote, her theme took on its own independent life, followed its own logic, presented its own demands. The dam that for years had blocked the compassionate heart and the creative mind was broken. The deep feelings, the pent-up thoughts and dreams of seventeen years came roaring through the breach.

The first installment of "Uncle Tom's Cabin; or, Life Among the Lowly," appeared in *The National Era* on June 5, 1851. After that the story came out in weekly installments running almost without interruption until March 1852. Harriet did occasionally skip a week when she fell behind in the grueling and apparently unending job of writing for a weekly deadline. These delays brought anguished protests from her readers.

Before Harriet's work was one-third done she made arrangements with John P. Jewett of Boston to have her story published as a novel. *Uncle Tom's Cabin* was given to the world in book form on March 20, 1852. Jewett was rather frightened by the risk that he was taking in putting out so bulky a novel by so little known a woman author. But his fears soon vanished. The first printing of the *Cabin* was a mere five thousand copies, but these were grabbed up in two days. The public's appetite for the book seemed to be insatiable. By March 1853, one year after publication, three hundred thousand copies had been sold in the United States alone. By the time the Civil War broke out eight years later the figures for both American and British sales ran into the millions. *Uncle Tom's Cabin* was soon translated into forty foreign languages and was being read by people all over the world. Very few books in the history of modern literature have won such instant and such universal popularity.

Uncle Tom's Cabin made Harriet America's leading literary figure. Not since 1776 when Tom Paine published *Common Sense*, calling for independence from Great Britain, had a piece of writing made so deep an impression upon the public. In 1853 an abridged edition for children came out, entitled *A Peep Into Uncle Tom's Cabin*, and that same year there were Welsh and German versions specially for immigrants. Tom songs became popular; and there was also a card game, Uncle Tom and Little Eva, in which the winning player was the one who first brought together a complete suit consisting of all the members of a slave family. A stage show produced by George Aiken played to packed audiences in Troy, New York, for one hundred nights, and traveling players were soon making their living from Tom shows all over the North. These, too, popularized the book and helped to boost its sales.

For the first time in their lives tens of thousands of Americans, regardless of age, race, creed, or sex, began to read a story that set forth vividly the human horror of slavery and exposed the inhumanity of those who profited by it. People reacted to the message with anger, shock, and tears. It was a moment of truth that would not occur again until February 1977 when Alex Haley's *Roots* flashed before millions on the nation's TV screens.

Harriet's creation was both bold and unique. No American writer before her had ever attempted a novel about slavery or anything that even remotely foreshadowed the *Cabin*. Of course, when the *Cabin* appeared there was already a great deal of antislavery literature in America; but most of this was in the form of antislavery tracts or pamphlets. These lectured the reader about the evils of slavery and gave the reasons why as a system of exploitation it defied the laws both of God and man. There were, too, a number of antislavery poems by people like John Greenleaf Whittier and Henry Wadsworth Longfellow which denounced slavery and those who defended it.

In addition to these antislavery poems and tracts there was a growing literature composed by fugitives and runaways themselves and published with the help of northern abolitionists and antislavery societies. The most famous of such memoirs, in which ex-slaves told of the horrors they had personally experienced and of their lives in bondage, was Frederick Douglass' *Narrative*. Josiah Henson's *Story of His Own Life* was another important work of the same type. Harriet had met Henson in Boston at Edward's house in 1850. A slave of saintly character, Henson had succeeded in fleeing from Maryland and finding his way to Canada. Harriet drew heavily upon his personality and his experience in order to create the character of Uncle Tom.

Writings like those of Douglass and Henson were often moving and informative accounts of the life and sufferings of an individual or a family, but they lacked the scale of Harriet's canvas and the sweeping vision of an entire social system which she set before the reader. The same was true of Richard Hildreth's *The Slave*, a fictionalized account of a slave's life written by a white historian and published in 1836.

Harriet's work was extraordinary not only because it was a new and pioneer type of novel but because it was written by a woman. Until 1852 few American women had broken the barriers of convention that forbade women to write about anything so real and so brutal as slavery. Angelina and Sarah Grimké had written about slavery and had agitated against it. Lydia Maria Child had edited an antislavery newspaper and had published her own antislavery tracts. But the most popular women writers wrote polite or conventional novels in which discussion of the topic of slavery was taboo. The most famous of such women novelists, in Harriet's time, was Catharine Maria Sedgwick, who wrote polite tales of upper-class life in New England.

For a woman to depart so boldly from custom took both courage and conviction. It is part of Harriet's supreme achievement that she dared to give a bold and scorching expression to her feelings as a woman and a mother when she saw innocent and often defenseless human beings ground up or torn to pieces by the workings of slavery. "I wrote as I did," she said in 1853, "because as a woman, as a mother, I was oppressed and broken-hearted with the sorrow and injustice I saw, because as a Christian I felt the dishonor to Christianity, because as a lover of my country I trembled in the coming day of wrath. It is no merit in the sorrowful that they weep, or in the oppressed and smothering that they gasp and struggle, nor to me that I *must* speak for the oppressed—who cannot speak for themselves.". . .

. . . At the end of her book, Harriet emerges from her role as a writer about slavery and speaks directly to her audience. What, she asks, can ordinary people do, faced as they are with the horrors that she has described? "There is one thing that every individual can do," she points out; "they can see to it that *they feel right*." Americans must stop turning their backs on slavery, treating it with indifference, or even apologizing for it. They must learn to use their hearts, to feel pity and compassion for the victims of the system, and to think of the wrongs done to these people as wrongs done to themselves.

Receive the black strangers, she goes on, into our Christian churches, educate them. Then help them to return to Africa "where they may put into practice the lesson they have learned in America." Only so can the Union be saved, for the whole American people is involved in the crime of slavery, not just a portion of them. We must purge ourselves, she says, of this injustice, or there will be a day of reckoning and a day of vengeance. The judgment of God will be upon us.

To understand the nature of Harriet's achievement it is helpful to compare *Uncle Tom's Cabin* with the Fourth of July address that [abolitionist William Lloyd] Garrison had delivered twenty-three years before in Edward Beecher's Boston church.

Garrison warned the American people, in that speech, that slavery had become a mortal threat to the American union; that either slavery must go, or the American people and their Republic would face destruction. Harriet's message in the *Cabin* was the same. "You must," she told the people, "feel in your hearts the horror and evil of slavery, and you must abolish it; if not, you will face a day of reckoning compared with which a thousand cholera epidemics will be as nothing."

There were a number of important differences in the reception of Harriet's message and Garrison's. Garrison, and the abolitionists who followed him, spoke to limited audiences; their books and pamphlets and newspapers reached, relatively speaking, only a handful of people. The abolitionists, too, often paid a heavy price for daring to discuss in public a topic that powerful and wealthy leaders had decided was taboo. Theodore Weld was driven from Lane, and James G. Birney from Kentucky; Garrison himself nearly lost his life at the hands of a lynch mob in Boston in 1836; Elijah Lovejoy was killed at Alton, Illinois, the following year.

Harriet, too, might have been afraid of rock-throwing or threats upon her life or demands that she be thrown in jail. What is striking about her book is its magnificent audacity. She took hold of a forbidden subject and explored it boldly. She wrote an antislavery tract that, for the first time in the history of the country, reached the homes and touched the hearts not of a few, but of millions. She made antislavery thinking the common property of every family in the land.

In the *Cabin* Harriet handed down a blunt but deeply considered Christian judgment upon slavery and all its works. This, of course, was in itself not new: since colonial times people had been attacking slavery as a social evil that mocked the laws of God and the rights of man. Harriet, indeed, like so many of the writers who went before her, was a Christian moralist. But the *form* of her attack was so different from theirs as to be revolutionary; she was the first person to write a truly effective novel about slavery, rather than just a sermon, or an exposé, or a tract.

This novelistic form was vital to the success of Harriet's work. She painted a series of scenes into which she introduced real and highly articulate people—they laugh, groan, fight, mock, lament, and talk to each other. These scenes are so vividly constructed that Harriet carries us in imagination from one end of the Union to the other. By this means she shows us slavery in its everyday operation. We see how the system takes living, breathing people, how it grinds them up body and soul, and destroys them. She shows how the law of slavery violates Christian law with respect to the *human* use of human beings: do unto others as you would that they should do unto you. This law, she reminds us, is the very bedrock of our American faith.

Harriet's message, that slavery is wrong and must be abolished, came at a critical moment in the history of the United States. Public opinion, spurred by the war with Mexico and the Fugitive Slave Act of 1850, was beginning to awaken to the fact that the abolitionists were right, that the slave masters of the South and the slave empire that they ruled had taken the place of the British Empire as the major enemy of the American people, of their democratic institutions and of their free-labor economy. Harriet's book was a response to this new mood, but it was also an independent contribution to the antislavery cause of the first magnitude. The *Cabin* not only reflected the American mood, but it speeded up that lightning change or revolution in public opinion, which slaveholders had foreseen and which they so much feared.

There was yet another important difference between *Uncle Tom's Cabin* and Garrison's 1829 address. Garrison had proclaimed the new and radical doctrine that black people were American citizens, that they had as much right as any white person to be in the United States and to own and inherit the American soil upon which they had labored so long and so painfully without pay. This was a message that Harriet Stowe never fully absorbed. She remained for many years a colonizationist; one, that is, who believed that black people had no right to stay in America, that they ought to be returned to Africa.

From Harriet's day till our own a number of black leaders like Martin Delaney and Marcus Garvey have taken the same position. They have contended that black people ought to return to Africa because winning true equality in the United States is impossible and even to dream of this is a delusion. But white colonizationists, on the whole, have been racists; they have contended that America ought to be reserved for the Anglo-Saxon race, and that there is no place in it for "lesser breeds" like Africans. In the *Cabin* Harriet sometimes refers to black people in the condescending tones of white superiority. There is some nonsensical talk about African "docility of heart," childlike simplicity of affection, and so on. We in the twentieth century find this both unacceptable and offensive.

In being a colonizationist Harriet was not at all unusual—both Thomas Jefferson and Abraham Lincoln held identical views. Colonizationists never denied that slavery was wrong; they only insisted that the future of blacks as free people lay not in the United States but under an African sky. The racism behind this notion of the future of black Americans is a fault in Harriet's book; but it does not diminish at all the central and revolutionary thrust of the *Cabin*. The *Cabin* was a call to all Americans to place themselves in harmony with their own Declaration of Independence, and to face the fact that the holding of human beings in bondage is wrong. The *Cabin* was a trumpet blast announcing the day of judgment and the end of the world—the world of slavery. In writing this book Harriet saw herself as a messenger of God bearing tidings both of doom and joy. She announced, and she demanded, a revolution in American public opinion.

10

EQUAL PROTECTION OF THE LAWS

History demonstrates that those who want their rights have to demand them. White abolitionists like Harriet Beecher Stowe made their moral point and eventually helped scrub the stain of slavery from the national standard. But then what? The newly freed slaves, most of them illiterate and ignorant of the skills of self-support, had to find their place in the fabric of American life. That story would unfold for a century, which is approximately how long it took blacks to move from their theoretical right to vote to actually voting on a widespread, organized basis.

One prophet who led the way after the carnage of the Civil War was Sojourner Truth, a tall, gaunt, gray-haired woman who wore a sunbonnet and spoke like a clarion. Born a slave in New York's Hudson Valley, she never learned to read or write. Yet she heard God speak to her, telling her to go out and be "a sign unto the people." She began "testifying of the hope that's in me." She took the name Sojourner, she said, " 'cause I'm to travel up and down the land," and Truth because, as she said to her God, "Your name is truth." There was no stopping her. She stood up for her own people to all the powers that were, including a great president and his tarnished successor. Along the way Sojourner Truth bore witness to the rights of women, black and white, as children of God and citizens of the United States.

Sojourner Truth and the Freedmen

by Hertha Pauli

The turn was near. John Brown took the sword and perished by the sword, and Frederick Douglass, having tried in vain to dissuade the old man from his suicidal raid on Harper's Ferry, barely escaped arrest for complicity and had to flee abroad once more. But the year was 1859; the tide of events rushed on to Lincoln's nomination

From Hertha Pauli, *Her Name Was Sojourner Truth* (New York: Avon, 1976), pp. 194–200, 210–17, 220–30.

and election, to secession and war. John Brown's body lay a-mouldering in the grave, but his soul went marching on. Anti-slavery men quivered with impatience. Now, would the monster be crushed? Their press chided Lincoln for temporizing on emancipation, on the use of Negro troops. Douglass, back from England, joined in the strictures.

"Wait, child," counseled Sojourner. "It takes a while to turn about a great ship of state."

Waiting was hard, after so many years of it, and when the longed-for word finally came, it called for more patience. An emancipation proclamation was issued in September, 1862, but not to take effect for a hundred days; even after the New Year it should apply only to the states "then in rebellion." The oft-disillusioned could scarcely believe that the New Year might bring freedom. What if the war ended sooner? If the rebels quit before the year's end, would they keep their human chattels next year, and forever?

"Seek ye first the kingdom of God, and his righteousness, and all these things shall be added unto you," Sojourner answered from Scripture. Sufficient unto her day was the evil thereof.

That fall, with Josephine Griffing, she held meetings in the northern counties of Indiana. Indiana was Copperhead country, so livid with anti-war and anti-Negro feeling that the legislature had barred non-resident colored persons from the state. Sojourner was arrested repeatedly, but Mrs. Griffing convinced every judge that the law was unconstitutional. Their associates were prosecuted for encouraging Sojourner to remain. Arriving in Steuben County for a meeting in the town hall of Angola, she was yelled at, "Down with you! We think the niggers have done enough! We won't have you speak! Shut your mouth!"

"The Union people will make you shut your mouths," she yelled back.

She stayed with a family in Pleasant Lake, five miles from Angola. On the eve of the meeting her host was arrested for entertaining her, and two ladies hurried to warn Sojourner. She got into their chaise, expecting to be driven to their home; when they headed for a hide-out in the woods, she balked. "I'd sooner go to jail," she said, and indeed, a constable promptly appeared with a warrant for her arrest.

On his heels came a captain of the Union home guard. "She is my prisoner," he announced, producing orders to take her into custody. The fife and drum of a home guard unit was heard down the street.

The constable looked disgusted. "I ain't going to bother my head with niggers; I'll resign my office first," he said and vanished as the handful of guardsmen marched up, cheering lustily for Sojourner and the Union. The captain promised to escort her to the meeting—if there was a meeting. It seemed doubtful, for the Copperheads had threatened to burn down the town hall if she tried to speak in it.

"Then I'll speak on the ashes," said Sojourner.

The ladies thought she had better wear uniform. They found her a red, white, and blue shawl with apron to match and put a cap with a star on her head, and a star on each shoulder. "I could scare myself," she said after a glance at the mirror. She refused to take a sword or pistol: "The Lord will preserve me without weapons. The truth is powerful and will prevail."

In the street she found a carriage waiting. The captain and some gentlemen got in with her, the home guard marched alongside, and the Loyal League of Pleasant Lake brought up the rear. Sojourner gripped a white satin banner the ladies had given her, with the inscription, "Proclaim Liberty Throughout the Land," and as the procession entered Angola, she saw the town hall ringed by a huge crowd. "I felt I was going against the Philistines," she said later, "and I prayed God to deliver me out of their hands. But when the rebels saw such a mighty host coming, they fled, and by the time we got there they were scattered over the fields like a flock of scared crows, and not one was left but a small boy who sat on the fence crying, 'Nigger, nigger!' "

After the meeting her friends took her to the squire's home for safety, but in Angola she had no more trouble. She was threatened, heckled, and arrested elsewhere—"at all our meetings," Mrs. Griffing wrote to the *Anti-Slavery Standard*, "we have been told that armed men were in our midst and had declared they would blow out our brains." No meeting was canceled, and Sojourner's banner waved at every one.

"What business are you now in?" she was asked once, by a man who knew her from New York.

"In New York," she told him, "my business was scouring brass door knobs; now I go about scouring copperheads."

She scoured them until winter, when she fell ill. The long wait was drawing to a close, and Freedom Day came near enough to grasp. On New Year's Eve, Negro churches and lodge halls were crowded all over the land; in Boston's Tremont Temple William Lloyd Garrison sat in the balcony, weeping, while Frederick Douglass led the singing on the floor: "Blow ye the trumpets, blow! The year of jubilee has come . . ."

Battle Creek, too, saw rejoicing by the fugitives who had settled in shacks at the ends of the streets. There was "Old Agnes," who owed her life to the mercy of her master's hounds; there was "Old Nancy," whose growing son had no wish to join the Union army; there were a mother and daughter whom chance had reunited in Battle Creek, after long years. Singing paeans, they marched through the frozen town.

Sojourner was at the Merritts' again—bedridden, unable to help in the house, feeling hopelessly dependent. She thought of the aged who were now to go free, and she wondered about the lucky ones who had been cared for by kind masters rather than set adrift like Mau-Mau and Baumfree. Free people worked or paid for their keep, and the oldsters had no money, nor had they strength left to work. The Merritts were kindness itself, but every trifle Sojourner had to accept nowadays reminded her painfully of old age in bondage.

A young woman sat by her bedside, writing a letter. "From Phebe M. Stickney"—the Merritts' daughter had married the year before—"to Joseph A. Dugdale, Mount Pleasant, Iowa . . ."

"At the request of our dear friend, Sojourner Truth," Mrs. Stickney wrote to the Quaker who had been Sojourner's host on the prairie across the Mississippi River, "I write to thee and thine to solicit a little assistance for her. She is now with us, and has many friends, and all are trying to do a little for her. She is this winter quite feeble, not able, by selling her book, to supply herself with the many little comforts that an aged and feeble person needs . . ."

She could not explain her reluctance to take what the friends in Battle Creek were so persistently offering. The voice she had heard all her life had work for her still—yet how to do it, so dependent upon white people as if she had never been free? She thought of her friends elsewhere. "Uncle Joe" Dugdale and others would surely help pay for her needs till she could work again; there was a world of difference, to Sojourner, between asking friends for assistance and inflicting your infirmity upon them like an outworn slave. "Help me live a little longer to praise God and speak to the people in this glorious day of 'mancipation . . ."

Mrs. Stickney put the exact words into her letter. "I write this with Sojourner at my side," she concluded, "and at her request. She is very poorly, and probably will not live long."

"You sent the ravens to feed 'Lijah in the wilderness; now send the good angels to feed me while I live on thy footstool . . ."

Alone in her barn, Sojourner talked to her God. One day, Phebe Stickney came with mail. One by one, she opened and read the letters. Friend Dugdale's reply, "I never remember to have regretted more that I had so little at command to bestow," was accompanied by greenbacks, and his Iowan neighbors had followed his example.

Sojourner lifted her weary eyes. "Lord, I knew thy laws was sure, but I didn't think they'd work so quick!"

To everyone's surprise, the next week's *Anti-Slavery Standard* contained Phebe's letter to Dugdale. It was not her doing; friends from Pennsylvania had responded to her plea and sent it in. Contributions could be addressed to the Stickneys in Battle Creek, the editor added. It sufficed to keep them coming from East and West.

"I tell you, child, the Lord manages everything," Sojourner explained to the young woman. "You see, when you wrote that letter you didn't think you was doing much; but I tell you, dear lamb, when a thing is done in the right spirit, God takes it up and spreads it all over the country."

Among the senders were Oliver Johnson, the *Standard* editor who had welcomed Sojourner to Ohio, and Samuel Hill who had befriended her in Northampton, and Mrs. Griffing who was now in Washington, working for Freedmen's Aid. "Sojourner," wrote Gerrit Smith, "the God whom you so faithfully serve will abundantly bless you; he will suffer you to lack nothing either in body or soul . . ."

She threw up her hands. "The Lord bless the man! His heart is as big as the nation—if he hadn't sent a penny, his words would feed my soul, and that's what we all want."

The surprises mounted. When the *Standard* of March 25 arrived, Mrs. Stickney brought it to the barn with all signs of excitement. Spread over the whole back page was an article that said, "From the Atlantic Monthly for April," over the title: "Sojourner Truth, the Libyan Sibyl," by Harriet Beecher Stowe! Almost ten years had gone by since their first and last meeting, but Mrs. Stowe had not forgotten anything. Word by word, as Phebe read from the printed page, the colloquies at Andover came back, from the moment of arrival to Sojourner's departure "as a wave of the sea."

"Her memory still lives in one of the loftiest and most original works of modern art," continued Mrs. Stowe who had visited Rome, some years back, and there told Sojourner's history to the American sculptor, William Wetmore Story. The marble statue inspired by her account had been judged the most impressive work at the 1862 World's Exhibition in London. It was called *Sibilla Libica*, the Libyan Sibyl.

Sojourner shook her head. Could she be that? Nowhere in Scripture was mention made of a sibyl. She pronounced it "symbol," and when Phebe wished to read the article over, she became impatient: "Oh, I don't want to hear about that old symbol. Read me something that's going on now, something about this great war!"

Hearing her grandson described as an "African Puck" did not please her, either. James was no longer the giggly child of Andover. Grown up into a tall, able-bodied lad, he had gone to answer a call sounded by Frederick Douglass: "MEN OF COLOR, TO ARMS!" At last, the nation had unchained "her powerful black hand." On every highway men were making their way eastward to join the new colored units, and the nineteen-year-old from Battle Creek had just enlisted in the 54th Massachusetts Volunteer Infantry, Colonel Robert Gould Shaw commanding.

"We are the valiant soldiers who've enlisted for the war," Sojourner hummed to the tune of "John Brown's Body." Whatever she sang now would fit itself to this tune that was sweeping the land. Her voice regained its vigor. Her careworn face lit up on hearing names she knew. "They're appointed to God," she said of abolitionists commanding Negro troops, of feminist ladies gone south to care for slaves escaping through the lines—"contrabands," the Army termed them. She was aglow with her old fire. If only she were younger and as strong as when Olive Gilbert had been sitting in Phebe Stickney's place! What had Olive said she might have been? "Another Joan of Arc"—that was it. "I'd be on hand as the Joan of Arc," she told Phebe, "to lead the army of the Lord. For now is the day and the hour for the colored man to save this nation.". . .

The leaves on the Maryland hills had yellowed when Sojourner and her grandson came to Washington. She had never seen it before. In all her travels she had not set foot in slaveholding territory, and the capital had not long been free soil. But what impressed her was not what impressed other visitors: the Capitol dome, the ankle-deep mud on Pennsylvania Avenue, or the prevalence of uniforms and the grim ring of forts. Victories—Sherman's in Georgia, Sheridan's in the Shenandoah Valley—were the talk of the town, but Washington still felt as if one could see the front.

Sojourner saw her people.

In her born days she had not seen so many. There were few colored soldiers in Washington and vicinity, no colored regiments in camps such as she had been visiting, but here a colored host roamed the city. Decently clad or in rags, in the faded finery of some master or mistress or in the coarse, sweat-stained togs of the field, dark faces seemed to be everywhere. Only a fraction were Washington Negroes. The bulk were "contraband of war." The ingenious label, devised to free the early wartime runaways for trench-digging, had stuck to the deluge that followed. All through the war they kept pouring into the city where "Massa Linkum" lived and they were free—free to live in shanty towns, to be herded into camps, to be locked up in the "Blue Jug," the dismal county jail. Sojourner could soon tell the contrabands. They had a dreamy unawareness of time as if a pause had come in their lives, as if they were facing an abyss and dared not look. They were strangers in a strange land, hungry, thirsty, ragged, homeless.

She saw bands of children prowl the streets, children who pilfered and robbed to live, were caught, jailed, released, and went back to stealing. She saw what was called "home" by the contrabands who had come early during the war: teeming shacks, often built atop one another—near the Washington Canal a hundred families, three to ten persons each, lived in a space 50 yards square. The rooms were windowless, some accessible only through others, so no light at all got in. The roofs leaked. The stench from beneath the few rotten floor boards was worse than in the cellar of Sojourner's childhood. The filth was indescribable. Washingtonians knew the spot as "Murder Bay."

Sojourner stayed with a friend, a feminist and abolitionist from way back; in the old days a mob had wrecked Jane Swisshelm's paper in Minnesota, and after the outbreak of war she had nursed in field hospitals until the Army Nurse Corps came into being. At fifty she was busier than ever. The veterans of the great cause did not rest after emancipation. Frances Gage, back from South Carolina, had left on a speaking tour for Freedmen's Aid; Laura Haviland was trouble-shooting in Louisiana; Lucy Colman, Sojourner's companion in Ohio, served as a gadfly to Washington bureaucrats—"Somehow," she boasted, "if anything was to be done for any special colored person, everyone knew I was the one to do it." And Josephine Griffing was the freedmen's angel in the capital, the one who organized relief, the one who found work. Week after week she took small groups to Philadelphia or New York, paying their fare and feeding them until they started in their jobs as free people.

As the stream of contrabands swelled, camps were set up on North Tenth Street, on Mason's Island in the Potomac, finally at Arlington Heights across the river, where the men were put to tilling the farms around the pillared mansion of Robert E. Lee. The Arlington camp was named Freedman's Village. Many called it Freedom Village. The superintendent, Captain Carse, a man as dedicated as the women volunteers, arranged for crafts to be taught and a school, a church, a hospital, a home for the aged to be set up—the camp, laid out around a small park, could have been a model miniature city if the incoming tide had not continually overflowed its bounds and overtaxed its facilities. Bewildered, uncertain, without possessions other than their bodies, without resources other than hands and legs accustomed to move only at a master's bidding, the freedmen poured in. Young men went into the Army; the women and children, the crippled and the aged remained. They kept coming and coming.

Sojourner moved out of Mrs. Swisshelm's. After a week on Mason's Island, holding meetings for the people there, she went to Arlington and found she was needed. The contrabands at Freedman's Village were not the strong and the strong-willed, those who had escaped in former years and had since had a taste of the free world. These, until now, had never left a plantation except to be sold to another plantation; their world was the cotton field, the cabin, and the coffle. Their habits were dirty. Their children wallowed naked in the mud. But the word God, on Sojourner's lips, still had a sound all its own.

It was Sunday; she held a meeting. From all over the camp they came to listen, to look at the tall woman who stood on the platform wearing a turban of spotless white, who was one of them and yet so different. She preached on cleanliness. "Be clean," she demanded as a start. "Cleanliness is next to godliness!"

They flocked about her after the sermon, to hear more, listening as to an oracle.

The superintendent asked her to stay at the Village. She had, of course, come to Washington to see Mr. Lincoln, but this proved to be more difficult than she had thought. One did not simply call on the President. One needed an appointment, and Captain Carse was unable to get one for her. The war, the government, and the election that was only a few weeks off kept Mr. Lincoln too busy. The captain advised asking Mrs. Colman. If anyone in Washington could wangle it, she was the one.

In mid-October Sojourner saw the President, but at a distance. The State of Maryland had abolished slavery, and the colored people in Washington and environs were celebrating. Sojourner was one of the speakers. Afterwards, when a torchlight procession with banners marched behind a brass band to the White House lawn, she went along. The crowd cheered itself hoarse until the French doors opened and a man came out on the portico.

In the flickering light of the torches Sojourner saw a gaunt figure—not unlike her own, but taller—and a drawn, deeply lined face. "I have to guess, my friends, the object of this call which has taken me quite by surprise this evening," said the President.

"The emancipator of Maryland, sir," someone shouted.

Lincoln smiled. "It is no secret that I have wished and still do wish mankind everywhere to be free."

"God bless Abraham Lincoln!" The cheers rose to the portico, and Sojourner kept looking at the doors that had closed behind the gaunt man. Freedom, like God, must be all over . . .

It was for 8 A.M. on Saturday, October 29, that Mrs. Colman finally obtained a White House appointment for herself and Sojourner. The two arrived to find about a dozen callers waiting, among them two other colored women. The door to the President's room was open. Waiting her turn, Sojourner enjoyed hearing him converse with others, and it occurred to her that he was as friendly to his colored visitors as to the whites—indeed somewhat friendlier. One of the colored women, a soldier's wife, was sick and due to be evicted for being behind in her rent. The President listened attentively, and there was kindness and concern in his voice as he told the woman where to turn for help and asked Mrs. Colman to assist her.

Lucy Colman gave the woman some instructions and turned back to the President. "I am happy to say to you, sir, that I haven't come to ask any favor. My business is simply to present Sojourner Truth, who has come all the way from Michigan to see you."

Abraham Lincoln rose and gave Sojourner his hand, with a bow. "I am pleased to see you."

"Mr. Lincoln," she said, "I'd never heard tell of you before they put you up for president."

"But I had heard of you," he said, smiling.

"And when you took your seat," she went on, "I feared you'd be torn to pieces. I likened you unto Daniel, who was thrown into the lions' den—and if the lions didn't tear you to pieces, I knew it would be God that saved you. And I said if he spared me, I'd see you before the four years expired, and he'd done so, and now I'm here to see you for myself."

He congratulated her on being spared. When she called him "the best president who's ever taken the seat," he replied that she was probably referring to his Emancipation Proclamation, but his predecessors, Washington in particular, had been just as good and would have done just as he had, if the time had come. "If the people over there," he said, pointing across the Potomac, "had behaved themselves, I couldn't have done what I have; but they didn't, which gave me the opportunity to do these things."

"Thank God," she said with fervor, "that you were the instrument chosen by him and the people to do it."

He opened a silver-mounted box and showed her a book, which she recognized as a Bible even though the gold plate on the cover bore a slave with the shackles dropping off his hands in a cotton field. Lincoln turned the book around; on the back cover was another gold plate, with an inscription.

Mrs. Colman rushed to read it aloud: "To Abraham Lincoln, President of the United States, the friend of universal freedom, by the loyal colored people of Baltimore, as a token of respect and gratitude. Baltimore, July 4, 1864."

Sojourner examined the gift and had to think of the laws that made it a crime to teach the givers to read it. "And for what?" she asked. "Let them answer who can."

As if to answer, the President reached for her "Book of Life." The hand that had signed the death warrant of slavery wrote a few words, and she heard him say, writing "For Aunty Sojourner Truth, October 29, 1864. A. Lincoln." Then he rose, took her hand, and told her that he would be pleased to have her call again.

Her time had run out. And so, before she had a chance to call again, would Mr. Lincoln's.

A week after the election, Sammy took down a letter for his grandmother, to friends up north. "Abraham Lincoln, by the grace of God President of the United States for four years more," she began a detailed description of her White House visit. And she summed up: "I must say, and I am proud to say, that I never was treated by anyone with more kindness and cordiality than by that great and good man. I felt I was in the presence of a friend."

She was now at Freedman's Village and had found things as well as expected. "I think I can be useful and will stay. The captain in command of the guard has given me his assistance, and by his aid I have got a little house, and will move into it tomorrow. Will you ask any of my friends to send me a couple of sheets and a pillow?"

Her job was to keep the new arrivals

out of the filth and crime and degradation of their predecessors in the slums of Washington. The job began in the home, and the women who would have to make the homes did not know how. They had been taught to pick cotton, not to keep house; they could handle a hoe, but not a needle or a skillet. Yet Sojourner, walking about the camp to instruct them in domestic duties, found them eager to learn. "They want to learn the way we live in the North," she reported. "I am listened to with attention and respect, and from all things, I judge it is the will of both God and the people that I should remain."

She wanted the *Standard* sent to her in care of Captain Carse, for the freedmen liked to hear what was happening in the new world they had entered—how the war was going, and what would be done for them. "Sammy, my grandson, reads for them. We are both well and happy, and feel that we are in good employment," she assured her friends.

In December a document came from up north.

> New York, Dec. 1, 1864
>
> This certifies that The National Freedman's Relief Association has appointed Sojourner Truth to be a counselor to the freed people at Arlington Heights, Va., and hereby commends her to the favor and confidence of the offices of government, and of all persons who take an interest in relieving the condition of the freedmen, or in promoting their intellectual, moral, and religious instruction. . . .

"They have to learn to be free," Sojourner put it. The need was obvious. Daily she found women in tears or stony grief, or rattling the bars of the guardhouse—women whose children had been spirited off to Maryland. The law abolishing slavery in Maryland was still being fought in the courts, and in the meantime many of her slaveholders felt entitled to make up for their absconding property. As grown blacks might cause trouble, they preferred the children playing in the fields about the camp. They took what came to hand; one could not tell the pickaninnies apart, anyway. If the dams squawked, one locked them up for disturbing the peace.

Captain Carse shrugged: his authority was confined to Freedman's Village. There he had to keep order. He pitied the women, but they must not make a fuss in his camp.

Make a fuss! Voices from the past rang in Sojourner's ear—Mrs. Dumont's, Mrs. Gedney's. Then her own son had been sold away, and the law had brought him back. She told the mothers that they were free and had rights; they could bring the robbers to justice. "The law is with you," she insisted.

The freedwomen gaped. They knew there was no more selling down the river, no more toiling for masters—but the law? They knew about the law. Where they came from, it was called the Black Code. It set less store by a free Negro than by a slave. Bring white men to justice? They shuddered at the idea.

Sojourner talked to some soldiers she knew as good anti-slavery men, and the next time the kidnappers struck, a posse pursued them. Caught, they denied that the cowering little blacks in their company came from the camp. Sojourner recalled the Kingston courthouse, the book she had sworn by, without knowing what it was, that her son was her son.

She rounded up the frightened mothers. "The law is with you; get behind it!"

Trembling, they swore out warrants and received their children.

The exasperated Marylanders turned upon Sojourner. "We'll have you put in the guardhouse, you old . . ."

"If you try to put me in the guardhouse, I'll make the United States rock like a cradle," she threatened back. . . .

Her hospital work did not take up all her time. She held meetings in Washington, spoke in churches, kept making friends, and was asked once to find a congressman to present a feminist petition drawn up by a new associate editor of the

Standard, a young woman named Susan B. Anthony. The burning issue of the day was Negro suffrage—"I hear so much about colored men getting their rights," she said, "but not a word about the colored women." She went to a New York equal rights convention, as Elizabeth Cady Stanton's house guest, and addressed the fashionable audience at the Church of the Puritans as "chillun," like everybody else.

"I call you chillun, because you are somebody's children, and I'm old enough to be the mother of all that's here. I want women to have their rights, and while the water is stirring I'll step into the pool. Now that there's a stir about colored men's rights is the time for women to get theirs. I'm sometimes told, 'Women ain't fit to vote; don't you know a woman had seven devils in her?' Seven devils ain't no account. A man had a legion in him."

The hall roared.

In Mrs. Stanton's parlor she explained her reasoning. "You never lose anything by asking everything. If you bait this suffrage hook with a woman, you'll surely catch a black man." She gathered up her bag and shawl. "There's a great deal in that philosophy, chillun. Now I must go and take a smoke . . ."

She smoked a pipe and blamed the habit on race prejudice: on railway trains she had been sent into the smoking car so often, she had taken it up in self-defense. She now traveled much for the purpose of placing freedmen in jobs. Families wanting to go north were sent to her, as were requests for young, strong, willing workers, trained domestics in particular. But matching supply and demand was no easy task. There was the red tape of Bureau regulations to be overcome, and the natural fear of dispersal in a strange environment, and the politicians' desire to keep the newly enfranchised where their votes would do the most good. . . .

One day, without warning, she quit her jobs in Washington and left the capital as she had once left New York. She was busy, beloved, yet more and more discontented. The "sable host" in the camps would not diminish. Hundreds were placed by her, thousands by others—it made hardly a dent. For the old and infirm, for the children growing up in wickedness, there was no chance, no hope of learning "the way we live in the North." The Bureau fed them, but they had no future. In the South she had seen them living in their old cabins, toiling for their old masters, cowed as before, torn between a longing to leave and the dread of a lonely, friendless new life on their own. Some day, too, the government was bound to tire of supporting those in Washington. Where could they go?

Sojourner went home [to Battle Creek] with Sammy. . . .

In these months on the prairie, a plan had ripened in her. What did white folks do who had no chance in the East? They went west. What was done about the Indians? They got government land in the West, sometimes with housing. The railroads got land in the West every day, to create new wealth for the country. Why should the freedmen not have this chance to enrich the country by supporting themselves, to escape from slavery's backwash without being scattered all over?

She left children and grandchildren in Battle Creek and took to the road once more, to proclaim her idea. . . .

It was in Brooklyn that Sojourner's idea evolved into a project. Theodore Tilton explained to her why those who would like it lacked the power to carry it out, while those who had power were apt to view it with indifference. A petition, with signatures enough to impress the politicians, was the answer.

Sojourner had put her mark to many petitions. After all, what were they but prayers—prayers to human authority? She had always stood on praying ground. Mr. Tilton helped her with the wording:

To the Senate and House of Representatives, in Congress assembled:

Whereas, From the faithful and earnest representations of Sojourner Truth (who has personally investigated the matter) we believe that the freed colored people in and about Washington, dependent upon government for support, would be greatly benefited and might become useful citizens by being placed in a position to support themselves: We, the undersigned, therefore earnestly request your honorable bodies to set apart for them a portion of the public land in the West, and erect buildings thereon for the aged and infirm, and otherwise legislate so as to secure the desired results.

The crusade began quietly, in the homes of friends in Philadelphia. Lucretia Mott, the grand old lady of the cause, signed the petition and offered encouragement. Anna Dickinson, a young woman whose wartime speeches as a teen-ager had set the North ablaze, signed and replenished Sojourner's supply of "shadows." A doctor promised to forward her back pay, which General Howard had finally pried out of the Treasury—fifteen dollars a month for two years—to William Merritt in Battle Creek on account of her mortgage. She traversed New Jersey: "On Saturday, January 1st, 1870, our house received a new baptism through Sojourner Truth," wrote her hosts at Vineland. She went on to New England, and in February, at a mass meeting in Providence, she took her petition to the public.

In plain Quaker garb, bent only slightly with age, her voice first husky, but clearing fast, she pleaded the cause of her people. They could not take care of themselves, she assured her listeners: "Why, you've taken that all away from them. They've got nothing left." They were doomed in the South: "I know the good people in the South can't take care of the Negroes as they ought to, 'cause the rebels won't let them." But the nation had grown wealthy on the Negroes' toil. They had earned help. "We've earned land enough for a home, and it would be a benefit for you all, and God would bless the whole of you for doing it. How can you expect to do good to God, if you don't learn first to do good to each other?"

The whole audience sighed.

Wendell Phillips was present; he had lately opened some of his own speeches with a line heard from Sojourner: "Children, I've come here tonight like the rest of you, to hear what I've got to say . . ." And he inscribed her book: "Blessings on thee, my good old friend."

Flushed with success, she headed straight for Washington, to let the government go to work on her program. "I thank my God that I have met Sojourner Truth," wrote someone along her way. . . .

[On March 30, 1870, the Fifteenth Amendment was ratified, forbidding the United States or any state from denying or abridging the right to vote "on account of race, color, or previous condition of servitude." On the occasion, Sojourner Truth went to the White House and met President Grant.]

She visited the Capitol. The corridors rustled with subdued excitement. Pages stared in disbelief. Wide-eyed clerks peered out of office doors along her way to the Chamber. The stir had nothing in common with the hostile mutters of old; what she felt around her, what she felt herself, was wonder at the change that had come to pass in ten years.

"It was an hour not soon to be forgotten," a Washington Sunday paper said of the scene that ensued,

for it is not often even in this magnanimous age of progress that we see reverend senators—even him that holds the second chair in the gift of the Republic—vacate their seats in the hall of State, to extend the hand of welcome, the meed of praise, and substantial blessings, to a poor negro woman. . . . It was as refreshing as it was strange to see her who had served in the shackles of slavery in the great State of New York for a quarter of a century before a majority of the senators were born now holding a levee with them in the marble room, where a decade ago she would have been spurned from its outer corridor by the lowest menial. . . . Truly, the spirit of progress is abroad in the land, and the leaven of love is working in the hearts of the people, pointing with unerring certainty to the not far distant future, when the ties of affection shall cement all nations, kindreds and tongues into one common brotherhood . . .

The two senators from Michigan, one a millionaire merchant from Detroit, hovered about her like guardian angels. Fourteen, all told, signed her book, and when the names were read back to her, she could count one from her native New York, one from Indiana, where she had been jailed so many times, and five from the South—including one who had inscribed himself, "H. R. Revels, Senator, Miss., Colored."

Only one asked about her plan for the freedmen. It was a man as tall as she, with a mane of white hair over a lined, leonine face, who invited her to his office to discuss her ideas in more courtly fashion than she had ever seen a gentleman treat a lady. He signed her book not like the rest, with name and state only, but wrote:

Equality of rights is the first of rights.

Charles Sumner,
Senate Chamber, April 26, 1870.

Sojourner knew the tall man. The senior Senator from Massachusetts was a familiar figure in Washington; she had seen him in Lafayette Square, faultlessly dressed, walking to or from the simple home on the corner of Vermont Avenue in which no one suspected the art treasures massed inside. She had seen him walk—he never rode—to Capitol Hill, though she had no clear picture of what he was doing there as chairman of the Committee on Foreign Relations. But she knew he had borne the brunt of the battle against slavery for twenty years, had fought it wherever he found it, in every form, under every disguise, on any issue. In Massachusetts she had not known either that he, more than any one man, had welded the state to the cause, that he had broken up the alliance between Southern cotton planters and Northern cotton manufactures, "the lords of the lash and the lords of the loom." She had known only a story people told about him: when someone said he was forgetting the other side of the question, Sumner thundered, "There is no other side!"

His friendly concern with her plan came as no surprise to Sojourner. He advised her, as others had, to get a great many more signatures to her petition than she had gathered thus far, and even then he seemed not to hold much hope for an effort to aid neither veterans nor industries nor railroads, only former slaves. But he did not discourage her. Prospects of failure never daunted the man of whom a friend would soon say, "I don't suppose Charles Sumner knew what fear was."

He went on to talk of his own fight of the time: for a civil rights bill that would achieve his goal of "absolute human equality, secured, assured, and invulnerable." His chances were not too good, either. There were not votes enough to pass the bill as written, but he would not have it watered down—in fact, he had to die before it could become law in 1875, in a form that even Southerners admitted they could "live with." While Sumner lived, he preferred to keep "his bill" unpassed but unweakened, as a goad to the national conscience.

Meanwhile, he worked to better things piecemeal. Sojourner's visit was an occasion for reminiscing, for they had been comrades-in-arms in a skirmish of the great campaign: in the fight over the streetcars in the nation's capital.

Wartime Washington had restricted Negroes to special Jim Crow cars. Whites often occupied the seats in these, too, leaving the colored with standing room only—a situation accepted by the newly freed, but not by Sojourner. She complained to the president of the street railway, and Senator Sumner used her complaint to get Congressional action banning segregated public transport in the District of Columbia.

But the law did not enforce itself. It had to be made effective in the streets, and local Negroes feared to test its power. Sojourner "got behind it." Her every trip to Washington was marked by running fights with streetcar drivers, conductors, and infuriated passengers. When a driver ignored her signal, she yelped, "I WANT TO RIDE!" in a voice that stopped traffic. Or she got on by surprise, resisted attempts to eject her, and rode farther than she had to, so as to make the most of her experience. "Bless God! I've had a ride," she would exclaim when she got off.

One day, returning from Georgetown with Laura Haviland, she kept walking as her friend signaled to a streetcar. The driver stopped. Mrs. Haviland got on slowly. Suddenly Sojourner wheeled and jumped aboard also.

"Conductor! Do niggers ride in these cars?" a man bristled.

The conductor tried to put Sojourner off, dislocating her shoulder in the process, but she held fast. Mrs. Haviland protested. The conductor shouted at her, "Does she belong to you, lady?"

"No," said the lady. "She belongs to humanity."

11

OBTAINING EQUAL RIGHTS

Ella Baker has been organizing civil-rights actions for more than fifty years—and you've never heard of her. Her story proves that stirring declarations and inspirational speeches are only half the task of a political leader. The other half is organization: turning that inspiration into genuine change. That takes a special kind of talent and incredible persistence. Ella Baker has the knack and the staying power. Back in 1957, the Reverend Martin Luther King, Jr., asked her to organize the national office and the mass meetings of the new Southern Christian Leadership Conference. But, she says, "You didn't see me on television, you didn't see news stories about me. The kind of role that I tried to play was to pick up pieces or put together pieces out of which I hoped organization might come." In 1980 she was still going strong, counseling civil-rights activists who came to her for advice. If there has been a civil-rights revolution in this country, Ella Baker is one who made it happen.

Ella Baker Organizes for Civil Rights

by Ellen Cantarow and Susan Gushee O'Malley

Ella Baker began her work for the NAACP as a field organizer, someone who travels to different cities, towns, and rural areas trying to recruit new people to an organization and raise money. How does a field organizer begin? When you go to a place you

---

From Ellen Cantarow and Susan Gushee O'Malley, "Ella Baker: Organizing for Civil Rights," in *Moving the Mountain: Women Working for Social Change*, ed. Ellen Cantarow (Old Westbury, Conn.: Feminist Press, 1980), pp. 69–93.

don't know, how do you find people who will introduce you into the community? How do you help the fearful overcome their fear and sign up for work? How do you persuade the well-off that they have a kinship with the poor? Out of such questions, the following reminiscences flow.

The first aspect of being on the field staff was to help. You helped raise money. You conducted membership campaigns in different areas. A new person coming on the field would learn how to campaign, and then you would be sent to smaller territory. I started in Florida. I'd never been there before.

The NAACP had a roster of people who were in contact, who were members. And so when you go out in the field, if they had a branch, say, in Sanford or Clearwater, Florida, you had been in correspondence there. So you make your contact with the person in Tampa who's said to the community, "Miss so-and-so's coming in." And so you go down, and they have provided some space in somebody's church or office or somewhere you had access to a telephone.

Where did people gather? They gathered in churches. In schools. And you'd get permission. You'd call up Reverend Brother so-and-so, and ask if you could appear before the congregation at such-and-such a time. Sometimes they'd give you three minutes, because, after all, many people weren't secure enough to run the risk, as they saw it, of being targeted as ready to challenge the powers that be. And they'd say, "You have three minutes after the church service." And you'd take it. And you'd use it, to the extent to which you can be persuasive. It's the ammunition you have. That's all you have.

We dealt with what was most pressing for a given section. For instance, Harry T. Moore was one of three black principals in Florida who was fired when they began to talk in terms of equal pay. The differential between black and white teachers was tragic, to say the least. Many times, money had been "appropriated" for black education and it had been diverted to other sources. And, of course, there wasn't headlines on that, they just didn't *get* there, see.

Harry T. Moore's house was bombed from under him one night. And he was killed as a result. This particular night, I think it was Christmas eve, '46, dynamite was placed under his bedroom. He and his wife were blown to smithereens. There were a lot of people whom Harry T. Moore had benefited. We talked to them. He helped them get their pay when they had worked and didn't get paid. So you could go into that area of Florida and you could talk about the virtue of NAACP, because they knew Harry T. Moore. They hadn't discussed a whole lot of theory. But there was a *man* who served *their* interests and who *identified* with them.

On what basis do you seek to organize people? Do you start to try to organize them on the fact of what *you* think, or what they are first interested in? You start where the *people* are. Identification with people. There's always this problem in the minority group that's escalating up the ladder in this culture, I think. Those who have gotten some training and those who have gotten some material gains, it's always the problem of their not understanding the possibility of being divorced from those who are not in their social classification. Now, there were those who felt they had made it, would be embarrassed by the fact that some people would get drunk and get in jail, and so they wouldn't be concerned too much about whether they were brutalized in jail. 'Cause he was a *drunk*! He was a so-and-so. Or she was a streetwalker. We get caught in that bag. And so you have to help break that down without alienating them at the same time. The gal who has been able to buy her minks and whose husband is a professional, they live well. You can't insult her, you never go and tell her she's a so-and-so for taking, for *not* identifying. You try to point out where her interest lies in identifying with that other one across the tracks who doesn't have minks.

How do you do that? You don't always succeed, but you try. You'd point out what had happened, in certain cases, where whole communities were almost destroyed by police brutality on a large scale. They went and burned down the better homes. In Tampa, Florida, I met some of those people whose homes were burned down. These were people I'd call middle class. The men got the guns, and they carried their womenfolk and the children into the woods. And they stood guard. Some stood guard over the people in the woods, and they stood guard over their homes and property, ready to shoot. So what you do is to cite examples that had taken place somewhere else. You had to be persuasive on the basis of fact. You cite it, you see. This can happen to *you*. Sometimes you're able to cite instances of where there's been a little epidemic, or an outbreak of the more devastating kinds of disease. You point out that those of us who live across the railroad track and are in greater filth or lack of sanitation can have an effect on you who live on the other side, 'cause disease doesn't have such a long barrier between us, you see. As long as the violations of the rights of Tom Jones could take place with impunity, you are not secure. So you helped to reestablish a sense of identity of each with the struggle.

Of course, your success depended on both your disposition and your capacity to sort of stimulate people—and how you carried yourself, in terms of not being above people. And see, there were more people who were not economically secure than there were economically secure people. I didn't *have* any mink—I don't have any now—but you don't go into a group where minks are prohibitive in terms of getting them and carry your minks and throw 'em around. Why, they can't get past *that*. They can't get past the fact that you got minks and they don't have mink. And see, I had no problems 'cause I didn't have none. Nor did I have aspirations for these things.

I remember one place I got a contribution for a life membership in the NAACP, which was five hundred dollars then, was from a longshoremen's union. They remembered somebody who had been there before from the NAACP, with a mink coat. When they gave this five-hundred-dollar membership, somebody mentioned it. See, they had resented the mink coat. I don't think it was the mink coat that they really resented. It was the *barrier* they could sense between them and the person in the coat. See, you can have a mink coat on and you can identify with the man who is working on the docks. If you got it, if you *really* identify with him, what you wear won't make a damn bit of difference. But if you talk differently, and somehow talk down to people, they can sense it. They can feel it. And they know whether you are talking *with* them, or talking *at* them, or talking *about* them.

If you feel that you are part of them and they are part of you, you don't *say* "I'm-a-part-of-you." What you really do is, you point out something. Especially the lower-class people, the people who'd felt the heel of oppression, see, they *knew* what you were talking about when you spoke about police brutality. They *knew* what you were speaking about when you talked about working at a job, doing the same work, and getting a differential in pay. And if your sense of being a part of them got over to them, they appreciated that. Somebody would get the point. Somebody would come out and say, "I'm gon' join that darn organization." As an example, I remember in someplace out of St. Petersburg, Florida, the first time I'd ever been to the Holy and Sanctified church. We had a good response. One lady came out and all she could say was how my dress was the same as hers. Now, she didn't know how to deal with issues. But she identified. And she joined.

And, then you have to recognize what people *can* do. There're some people in my experience, especially "the little people" as some might call them, who never could explain the NAACP as such. But they had the knack of getting money from John Jones or somebody. They might walk up to him: "Gimme a dollar for the NAACP." And maybe because of what they had done in relationship to John Jones, he'd give the dollar. They could never tell anybody what the program of the Association was. So what do you do about that. You don't be demeaning them. You say, well here is Mrs. Jones, Mrs. Susie Jones, and remember last year Sister Susie Jones came in with so much. And Sister Susie Jones would go on *next* year and get this money. Now, somewhere in the process she may learn some other methods, and she may learn to articulate some of the program of the Association. But whether she does or not, she *feels* it. And she transmits it to those she can talk to. And she might end up just saying, "You ain't doin' nothin' but spendin' your money down at that so-and-so place." She may shame him. Or she may say, "Boy, I know your mama." And so you start talkin' about what the mothers would like for them to do. So you do it because there's mama, mama's callin'. See, somewhere down the line this becomes important to them. At least these are the ways I saw it. And I think they respond.

DAILY FUNDAMENTALS

How did I make my living? I haven't. I have eked out existence.

—*Ella Baker.*

We asked Ella Baker how she had earned her living. We also asked about childrearing. She told us, "I didn't have any children, I didn't beget any. I wasn't interested, really, in having children *per se*. I didn't have all the advantages young ladies have now, protecting themselves from pregnancy. But it just didn't happen." We asked her how long she had had her niece, and she replied, laughing, "Through college. She's still living, she's raising me now."

In school, I waited tables and had charge of a chemistry laboratory, and that provided a certain amount of money to help pay tuition, because my parents had three children in boarding school at the same time and no real money. The summer after school, I worked in a hotel—we called it "a roadhouse." A rich lady had this place, and she decided I was to be the one to wait on her table.

'Course we organized the group that was working out there that summer. We started out with a guy named Uncle Charlie. I don't know what his nationality was—we were all mixed up in nationality—but he had the entertainment. There was a girl who had a very beautiful voice, and I usually would announce things. But if something came up that I didn't like, I'd react to it. I retained what I called my essential integrity. I neither kowtowed nor felt it necessary to lord it over anyone else. If I were, let's call it the head waitress, I didn't find it necessary to lord it over the man who washed dishes in the kitchen. Somewhere down the line I had a deep sense of my being part of humanity, and this I've always tried to preserve.

At various times, I worked for newspapers. I used to send in some stories to the black newspapers, and sometimes I'd get paid. I worked with a couple of newspapers of short vintage which were black-based, an American West Indian newspaper I think was the first one here in New York. When George Schuyler organized the *Negro National News*, I was the office manager there. A lot of the young black columnists you see now in the black press were youngsters then, and they came through there.

Then I was with the WPA workers' education, the consumer education project. I got top salary. I was a teacher and teachers were paid more than some of the others. Then the NAACP paid me. At first, all of two thousand dollars a year, which maybe at that stage people could live on.

I had to resign from the NAACP in 1946 because I had taken on the responsibility of raising a niece, and I knew I could not travel as widely when I took her. She was about seven or eight then.

I think today, people's concept of political organizing is like you're really out there night and day doing it all. See, young people today have had the luxury of a period in which they could give their all to this political organizing. They didn't have to be bothered by a whole lot of other things. But most of those who are older put it in with the things that they had to do.

THE BEGINNINGS OF THE MOVEMENT

He pulled up the top and reached for a bottle. "That'll be a nickel," he said. "You drink it here."

"But . . . but . . . I don't want a Coke from the bottle. I want to sit up there and drink my Coke from a glass. Why do I have to drink it here?" The man looked at me. Something was wrong. I didn't know what, but something. A fear swelled within me, the fear of the unknown. . . .

"You have to drink your Coke back here. You can't sit on these stools."

"But . . . why?" By this time I had the cold Coca-Cola in my hands. It was very wet and very cold and I felt myself turning cold like the bottle of Coke. Something dreadful was wrong and I could not understand why I was crying, what was the matter, who this man was, what right he had to tell me where I had to drink my Coke, why I couldn't sit on the stool. . . .

"Well, don't you know?"

"Know what?"

"Boy, you're a nigger," he said in a flat voice.

"A what?" I asked. I heard him and I didn't hear him because I didn't really understand the word.

"A nigger, and Negroes don't sit on the stools here."

—*James Forman, description of a childhood experience in the 1940s,* The Making of Black Revolutionaries *(1972).*

Black resistance to oppression began in the ships that brought West Africans to America to be slaves. There were small, personal acts—the handing down of language, tradition, and memories among friends, and from parents to children. There were large, public acts, like mutinies on slave ships. From slavery days through the 1940s, where the previous part of Ella Baker's story left off, black women and men took individual and group stands against government, masters, and employers. They sang their sorrow and asserted the facts of their lives in the blues. They established organizations, like the National Association for the Advancement of Colored People, for legal and political action.

There have been times when the grassroots movement has been more visible than others, and periods when it has seemed to disappear altogether. Such a time of "disappearance" was the decade between the mid-forties and fifties. There were no *visible* signs of life—few group protests or mass demonstrations. There was a cold war on, not only against communism but against the idea that ordinary people might change the course of history.

But even during a time like the cold war, people were still active and kept ideals and commitment alive. Take a man named Amzie Moore, long-time friend and NAACP associate of Ella Baker, who returned from the segregated Armed Forces of World War II to the heart of Mississippi—a terror state for southern blacks. There, he initiated a drive, one of the first since the 1870s, to register black people to vote. Amzie Moore and others like him are not in history books even now. But they made contact with people around them. And when the black students of the late fifties and early sixties decided to take action in the South, it was to people like Amzie Moore and the black dentist Ella Baker mentions below, that they went for advice.

The shockwave that caused a visible crack in the cold war glacier began in 1955. In Montgomery, Alabama, a black woman named Rosa Parks refused to yield her bus seat to a white passenger. Parks, secretary of the Alabama NAACP, was arrested. Like lunch counters, drinking fountains, swimming pools, toilets, and other public facilities, buses had been segregated in the South by custom since slavery. They had been segregated by law since 1896, when the Supreme Court, in a decision that would set back black civil rights for sixty years, declared "the enforced separation of the two races" the law of the land. On Rosa Parks's arrest, Montgomery's black citizens started a 381-day boycott of the city's buses. For over a year, they walked. As they were the city's main users of the bus system, they brought public transportation to a halt.

The Southern Christian Leadership Conference was founded in 1957 by Martin Luther King and other ministers, on the heels of the Montgomery bus boycott. The founders of SCLC knew that if a mass movement is to grow from a single gesture of protest, people must *keep on* acting and demonstrating. The organization's original idea of how to keep the movement going was a crusade for citizenship—voter registration. But voter registration did not become a reality until some five years later. And then, it did not come by way of SCLC, but from a very different group, the Student Nonviolent Coordinating Committee.

Instead, sit-ins became the main actions of the movement, beginning in 1960, when four freshmen from A & T College in Greensboro, North Carolina, sat down at a Woolworth's lunch counter to challenge segregation. The sit-ins spread in waves across the South, involving thousands of black students and some whites. The philosophy behind the sit-ins was "nonviolent direct action." The decision to take direct action—to sit in, demonstrate, picket segregated facilities—sprang from the realization that it would take more than going through the orderly channels of government to combat racism. As direct action protests were met with violence by police and white hoodlums and mobs, the evidence of racism was displayed graphically on front pages of newspapers and on television screens.

When SNCC was founded, the members of the Student Nonviolent Coordinating Committee believed that their actions must always be taken in a spirit of love and forgiveness. "Love," asserted the SNCC credo adopted in April 1960, "is the central motif of nonviolence. . . . Such love goes to the extreme; it remains loving and forgiving even in the midst of hostility. It matches the capacity of evil to inflict suffering with an even more enduring capacity to absorb evil, all the while persisting in love." Translated in deeds, the philosophy meant that if police came to arrest you, you did not resist, you simply went limp. If, at a demonstration or elsewhere, someone attacked you, you fell to the ground, protecting your most vulnerable parts by drawing your knees up to your chest, and protecting your head by cupping your hands over it.

To remain nonviolent in the face of violence required a great deal of training and discipline. "Nonviolent direct action" was a Christian idea, Ella Baker explains. "For a long time the church had been the center of whatever activity or leadership for change there was in the black community. I think the reason they were able to be so disciplined, the earlier sit-inners, was because they were for the most part church-oriented."

From 1960 to 1965, many black and white civil rights activists and black citizens were teargassed, clubbed, shot, poked with electrically-charged cattle prods, and tortured in jail. Some people were brutally murdered, including three young student activists, Michael Schwerner, James Chaney, and Andrew Goodman. On a quiet Sunday morning in Birmingham, Alabama, in 1963, whites bombed a church. Four young black girls, aged eleven to fourteen, were killed.

Many—Ella Baker was one—recoiled at the thought of not defending themselves when attacked.

> I frankly could not have sat and let someone put a burning cigarette on the back of my neck as some young people did. Whether this is right or wrong or good or bad, I have already been conditioned, and I have not seen anything in the nonviolent technique that can dissuade me from challenging somebody who wants to step on my neck. If necessary, if they hit me, I might hit them back.

In fact, a turning point in the civil rights movement came in the mid-sixties as the notion of a more militant "black power" movement superseded the early movement of nonviolent civil disobedience. But that movement of nonviolent direct action shook the nation to its foundations in the early sixties. And the idea of revolution—a radical change in the way a nation is governed, a faith in the power of the oppressed majority to change the way things are done in a country—was reborn in the United States in this stubborn, daring, Christian wave of sit-ins. We asked Ella Baker: Had the sit-ins seemed revolutionary to her? How had they come to be?

> I guess revolutionary is relative to the situations that people find themselves in, and whatever their goals are, and how many people are in agreement that this is a desired goal. The original four kids who sat down in Greensboro, North Carolina, I'm confident that they had little or no knowledge of the revolutionary background that people talk about when they speak of changing the society by way of socialism or communism. They were youngsters who had a very simple reaction to an inequity. When you're a student with no money, and you go buy what you need like your paper or your pencils, where do you go? The five-and-ten-cent-

store. At least you could then, because the prices were not quite as disproportionate as they are now. These two had been talking with a dentist, a black dentist who apparently had some experience with the earlier days of the formation of the Congress of Racial Equality (CORE). They were able to talk with him about their frustrations, going in there, spending all their little money, and yet not being able to sit and buy a five-cent Coke. That was a rather simple challenge as you look back. They decided they were going to do something about it, and so they sat down. Then some others followed their actions. A sister who had a brother in school in another town, her town had already sat in. She might call and ask, why doesn't his school sit in? This was the communication link, plus the media. They sat, and the others came and sat, and it spread. I guess one of the reasons it spread was because it was simple, and it struck home to a lot of young people who were in school.

It hadn't gone on so long before I suggested that we call a conference of the sit-inners to be held in Raleigh. It was very obvious to the Southern Christian Leadership Conference that there was little or no communication between those who sat in, say, in Charlotte, North Carolina, and those who eventually sat in at some other place in Virginia or Alabama. They were motivated by what the North Carolina four had started, but they were not in contact with each other, which meant that you couldn't build a sustaining force just based on spontaneity.

My estimate was that the conference would bring together a couple hundred of the young leadership. I had not hoped for such large numbers of adults who came. These adults were part and parcel of groups such as the Montgomery bus boycott. They also may have been relating to the organizing first steps of SCLC, which had been officially established but had not expanded very much.

We ended up with about three hundred people. We had insisted that the young people be left to make their own decisions. Also, we provided for those who came from outside the South to meet separately from those who came from the sit-in areas, because the persons who came from, say, New York, frequently had had wider experience in organizing and were too articulate. In the initial portion of the conference, the southern students had the right to meet, to discuss, and to determine where they wanted to go. It wasn't my idea to separate the northern and southern students. I hesitated to project ideas as pointedly as that, but those who had worked closely with me knew that I believed very firmly in the right of the people who were under the heel to be the ones to decide what action they were going to take to get from under their oppression. As a group, basically, they were the black students from the South. The heritage of the South was theirs, and it was one of oppression. Those who came from the other nineteen schools and colleges and universities up North didn't have the same oppression, and they were white. They were much more erudite and articulate, farther advanced in the theoretical concepts of social change. This can become overwhelming for those who don't even understand what you're talking about and feel put down.

The Southern Christian Leadership Conference felt that they could influence how things went. They were interested in having the students become an arm of SCLC. They were most confident that this would be their baby, because I was their functionary and I had called the meeting. At a discussion called by the Reverend Dr. King, the SCLC leadership made decisions who would speak to whom to influence the students to become part of SCLC. Well, I disagreed. There was no student at Dr. King's meeting. I was the nearest thing to a student, being the advocate, you see. I also knew from the beginning that having a woman be an executive of SCLC was not something that would go over with the male-dominated leadership. And then, of course, my personality wasn't right, in the sense I was not afraid to disagree with the higher authorities. I wasn't one to say, yes, because it came from the Reverend King. So when it was proposed that the leadership could influence the direction by speaking to, let's say, the man from Virginia, he could speak to the leadership of the Virginia student group, and the assumption was that having spoken to so-and-so, so-and-so would do what they wanted done, I was outraged. I walked out.

SNCC AND VOTER REGISTRATION

The issue is power. We control the state and we're not going to allow any Negras to run Alabama and take our power from us. . . . If we allow the Negras to crack our power in any way, this is an invitation to further weaken it. Why, in the county where my friend lives, the Negras are nine to one and his father is sheriff of that county. Do you think if the Negras had the right to vote that they would elect his father as sheriff? We got the power and we intend to keep it.

—*Statement by John Patterson, son of the then governor of Alabama, at the 1956 national meeting of the National Student Association, quoted by James Forman,* The Making of Black Revolutionaries (*1972*).

Ella Baker left the Southern Christian Leadership Conference in August 1960, and went to work for the Student Nonviolent Coordinating Committee. She earned money working part-time for the YWCA in Atlanta. But she spent most of her days staffing the tiny SNCC office—which she had found space for through black businessmen friendly to the cause—on Auburn Avenue in Atlanta, Georgia. She worked there with two young people, Jane Stembridge, a white student from Georgia, who was studying theology in New York City, and Bob Moses, a black teacher in his midtwenties from New York.

The Student Nonviolent Coordinating Committee started by coordinating and continuing the sit-ins. In 1961, "freedom rides" began, to test rulings by the Supreme Court and the Interstate Commerce Commission that transportation between states could not be segregated. In May of 1961, the Congress of Racial Equality united with SNCC to have black and white activists ride a bus together from Washington to New Orleans. The bus ride was catastrophic. In Anniston, Alabama, on Mother's Day, the bus was surrounded by a white mob and fire-bombed. It burned to a shell, and several riders were hospitalized. Further south, in Birmingham, the riders were surrounded by a mob of men brandishing iron bars. The men attacked, chased, and beat several riders bloody and unconscious. Nevertheless, SNCC continued coordinating freedom rides, and the riders used nonviolent resistance in the face of ceaseless brutality and jailings.

The most important step SNCC took during its first year of existence was to make voter registration its main activity. Except for the early 1870s, when blacks had momentarily gained the vote and even elected some local officials and congressmen, black voting in the South had been stifled.

Trying to register people to vote might seem today an obvious way to combat discrimination. But the proposal touched off furious debate in the Student Nonviolent Coordinating Committee. On one side of the argument were the supporters of voter registration. On the other side were people who feared that in only registering people to vote, SNCC would lose the spiritual fervor of nonviolent direct action. By comparison with the direct confrontations with white mobs and police, voter registration seemed a narrow, legalistic activity. Those who argued for the voting drive said that denial of the opportunity to vote was so blatantly unjust that the registration campaign was absolutely necessary. And in the campaign, they said, there would still be plenty of opportunity for nonviolent direct action.

The structure of SNCC finally got hammered out by having long meetings that would last from six in the evening through early morning, or maybe all day. The first time I ever remember having a charley horse in my leg was after thirty hours that I had been more or less sitting in the same sort of cramped position. Because I felt if we had a table, that the first priority would be for the young people to sit there. I had no ambition to be in the leadership. I was only interested in seeing that a leadership had the chance to develop.

The worst conference I remember was at Highlander Folk School. The issue that surfaced was a debate between the group that believed in nonviolence against the group that wanted to introduce political action, get people registered to vote. The nonviolent faction was adamant against political action. My feeling was that you would have to deal with the political action because of the denials that had obtained. See, people had not been free all along to be political, and there was a concerted action on the part of the powers that be to prevent blacks from participating in politics or even having the chance to register and vote.

When those who advocated going into voter registration spoke, those who were more highly indoctrinated in the nonviolent approach objected that they didn't want just to go into voter registration. They broke up into a kind of fight—a pulling apart. I never intervened between the struggles if I could avoid it. Most of the youngsters had been trained to believe in or to follow adults if they could. I felt they ought to have a chance to learn to think things through and to make the decisions. But this was a point at which I did have something to say. I hope I helped point out that the people who they were most concerned about lived in areas where they had no political influence; they could not exercise their political right to register and vote without intimidation. This in itself was a justification for whatever political action was being proposed. If they went into these deeply prejudiced areas and started voter registration, they would have an opportunity to exercise nonviolent resistance. It worked out that they began to see that those who went in for voter registration would be challenged so that they would have to endure violence—and resort to the nonviolent concept. So they began to talk in terms of this, and that's how they got into a voter registration program.

Bob Moses started a program of voter registration in McComb, Mississippi, and one of the young men was pistol-whipped, I believe. And then, one of the young high school students who had demonstrated, Brenda Travis, was put into reform school, and things developed from there. And they began to see that they wouldn't have to abandon their nonviolence. In fact, they would be hard put to keep it up.

The National Association for the Advancement of Colored People had not developed to the point of sending out people to the hinterlands to actually have voter registration and leadership clinics and to test the barriers. It was the SNCC people who tested them. An NAACP president, in one particular NAACP town, wanted somebody to come down and hold registration clinics—helping people know what they had to do to qualify, what kind of questions they would be asked, and what kind of difficulties they would encounter. Out of that setting the first of the persons was sort of indoctrinated to go and register and buck the system in those deep places. A couple of other SNCC people went down, and one of them got shot. That was the beginning of the Mississippi thrust, the real Mississippi thrust.

THE MISSISSIPPI THRUST

Gulfport, July 8
There is no such thing as a completed job until every-one *is registered. When you cheat and take a lunch hour . . . you suddenly find yourself reviewing a failure or a success to discover the whys: maybe I should have bullied him slightly, or maybe I should have talked less—and relied on silences. Did I rush him? Should I never have mentioned registering at all, and just tried to make friends and set him at ease? It goes on and on.*

—From a letter by a northern student registering voters during Mississippi Summer, 1964.

One of the high points of the voting campaign was Mississippi Summer. It was organized by Bob Moses and the Council of Federated Organizations (COFO), which was made up of the Student Nonviolent Coordinating Committee, the Southern Christian Leadership Conference, the Congress of Racial Equality, and the National Association for the Advancement of Colored People. Northern students were asked to go South to help in the voter registration activities. Mississippi Summer was part of the revival of radical spirit among young whites in America. Many white students went down to Mississippi that summer. None remained unchanged by the experience. Many became active shortly thereafter in the movement against the war in Vietnam and in the women's liberation movement.

After Mississippi Summer, the Student Nonviolent Coordinating Committee decided to organize a separate political party in Mississippi—the Mississippi Freedom Democratic Party (MFDP). The MFDP was set up in 1964 as an alternative for blacks to the regular Democratic party. In most regular party districts, blacks were prevented from voting. Some whites as well as blacks voted for the MFDP, which sent its delegates to the Democratic convention of that year in Atlantic City. Though these delegates had proof that they had received more votes than the regular Democratic party delegates, the party refused to seat them as Mississippi delegates.

My basic role was, I insisted on being available when SNCC was having crisis meetings. Where they were going, I had been. In terms of going to Mississippi, in terms of trying to reach leadership people in certain areas, most of them I knew. The students would come to me and ask me, if you're going to Mississippi, what? Or who? I had worked with the National Association for the Advancement of Colored People, I had worked with the Southern Christian Leadership Conference, I knew people in all of the sections of the South. When Bob Moses went to Mississippi, I sent him to Amzie Moore, who had been one of the earlier pioneers and had suffered reprisals from his voter registration effort. I had helped to raise money here in New York City for Amzie Moore. I had gone down there and stayed with them and helped with meetings, so I knew the person. I knew he knew the state, and so Bob Moses was able to have an entrée. Here was a man who had never been to Mississippi, and he had somewhere to sleep, to eat, and he had somebody who knew something that could be useful.

Then maybe it was a question of helping to write and talk over certain things—what should be the approach? What should we do? I also went around to the campuses that had Ys. I would deal inevitably with the question, what is SNCC doing? Who are the students who had done these things? Because it tends to follow, that when you're young, especially if you see somebody out there doing something, challenging a system that you say you are concerned about, it makes you a little uneasy, or at least maybe inspires you.

Why '64? Why that summer? The Student Nonviolent Coordinating Committee debated it very pointedly, and they came to the conclusion that it was a necessary political move to invite white students to participate in the program. They were very aware that when a black person got brutalized for attempting to register to vote, this was nothing new, it had been done before. But when the son of a governor or the daughter of a congressman or the daughter and son of people up North who could give money and who had some political clout got involved, it was a challenge to the powers that be.

As for the Mississippi Freedom Democratic Party, my thinking was along these lines. The people who were black in Mississippi, if they were going to organize and have any clout at that stage of the game in the Democratic setup, should have the opportunity to organize themselves to do what they thought they ought to do. And if they wanted to become a Mississippi Freedom Democratic Party, then it was my role to help support that.

I was asked to keynote the Mississippi Freedom Democratic Party's convention in Jackson, preparatory to their going to the Democratic convention in Atlantic City. I also was sent to Washington, where the MFDP decided to set up an office which had in it people who were going out to the hinterlands, carrying the challenge to the Democratic delegates who were going to the convention. They were able to secure commitments from the delegates to support the MFDP's challenge to be seated. President Johnson, of course, was the only person who controlled the '64 convention. He had it in his complete control, and he did not permit anything to come up on the floor, which meant that nothing really did surface.

The MFDP delegates carried up all these files which showed that thousands of people had evidenced their interest in registering to vote by going to beauty parlors and barber shops, churches, or wherever else they could set up a registration booth. This was to counter the prevailing concept that Negroes weren't interested in registering. Great fruit came of it in terms of arousing the people and getting them involved, like Mrs. Johnson of Greenwood and like Mrs. Hamer. There's a woman that had been a timekeeper on a plantation for sixteen or more years, and when she attempted to register to vote she lost her job, her husband lost his, and then she was badly beaten.[1]

SOMEBODY CARRIES ON

It's not hard to interpret what our parents mean by a better world. You know, go to school, son, and get a good education. And what do you do with this? You get a degree, you move out into some little community housing project, you get married, five kids and two cars, and you don't care what's happening. . . . So I think when we talk about growing up in a better world, a new world, we mean changing the world to a different place.

—Cordell Reagan, a nineteen-year-old Student Nonviolent Coordinating Committee activist, in the early 1960s.

Although the Mississippi Freedom Democratic Party did not get its delegates seated at the national convention, many local MFDP leaders were elected to office in Mississippi, and MFDP efforts resulted in the 1967 election of the first black state legislator since Reconstruction, Robert Clark. Founders and members of the Mississippi Freedom Democratic Party, like Ella Baker, have kept on, persistent in their efforts to make a better world. For a number of years, Ella Baker was on the staff of the Southern Conference Educational Fund (SCEF), an organization formed to encourage black and white people to work together in the South, and led for many years by Carl and Anne Braden. Ella Baker remains active in New York City, where she is an adviser to many liberation and human rights groups. She also speaks publicly. She has been particularly active in groups supporting freedom struggles in Zimbabwe (Rhodesia) and South Africa. We asked her: What happened to others in the civil rights movement? And how do you keep going?

I think a number of things happened. The people endured with more sense about what they were involved in. They at least survived with knowledge, and out of it has come various kinds of—let's call it adequate leadership. People are more easily alerted to whether they are getting unusual oppression, and they'll do something. They're quicker to respond now. They would be much less willing to settle for what they had endured before, and they would be more likely to actually go to the Nth degree in revolt, if the pressure of the past were reinstated.

You see, today, they are living in what we call a normal society. The same kinds of denials that we have up here in the North, to one degree or another they have down there. But the major pressures, the things that they consider the most oppressive, are lifted. I mean, you don't ride Jim Crow.[2] You can even go as far as boycotting the stores, which has gotten the NAACP in deep water. But the people have taken action. They can elect the people they want to elect whether they turn out to be good or not. And they can make the usual mistake of feeling that you can trust those in power, because they have given you a little power. Whether that's good or bad, I'm not in a position at this stage to talk too pointedly about. It's no worse than it is anywhere else. You see, I have grave reservations about what can be accomplished, anyway, by established political parties.

Maybe there will be a new revolution. I don't think there's going to be one anytime soon, to be honest—I mean among blacks nor whites in this country. The best country in the world, you hear them say. I guess it may be, I haven't lived anywhere else. But it's not good enough as far as I'm concerned. But I'm not good enough for the task.

I keep going because I don't see the productive value of being bitter. What else *do* you do? Do you get so bitter that you give up, and when young people come and want to talk to me, to hear about the past and learn from it, am I to say, "Oh, forget it, go on about your business, I'm bitter." You *can* just say, the heck with it. I'll break off and do what I need to do. Those of us who have responsibilities of children and family, somebody's got to provide some food for them, so you might decide to concentrate on getting that. I can stand that. But if people begin to place their values in terms of how high they get in the political world, or how much worldly goods they accumulate, or what kind of cars they have, or how much they have in the bank, that's where I begin to lose respect.

To me, I'm part of the human family. What the human family will accomplish, I can't control. But it isn't impossible that what those who came along with me went through, might stimulate others to continue to fight for a society that does not have those kinds of problems. Somewhere down the line the numbers increase, the tribe increases. So how do you keep on? I can't help it. I don't claim to have any corner on an answer, but I believe that the struggle is eternal. Somebody else carries on.

NOTES

1. While Ella Baker is a behind-the-scenes figure, Fannie Lou Hamer was a public orator. She was the keynote speaker for the MFDP at Atlantic City in 1964. In 1977, she died of cancer, after having worked in a cooperative farm movement among blacks in Sunflower County, Mississippi.

2. Jim Crow is a term for segregation laws. It comes from the name of a character who scraped and shuffled in minstrel (song and dance) shows in pre–Civil war days.

12

THE CITIZEN AND THE LAW

More and more women are going to law school—partly because new laws demand they get a chance. When they graduate, significant numbers now go into trial work. There the new woman lawyer has to find her way in what has traditionally been a man's world, the world of the courtroom, where highly complex rules, written and unwritten, guide the argument by which guilt or innocence is determined. The essence of that system is the "adversary process," an artificial contest about law and evidence, out of which justice is meant to emerge. The stereotype of the woman shrinking from controversy does not fit the courtroom scene. Among many other victories, the new women lawyers are demonstrating that women can not only plead but also fight.

The courtroom is a major institution in our political system. The shape of criminal law itself has often been a hot political issue; politics produces law. It is in the courtroom that the rights of the individual meet the demands of the community for security and justice. Average citizens—and especially disadvantaged citizens—encounter the law in the courts every day. What goes on there suddenly becomes extremely important when a citizen gets involved with the law. At that point, he or she needs help. Alexandra Cury and Pamela Chepiga know how to give it.

Women Attorneys in Defense and Prosecution

A WOMAN ATTORNEY FOR THE DEFENSE

by Mitchell Pacelle

Last August, when assistant Florida state attorney David Ranck strode into Dade County felony court to prosecute a burglary case, he was sure the state had an airtight case. On trial was John Green, a 22-year-old from Miami's black ghetto who had been arrested for breaking into a liquor store. The defendant was allegedly caught in the act and photographed at the scene.

Looking back on the trial, Ranck admits that he wasn't prepared for Alexandra Cury, the 27-year-old trial lawyer from the Dade County public defender's office who was representing Green. Cury told the jury

---

From Mitchell Pacelle, "The Joyce Davenport of Dade County," *American Lawyer*, May 1984, pp. 99ff.

that her client had been framed. Green testified that he and a friend were walking home from a disco when police officers grabbed them, beat them up, brought them into the liquor store, and arrested them for burglary.

The police, however, said that they followed Green and two accomplices into the liquor store through a hole in the roof, caught the defendant hiding in a bathroom, and radioed for support. The arresting officers testified that they could not leave the building because a security gate in front of the doorway was padlocked from the outside, and that they were not carrying handcuffs. The back-ups allegedly passed handcuffs through the security bars to the officers inside, then broke open the bars to release the officers and the suspects. The state had photographs of the suspects standing behind the bars, handcuffed.

In her cross-examination of the arresting officers, Cury says she "made a real point of asking, 'You passed [the cuffs] through the bars?' [The police responded,] 'Yeah, yeah, yeah.' " In her closing argument, Cury established that the "bars" in front of the doorway were actually a metal screen. "I held up a photo and the mesh looked like this," says Cury, holding her thumb and forefinger about one-half inch apart. "There's no way they could have passed the handcuffs through."

She also used the same photo to suggest that the police were lying on another point. "The police testified that they used no force," says Cury. She instructed the jury to examine the photo closely. "You couldn't see it very well, but I really looked. . . . My client had this shiner, a huge black eye." Cury told the jury that if the police were willing to lie about using force and passing the cuffs between the bars, they would be willing to lie on other points. The jury voted for acquittal. "It was a miracle," Cury recalls.

Prosecutor Ranck admits ruefully, "She kicked my ass from one end of the courtroom to the other." Cury's defense, says Ranck, "never occurred to me because it was so ludicrous. God-damn, she sold it to the jury." Ranck continues, "I was shocked by the verdict. I had gone in and talked to the judge, and he said he would have convicted the guy in ten seconds."

"She's one of those very zealous trial lawyers. Her avowed purpose is to get her man out of jail," says Robert Kaye, a Dade County judge described by both defense lawyers and prosecutors as prosecution-oriented. "The comment around here is that she's the Joyce Davenport of Dade County," he says, referring to the heroine of television's "Hill Street Blues."

Cury has heard the comparison before. Prosecutors bemoan the vigor with which she argues her clients' not-guilty pleas. Prosecutor Jeffrey Swartz, division chief of the robbery task force unit, remembers Cury's stinging frontal attacks on his and other prosecutors' witnesses during her first year in felony court. "She was just openly, consistently calling the state's witnesses liars, even at plea-bargaining sessions," he says. At an age when many Wall Street litigators are hungering for their first opportunity to stand up in court, Cury posts an impressive three-year trial record. After graduating from the University of Virginia law school in the summer of 1981, she joined the public defender's office at a salary of $17,500 (she now earns $30,000) and was admitted to the bar that October. She immediately began a three-month stint in misdemeanor court, during which she tried eight jury trials, won acquittals in all, and was promptly promoted to felony court.

In 1982 and 1983 Cury tried 37 felony jury trials, resulting in 20 acquittals, 13 convictions, some on lesser charges, and four mistrials. Her two-year nonconviction rate of 63 percent tops the office's overall rate, which head public defender Bennett Brummer estimates is 45 to 50 percent. In 1983 alone, Cury defended about 250 clients who faced charges ranging from burglary to rape to first-degree murder.

Approximately 50 of these cases washed out before trial. Of the remaining defendants, 21 pleaded not guilty in front of a jury and the rest plea-bargained. Cury estimates that eight trials a year is the average for a public defender.

Cury is among the 50-odd "pit lawyers" (staff attorneys) in the Dade County public defender's office, which handled more than 8,100 felony cases last year, including 78 capital cases. Almost without exception, all trials are jury trials, says Brummer, because "we consider bench trials a slow guilty plea." The lure of lucrative private work, particularly drug defense, keeps the average attorney in the office for just three years. For those who stay on, however, the position offers a fast track to major trial work.

Cury's ultimate goal—her professional mission—is to do capital-punishment defense work full-time. "If anyone needs help, it's the ones who are confronting the possibility of state execution," says Cury. "And there are not a great number of competent attorneys that are practicing capital defense law." She is presently closing in on her goal, and is assisting senior public defenders in two capital cases that are scheduled to come to trial this summer.

Like her fellow assistant public defenders, Cury tries cases in front of the same judge for periods of six months or more and spends one week of every three in the courtroom. Last year she was assigned to Judge Kaye's court—called a "war court" by public defenders because of Kaye's alleged pro-prosecution bias. Although Kaye and Cury clashed often, Cury did well with the juries in Kaye's court, scoring, in the seven cases she argued, four acquittals, a hung jury, and two convictions.

Cury's "biggest problem was that she thought everyone was innocent," says Kaye. "Ask any defense lawyer and they'll tell you that ninety-nine percent are guilty." Cury, on the other hand, estimates that "some twenty percent of those people charged with crimes are innocent."

She says she likes to use voir dire to remind jurors of the central tenet of the justice system. She challenges potential jurors, "When you see someone riding in the back of the police car, isn't it your natural inclination to ask yourself, 'Wonder what he did?' not 'Wonder if he did anything?' You're asked to leave those natural feelings outside this courtroom. Can you do it???"

Cury adds that although she is often able to determine whether her own clients are guilty, her job is not to judge them, but to "tell [clients] what they're up against, ask them their personal histories, [and] tell them what their possible defenses are."

When she goes to trial, Cury believes in her clients so completely that she blames herself for all guilty verdicts and "regrets them forever," she says. "You get up in closing argument and you argue to a jury, 'He's not guilty. He didn't do it. It didn't happen that way.' And when the jury votes guilty, they've said that you haven't done your job and that they didn't believe you. You've put your credibility on the line . . . and the jury has condemned you."

Cury has also been known to put her emotions on the line during a trial. In her first case in felony court, tried in April 1982, Cury defended a 16-year-old boy charged with breaking into the home of a friend, a 38-year-old retarded man, and robbing him at gunpoint. On cross-examination, Cury established that the victim had let her client into the house and that there was reason to believe the gun was a toy. In an emotional closing argument, Cury began to cry. "The thing that makes her most successful is that she really believes in her clients," says assistant state attorney Robert Scola, who prosecuted the case. "[But] if she can raise tears for this thing," he complains, "what's she going to do when she represents the guy who has six kids and is charged with rape?"

Cury admits that she may have been overzealous in her first felony trials, but says the tears were sincere. "I would prefer that not to happen," she explains. "You run a certain risk of losing control." The jury convicted her client of simple trespassing and sentenced him to one year in jail.

Eleven months later, in March 1983, Cury was handling a rape case, which she considers to have been one of her most interesting assignments. Her client was a 50-year-old man charged with raping the 22-year-old daughter of the woman he had been living with for a number of years. Cury argued that the daughter, who was mentally disabled and suffered from cerebral palsy, had had sex with someone else and then blamed Cury's client. It came out in trial that on two previous occasions the daughter "had accused her mother's boyfriends of attacking her in order to get rid of them," Cury explains.

The most crucial moment in the case was Cury's cross-examination of the young woman. Prosecutor Jeffrey Swartz, who expected Cury to be aggressive, says he was surprised when Cury questioned the woman carefully and delicately. The victim broke into tears anyway, and a recess was called, during which Cury learned that a witness coordinator—a nonlawyer employed by the state to prepare witnesses—had been coaching the young woman from the back of the room. Cury moved for a mistrial, and although the judge refused, the coordinator left the courtroom for the rest of the cross-examination.

Cury delegated the closing argument to a third-year law student, an intern who was trying the case with her, reserving the half-hour rebuttal for herself. "The intern made his closing argument," Cury recalls, "then the prosecution stood up and said, 'We waive,' so that I wouldn't have the last closing argument. I went crazy. I was miserable." Cury went sidebar with the judge and prosecutor for 15 minutes, but her arguments were fruitless. "I came back to the table and stomped my foot. I was angry with myself."

Swartz believes that the jury finally acquitted Cury's client because it thought Swartz, by waiving his closing argument, was throwing up his hands in defeat. "I was somewhat taken aback by the quickness of the verdict," says Swartz. The jury deliberated for approximately an hour, Cury recalls.

The trial left Swartz with mixed feelings about Cury. Her self-control during cross-examination impressed him, but her later outburst annoyed him. "She had a tendency to wear her feelings for her clients on her sleeves," says Swartz. He chalks it up to her inexperience: "As a young lawyer I would believe any police officer that walked in the door. She would believe any client."

To Cury's mind, the jury acquitted because she suggested a credible alternative to the state's theories. "[Many defense lawyers] create unreasonable theories. I hear defense lawyers make incredible arguments all the time," Cury says. "Sometimes my behavior and my emotions are overstated, but I don't think my theories are."

Cury has aspired to be a criminal defense lawyer since she was 11 or 12. As a teenager in her hometown of Jacksonville, she worked after school doing office chores for a criminal defense and civil rights lawyer. She worked for the ACLU National Prison Project during her first summer break from law school, and the next year was a summer associate at the Houston defense firm Schaffer, Lambright & Ramsey.

After law school, her commitment to fighting capital punishment pointed her toward Texas and Florida, the two states with the largest death row populations. Texas was ruled out because it doesn't have a public defender program. Dade County, however, has a public defender's office that assigns capital cases to lawyers with only five or six years of experience. "That's an awfully short time," Cury remarks. "What corporation entrusts its legal affairs to a five-year law school graduate? In the scale of things, what responsibility is more awesome?"

A typical day for Cury, when she is not in trial, is spent taking depositions and researching and writing motions. She frequently leaves the office to interview clients in prison or photograph the crime site. Trial weeks are more hectic. After working through the weekend, Cury is in her office by 7:30 A.M. Monday. She is then ready to mobilize when the judge chooses which case he will hear that week. On Tuesday, the trial begins. Typically, she presents her opening arguments on Wednesday and her final rebuttal on Thursday. Thursday afternoon the jury reaches a verdict and the case closes.

Cury counts herself among "the crew that love their work." She regularly sits in on her colleagues' trials, takes notes, and, in the hallways during recesses, offers critiques. In the evenings, she joins the "skull sessions" in which she and other public defenders review trial preparation and strategy. One strategy that she has adopted from her colleagues is rarely calling witnesses. In Florida, if the defense calls no witnesses (except the defendant) and introduces no evidence, it presents the first closing argument and the final rebuttal. For this reason, Cury calls defense witnesses only to present alibis. "I believe the last word with the jury is really important," she says. "I don't like to give it up."

Cury's 100 percent, no-compromise style of advocacy has won her points with the defense bar. She first worked alongside private lawyers last December when she represented a Colombian woman who had been arrested with three others after they sold a kilo of cocaine to undercover police officers. Cury's client, who allegedly introduced the officers to the suppliers, was charged with trafficking. The three other defendants hired private counsel.

Miami solo practitioner William Clay, a former public defender whose criminal defense practice is two-thirds drug defense, represented one of the defendants. Clay calls the case "about as intense a criminal case as you can envision," primarily because the codefendants were expected to trade accusations in front of a jury, which leads to conflicting interests among the defense lawyers. "When there's a possibility of a shootout between defendants, weaker defense lawyers might decide to acquiesce to the tactics of the older, more experienced defense lawyers," says Clay.

Cury did nothing of the kind. Because her client was in jail, she filed a speedy-trial demand, despite the fact that Clay's client and one other were out on bond and in no hurry to go to trial. Her argument to the jury was anything but acquiescent, Clay recalls. "Alex's position was, 'Someone is guilty of trafficking here, but it's not my client.' She is absolutely not intimidated by anyone," he says. "There's no doubt in my mind that Alex Cury is one of the toughest young lawyers around."

As Cury finishes her third year in the public defender's office, she claims that setting up a private practice on the order of Clay's is out of the question. "In order to run an office, you're going to have to take some high-paying clients. If I still wanted to do capital defense work, I'd have to represent some big drug dealers," she says. "The economics of it don't appeal to me at all."

A WOMAN ATTORNEY FOR THE PROSECUTION

by Robin Reisig

Pamela Rogers Chepiga, 33, remembers herself as a shy studious law student who hated debating and planned to become a tax lawyer. "I had fairly well dismissed the

From Robin Reisig, "The Improbable Rise of Pamela Chepiga," *American Lawyer*, May 1984, pp. 102 ff.

notion of becoming a litigator," she recalls. "I didn't view my personality as sufficiently outgoing, aggressive, or combative." Given these qualities, Chepiga would seem an unlikely candidate to direct what is widely regarded as the toughest white-collar-crime enforcement team in the country.

Yet in December 1982, she was named chief of the securities and commodities fraud unit in the U.S. attorney's office of New York's Southern District. Under previous heads, the unit obtained the five pending indictments against financier Robert Vesco, pressed such major actions as the OPM leasing swindle, and prosecuted the late Carmine Tramunti for stock manipulation involving organized crime money.

Chepiga now oversees the roughly 50 cases handled by the unit at a given time and works closely with the local administrators of the Securities and Exchange Commission and the Commodities Futures Trading Commission. About a dozen investigators from the SEC, Post Office, and Internal Revenue Service are stationed at the unit under her supervision. In addition to administrative work, which consumes about a quarter of her time, Chepiga is continuing to develop and try her own cases. Her annual salary is $54,600.

Chepiga was "selected from the best of the best," says her boss, U.S. attorney John Martin, Jr., who describes her as a "superb attorney." "She is someone whose judgment you would look to and rely on," adds Patricia Hynes, who was the unit's executive assistant U.S. attorney until she joined Milberg Weiss Bershad Specthrie & Lerach as a partner early this year.

To at least one of her teachers at Fordham law school, U.S. district judge John Sprizzo, Chepiga did not at first seem to be star litigator material. She rarely spoke up in class, recalls Sprizzo, who was surprised when she turned in what he describes as "really extraordinary" exams. Chepiga had to perform well. Her full scholarship at law school depended on her staying in the top tenth of her class.

The daughter of an engineer who died when she was eight, Chepiga had attended a small, Catholic girls' school in Brooklyn before graduating cum laude from Fordham University at the age of 20. She went on to finish fifth in her law school class in 1973. Sprizzo, who says she was the best student he had in his four years as a teacher, urged her to become a litigator. At his suggestion, she worked as an assistant in the U.S. attorney's office during her last year in law school. Sprizzo also introduced her to such well-known veterans of the Southern District as Peter Fleming, Jr., of New York's Curtis, Mallet-Prevost, Colt & Mosle, where Sprizzo was then of counsel.

"Fleming said he was always nervous before he went into court," Chepiga recalls. "He said perhaps it was a good idea to stop being a trial lawyer when one stopped being nervous. It gave you an edge." Fleming's confession, Chepiga says, convinced her to become a litigator. "If such a polished trial lawyer admitted being nervous before going into a courtroom, I thought perhaps it was something I could handle. John Sprizzo and Peter Fleming made me realize that my preconceived notions of a good trial lawyer were more Perry Mason-ish than real," she adds.

Chepiga's goal from then on was a slot on the elite corps of the criminal division in the U.S. attorney's office. She chose not to apply there directly, however, after completing a two-year clerkship with U.S. district judge Kevin Thomas Duffy in 1975. Instead, Chepiga trained for two years as a litigation associate at New York's Hughes Hubbard & Reed to gain extra speed and skill in drafting briefs. The preparation apparently paid off. In her five and a half years at the criminal division—where she tried cases in both the official corruption unit and securities and commodities fraud unit—Chepiga has lost only one of her fifteen trials, a perjury case that grew out of her first full criminal prosecution in 1977.

During her first full trial, Chepiga

helped prosecutor Jed Rakoff retry and convict two promoters of Industries International of fraudulently inflating the value of the company's stock. "She kept coming up with one brilliant idea after another," says Rakoff, now a partner at New York's Mudge Rose Guthrie & Alexander. Chepiga suggested the trial judge give a preliminary charge to the jury explaining the law on the criminal offense of knowingly selling unregistered stock.

The idea of such a preliminary charge sounds obvious, but, according to Rakoff, no one in the unit had heard of its being used in a criminal case. "I had enough good sense to follow her advice," Rakoff explains. Rakoff says he had expected the retrial to be more difficult than the first, which had ended in a mistrial when a juror had a heart attack during deliberations. But, he adds, largely due to Chepiga's suggestions, it took three instead of eight weeks to try, and the jury voted for conviction after only a few hours. (The first jury had been undecided after four days.)

Chepiga's most celebrated and controversial case was the successful 1980 mail fraud prosecution of Jack Bronston, a former state senator and partner at New York's Rosenman Colin Freund Lewis & Cohen. Bronston was accused of having breached his fiduciary duty by lobbying to get a client the franchise for New York City's bus-stop shelters, even though his law firm represented investors in a competing company. He was sentenced to four months in jail and fined $2,000 plus court costs. Several publications praised Chepiga and her co-counsel Hynes for a gutsy, skillful performance, but some attorneys criticized the decision to prosecute. "It was an overextension of the rather vague mail fraud statute to something that, while improper, was arguably not criminal," asserts Columbia law school professor John Coffee, Jr.

Chepiga still defends the decision, arguing that if an unknown lawyer had ignored such a conflict, it would have been "less offensive. But here," she contends, "when Bronston actually has the nerve to write on Senate stationery and note in his diary that this is to be billed to [the client], it's reprehensible!"

Chepiga's most recent trial involved the promoters of Tellco, a company that lured investors into buying worthless promissory notes. Chepiga's damning pre-trial presentation of the case caused three of the four defendants to plead guilty, according to New York solo practitioner Henry Putzel III, who represented one of the three. Charles Weintraub, a solo practitioner who represented the only defendant to go to trial, says regretfully that Chepiga "showed a very fine sense of judgment" in her prosecution. Weintraub had banked on Chepiga's calling a witness who had supplied strong evidence to the SEC. Weintraub says that the witness, "not being lily white himself, " would have given him an opportunity "to score points." Instead, Chepiga relied solely on the testimony of victims, a strategy Weintraub says helped win her a conviction.

For all her talk of shyness and nervousness, Chepiga appears more composed, in or out of the courtroom, than most lawyers. In 1982 she and SEC investigator Robert Brehme interviewed more than 100 witnesses to develop a perjury charge into a much broader securities fraud action against suspended New Jersey lawyer John Surgent, Jr., who ran World Gambling Corporation. The indictment charged Surgent with having bought World Gambling stock in the name of a mechanic while manipulating the value of the company's shares. Shortly before the trial, Chepiga learned of the death of their star witness, the mechanic, in a 10 A.M. phone call from a codefendant's attorney who had been trying unsuccessfully to plea bargain for his client in exchange for testimony. The attorney presumed, says Chepiga, that the prosecutors would now be forced to reduce the charges against his client. Chepiga and Brehme spent the next 12 hours poring over the other evidence in the case. By 10 P.M. they decided they didn't need to plea bargain. "There was no wasted time, no wasted effort," marvels Brehme. "Nothing threw her."

"I see no point in being upset," says Chepiga, who has a disposition some might find bafflingly calm. "It may take less energy to be serene. It's more productive."

But what makes Chepiga an unusually effective prosecutor, observers say, is her ability to focus attention on the victims of a case and to convey a sense of outrage to a jury. Audrey Strauss, her former unit chief and now an associate at Mudge Rose, describes watching Chepiga sum up the Tellco case last October: "To see her, with all her integrity and purity, conveying the enormity of the defendant's crimes with such emotion in her voice—she could have convicted anyone."

Chepiga's courtroom style reflects the way in which she has managed to overcome her natural shyness. "I had viewed litigation as an exercise in debate," she says. "It isn't. It's advocacy. When you've prepared your case, and it's a cause you believe in, you can absolutely turn on in the courtroom."

Chepiga now has the power, along with the U.S. attorney and the chief of the criminal division, to decide which cases her unit will prosecute. She plans to attack what she says is a resurgence of the traditional shell game, in which manipulators take over a dormant company, pretend it is active, and manipulate its stock price for quick profits. She will also step up investigations of the rising number of corporate record falsifications, in which companies seek to hide their true profits and losses.

Chepiga puts in nine- to fifteen-hour days at her new office at the criminal division, depending on whether she's in a trial. But she says she tries to get home by 7 P.M. to be with her two-year-old son, Geoffrey, who has developed the habit of staying up until midnight to be with his parents. Her husband, Michael, who was an aspiring playwright and teacher, used to complain about her long hours. But, influenced by his wife and her lawyer friends, he now logs the same hours himself, as a litigation associate at New York's Simpson Thacher & Bartlett.

Chepiga took 12 weeks off in 1980 between the indictment and trial of the bus-shelter case to have her baby. Then, during the most publicized case of her career, she got between three and four hours of sleep a night while she was breast-feeding her son. Raising a child isn't difficult, says Chepiga: "The thing that gets cut is your sleep."

Few assistants last longer than four and a half years at the U.S. attorney's office, which is used by many as a stepping-stone to more lucrative careers in private practice. Chepiga has committed herself to staying at least 18 months at her new job. Although she says her next move will be to develop a civil and criminal trial practice at a law firm large enough to offer extensive support services, Chepiga is doubtful that such a career will prove as satisfying as her years as a prosecutor: "Most people find this the best job they've ever had. The elements of public service and excitement make it hard to replace."

13

GROUPS IN ACTION

A big political movement is born when many people begin to think they have the same problem. That awareness opens the way for a new political identity, a sense of shared experiences, attitudes, beliefs, and values, which deepen the bonds of unity and purpose. So it has been with the women's movement in the United States. Women had first to discover their common grievance and character, had to meet and talk themselves into mutual understanding. Until and unless such passions and perceptions get themselves established, no amount of money or technique of organization will suffice to make a movement.

From the start, women had to overcome nearly the full weight of their cultures. They had to get past the disdain, contempt, and condemnation the spokesmen of the status quo rained upon them. Women had to convince themselves that they were neither crazy nor blasphemous nor unfeminine when they insisted on their rights.

A pathbreaking book, *The Feminine Mystique* by Betty Friedan, played an important role in opening up those discoveries.

Invariably, a big political movement generates resistance. The women's movement is no exception. Perhaps the most powerful resistance came from other women who, far from seeing the new way as a liberation, saw it as a threat to their own way of life. Phyllis Schlafly argued that women who wanted to succeed should steer clear of the complainers and focus on "positive" achievement. Her book, *The Power of the Positive Woman*, sought to mobilize women against the movement's tide.

Betty Friedan's Ideas for a New Women's Movement

by Betty Friedan

THE PROBLEM THAT HAS NO NAME

The problem lay buried, unspoken, for many years in the minds of American women. It was a strange stirring, a sense of dissatisfaction, a yearning that women suffered in the middle of the twentieth century in the United States. Each suburban wife struggled with it alone. As she made the beds, shopped for groceries, matched slipcover material, ate peanut butter sandwiches with her children, chauffeured Cub Scouts and Brownies, lay beside her husband at night—she was afraid to ask even of herself the silent question—"Is this all?"

For over fifteen years there was no word of this yearning in the millions of words written about women, for women, in all the columns, books and articles by experts telling women their role was to seek fulfillment as wives and mothers. Over and over women heard in voices of tradition and of Freudian sophistication that they could desire no greater destiny than to glory in their own femininity. Experts told them how to catch a man and keep him, how to breastfeed children and handle their toilet training, how to cope with sibling rivalry and adolescent rebellion; how to buy a dishwasher, bake bread, cook gourmet snails, and build a swimming pool with their own hands; how to dress, look, and act more feminine and make marriage more exciting; how to keep their husbands from dying young and their sons from growing into delinquents. They were taught to pity the neurotic, unfeminine, unhappy women who wanted to be poets or physicists or presidents. They learned that truly feminine women do not want careers, higher education, political rights—the independence and the opportunities that the old-fashioned feminists fought for. Some women, in their forties and fifties, still remembered painfully giving up those dreams, but most of the younger women no longer even thought about them. A thousand expert voices applauded their femininity, their adjustment, their new maturity. All they had to do was devote their lives from earliest girlhood to finding a husband and bearing children.

By the end of the nineteen-fifties, the average marriage age of women in America dropped to 20, and was still dropping, into the teens. Fourteen million girls were engaged by 17. The proportion of women attending college in comparison with men dropped from 47 per cent in 1920 to 35 per cent in 1958. A century earlier, women had fought for higher education; now girls went to college to get a husband. By the mid-fifties, 60 per cent dropped out of college to marry, or because they were afraid too much education would be a marriage bar. Colleges built dormitories for "married students," but the students were almost always the husbands. A new degree was instituted for the wives—"Ph.T." (Putting Husband Through).

Then American girls began getting married in high school. And the women's mag-

---

From Betty Friedan, *The Feminine Mystique* (New York: Norton, 1983, 1974, 1973, 1963), pp. 11–27, 80–102.

azines, deploring the unhappy statistics about these young marriages, urged that courses on marriage, and marriage counselors, be installed in the high schools. Girls started going steady at twelve and thirteen, in junior high. Manufacturers put out brassieres with false bosoms of foam rubber for little girls of ten. And an advertisement for a child's dress, sizes 3–6x, in the *New York Times* in the fall of 1960, said: "She Too Can Join the Man-Trap Set."

By the end of the fifties, the United States birthrate was overtaking India's. The birth-control movement, renamed Planned Parenthood, was asked to find a method whereby women who had been advised that a third or fourth baby would be born dead or defective might have it anyhow. Statisticians were especially astounded at the fantastic increase in the number of babies among college women. Where once they had two children, now they had four, five, six. Women who had once wanted careers were now making careers out of having babies. So rejoiced *Life* magazine in a 1956 paean to the movement of American women back to the home.

In a New York hospital, a woman had a nervous breakdown when she found she could not breastfeed her baby. In other hospitals, women dying of cancer refused a drug which research had proved might save their lives: its side effects were said to be unfeminine. "If I have only one life, let me live it as a blonde," a larger-than-life-sized picture of a pretty, vacuous woman proclaimed from newspaper, magazine, and drugstore ads. And across America, three out of every ten women dyed their hair blonde. They ate a chalk called Metrecal, instead of food, to shrink to the size of the thin young models. Department-store buyers reported that American women, since 1939, had become three and four sizes smaller. "Women are out to fit the clothes, instead of vice-versa," one buyer said.

Interior decorators were designing kitchens with mosaic murals and original paintings, for kitchens were once again the center of women's lives. Home sewing became a million-dollar industry. Many women no longer left their homes, except to shop, chauffeur their children, or attend a social engagement with their husbands. Girls were growing up in America without ever having jobs outside the home. In the late fifties, a sociological phenomenon was suddenly remarked: a third of American women now worked, but most were no longer young and very few were pursuing careers. They were married women who held part-time jobs, selling or secretarial, to put their husbands through school, their sons through college, or to help pay the mortgage. Or they were widows supporting families. Fewer and fewer women were entering professional work. The shortages in the nursing, social work, and teaching professions caused crises in almost every American city. Concerned over the Soviet Union's lead in the space race, scientists noted that America's greatest source of unused brain-power was women. But girls would not study physics: it was "unfeminine." A girl refused a science fellowship at Johns Hopkins to take a job in a real-estate office. All she wanted, she said, was what every other American girl wanted—to get married, have four children and live in a nice house in a nice suburb.

The suburban housewife—she was the dream image of the young American women and the envy, it was said, of women all over the world. The American housewife—freed by science and labor-saving appliances from the drudgery, the dangers of childbirth and the illnesses of her grandmother. She was healthy, beautiful, educated, concerned only about her husband, her children, her home. She had found true feminine fulfillment. As a housewife and mother, she was respected as a full and equal partner to man in his world. She was free to choose automobiles, clothes, appliances, supermarkets; she had everything that women ever dreamed of.

In the fifteen years after World War II,

this mystique of feminine fulfillment became the cherished and self-perpetuating core of contemporary American culture. Millions of women lived their lives in the image of those pretty pictures of the American suburban housewife, kissing their husbands goodbye in front of the picture window, depositing their stationwagonsful of children at school, and smiling as they ran the new electric waxer over the spotless kitchen floor. They baked their own bread, sewed their own and their children's clothes, kept their new washing machines and dryers running all day. They changed the sheets on the beds twice a week instead of once, took the rug-hooking class in adult education, and pitied their poor frustrated mothers, who had dreamed of having a career. Their only dream was to be perfect wives and mothers, their highest ambition to have five children and a beautiful house, their only fight to get and keep their husbands. They had no thought for the unfeminine problems of the world outside the home; they wanted the men to make the major decisions. They gloried in their role as women, and wrote proudly on the census blank: "Occupation: housewife."

For over fifteen years, the words written for women, and the words women used when they talked to each other, while their husbands sat on the other side of the room and talked shop or politics or septic tanks, were about problems with their children, or how to keep their husbands happy, or improve their children's school, or cook chicken or make slipcovers. Nobody argued whether women were inferior or superior to men; they were simply different. Words like "emancipation" and "career" sounded strange and embarrassing; no one had used them for years. When a Frenchwoman named Simone de Beauvoir wrote a book called *The Second Sex*, an American critic commented that she obviously "didn't know what life was all about," and besides, she was talking about French women. The "woman problem" in America no longer existed.

If a woman had a problem in the 1950's and 1960's, she knew that something must be wrong with her marriage, or with herself. Other women were satisfied with their lives, she thought. What kind of a woman was she if she did not feel this mysterious fulfillment waxing the kitchen floor? She was so ashamed to admit her dissatisfaction that she never knew how many other women shared it. If she tried to tell her husband, he didn't understand what she was talking about. She did not really understand it herself. For over fifteen years women in America found it harder to talk about this problem than about sex. Even the psychoanalysts had no name for it. When a woman went to a psychiatrist for help, as many women did, she would say, "I'm so ashamed," or "I must be hopelessly neurotic." "I don't know what's wrong with women today," a suburban psychiatrist said uneasily. "I only know something is wrong because most of my patients happen to be women. And their problem isn't sexual." Most women with this problem did not go to see a psychoanalyst, however. "There's nothing wrong really," they kept telling themselves. "There isn't any problem."

But on an April morning in 1959, I heard a mother of four, having coffee with four other mothers in a suburban development fifteen miles from New York, say in a tone of quiet desperation, "the problem." And the others knew, without words, that she was not talking about a problem with her husband, or her children, or her home. Suddenly they realized they all shared the same problem, the problem that has no name. They began, hesitantly, to talk about it. Later, after they had picked up their children at nursery school and taken them home to nap, two of the women cried, in sheer relief, just to know they were not alone.

Gradually I came to realize that the problem that has no name was shared by countless women in America. As a magazine writer I often interviewed women about problems with their children, or their marriages, or their houses, or their communities. But after a while I began to recognize the telltale signs of this other problem. I saw the same signs in suburban ranch houses and split-levels on Long Island and in New Jersey and Westchester County; in colonial houses in a small Massachusetts town; on patios in Memphis; in suburban and city apartments; in living rooms in the Midwest. Sometimes I sensed the problem, not as a reporter, but as a suburban housewife, for during this time I was also bringing up my own three children in Rockland County, New York. I heard echoes of the problem in college dormitories and semiprivate maternity wards, at PTA meetings and luncheons of the League of Women Voters, at suburban cocktail parties, in station wagons waiting for trains, and in snatches of conversation overheard at Schrafft's. The groping words I heard from other women, on quiet afternoons when children were at school or on quiet evenings when husbands worked late, I think I understood first as a woman long before I understood their larger social and psychological implications.

Just what was this problem that has no name? What were the words women used when they tried to express it? Sometimes a woman would say "I feel empty somehow . . . incomplete." Or she would say, "I feel as if I don't exist." Sometimes she blotted out the feeling with a tranquilizer. Sometimes she thought the problem was with her husband, or her children, or that what she really needed was to redecorate her house, or move to a better neighborhood, or have an affair, or another baby. Sometimes, she went to a doctor with symptoms she could hardly describe: "A tired feeling . . . I get so angry with the children it scares me . . . I feel like crying without any reason." (A Cleveland doctor called it "the housewife's syndrome.") A number of women told me about great bleeding blisters that break out on their hands and arms. "I call it the housewife's blight," said a family doctor in Pennsylvania. "I see it so often lately in these young women with four, five and six children who bury themselves in their dishpans. But it isn't caused by detergent and it isn't cured by cortisone."

Sometimes a woman would tell me that the feeling gets so strong she runs out of the house and walks through the streets. Or she stays inside her house and cries. Or her children tell her a joke, and she doesn't laugh because she doesn't hear it. I talked to women who had spent years on the analyst's couch, working out their "adjustment to the feminine role," their blocks to "fulfillment as a wife and mother." But the desperate tone in these women's voices, and the look in their eyes, was the same as the tone and the look of other women, who were sure they had no problem, even though they did have a strange feeling of desperation.

A mother of four who left college at nineteen to get married told me:

> I've tried everything women are supposed to do—hobbies, gardening, pickling, canning, being very social with my neighbors, joining committees, running PTA teas. I can do it all, and I like it, but it doesn't leave you anything to think about—any feeling of who you are. I never had any career ambitions. All I wanted was to get married and have four children. I love the kids and Bob and my home. There's no problem you can even put a name to. But I'm desperate. I begin to feel I have no personality. I'm a server of food and putter-on of pants and a bedmaker, somebody who can be called on when you want something. But who am I?

A twenty-three-year-old mother in blue jeans said:

> I ask myself why I'm so dissatisfied. I've got my health, fine children, a lovely new home, enough money. My husband has a real future as an electronics engineer. He doesn't have any of these feelings. He says maybe I need a vacation, let's go to New York for a weekend. But

that isn't it. I always had this idea we should do everything together. I can't sit down and read a book alone. If the children are napping and I have one hour to myself I just walk through the house waiting for them to wake up. I don't make a move until I know where the rest of the crowd is going. It's as if ever since you were a little girl, there's always been somebody or something that will take care of your life: your parents, or college, or falling in love, or having a child, or moving to a new house. Then you wake up one morning and there's nothing to look forward to.

A young wife in a Long Island development said:

I seem to sleep so much. I don't know why I should be so tired. This house isn't nearly so hard to clean as the cold-water flat we had when I was working. The children are at school all day. It's not the work. I just don't feel alive.

In 1960, the problem that has no name burst like a boil through the image of the happy American housewife. In the television commercials the pretty housewives still beamed over their foaming dishpans and *Time*'s cover story on "The Suburban Wife, an American Phenomenon" protested: "Having too good a time . . . to believe that they should be unhappy." But the actual unhappiness of the American housewife was suddenly being reported—from the *New York Times* and *Newsweek* to *Good Housekeeping* and CBS Television ("The Trapped Housewife"), although almost everybody who talked about it found some superficial reason to dismiss it. It was attributed to incompetent appliance repairmen (*New York Times*), or the distances children must be chauffeured in the suburbs (*Time*), or too much PTA (*Redbook*). Some said it was the old problem—education: more and more women had education, which naturally made them unhappy in their role as housewives. "The road from Freud to Frigidaire, from Sophocles to Spock, has turned out to be a bumpy one," reported the *New York Times* (June 28, 1960). "Many young women—certainly not all—whose education plunged them into a world of ideas feel stifled in their homes. They find their routine lives out of joint with their training. Like shut-ins, they feel left out. In the last year, the problem of the educated housewife has provided the meat of dozens of speeches made by troubled presidents of women's colleges who maintain, in the face of complaints, that sixteen years of academic training is realistic preparation for wifehood and motherhood."

There was much sympathy for the educated housewife. ("Like a two-headed schizophrenic . . . once she wrote a paper on the Graveyard poets; now she writes notes to the milkman. Once she determined the boiling point of sulphuric acid; now she determines her boiling point with the overdue repairman. . . . The housewife often is reduced to screams and tears. . . . No one, it seems, is appreciative, least of all herself, of the kind of person she becomes in the process of turning from poetess into shrew.")

Home economists suggested more realistic preparation for housewives, such as high-school workshops in home appliances. College educators suggested more discussion groups on home management and the family, to prepare women for the adjustment to domestic life. A spate of articles appeared in the mass magazines offering "Fifty-eight Ways to Make Your Marriage More Exciting." No month went by without a new book by a psychiatrist or sexologist offering technical advice on finding greater fulfillment through sex.

A male humorist joked in *Harper's Bazaar* (July, 1960) that the problem could be solved by taking away women's right to vote. ("In the pre–19th Amendment era, the American woman was placid, sheltered and sure of her role in American society. She left all the political decisions to her husband and he, in turn, left all the family decisions to her. Today a woman has to make both the family *and* the political decisions, and it's too much for her.")

A number of educators suggested seriously that women no longer be admitted to the four-year colleges and universities: in the growing college crisis, the education which girls could not use as housewives was more urgently needed than ever by boys to do the work of the atomic age.

The problem was also dismissed with drastic solutions no one could take seriously. (A woman writer proposed in *Harper's* that women be drafted for compulsory service as nurses' aides and baby-sitters.) And it was smoothed over with the age-old panaceas: "love is their answer," "the only answer is inner help," "the secret of completeness—children," "a private means of intellectual fulfillment," "to cure this toothache of the spirit—the simple formula of handing one's self and one's will over to God."[1]

The problem was dismissed by telling the housewife she doesn't realize how lucky she is—her own boss, no time clock, no junior executive gunning for her job. What if she isn't happy—does she think men are happy in this world? Does she really, secretly, still want to be a man? Doesn't she know yet how lucky she is to be a woman?

The problem was also, and finally, dismissed by shrugging that there are no solutions: this is what being a woman means, and what is wrong with American women that they can't accept their role gracefully? As *Newsweek* put it (March 7, 1960):

> She is dissatisfied with a lot that women of other lands can only dream of. Her discontent is deep, pervasive, and impervious to the superficial remedies which are offered at every hand. . . . An army of professional explorers have already charted the major sources of trouble. . . . From the beginning of time, the female cycle has defined and confined woman's role. As Freud was credited with saying: "Anatomy is destiny." Though no group of women has ever pushed these natural restrictions as far as the American wife, it seems that she still cannot accept them with good grace. . . . A young mother with a beautiful family, charm, talent and brains is apt to dismiss her role apologetically. "What do I do?" you hear her say. "Why nothing. I'm just a housewife." A good education, it seems, has given this paragon among women an understanding of the value of everything except her own worth.

And so she must accept the fact that "American women's unhappiness is merely the most recently won of women's rights," and adjust and say with the happy housewife found by *Newsweek*: "We ought to salute the wonderful freedom we all have and be proud of our lives today. I have had college and I've worked, but being a housewife is the most rewarding and satisfying role. . . . My mother was never included in my father's business affairs . . . she couldn't get out of the house and away from us children. But I am an equal to my husband; I can go along with him on business trips and to social business affairs."

The alternative offered was a choice that few women would contemplate. In the sympathetic words of the *New York Times*: "All admit to being deeply frustrated at times by the lack of privacy, the physical burden, the routine of family life, the confinement of it. However, none would give up her home and family if she had the choice to make again." *Redbook* commented: "Few women would want to thumb their noses at husbands, children and community and go off on their own. Those who do may be talented individuals, but they rarely are successful women."

The year American women's discontent boiled over, it was also reported (*Look*) that the more than 21,000,000 American women who are single, widowed, or divorced do not cease even after fifty their frenzied, desperate search for a man. And the search begins early—for seventy per cent of all American women now marry before they are twenty-four. A pretty twenty-five-year-old secretary took thirty-five different jobs in six months in the futile hope of finding a husband. Women were moving from one political club to another, taking evening courses in accounting or sailing, learning to play golf or ski, joining a number of churches in succession, going to bars alone, in their ceaseless search for a man.

Of the growing thousands of women currently getting private psychiatric help in the United States, the married ones were reported dissatisfied with their marriages, the unmarried ones suffering from anxiety and, finally, depression. Strangely, a number of psychiatrists stated that, in their experience, unmarried women patients were happier than married ones. So the door of all those pretty suburban houses opened a crack to permit a glimpse of uncounted thousands of American housewives who suffered alone from a problem that suddenly everyone was talking about, and beginning to take for granted, as one of those unreal problems in American life that can never be solved—like the hydrogen bomb. By 1962 the plight of the trapped American housewife had become a national parlor game. Whole issues of magazines, newspaper columns, books learned and frivolous, educational conferences and television panels were devoted to the problem.

Even so, most men, and some women, still did not know that this problem was real. But those who had faced it honestly knew that all the superficial remedies, the sympathetic advice, the scolding words and the cheering words were somehow drowning the problem in unreality. A bitter laugh was beginning to be heard from American women. They were admired, envied, pitied, theorized over until they were sick of it, offered drastic solutions or silly choices that no one could take seriously. They got all kinds of advice from the growing armies of marriage and child-guidance counselors, psychotherapists, and armchair psychologists, on how to adjust to their role as housewives. No other road to fulfillment was offered to American women in the middle of the twentieth century. Most adjusted to their role and suffered or ignored the problem that has no name. It can be less painful for a woman, not to hear the strange, dissatisfied voice stirring within her.

It is no longer possible to ignore that voice, to dismiss the desperation of so many American women. This is not what being a woman means, no matter what the experts say. For human suffering there is a reason; perhaps the reason has not been found because the right questions have not been asked, or pressed far enough. I do not accept the answer that there is no problem because American women have luxuries that women in other times and lands never dreamed of; part of the strange newness of the problem is that it cannot be understood in terms of the age-old material problems of man: poverty, sickness, hunger, cold. The women who suffer this problem have a hunger that food cannot fill. It persists in women whose husbands are struggling internes and law clerks, or prosperous doctors and lawyers; in wives of workers and executives who make $5,000 a year or $50,000. It is not caused by lack of material advantages; it may not even be felt by women preoccupied with desperate problems of hunger, poverty or illness. And women who think it will be solved by more money, a bigger house, a second car, moving to a better suburb, often discover it gets worse.

It is no longer possible today to blame the problem on loss of femininity: to say that education and independence and equality with men have made American women unfeminine. I have heard so many women try to deny this dissatisfied voice within themselves because it does not fit the pretty picture of femininity the experts have given them. I think, in fact, that this is the first clue to the mystery: the problem cannot be understood in the generally accepted terms by which scientists have studied women, doctors have treated them, counselors have advised them, and writers have written about them. Women who suffer this problem, in whom this voice is stirring, have lived their whole lives in the pursuit of feminine fulfillment. They are not career women (although career women may have other problems); they are women whose greatest ambition has been marriage and children. For the oldest of these women, these daughters of the American middle class, no other dream was possible. The ones in their forties and fifties who once had other dreams gave them up and threw themselves joyously into life as housewives. For the youngest, the new wives and mothers, this was the only dream. They are the ones who quit high school and college to marry, or marked time in some job in which they had no real interest until they married. These women are very "feminine" in the usual sense, and yet they still suffer the problem.

Are the women who finished college, the women who once had dreams beyond housewifery, the ones who suffer the most? According to the experts they are, but listen to these four women:

> My days are all busy, and dull, too. All I ever do is mess around. I get up at eight—I make breakfast, so I do the dishes, have lunch, do some more dishes, and some laundry and cleaning in the afternoon. Then it's supper dishes and I get to sit down a few minutes, before the children have to be sent to bed. . . . That's all there is to my day. It's just like any other wife's day. Humdrum. The biggest time, I am chasing kids.

> Ye Gods, what do I do with my time? Well, I get up at six. I get my son dressed and then give him breakfast. After that I wash dishes and bathe and feed the baby. Then I get lunch and while the children nap, I sew or mend or iron and do all the other things I can't get done before noon. Then I cook supper for the family and my husband watches TV while I do the dishes. After I get the children to bed, I set my hair and then I go to bed.

> The problem is always being the children's mommy, or the minister's wife and never being myself.

> A film made of any typical morning in my house would look like an old Marx Brothers' comedy. I wash the dishes, rush the older children off to school, dash out in the yard to cultivate the chrysanthemums, run back in to make a phone call about a committee meeting, help the youngest child build a blockhouse, spend fifteen minutes skimming the newspapers so I can be well-informed, then scamper down to the washing machines where my thrice-weekly laundry includes enough clothes to keep a primitive village going for an entire year. By noon I'm ready for a padded cell. Very little of what I've done has been really necessary or important. Outside pressures lash me through the day. Yet I look upon myself as one of the more relaxed housewives in the neighborhood. Many of my friends are even more frantic. In the past sixty years we have come full circle and the American housewife is once again trapped in a squirrel cage. If the cage is now a modern plate-glass-and-broadloom ranch house or a convenient modern apartment, the situation is no less painful than when her grandmother sat over an embroidery hoop in her gilt-and-plush parlor and muttered angrily about women's rights.

The first two women never went to college. They live in developments in Levittown, New Jersey, and Tacoma, Washington, and were interviewed by a team of sociologists studying workingmen's wives.[2] The third, a minister's wife, wrote on the fifteenth reunion questionnaire of her college that she never had any career ambitions, but wishes now she had.[3] The fourth, who has a Ph.D. in anthropology, is today a Nebraska housewife with three children.[4] Their words seem to indicate that housewives of all educational levels suffer the same feeling of desperation.

The fact is that no one today is muttering angrily about "women's rights," even though more and more women have gone to college. In a recent study of all the classes that have graduated from Barnard College,[5] a significant minority of earlier graduates blamed their education for making them want "rights," later classes blamed their education for giving them career dreams, but recent graduates blamed the college for making them feel it was not enough simply to be a housewife and mother; they did not want to feel guilty if they did not read books or take part in community activities. But if education is not the cause of the problem, the fact that education somehow festers in these women may be a clue.

If the secret of feminine fulfillment is having children, never have so many women, with the freedom to choose, had so many children, in so few years, so willingly. If the answer is love, never have women searched for love with such determination. And yet there is a growing suspicion that the problem may not be sexual, though it must somehow be related to sex. I have heard from many doctors evidence of new sexual problems between man and wife—sexual hunger in wives so great their husbands cannot satisfy it. "We have made women a sex creature," said a psychiatrist at the Margaret Sanger marriage counseling clinic. "She has no identity except as a wife and mother. She does not know who she is herself. She waits all day for her husband to come home at night to make her feel alive. And now it is the husband who is not interested. It is terrible for the women, to lie there, night after night, waiting for her husband to make her feel alive." Why is there such a market for books and articles offering sexual advice? The kind of sexual orgasm which Kinsey found in statistical plenitude in the recent generations of American women does not seem to make this problem go away.

On the contrary, new neuroses are being seen among women—and problems as yet unnamed as neuroses—which Freud and his followers did not predict, with physical symptoms, anxieties, and defense mechanisms equal to those caused by sexual repression. And strange new problems are being reported in the growing generations of children whose mothers were always there, driving them around, helping them with their homework—an inability to endure pain or discipline or pursue any self-sustained goal of any sort, a devastating boredom with life. Educators are increasingly uneasy about the dependence, the lack of self-reliance, of the boys and girls who are entering college today. "We fight a continual battle to make our students assume manhood," said a Columbia dean.

A White House conference was held on the physical and muscular deterioration of American children: were they being over-nurtured? Sociologists noted the astounding organization of suburban children's lives: the lessons, parties, entertainments, play and study groups organized for them. A suburban housewife in Portland, Oregon, wondered why the children "need" Brownies and Boy Scouts out here. "This is not the slums. The kids out here have the great outdoors. I think people are so bored, they organize the children, and then try to hook everyone else on it. And the poor kids have no time left just to lie on their beds and daydream."

Can the problem that has no name be somehow related to the domestic routine of the housewife? When a woman tries to put the problem into words, she often merely describes the daily life she leads. What is there in this recital of comfortable domestic detail that could possibly cause such a feeling of desperation? Is she trapped simply by the enormous demands of her role as modern housewife: wife, mistress, mother, nurse, consumer, cook, chauffeur; expert on interior decoration, child care, appliance repair, furniture refinishing, nutrition, and education? Her day is fragmented as she rushes from dishwasher to washing machine to telephone to dryer to station wagon to supermarket, and delivers Johnny to the Little League field, takes Janey to dancing class, gets the lawnmower fixed and meets the 6:45. She can never spend more than 15 minutes on any one thing; she has no time to read books, only magazines; even if she had time, she has lost the power to concentrate. At the end of the day, she is so terribly tired that sometimes her husband has to take over and put the children to bed.

This terrible tiredness took so many women to doctors in the 1950's that one decided to investigate it. He found, surprisingly, that his patients suffering from "housewife's fatigue" slept more than an adult needed to sleep—as much as ten hours a day—and that the actual energy they expended on housework did not tax their capacity. The real problem must be something else, he decided—perhaps boredom. Some doctors told their women patients they must get out of the house for a day, treat themselves to a movie in town. Others prescribed tranquilizers. Many suburban housewives were taking tranquilizers like cough drops. "You wake up in the morning, and you feel as if there's no point in going on another day like this. So you take a tranquilizer because it makes you not care so much that it's pointless."

It is easy to see the concrete details that trap the suburban housewife, the continual demands on her time. But the chains that bind her in her trap are chains in her own mind and spirit. They are chains made up of mistaken ideas and misinterpreted facts, of incomplete truths and unreal choices. They are not easily seen and not easily shaken off.

How can any woman see the whole truth within the bounds of her own life? How can she believe that voice inside herself, when it denies the conventional, accepted truths by which she has been living? And yet the women I have talked to, who are finally listening to that inner voice, seem in some incredible way to be groping through to a truth that has defied the experts.

I think the experts in a great many fields have been holding pieces of that truth under their microscopes for a long time without realizing it. I found pieces of it in certain new research and theoretical developments in psychological, social and biological science whose implications for women seem never to have been examined. I found many clues by talking to suburban doctors, gynecologists, obstetricians, child-guidance clinicians, pediatricians, high-school guidance counselors, college professors, marriage counselors, psychiatrists and ministers—questioning them not on their theories, but on their actual experience in treating American women. I became aware of a growing body of evidence, much of which has not been reported publicly because it does not fit current modes of thought about women—evidence which throws into question the standards of feminine normality, feminine adjustment, feminine fulfillment, and feminine maturity by which most women are still trying to live.

I began to see in a strange new light the American return to early marriage and the large families that are causing the population explosion; the recent movement to natural childbirth and breastfeeding; suburban conformity, and the new neuroses, character pathologies and sexual problems being reported by the doctors. I began to see new dimensions to old problems that have long been taken for granted among women: menstrual difficulties, sexual frigidity, promiscuity, pregnancy fears, childbirth depression, the high incidence of emotional breakdown and suicide among women in their twenties and thirties, the menopause crises, the so-called passivity and immaturity of American men, the discrepancy between women's tested intellectual abilities in childhood and their adult achievement, the changing incidence of adult sexual orgasm in American women, and persistent problems in psychotherapy and in women's education.

If I am right, the problem that has no

name stirring in the minds of so many American women today is not a matter of loss of femininity or too much education, or the demands of domesticity. It is far more important than anyone recognizes. It is the key to these other new and old problems which have been torturing women and their husbands and children, and puzzling their doctors and educators for years. It may well be the key to our future as a nation and a culture. We can no longer ignore that voice within women that says: "I want something more than my husband and my children and my home."

THE PASSIONATE JOURNEY

It was the need for a new identity that started women, a century ago, on that passionate journey, that vilified, misinterpreted journey away from home.

It has been popular in recent years to laugh at feminism as one of history's dirty jokes: to pity, sniggering, those old-fashioned feminists who fought for women's rights to higher education, careers, the vote. They were neurotic victims of penis envy who wanted to be men, it is said now. In battling for women's freedom to participate in the major work and decisions of society as the equals of men, they denied their very nature as women, which fulfills itself only through sexual passivity, acceptance of male domination, and nurturing motherhood.

But if I am not mistaken, it is this first journey which holds the clue to much that has happened to women since. It is one of the strange blind spots of contemporary psychology not to recognize the reality of the passion that moved these women to leave home in search of new identity, or, staying home, to yearn bitterly for something more. Theirs was an act of rebellion, a violent denial of the identity of women as it was then defined. It was the need for a new identity that led those passionate feminists to forge new trails for women. Some of those trails were unexpectedly rough, some were dead ends, and some may have been false, but the need for women to find new trails was real.

The problem of identity was new for women then, truly new. The feminists were pioneering on the front edge of woman's evolution. They had to prove that women were human. They had to shatter, violently if necessary, the decorative Dresden figurine that represented the ideal woman of the last century. They had to prove that woman was not a passive, empty mirror, not a frilly, useless decoration, not a mindless animal, not a thing to be disposed of by others, incapable of a voice in her own existence, before they could even begin to fight for the rights women needed to become the human equals of men.

Changeless woman, childish woman, a woman's place is in the home, they were told. But man was changing; his place was in the world and his world was widening. Woman was being left behind. Anatomy was her destiny; she might die giving birth to one baby, or live to be thirty-five, giving birth to twelve, while man controlled his destiny with that part of his anatomy which no other animal had: his mind.

Women also had minds. They also had the human need to grow. But the work that fed life and moved it forward was no longer done at home, and women were not trained to understand and work in the world. Confined to the home, a child among her children, passive, no part of her existence under her own control, a woman could only exist by pleasing man. She was wholly dependent on his protection in a world that she had no share in making: man's world. She could never grow up to ask the simple human question, "Who am I? What do I want?"

Even if man loved her as a child, a doll, a decoration; even if he gave her rubies, satin, velvets; even if she was warm in her house, safe with her children, would she not yearn for something more? She was, at that time, so completely defined as object by man, never herself as subject, "I," that she was not even expected to enjoy or participate in the act of sex. "He took his pleasure with her . . . he had his way with her," as the sayings went. Is it so hard to understand that emancipation, the right to full humanity, was important enough to generations of women, still alive or only recently dead, that some fought with their fists, and went to jail and even died for it? And for the right to human growth, some women denied their own sex, the desire to love and be loved by a man, and to bear children.

It is a strangely unquestioned perversion of history that the passion and fire of the feminist movement came from man-hating, embittered, sex-starved spinsters, from castrating, unsexed non-women who burned with such envy for the male organ that they wanted to take it away from all men, or destroy them, demanding rights only because they lacked the power to love as women. Mary Wollstonecraft, Angelina Grimké, Ernestine Rose, Margaret Fuller, Elizabeth Cady Stanton, Julia Ward Howe, Margaret Sanger all loved, were loved, and married; many seem to have been as passionate in their relations with lover and husband, in an age when passion in woman was as forbidden as intelligence, as they were in their battle for woman's chance to grow to full human stature. But if they, and those like Susan Anthony, whom fortune or bitter experience turned away from marriage, fought for a chance for woman to fulfill herself, not in relation to man, but as an individual, it was from a need as real and burning as the need for love. ("What woman needs," said Margaret Fuller, "is not as a woman to act or rule, but as a nature to grow, as an intellect to discern, as a soul to live freely, and unimpeded to unfold such powers as were given her.")

The feminists had only one model, one image, one vision, of a full and free human being: man. For until very recently, only men (though not all men) had the freedom and the education necessary to realize their full abilities, to pioneer and create and discover, and map new trails for future generations. Only men had the vote: the freedom to shape the major decisions of society. Only men had the freedom to love, and enjoy love, and decide for themselves in the eyes of their God the problems of right and wrong. Did women want these freedoms because they wanted to be men? Or did they want them because they also were human?

That this is what feminism was all about was seen symbolically by Henrik Ibsen. When he said in the play *A Doll's House*, in 1879, that a woman was simply a human being, he struck a new note in literature. Thousands of women in middle-class Europe and America, in that Victorian time, saw themselves in Nora. And in 1960, almost a century later, millions of American housewives, who watched the play on television, also saw themselves as they heard Nora say:

> You have always been so kind to me. But our home has been nothing but a playroom. I have been your doll wife, just as at home I was Papa's doll child; and here the children have been my dolls. I thought it great fun when you played with me, just as they thought it fun when I played with them. That is what our marriage has been, Torvald . . .
>
> How am I fitted to bring up the children? . . . There is another task I must undertake first. I must try and educate myself—you are not the man to help me in that. I must do that for myself. And that is why I am going to leave you now . . . I must stand quite alone if I am to understand myself and everything about me. It is for that reason that I cannot remain with you any longer . . .

Her shocked husband reminds Nora that woman's "most sacred duties" are her duties to her husband and children. "Before all else, you are a wife and mother," he says. And Nora answers:

> I believe that before all else I am a reasonable human being, just as you are—or, at all events, that I must try and become one. I know quite well, Torvald, that most people would think you right, and that views of that kind are to be found in books; but I can no longer content myself with what most people say or with what is found in books. I must think over things for myself and get to understand them . . .

It is a cliché of our own time that women spent half a century fighting for "rights," and the next half wondering whether they wanted them after all. "Rights" have a dull sound to people who have grown up after they have been won. But like Nora, the feminists had to win those rights before they could begin to live and love as human beings. Not very many women then, or even now, dared to leave the only security they knew—dared to turn their backs on their homes and husbands to begin Nora's search. But a great many, then as now, must have found their existence as housewives so empty that they could no longer savor the love of husband and children.

Some of them—and even a few men who realized that half the human race was denied the right to become fully human—set out to change the conditions that held women in bondage. Those conditions were summed up by the first Woman's Rights Convention in Seneca Falls, New York, in 1848, as woman's grievances against man:

> He has compelled her to submit to laws in the formation of which she has no voice. . . . He has made her, if married, in the eyes of the law, civilly dead. He has taken from her all right to property, even to the wages she earns . . . In the covenant of marriage, she is compelled to promise obedience to her husband, he becoming to all intents and purposes her master—the law giving him power to deprive her of her liberty, and to administer chastisement. . . . He closes against her all the avenues of wealth and distinction which he considers most honorable to himself. As a teacher of theology, medicine or law, she is not known. He has denied her the facilities for obtaining a thorough education, all colleges being closed against her. . . . He has created a false public sentiment by giving to the world a different code of morals for men and women by which moral delinquencies which exclude women from society are not only tolerated, but deemed of little account to man. He has usurped the prerogative of Jehovah himself, claiming it as his right to assign for her a sphere of action, when that belongs to her conscience and to her God. He has endeavored in every way that he could to destroy her confidence in her own powers, to lessen her self-respect, and to make her willing to lead a dependent and abject life.

It was these conditions, which the feminists set out to abolish a century ago, that made women what they were—"feminine," as it was then, and is still, defined.

It is hardly a coincidence that the struggle to free woman began in America on the heels of the Revolutionary War, and grew strong with the movement to free the slaves.[6] Thomas Paine, the spokesman for the Revolution, was among the first to condemn in 1775 the position of women "even in countries where they may be esteemed the most happy, constrained in their desires in the disposal of their goods, robbed of freedom and will by the laws, the slaves of opinion . . ." During the Revolution, some ten years before Mary Wollstonecraft spearheaded the feminist movement in England, an American woman, Judith Sargent Murray, said woman needed knowledge to envision new goals and grow by reaching for them. In 1837, the year Mount Holyoke opened its doors to give women their first chance at education equal to man's, American women were also holding their first national anti-slavery convention in New York. The women who formally launched the women's rights movement at Seneca Falls met each other when they were refused seats at an anti-slavery convention in London. Shut off behind a curtain in the gallery, Elizabeth Stanton, on her honeymoon, and Lucretia Mott, demure mother of five, decided that it was not only the slaves who needed to be liberated.

Whenever, wherever in the world there has been an upsurge of human freedom, women have won a share of it for themselves. Sex did not fight the French Revolution, free the slaves in America, overthrow the Russian Czar, drive the British out of India; but when the idea of human freedom moves the minds of men, it also moves the minds of women. The cadences of the Seneca Falls Declaration came straight from the Declaration of Independence:

> When, in the course of human events, it becomes necessary for one portion of the family of man to assume among the people of the earth a position different from that they have hitherto occupied. . . . We hold these truths to be self-evident: that all men and women are created equal.

Feminism was not a dirty joke. The feminist revolution had to be fought because women quite simply were stopped at a stage of evolution far short of their human capacity. "The domestic function of woman does not exhaust her powers," the Rev. Theodore Parker preached in Boston in 1853. "To make one half the human race consume its energies in the functions of housekeeper, wife and mother is a monstrous waste of the most precious material God ever made." And running like a bright and sometimes dangerous thread through the history of the feminist movement was also the idea that equality for woman was necessary to free both man and woman for true sexual fulfillment.[7] For the degradation of woman also degraded marriage, love, all relations between man and woman. After the sexual revolution, said Robert Dale Owen, "then will the monopoly of sex perish with other unjust monopolies; and women will not be restricted to one virtue, and one passion, and one occupation."[8]

The women and men who started that revolution anticipated "no small amount of misconception, misrepresentation and ridicule." And they got it. The first to speak out in public for women's rights in America—Fanny Wright, daughter of a Scotch nobleman, and Ernestine Rose, daughter of a rabbi—were called, respectively, "red harlot of infidelity" and "woman a thousand times below a prostitute." The declaration at Seneca Falls brought such an outcry of "Revolution," "Insurrection Among Women," "The Reign of Petticoats," "Blasphemy," from newspapers and clergymen that the faint-hearted withdrew their signatures. Lurid reports of "free love" and "legalized adultery" competed with phantasies of court sessions, church sermons and surgical operations interrupted while a lady lawyer or minister or doctor hastily presented her husband with a baby.

At every step of the way, the feminists had to fight the conception that they were violating the God-given nature of woman. Clergymen interrupted women's rights conventions, waving Bibles and quoting from the Scriptures: "Saint Paul said . . . and the head of every woman is man" . . . "Let your women be silent in the churches, for it is not permitted unto them to speak" . . . "And if they will learn anything, let them ask their husbands at home; for it is a shame for women to speak in the church" . . . "But I suffer not a woman to teach, nor to usurp authority over the man, but to be in silence; for Adam was first formed, then Eve" . . . "Saint Peter said: likewise, ye wives, be in subjection to your own husbands" . . .

To give women equal rights would destroy that "milder gentler nature, which not only makes them shrink from, but disqualifies them for the turmoil and battle of public life," a Senator from New Jersey intoned piously in 1866. "They have a higher and a holier mission. It is in retiracy to make the character of coming men. Their mission is at home, by their blandishments, and their love, to assuage the passions of men as they come in from the battle of life, and not themselves by joining in the contest to add fuel to the very flames."

"They do not appear to be satisfied with having unsexed themselves, but they desire to unsex every female in the land," said a New York assemblyman who opposed one of the first petitions for a married woman's right to property and earnings. Since "God created man as the representative of the race," then "took from his side the material for woman's creation" and returned her to his side in matrimony as "one flesh, one being," the assembly smugly denied the petition: "A higher power than that from which emanates legislative enactments has given forth the mandate that man and woman shall not be equal."[9]

The myth that these women were "unnatural monsters" was based on the belief that to destroy the God-given subservience of women would destroy the home and make slaves of men. Such myths arise in every kind of revolution that advances a new portion of the family of man to equality. The image of the feminists as inhuman, fiery man-eaters, whether expressed as an offense against God or in the modern terms of sexual perversion, is not unlike the stereotype of the Negro as a primitive animal or the union member as an anarchist. What the sexual terminology hides is the fact that the feminist movement was a revolution. There were excesses, of course, as in any revolution, but the excesses of the feminists were in themselves a demonstration of the revolution's necessity. They stemmed from, and were a passionate repudiation of, the degrading realities of woman's life, the helpless subservience behind the gentle decorum that made women objects of such thinly veiled contempt to men that they even felt contempt for themselves. Evidently, that contempt and self-contempt were harder to get rid of than the conditions which caused them.

Of course they envied man. Some of the early feminists cut their hair short and wore bloomers, and tried to be like men. From the lives they saw their mothers lead, from their own experience, those passionate women had good reason to reject the conventional image of woman. Some even rejected marriage and motherhood for themselves. But in turning their backs on the old feminine image, in fighting to free themselves and all women, some of them became a different kind of woman. They became complete human beings.

The name of Lucy Stone today brings to mind a man-eating fury, wearing pants, brandishing an umbrella. It took a long time for the man who loved her to persuade her to marry him, and though she loved him and kept his love throughout her long life, she never took his name. When she was born, her gentle mother cried: "Oh, dear! I am sorry it is a girl. A woman's life is so hard." A few hours before the baby came, this mother, on a farm in western Massachusetts in 1818, milked eight cows because a sudden thunderstorm had called all hands into the field: it was more important to save the hay crop than to safeguard a mother on the verge of childbirth. Though this gentle, tired mother carried the endless work of farmhouse and bore nine children, Lucy Stone grew up with the knowledge that "There was only one will in our house, and that was my father's."

She rebelled at being born a girl if that meant being as lowly as the Bible said, as her mother said. She rebelled when she raised her hand at church meeting and, time and again, it was not counted. At a church sewing circle, where she was making a shirt to help a young man through theological seminary, she heard Mary Lyon talk of education for women. She left the shirt unfinished, and at sixteen started teaching school for $1 a week, saving her earnings for nine years, until she had enough to go to college herself. She wanted to train herself "to plead not only for the slave, but for suffering humanity everywhere. Especially do I mean to labor for the elevation of my own sex." But at Oberlin, where she was one of the first women to graduate from the "regular course," she had to practice public speaking secretly in the woods. Even at Oberlin, the girls were forbidden to speak in public.

> Washing the men's clothes, caring for their rooms, serving them at table, listening to their orations, but themselves remaining respectfully silent in public assemblages, the Oberlin "co-eds" were being prepared for intelligent motherhood and a properly subservient wifehood.[10]

In appearance, Lucy Stone was a little woman, with a gentle, silvery voice which could quiet a violent mob. She lectured on abolition Saturdays and Sundays, as an agent for the Anti-Slavery Society, and for women's rights the rest of the week on her own—facing down and winning over men who threatened her with clubs, threw prayer books and eggs at her head, and once in midwinter shoved a hose through a window and turned icy water on her.

In one town, the usual report was circulated that a big, masculine woman, wearing boots, smoking a cigar, swearing like a trooper, had arrived to lecture. The ladies who came to hear this freak expressed their amazement to find Lucy Stone, small and dainty, dressed in a black satin gown with a white lace frill at the neck, "a prototype of womanly grace . . . fresh and fair as the morning."[11]

Her voice so rankled pro-slavery forces that the *Boston Post* published a rude poem promising "fame's loud trumpet shall be blown" for the man who "with a wedding kiss shuts up the mouth of Lucy Stone." Lucy Stone felt that "marriage is to a woman a state of slavery." Even after Henry Blackwell had pursued her from Cincinnati to Massachusetts ("She was born locomotive," he complained), and vowed to "repudiate the supremacy of either woman or man in marriage," and wrote her: "I met you at Niagara and sat at your feet by the whirlpool looking down into the dark waters with a passionate and unshared and unsatisfied yearning in my heart that you will never know, nor understand," and made a public speech in favor of women's rights; even after she admitted that she loved him, and wrote "You can scarcely tell me anything I do not know about the emptiness of a single life," she suffered blinding migraine headaches over the decision to marry him.

At their wedding, the minister Thomas Higginson reported that "the heroic Lucy cried like any village bride." The minister also said: "I never perform the marriage ceremony without a renewed sense of the iniquity of a system by which man and wife are one, and that one is the husband." And he sent to the newspapers, for other couples to copy, the pact which Lucy Stone and Henry Blackwell joined hands to make, before their wedding vows:

> While we acknowledge our mutual affection by publicly assuming the relationship of husband and wife . . . we deem it a duty to declare that this act on our part implies no sanction of, nor promise of voluntary obedience to such of the present laws of marriage as refuse to recognize the wife as an independent, rational being, while they confer upon the husband an injurious and unnatural superiority.[12]

Lucy Stone, her friend, the pretty Reverend Antoinette Brown (who later married Henry's brother), Margaret Fuller, Angelina Grimké, Abbey Kelley Foster—all resisted early marriage, and did not, in fact, marry until in their battle against slavery and for women's rights they had begun to find an identity as women unknown to their mothers. Some, like Susan Anthony and

Elizabeth Blackwell, never married; Lucy Stone kept her own name in more than symbolic fear that to become a wife was to die as a person. The concept known as "femme couverte" (covered woman), written into the law, suspended the "very being or legal existence of a woman" upon marriage. "To a married woman, her new self is her superior, her companion, her master."

If it is true that the feminists were "disappointed women," as their enemies said even then, it was because almost all women living under such conditions had reason to be disappointed. In one of the most moving speeches of her life, Lucy Stone said in 1855:

> From the first years to which my memory stretches, I have been a disappointed woman. When, with my brothers, I reached forth after sources of knowledge, I was reproved with "It isn't fit for you; it doesn't belong to women" . . . In education, in marriage, in religion, in everything, disappointment is the lot of woman. It shall be the business of my life to deepen this disappointment in every woman's heart until she bows down to it no longer.[13]

In her own lifetime, Lucy Stone saw the laws of almost every state radically changed in regard to women, high schools opened to them and two-thirds of the colleges in the United States. Her husband and her daughter, Alice Stone Blackwell, devoted their lives, after her death in 1893, to the unfinished battle for woman's vote. By the end of her passionate journey, she could say she was glad to have been born a woman. She wrote her daughter the day before her seventieth birthday:

> I trust my Mother sees and knows how glad I am to have been born, and at a time when there was so much that needed help at which I could lend a hand. Dear Old Mother! She had a hard life, and was sorry she had another girl to share and bear the hard life of a woman. . . . But I am wholly glad that I came.[14]

In certain men, at certain times in history, the passion for freedom has been as strong or stronger than the familiar passions of sexual love. That this was so, for many of those women who fought to free women, seems to be a fact, no matter how the strength of that other passion is explained. Despite the frowns and jeers of most of their husbands and fathers, despite the hostility if not outright abuse they got for their "unwomanly" behavior, the feminists continued their crusade. They themselves were tortured by soul-searching doubts every step of the way. It was unladylike, friends wrote Mary Lyon, to travel all over New England with a green velvet bag, collecting money to start her college for women. "What do I do that is wrong?" she asked. "I ride in the stage-coach or cars without an escort. . . . My heart is sick, my soul is pained with this empty gentility, this genteel nothingness. I am doing a great work, I cannot come down."

The lovely Angelina Grimké felt as if she would faint, when she accepted what was meant as a joke and appeared to speak before the Massachusetts legislature on the anti-slavery petitions, the first woman ever to appear before a legislative body. A pastoral letter denounced her unwomanly behavior:

> We invite your attention to the dangers which at present seem to threaten the female character with widespread and permanent injury. . . . The power of woman is her dependence, flowing from the consciousness of that weakness which God has given her for her protection. . . . But when she assumes the place and tone of man as a public reformer . . . her character becomes unnatural. If the vine, whose strength and beauty is to lean on the trellis-work and half conceal its cluster, thinks to assume the independence and overshadowing nature of the elm, it will not only cease to bear fruit, but fall in shame and dishonor in the dust.[15]

More than restlessness and frustration made her refuse to be "shamed into silence," and made New England housewives walk two, four, six, and eight miles on winter evenings to hear her.

The emotional identification of American women with the battle to free the slaves may or may not testify to the unconscious foment of their own rebellion. But it is an undeniable fact that, in organizing, petitioning, and speaking out to free the slaves, American women learned how to free themselves. In the South, where slavery kept women at home, and where they did not get a taste of education or pioneering work or the schooling battles of society, the old image of femininity reigned intact, and there were few feminists. In the North, women who took part in the Underground Railroad, or otherwise worked to free the slaves, never were the same again. Feminism also went west with the wagon trains, where the frontier made women almost equal from the beginning. (Wyoming was the first state to give women the vote.) Individually, the feminists seem to have had no more nor less reason than all women of their time to envy or hate man. But what they did have was self-respect, courage, strength. Whether they loved or hated man, escaped or suffered humiliation from men in their own lives, they identified with women. Women who accepted the conditions which degraded them felt contempt for themselves and all women. The feminists who fought those conditions freed themselves of that contempt and had less reason to envy man.

The call to that first Woman's Rights Convention came about because an educated woman, who had already participated in shaping society as an abolitionist, came face to face with the realities of a housewife's drudgery and isolation in a small town. Like the college graduate with six children in the suburb of today, Elizabeth Cady Stanton, moved by her husband to the small town of Seneca Falls, was restless in a life of baking, cooking, sewing, washing and caring for each baby. Her husband, an abolitionist leader, was often away on business. She wrote:

> I now understood the practical difficulties most women had to contend with in the isolated household and the impossibility of woman's best development if in contact the chief part of her life with servants and children. . . . The general discontent I felt with woman's portion . . . and the wearied, anxious look of the majority of women, impressed me with the strong feeling that some active measures should be taken. . . . I could not see what to do or where to begin—my only thought was a public meeting for protest and discussion.[16]

She put only one notice in the newspapers, and housewives and daughters who had never known any other kind of life came in wagons from a radius of fifty miles to hear her speak.

However dissimilar their social or psychological roots, all who led the battle for women's rights, early and late, also shared more than common intelligence, fed by more than common education for their time. Otherwise, whatever their emotions, they would not have been able to see through the prejudices which had justified woman's degradation, and to put their dissenting voice into words. Mary Wollstonecraft educated herself and was then educated by that company of English philosophers then preaching the rights of man. Margaret Fuller was taught by her father to read the classics of six languages, and was caught up in the transcendentalist group around Emerson. Elizabeth Cady Stanton's father, a judge, got his daughter the best education then available, and supplemented it by letting her listen to his law cases. Ernestine Rose, the rabbi's daughter who rebelled against her religion's doctrine that decreed woman's inferiority to man, got her education in "free thinking" from the great utopian philosopher Robert Owen. She also defied orthodox religious custom to marry a man she loved. She always insisted, in the bitterest days of the fight for women's rights, that woman's enemy was not man. "We do not fight with man himself, but only with bad principles."

These women were not man-eaters. Julia Ward Howe, brilliant and beautiful daughter of the New York "400" who studied intensively every field that interested her, wrote the "Battle Hymn of the Republic" anonymously, because her husband believed her life should be devoted to him and their six children. She took no part in the suffrage movement until 1868, when she met Lucy Stone, who "had long been the object of one of my imaginary dislikes. As I looked into her sweet, womanly face and heard her earnest voice, I felt that the object of my distaste had been a mere phantom, conjured up by silly and senseless misrepresentations. . . . I could only say, 'I am with you.' "[17]

The irony of that man-eating myth is that the so-called excesses of the feminists arose from their helplessness. When women are considered to have no rights nor to deserve any, what can they do for themselves? At first, it seemed there was nothing they could do but talk. They held women's rights conventions every year after 1848, in small towns and large, national and state conventions, over and over again—in Ohio, Pennsylvania, Indiana, Massachusetts. They could talk till doomsday about the rights they did not have. But how do women get legislators to let them keep their own earnings, or their own children after divorce, when they do not even have a vote? How can they finance or organize a campaign to get the vote when they have no money of their own, nor even the right to own property?

The very sensitivity to opinion which such complete dependence breeds in women made every step out of their genteel prison a painful one. Even when they tried to change conditions that were within their power to change, they met ridicule. The fantastically uncomfortable dress "ladies" wore then was a symbol of their bondage: stays so tightly laced they could hardly breathe, half a dozen skirts and petticoats, weighing ten to twelve pounds, so long they swept up refuse from the street. The specter of the feminists taking the pants off men came partly from the "Bloomer" dress—a tunic, knee-length skirt, ankle length pantaloons. Elizabeth Stanton wore it, eagerly at first, to do her housework in comfort, as a young woman today might wear shorts or slacks. But when the feminists wore the Bloomer dress in public, as a symbol of their emancipation, the rude jokes, from newspaper editors, street corner loafers, and small boys, were unbearable to their feminine sensitivities. "We put the dress on for greater freedom, but what is physical freedom compared to mental bondage," said Elizabeth Stanton and discarded her "Bloomer" dress. Most, like Lucy Stone, stopped wearing it for a feminine reason: it was not very becoming, except to the extremely tiny, pretty Mrs. Bloomer herself.

Still, that helpless gentility had to be overcome, in the minds of men, in the minds of other women, in their own minds. When they decided to petition for married women's rights to own property, half the time even the women slammed doors in their faces with the smug remark that they had husbands, they needed no laws to protect them. When Susan Anthony and her women captains collected 6,000 signatures in ten weeks, the New York State Assembly received them with roars of laughter. In mockery, the Assembly recommended that since ladies always get the "choicest tidbits" at the table, the best seat in the carriage, and their choice of which side of the bed to lie on, "if there is any inequity or oppression the gentlemen are the sufferers." However, they would waive "redress" except where both husband and wife had signed the petition. "In such case, they would recommend the parties to apply for a law authorizing them to change dresses, that the husband may wear the petticoats and the wife the breeches."

The wonder is that the feminists were able to win anything at all—that they were not embittered shrews but increasingly zestful women who knew they were making history. There is more spirit than bitterness in Elizabeth Stanton, having babies into her forties, writing Susan Anthony that this one truly will be her last, and the fun is just beginning—"Courage, Susan, we will not reach our prime until we're fifty." Painfully insecure and self-conscious about her looks—not because of treatment by men (she had suitors) but because of a beautiful older sister and mother who treated a crossed eye as a tragedy—Susan Anthony, of all the nineteenth-century feminist leaders, was the only one resembling the myth. She felt betrayed when the others started to marry and have babies. But despite the chip on her shoulder, she was no bitter spinster with a cat. Traveling alone from town to town, hammering up her meeting notices, using her abilities to the fullest as organizer and lobbyist and lecturer, she made her own way in a larger and larger world.

In their own lifetime, such women changed the feminine image that had justified woman's degradation. At a meeting while men jeered at trusting the vote to women so helpless that they had to be lifted over mud puddles and handed into carriages, a proud feminist named Sojourner Truth raised her black arm:

> Look at my arm! I have ploughed and planted and gathered into barns . . . and ain't I a woman? I could work as much and eat as much as a man—when I could get it—and bear the lash as well . . . I have borne thirteen children and seen most of 'em sold into slavery, and when I cried out with my mother's grief, none but Jesus helped me—and ain't I a woman?

That image of empty gentility was also undermined by the growing thousands of women who worked in the red brick factories: the Lowell mill girls who fought the terrible working conditions which, partly as a result of women's supposed inferiority, were even worse for them than for men. But those women, who after a twelve- or thirteen-hour day in the factory still had household duties, could not take the lead in the passionate journey. Most of the leading feminists were women of the middle class, driven by a complex of motives to educate themselves and smash that empty image.

What drove them on? "Must let out my pent-up energy in some new way," wrote Louisa May Alcott in her journal when she decided to volunteer as a nurse in the Civil War. "A most interesting journey, into a new world, full of stirring sights and sounds, new adventures, and an ever-growing sense of the great task I had undertaken. I said my prayers as I went rushing through the country, white with tents, all alive with patriotism, and already red with blood. A solemn time, but I'm glad to live in it."

What drove them on? Lonely and racked with self-doubt, Elizabeth Blackwell, in that unheard-of, monstrous determination to be a woman doctor, ignored sniggers—and tentative passes—to do her anatomical dissections. She battled for the right to witness the dissection of the reproductive organs, but decided against walking in the commencement procession because it would be unladylike. Shunned even by her fellow physicians, she wrote:

> I am woman as well as physician . . . I understand now why this life has never been lived before. It is hard, with no support but a high purpose, to live against every species of social opposition . . . I should like a little fun now and then. Life is altogether too sober.[18]

In the course of a century of struggle, reality gave the lie to the myth that woman would use her rights for vengeful domination of man. As they won the right to equal education, the right to speak out in public and own property, and the right to work at job or profession and control their own earnings, the feminists felt less reason to be bitter against man. But there was one more battle to be fought. As M. Carey Thomas, the brilliant first president of Bryn Mawr, said in 1908:

> Women are one-half the world, but until a century ago . . . women lived a twilight life, a half life apart, and looked out and saw men as shadows walking. It was a man's world. The laws were men's laws, the government a man's government, the country a man's country. Now women have won the right to higher education and economic independence. The right to become citizens of the state is the next and inevitable consequence of education and work outside the home. We have gone so far; we must go farther. We cannot go back.[19]

The trouble was, the women's rights movement had become almost too respectable; yet without the right to vote, women could not get any political party to take them seriously. When Elizabeth Stanton's daughter, Harriet Blatch, came home in 1907, the widow of an Englishman, she found the movement in which her mother had raised her in a sterile rut of tea and cookies. She had seen the tactics women used in England to dramatize the issue in a similar stalemate: heckling speakers at public meetings, deliberate provocation of the police, hunger strikes in jail—the kind of dramatic nonviolent resistance Gandhi used in India, or that the Freedom Riders now use in the United States when legal tactics leave segregation intact. The American feminists never had to resort to the extremes of their longer-sinned-against English counterparts. But they did dramatize the vote issue until they aroused an opposition far more powerful than the sexual one.

As the battle to free women was fired by the battle to free the slaves in the nineteenth century, it was fired in the twentieth by the battles of social reform, of Jane Addams and Hull House, the rise of the union movement, and the great strikes against intolerable working conditions in the factories. For the Triangle Shirtwaist girls, working for as little as $6 a week, as late as 10 o'clock at night, fined for talking, laughing, or singing, equality was a question of more than education or the vote. They held out on picket lines through bitter cold and hungry months; dozens were clubbed by police and dragged off in Black Marias. The new feminists raised money for the strikers' bail and food, as their mothers had helped the Underground Railroad.

Behind the cries of "save femininity," "save the home," could now be glimpsed the influence of political machines, quailing at the very thought of what those reforming women would do if they got the vote. Women, after all, were trying to shut down the saloons. Brewers as well as other business interests, especially those that depended on underpaid labor of children and women, openly lobbied against the woman's suffrage amendment in Washington. "Machine men were plainly uncertain of their ability to control an addition to the electorate which seemed to them relatively unsusceptible to bribery, more militant and bent on disturbing reforms ranging from sewage control to the abolition of child labor and worst of all, 'cleaning up' politics."[20] And Southern congressmen pointed out that suffrage for women also meant Negro women.

The final battle for the vote was fought in the twentieth century by the growing numbers of college-trained women, led by Carrie Chapman Catt, daughter of the Iowa prairie, educated at Iowa State, a teacher and a newspaperwoman, whose husband, a successful engineer, firmly supported her battles. One group that later called itself the Woman's Party made continual headlines with picket lines around the White House. After the outbreak of World War I, there was much hysteria about women who chained themselves to the White House fence. Maltreated by police and courts, they went on hunger strikes in jail and were finally martyred by forced feeding. Many of these women were Quakers and pacifists; but the majority of the feminists supported the war even as they continued their campaign for women's rights. They are hardly accountable for the myth of the man-eating feminist which is prevalent today, a myth that has cropped up continuously from the days of Lucy Stone to the present, whenever anyone has reason to oppose women's move out of the home.

In this final battle, American women over a period of fifty years conducted 56 campaigns of referenda to male voters; 480 campaigns to get legislatures to submit suffrage amendments to voters; 277 campaigns to get state party conventions to include woman's suffrage planks; 30 campaigns to get presidential party conventions to adopt woman's suffrage planks, and 19 campaigns with 19 successive Congresses.[21] Someone had to organize all those parades, speeches, petitions, meetings, lobbying of legislators and Congressmen. The new feminists were no longer a handful of devoted women; thousands, millions of American women with husbands, children, and homes gave as much time as they could spare to the cause. The unpleasant image of the feminists today resembles less the feminists themselves than the image fostered by the interests who so bitterly opposed the vote for women in state after state, lobbying, threatening legislators with business or political ruin, buying votes, even stealing them, until, and even after, 36 states had ratified the amendment.

The ones who fought that battle won more than empty paper rights. They cast off the shadow of contempt and self-contempt that had degraded women for centuries. The joy, the sense of excitement and the personal rewards of that battle are described beautifully by Ida Alexis Ross Wylie, an English feminist:

> To my astonishment, I found that women, in spite of knock-knees and the fact that for centuries a respectable woman's leg had not even been mentionable, could at a pinch outrun the average London bobby. Their aim with a little practice became good enough to land ripe vegetables in ministerial eyes, their wits sharp enough to keep Scotland Yard running around in circles and looking very silly. Their capacity for impromptu organization, for secrecy and loyalty, their iconoclastic disregard for class and established order were a revelation to all concerned, but especially themselves. . . .
>
> The day that, with a straight left to the jaw, I sent a fair-sized CID officer into the orchestra pit of the theatre where we were holding one of our belligerent meetings, was the day of my own coming of age. . . . Since I was no genius, the episode could not make me one, but it set me free to be whatever I was to the top of my bent. . . .
>
> For two years of wild and sometimes dangerous adventure, I worked and fought alongside vigorous, happy, well-adjusted women who laughed instead of tittering, who walked freely instead of teetering, who could outfast Gandhi and come out with a grin and a jest. I slept on hard floors between elderly duchesses, stout cooks, and young shopgirls. We were often tired, hurt and frightened. But we were content as we had never been. We shared a joy of life that we had never known. Most of my fellow-fighters were wives and mothers. And strange things happened to their domestic life. Husbands came home at night with a new eagerness. . . . As for children, their attitude changed rapidly from one of affectionate toleration for poor, darling mother to one of wide-eyed wonder. Released from the smother of mother love, for she was too busy to be more than casually concerned with them, they discovered that they liked her. She was a great sport. She had guts. . . . Those women who stood outside the fight—I regret to say the vast majority—and who were being more than usually Little Women, hated the fighters with the venomous rage of envy . . .[22]

Did women really go home again as a reaction to feminism? The fact is that to women born after 1920, feminism was dead history. It ended as a vital movement in America with the winning of that final right: the vote. In the 1930's and 40's, the sort of woman who fought for woman's rights was still concerned with human rights and freedom—for Negroes, for oppressed workers, for victims of Franco's Spain and Hitler's Germany. But no one was much concerned with rights for women: they had all been won. And yet the man-eating myth prevailed. Women who displayed any independence or initiative were called "Lucy Stoners." "Feminist," like "career woman," became a dirty word. The feminists had destroyed the old image of woman, but they could not erase the hostility, the prejudice, the discrimination that still remained. Nor could they paint the new image of what women might become when they grew up under conditions that no longer made them inferior to men, dependent, passive, incapable of thought or decision.

Most of the girls who grew up during the years when the feminists were eliminating the causes of that denigrating "genteel nothingness" got their image of woman from mothers still trapped in it. These mothers were probably the real model for the man-eating myth. The shadow of the contempt and self-contempt which could turn a gentle housewife into a domineering shrew also turned some of their daughters into angry copies of man. The first women in business and the professions were thought to be freaks. Insecure in their new freedom, some perhaps feared to be soft or gentle, love, have children, lest they lose their prized independence, lest they be trapped again as their mothers were. They reinforced the myth.

But the daughters who grew up with the rights the feminists had won could not go back to that old image of genteel nothingness, nor did they have their aunts' or mothers' reasons to be angry copies of man, or fear to love them. They had come unknowing to the turning-point in woman's identity. They had truly outgrown the old image; they were finally free to be what they chose to be. But what choice were they offered? In that corner, the fiery, man-eating feminist, the career woman—loveless, alone. In this corner, the gentle wife and mother—loved and protected by her husband, surrounded by her adoring children. Though many daughters continued on the passionate journey their grandmothers had begun, thousands of others fell out—victims of a mistaken choice.

The reasons for their choice were, of course, more complex than the feminist myth. How did Chinese women, after having their feet bound for many generations, finally discover they could run? The first women whose feet were unbound must have felt such pain that some were afraid to stand, let alone to walk or run. The more they walked, the less their feet hurt. But what would have happened if, before a single generation of Chinese girls had grown up with unbound feet, doctors, hoping to save them pain and distress, told them to bind their feet again? And teachers told them that walking with bound feet was feminine, the only way a woman could walk if she wanted a man to love her? And scholars told them that they would be better mothers if they could not walk too far away from their children? And peddlers, discovering that women who could not walk bought more trinkets, spread fables of the dangers of running and the bliss of being bound? Would many little Chinese girls, then, grow up wanting to have their feet securely bound, never tempted to walk or run?

The real joke that history played on American women is not the one that makes people snigger, with cheap Freudian sophistication, at the dead feminists. It is the joke that Freudian thought played on living women, twisting the memory of the feminists into the man-eating phantom of the feminine mystique, shriveling the very wish to be more than just a wife and mother. Encouraged by the mystique to evade their identity crisis, permitted to escape identity altogether in the name of sexual fulfillment, women once again are living with their feet bound in the old image of glorified femininity. And it is the same old image, despite its shiny new clothes, that trapped women for centuries and made the feminists rebel.

NOTES

1. See the Seventy-fifth Anniversary Issue of *Good Housekeeping*, May, 1960, "The Gift of Self," a symposium by Margaret Mead, Jessamyn West, *et al.*

2. Lee Rainwater, Richard P. Coleman, and Gerald Handel, *Workingman's Wife*, New York, 1959.

3. Betty Friedan, "If One Generation Can Ever Tell Another," *Smith Alumnae Quarterly*, Northampton, Mass., Winter, 1961. I first became aware of "the problem that has no name" and its possible relationship to what I finally called "the feminine mystique" in 1957, when I prepared an intensive questionnaire and conducted a survey of my own Smith College classmates fifteen years after graduation. This questionnaire was later used by alumnae classes of Radcliffe and other women's colleges with similar results.

4. Jhan and June Robbins, "Why Young Mothers Feel Trapped," *Redbook*, September, 1960.

5. Marian Freda Poverman, "Alumnae on Parade," *Barnard Alumnae Magazine*, July, 1957.

6. See Eleanor Flexner, *Century of Struggle: The Woman's Rights Movement in The United States*, Cambridge, Mass., 1959. This definitive history of the woman's rights movement in the United States, published in 1959 at the height of the era of the feminine mystique, did not receive the attention it deserves, from either the intelligent reader or the scholar. In my opinion, it should be required reading for every girl admitted to a U.S. college. One reason the mystique prevails is that very few women under the age of forty know the facts of the woman's rights movement. I am much indebted to Miss Flexner for many factual clues I might otherwise have missed in my attempt to get at the truth behind the feminine mystique and its monstrous image of the feminists.

7. See Sidney Ditzion, *Marriage, Morals and Sex in America—A History of Ideas*, New York, 1953. This extensive bibliographical essay by the librarian of New York University documents the continuous interrelationship between movements for social and sexual reform in America, and, specifically, between man's movement for greater self-realization and sexual fulfillment and the woman's rights movement. The speeches and tracts assembled reveal that the movement to emancipate women was often seen by the men as well as the women who led it in terms of "creating an equitable balance of power between the sexes" for "a more satisfying expression of sexuality for both sexes."

8. *Ibid.*, p. 107.

9. Yuri Suhl, *Ernestine L. Rose and the Battle for Human Rights*, New York, 1959, p. 158. A vivid account of the battle for a married woman's right to her own property and earnings.

10. Flexner, *op. cit.*, p. 30.

11. Elinor Rice Hays, *Morning Star, A Biography of Lucy Stone*, New York, 1961, p. 83.

12. Flexner, *op. cit.*, p. 64.

13. Hays, *op. cit.*, p. 136.

14. *Ibid.*, p. 285.

15. Flexner, *op. cit.*, p. 46.

16. *Ibid.*, p. 73.

17. Hays, *op. cit.*, p. 221.

18. Flexner, *op. cit.*, p. 117.

19. *Ibid.*, p. 235.

20. *Ibid.*, p. 299.

21. *Ibid.*, p. 173.

22. Ida Alexis Ross Wylie, "The Little Woman," *Harper's Magazine*, November, 1945.

Phyllis Schlafly's Alternative: "The Positive Woman"

by Phyllis Schlafly

The first requirement for the acquisition of power by the Positive Woman is to understand the differences between men and women. Your outlook on life, your faith, your behavior, your potential for fulfillment, all are determined by the parameters

---

From Phyllis Schlafly, *The Power of the Positive Woman* (New Rochelle, NY: Arlington House, 1977), pp. 11–27.

of your original premise. The Positive Woman starts with the assumption that the world is her oyster. She rejoices in the creative capability within her body and the power potential of her mind and spirit. She understands that men and women are different, and that those very differences provide the key to her success as a person and fulfillment as a woman.

The women's liberationist, on the other hand, is imprisoned by her own negative view of herself and of her place in the world around her. This view of women was most succinctly expressed in an advertisement designed by the principal women's liberationist organization, the National Organization for Women (NOW), and run in many magazines and newspapers and as spot announcements on many television stations. The advertisement showed a darling curly-headed girl with the caption: "This healthy, normal baby has a handicap. She was born female."

This is the self-articulated dog-in-the-manger, chip-on-the-shoulder, fundamental dogma of the women's liberation movement. Someone—it is not clear who, perhaps God, perhaps the "Establishment," perhaps a conspiracy of male chauvinist pigs—dealt women a foul blow by making them female. It becomes necessary, therefore, for women to agitate and demonstrate and hurl demands on society in order to wrest from an oppressive male-dominated social structure the status that has been wrongfully denied to women through the centuries.

By its very nature, therefore, the women's liberation movement precipitates a series of conflict situations—in the legislatures, in the courts, in the schools, in industry—with man targeted as the enemy. Confrontation replaces cooperation as the watchword of all relationships. Women and men become adversaries instead of partners.

The second dogma of the women's liberationists is that, of all the injustices perpetrated upon women through the centuries, the most oppressive is the cruel fact that women have babies and men do not. Within the confines of the women's liberationist ideology, therefore, the abolition of this overriding inequality of women becomes the primary goal. This goal must be achieved at any and all costs—to the woman herself, to the baby, to the family, and to society. Women must be made equal to men in their ability *not* to become pregnant and *not* to be expected to care for babies they may bring into the world.

This is why women's liberationists are compulsively involved in the drive to make abortion and child-care centers for all women, regardless of religion or income, both socially acceptable and government-financed. Former Congresswoman Bella Abzug has defined the goal: "to enforce the constitutional right of females to terminate pregnancies that they do not wish to continue."

If man is targeted as the enemy, and the ultimate goal of women's liberation is independence from men and the avoidance of pregnancy and its consequences, then lesbianism is logically the highest form in the ritual of women's liberation. Many, such as Kate Millett, come to this conclusion, although many others do not.

The Positive Woman will never travel that dead-end road. It is self-evident to the Positive Woman that the female body with its baby-producing organs was not designed by a conspiracy of men but by the Divine Architect of the human race. Those who think it is unfair that women have babies, whereas men cannot, will have to take up their complaint with God because no other power is capable of changing that fundamental fact. On some college campuses, I have been assured that other methods of reproduction will be developed. But most of us must deal with the real world rather than with the imagination of dreamers.

Another feature of the woman's natural

role is the obvious fact that women can breast-feed babies and men cannot. This functional role was not imposed by conspiratorial males seeking to burden women with confining chores, but must be recognized as part of the plan of the Divine Architect for the survival of the human race through the centuries and in the countries that know no pasteurization of milk or sterilization of bottles.

The Positive Woman looks upon her femaleness and her fertility as part of her purpose, her potential, and her power. She rejoices that she has a capability for creativity that men can never have.

The third basic dogma of the women's liberation movement is that there is no difference between male and female except the sex organs, and that all those physical, cognitive, and emotional differences you *think* are there, are merely the result of centuries of restraints imposed by a male-dominated society and sex-stereotyped schooling. The role imposed on women is, by definition, inferior, according to the women's liberationists.

The Positive Woman knows that, while there are some physical competitions in which women are better (and can command more money) than men, including those that put a premium on grace and beauty, such as figure skating, the superior physical strength of males over females in competitions of strength, speed, and short-term endurance is beyond rational dispute.

In the Olympic Games, women not only cannot win any medals in competition with men, the gulf between them is so great that they cannot even qualify for the contests with men. No amount of training from infancy can enable women to throw the discus as far as men, or to match men in push-ups or in lifting weights. In track and field events, individual male records surpass those of women by 10 to 20 percent.

Female swimmers today are beating Johnny Weissmuller's records, but today's male swimmers are better still. Chris Evert can never win a tennis match against Jimmy Connors. If we removed lady's tees from golf courses, women would be out of the game. Putting women in football or wrestling matches can only be an exercise in laughs.

The Olympic Games, whose rules require strict verification to ascertain that no male enters a female contest and, with his masculine advantage, unfairly captures a woman's medal, formerly insisted on a visual inspection of the contestants' bodies. Science, however, has discovered that men and women are so innately different physically that their maleness/femaleness can be conclusively established by means of a simple skin test of fully clothed persons.

If there is *anyone* who should oppose enforced sex-equality, it is the women athletes. Babe Didrickson, who played and defeated some of the great male athletes of her time, is unique in the history of sports.

If sex equality were enforced in professional sports, it would mean that men could enter the women's tournaments and win most of the money. Bobby Riggs has already threatened: "I think that men 55 years and over should be allowed to play women's tournaments—like the Virginia Slims. Everybody ought to know there's no sex after 55 anyway."

The Positive Woman remembers the essential validity of the old prayer: "Lord, give me the strength to change what I can change, the serenity to accept what I cannot change, and the wisdom to discern the difference." The women's liberationists are expending their time and energies erecting a make-believe world in which they hypothesize that *if* schooling were gender-free, and *if* the same money were spent on male and female sports programs, and *if* women were permitted to compete on equal terms, *then* they would prove themselves to be physically equal. Meanwhile, the Positive Woman has put the ineradicable physical differences into her mental computer, programmed her plan of action, and is already on the way to personal achievement.

Thus, while some militant women spend

their time demanding more money for professional sports, ice skater Janet Lynn, a truly Positive Woman, quietly signed the most profitable financial contract in the history of women's athletics. It was not the strident demands of the women's liberationists that brought high prizes to women's tennis, but the discovery by sports promoters that beautiful female legs gracefully moving around the court made women's tennis a highly marketable television production to delight male audiences.

Many people thought that the remarkable filly named Ruffian would prove that a female race horse could compete equally with a male. Even with the handicap of extra weights placed on the male horse, the race was a disaster for the female. The gallant Ruffian gave her all in a noble effort to compete, but broke a leg in the race and, despite the immediate attention of top veterinarians, had to be put away.

Despite the claims of the women's liberation movement, there are countless physical differences between men and women. The female body is 50 to 60 percent water, the male 60 to 70 percent water, which explains why males can dilute alcohol better than women and delay its effect. The average woman is about 25 percent fatty tissue, while the male is 15 percent, making women more buoyant in water and able to swim with less effort. Males have a tendency to color blindness. Only 5 percent of persons who get gout are female. Boys are born bigger. Women live longer in most countries of the world, not only in the United States where we have a hard-driving competitive pace. Women excel in manual dexterity, verbal skills, and memory recall.

Arianna Stassinopoulos in her book *The Female Woman* has done a good job of spelling out the many specific physical differences that are so innate and so all-pervasive that

> even if Women's Lib was given a hundred, a thousand, ten thousand years in which to eradicate *all* the differences between the sexes, it would still be an impossible undertaking. . . .
>
> It is inconceivable that millions of years of evolutionary selection during a period of marked sexual division of labor have not left pronounced traces on the innate character of men and women. Aggressiveness, and mechanical and spatial skills, a sense of direction, and physical strength—all masculine characteristics—are the qualities essential for a hunter; even food gatherers need these same qualities for defense and exploration. The prolonged period of dependence of human children, the difficulty of carrying the peculiarly heavy and inert human baby—a much heavier, clumsier burden than the monkey infant and much less able to cling on for safety—meant that women could not both look after their children and be hunters and explorers. Early humans learned to take advantage of this period of dependence to transmit rules, knowledge and skills to their offspring—women needed to develop verbal skills, a talent for personal relationships, and a predilection for nurturing going even beyond the maternal instinct.

Does the physical advantage of men doom women to a life of servility and subservience? The Positive Woman knows that she has a complementary advantage which is at least as great—and, in the hands of a skillful woman, far greater. The Divine Architect who gave men a superior strength to lift weights also gave women a different kind of superior strength.

The women's liberationists and their dupes who try to tell each other that the sexual drive of men and women is really the same, and that it is only societal restraints that inhibit women from an equal desire, an equal enjoyment, and an equal freedom from the consequences, are doomed to frustration forever. It just isn't so, and pretending cannot make it so. The differences are not a woman's weakness but her strength.

Dr. Robert Collins, who has had ten years' experience in listening to and advising young women at a large eastern university, put his finger on the reason why casual "sexual activity" is such a cheat on women:

A basic flaw in this new morality is the assumption that males and females are the same sexually. The simplicity of the male anatomy and its operation suggest that to a man, sex can be an activity apart from his whole being, a drive related to the organs themselves.

In a woman, the complex internal organization, correlated with her other hormonal systems, indicates her sexuality must involve her total self. On the other hand, the man is orgasm-oriented with a drive that ignores most other aspects of the relationship. The woman is almost totally different. She is engulfed in romanticism and tries to find and express her total feelings for her partner.

A study at a midwestern school shows that 80 percent of the women who had intercourse hoped to marry their partner. Only 12 percent of the men expected the same.

Women say that soft, warm promises and tender touches are delightful, but that the act itself usually leads to a "Is that all there is to it?" reaction. . . .

[A typical reaction is]: "It sure wasn't worth it. It was no fun at the time. I've been worried ever since. . . ."

The new morality is a fad. It ignores history, it denies the physical and mental composition of human beings, it is intolerant, exploitative, and is oriented toward intercourse, not love.

The new generation can brag all it wants about the new liberation of the new morality, but it is still the woman who is hurt the most. The new morality isn't just a "fad"—it is a cheat and a thief. It robs the woman of her virtue, her youth, her beauty, and her love—for nothing, just nothing. It has produced a generation of young women searching for their identity, bored with sexual freedom, and despondent from the loneliness of living a life without commitment. They have abandoned the old commandments, but they can't find any new rules that work.

The Positive Woman recognizes the fact that, when it comes to sex, women are simply not the equal of men. The sexual drive of men is much stronger than that of women. That is how the human race was designed in order that it might perpetuate itself. The other side of the coin is that it is easier for women to control their sexual appetites. A Positive Woman cannot defeat a man in a wrestling or boxing match, but she can motivate him, inspire him, encourage him, teach him, restrain him, reward him, and have power over him that he can never achieve over her with all his muscle. How or whether a Positive Woman uses her power is determined solely by the way she alone defines her goals and develops her skills.

The differences between men and women are also emotional and psychological. Without woman's innate maternal instinct, the human race would have died out centuries ago. There is nothing so helpless in all earthly life as the newborn infant. It will die within hours if not cared for. Even in the most primitive, uneducated societies, women have always cared for their newborn babies. They didn't need any schooling to teach them how. They didn't need any welfare workers to tell them it is their social obligation. Even in societies to whom such concepts as "ought," "social responsibility," and "compassion for the helpless" were unknown, mothers cared for their new babies.

Why? Because caring for a baby serves the natural maternal need of a woman. Although not nearly so total as the baby's need, the woman's need is nonetheless real.

The overriding psychological need of a woman is to love something alive. A baby fulfills this need in the lives of most women. If a baby is not available to fill that need, women search for a baby-substitute. This is the reason why women have traditionally gone into teaching and nursing careers. They are doing what comes naturally to the female psyche. The schoolchild or the patient of any age provides an outlet for a woman to express her natural maternal need.

This maternal need in women is the reason why mothers whose children have grown up and flown from the nest are sometimes cut loose from their psychological moorings. The maternal need in women can show itself in love for grandchildren, nieces, nephews, or even neighbors' children. The maternal need in some women has even manifested itself in an extraordinary affection lavished on a dog, a cat, or a parakeet.

This is not to say that every woman must have a baby in order to be fulfilled. But it is to say that fulfillment for most women involves expressing their natural maternal urge by loving and caring for someone.

The women's liberation movement complains that traditional stereotyped roles assume that women are "passive" and that men are "aggressive." The anomaly is that a woman's most fundamental emotional need is not passive at all, but active. A woman naturally seeks to love affirmatively and to show that love in an active way by caring for the object of her affections.

The Positive Woman finds somebody on whom she can lavish her maternal love so that it doesn't well up inside her and cause psychological frustrations. Surely no woman is so isolated by geography or insulated by spirit that she cannot find someone worthy of her maternal love. All persons, men and women, gain by sharing something of themselves with their fellow humans, but women profit most of all because it is part of their very nature.

One of the strangest quirks of women's liberationists is their complaint that societal restraints prevent men from crying in public or showing their emotions, but permit women to do so, and that therefore we should "liberate" men to enable them, too, to cry in public. The public display of fear, sorrow, anger, and irritation reveals a lack of self-discipline that should be avoided by the Positive Woman just as much as by the Positive Man. Maternal love, however, is not a weakness but a manifestation of strength and service, and it should be nurtured by the Positive Woman.

Most women's organizations, recognizing the preference of most women to avoid hard-driving competition, handle the matter of succession of officers by the device of a nominating committee. This eliminates the unpleasantness and the tension of a competitive confrontation every year or two. Many women's organizations customarily use a prayer attributed to Mary, Queen of Scots, which is an excellent analysis by a woman of women's faults:

> Keep us, O God, from pettiness; let us be large in thought, in word, in deed. Let us be done with fault-finding and leave off self-seeking. . . . Grant that we may realize it is the little things that create differences, that in the big things of life we are at one.

Another silliness of the women's liberationists is their frenetic desire to force all women to accept the title *Ms* in place of *Miss* or *Mrs*. If Gloria Steinem and Betty Friedan want to call themselves *Ms* in order to conceal their marital status, their wishes should be respected.

But that doesn't satisfy the women's liberationists. They want all women to be compelled to use *Ms* whether they like it or not. The women's liberation movement has been waging a persistent campaign to browbeat the media into using *Ms* as the standard title for all women. The women's liberationists have already succeeding in getting the Department of Health, Education and Welfare to forbid schools and colleges from identifying women students as *Miss* or *Mrs*.

All polls show that the majority of women do not care to be called *Ms*. A Roper poll indicated that 81 percent of the women questioned said they prefer *Miss* or *Mrs*. to *Ms*. Most married women feel they worked hard for the *r* in their names, and they don't care to be gratuitously deprived of it. Most single women don't care to have their name changed to an unfamiliar title that at best conveys overtones of feminist ideology and is polemical in meaning, and at worst connotes misery instead of joy. Thus, Kate Smith, a very Positive Woman, proudly proclaimed on television that she is "Miss Kate Smith, not Ms." Like other Positive Women, she has been succeeding while negative women have been complaining.

Finally, women are different from men in dealing with the fundamentals of life itself. Men are philosophers, women are practical, and 'twas ever thus. Men may philosophize about how life began and where we are heading; women are concerned about feeding the kids today. No woman would ever, as Karl Marx did, spend years reading political philosophy in the British Museum while her child starved to death. Women don't take naturally to a search for the intangible and the abstract. The Positive Woman knows who she is and where she is going, and she will reach her goal because the longest journey starts with a very practical first step.

Amaury de Riencourt, in his book *Sex and Power in History*, shows that a successful society depends on a delicate balancing of different male and female factors, and that the women's liberation movement, which promotes unisexual values and androgyny, contains within it "a social and cultural death wish and the end of the civilization that endorses it."

One of the few scholarly works dealing with woman's role, *Sex and Power in History* synthesizes research from a variety of disciplines—sociology, biology, history, anthropology, religion, philosophy, and psychology. De Riencourt traces distinguishable types of women in different periods in history, from prehistoric to modern times. The "liberated" Roman matron, who is most similar to the present-day feminist, helped bring about the fall of Rome through her unnatural emulation of masculine qualities, which resulted in a large-scale breakdown of the family and ultimately of the empire.

De Riencourt examines the fundamental, inherent differences between men and women. He argues that man is the more aggressive, rational, mentally creative, analytical-minded sex because of his early biological role as hunter and provider. Woman, on the other hand, represents stability, flexibility, reliance on intuition, and harmony with nature, stemming from her procreative function.

Where man is discursive, logical, abstract, or philosophical, woman tends to be emotional, personal, practical, or mystical. Each set of qualities is vital and complements the other. Among the many differences explained in de Riencourt's book are the following:

> Women tend more toward conformity than men—which is why they often excel in such disciplines as spelling and punctuation where there is only one correct answer, determined by social authority. Higher intellectual activities, however, require a mental independence and power of abstraction that they usually lack, not to mention a certain form of aggressive boldness of the imagination which can only exist in a sex that is basically aggressive for biological reasons.
>
> To sum up: The masculine proclivity in problem solving is analytical and categorical; the feminine, synthetic and contextual. . . . Deep down, man tends to focus on the object, on external results and achievements; woman focuses on subjective motives and feelings. If life can be compared to a play, man focuses on the theme and structure of the play, woman on the innermost feelings displayed by the actors.

De Riencourt provides impressive refutation of two of the basic errors of the women's liberation movement: (1) that there are no emotional or cognitive differences between the sexes, and (2) that women should strive to be like men.

A more colloquial way of expressing the de Riencourt conclusion that men are more analytical and women more personal and practical is in the different answers that one is likely to get to the question, "Where did you get that steak?" A man will reply, "At the corner market," or wherever he bought it. A woman will usually answer, "Why? What's the matter with it?"

An effort to eliminate the differences by social engineering or legislative or constitutional tinkering cannot succeed, which is fortunate, but social relationships and spiritual values can be ruptured in the attempt. Thus the role reversals being forced upon high school students, under which guidance counselors urge reluctant girls to take "shop" and boys to take "home economics," further confuse a generation already unsure about its identity. They are as wrong as efforts to make a left-handed child right-handed.

THE FIVE PRINCIPLES

When the women's liberationists enter the political arena to promote legislation and litigation in pursuit of their goals, their specific demands are based on five principles.

1. They demand that a "gender-free" rule be applied to every federal and state law, bureaucratic regulation, educational institution, and expenditure of public funds. Based on their dogma that there is no real difference between men and women (except in sex organs), they demand that males and females have identical treatment always. Thus, if fathers are not expected to stay home and care for their infant children, then neither should mothers be expected to do so; and, therefore, it becomes the duty of the government to provide kiddy-care centers to relieve mothers of that unfair and unequal burden.

   The women's lib dogma demands that the courts treat sex as a "suspect" classification—just as race is now treated—so that no difference of treatment or separation between the sexes will ever be permitted, no matter how reasonable or how much it is desired by reasonable people.

   The nonsense of these militant demands was illustrated by the Department of Health, Education and Welfare (HEW) ruling in July, 1976, that all public school "functions such as father-son or mother-daughter breakfasts" would be prohibited because this "would be subjecting students to separate treatment." It was announced that violations would lead to a cutoff of federal assistance or court action by the Justice Department.

   When President Gerald Ford read this in the newspaper, he was described by his press secretary as being "quite irritated" and as saying that he could not believe that this was the intent of Congress in passing a law against sex discrimination in education. He telephoned HEW Secretary David Mathews and told him to suspend the ruling.

   The National Organization for Women, however, immediately announced opposition to President Ford's action, claiming that such events (fashion shows, softball games, banquets, and breakfasts) are sex-discriminatory and must be eliminated. It is clear that a prohibition against your right to make any difference or separation between the sexes anytime anywhere is a primary goal of the women's liberation movement.

   No sooner had the father-son, mother-daughter flap blown over than HEW embroiled itself in another controversy by a ruling that an after-school choir of fifth and sixth grade boys violates the HEW regulation that bars single-sex choruses. The choir in Wethersfield, Connecticut, that precipitated the ruling had been established for boys whose "voices haven't changed yet," and the purpose was "to get boys interested in singing" at an early age so they would be willing to join coed choruses later. Nevertheless, HEW found that such a boy's chorus is by definition sex discriminatory.

   The Positive Woman rejects the "gender-free" approach. She knows that there are many differences between male and female and that we are entitled to have our laws, regulations, schools, and courts reflect these differences and allow for reasonable differences in treatment and separations of activities that reasonable men and women want.

   The Positive Woman also rejects the argument that sex discrimination should be treated the same as race discrimination. There is vastly more difference between a man and a woman than there is between a black and a white, and it is nonsense to adopt a legal and bureaucratic attitude that pretends that those differences do not exist. Even the United States Supreme Court has, in recent and relevant cases, upheld "reasonable" sex-based differences of treatment by legislatures and by the military.

2. The women's lib legislative goals seek an irrational mandate of "equality" at the expense of justice. The fact is that equality cannot always be equated with justice, and may sometimes even be highly unjust. If we had absolutely equal treatment in regard to taxes, then everyone would pay the same income tax, or perhaps the same rate of income tax, regardless of the size of the income.

   If we had absolutely equal treatment in regard to federal spending programs, we would have to eliminate welfare, low-income housing benefits, food stamps, government scholarships, and many other programs designed to benefit low-income citizens. If we had absolutely equal treatment in regard to age, then seventeen-year-olds, or even ten-year-olds, would be permitted to vote, and we would have to eliminate Social Security unless all persons received the same benefits that only those over sixty-two receive now.

   Our legislatures, our administrative departments, and our courts have always had and still retain the discretion to make reasonable differences in treatment based on age, income, or economic situation. The Positive Woman believes that it makes no sense to deprive us of the ability to make reasonable distinctions based on sex that reasonable men and women want.

3. The women's liberation movement demands that women be given the benefit of "reverse discrimination." The Positive Woman recognizes that this is mutually exclusive with the principle of equal opportunity for all. Reverse discrimination is based on the theory that "group rights" take precedence over individual rights, and that "reverse discrimination" (variously called "preferential treatment," "remedial action," or "affirmative action") should be imposed in order to compensate some women today for alleged past discriminations against other women. The word "quotas" is usually avoided, but it amounts to the same thing.

   The fallacy of reverse discrimination has been aptly exposed by Professor Sidney Hook. No one would argue, he wrote, that because many years ago blacks and women were denied the right to vote, we should now compensate by giving them an extra vote or two, or by barring white men from voting at all.

   But that is substantially what the women's liberationists are demanding—and getting by federal court orders—in education, employment, and politics when they ask for "affirmative action" to remedy past discrimination.

   The Positive Woman supports equal opportunity for individuals of both sexes, as well as of all faiths and races. She rejects the theories of reverse discrimination and "group rights." It does no good for the woman who may have been discriminated against twenty-five years ago to know that an unqualified woman today receives preferential treatment at the expense of a qualified man. Only the vindictive radical would support such a policy of revenge.

4. The women's liberation movement is based on the unproven theory that uniformity should replace diversity—or, in simpler language, the federalization of all remaining aspects of our life. The militant women demand that *all* educational institutions conform to federally determined rules about sex discrimination.

   There is absolutely no evidence that HEW bureaucrats can do a better or fairer job of regulating our schools and colleges than local officials. Nor is there any evidence that individuals, or women, or society as a whole, would be better off under a uniform system enforced by the full power of the federal government than they would be under a free and competitive system, under local control, using diverse methods and regulations. It is hard to see why anyone would want to put more power into the hands of federal bureaucrats who cannot cope with the problems they already have.

   The militant women demand that HEW regulations enforce a strict gender-free uniformity on all schools and colleges. Everything from sports to glee clubs must be coed, regardless of local customs or wishes. The militants deplore the differences from state to state in the laws governing marriage and divorce. Yet does anyone think our nation would be improved if we were made subject to a national divorce law devised by HEW?

The Positive Woman rejects the theory that Washington, D.C., is the fountainhead of all wisdom and professional skill. She supports the principle of leaving all possible control and discretion in the hands of local school and college officials and their elected boards.

5. The women's liberation movement pushes its proposals on the premise that everything must be neutral as between morality and immorality, and as between the institution of the family and alternate lifestyles: for example, that homosexuals and lesbians should have just as much right to teach in the schools and to adopt children as anyone else; and that illegitimate babies and abortions by married or single mothers should be accepted as normal behavior for teachers—and funded by public money.

A good example of the rabid determination of the militant radicals to push every law and regulation to the far-out limit of moral neutrality is the HEW regulation on sex discrimination that implements the Education Amendments of 1972. Although the federal statute simply prohibits sex discrimination, the HEW regulation (1) requires that any medical benefit program administered by a school or college pay for abortions for married and unmarried students, (2) prohibits any school or college from refusing to employ or from firing an unmarried pregnant teacher or a woman who has had, or plans to have, an abortion, and (3) prohibits any school or college from refusing admission to any student who has had, or plans to have, an abortion. Abortion is referred to by the code words "termination of pregnancy."

This HEW regulation is illogical, immoral, and unauthorized by any reasonable reading of the 1972 Education Act. But the HEW regulation became federal law on July 18, 1975, after being signed by the president and accepted by Congress.

The Positive Woman believes that our educational institutions have not only the right, but the obligation, to set minimum standards of moral conduct at the local level. She believes that schools and colleges have no right to use our public money to promote conduct that is offensive to the religious and moral values of parents and taxpayers.

NEUTERIZING SOCIETY

A basic objective and tactic of the women's liberationists is to neuterize all laws, textbooks, and language in newspapers, radio, and television. Their friends in state legislatures are ordering computer printouts of all laws that use such "sexist" words as *man*, *woman*, *husband*, and *wife*. They are to be expunged and replaced with neuter equivalents. Some state legislators have acquiesced rather than face charges of "sexism." Others have rejected this effort and labeled it the silliness that it is.

The feminists look upon textbooks as a major weapon in their campaign to eliminate what they call our "sex-stereotyped society" and to restructure it into one that is sex-neutral from cradle to grave. Under liberationist demands, the Macmillan Publishing Company issued a booklet called "Guidelines for Creating Positive Sexual and Racial Images in Educational Materials." Its purpose is to instruct authors in the use of sex-neutral language, concepts, and illustrations in order to conform to the new Macmillan censorship code. (The McGraw-Hill Book Company has issued a similar pamphlet, "Guidelines for Equal Treatment of the Sexes.")

Henceforth, you may not say *mankind*, it should be *humanity*. You may not say *brotherhood*, it should be *amity*. *Manpower* must be replaced by *human energy*; *forefathers* should give way to *precursors*. *Chairman* and *salesman* are out; and "in" words are *chairperson* and *salesperson*.

You are forbidden to say "man the sailboat." The acceptable substitute is not given; presumably it is "person the sailboat." You must not say "the conscientious housekeeper dusts *her* furniture at least once a week"; you must say "*the* furniture," because otherwise you would imply that the housekeeper is a woman—and that would be intolerable. You may not say "the cat washed herself"; it must be "the cat washed itself," because it would be sexist to imply that the cat is female.

The section forbidding sexism in textbook illustrations is even more amusing. According to the Macmillan guidelines, males must be shown wearing aprons just as often as females. Father should be pictured doing household chores and nursing a sick child, mother working at her desk while dad clears the dining-room table, little girls reaching toward snakes instead of recoiling from them, boys crying or preening in front of a mirror, and fathers using hair spray.

Women must be shown participating actively "in exciting worthwhile pursuits," which, by apparent definition, do not include being a homemaker. The guidelines warn that books will not be tolerated that indicate that "homemaking is the true vocation for a woman."

The Macmillan guidelines reach the height of absurdity when they deliver a stern rebuke to the history book that refers to Sacajawea as "an amazing Shoshoni Indian woman" because she led the Lewis and Clark expedition through the Rockies "with a young baby strapped to her back." According to the Macmillan guidelines, the use of the word *amazing* is intolerable sexist propaganda that perpetuates "the myth of feminine fragility." It is a pity that our school children can no longer be told that Sacajawea was "amazing" because the historical fact is that her physical accomplishment was unique.

The Macmillan guidelines reserve their most stinging rebuke for the four-letter word *lady*, terming it "distasteful" specifically because it connotes "ladylike" behavior.

The Macmillan guidelines are not only a good source of laughs, but are a healthy exposure to the hypocrisy of the liberals who pilloried the West Virginia parents who tried to censor obnoxious four-letter words from their children's textbooks. It all depends on which four-letter words you want to censor.

Baby-care doctor Benjamin Spock was one of those whom the feminists targeted as obnoxious because of the alleged "sexism" in his bestselling baby books. His principal offense was that, in advising mothers how to care for their babies, he repeatedly used the pronoun *he* instead of *she*. Obviously, it would be a semantic hurdle of significant magnitude to write a baby book and say "he or she" every time the author refers to the baby. Until women's liberationists became so vocal, normal mothers understood that *he* is used in the generic sense to mean babies of both sexes.

The feminists continued their campaign against Dr. Spock's "sexism" until they finally convinced him that modern liberated society should treat males and females exactly the same. In his latest book he eliminated "sexist" language. The only trouble was, Dr. Spock bought the whole bag of "liberation." He walked out on his faithful wife Jane, to whom he had been married for forty-eight years, and took up with a younger woman. Dr. Spock was truly "liberated" from traditional restraints.

It is no gain for women, for children, for families, or for America to propel us into a unisex society. Our strength is in our diversity, not in our sameness. . . .

14

COALITION STRATEGIES

Many supporters of the civil-rights movement were puzzled—and not a few chagrined—when Martin Luther King and other leaders began to talk about and work for rights much more broadly defined than those of black Americans alone. King developed a profound concern for peace and economic justice—not as contradictions of or replacements for the civil-rights struggle, but as natural and indeed necessary elements of it.

As the women's movement developed, a similar pattern emerged. Gaining the right to vote had been a giant leap forward; the fight for the Equal Rights Amendment, yet to succeed, had concentrated on the specific goal of equal rights for women. But increasingly, movement leaders came to see the larger dimensions of the struggle: the sense in which the women's-rights movement was a human-rights movement aimed at a male humanization too; the perception that women everywhere on the globe and in every social class should share in the new vision; the understanding (or reunderstanding) that the modern movements for blacks' civil rights and women's rights are linked, historically and logically. Thus, in many ways the growing organization of women (as in NOW) contributed significantly to the struggle for the rights of all humankind. At Houston in November 1977, the First National Women's Conference brought those organizational and cultural forces together. The feminist leader and editor of *Ms.*, Gloria Steinem, analyzes this historic event.

The First National Women's Conference

by Gloria Steinem

Were our State a pure democracy there would still be excluded from our deliberations women who, to prevent deprivation of morals and ambiguity of issues, should not mix promiscuously in gatherings of men.

—Thomas Jefferson

In 1972 the United Nations declared 1975 to be the official International Year of the Woman. Among the world's women themselves, reaction was not all good. Was this like the International Year of the Handicapped? Or was it an admission that everything else was the Year of the Man?

Nonetheless, most governments began to collect statistics to present at the International Women's Year Conference in Mexico City, and that was a worthwhile result in itself. In some countries, this was the first time that research had been focused on the status of females. Many individual women and their organizations decided to use this world spotlight as an opportunity to meet each other and to further the cause of equality in any way they could. In this country, President Ford appointed an International Women's Year Commission of thirty-nine members to round up statistics and recommendations, and to travel to Mexico City as delegates. Thousands of individual American women also went there to take part in the unofficial events that often outnumbered and overshadowed the official ones. By the end of those few days, at least one other world conference had been called for, and Women's Year had become Women's Decade.

For most official and unofficial Americans, this was the first, mind-expanding experience of a massive multicultural women's meeting. It was also a source of learning. The range of women's concerns was both culturally diverse and amazingly similar on the basic problems of women in male-dominant societies. The nationalist divisions among women who otherwise agreed on those basics were destructive and embittering. And, like the women of most countries, the female half of the United States was represented by a delegation and an official national agenda that might or might not be what we had in mind. Despite many presidential commissions and other goodwill efforts to "study" American women, no one had ever asked us.

It was this desire to work out women's own agenda of issues, goals, and timetables that had motivated Congresswomen Bella Abzug and Patsy Mink earlier in 1975 when they drafted and got support from other congresswomen for Public Law 94–167—a proposal for a public, government-funded conference in every state and territory that would identify issues and elect delegates to a U.S. National Women's Conference. As a kind of Constitutional Convention for women and a remedy for the founding fathers who had excluded all women from the first one, this national elected body would then recommend to Congress and the president those changes in laws, government procedures, and the Constitution itself that would remove barriers to women's equality.

After Mexico City, there was enough enthusiasm and international publicity to lobby this bill through. Of course, Congress didn't pass and fund it until too late for the 1976 Bicentennial year in which the conference was supposed to happen, and its modest requested appropriation of ten million dollars was cut to five million dollars: less than the cost of sending one postcard to every adult woman. Nonetheless,

From Gloria Steinem, *Outrageous Acts and Everyday Rebellions* (New York: Holt, Rinehart & Winston, 1983), pp. 279–91.

a new International Women's Year Commission was appointed by President Carter, this time for the purpose of carrying out the complex process of convening a representative conference in every state and territory and electing delegates proportionate to populations.

Thanks to the enthusiasm, energy, and sacrifice of women who responded and spent months of outreach and organizing within their own states, some of those fifty-six two-day conferences were attended by as many as twenty thousand women and interested men. They were the biggest and most economically and racially representative statewide political meetings ever held. The result was not only the identification of barriers to equality in twenty-six areas, from arts and humanities to welfare, but the election of two thousand delegates who were the first (and still the only) national political representatives in which family incomes of less than twenty thousand dollars a year, racial minorities, and all ages over eighteen were represented in proportion to their real presence in the population.

Once in Houston where the First National Women's Conference was held in November 1977, fifteen thousand participants, including observers from other countries, joined the two thousand voting delegates. A careful debate and balloting procedure allowed four days of discussion and voting on each of the twenty-six areas recommended by state conferences.[1] Though anti-equality women and men also rallied in protest in another part of Houston, led by right-wing Congressman Robert Dornan and anti-ERA activist Phyllis Schlafly, their views were fairly, perhaps disproportionately, represented among the voting delegates themselves. In some states, calculated and disproportionate flooding of the conferences by such groups as Mormons, fundamentalist Baptists, and, in Mississippi, the Ku Klux Klan had produced elected delegates whose positions did not match their states' majority opinions in elections and public opinion polls. Nonetheless, resolutions were passed that were pro-equality and, according to post-Houston national opinion polls, did have the majority support of Americans, women and men.

As journalist Lindsy Van Gelder reported from Houston, "It was like a supermarket check-out line from Anywhere, U.S.A., transposed to the political arena: homemakers and nuns, teenagers and senior citizens, secretaries and farmers and lawyers, mahogany skins and white and café au lait. We were an all-woman Carl Sandburg poem come to life."

Certainly the Houston conference itself was more representative by race, class, and age than either the U.S. House of Representatives or the Senate, and more democratic in its procedures—from allowing floor debate, amendments, and substitute motions to encouraging voting by individual conscience rather than by geographical blocks or for political reward—than the national presidential conventions that were its closest models. The long and complex process leading up to Houston was often frustrating and never perfect, but its impressive results surprised many Americans, including some of the women who had worked hardest to make it happen.

This mammoth project begins to sound unprecedented, and there are many factual ways in which that is true. But comparable events *have* happened in the past. Women have taken action against the political systems of male dominance for as many centuries as they have existed, and some of those actions have been at least as impressive and, in their own contexts, more courageous. If we are to be successful in preserving the spirit of Houston, we should be aware that similar changeful, challenging, women-run events have been unrecorded, suppressed, ridiculed, or met with violence in the past.

As a student learning American history from the textbooks of the 1950s, I read that white and black women had been "given" the vote in 1920, an unexplained fifty years after black men had been "given" the vote as a result of a civil war fought on their behalf. I learned little about the many black people who had risen up in revolt and fought for their own freedom, and nothing about the more than one hundred years of struggle by nationwide networks of white and black women who organized and lectured around the country for both Negro and women's suffrage at a time when they were not even supposed to speak in public. They lobbied their all-male legislatures, demonstrated in the streets, went on hunger strikes and went to jail, and opposed this country's right to "fight for democracy" in World War I when half of American citizens had no political rights at all. In short, I did not learn that several generations of our foremothers had nearly brought the country to a halt in order to win a legal identity as human beings for women of all races.

At least the right to vote was cited in history books, however, as one that American women had not always enjoyed. Other parts of that legal identity—the goal of this country's long, first wave of feminism—were not mentioned. How many of us learned what it meant, for instance, for females to be the human property of husbands and fathers, and to die a "civil death" under the marriage laws? It was a condition of chattel so clear that the first seventeenth-century American slaveholders simply adopted it, as Gunnar Myrdal has pointed out, as the "nearest and most natural analogy" for the legal status of slaves.[2] As young students, how many of us understood that the right of an adult American female to own property, to sue in court, or to sign a will; to keep a salary she earned instead of turning it over to a husband or father who "owned" her; to go to school, to have legal custody of her own children, to leave her husband's home without danger of being forcibly and legally returned; to escape a husband's right to physically discipline her; to challenge the social prison of being a lifelong minor if she remained unmarried or a legal nonperson if she did marry—how many of us were instructed that all of these rights had been won through generations of effort by an independent women's movement?

When we studied American progress toward religious freedom, did we read about the many nineteenth-century feminists who challenged the patriarchal structure of the church, who dared question such scriptural rhetoric as the injunction of the Apostle Paul to "Wives, submit yourselves unto your husbands as unto the Lord"? Were we given a book called *The Woman's Bible*, a scholarly and very courageous revision of the scriptures undertaken by Elizabeth Cady Stanton?

If we read about religious and political persecution in America, did we learn that the frenzy of the New England witch trials, tortures, and burnings were usually the persecutions of independent or knowledgeable women, of midwives who performed abortions and taught contraception, of women who challenged the masculine power structure in many ways?

When we heard about courageous people who harbored runaway slaves, did they include women like Susan B. Anthony, who scandalized and alienated abolitionist allies by helping not only black slaves, but runaway wives and children who were escaping the brutality of white husbands and fathers who "owned" them?

Of course, to record the fact that both blacks and women were legal chattel, or that their parallel myths of "natural" inferiority were (and sometimes still are) used to turn both into a source of cheap labor, is not to be confused with equating these two groups. Black women and men often suffered more awful restrictions on their freedom, a more overt cruelty and violence, and their lives were put at greater risk. To teach a white girl child to read might be condemned as dangerous and even sinful, but it was not against the law, as it was for blacks in many slave states of the South. White women were far less likely than black slaves to risk their lives or be separated from their children, and particularly less so than black women who were forced to be breeders of more slaves as well as slaves themselves. Angelina Grimke, one of the courageous white southern feminists who worked against both race and sex slavery, always pointed out that "We have not felt the slaveholder's lash . . . we have not had our hands manacled."[3]

Nonetheless, white women were sometimes tortured or killed in "justified" domestic beatings or sold as indentured workers as a punishment for poverty, or for a liaison with a black man, or for breaking a law of obedience. Hard work combined with the years of coerced childbearing designed to populate this new land may have made white women's life expectancy as low as half that of white men. Early American graveyards full of young women who died in childbirth testify to the desperation with which many women must have sought out midwives for contraception or abortion. The most typical white female punishment was humiliation, the loss of freedom and identity, or to have her health and spirit broken. As Angelina Grimke explained, "I rejoice exceedingly that our resolution should combine us with the Negro. I feel that we have been with him; that the iron has entered into our souls . . . our *hearts* have been crushed."[4]

But why did so many of my history books assume that white women and blacks could have no issues in common, so much so that they failed to report on the real coalitions of the past? Historians seem to pay little attention to movements among the powerless. Perhaps the intimate, majority challenge presented by women of all races and men of color was (and still is) too threatening to the power of a white male minority.

Certainly, the lessons of history were not ignored because they were invisible at the time. Much of the long struggle for black and female personhood had been spent as a functioning, conscious coalition. ("*Resolved*. There never can be a true peace in this Republic until the civil and political rights of all citizens of African descent and all women are practically established."[5] That statement was made by Elizabeth Cady Stanton and passed at a New York convention in 1863.) Like most early feminists, Stanton believed that sex and race prejudice had to be fought together; that both were "produced by the same cause, and manifested very much in the same way. The Negro's skin and the woman's sex are both [used as] *prima facie* evidence that they were intended to be in subjection to the white Saxon man."[6] Frederick Douglass, the fugitive slave who became an important national leader of the movement to abolish slavery and to establish the personhood of all females, vowed in his autobiography that, "When the true history of the antislavery cause shall be written, women will occupy a large space in its pages, for the cause of the slave has been peculiarly women's cause."[7] When Douglass died, newspapers reported a national mourning for him as a "friend of women" as well as an abolitionist pioneer. And there were many more such conscious statements and obvious lessons.

If more of us had learned the parallels and origins of the abolitionist and suffragist movements, there might have been less surprise when a new movement called "women's liberation" grew from the politicization of white and black women in the civil rights movement of the 1960s. Certainly a familiarity with the words of Frederick Douglass might have prevented some of the white and black men in both the civil rights and peace movements from feeling that their dignity depended on women's second-classness, or from seeing that they themselves were sometimes waging a sexual war against women, in Vietnam villages and at home. If women had been taught that feelings of emotional connection to other powerless groups were logical—that women also lacked power as a caste, and that we might feel understandably supportive when peace or civil rights sit-ins rejected violence as proofs of manhood—certainly I and many other women of my generation would have wasted less time being mystified by our odd and frequent sense of identification with all the "wrong" groups: the black movement, migrant workers, or with male contemporaries who were defying the "masculine" role by refusing to fight in Vietnam.

As it was, however, suffragists were often portrayed as boring, ludicrous bluestockings when they were in history books at all: certainly no heroines you would need in modern America where we were, as male authorities kept telling us resentfully, "the most privileged women in the world." Some of us were further discouraged from exploring our real human strengths by accusations of Freudian penis envy, the dominating-mother syndrome, careerism, a black matriarchy that was (according to some white sociologists) more dangerous to black men than white racism, plus other punishable offenses. Men often emerged from World War II, Freudian analysis, and locker rooms with vague threats that they would replace any uppity women with more subservient ones—an Asian or European war bride instead of a "spoiled" American, a "feminine" white woman to replace a black "matriarch," or just some worshipful young "other woman."

There were many painful years of reinventing the wheel before we relearned the lessons that our foremothers could have taught us: that a false mythology of inferiority based on sex and race was being used to turn both groups into a support system. Limited intellectual ability, childlike natures, special job skills (always the poorly paid ones), greater emotionalism and closeness to nature, an inability to get along with our own group, chronic lateness and irresponsibility, happiness with our "natural" place—all these similar arguments were used against women of every race and men of color.

"The parallel between women and Negroes is the deepest truth of American life, for together they form the unpaid or underpaid labor on which America runs."[8] That was Gunnar Myrdal writing in 1944 in a rather obscure appendix to his landmark study on racism, *An American Dilemma*. Even in the sixties when I discovered those words (and wished devoutly that I had read them years before), I still did not know that Susan B. Anthony had put the issue even more succinctly almost a century before Myrdal. "Woman," she said, "has been the great unpaid laborer of the world."[9]

The current movements toward racial and sexual justice have had some success in pressuring for courses in women's history, black history, the study of Hispanic Americans, Native Americans, and many others, but these subjects still tend to be special studies taken only by those with the most interest and the least need. They are rarely an integrated, inescapable part of the American history texts read by all students.

And if the recent past of our own country is still incomplete for many of us, how much less do we learn about other countries and more distant times?

What do we know about the African warrior queens of Dahomey, for instance, who led their armies against colonial invaders? Or the market women of modern West Africa who run the daily businesses of their countries? If we know little about the relationship of the witch hunts of New England to patriarchal politics, how much less do we know about the more than eight million women who were burned at the stake in medieval Europe, clearly as an effort to wipe out remains of a pre-Christian religion that honored the power of women and nature? If we know not even Stanton's *Woman's Bible* of the nineteenth century, what about the first-century texts of the Bible itself that show a much less patriarchal version of Christ's teachings? If the exceptional American women who were explorers, outlaws, ranchers, pirates, publishers, soldiers, and inventors are only just being rediscovered, what about those Native American nations and tribes that honored women in authority far more than the "advanced" European cultures that invaded their shores?

How are we to interpret the discovery that many of the "pagan idols," "false gods," and "pagan temples" so despised by Judeo-Christian tradition and the current Bible were representations of a female power: a god with a womb and breasts? How will our vision of prehistory change now that archaeologists have discovered that some skeletons long assumed to be male—because of their large-boned strength or because they were buried with weapons and scholarly scrolls—are really female? (In America, the famous archaeological find described as the Minnesota Man has recently been redesignated the Minnesota Woman. In Europe, the graves of young warriors killed by battle wounds have turned out to contain the skeletons of females.) Now that we are beginning to rediscover the interdependency of sexual and racial caste systems in our own nation's history, and the parallels in modern forms of job discrimination, will political-science courses begin to explain that a power structure dependent on race or class "purity"—whether it is whites in the American South and South Africa or Aryans in Nazi Germany—must place greater restrictions on the freedom of women in order to perpetuate that "purity"? Will we finally be allowed to confront these caste systems together, and therefore successfully in the long run, instead of facing constant divide-and-conquer tactics in the short run?

Such revolts against birth-based caste systems have always been international, and contagious. Anticolonial movements against external dominations of one race by another have deepened into movements against internal dominations based on racial or sexual caste. Together, they are the most profound and vital movements of this century and the last. They are changing both our hopes for the future and our assumptions about the past.

But some revelations about the past can be both rewarding and angering. It seems that our ancestors knew so much that we should not have had to relearn.

Among the resolutions in the National Plan of Action adopted at Houston, for instance, there are many echoes of the first wave of American feminism. The high incidence of battered women, the inadequacy of laws to protect them, and the reluctance of police to interfere—all those facts struck many Americans as shocking new discoveries. If we had known more about the history of a husband's legal right to "own" his wife, and therefore to "discipline" her physically with the explicit permission of the law, we could have uncovered this major form of violence much sooner. A wife's loss of her own name, legal residence, credit rating, and many other civil rights might have seemed less "natural" and inevitable if we had known that our marriage laws were still rooted in the same common-law precedent ("husband and wife are one person in law . . . that of the husband"[10]) that nineteenth-century English and American women had struggled so hard to reform. We would have been better prepared for arguments that the Equal Rights Amendment would "destroy the family" or force women to become "like men" if we had known that the same accusations, almost word for word, were leveled against the suffrage movement. (The possibility of two political opinions in one family was said to be a sure way to destroy it. Our own foremothers were called "unsexed women," "entirely devoid of personal attraction," who had only been "disappointed in their endeavors to appropriate breeches," all because they wanted to vote and own property.) Even the charge that the ERA would be contrary to states' rights and constitute a "federal power grab" is a repeat of the argument that a citizen's right to vote should be left entirely up to the states; a stumbling block that caused suffragists to proceed state by state, and to delay focusing on a Nineteenth Amendment to the Constitution for many years.

In a way, the unity represented by the minority women's resolution—perhaps the single greatest accomplishment of the Houston Conference, because it brought together all Americans of color for the first time, from Asian to Puerto Rican—was also the greatest example of the high price of lost history. After all, black women had been the flesh-and-blood links between abolition and suffrage; yet they had suffered from double discrimination and invisibility even then. ("There is a great stir about colored men getting their rights," warned Sojourner Truth, the great black feminist and antislavery leader, "but not a word about colored women."[11]) When American male political leaders destroyed the coalition for universal adult suffrage by offering the vote to its smallest segment—that is, to black males—but refused the half of the country that was female, black women were forced to painfully and artificially slice up their identities. They could either support their brothers in, as the slogan of the era put it, "the Negroes' hour," even though no black woman was included; or, like Sojourner Truth, they could advocate "keeping the thing going . . . because if we wait till it is still, it will take a great while to get things going again."[12] Once it was clear that black men were going to get the vote first, no matter what any woman said, black women were further isolated by some white suffragists who, embittered by the desertion of both white and black male allies, began to use the racist argument that the white female "educated" vote was necessary to outweigh the black male "uneducated" vote. Divisions deepened. Sojourner Truth's prediction that it would "take a great while to get things going again" if the two great parallel causes were divided turned out to be true. It was a half century . . . , and many years after Sojourner Truth's death, before women of all races won the vote.

Even so, many scars of the rift between white and black women remain. So does the cruel and false argument that black women must suppress their own talents on behalf of black men, thus weakening the black community by half. White male "liberals" had tried a divide-and-conquer tactic by separating out black men, and, in many sad ways, they won.

When the first reformist prelude to feminism started up again in the early and mid sixties, it was largely a protest of middle-class white housewives against the "feminine mystique" that kept them trapped in the suburbs. For black women who often had no choice but to be in the labor force, that was a life-style that some envied and few could afford. Only after the civil rights movement and feminism's emergence again in the later sixties—after the analysis of all women as a caste, not just as a privileged and integrationist few—did the organic ties between the movements against racial and sexual caste begin to grow again. In spite of enduring racism in society, in spite of an economic and social structure that exploits racial divisions among women and also manufactures social and economic tensions between black women and men, the women's movement has become the most racially and economically integrated movement in the country—and even so, it is not integrated enough. Despite the enduring argument that male supremacy is a social norm to which all should aspire, the black movement and its political leaders now include a few more women than do their white counterparts—but even so, there is far from a balance.

For this wave of feminism, Houston was the first public landmark in a long, suspicion-filled journey across racial barriers. At last there were enough women of color (more than a third of all delegates and thus a greater proportion than the population) to have a strong voice. There were not only black women, but Hispanic women (from Chicana to Puerto Rican, Latina to Cuban) as the second largest American minority, Asian Pacific women, Alaskan Native, and American Indian women from many different nations, who themselves were often meeting for the first time. But how much less perilous this journey would have been if we had maintained the bridges of the past; if we had not had to build new roads to coalitions through what seemed to us an uncharted wilderness.

For myself, Houston and all the events surrounding it have become a landmark in personal history, the sort of milestone that divides our sense of time. Figuring out the date of any other event now means remembering: Was it before or after Houston?

The reason has a lot to do with learning. In retrospect, I realize that I had been skeptical about the time and effort spent on this First National Women's Conference. Could a government-sponsored conference really be populist and inclusive? Even after the state conferences made clear that the combination of public and private outreach was working, I still feared the culmination in Houston as if it were an approaching trial. Would this enormous meeting attract national and international attention, only to highlight disorder? Would the anti-equality counterconference be taken as proof that "women can't get along"? As a member of the new International Women's Year Commission appointed by President Carter, I had worked throughout that year of state conferences and preparation, but as their culmination in Houston came closer, I still would have given anything to stop worrying, avoid conflict, stay home, or just indefinitely delay this event about which I cared too much.

I thought my fears were rational and objective. They were not.

Yes, I had learned, finally, that *individual women* could be competent, courageous, and loyal to each other. Despite growing up with no experience of women in positions of worldly authority, I had learned that much. But I still did not believe that *women as a group* could be competent, courageous, and loyal to each other. I didn't believe that we could conduct large, complex events that celebrated our own diversity. I wasn't sure that we could make a history that was our own.

But we can. Houston taught us that. The question is: Will this lesson be lost again?

—1979

NOTES

1. For a full text of this National Plan of Action, see Caroline Bird, *What Women Want: The National Women's Conference* (New York: Simon and Schuster, 1979).
2. Gunnar Myrdal, *An American Dilemma* (New York: Harper and Brothers, 1944), 1073.
3. Angelina Grimke, in Elizabeth Cady Stanton et al., *The History of Woman Suffrage*, Vol. II. (Rochester: Charles Mann, 1899).
4. Ibid.
5. Ibid.
6. Ibid.
7. *The Life and Times of Frederick Douglass* (New York: Collier, 1962), p. 469.
8. Myrdal, 1077.
9. Susan B. Anthony, in Stanton, Vol. I.
10. Blackstone, *Commentaries*.
11. Sojourner Truth, in Stanton, Vol. II, 193.
12. Ibid.

15

PUBLIC OPINION

No one, we may confidently assert, is born with political opinions. Therefore, there is nothing inherent, nothing genetically natural, about the markedly different attitudes our culture assigns to men and women. Sexism is learned. It is the most significant dimension of American public opinion affecting the future of women, including their political future. Because sexism is learned, we may suppose it can be unlearned. That is the goal of Letty Cottin Pogrebin in the following selections from her book *Growing Up Free*.

Prescriptions for changing sexist attitudes will vary, but at least two of the teaching agencies involved will likely be television and schools. Evidence indicates that a great many American children spend a great deal of time watching television—or at least sitting in the same room with a turned-on set. Probably the average child spends nearly as much time with TV as in school. The *effect* of all that exposure is a complex matter. Clearly children do not take in and adopt all the messages they get from television or their teachers. But when the attitude conveyed is pervasive and persistent, it sticks. Thus it is with sexism. Sexism shapes the recruitment and advancement of those who govern. As sexism changes, those patterns will also change.

Sexism in American Culture

by Letty Cottin Pogrebin

Before we begin, please try to absorb these staggering numbers. Without them you'll surely accuse me of exaggerating TV's effect on children.

From Letty Cottin Pogrebin, *Growing Up Free: Raising Your Child in the 80's* (New York: McGraw-Hill, 1980), pp. 393–409, 492–99, 507–11.

- More American homes have television than have heat or indoor plumbing.
- The average TV set is turned on for 6½ hours per day.
- Most children begin watching television at 2.8 *months* of age.
- Three- to five-year-olds watch TV 54 hours a week.
- By the time a child enters kindergarten, she or he has spent more time in the TV room than a four-year college student spends in the classroom.
- By the time a child graduates from high school, he or she will have spent less than 12,000 hours in front of a teacher and more than 22,000 hours in front of a television set.
- By age seventeen, each child has seen 350,000 commercials.

What can one say about a nonhuman presence that, in some children's lives, outpulls parents, teachers, and peers put together. TV is not just an object giving forth words and pictures; it's a force with the status and persona of a friend.

When children aged four to six were asked "Which do you like better, TV or Daddy? TV or Mommy?" 20 percent preferred television to their mothers and 44 percent liked it better than their fathers. Another survey found junior high school students believe television more than parents, teachers, friends, books, radio, or newspapers.

What are they believing *in*?

The answer seems to be sex role propaganda, materialism, and violence.

SEX ROLE PROPAGANDA

Since there's no sex difference in television viewing habits by gender, both girls and boys are absorbing TV's version of both sex roles to an equal degree. For example, a girl learns that women seek men's approval by cooking "man-pleasing" meals, and at the same time, boys learn that men can expect to be fed and served.

Because young children have scant life experience against which to compare television's "reality," they more or less swallow it whole—especially since it comes with the implied sanction of parents and society-at-large. After all, grownups bought the set and grownups are clearly in charge of what's televised, so at both ends of the tube, adult authority seems to underwrite TV's output. And here is what's put out:

Cartoons

In this most frankly child-oriented of all entertainments, males outnumber females up to four to one. Cartoon daddies are ambitious, aggressive, adventurous, and employed, while cartoon mommies are passive, timid, emotional, and almost exclusively domestic. Rated on a forty-point personality chart, both sexes make a strong showing in all the stereotype categories, from boy-is-brave to female-is-fragile.

Public Television

The Task Force on Women in Public Broadcasting, which studied one week of children's programs televised on PBS, found that overall, male characters exceeded females by two to one on every show but *Electric Company*.

Sesame Street, so widely hailed by educators, came in with a three-to-one ratio, and the males were far more likely than the females to be interestingly and gainfully employed. The authors of the report are concerned

> because of the relationship of occupational role models with sex-role identification. "Sesame Street" in particular was designed so that children could "model" or learn behavior from what they see on television. . . . Therefore, the numbers of occupational roles presented to

children, as well as the kind of roles, are important as sources of learning.

I sampled a "Sesame Street" program and turned up these boners (along with some admittedly fine features):

- Susan says, "Maybe I can get my husband to take me to the movies tonight," suggesting that she is financially or physically incapable of going herself. (Reverse it and give Gordon the line to see how it signals dependency.)
- Two boys and one girl seem to be assembling a wooden box cart, but actually the boys are doing all the work while the girl is scampering around them trying to get in on it. Finally she gives up, clasps her hands behind her back and stands in the classic female posture—watching from the sidelines.
- A black boy narrates the events of his day. (Dad goes off to work; Mom shops and watches Son in the playground; Dad comes home, gets a big welcome, sits down to the dinner Mom cooked. Then Mom washes the dishes while Dad and Son draw pictures until bedtime. Dad reads Son a story.) It's admirable to show a black man as a worker, family man, and involved father, but the black woman is, to say the least, one-dimensional. Certainly, the cure for race stereotypes is not sex stereotypes.

Soap Operas

With fifteen million kids tuned in, preschool, during lunchtime, vacations, and sick days, the soap opera qualifies as children's programming. And although there has been some improvement it is still pretty traumatic programming.

A N.O.W. survey found that 15 percent of the female characters on the "suds" were portrayed as mentally and physically ill. These women share the screen with miraculously successful men, 60 percent of whom hold professional jobs, and with other women who either stay home worrying about divorce, disease, incest, and infidelity, or hold jobs in nursing or office work.

At best "women past thirty are depicted as sexual beings, desired and desiring." At worst, pregnancy seems to be the soap opera's ubiquitous plot device. (There are plenty of doctors and nurses in these stories but apparently they're ignorant of contraception.) Women who pursue careers or express personal autonomy are punished with sterility, miscarriage, tragic abortions, or an impotent mate.

> Normal women stay home and have babies . . . the birth rate on daytime TV seems to rival that of Latin America! . . . Strong impressions are conveyed here: pregnancy will save your marriage; motherhood will fulfill you; bearing a man's child will make you supremely important to that man.

In other words, Girls Are Meant to Be Mothers.

For all this obsession with childbearing, children themselves are virtually absent from the soaps except as behind-the-scenes pawns in their parents' melodramas.

These sob stories may offer misery-loves-company solace to isolated housewives. But the kid who's sick in bed with the TV on is getting an even sicker message about what men and women say and do to each other in the grown-up world.

Prime-Time Programs

In case you haven't noticed, not all kids are asleep during adult viewing hours. Fact is, even between 10:30 and 11 P.M., five million children under twelve are still glued to the set. What they and millions more have seen of an evening is a parade of brainless wives, dumb-but-pretty secretaries, sex kittens, Big Momma blacks, rape victims, floor waxers, and other cardboard characters who either shill for the status quo or perpetrate lies about women. After a year monitoring sixteen adventure and situation comedy shows, a Princeton group found, for example, that women characters were twice as likely as men to be incompetent. On a broader scale, the U.S. Civil Rights Commission accused the networks of systematic sex and race stereotyping. One sample: the Commission's 1979 report found white males account for nearly 63 percent of all TV roles but only 40 percent of the U.S. population.

The networks aren't exactly in a ratings war over who has more nonsexist male characters either. One study found only three instances of nurturant men in fifty-eight half-hour programs.

Commercials

Where life is measured in thirty-second "spots," there is one reigning star: Dirt. Pitted against Dirt is the Hysterical Housewife caught in the act of battling those grimy collars, gritty floors, greasy dishes, and clogged drains that have brought shame upon her house and reputation.

The plot thickens. Neighbors compete for a wash that is "cleaner than clean." Mothers and daughters gossip about "telltale gray." Friends destroy the perfect bridge party by noticing water spots on the stemware.

But a germ-free bathroom can restore a wife's peace of mind. Outwitting the "Ring Around the Collar" Patrol can save her marriage, and soft, sweet-smelling baseball uniforms can endear her to her children. ("Your Mom sure does love you because she uses Final Touch.")

Who helps H. H. clean up her act so well? Janitor in a Drum, the White Knight, Mr. Clean, and a chorus of knowing male voices who instruct from afar. (Josephine the Plumber, who has never so much as changed a washer, is expected to get right at the sink stains herself.)

A housewife who successfully tames Dirt still runs the risk of disaster at mealtimes. Her mother-in-law might find her spaghetti sauce thin, her kids might not like her green beans, and worst of all, her husband might commit coffee infidelity: accept a second cup from another woman's pot!

It's easy and fun to mock commercial messages, but how many realize that the real mockery is of us, the millions who are molded and moved by their sex role propaganda:

- Women's products are *essential* to her "femininity." Men's products only *add* to his appeal.
- A man's voice can sell a woman bras or feminine deodorant because male approval is supposed to motivate and reassure women. A woman's voice never sells a man's product unless she's purring the sexual tease.
- Women's self-improvement is hinged to others. ("No headache is going to make me snap at my child.") Men do things for themselves. (*The Wall Street Journal* is for the "man on the move.")
- Men care about how something is made, how it works, and whether it will last; women care only about how it looks.
- "Here's to good times . . ." Beer "quenches a man's thirst" because "one crack at life is all a man gets." Beer is a masculine beverage drunk by men in locker rooms and taverns despite the marketing fact that most beer is bought by women for home consumption.
- Tea is a "feminine" drink—though British men seem unaware of it. In America, if you want to get a man to drink tea, you need a sports hero to tell him it's okay. Then, for good measure, you need sexual innuendo: "Don Meredith is a Lipton Tea lover."
- Men take no-nonsense showers; women take narcissistic baths. That's because men have to get on with all the important things but women can soak in the tub.
- Women will buy products even if you show them as scatterbrained fools who squeeze the Charmin and panic over "housitosis." Men must be sold on the facts.
- If dirt and food are "feminine," travel and locomotion are in the men's column. Airlines are "the wings of man," but they offer "take me along" rates for the wife. Men are on camera when the commercial touts engine construction or on-time schedules; women sell the lure of sexy faraway places.

- Automobiles named for animals (Cougar, Pinto) and weapons (Dart, Javelin) are transparent virility symbols. Although women bought 42 percent of the first million Mustangs sold, it wasn't until 1977 that Ford briefly ran its "women's commercial": *Mustang gives me the feeling I can be everything a woman can be.*

New York N.O.W. studied 1,241 commercials and found only 0.3 percent of the women in them leading independent lives. That's only 3 full human beings in a 1,000. What are our children learning about womankind from the other 997 clean freaks and food fetishists? And are we letting them believe that love and intimacy can be summed up by "Good coffee is grounds for marriage"?

News

In a one-month survey of three local California stations, the American Association of University Women watched 5,353 straight news stories and counted only 523 that included women at all—most of whom were victims of kidnaps, rapes, murders, and disaster.

My own seven-month study of network news turned up serious inadequacies in their supposed "public service":

- General interest stories (energy or employment, for instance) are reported as if they affect only men. Rarely are women experts asked to comment, or women-in-the-street asked their reactions to events other than fashion or gossip.
- Networks devote more time to either sports or weather than to activities of 53 percent of the population.
- They sensationalize women's stories. (Coverage of a women's equality march focuses on the one man carrying a "male chauvinist pig" banner, or the one woman wearing a helmet and combat boots.) Thus girls are unlikely to see women activists as role models, and boys' schoolyard ridicule of "tomboys" and "women's libbers" is reinforced.
- Networks undervalue events that would be given historic weight if men, not women, were the subjects. For example, they ignored the formation of the Coalition of Labor Union Women. Had men representing fifty-eight separate trades gotten together across union and industry loyalties, it would have been the top story of the day.
- They label women by maternal status. Golda Meir was always "grandmotherly," but Menachim Begin, of similar age and type, was never "grandfatherly."
- Feature stories favor women who are attached to prominent men (Margaret Trudeau, former Canadian "first lady," rather than Margaret Atwood, the Canadian novelist).
- They emphasize conflict and ignore harmony. Two women arguing instantly attracts the camera. Two hundred women forging a coalition can't get ten seconds.
- They "lighten" the news at women's expense. (The low point of this genre was Tex Antoine's comment on a rape report: "If rape is inevitable, relax and enjoy it," a comment Antoine regretted only when he learned the victim was a child.)

News is supposed to be the only acre of the "wasteland" that prides itself on fairness and objectivity, yet both its *subject* and its *target viewer* are almost always male. Two examples:

- After announcing that Princeton University's valedictorian *and* salutatorian were both women, NBC's commentator smirked: "If it's any comfort to male chauvinists, the valedictorian at least is the *daughter* of a Princeton man!"
- At CBS, one newscaster hoped out loud that the "women around your house" aren't kicking up trouble like those on the news.

I somehow doubt that the networks would let its people reassure whites that the black-looking valedictorian is at least the child of a white man, or hope that the "blacks around your neighborhood" don't kick up trouble.

If children cannot get gender-blind objectivity and fairness on the news, then it's questionable whether TV has it to give.

Sports

Men's sports dominate the imagination of America partly because men's sports dominate the small screen. There's no telling what passionate devotees of women's sports we might be if women's games were telecast as extensively as men's; or what sports jobs women might hold if not for sexist ridicule, such as this from KING–TV, Seattle:

> The New York State Supreme Court goofed today. They ruled that a 41-year-old housewife from Queens can be an umpire in professional baseball. . . . Assuming Mrs. Gera is a lady, her position isn't behind the plate in baseball, but behind the plate in the kitchen provided by her frustrated husband.

Bernice Gera, a graduate of an accredited U.S. school for umpires, eventually quit baseball rather than stand the harassment she got on and off the field.

Girl athletes may quit before they begin unless networks and local sports departments do better than they did early in the seventies when NBC devoted 365 hours to men's sports and 1 hour to women, and CBS managed 10 women's sports hours to 260 for the men.

Game Shows

A network vice president explains how the game show is tuned to the housewife's cleaning routine:

> That's why we have buzzers and chimes and bells that tell her each step of the progress of the game . . . so she can rush back into the room for the jackpot question. By the time late morning or afternoon rolls around, the chores are finished . . . and she can sit down, relax and watch her serials!

What does this pragmatic programming mean for the young child who is at home with the homemaker?

Since the quiz questions are usually too sophisticated to be even subliminally educational for preschoolers, what children absorb is the sex role "theater" of the game shows: the bells and buzzers, the frantic contenders, manufactured tension, and outlandish prizes; the fact that most of the contestants are women and all of the hosts are men.

"The MC has to be in charge," says a CBS V.P. "When a female does this, somehow it doesn't work."

After a while it might "work"—if the image of a female in charge was ever allowed to register on the retina long enough. But game shows prefer to use women at their least "in charge" and most childish—squealing, jumping up and down, begging, performing for a prize—while the MC teases and comforts like a dog trainer.

As contestant after contestant introduces herself as "just a housewife" or "mother of five" (who else can be at a TV studio at 10 in the morning?), children conclude that homemakers can't buy their own prizes; things must be given to them or won by chance with the benign assistance of Big Daddy.

How Children Are Affected

> It's not the church which interests me, but the congregation. . . . A television set without viewers doesn't interest me.
>
> —*Jerzy Koszinski*

What about the littlest congregation? How do we know if television's sex role propaganda is sinking in or leaving scars?

First, listen to your kids recite advertising jingles verbatim (how much poetry do they know by heart?) and think about the sheer mass of rote learning involved. From Davy Crockett hats in my youth to the family tree fads inspired by *Roots*, from Farrah Fawcett's hairstyle to The Fonz's

"Aaaayyy," television's awesome power to teach and children's susceptibility to imitation cannot be missed.

Advertisers have always understood the power of "role models" to affect behavior, even if parents haven't. Bacon and eggs were banned from breakfast scenes in one show because its sponsor, a cereal manufacturer, knew kids would follow the hero's example and eat bacon and eggs. Years ago, the cigarette sponsor of a crime show instructed scriptwriters not to show "any disreputable person" smoking. Cigarettes were for the good guys.

If children copied only the *style* of their heroes, I'd be unconcerned, but they model the *behavior*, and as we've seen, heroes free of sex stereotyped behavior are few and far between. Thus, kids transform idealized sexist behavior into future aspirations.

Heavy viewers, aged three to twelve, held more stereotypical views of occupational sex roles than did light viewers of TV. In another study, when eight-to-eleven-year-olds were asked "Are there any people on TV that you want to be like when you grow up?" boys named more TV characters as models than did girls—which makes sense, given television's more frequent and more positive male characters. Boys often explained their choices on the basis of strength or toughness; girls chose a role model because she was "pretty" or "dressed nice"—probably the most favorable attributes that one could ascribe to TV's women.

Nevertheless, the main finding of this study is remarkably encouraging: after exposure to five somewhat counter-stereotypical women (the school principal on *Lucas Tanner*, the police officers on *Get Christie Love* and *Police Woman*, the park ranger on *Sierra*, and the TV producer on *Mary Tyler Moore*), children of both sexes were much more likely to say it was appropriate for girls to try for such jobs.

In a comparable experiment, children shown some specially prepared commercials that portrayed women in traditionally male jobs later endorsed those occupations as suitable for women; kids who saw standard commercials did not.

Before it went into reruns, *All in the Family*, the most provocative adult program on TV, was also the program with the largest young audience: every show was seen by nine million kids under twelve. A researcher interviewed 320 representative children about their favorite characters on the show. The top draws were Archie, because he "yells at Edith when she acts so stupid," Edith, because "she was nice no matter how mad Archie got," and Gloria, because she was "pretty" and "nice."

The study concluded that what had the greatest impact on most children was not the moral/ethical lessons that were the focus of the show, but the physical appearance of the characters, the role stereotypes, and the comedy behavior associated with them.

MATERIALISM: SEXISM'S FINANCIAL PAYOFF

A drawing in a children's book shows a little girl basking in the light of a boy's homemade lamp. The picture is captioned: "Boys invent things. Girls use what boys invent."

In rather more elaborate form, this is the principle that supports the economy of a patriarchal society. "Boys invent things, girls use them" extrapolates to a larger economic principle: "Men make things; women buy them." Men are the producers, women the consumers. The only production culturally approved for women is reproduction; women and their "product," children, together make a market of users for the things that men produce.

The number of commercials directed at women far exceeds those directed at men.

Advertisers estimate that women do up to 85 percent of the purchasing in America. And they *know* that the modern housewife buys more than the woman who works outside the home. That's why the sex role formula means to keep each woman isolated in her nuclear household, feeling inadequate to her cleaning tasks, wondering if she's as good a wife and mother as the next woman, and worrying about her fading looks. The only way to "do" something about her problems is to *buy* the promised solutions: Youth in a cream, fulfilment in a can, love in a brand name. Ad men characterize spending as "decision-making" in the supermarket and "accomplishment" at the cash register.

Despite convenience foods and labor-saving devices, as we've noted, the homemaker spends more hours at housework and shopping today than sixty years ago. "The housewife is urged to find new crevices to clean and higher standards of innovation and creativity against which to measure her domestic abilities."

Women in the labor force spend less than half as much time at housework as housewives and don't, as a general rule, live less hygienic or civilized lives. However, these women who clean less compulsively use fewer products and spend less money.

So advertisers glamorize homemaking, to make it a noble and "natural" calling, to create a full-time job out of keeping the self and others clean and fed. How? Romanticize routine, the thrilling waxed floor and so on, and if you're lucky, a woman won't realize she's working up to 99 hours a week without pay, and probably without much appreciation either.

The mercantile payoff of TV's sex role images is the manufacture of a class of female people who labor "for love," stay out of the job marketplace, and buy the products that make the male-run economy run so well without them.

What has all this to do with children?

Like many women, children are not producers. Linked to women by the caretaking relationship and by their shared "weakness" (embodied in the rescue call "women and children first"), kids are seen by advertisers as conduits to mothers.

In Vance Packard's words, children are "consumer-trainees." If they can be taught to *want* things, to *need* things, to spend and to make their mothers spend, they are useful to men's economy. The cynicism is not my own. Listen to an adman's view:

> When you sell a woman on a product and she goes into the store and finds your brand isn't in stock, she'll probably forget about it. But when you sell a kid on your product, if he can't get it, he will throw himself on the floor, stamp his feet and cry. You can't get a reaction like that from an adult.

Mothers succumb to kids' entreaties because, as we have seen, a mother's role is to make her children happy. To reach her through her persuasive child consumer, sponsors buy time on cartoon shows and children's programs that give advertisers a clear path to the child's psyche.

> Before the advent of television, it was almost impossible for an advertiser or a salesman to reach a young child without first encountering a protective adult. Door-to-door selling was dealt with by a parent, the salesman was barred from the classroom and magazine and newspaper ads were beyond the comprehension of most children under the age of nine or ten. With television, however, all this has changed.

The "talking furniture" that babysits for children, that supposedly makes Mom's day easier and kids' lives livelier, is actually a shill for man's economic gain. The show excuses the sell. *We'll be right back after this word . . .*—and the word is exploitation.

> The exploitation of children's appetites brought the networks nearly a quarter of their total profits for the year.

Mothers knock themselves out planning nutritional meals, schools teach balanced diets, health experts warn of empty calories and mood-altering additives, but television beats them all with a few well-chosen words about Choco Puffs.

Exploitation of dissatisfaction is another "consuming" device: making children dissatisfied with their toys and other possessions means parents will feel guilty about not providing what the child wants and what kids on television have. The pressure is felt most by the "masculine" provider. Fathers have to work harder and spend beyond their means to alleviate the dissatisfaction. Then the materialism that makes them work longer hours also requires them to buy more things to make up for their increased absences and to prove their love, materially. Dissatisfaction is bad for family life, but oh so good for business.

Exploitation of feelings of inferiority has the same result: "Step right up, ladies, your natural skin, hair, and everything you do are inadequate, but luckily, perfection is yours for a price while supplies last."

That message is brought to you by the same people who promise children "strength, energy, athletic prowess, almost anything short of sexual satisfaction for the use of certain products."

All children feel small, insufficient, and overwhelmed by events beyond their control. By suggesting that a toy or snack can bestow power or make children happy, commercials teach the First Commandment of a materialistic society: *You are what you own*. With television's help, the lesson will last a lifetime.

Advertisers' argument that commercials give children an education in consumerism collapses in the face of reason. If kids can't touch, taste, or try advertised products, and haven't lived long enough to compare products on claims alone, how are they learning good buying habits?

When they do buy something and it falls short of its video glories, as too often is the case, they've learned only that grown-ups are free to deceive children and that people are allowed to make things that don't work and aren't good for you. Children are not educated into the consumer economy, they're educated to be cynics and spenders in the profitable land of patriarchy.

VIOLENCE: SEXISM'S "HIT MAN"

If commercials are the appetizer and dessert of each TV time slot, violence is its main course, the meat and potatoes that make the sponsor's message stick to your ribs. "To the advertiser, violence equals excitement equals ratings."

How much violence? Three in ten programs are "saturated" with it or the threat of it; cartoons contain an average of one aggressive act per minute; and overall, an hour of children's "entertainment" contains six times more violence than an hour of adult fare. It adds up to some "18,000 murders and countless detailed incidents of robbery, arson, bombing, forgery, smuggling, beating and torture" seen by each American child between birth and eighteen.

The blood and bullets have attracted a lot of attention—from the White House Task Force on the Media, to the Surgeon General's Scientific Advisory Committee on Television and Social Behavior, to parent and child advocacy groups locally and nationally, all of whom have lobbied, held hearings or issued reports that made headlines—even on television.

Meanwhile, the networks issued denials, recruited educational advisors, appointed special vice presidents for children's programming, and declared themselves serious about self-regulation. They were very showy throughout the seventies about their "commitment" to children's well-being.

Yet in March 1977, Dr. George Gerbner, who tallies the annual *Violence Profile*, told

Congress that all three networks showed more incidents of extreme violence during the previous year than in any of the preceding ten years; in fact the percentage of programs showing violent acts "rose to the highest on record." At the close of the seventies, sex was edging out violence in prime time. But whether [the] annual violence quotient rises or falls by a few points, the basic tolerance and justifications of violence persist—and most parents don't like it.

Who's at fault? Advertisers say they're only paying for what people want to see. Producers say they need "action" or viewers get bored. The networks say, in effect, just because violence riddles the tube doesn't mean children are adversely affected or moved to commit violence. Some even claim TV action has a cathartic effect. But child specialists find it disturbs and upsets kids:

> They cannot understand why Tom keeps hitting Jerry; they worry about how much it hurts. As a result they themselves feel confused and vulnerable.

Children who watch many hours of TV suffer an increase in nightmares, fears, and appetite disturbances. They develop greatly distorted ideas about death and suffering. Their behavior is altered in small and large ways. They become insensitive to the sight of someone being hurt. They use violent scenarios as a guide for their own actions when playing with others. They are capable of reproducing hostile acts exactly as they saw them on TV eight months earlier. When given the opportunity to either help or hurt a child in need, kids were more likely to *hurt* after seeing a fighting scene than after seeing an exciting sports event. And an appalling number of juvenile crimes—torture, kidnappings, rapes, and murders—have been traced to events portrayed on television dramas.

Most sobering of all, I think, is this fact that affects all children, not just the criminal few: Kids who watch four or more hours of TV a day tend to overestimate the number of violent crimes that happen in real life and exaggerate the danger of their own victimization. Children needn't mimic violence to be damaged by it; they are wounded spiritually by the *fear* of violence and the suspicion that they are unsafe in our world.

One sex is influenced more than the other:

> A boy's television habits at age eight are more likely to be a predictor of his aggressiveness at age eighteen or nineteen than his family's socioeconomic status, his relationship with his parents, his IQ or any other single factor in his environment.

Correlations between aggressiveness and TV-watching do not hold for girls. Why? Because although television teaches both sexes how to be aggressive, boys learn that men are rewarded for it while girls learn that women are punished for it.

When television's female characters are involved in violent situations, their usual role is victim. In the relatively few instances when women are aggressors, they are less successful than men and less likely to get away with it. As victims, they are more likely to be single than married. As villains, they are more often working women than housewives.

Kids get the message, the moral, and the role models all rolled into one. The most powerful characters on television are males who are young, white, middle class, single, involved in violence and not only not punished for it, but usually rewarded with admiration and possessions—including beautiful women. Independent women end up victims of violence; married women and housewives who fulfill their proper role are spared some death and villainy. Violence by bad guys is punished because it's unjustified. Violence by good guys is justified ". . . for reasons of vengeance or self-defense or both."

Violence does pay when you're a good guy defending your manhood—or when you're a vast patriarchal institution like television, defending your team's social order.

Violence is the "hit man" for sexism, the last-ditch defender of the status quo, the gold coin of man's realm. To devalue it is to divest men of their ultimate advantage over women: that is, when all other power politics fail, a man has his muscles.

The mere capability of inflicting physical pain upon the female lies like a sleeping tiger in the male body—even in those who never batter, rape, or kill. But on behalf of all *man*kind, television lets the tiger off the leash, reminding us that it's there and showing us what happens to female pussies and housecats who overstep their bounds. . . .

TEXTBOOKS

Problems arise when instructional materials have sexism as their subtext, when they omit women's past achievements, misrepresent present options for both sexes, and when they call sex stereotypes "right" answers. A sampling:

> *History text*: beginning in 1492, not one woman is mentioned for the first 150 years of American history.
>
> *A music book* for primary grades contains these sex-specific ditties:
>
> *Boys' March*
>
> *I am a boy, marching along*
> *When I grow up, I will be strong*
> *I'll be a man for the world to see*
> *building a home, for my family.*
> *I'm a boy. I'm a boy, a fine boy.*
>
> *Girls' Ballet*
> *Girls like to dance a waltz, a ballet,*
> *Girls like to skip or gracefully sway.*
> *Girls like to play dress up and pretend.*
> *Girls like a party and girls like a friend.*
> *Because I'm a girl, I whirl and whirl.*
>
> *Kindergarten reading readiness text* shows a boy saying "I can cut," "I can dig," and a girl saying "I can dust," "I can mop."
>
> *Advice in a secretarial manual* supposedly for use by both sexes: "Wear fresh lingerie always."
>
> *Mental health text*: "A boy who does not have much athletic ability compensates by developing his hobby of photography. A girl who worries about being awkward joins a Y class in modern dance so that she will become more graceful."
>
> *World history*: in 877 pages of a book called, appropriately, *Men and Nations*, five pages are devoted to Napoleon III, described as a "mediocrity" (not to be confused with Napoleon I), while Queen Elizabeth I, called "one of the greatest of English rulers," gets one paragraph.
>
> *Ecology book*: Rachel Carson, the only woman in the book, is described as "bright and pretty" and "modest and gracious" when she takes on the chemical industry.
>
> *Vocational interest inventory*: Boys: would you like to "travel to outer space" or "explore the bottom of the ocean?" Girls: would you rather "marry a rancher" or "marry a corporation president?"
>
> *Government text, high school*: the index lists 246 men and 9 women. One of the 9, "Mrs. Ulysses S. Grant," is represented on page 243 by a picture of her inaugural gown.
>
> *Third-grade math*:
> Mary's way: $2 + 2 + 2 + 2 + 2 + 2 = 12$
> Jack's way: $2 \times 6 = 12$

Some of the bias is gratuitous. Math problems have boys computing large sums, distances, and speed while girls (when they are not doing math the dumb way) are measuring dress fabric, adding the grocery bill, and learning fractions via pie slices. Whatever the educational intent, the problems add up to boys make rockets, girls make dessert; his eye is on the stars, hers is on the oven.

Some textbooks push sex roles flagrantly: "home economics" speaks to the housewife-mother, "family life" portrays the life of the (usually white, usually middle-class) nuclear family, "health and sex education" assumes an aggressive male and a passive female, and "career" materials seem years behind occupational realities.

And some textbooks—especially in science and history—commit the sin of omission, neglecting female contributions almost to the vanishing point. Other than Eleanor Roosevelt, Harriet Beecher Stowe, Betsy Ross, and Helen Keller, if ten great women and their achievements can be found in a sixth-grade history book, it's a bonanza.

One searches in vain for a book that gives full credit to Marie Curie without giving equal or more credit to her husband, Pierre; or for an accurate portrayal of Maria Mitchell and other women astronomers or inventors; for a high school text that pays serious attention to the suffrage movement and the long parallels between racism and sexism in this country; or the courageous battle for the right to contraception and reproductive freedom (which has revolutionized modern life); or the changing roles of women and men in families, business and government.

Title IX does not prohibit the publication or use of biased textbooks, for fear of tampering with publishers' First Amendment rights. So it's up to us to identify objectionable materials, bring them to the attention of teachers and administrators, and pressure publishers to produce texts that are nonsexist, nonracist, creative, and accurate. . . .

CURRICULUM

A school's curriculum, meaning course content and recreational programs, can make equality either an imperative or an impossibility, depending on what information and skills are taught to which students in what facilities and with how many resources.

Most public schools are coeducational. (Title IX and a Supreme Court decision permit sex-segregated schools as long as the education they provide is "separate but equal," but most previously single-sex schools have voluntarily integrated their enrollment.) "Coeducational" does not, however, seem to mean equal-educational. In 1977, the government found nearly two-thirds of the nation's schools had "failed to meet legal requirements for banning sex discrimination in classes and activities." And a 1979 report ranking schools in all fifty states still found "galloping apathy toward the needs of today's girls."

Consider a few past complaints:

- Five- and six-year-olds were placed in sex-segregated classes in a coed school on the theory that girls' presence may be detrimental to boys.
- Elementary school boys could choose from nine different sports, girls from only four—among them, "slimnastics."
- Three junior high school girls were refused admission to the school's carpentry class.
- While all the boys' teams were outfitted to the letter, the thirty-six-member girls' field hockey team had to share eleven pairs of shoes and twelve warm-up suits.
- An assignment in the girls' home economics curriculum: washing the boys' football uniforms.

While these inequities are dramatic and concrete, others take the form of subtle tracking and gender type-casting.

The Making of Math Phobia

Studies show that more boys than girls have been math-encouraged at home, yet in elementary school, girls do about as well in math as boys. Until eighth grade or so. Then, when math begins to be typecast as "masculine" and math talent marks a girl as "unfeminine," math participation and performance dip precipitously. By high school graduation, only 8 percent of girls have four years of math to their credit, compared to 57 percent of boys.

A curriculum that does not take this socioemotional phenomenon into account, and compensate for it, is by inaction teaching girls "math anxiety." This is not a cute deficiency but rather a severe handicap. High school math is the "critical filter" for many satisfying careers. For instance, the four-year high school math sequence is required for admission to courses that in turn "are required for majoring in every field at the University of California except the traditional female (and hence lower-paying) fields." Math proficiency adds 36 percent to a girl's future income.

Teachers seem to recognize this when it comes to counseling boys to take advanced math "because they'll probably need it." But sex stereotypes clog the critical filter and advisors tend to coddle girls with, "Oh well, you're probably not going to be a physicist, so why ruin your grade average?"

I myself was a sweaty-palm victim of math anxiety. I took a "Mind Over Math" course when I was in my thirties, and discovered, some twenty years too late, to trust my "math intuition," to check my findings against the "reasonableness test," and to give up two beliefs drummed into me as a girl: "If it's not difficult, it's not math," and "Girls have no head for figures."

Until the curriculum gets rid of these beliefs and gives every girl the psychic and academic keys to math confidence, too few will discover that numbers can be as agreeable as words—and up to twice as profitable.

Science, Too

Much that can be said of math may be said of science, too. Several have said it, *and* done something about it, adding women's scientific accomplishments to the male-focus of the curriculum, and sponsoring conferences and counseling to dispel myths about women in scientific and technical careers. The National Science Foundation, for example, brings women chemists, physicists, and biologists into tenth-grade classrooms to motivate girls, help them pinpoint their interests, and to serve as role models for the "normalcy" of the scientific female.

Humanities for the Other Half of Humanity

If female deprivation centers on the math-science curriculum, boys are most likely missing out in the humanities. Under the flag of sexism, many have picked up the impression that English courses and foreign languages are "feminine," that accents (especially French) are fey, and that literature is for "ladies," not for life.

Because it is well known that boys do poorly on tasks they believe to be "girlish" (since the "opposite" sex should do "opposite" things), the responsive curriculum will use radical methods to attract boys to poetry, and expose them to writers of both sexes, to literary careers, work opportunities for the bi-lingual, and the superior pleasures of foreign travel when one speaks the native tongue.

Social Relations: Teaching "to Live" as Well as "to Know"

Sex education and family life courses are the curriculum areas where sex role training can be most pernicious. Common complaints:

- Experts from fifteen countries recommend sex education be designed for "the enhancement of life and personal relationships" and not just for dealing with "procreation or sexually transmitted diseases." They also agree that the cult of male dominance "makes it difficult to introduce the idea of sexual enjoyment for both partners."

- "Despite the fact that most students are single and nonengaged, the present focus of most family/sex education courses at this age is not on dating but on marriage."
- Student: "I'm tired of watching that ovum come bouncing down the fallopian tube; I want to know how girls feel about petting."
- Kids get "the miracle of new life," love, monogamy, marriage, intercourse for procreation, and pollination of flowers. What kids need is masturbation, the clitoris, venereal disease, homosexuality, contraception, and a clear connection between penis-in-vagina and teenage pregnancy.
- Student: "I already know all about girls. I want to know about boys and what they think about us. Why can't boys and girls have sex ed together so we can ask each other questions?"

At best, sex education is given once a week for 45 minutes. When we realize that human sexuality plays a far larger part in a person's life than basketball or British dynasties—and when we remember the data on parental silence and children's ignorance . . .—the low priority of sex education becomes a shameful failure of the school system. We need more sex ed and better sex ed. What is taught now in many classes makes the information kids pick up in the streets seem sage by comparison. Courses present sex as pathology, biology, or mythology; the male urge is the female's responsibility; V.D. is something girls carry and boys get; the girl does not "do," she is "done to."

Family life courses offer a prudish, moralizing view of marriage. Child care remains women's work and the parent role is seen as a biological inevitability, not an option and not an aptitude. Many still portray "the family" as Mommy-Daddy-baby; the props are an apron for her and a briefcase for him; everyone goes to church; and divorce is an unfortunate thing that happens to "other people."

TEACHER ATTITUDES

The teachers' sex role ideology is the third potential sore spot in the hidden curriculum. Most teachers perceive girls and boys as "significantly different" before any particular girl or boy takes a seat in the classroom. As a result, not surprisingly, studies also show that "boys and girls do not necessarily have similar experiences in the same classroom."

Like most of us, teachers who are not conscious of the damaging effects of sex stereotypes tend to act on them. But unlike most of us, in the course of a career, a teacher influences hundreds or even thousands of children.

Ask a third-grade teacher, say, to picture a normal child who is disruptive . . . loves to read . . . likes to help Mommy . . . would make a good audio-visual assistant . . . and the images that come to mind will very likely be sex-specific in each case. Teachers often make class jobs gender-linked and segregate girls and boys in line-ups, spelling bees, and study projects, giving official sanction to the destructive us–them dichotomy. . . .

Classroom events pay sex role dividends in maturity. Being placed on the "girls' line" becomes a mortifying punishment for a boy, and in later life a man finding himself in a female group, no matter how elite the women, feels a diminution of his status. Similarly, being excluded from audio-visual or other "boys' jobs" trains girls to accept discriminatory hiring as women's lot.

What the teacher does or says is not trivial. It is authoritative and *educational*. Everything matters. Everything sinks in. Yet, just as school cafeteria workers didn't realize "that they were automatically serving the boys bigger portions" until they were observed, teachers do not realize all the ways they treat the sexes differently.

- *Math teacher*: "Girls, you'll never be able to follow a recipe if you don't learn fractions."

- *Fifth-grade teacher* (ignoring that several girls tower over boys in the class): "May I have two strong boys to carry the chairs."
- *Industrial arts*: "After I show everyone how to do this, the boys will help the girls get it right."
- *Girl in a chemistry class*: "When my experiment exploded, my teacher said, 'Isn't that just like a girl.' But I know for a fact that last semester all the explosions were caused by boys."
- *On a class field trip*, passing a car junkyard, a male teacher quipped: "There's women's greatest contribution to the world."
- *Letter from principal to parents*: "The girls are permitted to wear slacks under a dress for our physical education program *only*. I'm all for equality, but I think girls should look like girls—and if that means skirts or dresses, so be it." (Incidentally, discriminatory dress codes are illegal under Title IX.)
- *When a high school history teacher* suggested a Women's Studies course be introduced into the curriculum, her (male) department chairman protested, "But when will the students get *real* history?"

Observers in many classrooms have found more subtle but even more damaging forms of sex bias than these teachers verbalize. Remember the reasoning . . . that gives rise to the cult of sex differences: *the two sexes are different . . . the two sexes are opposites . . . one sex is better than the other*. Since teachers have been found to subscribe to the first two tenets, inevitably they subscribe to the third. However, they split up their perception of "better": they think girls are better behaved, but boys have better brains, bodies, and value in society.

This means that although girls seem to be teachers' pets, preferred by predominantly women teachers in the supposedly "feminizing" environment of the school, it is actually boys who are favored because of teachers' more deeply held beliefs about male worth. Conventional sex role ideology may make them think of a boy as "the student who gives teachers trouble," but it also makes them give a boy more attention, more help, and more *teaching*. One educator explains:

> Because girls are considered to be neater, better-behaved, and harder-working, teachers assume that they are already doing the best they can. Because boys are considered to be sloppier and less diligent by nature, teachers tend to tell them, "You can do better. You're just not trying hard enough." The boys believe it. They do try harder, and do better.

Studies have shown that from nursery school on, teachers (most, not all of course) shape children's learning styles and dependence behaviors differently according to sex. They talk to boys more than girls and interact more with boys, whether "asking questions, criticizing, accepting or rejecting ideas, giving approval and disapproval," or listening to them. Girls volunteer answers more often than boys but are called on less often.

Teachers do a task for a girl, but give boys *eight* times as much detailed instruction in how to solve problems for themselves.

Teachers interact with boys wherever they may be in the classroom, which lets boys move about independently without risking neglect, but teachers respond to girls mainly when they are nearby, which inspires clingy, help-seeking dependency.

Teachers have clearer perceptions of boys' characteristics and abilities than of girls'. They spend more time with boys than girls, including in cooking and sewing classes. They have different expectations of the two sexes in line with gender stereotypes.

In a shop class, for instance, girls started the term full of confidence but ended up turned off—"not because girls couldn't learn to enjoy working with their hands, but because, by and large, the teachers treated them as *though* they couldn't." Teacher preconceptions become student profiles.

> Teachers generally prefer males to females, and they like children who fit sex stereotypes better than those who do not. In one survey, teachers said they like male students because they were more outspoken, active, willing to exchange

ideas, honest and easy to talk to. The only characteristic that endeared female students to them was their lower frequency of disciplinary problems.

Most male teachers show the same patterns and attitudes as female teachers except that they also give boys more leadership positions than girls. In any case, whether the differentiated attention is outright favoritism or comes in the form of "control messages" given to boys in "harsh and angry tones," it is still more attention. It results in an "increase in independent, autonomous behavior by boys."

With all this research data in mind, let's put a few ironies in the fire. Most of the national concern among educators seems focused on boys' being discriminated against, not girls'. The big worry is about boys' stultified physical activity and boys' reading problems in the early grades, not girls' total educational swindle and lifelong math and science handicap. The cures proposed range from paying men more money to attract them to early childhood teaching where they are in short supply (with no concomitant proposal to attract women to college teaching where *they* are under-represented), to single-sex classes in the early grades.

Although nurturant males in early childhood education could provide wonderful male role models, that cure begs the question. If women teachers "feminize" (*i.e.*, weaken, make dependent, squelch the spirit of) boys, aren't they also visiting that harm on girls? If it's not good for boys, why is it all right for girls? And if it is the result of female socialization, why not change the socialization rather than the sex of the teacher?

The answer is to stop "feminizing" anyone (because "feminizing" has come to mean weakness and dependency). And that cannot happen with the second prescription, single-sex classrooms. Besides rigidifying the old us–them division, you get all-girl classes whose teachers like to "orient" instruction to the supposed interests of the girls. As one teacher proudly illustrated the point: "The other day, they counted by tens up to a hundred by shaking up an instant pudding mix."

With all the talk about boys' needs, the fact is that one item on patriarchy's hidden agenda is to teach boys better. That's why, by junior high, boys manage to catch up and surpass girls.

- *Item*: In math, social studies, and science, both sexes are equally proficient at age nine. By thirteen, the girls drop back.
- *Item*: In reading and literature, girls outscore boys until age seventeen, then fall behind.
- *Item*: More girls than boys take the College Boards, but more boys than girls go to college. Girls' high school grade average is higher than boys', but boys score higher on the scholastic aptitude test. (Boys learn to aspire, strive, compete; girls learn to give up.)
- *Item*: Girls most often plan to study education, nursing, and social sciences; boys decide to study biology, business, and engineering. (Do these occupational choices just *happen* to parallel teachers' sex stereotypes and schools' sex-typed courses?)

The only areas in which females continue to outperform males throughout life are writing ability and music.

It is the function of a sex role stereotype to create self-fulfilling prophecies. . . . We've seen that school subjects are gender-linked, and we know that children concentrate on subjects that are gender-appropriate rather than risk sex role conflict. Since sex role *standards* are known long before the age at which sex differences in *performance* appear, the sad truth is that *standards influence performance*. Sixth graders think spatial relations performance is "masculine," but the difference in male and female aptitudes doesn't show up until ninth grade—the *stereotype* of male superiority preceded the *fact* of male superiority by three years!

16

THE MASS MEDIA

Public opinion is profoundly shaped by the mass media for at least three large reasons. First, nearly everything the public learns about politics and government they get from the media. Very few citizens have the chance to observe politicians in action at first hand. Second, journalists must pick the major stories of the day, which amount to only a tiny fraction of the day's happenings. They decide what news is. And third, because the audience for news must be attracted—not coerced—into paying attention, the journalist has to make it interesting. He or she has to impose order on the jumble of events, and then shape the content in dramatic fashion. Therefore, journalists are, and have been for many years, key political actors in the choice of rulers and the choices rulers make.

Women play an increasingly important part in journalism. Back in the nineteenth century, Sarah Josepha Hale managed a national magazine, and in Woodrow Wilson's time Ida Tarbell, the investigative reporter, was one of the best-known journalists in the country. Today television news employs many women in both visible and off-camera roles. Politicians pay enormous sums to get on television, and they spend long hours plotting how to gain the attention of the television journalists who will shape their story for the voters at home. One of those sought-out stars of the network news—and the first woman star—was Barbara Walters. For a time, many a national politician yearned for a chat with her—and her millions of watching friends.

Barbara Walters Anchors the News

by Barbara Matusow

Walters had worked her way up in television news against great odds. When she started out in the 1950s, so few women rose above the level of secretary or re-

From Barbara Matusow, *The Evening Stars: The Making of the Network News Anchor* (Boston: Houghton Mifflin, 1983), pp. 168–74, 178–88.

searcher that few even developed professional aspirations. But Walters was unusually tenacious and hard-working, and she was determined to be noticed. She was also fascinated by celebrities, having grown up around show business personalities as the daughter of Lou Walters, a well-known nightclub proprietor and founder of New York's Latin Quarter. After her graduation from Sarah Lawrence College in 1954, her first ambition was to be an actress, but too many disappointing auditions convinced her to turn elsewhere. Through her father's connections, she landed a job in the publicity department of NBC. That led to a training program in television production, followed by a succession of writing and producing jobs—interspersed with bouts of unemployment. Finally, in 1961, she found a secure berth as a writer-producer on the "Today" show.

"Today" had a format that devoured material, and Walters, who never lacked for ideas, contacts, or energy, soon progressed from writing for others to filming her own reports as "the 'Today' show reporter." She rarely appeared on the set with host Dave Garroway, however. That was an honor reserved for the " 'Today' girls," a succession of actresses and models, including Estelle Parsons, Betsy Palmer, Florence Henderson, and former Miss America Lee Ann Meriwether. Their function was to handle the lighter topics, such as food and fashions, and to add a decorative, feminine note to the proceedings. Evidently it was not an easy role to fill; a total of thirty young women came and went in the first thirteen years of the program. Many of them departed in tears, complaining of harsh treatment by Garroway or other members of the predominantly male staff.

Walters's big break came in 1964, when the " 'Today' girl" of the era, Maureen O'Sullivan, was fired. Coming in the midst of the Democratic national convention in Atlantic City, it left the producers with no time to find another "name," so they reluctantly agreed to give Walters a thirteen-week tryout. (She had applied for the job on two previous occasions but was turned down.) Walters had the support of host Hugh Downs; he quickly let it be known that she was a welcome addition to the cast—"the best thing that's happened to this show in a long time," he said. The audience liked her, too, in spite of the fact that she had a lisp and a sometimes abrasive manner. "I was very serious and didn't have an easy on-air manner," Walters recalls, "but the audience knew me as a reporter and accepted me, and so it worked well. I keep thinking of what Jack Benny once said, 'If they like you, nothing can stop them from liking you, and if they don't like you, nothing can make them like you.' And for whatever reason, the audience accepted me."

If Walters was less of a glamor girl than her predecessors, she was still expected to stick to the women's beat, which bored her. The only way she could do interesting things was to go out and film on her own. Thus it was that she developed her specialty, the celebrity interview. She discovered that, with hard work and perseverance, she could snare such elusive subjects as Princess Grace of Monaco, Britain's Prince Philip, Rose Kennedy, Ingrid Bergman, Fred Astaire, and Rex Harrison. She also discovered that it was helpful to know these people socially, that they were frequently willing to do her favors, celebrity to celebrity. As she became better known herself, her subjects became curious about *her*, so it grew easier to draw them out.

She proved as adept at handling serious subjects as she was at celebrity chitchat. An interview in 1968 with then–Secretary of State Dean Rusk (also a Barbara Walters fan) was deemed so impressive it ran as a series over five days. Not everyone liked Walters's style, of course, but many were fascinated with her unorthodox, sometimes daring approach, bringing up subjects that other interviewers wouldn't dream of broaching. Who but Barbara Walters would have asked Mamie Eisenhower if she was aware of the rumors that she drank, or probed Lady Bird Johnson's feelings about her late husband's reputation as a womanizer? Walters could put guests in their place occasionally, too. Once, after eliciting little more than bored grunts from Warren Beatty, she ended the interview by throwing up her hands and saying, "Oh, let's just forget the whole thing."

All in all, the Downs years were a boon to Walters. Though he held center stage on "Today," Downs gave her plenty of latitude. She was becoming one of the most sought-after speakers on the lecture circuit, and her book, *How to Talk to Practically Anybody About Practically Anything*, was a best-seller. NBC seemed to give no thought to elevating her to the role of co-host, but she and her agents were quietly laying their plans.

In 1971, after Hugh Downs left the "Today" show and Frank McGee took over as host, Walters was reminded of how precarious her professional situation still was, despite her rise as the pre-eminent woman in television news. McGee had been a member of the ill-fated troika experiment on the NBC Nightly News, and he regarded the shift to "Today" as a demotion. "He never really accepted the fact that he had to do the morning show," says Walters, "and he certainly didn't like sharing it with a woman, especially not one who did serious interviews." McGee arranged with the producers to pick his interviews; Walters was handed the leftovers. He also had the right to decide whether or not Barbara could participate in *his* interviews. It was understood that if she *was* allowed to join in, he asked the first question. Once again, the only way to assure herself a featured role on the program was to pursue big names and high government officials and film them outside the studio.

NBC had finally taken notice of her "star" quality, however, and she began receiving occasional prestige reporting assignments, such as President Ford's trip to China. One of only three female reporters on the trip, Walters impressed a number of NBC executives there with her dedication and professionalism. "Barbara was tops," says Lee Hanna, who was vice president of news programming at the time. "She worked about fifteen or sixteen hours a day in China, and she had marvelous contacts. Even if it wasn't her assignment and had nothing to do with her, you could count on her to get on the phone and check a story out."

Walters worked hard to cultivate her contacts, which she did in a highly personal fashion that differed from the way most reporters operate. Former White House press secretary Jody Powell says she uses the tactics of a skilled politician. "She remembers to ask about your children, and she has a habit of telephoning with little messages of congratulations or condolences, depending on whether something good or bad has happened." The day after Carter was defeated for re-election in 1980, for example, Walters called to wish Powell well, which impressed him. "These gestures, however sincere they are, can't help but make an impression over the long haul. I'd have to say they're effective."

But Walters did not rely solely on personal gestures and flattery to cultivate the powerful; she was resourceful, as well. At the Conference of Non-Aligned Nations in Cuba, she wanted to line up interviews with King Hussein of Jordan, Yasir Arafat, and Fidel Castro, but tight security kept her from getting near the principals. Her solution was to send them notes. To King Hussein she wrote. "Dear Your Majesty. Can we confirm our interview? I'm sitting in the press gallery in a pink blouse. Wave if you can see me. Barbara Walters." A messenger delivered the notes to the three leaders, who, upon receiving them, could be seen scanning the press box—and waving. She got her interviews.

If the definition of a journalist is someone who recognizes a news story, knows how to go after the facts and present them effectively, Walters certainly qualifies. But in television, reporters are not thought to have "paid their dues" unless they have spent long years in the field, trudging through rain and snow, covering natural disasters, or enduring endless "stakeouts" in front of courthouses or embassies. These are unpleasant, exhausting, dirty assignments—performed for years almost exclusively by men—and any reporter who has not done enough of them is unlikely to be regarded as a card-carrying journalist by other members of the profession. Surviving these rigors is no real proof of editorial ability, but the tradition persists. Walters had handled many field assignments throughout her career, but most of her experience in television was spent inside a studio, interviewing guests—generally deemed to be a lower order of journalism. Even within the NBC News hierarchy, a number of executives didn't take her seriously as a newswoman, in spite of her proven editorial abilities. Her colleague, Frank McGee, certainly did not accept her as an equal, treating her with icy condescension. He seldom spoke to her off camera, but if he did pay her a compliment after a particularly good effort, it was apt to be something cutting like, "We'll make a journalist out of you yet, Barbara." Walters and McGee were too professional to let their antagonism surface on the air, however; after McGee died of cancer in 1974, Walters even got letters expressing sympathy for her losing such a close friend. She was always careful not to seem too aggressive in relation to McGee and other male partners. "I was always a little reticent," she admits, "even a little subservient, because I felt that was the best way to be, that it was the most comfortable for the men, and I guess the most comfortable for the audience."

Despite the fact that McGee's illness was no secret, the network was unprepared to replace him when he died. Again, it did not seem to have occurred to anyone to give Walters a chance at the top spot on the program. But in her contract was a clause, forgotten by NBC, that stipulated that if Frank McGee ever left the show, she was to become a co-host. "Nobody expected Frank to leave the show, I guess, and maybe they figured he'd be there for ten years, and they'd worry about it later. Then he died, and I remember they put out all kinds of statements saying they were looking for a new host. And my agents and I very quietly said 'co-host.' NBC said, 'Co-host, co-host? What do you mean, co-host?' But it was in the contract, and that's how—quite literally, over Frank McGee's dead body—I became co-host of the 'Today' show."

Walters's hand was now immeasurably strengthened. Although she did not have veto power over her new partner, she was deeply involved in the selection process, a protracted affair that saw a long procession of NBC newsmen auditioning for the job—Garrick Utley, Tom Brokaw, Douglas Kiker, Bill Monroe, Edwin Newman, Jess Marlow, Floyd Kalber, Tom Snyder. In the end, Walters got the person she wanted: Jim Hartz, a lanky, laid-back, thirty-four-year-old from Oklahoma. A rising star in the NBC firmament in those days, Hartz was also an aviation buff, replacing McGee as the network's premier space expert. With Hartz co-anchoring on "Today," the tension on the set disappeared, much to the relief of the staff. The executive producer, Stuart Schulberg, told a reporter that Hartz brought a "warm, sane, stable quietude to 'Today.' " But "quietude" may not have been what viewers were looking for at that hour; the program lost a sizable number of viewers during the Walters-Hartz era—some of them lured away by ABC's new morning program, "Good Morning America," and its folksy host, David Hartman.

Walters, who had wanted to move on to other things for some time, now felt a certain urgency about leaving "Today," before her reputation as a major box office attraction became seriously damaged.

The one job she wanted at NBC, however—co-anchor of the evening news—was closed to her. Chancellor would not agree to it, and a number of executives did not think it was a good idea in any case. Yet NBC was desperately anxious to keep her, eventually offering her as much money as ABC and a promise that she would receive "first consideration" if the network decided to pair Chancellor with someone else.

ABC had no such reservations about using Walters as a co-anchor on the ABC Evening News, but it took a good deal of arm-twisting before Harry Reasoner agreed. He had gained sole custody of the program only a few months earlier and made no secret of the fact that he was hoping to become the next Walter Cronkite. Nor was Walters willing to be harnessed to someone who did not want to work with her; she insisted there could be no deal unless Reasoner gave his wholehearted acceptance. The ABC executives hovered over them like old-fashioned matchmakers, arranging lunches, dinners, and other occasions where the two could become better acquainted. [ABC News vice president William] Sheehan also had a series of separate meetings with Reasoner to extol the benefits of the dual anchor arrangement. Reasoner finally agreed, reluctantly and conditionally. If, after eighteen months of trying in good faith to make the arrangement work, he still was unhappy, Sheehan promised to let him out of his contract.

Walters knew that Reasoner's acceptance was grudging, but she was optimistic. "I thought, I've been able to work with anybody, and I'll be able to work with Harry. I liked Harry, and I admired his work. And I sort of liked the combination. He was sort of gruff and amusing, and I was a little harder as a personality. I thought we could work together, and I really had high hopes about it." Mindful of her experiences with Frank McGee, however, she insisted on contractual guarantees that all assignments be split evenly between her and Reasoner.

The one issue that didn't prove troublesome was the money, in spite of the fact that her salary demand—an unnegotiable $1 million—was almost twice the going rate. ABC–TV president Fred Pierce was so eager to sign her that he devised a plan for splitting the cost of her salary between the entertainment and news divisions; she would be paid $500,000 for anchoring, and another $500,000 for producing and hosting four entertainment specials a year. (ABC also agreed to increase Harry Reasoner's salary from $400,000 to $500,000 so that both stars would be paid equally for their duties as newscasters.)

It was Walters's other demands, which were so lengthy, complicated, and in some cases unprecedented, that took weeks to resolve. The last week, when negotiating sessions continued around the clock, three suites were rented on the sixteenth floor of the Essex House in Manhattan—one for the ABC team, one for Walters's agents, and one that could be used by either side as a place to caucus. . . .

Out in the field, covering presidential trips and other major stories, she traveled with an entourage and she demanded—and usually received—special treatment. A White House aide in the Carter administration recalls an incident at the Nile Hilton, when he found two ABC photographers and a producer sleeping in the hall of the overcrowded hotel. After a word to the hotel manager, an empty three-bedroom suite was discovered and the aide went off, thinking the ABC party had been taken care of. A couple of hours later, however, he found them sleeping in the hall again; Walters had taken over the suite for her own use. "She was always treated differently from the other reporters," the aide says. "You always saw her with the Sadats and people like that. She never hung around with the rest of the press."

The boys on the bus, as writer Tim

Crouse dubbed the press corps in his book about reporters on the presidential campaign trail, observed the fuss surrounding Walters and despised her for it. Some were scandalized during a trip to India when she got into a shouting match with the prime minister's aide, demanding that an interview he had set up for her be switched from Sunday to Monday because she couldn't get any airtime on Sunday. "I'm Number One," she shouted, pointing her finger at the Indian. "In America, I'm Number One." The boys on the bus don't always behave like gentlemen themselves, but when a highly paid, highly visible, and not very welcome woman conducts herself that aggressively, she sets herself up to become an object of hatred.

Many newspeople also disliked her interviewing style, which became increasingly personal over the years. There was the time she implored Jimmy Carter at the end of an interview, "Be good to us, Mr. President, be kind." In trying to erase her image as an abrasive interviewer, she became almost abject at times. In a parody in *TV Guide* comparing the way a number of well-known television personalities would interview a Martian invader, the writer imagined Walters saying, "Tell us, Mr. 240X3—May I call you Gkjrfc?—tell us, please—and forgive me for asking this, but I must—what makes a man, or whatever, like yourself—now please don't hate me for asking this, sir, or whatever, but . . ."

When interviewing men, she often let a seductive, even sexual tone creep into her voice. "I love to flirt and be flirted with," she wrote in her book. "One of my favorite interviews was with the actor, Oskar Werner. I began on the air by commenting that I had read that he was a very difficult person. He gazed at me with luxuriant sleepiness for a moment and then asked softly, 'But how do you know? We never even had an affair.' I forget how the rest of the interview went." It doesn't seem to have occurred to her that such an open use of her femininity might be unprofessional. "When she first meets politicians, she comes on with them," notes Gerald Rafshoon, who served as Jimmy Carter's media adviser. "Her manner says, 'Don't worry, I'm your friend.' They all fall for it." Politicians also felt they could trust her not to bear down too hard. During the 1980 campaign, when Carter was being charged with "meanness," Rafshoon decided it would be helpful to address the issue head-on by means of a television interview, preferably with Walters. "She's very good about fighting with the producers for time. And the other reason we decided on her was that she's more reflective, less prosecutorial. She would be willing to discuss the issue with us and give the President more of a chance to say what was on his mind. Besides, he felt comfortable with her."

While Walters's methods worked very well with presidents, it was her peers in the media, in both print and broadcasting, who would judge her and influence the public's perception of her. She never understood that she had to play to *them* as well as to the world leaders and others she hoped to interview.

It must be acknowledged, of course, that most of Walters's critics were men, none of whom would dare suggest that she was unqualified to become the anchor because she was a woman. Yet sexism was still a fact of life in network news in 1976; whatever gains women made until then had been accomplished over the strong objections of the majority of their male colleagues.

Stretching back at least to the nineteenth century, women had been unwelcome in the newsroom, partly because they spoiled the clubhouse atmosphere and partly because of paternalism. In the 1860s, for example, big-city editors complained of the need to provide escorts for female employees who worked late. By the turn of the century, only a few women had managed to make names for themselves, including

Elizabeth Cochrane ("Nellie Bly"), who became famous for her stunt reporting for the *New York World*, and the great investigative reporter, Ida Tarbell.

Not until the 1930s, a decade in which the "independent female" had a certain vogue, did notable female journalists emerge in substantial numbers. Among them were Hearst reporter Dorothy Kilgallen, financial writer Sylvia Porter, *Life* magazine cover photographer Margaret Bourke White, famed columnist and radio commentator Dorothy Thompson, and the inimitable Mary Margaret McBride, whose radio interview show on NBC was a must-stop for book authors and politicians. Eleanor Roosevelt contributed to the advancement of women journalists in the thirties, too, by barring men from her regular Monday morning press briefings—a move that forced several major dailies and the wire services to hire females.

The acute shortage of manpower during World War II served to further lower resistance to hiring women reporters. A few were even permitted to serve as war correspondents. But the end of the war brought a reappearance of the old pattern of one woman to a newsroom, and the lone woman's job was usually to cover "the woman's angle." Editors used the same old reasons for excluding females, according to Marian Marzolf, whose book, *Up from the Footnote*, traces the history of women in journalism. She quotes editors as saying they preferred to hire men because "assignments would take them where I wouldn't want any lady relative of mine to go after nightfall." Other reasons given by editors included:

> Women get married and quit just about the time they're any good to you . . . women expect special consideration . . . women lack the all-round grasp of affairs it takes to operate on these jobs . . . women lack evenness of temperament, dependability, stability, quickness, range, understanding, knowledge, insight.

Women advanced even more slowly in broadcasting than in newspapers. After World War II, when the switch from radio to television was taking place, many women moved into good jobs as producers, writers, directors, and engineers, but *not in news*. After Pauline Frederick was hired by ABC in 1948, she remained the sole female hard news reporter on network news for the next twelve years. Editors didn't like to use her on the air, she had been told, because a woman's voice lacked authority, a belief that persisted for a long time. As late as 1971, NBC's Reuven Frank told a reporter, "I have the strong feeling that audiences are less prepared to accept news from a woman's voice than a man's." Yet the public accepted Frederick very well; she became famous for her coverage of the United Nations, first as a correspondent for ABC, then with NBC. In the 1960s, visitors to the U.N. invariably asked their guide two questions: "Where did Khrushchev bang his shoe?" and "Do you ever see Pauline Frederick?"

As the sixties progressed, a handful of female newscasters achieved short bursts of prominence. Nancy Dickerson scored several "firsts" as a correspondent for NBC; in 1963, she anchored a daily five-minute newscast called "Nancy Dickerson with the News," and the following year, she became the first woman to serve as a floor reporter at the political conventions. Marlene Sanders, who joined ABC in 1964, also received some anchoring assignments, but she recalls facing a continuous struggle with editors who insisted on assigning her to "women's" stories. Still, the principle of one woman to a newsroom was disappearing, which represented progress. And off camera, more women were being hired as producers, researchers, and production assistants, setting the stage for their later rise.

It took the women's movement in the early 1970s, however, to force the networks to put more women on the air. Several successful antidiscrimination suits were filed against network-owned-and-operated stations, and in 1971, the Federal Communications Commission began requiring stations to file affirmative action plans for women as a condition for license renewal. By 1974, the three networks had added about a dozen women reporters, and all were actively trying to recruit more. Not many of these women were well known to the public yet, though. At CBS, it was still considered an event when one of the three women in the Washington bureau, Marya McLaughlin, Connie Chung, or Lesley Stahl, made an appearance on the Evening News. Only Stahl, nicknamed Brenda Starr by her CBS colleagues for her aggressiveness, was achieving anything close to real prominence at the time. Assigned to cover the Watergate break-in because most of the other Washington bureau reporters were out of town and the story was considered minor, she couldn't be removed later because she had become so expert. Yet it was Daniel Schorr who handled the story for the Evening News; Stahl's main outlet, besides radio, was the CBS Morning News. . . .

. . . Walters was nearly crushed by the negative reviews her own performance received. "I couldn't bear to pick up a paper for a year," she told her old colleague from the "Today" show, Gene Shalit, in an interview for *Ladies' Home Journal*. "I felt as though I were drowning. . . . Every day at three o'clock the papers would be delivered, and there would be another blast. Tears would come to my eyes and I would blot my eyes so the mascara wouldn't run, and go on the air." Her boss, Bill Sheehan, and other supporters tried to comfort her, but to no avail. "She was irrational to the point of hysteria about anything that appeared in the press," says Sheehan. "She couldn't handle it at all. There was no way to convince her to sit back and let it roll over."

There is no question that the negative stories hurt her with the public. Soon after ABC announced that Walters had been hired to co-anchor the Evening News, so many unfavorable letters arrived that a form letter had to be devised:

Dear _______:

We feel that the new co-anchor format with Barbara Walters and Harry Reasoner will add a very exciting dimension to newscasting, and we hope you will decide to continue to be one of our viewers. In that connection, we do ask that you keep an open mind and tune in for a reasonable period before making your decision.

Sincerely yours.

Walters was also unprepared for the depth of Reasoner's hostility. Contrary to the stories that circulated, there were never any public scenes, no personal confrontations or childish behavior. It was more subtle than that. "Harry ignored her," says Sheehan, "and it made her tight. It really affected her performance." From the start, Reasoner viewed being teamed up with Walters as a no-win arrangement. If the ratings went up, *she* would get the credit. If they went down, he would share the blame. As the wave of negative press stories swelled, he realized that his own credibility could be damaged by association with her. Every night after the program, he and his pals—Reasoner's little band of merry men, as one correspondent tagged them—gathered at the bar of the Café des Artistes, a restaurant across the street from ABC News. There they would vie with one another in ridiculing her, a ritual of which she became aware.

As the animosity between the two increased, little remarks that might have been harmless were interpreted as hostile jabs. Once, evidently in an effort to appear a little warmer on the air, Walters remarked of Henry Kissinger, "You know, Harry, Kissinger didn't do too badly as a sex symbol in Washington." Reasoner, who prides himself for being quick on the uptake, replied, "Well, you would know more about that than I would." Regardless of how the remark was intended, it was widely interpreted as a putdown, both by the press and by insiders at ABC. Bob Siegenthaler, who produced the program during that era, remembers how things got blown out of proportion. "I remember the corrosive nature, not so much of the publicity, but of their friends. There was a constant procession of meddlers who would go in and say, 'She's doing this to you.' 'He's doing that to you.' 'How about that Kissinger remark?' They were just a bunch of tattletales, fanning the flames."

Reasoner denies he was ever cruel to Walters. "I wasn't opposed to Barbara as a person or Barbara as a woman. It seemed to me inevitable that hiring her would be perceived as a stunt and would be treated that way by the print press. I told her that three weeks before she joined. I also told her she would find problems with the way ABC was going. As I've said before, we were the least of each other's problems."

Nevertheless, a bitter contest for airtime developed between them. The "Barbara Walters segment," which reverted to her old standby, the big-name interview, put her in direct competition with Reasoner, who had a personal vehicle of his own called "The Reasoner Report"—film essays that ran from four to six minutes, covering everything from spring training to the price of real estate in Los Angeles. Considering that only twenty-two minutes are left for news after subtracting time for commercials, there was bound to be trouble. According to Siegenthaler, it was a constant tug of war. "Harry wanted to do second-line stories—something like the House Select Committee on Interstate Commerce, which you can handle a number of ways. You can cover it as a twenty-second 'reader' by the anchor or as a two-minute film report. Harry would tend to say, 'Let's put on Joe Smith, congressional correspondent.' Barbara would say, 'Let's save the time and use it for an interview.' " The unlucky Siegenthaler would get to break the ties.

Part of the trouble lay in the fact that both anchors and ABC expected the Evening News to be expanded to forty-five minutes—it was the assumption underlying all of the discussions before Walters joined ABC—but at the last minute, in fact, the day that Walters signed her contract, the affiliates reversed their decision to give up the needed time to the network. With a forty-five-minute newscast, the competition for airtime between the two anchors would have been less acute, and, as local stations discovered when they expanded their own local news broadcasts, there would have been more room for feature material. It was difficult for Walters to do the kind of lengthy, highly personalized interview she excelled at within the confines of the half-hour Evening News.

To make the competition for airtime even more intense, a number of "soft" features, including a wildlife expert and a psychologist, were added to the mix—features originally designed to help fill the forty-five-minute format but retained after the plan fell through. Inevitably, the time they took up, together with Walters's interviews and the occasional "Reasoner Reports," made ABC's other reporters feel their work was being crowded off the air. To the disgruntled correspondents, Walters symbolized a perversion of the news process, and in a sense they were right. It was not that she was unqualified for the job. Assuming that it takes a journalist to read the news—an arguable point—her news credentials were certainly good enough. But her interviews with famous people like Henry Kissinger and Anwar Sadat were often designed more as a showcase for her than as a vehicle to elicit information. Even so, there was nothing intrinsically harmful about such interviews, nor for that matter about the wildlife expert or the psychologist, so long as they did not displace legitimate news. But the staff thought they did just that, and loathed Walters for it.

If the reporters had had a chance to get

acquainted with Walters, who is charming and thoughtful with intimates, they might not have objected to her presence on the program quite so strongly. But Walters, a surprisingly shy person for all her on-camera toughness, has never been one to fraternize much with the troops and is not given to easy camaraderie. She is also famous for not remembering people she has worked with. She once spent a week in Cuba with an ABC crew interviewing Castro—an experience that generated great esprit de corps among all those involved because they felt they were making history together. A few months later, however, when she bumped into the cameraman, Vinnie Gaito, in Washington, she responded to his greeting with a blank stare. Gaito, a popular veteran of the network, was furious when he heard her whisper to a nearby producer, "Who is that guy, anyway?"

Part of the trouble is that Walters gets so wrapped up in what she is doing that she seems oblivious of others. Yet many people who work with her long enough find her warm and endearing. "The only problem I ever had was that she was hard to get to," says John Miller, a writer who knew her on the "Today" show. "She would be busy with her other program or lunching with important people. However, she could be an extremely concerned human being. I was feeling down in the dumps at one point over my divorce, and she was very solicitous when she heard what I was going through. Basically, she is a good egg."

Unfortunately for Walters, it took a while for people at ABC to see that side of her. Initially, she spent a lot of time behind closed doors with ABC executives, alternately heartsick and angry about her situation.

Within the industry, ABC News once again became the butt of malicious jokes. Even the public began to mimic her, thanks in part to Gilda Radner's "Barbara Wa-Wa" act on "Saturday Night Live." At ABC, an air of defeatism hung over the enterprise, almost from the start. Bill Sheehan, the man who hired Walters, believes the Reasoner-Walters combination was never given a chance to succeed. "ABC made its decision to drop them much too fast," he says. "They went on the air in October and by January, everybody was saying it wouldn't work."

Strong ammunition for this negative view came from an audience study conducted for ABC the following year by the consulting firm of Frank Magid and Associates. The conclusions, based on discussions with the so-called focus groups, did not mince words. "Many viewers are not comfortable watching her deliver the news. Much of this discomfort has to do with the aura that surrounds Barbara Walters at the present time, an aura that was perpetuated by the press regarding her switch to ABC. . . . Viewers often volunteered that she is not worth the money she is being paid, that she appears lofty, 'stuck-up,' extremely difficult to understand and follow, has a bad voice, is not able to effectively handle the anchor responsibilities, and quite simply, is not the type of personality that viewers can relate to as an individual. The only area in which Barbara Walters is thought to be efficient is interviewing, and many feel she excels in this capacity. Nevertheless, many questioned her function as a newscaster." The report added that viewer discontent with Walters as an anchor colored their acceptance of ABC News as a whole. "[Focus group] members' perceptions of her so overshadowed the entirety of ABC News, that in many instances, Walters and ABC [were] spoken of synonymously."

Reaction to Reasoner among the focus groups was much more positive. "Reasoner is liked, trusted, and viewers are comfortable watching him. As has been the case in prior research, he falls just short of making the kind of impact on viewers that Walter Cronkite does." The irony of these conclusions, as ABC's executives saw it, was that

Walters had been doing everything in her power to make the dual anchor work, while Reasoner was doing his utmost to undermine it. She would have to be replaced, but nobody wanted to make *her* look like the scapegoat.

Reasoner *was* behaving badly. Never inclined to work too hard under any circumstances, he began to grow more distant from the operation, acting temperamental and uncooperative. He would generally arrive about eleven o'clock in the morning, look at the wires, then go out for a long, invariably liquid lunch with his old pals from CBS. Back at ABC, he would retire to his office for a nap. At about five o'clock, he would check the script that had been written for him, and at ten past five, three or four of his buddies would join him for a round of drinks known as "fivesies." He used to tell friends that having a drink before he went on the air made him talk better.

Despite all the gossip about his fondness for the bottle—some of the stories put out intentionally by ABC executives when it became apparent that Reasoner wanted out of his contract—his drinking never seemed apparent on the air. However, his lack of interest became more and more evident. Reasoner acknowledges that he was partly to blame for the debacle at ABC. "By 1975," he says, "the fun had gone out of it. I got fat and lazy, and between management and me, we screwed up. There was a lot of turmoil in my personal life at that time, and I was tired of anchoring. I didn't give it my full shot. I should have. In any case, it probably came across on the air."

17

THE RIGHT TO VOTE

It can be argued that the right to vote—and to have that vote count in the operation of the government—is the essential democratic right. Freedom of speech, for example, would mean considerably less if speech were not followed by the act of voting. Yet early in the women's movement the right to vote was seen by some as secondary, particularly after women were left out of the Fifteenth Amendment, which declared (but did not implement) the voting rights of blacks. Elizabeth Cady Stanton, for example, thought that women suffered more from marital and social restrictions than from political discrimination. At the famous Seneca Falls Convention of 1848, the "sacred right to the elective franchise" was the only one of twelve resolutions that did not receive unanimous support; it passed by a small majority. In time, the right to vote would become the core demand of the women's movement, and would at last be embodied in the Constitution.

The convention at Seneca Falls, New York, a dozen years before the Civil War, brought together a flock of earnest and distinctly offbeat women and men who believed the time had come to speak out. The original plan was to bar men from the first day's proceedings, but they came and were included; one of them chaired the meeting. While preparing the agenda, the convention's instigators had trouble deciding how to focus their concerns. Then one of them picked up the Declaration of Independence and read it aloud. The "Declaration of Sentiments" the meeting produced, and the concomitant resolutions, were very widely published—mainly to be ridiculed and damned in the press. Frederick Douglass, who helped lead the convention, noted in his newspaper that "a discussion of the rights of animals would be regarded with far more complacency by many of what are called the *wise* and the *good* of our land, than would be a discussion of the rights of women." Yet soon after Seneca Falls, similar conventions took place in Ohio, Massachusetts, Indiana, Pennsylvania, and elsewhere in New York. And long after Seneca Falls, when the right of women to vote became a matter of life and death to some, the early courage of these pioneer mavericks would light some very dark days.

Declaration and Resolutions of the Seneca Falls Convention

by Elizabeth Cady Stanton, Susan B. Anthony, and Matilda Josephine Gage

When, in the course of human events, it becomes necessary for one portion of the family of man to assume among the people of the earth a position different from that which they have hitherto occupied, but one to which the laws of nature and of nature's God entitle them, a decent respect to the opinions of mankind requires that they should declare the causes that impel them to such a course.

We hold these truths to be self-evident: that all men and women are created equal; that they are endowed by their Creator with certain inalienable rights; that among these are life, liberty, and the pursuit of happiness; that to secure these rights governments are instituted, deriving their just powers from the consent of the governed. Whenever any form of government becomes destructive of these ends, it is the right of those who suffer from it to refuse allegiance to it, and to insist upon the institution of a new government, laying its foundation on such principles, and organizing its powers in such form, as to them shall seem most likely to effect their safety and happiness. Prudence indeed, will dictate that governments long established should not be changed for light and transient causes; and accordingly all experience hath shown that mankind are more disposed to suffer, while evils are sufferable, than to right themselves by abolishing the forms to which they were accustomed. But when a long train of abuses and usurpations, pursuing invariably the same object evinces a design to reduce them under absolute despotism, it is their duty to throw off such government, and to provide new guards for their future security. Such has been the patient sufferance of the women under this government, and such is now the necessity which constrains them to demand the equal station to which they are entitled.

The history of mankind is a history of repeated injuries and usurpations on the part of man toward woman, having in direct object the establishment of an absolute tyranny over her. To prove this, let facts be submitted to a candid world.

He has never permitted her to exercise her inalienable right to the elective franchise.

He has compelled her to submit to laws, in the formation of which she had no voice.

He has withheld from her rights which are given to the most ignorant and degraded men—both natives and foreigners.

Having deprived her of this first right of a citizen, the elective franchise, thereby leaving her without representation in the halls of legislation, he has oppressed her on all sides.

He has made her, if married, in the eye of the law, civilly dead.

He has taken from her all right in property, even to the wages she earns.

He has made her, morally, an irresponsible being, as she can commit many crimes with impunity, provided they be done in the presence of her husband. In the covenant of marriage, she is compelled to promise obedience to her husband, he becoming, to all intents and purposes, her master—the law giving him power to deprive her of her liberty, and to administer chastisement.

He has so framed the laws of divorce, as to what shall be the proper causes, and in case of separation, to whom the guardianship of the children shall be given, as to be wholly regardless of the happiness of women—the law, in all cases, going upon a false supposition of the supremacy of man, and giving all power into his hands.

After depriving her of all rights as a married woman, if single, and the owner of property,

---

From Elizabeth Cady Stanton, Susan B. Anthony, and Matilda Josephine Gage, eds., *History of Woman Suffrage* (New York: Arno; *New York Times*, 1969), pp. 70–73.

he has taxed her to support a government which recognizes her only when her property can be made profitable to it.

He has monopolized nearly all the profitable employments, and from those she is permitted to follow, she receives but a scanty remuneration. He closes against her all the avenues to wealth and distinction which he considers most honorable to himself. As a teacher of theology, medicine, or law, she is not known.

He has denied her the facilities for obtaining a thorough education, all colleges being closed against her.

He allows her in Church, as well as State, but a subordinate position, claiming Apostolic authority for her exclusion from the ministry, and, with some exceptions, from any public participation in the affairs of the Church.

He has created a false public sentiment by giving to the world a different code of morals for men and women, by which moral delinquencies which exclude women from society, are not only tolerated, but deemed of little account in man.

He has usurped the prerogative of Jehovah himself, claiming it as his right to assign for her a sphere of action, when that belongs to her conscience and to her God.

He has endeavored, in every way that he could, to destroy her confidence in her own powers, to lessen her self-respect, and to make her willing to lead a dependent and abject life.

Now, in view of this entire disfranchisement of one-half the people of this country, their social and religious degradation—in view of the unjust laws above mentioned, and because women do feel themselves aggrieved, oppressed, and fraudulently deprived of their most sacred rights, we insist that they have immediate admission to all the rights and privileges which belong to them as citizens of the United States.

In entering upon the great work before us, we anticipate no small amount of misconception, misrepresentation, and ridicule; but we shall use every instrumentality within our power to effect our object. We shall employ agents, circulate tracts, petition the State and National legislatures, and endeavor to enlist the pulpit and the press in our behalf. We hope this Convention will be followed by a series of Conventions embracing every part of the country.

The following resolutions were discussed by Lucretia Mott, Thomas and Mary Ann McClintock, Amy Post, Catharine A. F. Stebbins, and others, and were adopted:

WHEREAS, The great precept of nature is conceded to be, that "man shall pursue his own true and substantial happiness." Blackstone in his Commentaries remarks, that this law of Nature being coeval with mankind, and dictated by God himself, is of course superior in obligation to any other. It is binding over all the globe, in all countries and at all times; no human laws are of any validity if contrary to this, and such of them as are valid, derive all their force, and all their validity, and all their authority, mediately and immediately, from this original; therefore,

Resolved, That such laws as conflict, in any way, with the true and substantial happiness of woman, are contrary to the great precept of nature and of no validity, for this is "superior in obligation to any other."

Resolved, That all laws which prevent woman from occupying such a station in society as her conscience shall dictate, or which place her in a position inferior to that of man, are contrary to the great precept of nature, and therefore of no force or authority.

Resolved, That woman is man's equal—was intended to be so by the Creator, and the highest good of the race demands that she should be recognized as such.

Resolved, That the women of this country ought to be enlightened in regard to the laws under which they live, that they may no longer publish their degradation by declaring themselves satisfied with their present position, nor their ignorance, by asserting that they have all the rights they want.

Resolved, That inasmuch as man, while claiming for himself intellectual superiority, does accord to woman moral superiority, it is pre-eminently his duty to encourage her to speak and teach, as she has an opportunity, in all religious assemblies.

Resolved, That the same amount of virtue, delicacy, and refinement of behavior that is required of woman in the social state, should also be required of man, and the same transgressions should be visited with equal severity on both man and woman.

Resolved, That the objection of indelicacy and impropriety, which is so often brought against woman when she addresses a public audience, comes with a very ill-grace from those who encourage, by their attendance, her appearance on the stage, in the concert, or in feats of the circus.

Resolved, That woman has too long rested satisfied in the circumscribed limits which corrupt customs and a perverted application of the Scriptures have marked out for her, and that it is time she should move in the enlarged sphere which her great Creator has assigned her.

Resolved, That it is the duty of the women of this country to secure to themselves their sacred right to the elective franchise.

Resolved, That the equality of human rights results necessarily from the fact of the identity of the race in capabilities and responsibilities.

Resolved, therefore, That, being invested by the Creator with the same capabilities, and the same consciousness of responsibility for their exercise, it is demonstrably the right and duty of woman, equally with man, to promote every righteous cause by every righteous means; and especially in regard to the great subjects of morals and religion, it is self-evidently her right to participate with her brother in teaching them, both in private and in public, by writing and by speaking, by any instrumentalities proper to be used, and in any assemblies proper to be held; and this being a self-evident truth growing out of the divinely implanted principles of human nature, any custom or authority adverse to it, whether modern or wearing the hoary sanction of antiquity, is to be regarded as a self-evident falsehood, and at war with mankind.

At the last session Lucretia Mott offered and spoke to the following resolution:

Resolved, That the speedy success of our cause depends upon the zealous and untiring efforts of both men and women, for the overthrow of the monopoly of the pulpit, and for the securing to woman an equal participation with men in the various trades, professions, and commerce.

18

LOBBYING FOR THE VOTE

It is ironic that "The Battle Hymn of the Republic," anthem of the North in the Civil War, has become a favorite selection of southern choirs. Perhaps as ironic is the song's adoption by religious conservatives, many of whom fulminate against women's rights. The author of that booming hymn, published in 1862, was Julia Ward Howe, ardent feminist of the late nineteenth century. It was her first literary success, after many efforts. President Lincoln, it is said, wept when he first heard it.

Julia Ward Howe was born when James Monroe was president and died when William Howard Taft held office. A little over five feet tall, always dressed in white-trimmed black with a lace cap, she peered at her audience over silver-rimmed glasses and spoke in a crisp Boston accent. Sometimes depressed, she prayed "for weight and earnestness of purpose" because "I am too frivolous and frisky."[1] She wrote passionate, if ponderous, poetry. But then she found the women's movement, and "there was a visible change; it gave a new brightness to her face, a new cordiality in her manner, made her calmer, firmer; she found herself among new friends and could disregard old critics."[2] Before she died at ninety-one, Julia Howe became an indefatigable woman's-club supporter, founding clubs everywhere she went. But it was as a champion of suffrage that she excelled, and for the last forty years of her life she was one of the leaders of this cause. She gave the following speech at a suffrage hearing before the Massachusetts legislature. When the little general of the movement finally died, four thousand singers boomed out "The Battle Hymn of the Republic" in Boston's Symphony Hall.

[1] Edward T. James, ed., *Notable American Women: A Biographical Dictionary* (Cambridge, MA: Belknap Press of Harvard Univ., 1973), p. 228.

[2] *Ibid*, p. 227.

Julia Ward Howe Addresses the Massachusetts Legislature

edited by Florence Howe Hall

I wish that the remonstrants were as happy as I feel myself to be in the faith which I have in my own sex.

I once thought as they do, that women should not be trusted with the ballot. I knew little about women in those days, and less about the principles upon which governments are founded, at least, the principles recognized in our Declaration of Independence, which sets before the world the fact that all men are born free and equal, and entitled to certain inalienable rights.

I knew then the women of society as technically so-called, and the subordinates with whom all of us have to do. I liked or disliked individuals of my own sex, but of women as a class, as half of the human race, I had very little knowledge. In years which have passed since that time, I have seen much of the rank and file of women, and I confess that my opinion of them, as regards mental capacity and moral character, has steadily risen with the increase of my knowledge. When a hundred thousand of them throughout the country band together to further the cause of temperance, I know that they are neither vicious disturbers of the peace, nor ignorant fanatics. When fifty thousand of them in Massachusetts petition for suffrage, I know that their signatures do not come from slums and liquor saloons, but from honest homes and honest hearts. And I know, and you know, that the men who have championed their cause are among the foremost of those who have given fame and glory to their country and their age.

But a deeper principle than the doubt regarding their own sex underlies the plea of the remonstrants. This is, the disbelief in suffrage itself. One of their cries is that they do not want to see the ignorant vote doubled. They believe that ignorance and vice govern the country already, and that a crowd of unconvicted felons who already besiege the polls will, if suffrage is granted to women, only bring with them a corresponding crowd of female roughs and toughs. On this point, I desire to appeal to you, gentlemen. You were chosen and sent here by the rank and file of the community. Were you the choice of ignorant voters? Did the vicious element of the community come to the front in your election? If, with others, the hod carrier, the railroad hand, the factory operative, had power to elect a decent and creditable legislature, why should not the school teachers and shop girls and servant maids of Boston, with all these ladies to help them, be able to do as well?

In pleas like those I have mentioned one great truth is left out. Christ hinted at it when he called his disciples the salt of the earth. The masses of men are necessarily ignorant of much that it concerns them to know. They need experts in every sort to think and act for them. They cannot move without leaders. Our system of government allows them to choose their own leaders. And when they have hit upon a blind leader of the blind who has gone with them into the ditch, they don't choose him a second time.

From Florence Howe Hall, ed., *Julia Ward Howe and the Woman Suffrage Movement* (New York: Arno; *New York Times*, 1969), pp. 190–97.

Can any one doubt to-day that women are as well able to choose their leaders, ay, and to choose them from among their fellow-women, as men are? We do not want to-day for these leaders of our own sex, reformers who understand principles, students of history, philosophy and political economy, often more willing than men are to devote their energies to the elevation of their kind. Look at the college settlements in the slums of great cities—look at the countless charities in which the women are the ministering angels—look at the devoted missionary women who take their lives in their hands, and visit the uttermost parts of the earth, to redeem their own sex from brutality, slavery, and ignorance of all that distinguishes the divine human from the human brute. No, gentlemen, men do not vote out of their vice and ignorance, but out of their best knowledge, when they are free to use it. Do not doubt that women will do the same thing.

The preamble published by the remonstrants goes out of the direct way, in order to reprobate the use which the women of Massachusetts have made of the school vote. Their objection to the school franchise is stated to be that so few have used it. Their objection to the municipal franchise is that so many would use it. They see danger in the vote of the few and in the vote of the many. If they consider the vote dangerous on account of its smallness, why don't they increase it by voting themselves? If, in their view, this vote has sometimes followed a mistaken lead, can you affirm that male voters have never done so? To deny the franchise because it is capable of leading to mischievous action, would be like standing beside a new-born babe and saying: "It will probably be a sinner, let us hinder it once and for all."

As to the plea of want of time, many things prove it to be futile. You, ladies, have time for embroidery, music, painting. You have time for theatre-going, for attending concerts and rehearsals, afternoon teas—for entertainments which require much care and forethought. You have time enough to follow the fashions of dress with minute care and attention. How important you esteem these to be, we well know. Your entertainments are a sort of dress parade, in which every line, every color, every bit of lace or ribbon, must have a certain set, must be up to date. City elections come once a year and last one day. Could you not spare one hour of one day in the year for your country's good?

They know not what they do.

Many of the women who join us in petitioning for suffrage are women who earn their own living, often supporting their families, including an aged father or impecunious husband. They teach, write, sew, cook, do their own housework and care for their children, and they know that they could find the little time required to give their vote. You, ladies, do not cook your dinners nor make your own clothes, nor sweep and dust your mansions, nor sit at the weary desk of the teacher day in and day out, and yet you have not time to vote. And because you have not, you with your delicate fingers would wring from the hard hand of labor its only guarantee of freedom?

19

THE FIGHT FOR WOMEN'S SUFFRAGE

On August 18, 1920, the Nineteenth Amendment to the Constitution of the United States was ratified. It stated: "The right of citizens of the United States to vote shall not be denied or abridged by the United States or by any state on account of sex." Women had won the right to vote, one hundred twenty-nine years after the ratification of the Bill of Rights.

That women can vote now seems as natural as that the sun can shine. Lest we forget what it took to reach that easy assumption, let us consider Alice Paul. What she did speaks louder than what we can say about it.

Alice Paul Goes to Jail

by Doris Stevens

The special session of the 65th Congress, known as the "War Congress," adjourned in October 1917, having passed every measure recommended as a war measure by the President.

In addition, it found time to protect by law migratory birds, to appropriate forty-seven million dollars for deepening rivers and harbors, and to establish more federal judgeships. No honest person would say that lack of time and pressure of war legislation had prevented its consideration of the suffrage measure. If one-hundredth part of the time consumed by its members

From Doris Stevens, *Jailed for Freedom* (New York: Boni & Liveright (original publisher); W. W. Norton Co., 1920), pp. 210–28.

in spreading the wings of the overworked eagle, and in uttering to bored ears "home-made" patriotic verse, had been spent in considering the liberty of women, this important legislation could have been dealt with. Week after week Congress met only for three days, and then often merely for prayer and a few hours of purposeless talking.

We had asked for liberty, and had got a suffrage committee appointed in the House to consider the pros and cons of suffrage, and a favorable report in the Senate from the Committee on Woman Suffrage, nothing more.

On the very day and hour of the adjournment of the special session of the War Congress, Alice Paul led eleven women to the White House gates to protest against the Administration's allowing its lawmakers to go home without action on the suffrage amendment.

Two days later Alice Paul and her colleagues were put on trial.

Many times during previous trials I had heard the District Attorney for the government shake his finger at Miss Paul and say, "We'll get you yet. . . . Just wait; and when we do, we'll give you a year!"

It was reported from very authentic sources that Attorney General Gregory had, earlier in the agitation, seriously considered arresting Miss Paul for the Administration, on the charge of conspiracy to break the law. We were told this plan was abandoned because, as one of the Attorney General's staff put it, "No jury would convict her."

However, here she was in their hands, in the courtroom.

Proceedings opened with the customary formality. The eleven prisoners sat silently at the bar, reading their morning papers, or a book, or enjoying a moment of luxurious idleness, oblivious of the comical movements of a perturbed court. Nothing in the world so baffles the pompous dignity of a court as non-resistant defendants. The judge cleared his throat and the attendants made meaningless gestures.

"Will the prisoners stand up and be sworn?"

They will not.

"Will they question witnesses?"

They will not.

"Will they speak in their own behalf?"

The slender, quiet-voiced Quaker girl arose from her seat. The crowded courtroom pressed forward breathlessly. She said calmly and with unconcern: "We do not wish to make any plea before this court. We do not consider ourselves subject to this court, since as an unenfranchised class we have nothing to do with the making of the laws which have put us in this position."

What a disconcerting attitude to take! Miss Paul sat down as quietly and unexpectedly as she had arisen. The judge moved uneasily in his chair. The gentle way in which it was said was disarming. Would the judge hold them in contempt? He had not time to think. His part of the comedy he had expected to run smoothly, and here was this defiant little woman calmly stating that we were not subject to the court, and that we would therefore have nothing to do with the proceedings. The murmurs had grown to a babel of conversation. A sharp rap of the gavel restored order and permitted Judge Mullowny to say: "Unfortunately, I am here to support the laws that are made by Congress, and, of course, I am bound by those laws; and you are bound by them as long as you live in this country, notwithstanding the fact that you do not recognize the law."

Everybody strained his ears for the sentence. The Administration had threatened to "get" the leader. Would they dare?

Another pause!

"I shall suspend sentence for the time being," came solemnly from the judge.

Was it that they did not dare confine Miss Paul? Were they beginning actually to perceive the real strength of the movement and the protest that would be aroused if she were imprisoned? Again we thought perhaps this marked the end of the jailing of women.

But though the pickets were released on suspended sentences, there was no indication of any purpose on the part of the Administration of acting on the amendment. Two groups, some of those on suspended sentence, others first offenders, again marched to the White House gates. The following motto:

THE TIME HAS COME TO CONQUER OR SUBMIT; FOR US THERE CAN BE BUT ONE CHOICE—WE HAVE MADE IT.

a quotation from the President's second Liberty Loan appeal, was carried by Miss Paul.

Dr. Caroline E. Spencer of Colorado carried:

RESISTANCE TO TYRANNY IS OBEDIENCE TO GOD.

All were brought to trial again.

The trial of Miss Paul's group ran as follows:

Mr. Hart: (Prosecuting Attorney for the Government): Sergeant Lee, were you on Pennsylvania Avenue near the White House Saturday afternoon?

Sergeant Lee: I was.

Mr. Hart: At what time?

Lee: About 4:35 in the afternoon.

Hart: Tell the court what you saw.

Lee: A little after half-past four, when the department clerks were all going home out Pennsylvania Avenue, I saw four suffragettes coming down Madison Place, cross the Avenue and continue on Pennsylvania Avenue to the gate of the White House, where they divided two on the right and two on the left side of the gate.

Hart: What did you do?

Lee: I made my way through the crowd that was surrounding them and told the ladies *they were violating the law by standing at the gates*, and wouldn't they please move on?

Hart: Did they move on?

Lee: They did not; and they didn't answer either.

Hart: What did you do then?

Lee: I placed them under arrest.

Hart: What did you do then?

Lee: *I asked the crowd to move on.*

Mr. Hart then arose and summing up said: "Your Honor, these women have said that *they will picket again*. I ask you to impose the maximum sentence."

Such confused legal logic was indeed drôle!

"You ladies seem to feel that we discriminate in making arrests and in sentencing you," said the judge heavily. "The result is that you force me to take the most drastic means in my power to compel you to obey the law."

More legal confusion!

"Six months," said the judge to the first offenders, "and then you will serve one month more," to the others.

Miss Paul's parting remark to the reporters who intercepted her on her way from the courtroom to begin her seven months' sentence was:

"We are being imprisoned, not because we obstructed traffic, but because we pointed out to the President the fact that he was obstructing the cause of democracy at home, while Americans were fighting for it abroad."

I am going to let Alice Paul tell her own story, as she related it to me one day after her release:

It was late afternoon when we arrived at the jail. There we found the suffragists who had preceded us, locked in cells.

The first thing I remember was the distress of the prisoners about the lack of fresh air. Evening was approaching, every window was closed tight. The air in which we would be obliged to sleep was foul. There were about eighty negro and white prisoners crowded together, tier upon tier, frequently two in a cell. I went to a window and tried to open it. Instantly a group of men, prison guards, appeared; picked me up bodily, threw me into a cell and locked the door. Rose Winslow and the others were treated in the same way.

Determined to preserve our health and that of the other prisoners, we began a concerted fight for fresh air. The windows were about twenty feet distant from the cells, and two sets of iron bars intervened between us and the windows, but we instituted an attack upon them as best we could. Our tin drinking cups, the electric light bulbs, every available article of the meagre supply in each cell, including my treasured copy of Browning's poems which I had secretly taken in with me, was thrown through the windows. By this simultaneous attack from every cell, we succeeded in breaking one window before our supply of tiny weapons was exhausted. The fresh October air came in like an exhilarating gale. The broken window remained untouched throughout the entire stay of this group and all later groups of suffragists. Thus was won what the "regulars" in jail called the first breath of air in their time.

The next day we organized ourselves into a little group for the purpose of rebellion. We determined to make it impossible to keep us in jail. We determined, moreover, that as long as we were there we would keep up an unremitting fight for the rights of political prisoners.

One by one little points were conceded to quiet resistance. There was the practice of sweeping the corridors in such a way that the dust filled the cells. The prisoners would be choking to the gasping point, as they sat, helpless, locked in the cells, while a great cloud of dust enveloped them from tiers above and below. As soon as our tin drinking cups, which were sacrificed in our attack upon the windows, were restored to us, we instituted a campaign against the dust. Tin cup after tin cup was filled and its contents thrown out into the corridor from every cell, so that the water began to trickle down from tier to tier. The District Commissioners, the Board of Charities, and other officials were summoned by the prison authorities. Hurried consultations were held. Nameless officials passed by in review and looked upon the dampened floor. Thereafter the corridors were dampened and the sweeping into the cells ceased. And so another reform was won.

There is absolutely no privacy allowed a prisoner in a cell. You are suddenly peered at by curious strangers, who look in at you all hours of the day and night, by officials, by attendants, by interested philanthropic visitors, and by prison reformers, until one's sense of privacy is so outraged that one rises in rebellion. We set out to secure privacy, but we did not succeed, for, to allow privacy in prison, is against all institutional thought and habit. Our only available weapon was our blanket, which was no sooner put in front of our bars than it was forcibly taken down by Warden Zinkhan.

Our meals had consisted of a little almost raw salt pork, some sort of liquid—I am not sure whether it was coffee or soup—bread and occasionally molasses. How we cherished the bread and molasses! We saved it from meal to meal so as to try to distribute the nourishment over a longer period, as almost every one was unable to eat the raw pork. Lucy Branham, who was more valiant than the rest of us, called out from her cell, one day, "Shut your eyes tight, close your mouth over the pork and swallow it without chewing it. Then you can do it." This heroic practice kept Miss Branham in fairly good health, but to the rest it seemed impossible, even with our eyes closed, to crunch our teeth into the raw pork.

However gaily you start out in prison to keep up a rebellious protest, it is nevertheless a terribly difficult thing to do in the face of the constant cold and hunger of undernourishment. Bread and water, and occasional molasses, is not a diet destined to sustain rebellion long. And soon weakness overtook us.

At the end of two weeks of solitary confinement, without any exercise, without going outside of our cells, some of the prisoners were released, having finished their terms, but five of us were left serving seven months' sentences, and two, one month sentences. With our number thus diminished to seven, the authorities felt able to cope with us. The doors were unlocked and we were permitted to take exercise. Rose Winslow fainted as soon as she got into the yard, and was carried back to her cell. I was too weak to move from my bed. Rose and I were taken on stretchers that night to the hospital.

For one brief night we occupied beds in the same ward in the hospital. Here we decided upon the hunger strike, as the ultimate form of protest left us—the strongest weapon left with which to continue within the prison our battle against the Administration.

Miss Paul was held absolutely incommunicado in the prison hospital. No attorney, no member of her family, no friend could see her. With Miss Burns in prison also it became imperative that I consult Miss Paul as to a matter of policy. I was peremptorily refused admission by Warden Zinkhan, so I decided to attempt to communicate with her from below her window. This was before we had established what in prison parlance is known as the "grape-vine route." The grape-vine route consists of smuggling messages oral or written via a friendly guard or prisoner who has access to the outside world.

Just before twilight, I hurried in a taxi to the far-away spot, temporarily abandoned the cab and walked past the dismal cemetery which skirts the prison grounds. I had fortified myself with a diagram of the grounds, and knew which entrance to attempt, in order to get to the hospital wing where Miss Paul lay. We had also ascertained her floor and room. I must first pick the right building, proceed to the proper corner, and finally select the proper window.

The sympathetic chauffeur loaned me a very seedy looking overcoat which I wrapped about me. Having deposited my hat inside the cab, I turned up the collar, drew in my chin and began surreptitiously to circle the devious paths leading to a side entrance of the grounds. My heart was palpitating, for the authorities had threatened arrest if any suffragists were found on the prison grounds, and aside from my personal feelings, I could not at that moment abandon headquarters.

Making a desperate effort to act like an experienced and trusted attendant of the prison, I roamed about and tried not to appear roaming. I successfully passed two guards, and reached the desired spot, which was by good luck temporarily deserted. I succeeded in calling up loudly enough to be heard by Miss Paul, but softly enough not to be heard by the guards.

I shall never forget the shock of her appearance at that window in the gathering dusk. Everything in the world seemed black-gray except her ghost-like face, so startling, so inaccessible. It drove everything else from my mind for an instant. But as usual she was in complete control of herself. She began to hurl questions at me faster than I could answer. "How were the convention plans progressing?" . . . "Had the speakers been secured for the mass meeting?" . . . "How many women had signed up to go out on the next picket line?" And so on.

"Conditions at Occoquan are frightful," said I. "We are planning to . . ."

"Get out of there, and move quickly," shouted the guard, who came abruptly around the corner of the building. I tried to finish my message. "We are planning to habeas corpus the women out of Occoquan and have them transferred up here."

"Get out of there, I tell you. Damn you!" By this time he was upon me. He grabbed me by the arm and began shaking me. "You will be arrested if you do not get off these grounds." He continued to shake me while I shouted back, "Do you approve of this plan?"

I was being forced along so rapidly that I was out of range of her faint voice and could not hear the answer. I plead with the guard to be allowed to go back quietly and speak a few more words with Miss Paul, but he was inflexible. Once out of the grounds I went unnoticed to the cemetery and sat on a tombstone to wait a little while before making another attempt, hoping the guard would not expect me to come back. The lights were beginning to twinkle in the distance and it was now almost total darkness. I consulted my watch and realized that in forty minutes Miss Paul and her comrades would again be going through the torture of forcible feeding. I waited five minutes—ten minutes—fifteen minutes. Then I went back to the grounds again. I started through another entrance, but had proceeded only a few paces when I was forcibly evicted. Again I returned to the cold tombstone. I believe that I never in my life felt more utterly miserable and impotent. There were times, as I have said, when we felt inordinately strong. This was one of the times when I felt that we were frail reeds in the hands of cruel and powerful oppressors. My thoughts were at first with Alice Paul, at that moment being forcibly fed by men jailers and men doctors. I remembered then the man warden who had refused the highly reasonable request to visit her, and my thoughts kept right on up the scale till I got to the man-President—the pinnacle of power against us. I was indeed desolate. I walked back to the hidden taxi, hurried to headquarters, and plunged into my work, trying all night to convince myself that the sting of my wretchedness was being mitigated by activity toward a release from this state of affairs.

Later we established daily communication with Miss Paul through one of the charwomen who scrubbed the hospital floors. She carried paper and pencil carefully concealed upon her. On entering Miss Paul's room she would, with very comical stealth, first elaborately push Miss Paul's bed against the door, then crawl practically under it, and pass from this point of concealment the coveted paper and pencil. Then she would linger over the floor to the last second, imploring Miss Paul to hasten her writing. Faithfully every evening this silent, dusky messenger made her long journey after her day's work, and patiently waited while I wrote an answering note to be delivered to Miss Paul the following morning. Thus it was that while in the hospital Miss Paul directed our campaign, in spite of the Administration's most painstaking plans to the contrary.

Miss Paul's story continues here from the point where I interrupted it.

From the moment we undertook the hunger strike, a policy of unremitting intimidation began. One authority after another, high and low, in and out of prison, came to attempt to force me to break the hunger strike.

"You will be taken to a very unpleasant place if you don't stop this," was a favorite threat of the prison officials, as they would hint vaguely of the psychopathic ward, and St. Elizabeth's, the Government insane asylum. They alternately bullied and hinted. Another threat was "You will be forcibly fed immediately if you don't stop"—this from Dr. Gannon. There was nothing to do in the midst of these continuous threats, with always the "very unpleasant place" hanging over me, and so I lay perfectly silent on my bed.

After about three days of the hunger strike a man entered my room in the hospital and announced himself as Dr. White, the head of St. Elizabeth's. He said that he had been asked by District Commissioner Gardner to make an investigation. I later learned that he was Dr. William A. White, the eminent alienist.

Coming close to my bedside and addressing the attendant, who stood at a few respectful paces from him, Dr. White said: "Does this case talk?"

"Why wouldn't I talk?" I answered quickly.

"Oh, these cases frequently will not talk, you know," he continued in explanation.

"Indeed I'll talk," I said gaily, not having the faintest idea that this was an investigation of my sanity.

"Talking is our business," I continued, "we talk to any one on earth who is willing to listen to our suffrage speeches."

"Please talk," said Dr. White. "Tell me about suffrage; why you have opposed the President; the whole history of your campaign, why you picket, what you hope to accomplish by it. Just talk freely."

I drew myself together, sat upright in bed, propped myself up for a discourse of some length, and began to talk. The stenographer whom Dr. White brought with him took down in shorthand everything that was said.

I may say it was one of the best speeches I ever made. I recited the long history and struggle of the suffrage movement from its early beginning and narrated the political theory of our activities up to the present moment, outlining the status of the suffrage amendment in Congress at that time. In short, I told him everything. He listened attentively, interrupting only occasionally to say, "But, has not President Wilson treated you women very badly?" Whereupon, I, still unaware that I was being examined, launched forth into an explanation of Mr. Wilson's political situation and the difficulties he had confronting him. I continued to explain why we felt our relief lay with him; I cited his extraordinary power, his influence over his party, his undisputed leadership in the country, always painstakingly explaining that we opposed President Wilson merely because he happened to be President, not because he was President Wilson. Again came an interruption from Dr. White, "But isn't President Wilson directly responsible for the abuses and indignities which have been heaped upon you? You are suffering now as a result of his brutality, are you not?" Again I explained that it was impossible for us to know whether President Wilson was personally acquainted in any detail with the facts of our present condition, even though we knew that he had concurred in the early decision to arrest our women.

Presently Dr. White took out a small light and held it up to my eyes. Suddenly it dawned upon me that he was examining me personally; that his interest in the suffrage agitation and the jail conditions did not exist, and that he was merely interested in my reactions to the agitation and to jail. Even then I was reluctant to believe that I was the subject of mental investigation and I continued to talk.

But he continued in what I realized with a sudden shock, was an attempt to discover in me symptoms of the persecution mania. How simple he had apparently thought it would be, to prove that I had an obsession on the subject of President Wilson!

The day following he came again, this time bringing with him the District Commissioner, Mr. Gardner, to whom he asked me to repeat everything that had been said the day before. For the second time we went through the history of the suffrage movement, and again his inquiry suggested his persecution mania clue? When the narrative touched upon the President and his responsibility for the obstruction of the suffrage amendment, Dr. White would turn to his associate with the remark: "Note the reaction."

Then came another alienist, Dr. Hickling, attached to the psychopathic ward in the District Jail, with more threats and suggestions, if the hunger strike continued. Finally they departed, and I was left to wonder what would happen next. Doubtless my sense of humor helped me, but I confess I was not without fear of this mysterious place which they continued to threaten.

It appeared clear that it was their intention either to discredit me, as the leader of the agitation, by casting doubt upon my sanity, or else to intimidate us into retreating from the hunger strike.

After the examination by alienists, Commissioner Gardner, with whom I had previously discussed our demand for treatment as political prisoners, made another visit. "All these things you say about the prison conditions may be true," said Mr. Gardner, "I am a new Commissioner, and I do not know. You give an account of a very serious situation in the jail. The jail authorities give exactly the opposite. Now I promise you we will start an investigation at once to see who is right, you or they. If it is found you are right, we shall correct the conditions at once. If you will give up the hunger strike, we will start the investigation at once."

"Will you consent to treat the suffragists as political prisoners, in accordance with the demands laid before you?" I replied.

Commissioner Gardner refused, and I told him that the hunger strike would not be abandoned. But they had by no means exhausted every possible facility for breaking down our resistance. I overheard the Commissioner say to Dr. Gannon on leaving, "Go ahead, take her and feed her."

I was thereupon put upon a stretcher and carried into the psychopathic ward.

There were two windows in the room. Dr. Gannon immediately ordered one window nailed from top to bottom. He then ordered the door leading into the hallway taken down and an iron-barred cell door put in its place. He departed with the command to a nurse to "observe her."

Following this direction, all through the day once every hour, the nurse came to "observe" me. All through the night, once every hour she came in, turned on an electric light sharp in my face, and "observed" me. This ordeal was the most terrible torture, as it prevented my sleeping for more than a few minutes at a time. And if I did finally get to sleep it was only to be shocked immediately into wide-awakeness with the pitiless light.

Dr. Hickling, the jail alienist, also came often to "observe" me. Commissioner Gardner and others—doubtless officials—came to peer through my barred door.

One day a young interne came to take a blood test. I protested mildly, saying that it was unnecessary and that I objected. "Oh, well," said the young doctor with a sneer and a supercilious shrug, "you know you're not mentally competent to decide such things." And the test was taken over my protest.

It is scarcely possible to convey to you one's reaction to such an atmosphere. Here I was surrounded by people on their way to the insane asylum. Some were waiting for their commitment papers. Others had just gotten them. And all the while everything possible was done to attempt to make me feel that I too was a "mental patient."

At this time forcible feeding began in the District Jail. Miss Paul and Miss Winslow, the first two suffragists to undertake the hunger strike, went through the operation of forcible feeding this day and three times a day on each succeeding day until their release from prison three weeks later. The hunger strike spread immediately to other suffrage prisoners in the jail and to the workhouse. . . .

One morning [Miss Paul's story continues] the friendly face of a kindly old man standing on top of a ladder suddenly appeared at my window. He began to nail heavy boards across the window from the outside. He smiled and spoke a few kind words and told me to be of good cheer. He confided to me in a sweet and gentle way that he was in prison for drinking, that he had been in many times, but that he believed he had never seen anything so inhuman as boarding up this window and depriving a prisoner of light and air. There was only time for a few hurried moments of conversation, as I lay upon my bed watching the boards go up until his figure was completely hidden and I heard him descending the ladder.

After this window had been boarded up no light came into the room except through the top half of the other window, and almost no air. The authorities seemed determined to deprive me of air and light.

Meanwhile in those gray, long days, the mental patients in the psychopathic ward came and peered through my barred door. At night, in the early morning, all through the day there were cries and shrieks and moans from the patients. It was terrifying. One particularly melancholy moan used to keep up hour after hour, with the regularity of a heart beat. I said to myself, "Now I have to endure this. I have got to live through this somehow. I'll pretend these moans are the noise of an elevated train, beginning faintly in the distance and getting louder as it comes nearer." Such childish devices were helpful to me.

The nurses could not have been more beautiful in their spirit and offered every kindness. But imagine being greeted in the morning by a kindly nurse, a new one who had just come on duty, with, "I know you are not insane." The nurses explained the procedure of sending a person to the insane asylum. Two alienists examine a patient in the psychopathic ward, sign an order committing the patient to St. Elizabeth's Asylum, and there the patient is sent at the end of one week. No trial, no counsel, no protest from the outside world! This was the customary procedure.

I began to think as the week wore on that this was probably their plan for me. I could not see my family or friends; counsel was denied me; I saw no other prisoners and heard nothing of them; I could see no papers; I was entirely in the hands of alienists, prison officials and hospital staff.

I believe I have never in my life before feared anything or any human being. But I confess I was afraid of Dr. Gannon, the jail physician. I dreaded the hour of his visit.

"I will show you who rules this place. You think you do. But I will show you that you are wrong." Some such friendly greeting as this was frequent from Dr. Gannon on his daily round. "Anything you desire, you shall not have. I will show you who is on top in this institution," was his attitude.

After nearly a week had passed, Dudley Field Malone finally succeeded in forcing an entrance by an appeal to court officials and made a vigorous protest against confining me in the psychopathic ward. He demanded also that the boards covering the window be taken down. This was promptly done and again the friendly face of the old man became visible, as the first board disappeared.

"I thought when I put this up America would not stand for this long," he said, and began to assure me that nothing dreadful would happen. I cherish the memory of that sweet old man.

The day after Mr. Malone's threat of court proceedings, the seventh day of my stay in the psychopathic ward, the attendants suddenly appeared with a stretcher. I did not know whither I was being taken, to the insane asylum, as threatened, or back to the hospital—one never knows in prison where one is being taken, no reason is ever given for anything. It turned out to be the hospital.

After another week spent by Miss Paul on hunger strike in the hospital, the Administration was forced to capitulate. The doors of the jail were suddenly opened, and all suffrage prisoners were released.

With extraordinary swiftness the Administration's almost incredible policy of intimidation had collapsed. Miss Paul had been given the maximum sentence of seven months, and at the end of five weeks the Administration was forced to acknowledge defeat. They were in a most unenviable position. If she and her comrades had offended in such degree as to warrant so cruel a sentence (with such base stupidity on their part in administering it), she most certainly deserved to be detained for the full sentence. The truth is, every idea of theirs had been subordinated to the one desire of stopping the picketing agitation. To this end they had exhausted all their weapons of force.

From my conversation and correspondence with Dr. White, it is clear that as an alienist he did not make the slightest allegation to warrant removing Miss Paul to the psychopathic ward. On the contrary he wrote, "I felt myself in the presence of an unusually gifted personality" and "she was wonderfully alert and keen . . . possessed of an absolute conviction of her cause . . . with industry and courage sufficient to avail herself of them [all diplomatic possibilities]. He praised the "most admirable, coherent, logical and forceful way" in which she discussed with him the purpose of our campaign.

And yet the *Administration put her in the psychopathic ward and threatened her with the insane asylum*.

An interesting incident occurred during the latter part of Miss Paul's imprisonment. Having been cut off entirely from outside communication, she was greatly surprised one night at a late hour to find a newspaper man admitted for an interview with her. Mr. David Lawrence, then generally accepted as the Administration journalist, and one who wrote for the various newspapers throughout the country defending the policies of the Wilson Administration, was announced. It was equally well known that this correspondent's habit was to ascertain the position of the leaders on important questions, keeping intimately in touch with opinion in White House circles at the same time.

Mr. Lawrence came, as he said, of his own volition, and not as an emissary from the White House. But in view of his close relation to affairs, his interview is significant as possibly reflecting an Administration attitude at that point in the campaign.

The conversation with Miss Paul revolved first about our fight for the right of political prisoners, Miss Paul outlining the wisdom and justice of this demand.

"The Administration could very easily hire a comfortable house in Washington and detain you all there," said Mr. Lawrence, "but don't you see that your demand to be treated as political prisoners is infinitely more difficult to grant than to give you the federal suffrage amendment? If we give you these privileges we shall have to extend them to conscientious objectors and to all prisoners now confined for political opinions. This the Administration cannot do."

The political prisoners' protest, then, had actually encouraged the Administration to choose the lesser of two evils—some action on behalf of the amendment.

"Suppose," continued Mr. Lawrence, "the Administration should pass the amendment through one house of Congress next session and go to the country in the 1918 elections on that record and if sustained in it, pass it through the other house a year from now. Would you then agree to abandon picketing?"

"Nothing short of the passage of the amendment through Congress will end our agitation," Miss Paul quietly answered for the thousandth time.

Since Mr. Lawrence disavows any connection with the Administration in this interview, I can only remark that events followed exactly in the order he outlined; that is, the Administration attempted to satisfy the women by putting the amendment through the House and not through the Senate.

20

WHAT VOTES CAN WIN

The *right* to vote is one thing; the *use* of that right is another. Gaining the suffrage did not automatically usher in utopia. What it did do, at first, was to wake up male politicians to the issues women had been specially concerned about, because women voters now could vote for their friends and against their enemies. But would they? The category *women* is a very large category. Politicians watched carefully how the votes of women broke out.

William Chafe traces the aftermath of the suffrage victory. Politics, it turned out, had to be worked on if it was to produce. The early political successes and failures of women voters helped shape the patterns of the national vote today, as votes cast by women emerge as distinctive in the total vote.

The Impact of Women's Suffrage

by William Henry Chafe

Politics, understandably, provided the first test of what the suffragists had won with the enactment of the Nineteenth Amendment. A half-century earlier, Elizabeth Cady Stanton and her followers had dismissed the vote as "not even half a loaf; . . . only a crust, a crumb." By 1920, however, such skepticism had been set aside, and the ballot was invested with the power to end sex prejudice and elevate the na-

From William Henry Chafe, *The American Woman: Her Changing Social, Economic, and Political Roles, 1920–1970* (London: Oxford University Press, 1972), pp. 25–47.

tion's morals. The change indicated the degree to which the woman's movement had come to view politics as the key to a just society. Female leaders claimed that extending the franchise would speed the passage of social-welfare legislation, enhance consumer protection, and reinforce the drive against bossism in America's cities. The nation, led by women, could proceed to solve its problems—peaceably and through the electoral process.[1]

The suffragists' hopes hinged on the assumption that female citizens—by virtue of their sex—would act as a cohesive force to bring about social change. Women were so different from men, the reformers believed, that once they had the vote, the entire political system would be transformed. Pure in spirit, selfless in motivation, and dedicated to the preservation of human life, female voters would remake society and turn government away from war and corruption. The deed was more difficult than the promise, however, for if women were to fulfill the expectations of female leaders, they had to vote together, organize on the basis of sex, and demonstrate a collective allegiance to common ideals and programs. The validity of suffragist claims thus turned ultimately on the question of whether women could create a separate "bloc" in the electorate, committed to a distinctive set of interests and values.

The few instances in which women had played an active role in politics provided some basis for speculation about the development of an independent female constituency. In Illinois, where the votes of the two sexes were counted separately, women gave the reform candidate for mayor of Chicago in 1915 almost as large a plurality as men gave the machine candidate. Massachusetts suffragists successfully mobilized a non-partisan coalition to defeat the anti-suffragist senator John Weeks in 1918. And in Columbus, Ohio, the Franklin County Suffrage Association helped upset the mayor of sixteen years by concentrating five hundred female volunteers in eleven key wards. The women campaigners registered 21,000 new voters, and their candidate won by 19,000.[2]

In addition, many women leaders rejected the regular party apparatus as a vehicle for expressing their ideals. The head of the Illinois Republican Women's Committee bolted her party in 1920 and led a campaign to unseat the Republican mayor of Chicago, William Thompson. Many of the most prominent spokesmen of the newly formed League of Women Voters urged women to avoid joining established political organizations. And Alice Paul of the National Women's Party threatened repeatedly to form an independent political force composed of females alone. The worst fears of party leaders seemed confirmed when Mary Garrett Hay, national vice-chairman of Republican women, strongly opposed the re-election of New York's senator James Wadsworth in 1920 because he had been a leader of the anti-suffrage forces in Congress. Hay's action, one reporter wrote, "exemplifies to the doubting element of both parties the dreaded third party, a petticoat hierarchy which may at will upset all orderly slates and commit undreamed of executions at the polls."[3]

Faced with such a spectre, politicians moved quickly to win the support of the new voters. The Democratic convention of 1920 incorporated twelve of fifteen League of Women Voters proposals in its national party platform, and the Republican convention endorsed five. The Republican presidential nominee, Warren Harding, invited prominent women leaders to his home and called for equal pay for women, an eight-hour day, passage of maternity and infancy legislation, and creation of a federal department of social welfare. Both parties appointed women as equal members of their respective national committees, and each named female aspirants to governmental positions.[4]

State politicians reacted with equal warmth to the potentially powerful new voters. By the end of 1921 twenty state legislatures had granted women the right to serve on juries. Other states passed night work laws and wage and hour legislation specifically designed to accommodate the wishes of female reformers. Michigan and Montana enacted equal-pay laws, Wisconsin approved a far-reaching equal rights bill, and lawmakers throughout the South showed a new flexibility toward social legislation. The Georgia assembly treated women lobbyists with unprecedented respect, and the Virginia legislature granted reform leaders eighteen of twenty-four requests, including a children's code, a child placement bill and a vocational education law.[5]

Congress, meanwhile, demonstrated its concern for women by acting expeditiously on maternity and infancy legislation, the primary demand of female reform organizations. The Sheppard-Towner bill, calling for an annual appropriation of $1,250,000 for educational instruction in the health care of mothers and babies, stirred immediate controversy when it was first introduced in May 1921. Opponents tried to kill the measure by calling it "federal mid-wifery" and "official meddling between mother and baby which would mean the abolition of the family." Supporters of the bill, however, responded with an impressive display of power. Under the banner "Herod Is Not Dead," *Good Housekeeping* documented the tragic toll in human life caused by maternal and infant illness and secured the endorsements of thirty-four governors. Harriet Taylor Upton, national vice-chairman of the Republican party, enlisted Harding's support by repeatedly holding out the threat of feminine retaliation at the polls. Representatives of women's reform groups lobbied intensively for the measure and offered dramatic testimony before legislative hearings. No one spoke with more fervor or greater authority than Florence Kelley, executive secretary of the National Consumers League. Citing the fact that a quarter of a million infants died each year in America, she inquired: "What answer can be given to the women who are marveling and asking, 'Why does Congress wish women and children to die?' " The *Journal of the American Medical Association* declared that the women had created "one of the strongest lobbies that has ever been seen in Washington."[6]

Faced with the unremitting pressure of female reform groups, Congress passed the bill. "If the members could have voted in the cloak room," one backer of the measure asserted later, "it would have been killed." As it was, the act passed with only seven dissenting votes in the Senate and thirty-nine in the House. "The Senators did not quite dare to turn it down," a former suffragist wrote. No other event demonstrated so dramatically the eagerness of politicians to win over the unknown quantity introduced into the electorate by the enactment of the Nineteenth Amendment. The statute represented precisely the kind of protection of human life which the suffragists had talked about as women's special concern. And it indicated the influence which women might exert on a continuing basis if they acted in a concerted way to express their wishes on issues and candidates.[7]

In subsequent years, female reformers enjoyed additional successes. Congress passed the Packers and Stockyards bill in 1921 designed to increase consumer protection; the Cable Act in 1922 reforming citizenship requirements for married women; the Lehlbach Act of 1923 upgrading the merit system in the civil service; and the Child Labor Amendment to the Constitution in 1924. Each bill was strongly supported by the Women's Joint Congressional Committee, an umbrella organization established by various female groups to coordinate legislative activity. If not every item desired by women activists was enacted, enough received some attention to sustain the hopes of female leaders.[8]

Beginning in mid-decade, however,

women's standing in the eyes of politicians dropped precipitously. A Congressional supporter urged the Women's Joint Congressional Committee to reduce its pressure for a home economics measure because Congress was tired of being asked to pass women's legislation. The Child Labor Amendment, which had engaged the energies of so many reform groups, failed ratification in the key states of Massachusetts and New York as Catholic bishops joined the opposition with claims that the amendment would destroy the sanctity of the home. Appropriations for the Women's Bureau and Children's Bureau were cut, and a two-year extension of the Sheppard-Towner Act was secured only by inserting into the new measure a written statement that the act would permanently expire on June 30, 1929. Congressmen seemed as intent on rebuffing the requests of female reformers in the second half of the decade as they had been in granting them during the first half.[9]

The abrupt reversal of fortune bewildered and demoralized women leaders. Just a few years before, their reform coalition had wielded considerable influence over Congress and state politicians. Now they were an embattled minority fighting a rearguard action against the destruction of programs already established. To some extent, the decline could be attributed to a conservative shift in national affairs. In the 1924 elections, the voters had flocked to the candidacy of Calvin Coolidge and rejected the Progressive challenge of Robert La Follette. The Supreme Court cut the ground from beneath many reform proposals by ruling against a federal child labor law and minimum-wage legislation for women. And a rash of red-baiting attacks had smeared women's organizations as Communist front groups.[10] Insofar as women's groups were part of a broader Progressive alliance, they were bound to suffer when reform became less popular than it once had been.

Fundamentally, however, women's political standing plummeted because the mass of female citizens failed to act in the cohesive and committed manner which the suffragists had predicted. The recognition which women had received in the years immediately after 1919 was based in large part on the claim that females would vote at the polls as a monolithic "bloc." With the passage of time, however, it became increasingly clear that no female bloc existed, that women in general voted like their husbands if they voted at all, and that enthusiasm among females for reform was limited at best. "Not one of the disasters has come to pass that four years ago glowered so fearsomely upon the politicians' trade," a reporter wrote in 1924. "Not a boss has been unseated, not a reactionary committee wrested from the old-time control. . . . Nothing has been changed." Other observers agreed. "I know of no woman today who has any influence or political power because she is a woman," Democratic Committeewoman Emily Newell Blair declared. "I know of no woman who has a following of other women. I know of no politician who is afraid of the woman vote on any question under the sun."[11]

The poor performance of women voters at the polls constituted the most crushing blow to suffragist hopes. Despite extensive efforts by the League of Women Voters to educate the new members of the electorate, women failed to exercise the franchise in substantial proportions. A low turnout in some states in the 1920 elections could be explained by the fact that the suffrage amendment was not ratified until August 1920. But in New York, where women had been given the franchise in 1917, females cast only 35 per cent of the total vote in 1920. In Illinois, where the suffrage had been granted in 1913, the figure was slightly higher, but only 46.5 per cent of the women eligible to vote went to the polls in contrast to 74.1 per cent of the men. Three years later, in the Chicago mayoralty election, women cast only 36 per cent of the vote, and they comprised 75 per cent of the eligible adults who were not registered. "Unless they have some personal or family contact with the political questions at issue," the Illinois *State Journal* concluded, "women do not vote."[12]

Equally devastating to suffragist predictions was the lack of evidence that women voted differently from men. Instead of becoming more and more solidified, a journalist commented in 1923, "the women's bloc . . . tends to become more and more disintegrated."[13] Occasionally, on issues like Prohibition or corruption in government, females voted in slightly larger proportions than men for the "moral" candidate; but in general, women voted according to their social and economic backgrounds and the political preference of their husbands rather than according to their sex.[14] Almost all the newspaper editors polled by the *Literary Digest* in 1924 reported that there was no distinction between the political behavior of men and women. Reform leaders had argued "passionately, if ignorantly" that females would use their ballot unselfishly for all mankind, Democratic national committeewoman Emma Guffey Miller noted, "but our first campaign taught us . . . that women were no more motivated by altruism or sense of historical perspective than men." [15]

In the aftermath of the Chicago mayoral election of 1923, Charles Merriam and Herbert Gosnell attempted to isolate the causes of female non-voting through interviews with those who had failed to go to the polls. Almost a third of the women surveyed pleaded general lack of interest in politics. Immigrant women, in particular, blamed ignorance of the balloting process and fear of embarrassment over language difficulties. The largest specific cause cited, however, was "disbelief in woman's voting." Over 11 percent of those interviewed stated that females should stay at home and leave politics to men. In addition, many of those who had intended to vote explained that they neglected to go to the polls at the last moment because their husbands had failed to remind them.[16]

Other observers noted the same tendency of women to defer to men when it came to politics. A *New York Times* reporter covering registration activities on the Lower East Side in 1920 commented that females comprised only one out of four new voters and that those women who did register were brought by their husbands. Sue White, a leading suffragist and Southern Democrat, explained that in her region women stayed away from politics because male party members insisted that government was a man's game. And the Minnesota League of Women Voters reported that female citizens in that state "were too timid to participate in an election where men folks made it plain that they were not wanted." The fact that most women were expected to concentrate on caring for the home further impeded their involvement in politics. Although the suffragists had argued that political activity was simply an extension of women's housekeeping role, a League of Women Voters official in New York noted that many women failed to vote owing to their absorption in homemaking. Women saw little relationship between their votes and the conduct of public policy, the *New York Times* observed, and hence felt no great urgency to go to the polls.[17]

Although much of the discussion of female voting behavior during the 1920's was impressionistic, subsequent research has confirmed the accuracy of earlier commentators on almost every point. A high degree of political participation, political scientists have concluded, depends at least in part on the presence of group pressures emphasizing the importance of the ballot, and the absence of cross-pressures discouraging political independence.[18] In the case of women, each variable worked against their voting in the same proportion as men. Despite the existence of organizations like the League of Women Voters, most women received little encouragement to vote. Unless they had supportive husbands, it was often just as easy not to go to the polls. More important, the whole notion of woman's place contradicted the idea of female political independence. The value of the vote, Angus Campbell has written, "is relevant to role beliefs that presume woman to be a submissive partner. Man is expected to be dominant in action toward the world outside the family; the woman is to accept his leadership passively." Studies of political behavior in the post–World War II period have shown that persons casting a vote for the first time generally follow the example of an authority figure in the family. Where disagreement exists, the new voter usually decides to abstain from political participation altogether.[19]

Projected backward in time, such observations help to explain why women during the 1920's either voted like their husbands or joined the ranks of those who with complete respectability ignored politics entirely. For females to vote at all required a substantial break from their conventional role. To ask that they oppose their husbands or fathers in the process entailed a commitment which only the most dedicated could sustain. As Emily Newell Blair observed in 1925, the very idea of a woman's bloc presumed the existence of a man's bloc as well; yet neither society nor the family could withstand the divisiveness of females fighting for one set of principles and males for another. The suffragists had anticipated that "women would organize along sex lines, nominate women, urge special legislation, and vote en masse." But such an expectation represented a "hallucination."[20] Women differed in emotions, ideals, and prejudices just as men did. They belonged to a variety of groups which held different political opinions. And their outlook was determined primarily by the social and economic backgrounds of their husbands. Ironically, the "special sex-cohesion" which women did manifest was negative rather than positive. Precisely because of the nature of sex roles, it was almost mandatory for wives and daughters to follow the lead of a male "authority figure" when they went to the polls.

The absence of a dramatic "woman's" issue of overriding proportions constituted a final obstacle to the realization of suffragist hopes. In the years before 1920, the vote had been equated with freedom and a substantial number of females had rallied to the suffrage banner. After the enactment of the Nineteenth Amendment, however, no issue of comparable dimension arose. Veterans of the suffrage fight found politics pale and uninspiring, Carrie Chapman Catt wrote, and missed the "exaltation, the thrill of expectancy, the vision which stimulated them in the suffrage campaign." The ballot had provided a "symbol" which united women, Anna Howard Shaw observed, but after the franchise was acquired, the symbol was lost.[21] Even if there had been a cause around which to mobilize female voters, it is unlikely that women would have responded with the same amount of commitment achieved in the suffrage fight. But without such an issue, there was almost no possibility of generating a sense of sex solidarity, or building an independent female constituency.

The problem of defining a separate "female" interest dominated the discussion of the League of Women Voters when it was formed in 1919 to provide organizational leadership for the newly enfranchised citizens. In the tradition of suffragist rhetoric, Carrie Chapman Catt exhorted the delegates to lead a "crusade that shall not end until the electorate is intelligent, clean and American."[22] When it came to specifics, however, the League faced a more difficult task. The central issue confronting the new group was whether it wished to integrate women within the existing political system or segregate them as an independent political force. Both alternatives had support. The whole goal of the suffrage campaign had been to liberate women so that they could join men as equals in the political and social institutions of the country. On the other hand, the fight had been waged on the premise that females had a special set of interests which distinguished them from men and made it necessary for them to have a separate voice. Each position thus represented a powerful segment of the woman's movement. Yet the two were mutually contradictory.

The debate over League policy toward partisan politics polarized the organization's leadership. Carrie Chapman Catt insisted that "the only way to get things done is to get them done on the inside of a political party." She urged women to participate directly in the political process and master party techniques. They would not be welcome, she predicted, but they had to try. "You will see the real thing in the center with the door locked tight. You will have a long hard fight before you get inside . . . but you must move right up to the center." Catt denounced the idea of sex segregation and even suggested that the word "women" be dropped from the League's title.[23] On the other side, however, equally powerful voices eschewed the policy of integration and condemned party politics as the tool of autocrats concerned only with self-aggrandizement. Prominent leaders like Jane Addams believed that unless women retained their identity as a separate interest group they would destroy the very principles which made them unique. Females were concerned with public service and high ideals, males with private profit and personal power. Consequently, if women accepted the discipline of regular party membership, they would violate their conscience and compromise their effectiveness.[24]

Anxious politicians interpreted the debate as a signal that the League intended to start a third party. President Harding warned against "organizing our citizenship into groups according to sex"; Mrs. Medill McCormick, an Illinois Republican leader, charged that the League was obstructing the enrollment of women into regular party groups; and the governor of New York denounced the organization as a "menace" to national life, a threat to traditional political allegiances.[25] In fact, however, there was little chance that women could be united under a single political banner. Females held too many diverse points of view and were too dependent on male leadership, to forge an alliance along sex lines. Moreover, League leaders themselves had neither the will nor the issues to create a third-party movement. Even those members who believed most vehemently in the existence of a separate woman's point of view rejected the idea of establishing an independent political organization. From their point of view, party politics by definition were unsavory.

In the end, the League resolved the conflict over its political role by compromise. Rather than create a new party, it determined to mobilize public opinion behind reform programs and to instruct women in the tasks of citizenship so that they could work more effectively within existing political organizations. "We have got to be nonpartisan and all-partisan," Catt said. Democratic and Republican women would work together for common ends, even while moving to the centers of their respective parties.[26] The League still failed to define the "common ends" which united women, however. It retained a diffuse belief that females, by virtue of their sex, had a special concern with issues like social welfare and education, but it was unable to give that concern a convincing focus, or to provide an institutional means by which women could express their interests in a cohesive way. The suffragists had assumed that women would automatically act together for a common set of principles, but their successors found it almost impossible to carry that assumption into practice.

Without a solid "woman's" issue around

which to rally female citizens, the League and other reform organizations lost much of the popular appeal which the suffragists had enjoyed. In Dade County, Wisconsin, a thousand women attended a meeting to learn about the ballot but only eleven joined the League of Women Voters. A local officer wrote that the League had not yet demonstrated its value or relevance. "Its reason for existence," she noted, "is far less compelling to the average woman than that of the suffrage organization." The Minnesota League complained that few women were willing to accept responsibility as county leaders, and by mid-1921 the organization in South Dakota was almost moribund. Other reform groups experienced similar problems. The Women's Trade Union League was torn by internal dissension over its future course of action, and the Federation of Women's Clubs—once a decisive voice in the Progressive coalition—abandoned politics entirely, choosing to emphasize home economics and the distribution of electrical appliances rather than political action.[27]

Individual female leaders, of course, continued to make distinguished contributions to a variety of causes. The peace movement proved especially compelling to suffragists like Carrie Chapman Catt and Jane Addams. Catt announced in 1925 that women could never be liberated until war was abolished, and thereafter devoted almost all of her energies to the Committee on the Cause and Cure of War, an organization which she founded. Jane Addams had been a leader of the Women's International League for Peace and Freedom since its beginning in 1915, and toward the last part of her life, spent an increasing amount of time in the effort to mobilize public sentiment on behalf of disarmament. Women peace advocates established an effective lobby in Washington and were directly responsible for the Nye investigation of the munitions industry in the early 1930's. Other women performed invaluable service in the cause of social-welfare legislation and more efficient government. Almost singlehandedly, Florence Kelley kept the fight for a Child Labor Amendment alive, and female reformers in the League of Women Voters and other organizations campaigned across the country for the establishment of the city manager form of municipal government.[28]

Despite such accomplishments, however, no group succeeded in galvanizing the mass of women—as women—into the effective force for change which female reformers had predicted. Five years after the passage of the Nineteenth Amendment, the highly cohesive popular constituency of the suffragists had disintegrated. At the height of its success, NAWSA boasted a membership of 2 million women. By mid-decade, however, the woman's movement had regressed to its earlier status as a small cadre of activists. The League of Women Voters claimed to represent all the former members of NAWSA, but in fact it kept only a fraction. Cleveland contributed 80,000 women to the suffrage fight, only 8,000 to the League.[29] Notwithstanding the claims of some leaders, most women showed no evidence of collective self-consciousness. They responded to public affairs as individuals rather than as members of a special group with a distinctive set of interests.

Without an independent power base of their own, female reformers became dependent on the favor of party officials for whatever influence they might exert. As long as politicians believed that women might constitute a cohesive bloc of voters, they were willing to make at least some positive response to the demands of female organizations. Once it became clear that the reformers had overstated their case, however, the concessions stopped. Male leaders appointed individual women who shared their point of view to party posts, but reformers were either excluded or kept in minor positions. The men retained control, and they preferred women who got down to the "practical things of politics," as Harry Hawes wrote Emma Guffey Miller, over the "visionary theorists" who headed the reform movement.[30]

The women chosen for elective position reflected party policy. Officeholding for females, the reporter Emma Bugbee observed in 1930, was primarily a "widow's game." Two-thirds of those who served in Congress from 1920 to 1930 succeeded their dead husbands, most for only a single term. Of the two woman governors, one—Nellie Ross—took over from her deceased spouse, and the other—"Ma" Ferguson—stood in for her husband in a successful attempt to circumvent a Texas constitutional provision prohibiting the state's chief executive from serving consecutive terms of office. No female officeholder during the 1920's served with special distinction. Most either accommodated male leaders, or remained in office for so brief a time that there was little opportunity to build influence.[31]

The career of Mary Norton exemplified the experience of most female politicians during the 1920's. Norton first came to the attention of local Democrats when she approached Frank Hague, mayor of Jersey City, for help in securing public funds for nursery school education. Two years later, after woman suffrage had passed, the mayor requested her to go on the Democratic state committee to assist in mobilizing the female vote. Norton told Hague that she had no interest in either politics or the suffrage, but her protestations were dismissed as irrelevant. No woman knew anything about politics, Hague said, and in any event the position of state committeewoman was an empty honor which required no work. Four years later, Norton was handpicked to represent Jersey City in Congress, a position which she held for twenty-six years. She later concluded that the leaders of her party wanted "the honor of sending the first woman of the Democratic party to Congress." More to the point was Mary Dewson's comment to party boss Jim Farley that "Mayor Hague did not want any rival in his field and felt safer with the Congressman from Jersey City a woman."[32] Although Norton performed with notable distinction in Congress during the 1930's and '40's, the manner of her selection demonstrated the desire of political leaders to choose female officeholders who were amenable to control by party bosses.

The appointment of Rebecca Felton as the first woman senator highlighted the disparity between the shadow and substance of female power. Mrs. Felton, an octogenarian from Georgia, was named in 1922 to fill a temporary vacancy caused by death. Her tenure lasted for approximately an hour and resulted from a temporary suspension of the rules permitting a postponement of the swearing in of Walter George, the regularly elected senator. For a few short minutes, one commentator wrote, "the woman senator held court . . . on the Senate floor in the midst of flowers and congratulations while national affairs awaited her exit." Once the honorary ritual was concluded, however, the male legislators returned to their seats and Mrs. Felton returned to Georgia. Womanhood had been acknowledged. In contrast, when Eleanor Roosevelt and other female liberals arrived at the 1924 Democratic convention with a series of proposals on the child labor amendment and other social-welfare measures, they were virtually ignored. Hour after hour, the women sat outside the Platform Committee hearings, hoping in vain that the Committee would listen to their plea and reconsider its rejection of a favorable resolution on the child labor amendment. The party leadership was ever ready with flowery honors. But when it came to the formation of party policy, woman's place remained that of an outsider.[33]

Significantly, the one occasion when women did succeed in gaining political influence occurred when Mrs. Roosevelt was an occupant of the White House and the President actively encouraged female participation in party affairs. Just as the Progressive era had provided a vehicle for advancement of the suffrage cause, the New Deal offered an opportunity for female social workers to put their principles to work through government service. As the Depression deepened, women reformers flocked to Washington to help manage the nation's emergency relief and social-welfare programs. Most of the women who came took professional positions in the WPA and other agencies, but some accepted political responsibilities as well. Among the latter was Mary Dewson, a leader of the National Consumers League and a close personal friend of the Roosevelts. Combining impeccable reform credentials with brilliant political instincts, Dewson assumed direction of women's work for the Democratic party in 1932 and succeeded for the first time in bringing women into the center of party councils.[34] Her experience proved that females could work effectively within the party system, even if they still lacked cohesion as a voting bloc.

Like most female reformers, Dewson was convinced that women differed fundamentally from men. Women wanted a better-ordered society and cared primarily about the "security of the home," she believed; men, on the other hand, sought power and individual distinction. In contrast to most reformers, however, Dewson placed her instincts about women's special nature at the service of a specific party. The political organization which first recognized the inherent differences between the sexes, she asserted, would benefit immeasurably. In the past, female politicians had failed to make any impact because they had aped men. The parties in turn had failed to recruit female supporters because they had not appealed to women's sexually distinctive interests. Dewson intended to correct that error by treating women as a special class and directing her attention to issues such as public welfare in which women had a specific interest.[35]

Education constituted the heart of Dewson's political strategy. "In 1932 we did not make the old-fashioned plea that our nominee was charming," she told an interviewer after the election. "Instead, we appealed to the intelligence of the country's women." Relying on what she called the "endless chain principle," Dewson urged women party members to be the "mouth to mouth, house to house interpreters of the New Deal" and its programs. Under her Reporter Plan, female party workers in each community were deputized to become expert on a New Deal program such as social security and to inform the electorate on a door-to-door basis of its importance for their lives. By 1936, 15,000 women Reporters were carrying the information they received from Washington to their local communities, ringing doorbells, explaining federal policies, and converting doubtful voters.[36]

In four years, Dewson transformed the Women's Division from a useless appendage of the Democratic party into a vital element in its continued success. When Jim Farley tried to cut the division's program in an economy move, the President enlarged it instead and gave Dewson added powers.[37] The Chief Executive's vote of confidence paid off in the 1936 election when over 60,000 female precinct workers canvassed the electorate. Local women's committees sponsored Radio Parties focusing on broadcasts by the President, and the Women's Division Rainbow Fliers—one-page pastel fact sheets on major New Deal accomplishments—constituted the principal literature distributed by the national party. Over 83 million fliers were circulated by the end of the campaign, each emphasizing how the New Deal helped the average person to save his home or to keep his family together.[38]

Through her efforts, Molly Dewson contributed significantly to the broadening of the Democratic constituency which occurred in the Roosevelt Administration. She directed her efforts not at solid party followers but at voters without a party affiliation. "There is a big group of people who are interested in issues and these are the ones that I want telling about what the New Deal is doing," she wrote. Despite Jim Farley's objections she dedicated herself to winning over intellectuals and independents. To widen the party's appeal she secured the President's approval of an Advisory Commission of New Dealers to be comprised primarily of independents, and in her own division she established special committees to deal with Negroes, educators, social workers, and writers. At a time when many party leaders still emphasized reliance on the old political machines, she helped to spearhead the New Deal's attempt to reach out beyond the established political structure and build new loyalties based on the issues.[39]

As a result of Dewson's achievement, women gained new recognition in party ranks. The 1936 Democratic convention passed a rule requiring that each delegate to the Platform Committee be accompanied by an alternate of the opposite sex, thereby ensuring fifty-fifty representation on the committee which had excluded Eleanor Roosevelt twelve years before. A *New York Times* reporter described the new rule as "the biggest coup for women in years," and Emily Newell Blair told a nationwide radio audience that for the first time female delegates were being treated as equals with men. Each day of the convention, the Washington *Times* noted, "the party leaders have recognized in some way the ability of women, and their value to the party." Seven of eight planks desired by the Women's Division were incorporated into the party platform, and Jim Farley named eight females as vice-chairmen of the national committee in an effort to establish parity with men.[40] In addition, women's patronage increased dramatically. Dewson later claimed that she "never cared much about the machinery of politics," but she knew enough to ensure that her own workers were rewarded for their efforts. Female party members were placed in nearly every department of government, and women's share of postmasterships shot up from 17.6 per cent in 1930 to 26 per cent from 1932 to 1938.[41]

The number of females appointed to policy-making posts testified most dramatically to the Roosevelt Administration's appreciation of women's talents. For the first time, women occupied the positions of Cabinet member (Frances Perkins), minister to a foreign country (Ruth Bryan Owen Rohde and Florence Jaffrey Harriman), and judge of the U.S. Circuit Court of Appeals (Florence Allen). Ellen Woodward, Hilda Smith, and Florence Kerr held executive offices in the WPA, and Lorena Hickok acted as Harry Hopkins' eyes and ears in trips across the country to observe the progress of the New Deal's relief program. At times, Washington seemed like a perpetual convention of social workers as women from the Consumers League, the Women's Trade Union League, and other reform groups came to Washington to take on government assignments. Mary Anderson, director of the Women's Bureau, recalled that in earlier years women government officials had dined together in a small university club. "Now," she said, "there are so many of them they would need a hall."[42]

The increased political role of women during the 1930's had a number of causes, but perhaps the most important was the dynamic leadership of Eleanor Roosevelt. As First Lady, Mrs. Roosevelt exercised an influence over public policy unparalleled in the history of the White House. The President relied on her for advice on a variety of issues and trusted her political judgment implicitly. Mrs. Roosevelt was charged with coordination of the women's campaign in 1932 and was asked to supervise the entire re-election effort in 1936. As the Chief Executive's personal representative, she toured the country repeatedly, surveying conditions in the coal mines, visiting relief projects, and speaking out for the human rights of the disadvantaged. Her travels enabled her to provide information on social and political questions which might not otherwise receive the President's attention, and more than one government project owed its existence to her interest and sponsorship.[43]

Not surprisingly, Mrs. Roosevelt played an instrumental part in persuading Mary Dewson and other social-welfare workers to become involved in government work. During her years in New York, she had participated actively in the endeavors of the Women's City Club and other civic organizations, and her own ability to combine public service with partisan political activity convinced doubtful female reformers that they could work within the party system without compromising their principles. Women throughout the administration looked upon her as a personal friend and as a "resident lobbyist" for their point of view. Her presence in the White House ensured that the voice of female reformers would not be ignored in government councils and that any grievances they felt would receive prompt and fair consideration at the highest level.[44]

The relevance of New Deal programs to the home and family also contributed to the increase in women's political activity. Throughout the 1920's, with the exception of the Sheppard-Towner bill and the Child Labor Amendment, politics had been dominated by issues essentially unrelated to women's primary sphere of responsibility. With the coming of the Great Depression, however, the actions of government affected every household in the land. Political decisions determined whether children would have new shoes, whether a mortgage would be foreclosed, whether a mother could feed her family. Government ceased to be extraneous to the concerns of the family but instead provided school lunches, aid to dependent children, and relief checks which helped the family to survive. Mary Dewson had devoted her entire life to such welfare measures, and with the encouragement of the President, she sought in every way possible to identify national politics with the "bread and butter" priorities of women in the home.

Nevertheless, it would be a mistake to conclude that under the Roosevelt Administration, the goals of the suffragists were suddenly realized. The women who honeycombed New Deal relief agencies came to Washington primarily because they were reformers, not because they were females. They shared a common commitment with men like Harry Hopkins, Aubrey Williams, and Harold Ickes to an issue-oriented politics and to greater federal involvement in social-welfare programs. For both male and female reformers, the New Deal represented an exciting, humane approach to the problems of government. Its appeal was based not on a distinctively "female" point of view, but on the attitude it brought to the solution of a grave national crisis. The influence which women such as Mary Dewson and Lorena Hickok acquired testified more to their long-standing participation in the social-welfare movement than to a belief that females deserved special recognition by virtue of their sex.[45]

Furthermore, the rise in women's political standing depended to a peculiar extent on their ties to the White House. Mary Dewson was the first to acknowledge the importance of her relationship with the Roosevelts. She had experienced no difficulty in getting started in politics, she recalled, "because FDR backed me." He alone among modern politicians had recognized that women had a contribution to make to politics. Dewson corresponded almost daily with Mrs. Roosevelt, and, when questions of great urgency arose, the First

Lady seated her next to the President at dinner so that she could persuade him to her point of view. Women's Division requests for help went in duplicate to the White House, often to be followed up by a personal note of endorsement from the President or his wife to the appropriate government or party official.[46] Dewson succeeded in implementing her educational program because at every critical juncture the President supported her. Significantly, when she retired from active politicking in 1937, her colleagues found it more difficult to see Jim Farley, let alone enlist his support for their demands.[47]

Even with the gains which had been made, therefore, women leaders still lacked the independent power to force equal recognition with men. The critical problem remained the absence of a politically cohesive female constituency. If women voters had formed a separate bloc in the electorate, female leaders could have backed up their claims with convincing threats of reprisal at the polls. Without such a bloc, however, they lacked a base of support and were forced to rely on the help of party leaders for whatever influence they acquired. Although it was likely that the mass of women became more politically conscious during the Depression, there was no evidence that they voted together or shared a distinctive approach to government. Thus the principal assumption of the suffragists still had no basis in reality. Indeed, in some ways the New Deal confirmed the failure of suffragist predictions, because it illustrated the extent to which women's success depended on the favor of those in power.

At least in part, the disappointing results of the suffrage experience could be traced to the inflated rhetoric of female leaders. By treating the Nineteenth Amendment as a panacea, the suffragists had raised hopes which could not be realized. Almost none of the measures adopted during the Progressive era accomplished the goals envisioned by its sponsors, and the suffrage was no exception. As one journalist observed in 1936, the Nineteenth Amendment, "like the secret ballot, the corrupt practices act, the popular election of senators, and the direct primary, promised almost everything and accomplished almost nothing."[48] In effect, the suffragists had demanded too much of the ballot. Political change occurred gradually, and it was unrealistic to expect that extending the vote to women would transform the nation's political and social institutions.

The basic problem, however, was that the suffrage failed to change the special status of women in relation to the wider society. In predicting that women would act together to spearhead a drive for social change, the suffragists had correctly assumed that all females shared a common experience based on their sex. But they failed to realize that, unlike some other minority groups, women were distributed throughout the social structure and had little opportunity to develop a positive sense of collective self-consciousness. More important, they underestimated the barriers obstructing the creation of such consciousness. One of the central experiences which women shared was their relationship with men, yet nothing did more to discourage the growth of an independent female constituency. As long as women were expected to follow the lead of their husbands and fathers in activities outside the home, it was hardly likely that they could act as a separate and autonomous segment within the electorate. Occasionally an issue like the suffrage focused overriding attention on the identity of women as women and generated a heightened sense of sex solidarity. But such issues emerged only rarely, and in the normal course of events women responded to political questions in the manner dictated by the men in their lives. Females did behave alike, but the sameness of their actions represented conformity to the role of helpmate rather than an assertion of their independence as a sex. Indeed, there was something contradictory about the whole notion of a female bloc. If the similarity of women's action was rooted in their subservience to men, once liberated from that "female" role, they would act as individuals, not members of a group.

In the end, therefore, it appeared that Elizabeth Cady Stanton had more correctly assessed the importance of the ballot than her twentieth-century successors. Discrimination against women was deeply rooted in the structure of society—in the roles women played, and in a sexual division of labor which restricted females primarily to the domestic sphere of life. Whatever else it accomplished, the suffrage did not alter that structure. Female leaders understandably believed that they had won a decisive victory with the acquisition of the franchise, but they made the mistake of mislabeling the nature of their accomplishment. The Nineteenth Amendment was a reform, not a revolution.

NOTES

1. Stanton's statement is quoted in William L. O'Neill, *Everyone Was Brave* (Chicago, 1969), p. 19.

2. Part III of an autobiographical typescript, Grace and Edith Abbott Papers, University of Chicago Library, Addenda II, Box 1; Stuart Rice, *Quantitative Methods in Politics* (New York, 1928), p. 177; E. O. Toombs, "Politicians Take Notice," *Good Housekeeping*, LXX (March 1920), pp. 14–15; "Much Surprised City Officials Ousted by Women," *Literary Digest*, LXVII (December 4, 1920), pp. 52–54; James Stanley Lemons, "The New Woman in the New Era: The Woman's Movement from the Great War to the Great Depression," unpublished doctoral dissertation, University of Missouri, 1967, pp. 142–43.

3. *New York Times*, March 30, 1920; August 14, 1920; February 17, 1920; April 7, 1922; July 24, 1920. See also "The Excursion," an account of the early history of the LWV in the Dorothy Kirchwey Brown Papers, the Arthur and Elizabeth Schlesinger Library on the History of Women in America (hereafter SL), Box 1; Olive H. P. Belmont, "Women as Dictators," *Ladies Home Journal*, XXXIX (September 1922); and clipping, n.d., Ethel Dreier Papers, Sophia Smith Collection, Smith College, Box 3.

4. *New York Times*, September 21, 1920; James Stanley Lemons, pp. 117–18, 136–37; Ida Harper, "The American Woman Gets the Vote," *Review of Reviews*, LXII (October 1920), pp. 380–84; League of Women Voters Press Release, July 2, 1920, in LWV Papers, Library of Congress, Series II, Box 6; and Mrs. Alvin Hirt to Helen M. Rocca, January 23, 1926, LWV Papers Box 43. The LWV platform for 1920 called for passage of maternity and infancy legislation, a federal department of education, federal aid for vocational training, regulation of marketing, a merit system in the civil service, and reform of citizenship qualifications for married women.

5. Lemons, p. 115; Anne F. Scott, "After Suffrage: Southern Women in the Twenties," *Journal of Southern History*, XXX (August 1964), pp. 304–6.

6. Lemons, pp. 232–35; "The Maternity and Infancy Measure," Elizabeth Hewes Tilton Papers, SL, Box 3; April 1956 history of the LWV, Brown Papers, Box 1; Josephine Goldmark, *Impatient Crusader* (Urbana, 1953), p. 9; Charles Selden, "Most Powerful Lobby in Washington," *Ladies Home Journal*, XXXIX (April 1920); and Clarke Chambers, *Seedtime of Reform* (Ann Arbor, 1967), p. 50.

7. See Lemons, p. 249; Chambers, p. 50; and an autobiographical typescript, Madeleine Doty Papers, Sophia Smith Collection, Smith College, Box 1.

8. Edna Kenton, "Four Years of Equal Suffrage," *Forum*, LXXII (July 1924), pp. 37–44; Mrs. H. V. Joslin to the Women's Joint Congressional Committee (WJCC), September 4, 1927, WJCC Papers, Library of Congress, Box 2; and minutes of WJCC Annual Meeting, November 19, 1923, and December 8, 1924, WJCC Papers, Box 6.

9. January 12, 1925, minutes of the WJCC, WJCC Papers, Box 6; Chambers, pp. 40–43; Lemons, p. 339; and "The Maternity and Infancy Measure," Tilton Papers. Another sign of the decline of women's influence as a pressure group was that from 1922 to 1935 only one state passed legislation granting women the right to serve on juries.

10. In the case of *Adkins* v. *Children's Hospital*, 261 U.S. 525 (1923), Justice George Sutherland declared that women's status had improved to such a point that protective legislation was no longer necessary. Needless to say, female reformers disagreed. The red-baiting attack had the support of many anti-suffragists and emanated from the Office of Chemical Warfare Services in the War Department. Women's organizations were depicted as being part of a "spider web" conspiracy to entrap women into service to the Communist cause. The LWV Papers, Box 31, and the Mary Anderson Papers, SL, Box 1 both contain voluminous information on the smear campaign.

11. Charles E. Russell, "Is Woman's Suffrage a Failure?" *Century*, CVII (March 1924), pp. 724–30; Emily Newell Blair, "Are Women a Failure in Politics?" *Harpers*, CLI (October 1925), pp. 513–22.

12. The estimate of New York's woman vote was made by Mary Garrett Hay in the *New York Times*, January 16, 1922. The Illinois figures are found in Stuart H. Rice and Malcolm Willey, "American Women's Ineffective Use of the Vote," *Current History*, XX (July 1924), pp. 641–47. The Chicago figures come from Charles Merriam and Herbert Gosnell, *Non-Voting* (Chicago, 1924), pp. ix, 7. The *State Journal* quotation is from "Why More Women Voters Don't Vote," *Literary Digest*, LXXXI (May 24, 1924), pp. 5–7.

13. Quoted in O'Neill, p. 264.

14. In 1920, for example, New Jersey women voters were reported to have turned out in large numbers where Prohibition was a significant issue. William Ogburn noted the same phenomenon in Portland, Oregon. But on the basis of extensive poll data, political scientists generally agree that there is no predictable or statistically meaningful connection between sex and voting habits or party affiliation. See William F. Ogburn, "How Women Vote, A Study of Portland, Oregon," *Political Science Quarterly*, XXXIV (September 1919), pp. 413–33; Seymour Martin Lipset, *Political Man* (New York, 1963), pp. 193, 260; Bernard Berelson, Paul Lazarsfeld, and William McPhee, *Voting* (Chicago, 1954), p. 320; Robert F. Lane, *Political Life* (Glencoe, 1959), p. 212; Angus Campbell, Gerald Gurin, and Warren Miller, *The Voter Decides* (Evanston, 1954), pp. 154–55.

15. "Why More Women Voters Don't Vote," *Literary Digest*; and "Recollections and Reflections of a Democratic Campaigner," *Bryn Mawr Alumnae Bulletin*, XIII (May 1933), in Emma Guffey Miller Papers, SL, Box 4.

16. Merriam and Gosnell, pp. 37, 39, 48, 164–67, 181–85, 188–92.

17. *New York Times*, October 17, 1920; Anne Scott, p. 314; Lemons, p. 84; *New York Times*, February 12, 1922, and November 8, 1922; and George Madden Martin, "American Women and Public Affairs," *Atlantic Monthly*, CXXXIII (February 1924), pp. 169–71.

18. Other variables include the relevance of government policies to the prospective voter and ready access to information on politics. See Lipset, pp. 182–229.

19. Political scientists agree that women vote less than men, that they have a lower sense of political efficacy, and that their lack of involvement is directly related to what Lipset calls traditional ideas of woman's place. See Lipset, pp. 209–11, 217, 222–23; Berelson et al., pp. 27, 41, 88–93; Angus Campbell, Philip Convers, and Donald Stokes, *The American Voter*, pp. 255–61; and Campbell et al., *The Voter Decides*, pp. 154–55, 191.

20. Blair, *op. cit.*

21. Carrie Chapman Catt, "What Have Women Done with the Suffrage," 1923 clipping, Catt Papers, Box 1. The Shaw comments are cited in O'Neill, p. 268. Lipset has noted that "a sharp break with a traditional political allegiance . . . by a group can occur only when some experience is perceived as clearly affecting the group's interests and requiring a new political orientation." The point being made here is that there was no transcendent issue during the 1920's which emphasized the distinctive identity of women as women in the same way that the suffrage had. See Lipset, pp. 203, 293.

22. Quoted in a survey of the first ten years of the LWV presented to the 33rd convention of the Massachusetts chapter on May 15, 1957, by Dorothy Kirchwey Brown, Brown Papers, Box 1; see also Mildred Adams, *The Right To Be People* (New York, 1967), p. 171.

23. See Helen Hill Miller, "Carrie Chapman Catt, The Power of an Idea," a pamphlet in the Catt Papers, Box 3; Lemons, p. 139; and *New York Times*, February 13 and 15, 1920. On February 17, 1921, Catt wrote Edna Gellborn and Elizabeth Hauser urging the League to eliminate the word "women" from the title and admit independent minded men in order to counter the charge that the League was fostering sex segregation. LWV Papers, Box 3.

24. For a discussion of the second point of view, see the Dreier Papers, Box 1; Marguerite Wells Papers, SL, Box 1 and Volume I. Dorothy Kirchwey Brown recounts the split between Addams and Catt in "The Excursion," Brown Papers.

25. *New York Times*, November 23, 1921; February 10, 1922; January 15, 1922; and Lemons, pp. 86, 152.

26. Helen Hill Miller, "Carrie Chapman Catt . . ." *op. cit.*; and "The Excursion.". . .

27. Margaret Schonger to Jessie Hooper, December 28, 1920, Jessie Hooper Papers, Wisconsin Historical Society, Box 1; Lemons, pp. 86, 187; O'Neill, pp. 261–62; and the minutes of the Executive Board Meeting, NWTUL, September 11–13, 1925, NWTUL Papers, Box 2.

28. Female involvement in the peace movement is treated in Dorothy Detzer, *Appointment on the Hill* (New York, 1948), and Gertrude Bussey and Margaret Tims, *The Women's International League for Peace and Freedom* (London, 1956). Florence Kelley's life is chronicled in Josephine Goldmark, *Impatient Crusader* (Urbana, 1953).

29. Lemons, p. 86.

30. See O'Neill, p. 267; and Harry Hawes to Emma Guffey Miller, November 9, 1924, Miller Papers, Box 1.

31. New York *Herald Tribune*, April 2 and 3, 1930, clippings, Catt Papers, Box 1; George E. Anderson, "Women in Congress," *Commonweal*, IX (March 13, 1929), pp. 532–34. A memorandum from Lorena Hickok to Mary Norton in October 1945 attributed

the failure of women in Congress to their unwillingness to serve for more than a single term and build seniority. Mary Norton Papers, Rutgers University Library, Box 1.

32. Draft of story by May F. Larkin in *Woman's Voice*, March 26, 1931; Mary Norton to Joseph McCaffrey, June 18, 1953, Norton Papers, Box 1; autobiographical typescript, Norton Papers, Box 6. See also Mary Dewson to Jim Farley, February 3, 1938, Mary Dewson Papers, Franklin Delano Roosevelt Library (hereafter FDRL), Box 9.

33. The commentator's statement is quoted in Lemons, p. 164. See also the *New York Times*, October 5 and 8, and November 16, 1922. Mrs. Roosevelt's experience is described in a 1940 issue of the *Democratic Digest*, clipping, Ellen Sullivan Woodward Papers, SL, Box 1.

34. There were two kinds of women, Emily Newell Blair wrote in 1933—those with a social-welfare point of view and those who were selfishly political. "Molly" was the rare exception who combined the best of both. Emily Newell Blair to Mary Dewson, July 28, 1933, Dewson Papers, FDRL, 1933 Volume on Women's Patronage.

35. Notes for a speech before the Kentucky Women's Clubs, April 1933, in Dewson Papers, FDRL, 1932 Campaign Volume; Mary Dewson, "Organizing the Woman Vote," *Women's Democratic News*, December 1932, in 1932 Campaign Volume; and form letter from Mary Dewson, May 14, 1936, Dewson Papers, FDRL, Box 5. Dewson's feelings about women's distinctiveness bore a remarkable resemblance to those of Marguerite Wells and other LWV officials.

36. Buffalo *Evening News*, January 12, 1933, clipping, Dewson Papers, SL, Box 1; Mary Dewson to Miss Hyde, July 27, 1932, Dewson Papers, FDRL, Box 1; "The Favored State Party Set-Up for Women," n.d., Dewson Papers, FDRL, Box 1; Mrs. James Wolfe to Emma Guffey Miller, April 10, 1936, Dewson Papers, FDRL, Box 2.

37. The President gave the Women's Division authority to increase its budget, enlarge its space at headquarters, and take over the *Democratic Digest*. See Mary Dewson to FDR, December 15, 1934, Dewson Papers, FDRL, Box 1; Mary Dewson to Jim Farley, December 21, 1935, in Democratic National Committee, Women's Division Papers, FDRL, Box 8.

38. "Work of the Women's Division, 1936 Campaign," Dewson Papers, SL, Box 2; "The Favored State Party Set-Up," *op. cit.*; Mary Dewson to Anna C. Struble, July 17, 1936, Dewson Papers, FDRL, Box 5; "Advance of Democratic Women," Dewson Papers, SL, Box 1.

39. Mary Dewson to Joseph McGrath, April 15, 1937, Dewson Papers, FDRL, Box 8; correspondence with Grace and Edith Abbott, Democratic National Committee, Women's Division Papers, FDRL, Boxes 1 and 8; Mary Dewson to FDR, December 1, 1934, Dewson Papers, FDRL, Box 1. Farley was very much opposed to Dewson's ideological approach, but she had the support of the President and other leading figures in the Administration.

40. Mary Dewson to Eleanor Roosevelt, June 19, 1936, Dewson Papers, FDRL, Box 3; the *New York Times* and Washington *Times* stories are cited in Volume II of "An Aid to the End," an autobiographical typescript, Dewson Papers, SL; Mrs. Blair's comments appear in a broadcast transcript in the Democratic National Committee, Women's Division Papers, FDRL, Box 22.

41. Mary Dewson to Lorena Hickok, November 21, 1952, in Dewson Papers, FDRL, Box 16. In letters to Farley throughout 1933 and 1934, Dewson pressed for patronage jobs. In a letter to Mrs. Roosevelt on April 27, 1933 (labeled "about the most important letter I ever wrote you"), she reiterated her plea for jobs. See Dewson Papers, FDRL, 1933 Volume on Patronage. The postal figures are cited in Mary Dewson to Jim Farley, May 18, 1938, Dewson Papers, FDRL, Box 9. The comparative figures come from Sophonisba P. Breckinridge, *Women in the Twentieth Century* (New York, 1933), p. 311.

42. Mary Anderson's comments are quoted in "An Aid to the End," Volume I, *op. cit.* Dewson declared that almost everyone she knew who was doing good work in her own field of regulating labor standards had come to Washington. Mary Dewson to Maud Wood Park, October 16, 1933, Dewson Papers, FDRL, 1932 Campaign Volume.

43. See, for example, Mrs. Roosevelt's letter to Mary Dewson on August 8, 1932, on staff set-up and organizational details for the women's campaign, Dewson Papers, FDRL, Box 1. In 1936 Mrs. Roosevelt instructed Jim Farley, Steve Early, Stanley High, and Mary Dewson to keep her and the President informed on the state of the campaign. Eleanor Roosevelt to Mary Dewson, July 16, 1936, Dewson Papers, FDRL, Box 3. Mrs. Roosevelt championed the cause of Negroes and other oppressed groups and took a direct role in sponsoring the subsistence settlements and Greenbelt communities under the New Deal. For a thorough and perceptive treatment of her activities during these years, see Joseph Lash, *Eleanor and Franklin* (New York, 1971). The Lash volume was published shortly before this book went to press, and for that reason it has not been used extensively here. Lash provides an abundance of additional material documenting Mrs. Roosevelt's role in helping the cause of women in politics and government.

44. See Mary Dewson to Herman Kahn, September 2, 1951, Dewson Papers, FDRL, Box 17; and Eleanor Roosevelt to Mary Dewson, September 1, 1936, Dewson Papers, FDRL, Box 4.

45. Dewson, for example, viewed politics as an extension of social work and declared that she had accom-

plished most for the objectives of social work "in the six political years under the leadership . . . of FDR." Thus while the women who came to Washington had a keen sense of themselves as women, they came basically because the Administration was pursuing reform objectives which they shared with men. In one sense, of course, their experience represented the ideal of equality. Women, as individuals, were playing an important part in determining national policy. But that was not the same thing as acting on behalf of all women to transform society to a specifically female way of looking at things. Mary Dewson to Jim Farley, August 27, 1937, Dewson Papers, FDRL, Box 9.

46. Mary Dewson to Lorena Hickok, n.d., 1953, Dewson Papers, FDRL, Box 16; Mary Dewson to Stephen Mitchell, May 17, 1953, Box 18; "An Aid to the End," Volume 1. Mrs. Roosevelt wrote Dewson on March 11, 1932, that "the nicest thing about politics is lunching with you on Mondays." For examples of Dewson using her influence with Mrs. Roosevelt, see her letter of January 18, 1936, urging Mrs. Roosevelt's help in getting good treatment for women at the 1936 Democratic convention, and the correspondence between the two women on patronage. Dewson Papers, FDRL, Box 4; and the 1933 Volume on Patronage.

47. See, for example, letters from Mrs. Earl Kitchen and Florence Whitney protesting the problems placed in the way of seeing Farley and getting his help. Dewson Papers, FDRL, Box 12; and volume labeled, "Letters, 1929–40."

48. John Gordon Ross, "Ladies in Politics," *Forum*, XCV (November 1936), p. 215. See also O'Neill, pp. 270–72.

21

POLITICAL PARTIES: THE NATIONAL CONVENTION

Democracy has yet to invent an instrument of government that can do what a political party does. For between the isolated, individual votes, and the institutions meant to represent and implement the citizens' will, yawns an enormous organizational gap. Without a party to pull together varying interests into a shared direction, each little group of like-thinking people would wander around bumping into other groups in aimless and unproductive confrontations. The party rallies groups on the basis of ideas—not necessarily large philosophies, more often formulas for cooperation.

As the previous selection showed, women had a hard time breaking into American political parties, those long-time bastions of the all-male boss. One access point turned out to be the national convention, where the party met to nominate candidates for President and Vice-President and to put together a platform to aid their chances. Supposedly the convention represented the party membership, but long after women's suffrage that remained a fiction. If women were represented, it was primarily by men, not by other women. In the late 1960's, pressure began to build for broader party representation, not only by women but also by young people and minorities who felt shut out by traditional party elites. By the 1980's, about half the delegates to the national convention of both parties were women. At long last, women had achieved the quantity of representation appropriate to their numbers in the electorate.

That by no means solved the problem. The political party is not an end in itself. It exists to shape what *government* does. And on that front, women have not been of a single mind. At the national party conventions, women found it necessary to join in the complex and shifting game of issue politics and coalition formation. As late as 1984, the configurations were still in rapid development.

The Women's Movement and the 1984 Democratic and Republican Conventions

by Jo Freeman

If I had any doubts about how profound an impact the women's movement has had on this country, they were assuaged by going to the 1984 Democratic Convention in San Francisco. If I then had any doubts about how far we still have to go, they were removed went I went to the 1984 Republican Convention. The major parties have often been criticized for offering no real choices to the American people. This year they offered a real choice on many things, not the least of which is their attitude toward women. It can be summed up very easily. The Democrats have adopted the feminist perspective on all public issues directly affecting women and take feminist concerns seriously. They may not put them all into practice. They may not be aware of all the ramifications of feminism. And they probably don't understand what feminism is really about. But at least on public issues, and the underlying assumptions behind them, they say the right things and don't do the wrong things. The Republican Party has gone in the opposite direction. Its public script is written by Phyllis Schlafly, and its practices are not ones she would disapprove of.

THE HISTORICAL CONTEXT

Although feminist issues have frequently been partisan in nature this is the first time that the Democratic Party has been so highly identified with feminists and feminist positions. Traditionally, the Republican Party was more likely to support those issues identified as feminist and the Democratic Party more likely to oppose them. Prior to the formation of the National Women's Political Caucus in 1971 what feminist pressure there was largely came from individuals, not organizations, and was largely aimed at getting political appointments for women, not changing public policy. NOW, founded only in 1966, lobbied the government but was not active within or on the parties. The National Women's Party, which had carried the burden and the banner of the Equal Rights Amendment since 1923, had members active in the parties but was not itself a force on them. Their members were more likely to be Republicans than Democrats because that party was traditionally thought to be the party of equal rights. The Suffrage Amendment was passed in 1919 by a Republican Congress, and 29 of the first 36 states to ratify it had Republican legislatures. As late as 1916 the Democrats favored state by state suffrage rather than a federal amendment. A Republican, Sen. Charles Curtis (R. Kan.), had been the ERA's first sponsor and Herbert Hoover was the only Presidential candidate to receive the NWP's endorsement (Curtis was his VP). Indeed, the only Democratic President who has ever publicly supported the ERA was Jimmy Carter.

Between the Suffrage Movement and the women's liberation movement the paramount feminist issue was the ERA. During most of its history it was perceived as a

---

Jo Freeman, "The Women's Movement and the 1984 Democratic and Republican Conventions," written especially for this book.

class issue as well. It was argued that requiring equal rights under law would favor upper class professional and executive women at the expense of working class women who needed legal protections in the form of laws which governed their working conditions and frequently restricted the hours they could work and the weight they could lift. Since the Democratic Party viewed itself as the party of the working man (sic), and virtually all labor unions opposed the ERA, all but a few politically active women in the Democratic party did so as well. This began to change after 1969, when Elizabeth Koontz was appointed to head the Women's Bureau by Nixon even though she was a Democrat. She had headed the National Education Association, which had supported the ERA. She persuaded many women union leaders to support the ERA and they in turn worked on the men.

After the Civil Rights Act passed in 1964 many working class women filed cases in federal court challenging their employers' right to deny them jobs or promotions based on restrictions in State protective laws. The courts consistently abolished these laws, and by so doing undermined the main opposition to the ERA. Although the AFL-CIO did not officially support the ERA until 1973 its opposition waned sufficiently after 1970 that the ERA ceased to be a partisan issue until Phyllis Schlafly formed STOP-ERA in 1973. What opposition there was to the other women's rights legislation passed in the early seventies was also not partisan in nature.

The first success within the major political parties of the contemporary, organized women's movement came with an increase in women delegates to the National Party Conventions between 1968 and 1972 of 13 to 40 percent for the Democrats and 17 to 30 percent for the Republicans. Its first failure was the refusal of the 1972 Democratic Convention to support a minority report to the Platform in favor of choice (which didn't even mention the word "abortion"). Without much fanfare both Democratic and Republican women succeeded in reinstating support for the Equal Rights Amendment into their party platforms. The Republican Party first supported it in 1940, but took out mention of the ERA in its 1964 and 1968 platforms. The Democratic Party, where the ERA had always been a much more controversial issue, did not support it until 1944, and took it out in 1960.

In 1972 individual feminists were equally active but a bit less powerless in the Republican than the Democratic Parties. Power in the Republican Party has been based on who you know and who you are while that in the Democratic Party is derived from who you represent. There were several strong feminists within the Republican Party who, because of their personal connections to important people, could influence the Party at least on those things which were not controversial (i.e., the ERA). Thus they were able to persuade the Platform Committee to include a more comprehensive plank on women than any previous ones, and to strengthen the rules slightly to urge the State parties "to endeavor to have equal representation" at future Conventions. Feminists within the Democratic Party had to build up a power base of women active in the Party whom they could legitimately claim to represent before they could have much of an impact. This wasn't accomplished until 1976. In 1972 their claims to representation were tenuous. However, one consequence of the much derided party reforms was to bring new activists into the Democratic Party who were also sympathetic to feminism. Thus, while the rules requiring demographic representation were weakened for the 1976 convention, the NWPC was able to locate supporters and begin building a base.

By the 1976 Conventions the stage had been set for major battles over women's issues by both Republicans and Democrats, but they were very different battles. In the Democratic Party feminists fought for power independently of other struggles going on within the Party. In the Republican Party feminists fought for the ERA as part of the contest between Reagan and Ford. In the Democratic Party, feminists lost their battle but won the war. Feminists in the Republican Party did the opposite.

The fight within the Democratic Party was over the "50–50" rule which mandated that from 1980 on all delegations would have to be half women. This change was proposed because there had been a sharp fall off of women delegates from 40 to 34 percent at the 1976 Convention. The Carter campaign controlled a majority of the votes and did not support the 50–50 rule. However, neither did it want a bloody floor fight in a year in which the Democrats sensed victory. After several days of negotiations Carter compromised by agreeing to *promote* equal division in future conventions. More important than victory was the opportunity feminists, in particular the NWPC, had to demonstrate their power and the legitimacy of their claim to represent Democratic women. It did this by joining with the Women's Caucus of the Democratic National Committee, headed by Koryne Horbal, to hold daily meetings open to both delegates and non-delegates to ratify the decisions reached in negotiations with the Carter campaign. NOW was an outsider to the negotiations and had few members as delegates, but its members did voice their support for a floor fight as non-delegates at the women's caucus meetings, and circulated a petition on the ERA for delegates to sign.

In winter of 1978 rules for the mid-term convention were changed to require equal division and at this meeting the Democratic National Committee, at the urging of Carter operatives, amended the 1980 convention "call" to also require it. They knew that if they didn't, equal division in each candidate's delegations would be an issue in 1980, when Carter faced potential opposition from Ted Kennedy. The Carter Administration pre-empted this issue by coopting it.

Feminists at the 1976 Republican Convention held only one meeting for delegates, the day before the Convention began. Its purpose was to provide information, not obtain ratification, and it was attended by few women delegates and a few more press. While Democratic politics are open, loud, and confrontational, those of the Republicans are closed, quiet and consensual. Thus feminist activity at the Republican Convention consisted of four women with close personal ties to the Ford campaign, who operated as the Republican Women's Task Force of the National Women's Political Caucus, quietly lobbying to retain the ERA in the Platform. The ERA won by only one vote in the relevant Platform subcommittee, but because Ford supported and Reagan opposed it Ford campaign operatives kept their members on the Platform Committee in line and the ERA was retained. Opponents did have enough votes for a minority report, but were dissuaded by Reagan operatives from bringing the ERA to the floor because he wanted floor fights only on two issues and removing the ERA was not one of them.

In 1980 there was a good deal of tension between feminists and both parties. In the Republican Party the Reagan campaign was completely in charge and none of the women involved in the Republican Women's Task Force of the NWPC had any personal ties to his campaign. Since Republicans don't organize caucuses, they had no alternative power base among the 36 percent of the delegates who were women. (Even if the Republican Party did have delegate caucuses it's doubtful the women would have been feminists. Schlafly's influence was quite strong by then.) Consequently feminist influence was negligible. The right had no trouble in removing the ERA from the Republican Platform and proposing a Constitutional amendment to ban abortion and a requirement that only federal judges who opposed abortion be appointed.

Despite these defeats Republican feminists are also Republican loyalists so several prominent supporters of choice and the ERA put together a Women's Policy Advisory Board to help sell Ronald Reagan to American women. This incurred the wrath of Phyllis Schlafly, who thought it was a feminist plot. She asked the Reagan campaign to abolish it and when that wasn't done, pulled her Eagle Forum supporters from their volunteer posts in numerous Reagan campaign offices, leaving some unable to get their phones answered. They were returned after a compromise in which one of her lieutenants, Elaine Donnelly, was put on the Women's Board and a separate Board on Family Policy was created for Schlafly supporters.

The tension within the Democratic party manifested itself in separate meetings for women delegates called by the Women's Caucus of the Democratic National Committee and a feminist coalition of NOW, the NWPC and prominent feminists such as Bella Abzug and Steinem. NOW had voted to not support Carter the year before because it was unimpressed with his efforts for the ERA. Even before this there had been quite an uproar when he fired Abzug from the Women's Advisory Commission so the Carter campaign just assumed all feminists were Kennedy supporters. The issue over which the confrontation between the Carter campaign and feminist forces was waged was Minority Report No. 10 to the Platform Committee—a proposal to deny Democratic Party funds to any candidate who did not support the ERA. This was one of several proposals drawn up by NOW for the Kennedy campaign. Many feminists thought it was a pretty silly issue, as the Democratic Party has little money to give candidates and was not known for enforcing a party line on any issue, but NOW argued that to reject No. 10 would play in the press as a rejection of the ERA.

Since several minority reports were to be debated on the floor the Carter campaign was not reluctant to engage in a public fight as it had been in 1976 and made no effort to negotiate a settlement. Instead Carter operatives "whipped down" the proposal (i.e., told their delegates not to support it) but women delegates, few of whom had gone to the feminist delegate meetings, revolted. The largest single group of Carter delegates at the 1980 Convention were members of the National Education Association. When they told the Carter campaign that they were going to support No. 10, Carter backed down. Tip O'Neill called for a voice vote of the Convention without debate and deemed it passed.

Whether what happened at the 1980 Conventions had any effect on the vote in November will never be established. Despite Reagan's repeated declaration that he supported equal rights for women he and the Republican Party were identified as anti ERA and the Democratic Party as pro ERA. That fall, for the first time in history, there was a statistically significant gap (8 percent) in the way men and women voted for President. More men voted for Reagan than for Carter while women evenly split their vote between the two. The gender gap continued throughout Reagan's Presidency and spread into attitudes toward the Republican Party. Surveys consistently showed that for every question in which Reagan's name appeared, women were more negative. The 1982 elections showed more women than men voted Democratic. The data do not show that this antagonism correlates with respondents' positions on the ERA and abortion.

THE 1984 DEMOCRATIC CONVENTION

The fact that feminists had displayed so much clout in 1980 gave them an inside spot in the 1984 race with the consequence that there was very little for them to do at the Convention itself. All the candidates trooped to San Antonio, Texas, in July 1983 to seek support from those attending the NWPC convention. When NOW announced it would endorse a Democratic Party candidate for President, it was courted by all. Six candidates were invited to address the NOW National Conference in October. Askew was not invited because of his anti-choice stand and Jackson had not yet declared his candidacy.

Although most observers expected Mondale to get the NOW endorsement, the officers drew up four criteria and met with five of the candidates—Mondale, Cranston, Glenn, Hart and Jackson. Each was also given lists of National Board members and State Chairs so he could lobby NOW. The four criteria were the 1) candidate's position on and priority of women's issues, 2) number of women in key staff positions, 3) willingness to select a woman Vice President, and 4) electability. There was some movement within NOW to withdraw the decision to endorse, but the NOW leadership felt strongly that endorsing Mondale was the way to go and persuaded everyone else to go along. At the December Board meeting an initial straw poll gave Mondale 25 votes to 12 for Cranston. A motion to endorse Mondale then passed by 32 to 5. Once the decision was made virtually no active NOW members supported any other Presidential candidate. The few who did largely supported Sonia Johnson in her bid for the Citizens Party nomination.

In the Spring representatives from feminist and women's organizations, and politically active women held several meetings to plan their actions at the convention. Although the platform had not been finalized it appeared that feminist minority planks would not be necessary because the Mondale campaign was prepared to give them everything they wanted. NOW Action Vice President Mary Jean Collins was appointed to the drafting committee by DNC Chair Chuck Manatt at the behest of the Mondale campaign and had "sign off" authority on all language of concern to NOW.

Therefore the incipient women's caucus decided that their focus should be on persuading Mondale to choose a woman Vice Presidential nominee, though they were uncertain on whether to force a floor fight should these efforts fail. Delegate surveys showed that there was considerable support for such a move and voter polls indicated that a woman would probably help the Democratic ticket more than hurt it. Therefore public and party officials were lobbied to put pressure on Mondale, helpful information was leaked to the press, and 150 delegates willing to be whips were identified and organized. It was also agreed that this time there would be only one women's caucus at the convention, at which everyone would be organized for the Vice Presidential selection. (Usually the Presidential candidate doesn't announce his VP choice until after formal nomination the third day of the convention.)

The coalition had a short list of acceptable women it thought Mondale should choose from but it had not singled one out. That was done by three Congresswomen, Barbara Mikulski (Md.), Mary Rose Oakar (Ohio) and Barbara Kennelly (Conn.), when they endorsed Geraldine Ferraro the night before the NOW National Conference in June. That conference passed a resolution to put the name of a woman in nomination for Vice President at the Democratic Convention "if necessary" without spelling out what that meant. Ferraro told the press that she would permit her name to be put into nomination as a "statement" if no other woman was nominated. On July 4, 23 feminists and elected women officials met with Mondale to add their support for a woman running mate.

After Mondale announced his choice of Geraldine Ferraro on July 12, the coalition dismantled their whip system. This upset the Jackson campaign as he had hoped it would be used to support his platform minority planks. A meeting of the women's caucus had voted favorably on Jackson's proposals, but it was not a binding vote, and was not solely by delegates. The women's caucus leadership felt its whips had been recruited solely to work on the Vice Presidential nomination and could not be directed elsewhere. NOW had also identified its delegates and independently organized some of them as whips. It did support Jackson's efforts but to no avail.

Because feminists got pretty much everything they wanted prior to the Democratic Convention, there wasn't much to do there except celebrate. Nonetheless a women's caucus met every day to listen to feminist speakers, the candidates, and to debate the minority planks. Throughout these meetings, I had the feeling that something was missing. There was so much celebration of Ferraro's nomination, and NOW, the most radical feminist group there, was so thoroughly incorporated into the mainstream, that the question of a future agenda was never broached. What was missing was a radical flank.

A good radical flank is an essential ingredient to steady social change. Someone, or something, who has nothing to gain by playing the insiders' game must regularly raise new issues and expound new analyses in order to pull the mainstream in a progressive direction. However a radical flank by itself moves very little. There must be people on the inside receptive to the message who can be persuaded to agitate from within. And those agitating on the outside must not be so alienated, or so radical, that they cannot deal with the political system at all.

Throughout most of the history of the women's movement there has been a good combination of insiders and outsiders. In the early days when all avowedly feminist groups were outsiders, there were plenty of closet feminists in influential positions in the government who could take advantage of the opportunities the newly emerging feminist constituency created. Similarly, the existence of small feminist groups, many of which were developing feminist analysis and applying it to new areas of life, provided a constant source of ideas and pressure on the more established national feminist organizations. In the mid seventies the small groups began to encapsulate into feminist communities and lose many of their connections to the larger feminist groups. Simultaneously, the national organizations demanded participation in the mainstream, and to judge by appearances at the 1984 Democratic Convention, have succeeded in becoming a working partner with at least the liberal portion of it.

But there is always a price for participating in the mainstream: one must abide by the inevitable requirement that one curb one's commitment to one's own agenda. The rules of the game require that one not make too many demands or ones that are too radical or that seriously conflict with the goals of other coalition groups. If the national organizations don't know this by now, they will find out eventually. Indeed, the NWPC does know the rules for insiders, which it implicitly followed by dismantling its whip system rather than permit it to be used by the dissident Jackson forces. The fact that NOW did not may mean that it has not yet learned the constraints of joining the mainstream, or may indicate that it thought it more desirable to earn points with Jackson forces. It may also reflect a residual attraction of the outsider role that NOW has played at past Democratic conventions; a role that permits allegiance to "principle" to take precedence over political exigencies. If so, what NOW must learn next is that one cannot be both an insider and an outsider; a mainstream participant and the radical flank. Both functions are important to achieving social change but they must be kept separate. Any person or organization trying to do both loses credibility and legitimacy. Thus, if NOW wants to be part of the mainstream what it and the rest of the women's movement needs most, in order to maintain pressure from within, is a good radical flank. It needs constant criticism, tempered with understanding of political reality, from outsiders.

By the end of the Democratic Convention I found myself both pleased and troubled. Pleased that committed feminists and a solid feminist agenda had been incorporated into the mainstream of the Democratic Party. And troubled that the absence of any radical flank would temper future progress. One month later I went to the Republican Convention in Dallas and came to a very different conclusion. In this country, in the mid 1980s, the Democratic Party *is* the radical flank.

THE 1984 REPUBLICAN CONVENTION

Both NOW and the NWPC had given up on the Republicans even before the Convention. They planned no actions. NOW sent executive Vice President Lois Reckitt as an observer. Kathy Wilson, President of the NWPC and a liberal Republican, gave a press conference and released a fifty-page document refuting Party claims that women are better off than they were four years ago. NOW and the NWPC made this decision because they felt the right had so thoroughly taken over the Republican Party that they could not get a hearing. That observation was certainly correct. Even the Republican Mainstream Committee, composed of a small group of liberal Republicans who sponsored Wilson's press conference as part of its convention program, was treated with disdain.

This year the Republican Party did not hold hearings on its Platform, but it did accept testimony one day prior to deliberations by the various subcommittees. (The Convention Committees meet the week before the Convention.) At these, persons testifying in opposition to key right wing planks found themselves barraged with questions about the Democratic ticket rather than the subject on which they testified. When Mary Louise Smith, former chair of the Republican National Committee and Mary Stanley, a long-term Reagan supporter from California who currently heads Republican activities in the NWPC, testified in favor of the ERA, they were cross-examined on Geraldine Ferraro's finances.

Yet by deciding to do nothing more at the Republican Convention NOW and the NWPC also declared that they would not participate in Party politics unless they could do so as insiders, or at least respected outsiders. In 1976 and 1980 NOW demonstrated outside the Convention while the RWTF acted, or tried to act, within. NOW was the radical flank, though its reluctance to accept this role was demonstrated in 1976 when NOW President Karen DeCrow acceded to the RWTF's request to leave town after the march in order not to contaminate the efforts of Republican feminists with the pinkish taint of radicalism that they said the NOW label meant in the Republican Party. NOW's and the NWPC's reluctance to insist on a feminist presence in the hostile Republican environment reinforced the Party's belief that both organizations are merely arms of the Democratic Party, and as such can be dismissed as irrevocably partisan.

Feminists may have been in hiding during the 1984 Republican National Convention, but the influence of the women's movement was pervasive. This influence was not seen in the content of the convention so much as in the quantity of attention paid to women. Although the Republican Party does not require that half of the delegates be women as the Democrats do, 48 percent of the delegates and 52 percent of the alternates were female. Betty Rendel, President of the independent National Federation of Republican Women, disavowed the Democratic quota system as "artificial, discriminatory and . . . a little silly," while describing the way in which Republican women were cajoled into running for delegate spots and men discouraged by top party leaders, including the President. She said Party leaders had to exert steady pressure to persuade men originally selected as delegates to step aside for the "envelope stuffers and precinct walkers."

One-third of the major speakers were women, including keynoter Katherine Davalos Ortega. With the exception of U.N. Ambassador Jeane Kirkpatrick, who got a longer and louder floor demonstration than any other speaker apart from Reagan even though she is a registered Democrat, their message was highly consistent. Each extolled President Reagan for appointing the "first woman to . . ." and then went on to say that she had not achieved her position because she was a woman but because of her exertions and her merit. The implication was that in the last four years the Republican Party has sprouted a lot of qualified women where none existed before.

For the first time the Republican Convention had a large booth in the press area solely to provide information on women. The Republican Women Information Services also set up interviews and sponsored or advertised receptions, luncheons and breakfasts aimed at women. The Women's Division of the Republican Party since its creation in April of 1983 has sponsored several projects aimed at women. These include the National Women's Coalition "of professional and activist women drawn from business, the arts, academia, the sports world and politics," numerous conferences and briefings to form women's networks, develop candidates and prepare speakers and the release of reams of material on what the Republican Party and Ronald Reagan have done for women.

Delegate surveys by several newspapers indicated that by and large, Republican women delegates took the same positions as did men. The two exceptions were a Constitutional amendment to prohibit abortions and the use of military force, which men favored more than women by a margin of ten percent. Women were also more favorably impressed by the women on a list of prominent politicians than were men—also by an average of ten percent.

Although the content was not what feminists would prefer, women and women's issues occupied a larger portion of the Platform than anytime since women got the vote. However, the slant was largely dictated by the Moral Majority and Phyllis Schlafly whose Eagle Forum supporters were much in evidence. Schlafly was the only person to come out of the decade-long ERA struggle with a personal power base. The Eagle Forum claims 60,000 members and all of its officers are appointed by Schlafly. Most of the planks relevant to women were discussed by the Human Resources Subcommittee. Schlafly sat on the National Security subcommittee but her lieutenant, Elaine Donnelly, acted as liaison between her and Human Resources member Jean Ashbrook of Oregon, who moved amendments in accordance with Schlafly's instructions.

The Equal Rights Amendment was not mentioned in either the draft or the final version of the Platform. Schlafly was not scheduled to speak against it, but decided spontaneously to do so when she discovered no else planned to either. She declared it as "dead as prohibition." Mary Louise Smith and Mary Stanley made a plaintive appeal that the ERA not be excluded. Smith said it was a paradigmatic conservative Republican issue. "Individual freedom and responsibility are at the soul of the women's movement and the Republican Party," she said. Stanley, with tears in her eyes, said she had been an active Republican all her life, as well as a feminist. Her Republican Party was the Party which supported the ERA, and she wanted it back.

She later said that the chair of the California Republican State Committee asked her to resign her position on it because she had made favorable comments about Democratic Vice Presidential nominee Geraldine Ferraro. She did not resign at that time, but eventually was convinced to do so.

Bill Hughes of Colorado moved to add a plank endorsing the ERA, but it failed for lack of a second. This effort was repeated on Thursday before the full Committee where it was defeated 15 to 76. Two other proposals, one to add sex to the equal protection clause of the 14th Amendment and another which merely recognized that many Party members supported the ERA, were also defeated. All motions to soften the hard-line pro-life language and the anti-comparable worth plank in the platform met similar fates. During a meeting of the full Platform Committee comparable worth was denounced as "a socialist idea" by Peggy Miller of West Virginia.

The final GOP Platform presents a very traditional image of the role of women. Most illustrative is that on welfare. Welfare, undefined, is accused of shattering "family cohesion," both "by providing economic incentives to set up maternal households and by usurping the breadwinner's economic role in intact families." The Republican Platform goes on to say that "the cruelest result was the *maternalization* of poverty, worsened by the breakdown of the family and accelerated by destructive patterns of conduct too long tolerated by permissive liberals." (Italics added).

Contained in these sentences are several assumptions, the most obvious and onerous of which is that the only proper family is one with a male breadwinner who does not share the role of economic provider. The Platform's redefinition of the feminization of poverty into the maternalization of poverty is not an idle choice of words but based on this assumption. When asked what were the solutions to this problem, a young but conservative male Congressman answered that this could be done by enforcing child support, and discouraging divorce and out-of-wedlock pregnancies. In effect he said that women should look solely to men for their economic sustenance, and not to themselves. They should also not expect government support to end discrimination and improve job opportunities.

Not surprisingly (since it was OK'd by NOW's Vice President), the Democratic Platform calls for "a renewed commitment to combat the feminization of poverty in our nation so that every American can be a productive, contributing member of our society." It says that what "young mothers" need is education, training, and quality child care and that what women in general should be guaranteed is not just "a place in the work force" but "an equal chance at a career leading to the board of directors." Unlike the GOP Platform, that of the Democrats supports pay equity, gay and lesbian rights, affirmative action, an end to discrimination in insurance, restoration of the Civil Rights Commission to independent status and strengthened enforcement of anti-discrimination laws.

There were no women's caucuses or any opportunity for women attending the convention, feminist or otherwise, to discuss the platform or any other issues. Republican Conventions rarely have caucuses. They have receptions. The two biggest events for women were the NFRW luncheon for Nancy Reagan, featuring Joan Rivers, and Phyllis Schlafly's fashion show. The latter attracted about 1,700 people who paid $50 each to watch the wives of prominent Republican men (including Mrs. James A. Baker, Mrs. Jesse Helms, Mrs. Jack Kemp, Mrs. Paul Laxalt and Mrs. Trent Lott, as they were listed in the program) and a couple prominent women (Cong. Barbara Vucanovich and Ambassador Jean Gerard) traipse down the aisle wearing the latest Texas fashions. They were applauded in accordance with the popularity of the men to whom they were attached. Jeane Kirkpatrick said a few words, and prominent Democrats (Mondale, Ferraro and Tip O'Neill) and feminists (Steinem and Abzug) were parodied in song and costume by Republican office holders.

Outside the hotel where this event was held Ladies Against Women, a Berkeley, California theater group, held its own fashion parade, a parody of campish fifties outfits. They held similar events outside all major Republican functions. Leaflets were passed out declaring them to be "a national group of grownup girls who have taken positions (ladylike, inferior positions) on all Republican planks." They urged that virginity be restored as a high school graduation requirement and that the gender gap be eliminated by repealing the "ladies vote."

The only other feminist presence in the entire Republican Convention was in the gift boutique four miles from the convention center, where Mary Stanley was selling buttons for the NWPC. Although business was slow due to the out-of-the-way location and the fact that delegates weren't free to shop until the third day of the proceedings, when the booths were scheduled to close, Stanley says she collected 200 names of pro-ERA Republican women. She said female delegates may not be speaking out but the most popular buttons in her stock, of which she sold several hundred, were "I want my party back," "GOP for the ERA" and "Women were not born Republicans, Democrats or Yesterday."

22

ELECTIONS

After suffrage, many political observers were surprised by the lack of distinctiveness in the women's vote. In the aggregate, women voted about as men did. Explanations abounded, from the dominance of husbands to the apathy of wives. But by 1980, sixty years after women got the vote, a distinctive female vote *did* seem to be emerging. Poll after poll picked up a widening difference between the voting patterns of the sexes. The 1982 elections and the polls of that year and beyond confirmed that a "gender gap" had appeared. Whether it would persist and grow or lapse and fade away was not yet apparent. But the study of voting—one of political science's most fascinating fields—took on new life.

Politicians used to be able to analyze public opinion without the hindrances or help of evidence. Every election year confident interpreters offered their unanchored explanations of what had really happened, many of them bizarre but unconfirmable. The public-opinion poll changed that. Elections were still subject to gross misinterpretation. But the facts the polls generated had to be dealt with, and those facts were being collected and interpreted in ever more sophisticated fashion. And the major economic, racial, and regional distinctions made room for a major distinction of gender. Though too late for Alice Paul, women's suffrage may have come to make a difference after all.

The New "Gender Gap"

by Bella Abzug with Mim Kelber

Ronald Reagan was declared the winner of the 1980 presidential election even before the polls had closed on the West Coast. At first glance the popular vote to-

From Bella Abzug with Mim Kelber, *Gender Gap* (Boston: Houghton Mifflin, 1984), pp. 89–98, 101–02, 104, 116–28.

tals and the Electoral College tally appeared to give Reagan an overwhelming victory, the much-heralded "mandate" that he quickly claimed as his own. Yet a closer look at the voting patterns reveals a different picture. Reagan won a scant majority—50.7 percent of the total vote—which represented only 30 percent of all Americans eligible to vote. Of those who voted for him, most gave an anti-Carter, not a pro-Reagan reason for doing so. According to the CBS/*New York Times* Election Day exit poll, 38 percent of those who voted for Reagan said they made their choice because "it's time for a change"; only 11 percent voted for him because "he's a real conservative." The NBC Election Day exit poll reported that fewer than half (49 percent) of those who voted for Reagan strongly supported him.

The most important story of the 1980 election results, though, was that a new and distinct political phenomenon—the gender gap—was revealed; it showed a marked difference between women and men in their candidate choice. While 54 percent of all male voters chose Reagan over Jimmy Carter, only 46 percent of women voters did so, a gender gap of 8 percent, the largest difference between women and men since the Gallup organization began compiling such data in 1952.[1]

On Election Day 1980, according to exit polls, nearly 46 million women went to the polls, and their votes were about evenly divided between the two major candidates: 46 percent for Reagan, 45 percent for Carter. Clearly, Reagan was not the first choice of a majority of American women voters. Although 21 million voted for him, when one adds the votes for Carter and the independent, John B. Anderson, the total shows that 25 million cast their ballots for a different presidential candidate.

Reagan's professionally cultivated charm and personality were insufficient to distract women from their serious concerns. Reagan and the majority of American women disagreed sharply on two fundamental issues: attitudes toward peace and the Soviet Union, and the Equal Rights Amendment, symbolizing the whole range of women's demands for equality. The ERA battle had been publicly fought at the 1980 Republican national convention, before a national TV audience. It was clear that the 1976 platform plank supporting ERA was deleted from the 1980 version at the behest of Ronald Reagan and delegates committed to his candidacy. Reagan was consistent in his opposition to the ERA. In both his unsuccessful primary campaign in 1976 and his winning 1980 effort, he tried to position himself as an advocate of equal rights for women, at the same time contending that a constitutional amendment was neither a necessary nor desirable mechanism for achieving this goal.

Women voters weren't fooled by Reagan's lip service to equality: fewer than one third of the women and only four out of ten men who supported the ERA chose Reagan. Even among self-identified Republican women, defections were notable: 8 percent voted for Carter and 5 percent for Anderson.

In the televised presidential debates sponsored by the League of Women Voters, Carter had tried to spotlight Reagan's aggressive foreign policy views. The hawkish image of Reagan—which his performance in the White House has fully borne out—seemed to take, even though the Republican candidate slickly softened his militaristic views sufficiently to cost Carter some female support. Even so, according to the CBS/*New York Times* Election Day exit poll, 59 percent of the women who disagreed with the statement that we "should be more forceful with the Soviet Union even at the risk of war" voted for Carter, and another 9 percent chose Anderson, leaving Reagan with just 29 percent of their votes.

There were other issues that divided the electorate. The NBC Election Day exit poll found that 62 percent of those who felt government spending on defense and the military should be increased voted for Reagan, while 57 percent of those who favored decreasing spending or keeping it at the same level voted for Carter. (Actually, Carter also favored more military spending, but not to the same extent as Reagan.) Furthermore, 68 percent of those who believed an effective President could control inflation voted for Reagan, while 67 percent of those who felt inflation was beyond the control of any President voted for Carter. Voters most concerned about America's position in the world, cutting federal taxes, and controlling inflation gave their votes to Reagan by a two-to-one margin. Carter received the overwhelming support of voters most concerned about ensuring peace and relations with Iran and Arab countries. On economic issues the CBS/*New York Times* exit poll found that those who viewed unemployment as the most important problem preferred Carter over Reagan, 51 percent to 40 percent, while those who cited inflation as the most important chose Reagan over Carter, 60 percent to 30 percent.

Significantly, in every area of the country, in all racial, demographic, and socioeconomic categories among women of almost every type, support for Reagan was lower than men's. His highest gender gap—17 percent, more than twice the national average—appeared among college graduates: 58 percent of the men chose Reagan, compared with only 41 percent of the women. The Reagan gender gap ran ahead of the national average in the South (11 percent), among Catholics (13 percent), professionals and union members (10 percent), the unemployed (13 percent), voters aged 18 to 21 (14 percent), and voters aged 30 to 59 (11 percent). Carter drew 84 percent of black women voters, a 7 percent margin over black men, and his biggest gender gap was the 19 percent difference in his support from Hispanic women (61 percent), compared with men (42 percent). Only among women in the West, among high school graduates, and among those over 60 years of age did Reagan's gender gap narrow to as little as 3 or 4 percent. Reagan received a majority of the female vote—and a scant majority at that—from women who lived in the West, Protestant women, women in professional or managerial occupations, and women over 60 years of age. According to political scientists Sandra Baxter and Marjorie Lansing in *Women and Politics*, "Women who identified themselves with the 'Moral Majority' or indicated that they were very religious were much more likely to vote for Reagan than were their less religious sisters," and the religious group included large numbers of older women. (See the chart, The Gender Gap, 1980 Election.)

Carter also had a problem with women voters. In the 1976 election, he had won 48 percent of the women's vote, roughly 3 percent less than Ford. By 1980 his rate of support had dropped to 45 percent. In considering Reagan, women were trying to decide what he might do. With Carter, they were evaluating his performance and obviously found it wanting. No longer did American women believe nor could Jimmy Carter prove to their satisfaction that he understood and would act on their concerns. Only 9 percent of the women interviewed in NBC's exit poll said they could trust Carter "to do what is right just about always," while 18 percent responded "almost never."

In 1976 both President Gerald Ford and Carter, then the challenger, supported the Equal Rights Amendment. In 1980 President Carter and challenger John Anderson were both pro-ERA, at least on the record, while Reagan was staunchly opposed. This gave Carter a distinct edge—55 percent of the vote from women and 47 percent of the vote from men who favored the ERA—

The Gender Gap, 1980 Election

R = Reagan *C = Carter* *A = Anderson*	MEN			WOMEN			REAGAN GENDER GAP[1]	CARTER GENDER GAP[2]
	R	C	A	R	C	A		
Percentage	54	37	7	46	45	7	− 8	+ 8
Region								
East	52	39	7	43	45	10	− 9	+ 6
Midwest	55	37	7	47	45	7	− 8	+ 8
West	56	31	10	53	38	8	− 3	+ 7
South	57	39	3	46	51	3	−11	+12
Background								
White								
Black		77			84			+ 7
Hispanic		42			61			+19
Religion								
Protestant	61	33		52	41		− 9	+ 8
Catholic	56	35		43	45		−13	+10
Jewish	39	41	17	31	53	13	− 8	+12
Occupation								
Professional	61	28	9	51	39	9	−10	+11
Blue Collar	49	44	4	41	50	5	− 8	+ 6
Union Members	47	45	6	37	54	8	−10	+ 9
Unemployed	41	49	8	28	61	8	−13	+12
Age								
18–21	48	41	8	34	51	13	−14	+10
22–29	46	39	11	41	45	12	− 5	+ 6
30–44	58	32	2	47	44	6	−11	+12
45–59	59	34	5	48	44	7	−11	+10
60 plus	55	40	4	51	43	5	− 4	+ 3
Education								
H.S. Graduate	52	45	2	48	45	5	− 4	0
College Graduate	58	29	11	41	44	13	−17	+15
Affiliation								
Democrat	25	67	8	17	76	7	− 8	+ 9
Republican	91	6	3	87	8	5	− 4	+ 2
Independent	63	25	12	51	34	15	−12	+ 9

[1] Reagan gender-gap column indicates lower percentage of support from women, compared with men.
[2] Carter gender-gap column shows higher percentage of support from women.

but what happened to the remaining votes? Eleven percent went to Anderson, four points above the 7 percent national average of the total vote that he received; the rest voted for Reagan, except for a few defectors to other third parties.

One explanation, of course, is that support for the ERA was not the "bottom line" issue in the decisions of some voters. Some of these women, fed up with Carter, believed Reagan would be a stronger President. A more significant reason, I believe,

WOMEN'S REGISTRATION AND VOTING RATES BY AGE AND BACKGROUND FOR 1980

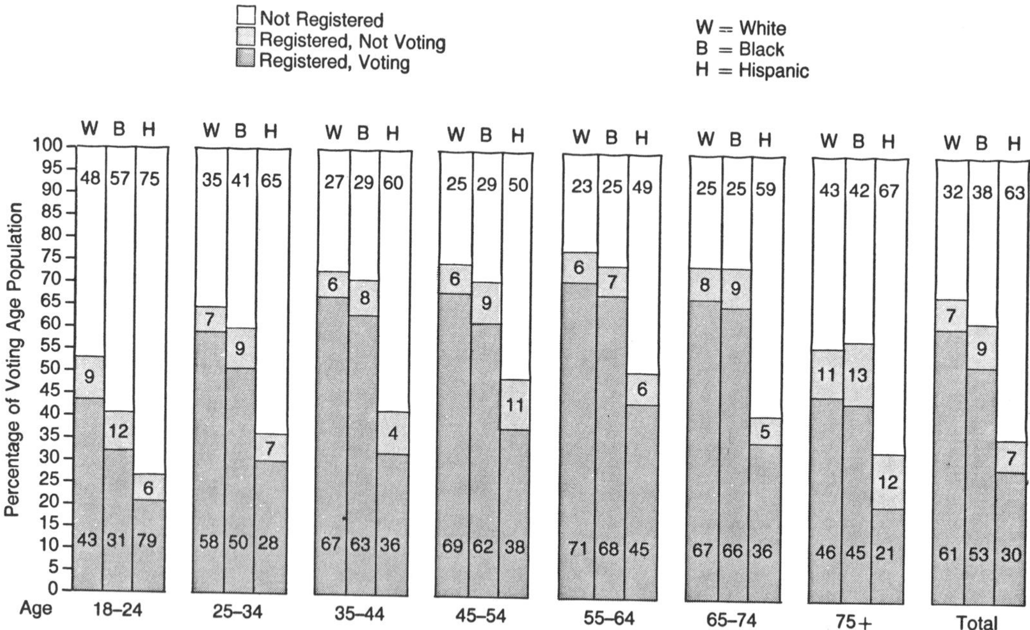

was that other women who defected from Carter were no longer content with words rather than action on this issue. Carter's waffling on abortion rights, his shift to a higher military spending policy that cut into women's programs, and his high-handed treatment of the National Advisory Committee on Women all took their toll. His economic policies were hardly more palatable to women than they were to men. Increasing unemployment threatened the slender hold low-seniority women had on their jobs, and rampant inflation caused hardships for women living on fixed incomes, those dependent on government benefits for the bulk of their income, and those living near or below the poverty line. A majority of these women are normally Democrats, and Carter retained most of their support, but at much lower levels than they had shown in 1976. On economic issues, Carter lost some support from blue-collar and union women as well. Although he won a majority of their votes, their rate of support had dropped significantly from 1976. Democrats, independents, and liberals, disaffected with Carter, gave Reagan his victory, not Republicans and conservatives.

According to the CBS/*New York Times* Election Day poll, Carter's support among Democrats dropped from 77 percent in 1976 to 66 percent in 1980, among independents from 43 percent to 30 percent, and among liberals from 70 percent to 57 percent. Reagan captured 54 percent of the independent vote, drew the support of 27 percent of liberal voters, and won 26 percent of the votes cast by Democrats.

John Anderson's independent candidacy siphoned off a large measure of support from Jewish, independent, professional, and younger voters and from self-identified liberals—both women and men—who had voted heavily for Carter in 1976. Although Anderson won just 7 percent of the nationwide vote, 13 percent of women with college degrees, 13 percent of Jewish women, and 13 percent of women voters under 21 years of age, and 12 percent of those aged 22 to 29 chose him. His 6 million votes were not enough to offset totally Reagan's 8.4 million plurality, but they more than accounted for the margin of difference between Reagan and Carter in fourteen states, thus explaining the Republican's Electoral College vote landslide.

Whether Anderson deserved the vote of women and liberals is a different question. During the campaign he did try to position himself as a "liberal" candidate on such issues as the ERA and peace, but his actual record as a Representative from Illinois was quite different. In Congress, for example, he was a conservative on economic issues; he had been a long-standing supporter of the Vietnam War, apologizing for his votes only after he got into the presidential contest; on ERA, he fell into the same "all talk and no action" category as Carter: he had never actually taken any effective steps to get it ratified in his home state, where some of the closest and most intensive vote battles had been fought in the legislature.

In 1980 the gender gap opened on presidential candidate preferences, but, happily, it closed in turnout rates. For the first time since 1944—when 12 million American men were absent on Election Day owing to armed service duty in World War II—women voted at the same rate as men. According to the U.S. Census Bureau, 59 percent of women and men eligible to vote actually did, but the women's voting rate was higher than men's among blacks, Hispanics, and in all age categories up to 55 years old. Because women are a majority—53 percent of the voting-age population—an equal turnout rate for both sexes means that far more women than men actually vote. In 1980, 6 million more women than men went to the polls. While the turnout rate for both sexes has been declining in all presidential elections since 1964, the percentage of women voters has been growing over the years, and in 1980 it equaled that of men.[2] This trend, coupled with the gender gap, strongly suggests that the women's vote will play an even more significant role in future elections, especially because there are now under way major registration and get-out-the-vote campaigns among women. . . .

1982: THE GENDER GAP WIDENS

Just before the 1982 election, *Ms*. magazine published an article entitled "Five Reasons to Vote, Any One of Which Should Be Enough." One reason cited was that "finally, belatedly, politicians and the media have discovered 'the women's vote.' If it doesn't materialize in 1982, how many more years before it's taken seriously again?" Well, it did materialize again in 1982, much to the delight of feminists and Democrats and to the chagrin of the White House and Republicans. In this nonpresidential election year, all 435 members of the House, one third of the U.S. Senate, 36 governors, and many state legislators were being voted on. For the first time since the mid-1960s, many more women than men voted Democratic in the congressional elections. Exit polls found an overall gender gap of 6 percent, with women favoring Democratic candidates over Republicans 53 percent to 47 percent. For men the reverse was true: 53 percent voted Republican and 47 percent Democratic. In specific races the gender gap was even greater, and in three gubernatorial contests the women's vote provided the winning margin.

According to a study by political scientists Arthur H. Miller and Oksana Malanchuk at the University of Michigan, "In all Congressional Districts combined, women voted only 6 percent more Democratic than did men . . . But in districts without an incumbent running for reelection, the gender gap was a full 16 percentage points." Although Democratic incumbents did well with both men and women, the researchers noted that reelected Republican incumbents received less support from women than from men.

While peace and women's rights issues were seen by poll analysts as important factors in the 1980 gender gap, in the 1982 midterm elections, after two years of Reagan rule, economic issues were emerging as a key explanation of the continuing gender gap. An April 1983 Census Bureau study reported that compared with the last nonpresidential election in 1978, a sharply higher proportion of the nation's jobless had voted in 1982. Voting turnout was also up among women (many in the ranks of the unemployed), blacks, government workers, and residents of middle western and north central states, areas that had been hard hit by the depression. Ann Lewis, political director of the Democratic National Committee, asserted that she felt the markedly higher turnout among the unemployed—who generally have a low voting rate—the women, and other groups materialized because these "people had been hurt and had reason to think there was worse on the way" from White House policies. . . .

Male Democratic candidates running against Republican women found that appealing to women voters on the basis of issues offset any advantage a woman candidate might normally have with voters of her own sex. In New Jersey, for example, Democratic Senate candidate Frank Lautenberg drew away women's support from Millicent Fenwick, and in Massachusetts, incumbent Democrat Barney Frank unseated incumbent Republican Margaret Heckler in a redrawn, heavily Democratic district, running ahead of her in the women's vote. . . .

In the wake of the 1982 elections, some commentators jumped to the conclusion that the gender gap represented nothing more than an automatic tendency among women voters to support Democratic candidates. That conclusion was not borne out by the facts. As the *Washington Post* reported in a postelection analysis, "The gender gap appears to favor candidates perceived to be more peace-oriented and more supportive of social programs." Those candidates were not always Democrats. In a Maine congressional race, for example, pro-choice Republican candidate John McKernan defeated his anti-choice Democratic opponent even though the Democratic ticket swept most of the other races in the state. The victorious new Congressman said, "My pro-choice position was a key factor in my election," thus dispelling the myth that a pro-choice stance is poison at the polls. . . .

Whether skeptics like it or not, the 1982 elections confirmed that the gender gap was alive and well. Some critics have cited preelection polls that predicted a higher gender gap than actually appeared on Election Day to downgrade the difference between the male and female vote, suggesting that gender-gap claims were overrated. This is an erroneous view. First, the actual gender gap of 6 percent was exactly the same as that which a Harris poll had found as early as April 1982. Second, in those states in which the gender gap did narrow, it was largely attributable to candidates who, after receiving polling data showing them in trouble with women voters, changed their campaign strategies and were able to win over the women. For example, Illinois Republican Governor James Thompson reacted to his early polls, which showed him trailing substantially with women voters, by airing television ads depicting himself as a "caring" governor and stressing such issues as education and the elderly. This strategy gave him a razor-thin victory over Democratic challenger Adlai Stevenson III in an election so close that a recount was necessary to determine the winner. Last, pollster Patrick Cadell reported his data as showing for the first time that "men converged toward women. Men have always been the lead group politically. This year showed that women can also lead."

In other words, as Election Day 1982 neared, men listened to their wives, daughters, and sisters and decided to change their votes, the reverse of what had been believed to be the traditional pattern.

The gender gap is both "something old" and "something new." In part, it represents the public expression of the values long held by women. As Maryland Congresswoman Barbara Mikulski said, "Women are recognizing that their private values are good enough to be their public values." Or, as I have often put it, "What's good for women is good for men, good for children, good for America." American female values are described by Carol Gilligan in her book *In a Different Voice* as the "ethic of care." She asserts that while men are mostly guided by a highly structured and abstract sense of equality and justice, women are more apt to be concerned with consequences, with immediate situations, and with personal relationships. "While an ethic of justice proceeds from the premise of equality—that everyone should be treated the same—an ethic of care rests on the premise of nonviolence—that no one should be hurt," she says. Congresswoman Barbara Kennelly, a Connecticut Democrat, makes the same point, remarking, "Men tend to say something is right or wrong. Women say, 'How can we help everyone?' "

It is not new for women to be more concerned than men about peace, preserving the environment, attending the needs of others, and nurturing people and the world we live in. These have long been women's socialized gender roles in the evolution of the family and society, roles that have been indispensable and at the same time sexually constricting. What is new is that the changing roles and attitudes of women have made them assert that their values should be equally shared by men, and that their ethic of care recognizes the legitimacy of women also caring about themselves as individuals. Women understand that they should operate out of self-interest (not selfishness, mind you, but enlightened self-interest), not just as protectors of others or as their sacrificial victims. Women have taken on new responsibilities—as single heads of households, as full-time workers outside the home, as coequal partners with spouses inside the home, and in joining together to seek equality and economic justice for all women.

The merging of their private values and public views has been charted in the opinion polls as well as in the voting booths, and there the gender gap assumes even larger dimensions than in the votes recorded in the 1980 and 1982 elections. The issues at the heart of the gender gap range from women's rights to their broader concerns about the economy, war and peace, the environment, and other issues related to their vision of a more rational, peaceful, and compassionate world.

As the following summary of recent polling data shows and as most analysts, including those in the White House, agree, President Ronald Reagan and the Republican Party were in deep trouble with women voters as 1984 approached. For the first time in history, there was a strong likelihood that the women's vote could and would defeat an incumbent President and oust his party from power.

WOMEN AND THE ECONOMY

Men and women express different priorities in the economic arena. Despite some improvements in the economy and a minor pickup in employment in the first half of 1983, the U.S. Labor Department reported that at the end of August 1983, the number of jobless aged sixteen and over was more than 10.6 million, compared with 6.7 million in January 1980, when Reagan took office. The overall unemployment rate for August 1983 was 9.5 percent, a shocking 20 percent for blacks, 12.9 percent for Hispanics, 23 percent for teen-agers, and 8 percent for women over age twenty; jobless rates were higher for black and Hispanic women than for whites. Although the overall unemployment rate was slightly lower for women than men, reflecting the huge layoffs in mass-production industries that traditionally employ larger numbers of men, almost twice as many females (4.2 million) as males (2.4 million) were considered labor market dropouts; women who needed jobs but could not find work had given up looking.

The social welfare program cuts that began under Carter and were continued much more deeply by Reagan as part of his plan to decimate all domestic and human services programs—the better to increase military spending—had a harsh impact on women workers, lower-middle-class women, and especially black and minority women who depended mainly on these programs not only for direct family assistance, but for job-training programs and, for upwardly mobile minority women, employment in related federal, state, local, and private-sector programs. Women's recognition of their economic vulnerability was undoubtedly an important factor in their negative views of Reaganomics.

In an interesting analysis of what he calls "the hidden agenda" of Reagan's "new class war," political scientist Steven P. Erie of the University of California at San Diego points out that in 1980 nearly one third of the nearly 38 million women in the nonagricultural labor force worked in human service jobs, compared with only 11 percent of the 47.5 million men then in the labor force.

"Social welfare employment was especially important for black women," he reported in a presentation to the annual meeting of the Women's Caucus for Political Science in September 1983. "In 1980, 39 percent of all black women were employed in the human services sector, compared with 30 percent of white women, 13 percent of black men, and 11 percent of white men. In terms of job growth between 1960 and 1980, a startling 59 percent of all new employment for black women occurred in social welfare fields, compared with 37 percent for white women, 24 percent for black men, and 22 percent for white women."

As Reagan's policies eliminated large numbers of these jobs and closed the escape hatch for women living in poverty, millions of other women—middle-class whites and minorities—were also confronted with the loss of their own jobs or unemployment among other members of their families. The result, a June 1983 CBS/*New York Times* poll showed, was widespread dissatisfaction among women with the administration's economic program and a growing gender gap. For example:

- Just 39 percent of the women, compared with 60 percent of the men, approved of Reagan's handling of the economy—a 21 percent gender gap.
- Only 21 percent of the women thought Reagan had done enough to reduce unemployment, while 34 percent of the men thought he had, a gender gap of 13 percent.
- A majority of women (54 percent), compared with 36 percent of men, thought Reagan had not done enough to bring down inflation—an 18 percent gender gap.
- Although men were equally divided on the question of whether or not the recession was over (47 percent thought it was, 48 percent did not), only 38 percent of the women believed it was over while 55 percent did not—a 9 percent gender gap.
- Only one in five women thought she had been personally helped by Reagan's economic program, while three out of ten men

thought they had—a gender gap of 10 percent.

- The views of men and women on their families' financial situations were mirror images of each other: 29 percent of the men, but 22 percent of the women, thought it had improved, while 22 percent of the men and 28 percent of the women thought it was worse.

Even more pessimistic views were recorded by a July 1983 Harris survey: 61 percent of the women, compared with 53 percent of the men, thought they and their families were then worse off than they had been when Reagan took office.

An August 1983 ABC poll showed roughly similar gender gaps in the way women and men viewed the economy, and also found women more skeptical that their hard work would be rewarded. Fewer women (57 percent) than men (68 percent) agreed with the statement that if you work hard in this country you will eventually get ahead. Four out of ten women did not think that was true, while only 29 percent of men disagreed.

By September 1983, a CBS/*New York Times* survey found that only 39 percent of women, compared with 50 percent of men, approved of the way Ronald Reagan was handling the economy; 48 percent of women and 44 percent of men disapproved.

A June 1983 poll taken for the National Republican Congressional Committee by Market Opinion Research of Detroit confirmed that women consistently take a more negative view of the Reagan administration's economic performance: it found that while 62 percent of the men said the economy was better than it had been one year ago, only 47 percent of the women felt that way, a fifteen-point gender gap. There was also sharp disagreement on whether "things are going in the right direction"—55 percent of men, compared with 39 percent of women, thought so; 51 percent of women and 36 percent of men thought the country was on the wrong track.

WOMEN AND PEACE

American men and women have registered the deepest division of opinion on the issues of war and peace, with women always taking the more pacific position. Willingness to fight in wars and to commit violence has been made the ultimate social test of manhood throughout history; the role of women has been more complex. Aggressive militarism has depended on the subordination and exploitation of women, who are needed to do society's work while the men are away at war and to validate the warmakers' propaganda rationalizations that they fight to save home, family, and country. Women have been complicitors in wars and have been used in armies as workers, nurses, logistical aides, and even as soldiers, but they have not been the primary makers of war or violence. Their traditional pacifism is often seen as an expression of motherly concern for the survival of their children, just as—in times of war—their willingness to send their sons (and sometimes their daughters) off to die is praised as the highest form of patriotism. But, historically, the tendency of women has been to favor peaceful solutions and to hate war. Some female peace leaders attribute this bent to biological reasons. Dr. Helen Caldicott, a pediatrician and leader of Women's Action for Nuclear Disarmament, says, "There's nothing more powerful than the instinct a mother feels for the preservation of her children" and describes the avoidance of a nuclear catastrophe as "the ultimate parenting issue." Others say that women have been socialized into the mothering and peacemaking role and, under certain conditions, are as capable as men of being warlike and violent.

On the whole, because of their exclusion from political power, government, and military leadership, women have no vested interests in war-making policies and institutions, and feel freer to express their opposition to war and aggression.

In 1983, the great majority of American women were opposed to the continuing arms race and the prospect of a nuclear war that could destroy all human life—men, women, fathers, mothers, children. Strengthening their antiwar stance was a growing recognition that the Reagan administration was choosing guns over butter, nuclear missiles over essential domestic programs. In March 1983 an ad hoc coalition of fifty-five major national women's organizations issued a report, *Inequality of Sacrifice: The Impact of the Reagan Budget on Women*, which charged that the administration's budget cuts would have "a devastating impact on women and their families at every stage of their lives." While concentrating on domestic issues, the coalition called on Congress to "look long and hard at the President's budget and help us find an alternative which will focus on our human infrastructures rather than just defense and public works." It cited a study by Employment Research Associates of Lansing, Michigan, which found that "every time the Pentagon budget goes up $1 billion, 9500 jobs disappear for American women." The coalition statement was symptomatic of a growing recognition in the women's movement that peace is a women's issue and that its goals of equity, economic justice, and feminist values cannot be achieved in a militaristic society.

Gender-gap differences on war and peace issues showed up long before the anti–nuclear war movement began. In an analysis of public opinion survey data from World War II to 1968, reported in Sandra Baxter and Marjorie Lansing's *The Invisible Majority*, Alfred Hero found that "females were more likely to view our entry into the two world wars and the Korean and Vietnam conflicts as a mistake than were males. Women have been more likely to support U.S. withdrawals from wars already entered into and less receptive to the idea of 'peacetime' conscription."

A 1952 University of Michigan survey reported a gender gap regarding the Korean conflict: almost half the men (48 percent), but fewer than one third of the women (32 percent), believed the United States had done "the right thing in getting into the fighting in Korea." Inversely, 45 percent of the women and 37 percent of the men believed "we should have stayed out." (The first electoral gender gap appeared in 1952, when women favored Dwight D. Eisenhower because he had pledged to end the Korean War.)

The gender gap was equally as marked in the Vietnam War period:

- In 1964 only 30 percent of the women, but 42 percent of the men surveyed felt we had done the right thing by getting involved in Vietnam; nearly twice as many men (38 percent) as women (21 percent) felt we should take a stronger stand.
- By 1969 nearly two thirds of the women (64 percent) labeled themselves doves, while fewer than half of the men (48 percent) did so.
- By 1972 Gallup found that 70 percent of the women, but only 54 percent of the men, favored troop withdrawal from Vietnam by the end of the year. (In a retrospective on the Vietnam War, a 1983 opinion poll found that only 16 percent of the men and 12 percent of the women replied that our involvement in Vietnam was "the right thing.")

Women react as strongly to threats of force and the risk of war as they do to war itself. For example, a January 1980 Gallup poll showed that only 30 percent of the women, compared with 43 percent of the men, favored using force to free the U.S. hostages in Iran.

Not only did November 1980 Election Day exit polls show a gender gap in women's perception of Reagan as a potential warmaker, but opinion polls taken during the Reagan presidency continued to show that women were more suspicious of Reagan's foreign policy, more concerned about the threat of nuclear war, and more opposed to the use of military force than men.

According to a June 1983 CBS/*New York Times* poll, only 35 percent of women, compared with 53 percent of men, approved of Reagan's handling of international issues. The same poll also found that a near majority of women (47 percent) answered yes to the question, "Regardless of your overall opinion of him, are you afraid Ronald Reagan might get us into war?"—up from 39 percent at the beginning of the year. Only 31 percent of the men held this view, for a gender gap of 16 percent. A majority of the women in this survey (56 percent) did not think Reagan had done enough to reach an agreement to reduce nuclear weapons, and only 39 percent of the women, compared with 49 percent of the men, believed Reagan "really means it" when he makes proposals for arms control.

An August 1983 ABC poll also showed women giving Reagan a higher negative rating on foreign affairs in general, on the Middle East, on the military budget, and on his nuclear weapons policy. Women were distinctly less supportive of his interventionist approach in Central America. Only 25 percent of women, compared with 39 percent of men, thought Congress should approve Reagan's request for more military/economic aid to Central America; 35 percent of women and 54 percent of men approved U.S. military exercises off the coast of Nicaragua; and only 12 percent of women and 29 percent of men approved U.S. overthrow of the Nicaraguan government.

A May 1982 CBS/*New York Times* poll found that 66 percent of women, but only 54 percent of men—a 12 percent gap—were afraid of a Vietnam-style involvement in El Salvador. In June 1983, when they were questioned again by the same polling group, only 24 percent of women, compared with 42 percent of men, favored sending combat troops to El Salvador. An August 1983 Gallup poll reported that 62 percent of the women, as against 48 percent of the men, believed we should not get involved in Central America.

A May 1982 CBS/*New York Times* poll also found that women were:

- less likely than men to think that development of the atomic bomb was a good thing (74 percent of the women and 56 percent of the men opposed its development—an 18 percent gender gap);
- more likely than men to think that the United States will get into a nuclear war (52 percent of the women and 33 percent of the men held this view—a 19 percent gap);
- less likely than men to trust the President to make the right decisions about nuclear weapons, by 14 percent;
- less likely than men to see any justification for a U.S. nuclear first strike, by 13 percent; and
- in favor of reducing tensions with the Soviet Union, by a 9 percent margin over men.

The Harris surveys have also found meaningful gender gaps and high levels of female dissatisfaction with Reagan on military issues. Their May 1983 data show that 64 percent of women—up from 51 percent in February 1983—worry that Reagan might get us into another war, while only 46 percent of men do, for a gender gap of 18 percent. Harris also found that men and women have different views on Reagan's big military budget. According to a June 1983 Harris survey, nearly three out of five women were opposed to building the MX missile system, and only about one in three were in favor. Men, on the other hand, were equally divided on the issue.

After the Soviet shooting down of Korean Air Lines Flight 007 in September 1983, a CBS/*New York Times* survey reported that although men and women gave equal levels of approval to Reagan's handling of the incident, women were less likely than men to say he should have taken stronger actions. Only 30 percent of women, compared with 41 percent of men, favored stronger action, and 52 percent of women against 44 percent of men agreed that "the risks of taking stronger action to punish the Russians are greater than any satisfaction it might give us." In the same poll, only 36 percent of women, compared with 46 percent of men, approved of the way Reagan was handling foreign policy; equal percentages of men and women, 40 percent, disapproved.

The day after more than two hundred U.S. marines were killed in Beirut, an October 24, 1983, ABC poll reported that 62 percent of women, compared with 34 percent of men, wanted American forces withdrawn from Lebanon.

Although President Reagan's popularity reportedly soared after the U.S. invasion of tiny Grenada, surveys disclosed continuing big differences of opinion between women and men. A November 1983 poll by the *New York Times* reported a twenty-three-percentage-point gender gap on this issue: 68 percent of men and 45 percent of women approved the invasion; 43 percent of women and 26 percent of men disapproved. On another issue, 49 percent of women feared Reagan might get the country into war, compared with 33 percent of men who felt that way, a sixteen-point gender gap.

WOMEN AND THE ENVIRONMENT

Nuclear energy concerns women nearly as much as the threat of nuclear war. A 1979 CBS/*New York Times* poll found that 49 percent of the women, compared to 32 percent of the men, opposed building more nuclear power plants. Hard times in the economy are not enough cause for women to soften their environmental protection concerns: in a September 1981 CBS/*New York Times* poll, 48 percent of the women, compared with 41 percent of the men, favored continuing environmental improvement programs regardless of the cost. An April 1983 CBS/*New York Times* poll found that the pro-environment position had gained ground with both sexes, with 58 percent of women and men supporting environmental protection.

The National Republican Congressional Committee's June 1983 survey, however, reported that "women are extremely harsh in their assessment of air and water pollution and toxic waste." Although the NRCC did not seek to evaluate public opinion of James Watt, the bane of environmentalists who was then Department of the Interior Secretary, its poll found that a majority of the public thought the problems of acid rain, toxic waste, and water pollution had become worse in the past three years, with more women than men holding this view.

What emerges in these and other polls is a general tendency among women to take more compassionate, more nurturing, and less violent positions than men, and to question and challenge government policies. (It should be noted, however, that on many issues of war and peace, a majority of men also favor peaceful solutions, albeit by considerably lower margins than women.) Women have a broad range of social concerns, as is evident in the results of a series of 1981 ABC/*Washington Post* polls:

- 73 percent of the women surveyed, compared with 61 percent of the men, believed the government should work to substantially reduce the income gap between the rich and poor;
- 56 percent of the women, but only 43 percent of the men, favored increased spending for Social Security (not surprising, since a majority of Social Security recipients are women);
- 61 percent of the women, but just 48 percent of the men, opposed the military draft; and

- 51 percent of the women, but only 35 percent of the men, favored banning possession of handguns, except by police and other authorized persons.

BAD NEWS FOR REPUBLICANS

The cumulative effect of the 1980 and 1982 elections, the public opinion polls, and its own June 1983 survey produced deep gloom in the Republican camp. The NRCC summary of the gender gap, as revealed in its own poll, reported: "Every subgroup of women is more negative towards President Reagan than their male counterparts. While the gender gap is indeed a significant problem for Reagan it is also a problem on the Congressional level. *The generic vote is more split by gender than ever . . . It is the worst it has ever been . . . and thus presents a real problem to Republican challengers and incumbents.*" (emphasis added)

The poll analysts had an explanation for the worsening gap: "This is partially due to partisanship," they said, "as women are 8½ percent more Democratic than men as measured in this study." They also singled out certain subgroups of women who "show an exaggerated tendency to disapprove of Reagan and the Party"; namely, black women, Jewish women, Catholic women, women who have less than a high school education, women who are divorced or separated, women who earn less than $15,000 a year regardless of marital status, single women regardless of age or education, and women over fifty-five years of age. (The change in attitudes among older women reflected their lingering fears about threats to Social Security.) And as if that weren't enough, the GOP analysts complained that women college graduates are "less supportive of Reagan and the Party than they should be, given their educational attainment."

Summing up, the Republican poll gave the dimensions of women's disagreements with Reagan policies: "In addition to Reagan approval, the gender gap is most striking on women's perceptions of the direction of the country, the generic vote, the President's handling of foreign affairs, the level of defense spending, the nuclear freeze, the fairness of personal income taxes, the increase of federal spending for day care centers."

The Republicans rightly recognized that their problem extends beyond Reagan. Women have been showing an increasing tendency to identify with the Democratic Party. More than 40 percent of all women, compared with 33 percent of all men, now call themselves Democrats. Because of this gender gap, women presently are a majority constituency within the Democratic Party, accounting for 60 percent or more of the vote in the party's nominating contests.

This gender gap in party affiliation is a recent development. From 1952 through the 1970s there were no statistically significant differences between men and women in terms of party preference. Virtually identical percentages of women and men chose the Republican and Democratic parties or labeled themselves independents. More recently, however, men have shifted away from the Democratic Party, becoming increasingly independent and slightly more Republican. For women the shift has been in the other direction: a decline within the Republican ranks as more women identify with the Democratic Party.

According to political scientists, the shift can be attributed in part to generational change. Older, apolitical women in the electorate are being replaced by younger women who are more likely to be Democrats. The reverse is true for men: older, traditionally Democratic men are being supplanted by younger men who are more apt to be Republican. Thus, the largest gender gap in party preferences appears between women and men in the eighteen-to-twenty-four age group, with women 11 percent more Democratic and men 10 percent more Republican.

Women and men are also in sharp disagreement on the question of which political party is more qualified to handle the problems facing our country. In a June 1983 CBS/*New York Times* poll, more women chose the Democratic Party as better able to deal with our current and future problems generally and to control inflation in particular. Men, on the other hand, selected the Republican Party. The gender gap on these issues ranged from 7 to 12 percent. Women and men agreed that the Democrats were more likely to "keep us out of war," with women rating the Democrats 3 percent higher than men. In an earlier CBS/*New York Times* poll on the issue of unemployment—cited by both sexes as by far the most important problem facing our country today—54 percent of the women and 50 percent of the men again chose the Democratic Party as better able to deal with the issue.

An in-house memorandum, which analyzed the ABC/*Washington Post's* July 21–August 1983 poll and earlier surveys, concluded that not only Reagan, but also his party, was "in trouble with women as 1984 approaches." The problem was not Reagan's personality. "As many women as men like Reagan personally," the memo observed, "but fewer women like his positions and programs. The gender gap is apparently more a result of substance, not style."

Although "the traditional 'feminist' issues such as abortion and the ERA play a role in hurting the President's image," the analysis said, "they do not totally explain it." Far more important to women, it concluded, are the economy and the conduct of international affairs.

NOTES

1. In both the 1952 and 1956 presidential elections, women gave Dwight D. Eisenhower 5 to 6 percent higher majorities than men. The distinction was attributed by Gallup to women's belief in 1952 that Eisenhower would end the war in Korea, and their subsequent approval of Eisenhower's refusal to involve the United States in the Suez Canal war, an interpretation that fits in with the higher value that women traditionally place on peace. From 1960 through 1972 Gallup found only marginal differences between male and female presidential choices. A 1976 Gallup poll showed women preferring President Ford by a 6 percent gender gap; a CBS News exit poll found no sex difference in the vote.

2. Reports on turnout rates vary because different standards and sources are used to calculate the vote. Although exit polls found that nearly 46 million women voted in 1980, the U.S. Census Bureau said that 49.3 million women voted. The Census Bureau statistics cited throughout this book are based on postelection surveys that ask respondents if they are registered to vote and whether they voted in the preceding election. More people say they vote than actually do. However, these data provide the most comprehensive information on a consistent and uniform basis from election year to election year and are the most reliable source available for measuring women's political participation against men's.

Actual registration and turnout statistics compiled by secretaries of state do not include breakdowns by gender. Because states have different standards concerning the kinds of data they compile and the methods they use to collect that information, drawing an accurate national picture from state records is extremely difficult. Voter surveys conducted by pollsters and political scientists may produce findings that differ from those of the Census Bureau because of variations in sample size, interview techniques, and other factors. Thus, use of the Census data provides the most consistent yardstick for measuring the voting behavior of women and men over the years. Although Asian/Pacific and Native Americans make up a significant proportion of the electorate in several states, the nationally aggregated data for these groups are not considered statistically reliable for analysis by sex.

23

THE IMAGE CAMPAIGN

The word *candidate* derives from the Latin for "one clothed in white," which is how ancient Romans running for office signaled their availability and/or ambition. George Washington, with his squirish garb, and Benjamin Franklin, appearing at the French king's court without a wig, both practiced political image-making. But today campaign cosmetology is a recognized profession; candidates ignore it at their peril. Even portraying one's real self accurately may require calculation. After all, it was Thomas Jefferson who wrote that "the whole of government is the *art* of being honest."

Women running in elections have to deal with special dimensions of the image game. On the one hand, in many constituencies a female candidacy is new—and thus news, which a candidate needs to attract. On the other hand, in many constituencies, a female candidate has to fight her way into, or find some new-built substitute for, a network of male relationships that seems to have been in place since the beginning of time; her image has to advance that cause. Just what the right image is, whether there is more than one of them, and how long any particular stereotype will last—these are questions without fixed answers.

As the following selection suggests, two core image concerns for women candidates are looks and aggression. Although these are hardly unique to politics, as womens' concerns they are especially salient there.

Women and the Arts of Media Politics

by Ruth Mandel

Who is the right woman for public leadership? Not this fat one. Not that loud one. She's just a housewife. No, she's too pushy. That gal's too pure. But she's too sexy.

From Ruth B. Mandel, *In the Running: The New Woman Candidate* (New Haven and New York: Ticknor & Fields, a Houghton Mifflin Company, 1981), pp. 33–48.

The seventies asked the country to begin recognizing that The Right Woman might be fiction. Many women were right for the job—and they were saying, "I'll take it."

By the end of the decade, however, still only a handful of women had acquired a political record and the political power to make their sex irrelevant either as a benefit or liability for creating a public image. Looking ahead to the 1980 election season, one writer asserted that "serious, direct, but nonabrasive women are gaining in popularity in and around politics these days." That notion of the right image could be hung in the dressing rooms of female candidates next to prevalent assumptions that women are especially honest, available, caring, and hardworking. Before she pastes and pins together an image to wear on the public platform, the woman running for office must come to terms at some level with the unsettling truth that many of the assumptions surrounding her are undergoing rapid change, and they are rife with contradictions. Among those contradictions and amidst change, she must move ahead—constructively utilizing how she is perceived by others, personally acknowledging who she sees herself to be, and thereby discovering the best ways to make a positive contribution in public life.

Standing in the campaign spotlight, men have image problems, too. There are limits on how far their appearance and demeanor can differ from what is expected at a given time in a given type of district. But these limits are less restrictive, with greater room for a variety of images because there is less doubt about men's basic suitability and competence as public leaders. Furthermore, since many men and few women have run for office, people are accustomed to a wider range of ages, sizes, and styles of behavior when it comes to males. One woman who took a race from her opponent was a 56-year-old Democrat who campaigned in 1976 against a 56-year-old Republican man for a seat in the New Hampshire state senate. He told a reporter for the *Concord Monitor* that he would make the better senator. "Why?" asked the reporter. The candidate responded jokingly, "Well, I'm a male and she's a female, for one." His wit may have been miscalculated for today's audience, and his reasoning may have been faulty for any day; but his basic assumption is supported by history and habit. The "right image" for a state senator or any other public official has been male.

Simply by virtue of announcing their political candidacies, women have been challenging that traditional image of who is appropriate to govern. Yet while the door to elective office did creak open during the seventies to make way for more members of the female sex than ever before, the passageway still seems narrow. Many a political woman has discovered a gulf between the self with whom she was familiar and other people's paper-cutout-doll image of a woman suited for candidacy. At issue are such items as her size, shape, manner of dress, facial features and expressions, tone and pitch of voice, and style of self-presentation, as well as the personal and professional history she brings to the podium.

The desirable image for political women seems to have been conceived as an idealized projection of womankind—a bit of everything that is pleasing, including many apparently contradictory characteristics. Emerging from the experiences of real women who collided with the platonic ideal is a long string of no-no's. They include: not too young, not too old; not too voluptuous, not too prissy; not too soft-spoken, not shrill; not too ambitious, not too retiring; not too independent, not too complaining about being excluded; not too smart, not uninformed. During the seventies one statewide candidate was urged to modify her "1950s college dean" image; a congressional candidate worked hard to counter a "suburban housewife" image; several women were advised to soften the "tough, hard old biddy" image; while others were advised to toughen up the "soft, sweet kitten" image. Bouncing between pillar and post with little space in between, women in politics found themselves pressed to mold and present an "I" who appealed to everyone's bias and offended no one, who approached a fantasy of "woman as candidate."

California legislative candidate Sabrina Schiller discovered that restrictions on what was acceptable were more rigid for women than for men. She reported: "I remember once walking a precinct and a woman said to me, 'I don't know if I want to vote for you. You're too young.' Then I realized I'm the same age as my opponent. Why am I too young and he's not? We're both 33." She was too young because, ideally, politicians are supposed to be "experienced" and "mature." At 33 he was and she was not, in the eyes of at least one district voter.

The age issue crops up often for the young female candidate, particularly in connection with related aspects of her nontraditional image. A candidate noted that her presence in the campaign was described repeatedly with references to her youth and stature—she being eight years younger and eight inches shorter than her male opponent. In an interview for television news, a woman campaigning in a special election for Congress in 1979 commented that among the problems she had encountered were her "youth and good looks." In contrast to the situation in everyday life, a woman's youthful looks are not often an asset on the campaign trail.

For women of any age, weight is a matter of concern because it frequently receives attention. In 1974, when she ran unsuccessfully for the Senate, Barbara Mikulski of Baltimore felt, "One of my problems is that I don't fit the image of a U.S. Senator. You know, an Ivy-League-looking male, over 50 and over six feet tall." Two years later, for her congressional campaign, Mikulski realized it would be impossible to turn a round, short, fuzzy-haired Polish woman from Southeast Baltimore into a Cary Grant overnight, so she did the next best thing: "I had to go on a seven-day fast, a vegetarian diet, and get an Italian boyfriend." Mikulski lost weight and drew on her diet for campaign material. "I told people it showed I could keep my mouth shut for a week. But it also showed them that when I make up my mind to do something, I can follow a goal."

In 1976 Bella Abzug dieted and lost forty pounds, but did not draw on that fact for campaign material. She treated the issue of appearance with a different twist, announcing that she did not fit the image of a U.S. Senator, but that she was what a Senator *should* look like.

One congressional candidate who lost weight specifically to avoid its use against her in the campaign was Pat Fullinwider of Arizona during her second challenge to House Minority Leader John J. Rhodes. When she first ran in 1974, she jokingly referred to herself as the "dumpy little housewife from Tempe." The press tagged her with that phrase, frequently describing her in print as "dumpy" while referring to her equally large opponent as "stoutish" or "solid." By 1976 she had lost weight and shed the "dumpy" tag, although at a candidates' night members of her own party introduced her as the one "who lost forty pounds and is beginning to look a lot better on television." An important aspect of the female candidate's credibility has to do with her appearance.

Most female candidates conscious about their physical images watch what they wear even more carefully than what they eat. Jewel Lansing experimented with wearing pants during her 1976 primary campaign for state treasurer of Oregon. She decided they were a liability after overhearing a bystander's comment during a parade in a blue-collar district of Portland. He looked her over and remarked, "Isn't it cute that this little girl is running for office." Cute little 46-year-old Lansing opted for matronly dresses after that experience. Another Oregonian who was even a decade older did wear pants during her legislative campaign, but deliberately chose to wear what she called "feminine colors" to avoid a "mannish image."

"You'd better not look too good," Texas candidate Nancy Judy said. Campaigning in a blue-collar district, she wore conservative clothes. "For six months I even wore turtlenecked evening dresses." At one contractors' meeting a builder told her she looked like "an uptight schoolmarm." "That was exactly the image I wanted to project to 99 percent of the people," Judy said. "You must be attractive enough so that men know there's a female there, but you can't make women feel threatened."

Handsome male candidates seem to benefit from their good looks in attracting campaign workers and voter support. For men seeking office, there hardly seems to be an issue of basic incompatibility between handsome looks and a fine mind. There certainly is no contradiction between the image of a striking masculine person and the image of a public leader. For the female candidate, on the other hand, it is problematic to be beautiful or glamorous; and there *is* a contradiction between the image of a striking feminine person and the image of a public leader. Oregon's Norma Paulus was 43 years old when she left the state legislature and won election as secretary of state. She had been fighting the "blond bombshell" image all of her political career. Her very first campaign brochure had proclaimed "NORMA PAULUS—Not just another pretty face!" Her advisors worried constantly about whether she was "too good-looking to get elected." As her campaign manager explained, "Being a blue-eyed blonde automatically means you don't have a brain in your head."

In a state legislative race in California in the mid-seventies a male incumbent was quoted as having said to an audience about himself and his female opponent, "Look, I lay it on the line to you. You can either elect a beautiful, young, attractive, energetic woman or you can elect a 60-year-old balding man." The implicit meaning of his irrelevant, self-denigrating remark, of course, was that glamorous young women are all well and good in their place, but not credible as candidates. On the other hand, outspoken and physically unattractive women often are hung with the other end of the rope. Overheard time and again among those reacting against women who stand up to speak up in public are remarks like, "She's too ugly to get a man, that's why she's out here doing this stuff." Motivations for behaving nontraditionally are suspect. Since women who can develop and fulfill their "proper" personhood do so on the basis of their physical appearance and in the context of private life with a man, those who behave otherwise must be compensating for their failures as true women by displacing their energies in inappropriate activities. Not too plain, not too too pretty—women must find the perfect in-between in constructing a public image.

Age, height and weight, clothing, and physical attractiveness are related to the underlying issue of being taken seriously. Women running for office attempt to establish an image of credibility as serious adults who can be trusted with the electorate's confidence. To some extent they are still perceived as interlopers or as misfits who wish to displace themselves from their natural settings in the home or behind the scenes in politics. Even where they are welcome, women are highly visible on the campaign platform as a new population of office seekers entering a man's world. Thus they are subject to closer scrutiny than the familiar white male candidate. Age and looks have always been popular criteria for judging a woman's worth. With a different twist, these measures operate forcefully in political life as well.

Regardless of age and physical appearance, a candidate's image must emit a competence which is rooted and thrives in her self-assurance as a knowledgeable political person and also as a woman. All female candidates must deal with how they present themselves as women. Whatever the particular circumstances, their sex is part of women's campaign consciousness. This is a truth sometimes not recognized fully by women who, because they are women, expend effort on underplaying and drawing attention away from their sex—a task no man must undertake. Constituents' ideas regarding how women should behave set the limits of the candidates' own behavior and create many of the obstacles they must overcome. Women must appear strong and assertive at the same time that they look and sound feminine; they must be tough with the opposition, but avoid seeming strident. They must somehow convince the public that they are knowledgeable and prepared to assume public leadership, and that their experiences as homemakers, mothers, teachers, consumers, citizen lobbyists, and volunteers are political assets.

During the 1976 legislative races in rural Minnesota, one woman's unsuccessful campaign encountered a number of the difficulties faced by female candidates as they pinched, poked, stretched, and twisted the clay of their individual personalities into an idealized image of political woman.

The perplexities of how to show what you've got—without taking off your gloves—concerned Minnesota's women candidates in 1976. Sue Rockne, a woman with flair and flamboyance, ran for state senate from a rural southeastern Minnesota district. She was determined to be a serious candidate with an acceptable image.

"Wherever I go, I highlight my competence," she said, explaining her campaign strategy. A graduate of Vassar College with a master's degree from the University of Chicago, she observed, "They don't expect facts, figures . . . even in coffee parties. I have to show I know more than they do."

Her direct, robust, even aggressive approach to issues and constitutents drew mixed reviews.

One supporter wrote in a letter to the editor in the *Cannon Falls Beacon*: "Those who know her best have observed her qualities of leadership, the knowledge and seriousness with which she approaches each issue, and her enthusiasm and vitality, qualities not commonly found in today's political world." The letter concluded, "Her academic training, her teaching experience, her years on the Zumbrota school board, and the positions she has held on numerous public boards and councils have, in my opinion, prepared her well for the office of state senator." Another fan wrote in the *Lake City Gazette*: "Sue Rockne is not only educated, articulate, and respected by state government officials and the voters of this area, Sue Rockne is experienced."

Her education and her experience did not help with those who disliked her aggressive style. Ken Pariseau, campaign manager for Steve Engler, her opponent, couched his criticism of her style this way: "She acts too much like a man . . . for a woman." He said, "Biologically, there's still a difference that's acceptable in the average mind. One expects a woman to be a little more refined."

Rockne concentrated on building her image as competent and experienced. But she tried not to overdo it, concerned about appearing "too" competent. She emphasized other, more conventional aspects of her life. Any mention of Vassar or the University of Chicago, any chronicling of her years of community service were usually buried after emphasis on such details of her life as "daughter of an Episcopalian minister . . . Sunday school superintendent and teacher for fifteen years . . . DFL[1] party worker for eighteen years."

Early in the campaign the *Rochester Post-Bulletin* carried her quip that she offered a "clear-cut alternative to that young, inexperienced gentleman." However, after noting similarities in stands on most issues (except abortion) between Rockne and Engler, the *Post-Bulletin*'s columnist observed that "age and sex may be the only differences between the two."

When she lost—and lost heavily—she and the media did not see eye to eye on the reasons for her defeat. She herself outlined some reasons: "One is being a woman. Two is being a DFLer, and number three is the abortion issue."

As a woman, she said, she discovered that "very definitely, the people of this district are not ready to be represented by a woman. They may want to work with a woman, but not be represented by one."

The *Red Wing Republican Eagle* took issue with this. In an editorial on 4 November 1976, it asked, "Why did Zumbrotan Sue Rockne fare so poorly against Engler, she who has been so active in public affairs, who carries a well-known political name and has such obvious ability?"

"Not we think because of Mrs. Rockne's sex by itself. . . . Our surmise," the editorial concluded, "is that, with Engler an attractive alternative, voters didn't want this particular woman. . . . Perhaps," it observed, "Sue's personality is a little strong, at least in contrast with the less vocal, easier going Steve."

Would it have been otherwise if Sue Rockne's opponent, Steve Engler, had been the one with the "strong" personality, and she had been quieter and more easygoing? Had she won, it seems unlikely that his defeat would have been attributed in part to a "personality" that "is a little strong."

The classic problem of the ambitious woman is how to be assertive enough to get what she wants without being charged as aggressive or unfeminine and thereby dismissed as abnormal. In politicians, the public favors those who will fight for their constituents. But a "fighting woman" is perceived as a contradiction in terms. Female candidates spend a good deal of time worrying about stepping over the fine line that separates the image of an acceptably assertive woman from that of an unacceptably aggressive woman. Most agree with Minnesota's Sue Rockne that aggressiveness in a woman is not perceived as an asset, yet all are conscious that the public likes a fighter who will champion the causes considered worthy by constituents. In rare instances a fighting woman does find an angry public willing to support her as a crusader. More often, however, women's experiences on the campaign trail have confirmed Bella Abzug's view that were she a man, those who dismiss her as "abrasive" and "aggressive" would instead describe her as a leader possessed with strength and courage.

It has been rumored that women are weaker than men and require masculine protection. Certainly differences between females and males in physical strength have shaped attitudes about weakness and strength in other human endeavors. Direct competition between females and males for high stakes has been virtually unknown. Therefore, very rarely have men been placed in the conflicting position of responding in public to challenges from women and at the same time restraining themselves from attacking the "weaker sex." On the women's side the dilemma is equally difficult. To assume a posture as challenger, confronter, attacker, she must adopt a mode of behavior she was brought up to consider inappropriate for members of her sex. Furthermore, when those whom she challenges are men, she is not only behaving counter to the ways acceptable for women, but she is doing so against the very human beings she has been told are stronger than she is and can defeat her in any direct competition.

In political campaigns these dilemmas are virtually unavoidable. Two or more candidates desire the same prize—a victory on election day. Whether opposing candidates are members of the same sex or members of opposite sexes, they are positioned during the campaign in direct competition with each other. They play out the struggle to win in public view. One of the biggest dilemmas any candidate with serious opposition must face is how much, how sharply, and how personally to cut down a rival. This is more of a problem for a challenger than an incumbent, as an incumbent usually runs on his or her record, and a challenger runs by denouncing that record. It is a problem because the public appreciates a fighter, but not a dirty fighter. In politics, what is and is not too dirty is a matter of opinion.

Opinions vary with time, place, and sex of candidate. Women are more immune from attack than men partly because of the fear which still exists in many parts of the country that the public will react adversely to attacks on women. A campaign manager whose male candidate was facing a female opponent said that his candidate was placed in a difficult position because "It's three times harder to run against a woman—we're halfway between liberation and old chauvinist standards." Women are supposed to be treated as equals; but, he said, "You can't go out and take her on. If you attack her, you're attacking a woman—and that won't go." In the mid-seventies, male opponents of Congresswomen Marjorie Holt and Gladys Spellman of Maryland felt that "attacking is a less desirable approach to take against a woman." As they perceived the situations, Holt's image as a "conservative white-gloves lady" and Spellman's ability to play "the hurt-female role" created a strategic problem for opponents. Holt herself has never felt protected, claiming that her opponents have not refrained from being abusive and from attempting to malign her personally. Both Spellman and Holt feel that as more women move into politics, if they are losing the protection of an imaginary pedestal, they are gaining the credibility properly accorded to serious political people.

A woman's major problem, however, is not in being attacked but in attacking. Attacks on an incumbent's record are frequently the only way in which an incumbent can be dislodged. Unless given a reason to alter their public officials, voters return incumbents to office because they prefer stability over change. Since women are far more likely to be challengers than incumbents, the double standard on attacks hurts them more than it helps.

In this case the double standard is one which says, "Men are acceptably aggressive, women are unacceptably shrill." Time and again women who went on the attack found their charges described in the press as "vicious," "mudslinging," and "negative." Other women avoided launching attacks because, as one candidate put it, "I'm just afraid that I'll come off as 'Superbitch' if I try."

The issue of whether a double standard operates in political life to reward men and punish women for similar behavior was discussed with greater frequency as the seventies wore on and more female candidates pondered how to win victories without losing votes for seeming too aggressive. They knew that one does not campaign successfully by sitting indoors and smiling, but rather by stepping outside and speaking up. They knew that competitive play is sometimes not polite. In a February 1979 *New York Times* article, a number of well-known political women spoke about the "double bind," with Gloria Steinem pointing out: "If you are assertive and aggressive enough to do the job, you're unfeminine and therefore unacceptable; if you're not aggressive, you can't do the job—and in either case, good-bye." New York City Council President Carol Bellamy noted, "Women are not supposed to be loud, and to some extent they are supposed to be deferential. . . . We are expected to be seen but not heard—and if heard, then in rather a limited way. There has to be much more measurement of a woman's personality—suppression, to a certain extent." Expressing a similar point of view, Bess Myerson, former Commissioner of Consumer Affairs for New York City, stated that the word "aggressive" is "one of the highest compliments you can pay a man . . . but with a woman it's a putdown. And ambitious: with a woman it becomes 'pushy,' and takes away her femininity."

If enmity is directed de facto against women who run hard to win, and if that enmity worries female candidates and their staffs to the extent that it ties their campaigns in knots, it is unlikely that even a small number of women will manage to win powerful leadership positions. "This power business" is something "men have been practicing for years, and the ones who succeed have got it down cold," observed New Jersey's Congresswoman Millicent Fenwick in the same *New York Times* article. She believes that women have to "keep [their] eyes and ears open" in order to avoid being "offensive" and to develop "the habit of limited aggression, which men have perfected: the good-humored, effective ways they've developed with such skill."

Commenting on the discussion about a double standard for women and men in public life, political consultant David Garth calls the issue a "cop-out" and says there is a "vast difference between being forceful and dynamic and being abrasive and obnoxious." He stresses that in order to survive in politics, any woman or man has to develop an acceptable style. Nonetheless, women's campaign experiences during the seventies suggest that in political personalities there seems to be a larger margin of tolerance for overpowering males than for bold and demanding females.

In 1976, the issue of attack strategies caused problems for women in Texas. Nancy Judy's congressional opponent, Jim Mattox, projected a feisty, street-fighter image. He emphasized this image by using words like "tough" and "fighter" in his campaign literature. "The public wants someone mean enough to say 'I don't like what you're doing,' and hit him in the mouth," is the way Mattox described the ideal candidate. Yet every time Nancy Judy attacked him for his voting record or campaign spending practices, he retaliated by saying she was "unladylike" or "vicious." In the meantime, he painted her as a suburban fatcat and a country-club Republican. Judy's family income was a modest $18,000, less than Mattox's. Nonetheless, she was unable to use his substantial salary and stock holdings to her advantage. Instead the overriding image of their 1976 campaign was that she was being negative.

Texas legislative candidate Billie Coopwood had the same problem. When a poll showed her behind 25 percent to her opponent's 75 percent, she went on the attack. The strategy boomeranged, and her media aide said later, "At the last, we couldn't turn around and be positive. Billie came off as strident and shrill." Her opponent, Gerald Hill, who did his attacking early so he could "take the high road" later, agreed with this estimate: "Attacking took away her natural advantage as a woman." Even the local newspaper, which did not endorse in this race, spoke positively of Hill and noted of Coopwood, "Her shrillness gives us pause." "Shrill" is a term rarely applied to men.

Republican Leon Richardson shared Coopwood's problem but to a lesser degree because she was armed with a great fear of "looking like a shrewish woman." Nonetheless, she felt she had to attack, and even her opponent's supporters viewed the charges as emanating not so much from her as from the Republican hierarchy. This perspective did not prevent incumbent state legislator Pike Powers from commenting later, "She was full of cheap shots. It hurt her. It sounded too shrill coming from a woman." He made it a point to stay aloof, emphasizing his performance, record, and seniority, and was the only one of three incumbents in his county to return to the legislature in Austin. One newspaper reporter speculated that Richardson's tough-talking manner might have unsettled people in the working-class part of the district: "She just isn't like the women in her district. They wouldn't consider running for office."

While cumulative experience strongly indicates that women lose favor—and perhaps elections—when they attack, at least some candidates feel they lose because they hold back. When two male opponents of Oregon's Caroline Wilkins were involved in a widely publicized mudslinging dispute during the primary, Wilkins refrained from criticizing them, and lost press publicity as a result. She said she refrained from commenting because, as former chairperson of the state's Democratic Party, she has always preached that Democrats should not go after their own. In retrospect she believes she could have won some political points and visibility by attacking them as "two turkeys."

Another Oregon candidate, Republican Virginia Vogel, had established a record as a city council member which her opponent for a state legislative seat constantly attacked. "I didn't retaliate," Vogel said. "That's just not my way of conducting a campaign." In retrospect Vogel believes her reluctance to strike back may have cost her the 1976 election, which she lost by only 365 votes.

Reports from campaigns also indicate that women aspiring to political careers encounter yet another tangle in the process of weaving an acceptable style. It appears when women holding lower-level positions set their sights on advancing to higher office. A nonaggressive, conventionally female image may be an asset in local races and even in contests for selected positions that have developed a tradition as "women's offices," but in running for highly competitive, powerful offices, a more aggressive stance may be required in order to create an image of forceful leadership.

Drastic changes in anyone's public image are difficult to fashion and, when accomplished, often produce problems of credibility. As one of Gloria Schaffer's supporters described the reaction to the "toughening" of her image during the 1976 U.S. Senate race in Connecticut: "Her image has been of a sweet, young, very personable, outgoing woman. When her literature came out with a tough image it was disorienting to those who knew her." It took several weeks for people to believe this is what the candidate would look like. Yet this toughening was also seen to be necessary. As another supporter explained, "Gloria's being pretty opens doors at the bottom, but closes them at the top."

Schaffer's image was "toughened" very deliberately. For the preceding eighteen years of her political career as state legislator and secretary of state she had always run as "Gloria," and her campaign color had been a bright pink. Her outside paid political advisors told her that if she wanted to be taken seriously as a candidate for the U.S. Senate, she would have to get rid of the "fluff." Therefore her Senate literature proclaimed in bold red and orange, "Schaffer for Senate." Her campaign photographs were shot to counter the "pretty blond lady" image. In fact, the photo used in her first leaflet made her look "so much like a bulldog" Schaffer made them do it over.

Bella Abzug did not need to toughen her image when leaving the House of Representatives to run for the Senate. In fact, many people thought she should tone it down. According to her campaign staff, Abzug did not consciously change her image, but ironically, many people thought she was trying to do so. More than one newspaper reporter wrote about the "new" Bella, who had "softened her often contentious manner." One of her chief congressional assistants, Harold Holzer, said these apparent changes were because "Bella is a person of many moods." In his view, all that the press remembers in between campaigns are her strongest statements and actions. As Abzug herself has pointed out, she "is an outspoken person and says things when they aren't in vogue." But in every campaign, Holzer said, the press is again exposed to a multi-faceted person and interprets this to mean Bella is deliberately changing her image.

Throughout her Democratic primary campaign for the Senate, Abzug aimed her specific attacks at her Republican opponent, incumbent Senator James Buckley, even though she was appalled that her main Democratic opponent, Patrick Moynihan, had been a staunch supporter of the Nixon administration. Two weeks before the primary, a reporter asked her if she would support Moynihan if he won. Firmly believing that she would be the winner, she replied that she could not support him unless he clarified his position on Richard Nixon. The press only reported her refusal to support, not the condition on which it was premised, and the party regulars who opposed her chortled that she had finally shown her true colors. *The New York Times* reported that "the nearly unanimous reaction of Democratic politicians" was that "after a year of the 'new' Bella biting her tongue and being nice, the 'old' Bella emerged . . . and got the 'new' Bella in trouble." It was not much of an attack that she was accused of making, and male politicians had made similar ones previously. Nonetheless, it gave her opponents in New York's Democratic Party just the occasion they sought to say that "battling Bella" would attack anyone who got in her way.

The press's stress on the tough side of her personality did have an unexpected dividend during 1976 in upstate New York, where Abzug was not personally known. Precisely because she had such a negative advance image, she came across well in person when people could see there was more to her than her press portrayal.

The following year, during the 1977 New York City mayoral primary, Abzug's television advertising played with some humor on several aspects of her personality. She appeared on screen announcing with a smile that she knew how to be "soft," then changed her facial expression and tone to state that she also knew how to be "tough." A male narrator spoke over the visual image to end the advertisement with a statement that New York City needed a "fighter." Defeated between 1976 and 1978 in senatorial, mayoralty, and congressional races by three men who could hardly be termed "soft-spoken," Bella Abzug more than any other female candidate has been seen as a warning about what happens when a woman cannot escape a negative image after having been labeled as "too ambitious" and "too aggressive."

In fact, guilt by association has plagued female candidates on a large scale in relation to what has become a negative image of political women based on a caricature of Bella Abzug. An outspoken forerunner for women seeking public office and a pioneer for women's rights, Abzug's aggressive style has been held up as a symbol of bad behavior, and her image as a fighter has caused some backlash for other women candidates. When Oregon's Rosemary Batori, a 62-year-old widow, took to wearing hats in the early weeks of her unsuccessful general election campaign for the state legislature in 1976, friends advised her that it might appear she was trying to imitate Abzug. After that, she left the hats at home. In 1979, Nevada State Senator Jean Ford attended a businessman's political-action breakfast wearing a white straw hat because "my hair looked absolutely awful." She encountered "several comments about 'Bella' being at breakfast," and concluded, "it would have been a better decision to forego the hat because it attracted too much attention."

Missouri's Mildred Huffman, a candidate in 1976 for secretary of state, overheard this remark while campaigning at a senior-citizen luncheon in a St. Louis suburb: an approving elderly citizen leaned over the table and commented to friends, "And she's not like Bella Abzug." Even a politician as well known locally as Maryland's Gladys Spellman, who served for twelve years on the Prince Georges county council before being elected to Congress in 1974, found herself confronted with

Abzug's image. "In 1974, I was a Bella Abzug. It was in those voters' minds a negative image I had to fight in Prince Georges County. The enmity was not at me personally, but at the image of women politicians."

In an article analyzing New York's primary races for the 1978 elections, a writer made the following observation about the candidacy of Brenda Feigen Fasteau for a state senate seat: "For her part, Feigen Fasteau's problem is the major hardship of most women candidates—trying to convince the voters she isn't another Bella Abzug." While it is true that no male politician would wish to be compared with Richard Nixon, the former President is associated with misuse of his office and criminal behavior. Abzug has been guilty of no abuses of power, and carries a record as an effective and courageous public official. It is difficult to call to mind an individual political man whose public image *alone* has been used so epidemically as a warning and a weapon as Abzug's.

NOTES

1. Democratic-Farmer-Labor: Minnesota's Democratic Party.

24

CONGRESS

Women have often been stereotyped as "ladies"—shy, gentle, cooperative, and dignified. Bella Abzug, congresswoman from New York, was none of the above. What she was was determined. Even as a freshman member of Congress, she set out to legislate change, such as an end to the war in Vietnam. To make that happen she first had to get on a committee from which she could speak and be heard on important issues, for she knew the modern Congress is basically a network of interlocking committees, not a forum for debating national policy. Abzug's method, direct confrontation and vigorous expostulation, did not always work for her in the Congress, where the social niceties rival those in the court of Louis XIV. She failed to gain a seat on her first-choice committee, Armed Services. But, as she recounts in her diary, Bella Abzug had her victories. She is still at it. (See Chapter 22 for her analysis of the gender gap.)

Her parents fled czarist Russia at the time of the Russo-Japanese War. Her father eventually managed the Live and Let Live Meat Market, but Bella was from early years a rebel, angered that women had to sit in the back rows of the balcony in her synagogue. She developed a direct approach and a hearty laugh. She also was elected class president in high school, student-body president at Hunter College, and editor of the *Law Review* at Columbia University. Elected to Congress, she wasted no time in moving on the issues.

If the House of Representatives was, in Bella Abzug's experience, a tradition-bound body, the Senate is more so. The Senate has been called "the most exclusive gentlemen's club in the world." When the first woman senator, Margaret Chase Smith, was sworn in on January 3, 1949, it was a bit like being the first black member of an all-white country club. Not only was she a woman, she was not even a college graduate, and she came from the underpopulated state of Maine. But respect preceded her. She had a good record as a Republican representative, so party leader Senator Robert A. Taft put her on the Republican Policy Committee. Before too long she even got a key to the bathroom reserved for the senators' wives, so she could quit standing in line with the tourists. On the floor she said little, dutifully read Washington's Farewell Address to the Senate on his birthday, and otherwise bided her time. The Associated Press named her Woman of the Year for 1949.

Meanwhile a morbid cloud of political paranoia was gathering in American politics. Its chief puffer-up was Senator Joe McCarthy, a raucous and unreliable—but rhetorically adroit—chaser of imaginary Communists. In too many quarters of the national community, fear was growing where trust had been. Senator Smith saw that happening and decided it was time to address it.

Bella Abzug Enters the House of Representatives

by Bella S. Abzug

January 21

After being officially sworn in on the Floor today, I came out to the Capitol steps, where I conducted my own ceremony for about a thousand women, friends and family, most of whom came down from New York for the occasion. Shirley Chisholm, the black Congresswoman from Brooklyn who is a friend of mine, administered an oath to me in which I pledged "to work for new priorities to heal the domestic wounds of war and to use our country's wealth for life, not death." A lot of other Congressmen came out to watch me being sworn in. It's a first, they tell me.

After I recited the pledge I gave a speech and then went back to the Floor where, as my first official act, I dropped a resolution in the hopper calling on the President to withdraw all American armed forces from Indochina no later than July 4 of this year. Twenty-eight other Congressmen and Congresswomen co-sponsored the resolution with me.

As far as I'm concerned, ending this dirty, immoral war is the most urgent thing this Congress has to do. President Nixon, with his phony "Vietnamization" schemes, is nothing but a wind-up, wind-down mechanical man who thinks he's fooling the American people. He and his pals in the Pentagon are full of lies and deceptions; they manipulate words as if they were playing parlor games instead of dealing in human suffering. They're making us live through a B-movie rerun of the Johnson script, which promised "no wider war" but brought just that.

Can you imagine telling us to rejoice because *only* forty American kids a week are getting killed over there now? This is going to be a no-hands war, Nixon says, and so what if it goes on? No ground troops, he says. Just hundreds of bombers dropping thousands of bombs on innocent villagers. Very clean, isn't it?

Well, if he thinks he's going to get away with it, he's nuts. Whether he knows it or not, the people are against him. They've had it. And so have I. That's why I've decided to fight for a seat on the House Armed Services Committee. It's not going to be easy, but it's the best way I can figure out to use my position to try to bust up the war from the inside.

January 22

The first time I officially raised the issue that I wanted a seat on the Armed Services Committee was at a dinner for the New York Congressional delegation a few weeks ago. Everybody seemed to approve, except for one guy by the name of John Rooney, from Brooklyn. He's a reactionary. While I was speaking, he was sitting there drinking beer, as he always is, and he got the notion to rib me a little.

I concluded my speech by saying, "I'm looking forward to your unanimous support in my bid for a seat on the committee, and that includes you too, John."

"Agriculture for you," he piped up.

From Bella S. Abzug, *Bella! Ms. Abzug Goes to Washington,* ed. Mel Ziegler (New York: Saturday Review Press, 1972), pp. 13–27, 39–41, 63–69.

"You start at the bottom. You stay at the bottom."

"John," I said. "I can't believe you would be so mean to a still unseated member of this delegation."

"Like I said," he went on. "You start at the bottom, you stay at the bottom—with your seat. And you got a pretty good seat."

Nonetheless, these guys, including John Rooney, know that I'm not up to any funny business in this thing. I've been thinking about a seat on Armed Services ever since the campaign. But you've got to understand a couple of things first, if you want to know what's involved in actually getting it.

First of all, the tradition down here is that new members, like myself, take what they get. They don't make a lot of noise; they don't ask for anything unreasonable; and they humbly go through the proper channels. In other words, we are expected to defer to the seniority system, which dictates that we shut up and listen to the tired old men who run this government.

Secondly, the House Armed Services Committee is not just another committee. I recall its chairman, Mendel Rivers, who died just before the session opened, once saying, "This is the most important committee in Congress. It is the only *official* voice the military has in the House of Representatives." He wasn't kidding. Armed Services is and always has been a special interest committee, loaded with reactionaries who, few questions asked, annually husband through in the neighborhood of $80 billion as a blank check for the military. Its hearings are largely held in secret, because almost everybody who testifies before it is either in the Army or pro-military. I doubt they've ever listened to a hostile witness. Last year, for instance, when the committee heard thirty-four witnesses on the $20 billion weapons procurement and research bill, all but one were from the Pentagon. The last was a Congressman in whose district the F-111 plane was built. Another series of hearings ran to three thousand pages of testimony from three hundred witnesses. Two hundred and ninety-eight of these witnesses worked for the Pentagon or within the military services. The other two represented the National Rifle Association.

The men who serve on the committee often represent areas with large defense establishments. They regard it as their special function to get their districts more and larger defense establishments. More defense contracts, more Army bases, more Naval bases, more war factories—they go on and on aggrandizing themselves and their districts while the American people are faced with the destruction of their economy, while the American people are driven to utter despair over this war. There are already so many defense establishments in places like South Carolina, where Mendel Rivers lived, that they used to say one more would sink the state into the sea.

The guy who's running the committee now, Edward Hébert, from Louisiana, is said to be less of a tyrant than Rivers, but he's made it clear that he intends to maintain the same symbiotic relationship between the committee and the Pentagon. In other words, under Hébert, the committee is going to continue representing the interests of the Pentagon instead of the interests of the American people.

Well, this is appalling! It should be an independently functioning committee of the legislative branch that exists to challenge the military—not to speak for it. Those admirals and generals and munitions-makers should have to answer for themselves, every step of the way. If I get on the committee, I'm going to raise tremendous objections to their requests for appropriations, to their cost overruns, to their never-ending need for this new weapon and that new weapon, and I'm going to get the hearings opened up so people can see what's going on.

January 23

One of the basic reasons that I'm claiming a right to a seat on the Armed Services Committee is that I'm a woman. A woman hasn't served on it since Margaret Chase Smith, and that was twenty-two years ago. I can't tell you how outrageous that is. Do you realize that there are 42,000 women in the military? Do you realize that about half the civilian employees of the Defense Department are women—290,000 of them at last count? And, as if that isn't enough, there are one and a half million wives of military personnel.

All this was the central point of a letter I sent today to Wilbur Mills, who's the chairman of the Democratic Committee on Committees, which will determine whether I get the seat on Armed Services. Believe it or not, the letter, which urged that I be appointed to the committee, has the unanimous backing of the New York Congressional delegation. Yes, even John Rooney.

The power structure is aware, however, that I have a pretty good argument on this woman thing, and they are not sitting idle. I read a newspaper column in which it was reported that Mendel Rivers, before he died, wanted Louise Day Hicks, the recently elected conservative Congresswoman from Boston, on the committee. "Dahhhling," he is reported to have said to her, "Ah want ya'll on mah committah."

Since I suspected a Tory plot to undercut me, I went to Mills a few weeks ago, before the session, and told him flatly that nobody was going to take the woman thing away from me. "If you guys want Louise," I said, "fine. Then we'll have two women on the committee."

January 27

I represented the Democrats in the "freshman class" at the annual political dinner of the Women's National Press Club, a very fancy affair attended by almost fifteen hundred people, including cabinet members, Senators, Congressmen and, of course, the press. The other speakers included Carl Albert, Hugh Scott, Jack Kemp, from upstate New York representing the freshmen Republicans, and Adlai Stevenson III, from Illinois, Lawton Chiles, from Florida, and James Buckley, representing the new Senators. We were all given instructions to be "funny" for two and a half minutes.

I broke them up with the story about what my older daughter, Egee, said on election night. Egee worked very hard for me during the campaign when my slogan was "This woman's place is in the House—the House of Representatives." After the results came in and we were in the middle of a victory celebration, she got up and told everybody, "Thank God we're getting her out of *our* house and into *their* House."

"After being in Washington for a week," I said, "I'm beginning to get the impression that a lot of fellows are feeling the same way as my daughter, except in reverse. 'God,' they're saying, 'if we could only get her out of *our* House and back into *theirs*.' "

Carl Albert spoke after me and he said, "I notice that we in the House have only half as many people here to speak for us as the Senate does. But, of course, we have Bella Abzug."

Then came Senator Buckley. At which point, even before he said a word, I intentionally stopped smiling, and froze my face to show great displeasure. I find nothing about that guy funny.

He started out his spiel by saying, "When I first received the invitation to speak here at the *Women's* National Press Club, I was shocked that I was to share the same platform with Bella Abzug, particularly as this is a sexist organization."

He went on with some other garbage. I forget exactly what it was, but it was ill-conceived humor, and in poor taste. Last week an invitation came to my office to attend a White House reception tomorrow for freshmen Congressmen. My staff and my friends have been pressing me about whether I intend to go or not, and up until tonight I couldn't make up my mind. It's not exactly the kind of thing that serves my ego. And who wants to listen to his pious idiocies? On the other hand, I have to admit I'm a little curious. After ten years of protesting on the sidewalk outside the place, you get to wondering what goes on inside.

Martin called tonight from New York to tell me he had his tuxedo cleaned for the occasion. He has said all along that if I was willing to go, he'd go too. But I think he's even more curious than I am, because, after all, he's a writer, and he's interested in experiencing different situations. Martin, incidentally, has published two novels—*The Seventh Avenue Story* in 1947 and *Spearhead* in 1960. He now works as a stockbroker.

So since he's got the tux ready, I told him to fly down and we'll go. I decided my own special reason for going will be to tell Nixon exactly how I feel about some things.

Tonight, as I was getting my hair done in the House Beauty Parlor, I was sitting under a hair dryer next to Louise Day Hicks, and the first thing she said to me was, "What are you going to wear tomorrow? Long or short?"

I decided to wear a short dress so I could also wear a hat. I didn't want to deprive the President of that great event. I figured I'd let him see me in my whole regalia.

Some kids from my office drove us over, but we had trouble finding the correct entrance to get in by car. Finally Martin and I just got out and walked up to the outside gate to make the approach by foot. I didn't want to be *too* late. You're supposed to arrive before the President does, and I figured it would look too much like a plan to upstage him if I arrived afterwards. I don't need any plans to upstage him. Anyhow, I wasn't planning on being smart-alecky.

So we got out of the car, passed the gate and started up the long walkway. Two or three times guards stopped us to demand, "Who goes there?" and we had to explain who we were. Everybody else was coming up in their limousines, Martin and I noted, while we the peasants arrived on foot. We felt there was something unintentionally symbolic about that.

When we finally got there, it was all red carpet and long gown and dapper people. With all the regalia, it actually looked more British than American to us. We got a big kick out of it. With the Marine band playing in the background, we started up the gold and marble steps and lo and behold . . .

There He Was. His Wife Too. Even though there wasn't a camera in sight, he had his makeup on. We got in the reception line, and then . . .

"Oh," he said. "I've been looking forward to meeting you."

"President Nixon," I said, unsmiling, "I want you to know that my constituents want you to withdraw from Vietnam and they're unhappy that you haven't."

Whereupon his hand stiffened up immensely and locked mine into what Martin described as an Indian hand wrestle.

"We're doing much better than our predecessors," he said.

"Well, your predecessors didn't do very well, but you're doing worse."

He stiffened up further, and his whole body became sort of rigid. "Yes, yes," he said, and pushed me on to Pat.

"Oh, I've been looking forward to meeting you," she chirped. "I've read all about you and your cute little bonnets."

In the course of the evening we met a lot of cabinet members and people on Nixon's staff. Martin cornered the Secretary of Commerce to chat about the stock market, which is in trouble. "I was lucky," the Secretary, Maurice Stans, told him. "I got this job and got out of it."

Almost everybody I met had seen me at the Women's National Press Club last night and they said they enjoyed me. They were a lot more relaxed than Nixon. Some of them even had a sense of humor. I was having a good time until at a certain point Senator Buckley walked up to me and held out his hand and said, "Hi, Bella."

"I don't shake your hand," I said.

"Why not?"

"Because I didn't like what you said about me last night."

"I was only kidding," he said. "I was trying to compliment you."

"Then you better get yourself another speechwriter."

All done with a smile, but I meant every word.

January 29

Just as I had hoped, my campaign to get a seat on the Armed Services Committee is taking on national proportions. I'm being interviewed all over the place by the press and radio and television, which is giving me the opportunity to drive home a number of points about the nature of the committee. In so doing, I'm stirring up pressure for change, and even if I don't succeed in getting seated on the committee, and I doubt I will, I'll have shaken them up and perhaps even made it possible for another liberal to get on.

Incidentally, those talk shows are something else. When I was on the "David Frost Show," the producer came out during the commercial and said I was being too rough on Nixon. Would I please let up, he asked. "What do you want me to talk about?" I said. "Tulips?"

I bumped into Ed Hébert on the Floor. I went up to him, put my hand on his shoulder and said, "Ed, look at how all this looks to the country. Here you are, the most hated committee, the committee that's taken our tax dollars and handed them over year after year to the military and here I am, considered probably the most opposite to you of all the people in Congress. Now, let's face it, you would show that you have great breadth and depth if you put me on your committee. Certainly, if you think you're right, you can take someone on who disagrees with you."

"You know it's not up to me, Bella," he said. "I have no objection to your being on the committee, but it's up to the Committee on Committees to put you there."

January 30

The news came late yesterday from Hugh Carey, our geographical zone leader on the Committee on Committees. He called and said, "Bella, I'm sorry, but you didn't make it. You got some votes, but not enough. A lot of people said there were already two Democrats and two Republicans from New York on the committee, and they didn't feel it was right to put any more New Yorkers on."

"What do you mean? These guys are great at making exceptions when the exceptions suit *them*. Let them make an exception and put me on the committee."

"Bella, you know they're not going to do it. Now what do you want me to do?"

"I don't give a damn what you do," I said furiously. "This is outrageous. You're like the rest of them. I don't care what you do. If I were you, I'd resign. You have no power."

"Look, Bella," he said. "I'm in the committee now and we're deciding. Will you consider any other committees?"

I had never listed any second or third choices, or even thought about them. I've been figuring that if I don't make Armed Services, I'll just conduct my own hearings on the military.

"Well, Bella, will you consider any other committees?" Carey pressed.

"Interstate and Foreign Commerce, *maybe*," I said, because this is the committee that regulates all the regulatory agencies and the alleged public services agencies that are killing us in this country. You know, Con Ed and the Telephone Company.

"Okay," he said. "Is there anything else you'll consider?"

"Banking and Currency, because it deals with housing, or Government Operations—*maybe*," I said. "So you'd better get back in there and get me on one of them. This geographical excuse for me not getting on Armed Services is baloney."

An hour or so later Carey called back.

"You got Government Operations," he said, "and you ought to be happy. It's the committee that is going to be handling Nixon's reorganization plan, and it's very rare for a freshman to get on it."

"That's a lot of baloney," I said. "You're not fooling me. Tell those guys that I never say die. As far as Armed Services is concerned, I'm not finished yet."

As soon as I hung up I called Carl Albert.

"Now look, Carl," I said. "Let me tell you something. You're the Speaker and you're the only one, really, to whom there is an appeal, and I want to tell you that there are three reasons from *your* point of view to have me on the Armed Services Committee." I then went into the business about the committee having no representation from the women or the cities, and the fact that it was a special interest group.

Then I went on to say, "Now what is this *new look* you're supposed to be representing in the Democratic Party. There's no *new look*! It's the same old sectional politics. Everybody who's in power is either from the South or the Southwest. Now, if you really want a *new look*, and if you really want to show people that the Democratic Party has the capacity to cope with change, then you'll do what I tell you to do. You'll take the one person who most represents change—the one who has the largest electoral mandate for change—and you'll put her on the Armed Services Committee. You'll overrule the old style! You'll show that you guys are willing to appreciate change, and people will appreciate you."

"Well, Bella," he said, "you're right—there is a desire for change and your arguments are very persuasive. Let me see what I can do."

I'm sure he was just putting me off. He's not going to do anything. My only hope now is to take the fight into the Democratic caucus next week, which has the power to reverse the Committee on Committees.

January 31

Paul Cowan, a reporter for *The Village Voice*, invited me to go with him this afternoon to meet a couple of nuns involved in the Justice Department's wild charges about a plot to kidnap Henry Kissinger and bomb government heating systems. A federal grand jury sitting in Harrisburg has issued a number of indictments naming the Berrigan brothers and others in the Catholic peace/resistance movement as conspirators or co-conspirators.

We went to an old brownstone in the West Nineties which houses the Religious Order of the Sacred Heart of Mary and there in a plainly furnished basement parlor I drank tea and talked with two remarkable women. Incidentally, neither one was dressed like a nun. They're part of the new breed of Catholic that is more concerned with substance than outward form.

Sister Elizabeth McAllister, the younger one, has actually been indicted and is out on bail. "I feel as though I'm trapped in a J. Edgar Hoover nightmare," she said. The other one, Sister Jogues Egan, is a really distinguished scholar and the former president of her order's Marymount College. She's fifty-two, white-haired and chic in a quiet way, and is considered part of the church establishment. She's an unindicted "co-conspirator" and has just spent a couple of days in Pennsylvania jails for refusing to testify before the grand jury. The jury's on a fishing expedition and apparently is now looking for testimony to justify the indictments it issued.

Like a lot of peace people who get thrown into jail for the first time, Sister

Jogues was so appalled by the conditions she found there that she wants to go into jail reform. As unbelievable as it may seem, she said, they took away her watch so she lost all sense of time and they also took away her Bible so she couldn't read. Then they had her cleaning toilets!

Unlike the Berrigans, she said, she had never wanted to commit any acts of civil disobedience because she didn't want to go to jail. But when she was called before the grand jury, she decided to refuse to answer their questions, insisting that her conscience bade her "obey a higher court than this one."

She and Sister Elizabeth said they were harassed for weeks before the indictments were handed down. Their phones were tapped and they'd get mysterious calls at all hours. It's really incredible what the FBI gets away with. That's one of the issues I must take on in Congress.

These women have guts—and humor. Just as I was leaving, Sister Elizabeth mentioned that she was especially annoyed at Henry Kissinger's having told the press that the nuns probably decided to kidnap him because they wanted a man. "So why would we pick Kissinger?" she asked.

February 1

I've been on the phone almost constantly the last day or so, trying to line up support for myself in the caucus, but I've been having a difficult time. Why? Because Les Aspin from Wisconsin and Michael Harrington from Massachusetts, both considered liberals and opponents of the Indochina war, have been appointed to the Armed Services Committee. While I consider their assignment a personal victory for myself, neither they nor anybody else in Congress represents the kind of activism and the kind of movement for change that I do. Nobody. I was firmly against this war when many of these "war critics" were enthusiastically presenting Johnson with his Gulf of Tonkin Resolution, and before that too. Ten years ago I was out in the streets protesting nuclear testing, organizing the mothers and other women of this country in a movement for peace and disarmament. It was largely because they were worried about the "mothers' vote" that the Senate ratified the partial nuclear test ban treaty. (Now they're going to have to worry about the "women's vote" too.)

I used to come down to Washington several times a year as a lobbyist for Women Strike for Peace. I would go from one Congressman to another, warning them, "You guys better do something about this war or we're not going to put you back in office." I'm no Joanna-come-lately, believe me. I've been here all along—outside. It's just that now there are enough people who feel the way I do so that they've been able to get me into Congress. I'm not going to betray them.

The more I look at this committee system, the more outrageous I realize it is. Of the grand total of twelve women in the House, five have been assigned to the Education and Labor Committee, which, for some reason or another, the gallant men around here are shaping into a female repository. Maybe they figure if they get us all in one place we'll cause less trouble.

Only one woman will serve on the very powerful Ways and Means Committee, and two on Appropriations. None of us has been assigned to the Rules Committee, the Judiciary Committee or, of course, the Armed Services Committee—as if the jurisdictions of these committees have nothing to do with 53 percent of the voting population in this country, which is female.

Besides women, New Yorkers are severely discriminated against. On the six major House committees, New York City's twenty Congressmen occupy only seven out of two hundred places. Only one Representative from the city is a committee chairman, and under the hideous seniority setup only four are high up enough on the list to have any hope of ever becoming chairmen.

So if you're a woman and a New Yorker too, watch out! Two years ago Shirley Chisholm from Brooklyn, not exactly the most pastoral of regions, was assigned to the Agriculture Committee. When she raised a fuss they shifted her to Veterans' Affairs. I don't know whether it's true or not, and I don't want to know, but this year it was reported in one of the papers that Shirley voted for Hale Boggs in the secret ballot against Morris Udall for Majority Leader. She did it, the article said, because "it was a deal, and the only way she could get on the committees she wanted to be on." She was assigned to the Education and Labor Committee. Believe me, if Shirley has to be driven to something like this, you can understand the degree to which the Tories have this place locked up. . . .

February 23

Like most nights, I worked in my Washington office until 10:30 (sometimes it's even later), signing mail, preparing for my committees, meeting with people and researching some upcoming projects. I grabbed a sandwich on the way home and ate it in the cab. It's my usual practice to either do that or get a quick bite in a local slop joint. I don't have time, as many of my colleagues seem to, for long lunches and dinners in the fine restaurants of this city.

Eating is only one of the things I don't have enough time for anymore. My family, unfortunately, is another. Luckily, it doesn't *require* a lot of time. Both Egee, who is twenty-one, and Liz, eighteen, are away at college and don't get in that often. As for Martin, he and I—even years before my election—were often so busy during the week that we didn't get to spend much time together anyway. We did, however, often have weekends to ourselves. Now we don't even have that. Weekends are the only time I'm in New York, and my schedule in my district is usually merciless.

The family plays a very important role in the lives of working women like me. The tough thing, of course, is trying to adjust the family situation to the realities of your life. You can't put either ahead of the other. There must be a balance, and you've got to strive to keep that balance. The family grows with it. The kids know that the mother is a woman, a wife and, in my case, a lawyer. A total person. It makes them better people.

Let's face it: Some of us have been and are more privileged than others. I, for instance, had a wonderful housekeeper, Alice Williams. To this day (she's now retired) she likes to tell me, "I all but had those kids." My husband, too, played a more domestic role than most do. He helped with the shopping and spent a great deal of time with the kids. I always tried to make it home for dinner every night, but often it was impossible. Once on a visiting day when the kids were very young and away at camp, I had an important trial and couldn't go. I felt so bad that I sent Martin, his mother, my mother and the housekeeper to substitute.

I don't mean to imply that I'm all guilt-ridden about being a working mother. I'm not. For the most part I rarely missed a school visiting day or school play. I have two great kids and a great husband. On the other hand, there are moments when I think back and say to myself, "I should have been more available." But what can you do? . . .

March 17

I got to the caucus at 8:15 A.M., all set with my hot little speech in my little hands, and a press release waiting upstairs. "Doc" Morgan was there when I arrived and he said, chomping on his cigar, "You're here so early."

"That's right."

"Well, I want you to know that I came just to hear you speak."

"Good," I said.

By 8:30 only a few people had arrived, and I began to get the feeling that the jig was up. It was apparent that the leadership, with its ploy of spreading the word that the vote was off, had gotten just what it wanted. Most people decided not to come. In the next few minutes a few more people trickled in, but we were still obviously far short of a quorum. Then—even before we got to any of the items on the agenda, including my speech—somebody asked for a quorum call. We only had 80 of the 127 heads we needed there, so Olin Teague, the caucus chairman, promptly declared the meeting adjourned.

We got screwed.

I headed right for Carl Albert and let him have it: "Now you listen to me, Carl," I said. "I'm sick and tired, because it's about time this caucus went on record against the war. The people want the war to end! And here you are, the Democratic leadership in the House, stifling a vote like this. What's the matter with you? I know why you're doing it, too, Carl. Because if you hadn't prevented this vote we would have won it, that's why, and that's what you're scared of."

"What do you mean by these charges?" he said angrily. "What you're saying is ridiculous. Anyway, how do you know how *the* people feel about this war?"

"Because I know how my constituents feel and how the people across this country feel. I go out there and I talk to them, and they tell me they want this war over. I also know how you feel about it too."

"You don't know how I feel."

"I sure do. You agree with Nixon. You support the war."

"How do you know that?"

"How do I know that? For one thing, when Nixon invaded Laos, you said it was a 'prudent' move. Well, if anything was ever a 'prudent' move, *that* sure wasn't, and neither was what you said."

By this time he was furious with me, really furious. "I don't like the way you're talking," he said, "and if you weren't a lady . . ."

"Being a lady has nothing to do with it, understand? I'm a Congresswoman with an electoral mandate, and I'm going to fulfill it."

"Well, I don't know why you're so angry with us. We've been very nice to you."

"What are you talking about? You've done *nothing* for me in this House. Nothing! You didn't give me a decent committee. You stopped this vote. If you had any damn political sense you'd know the only way to defeat Nixon is to have a vote which opposes his Vietnam policies."

"Well, lady, that's your opinion."

"Yes, that's *my* opinion," I said and walked away, disgusted.

This is my week for telling off the political power structure, I guess. About twenty people saw me shouting at Carl. I couldn't help noticing that a lot of them had secret smiles on their faces.

I started to storm out of the room, but instead I circled around for a moment. Albert's a real shrewdy. Something he said hit me. He said he'd been nice to me, and in a way I knew he was right. He was in New York when I was campaigning and made a point of being friendly and helpful. Even though when it really matters on political issues he's nowhere, I felt bad for what I had said to him, at least for the tone I had used.

He was watching me pacing around, and he came over to put his arm around me. He's a little fellow, so it was kind of funny. "Come on, Bella, let's go get a cup of coffee," he said.

"Look, Carl," I said in a much gentler tone of voice. "You know I'm trying to do my best. I've got a lot of things to offer this House, and if you'll only give me a chance, such as getting me on the Armed Forces Committee . . ."

"Well," he said, "I don't know if that's possible, but I've been thinking there may be a vacancy on the Joint Economics Committee—nothing definite—but if there's room, would you like to come on it?"

"Yeah," I said. And then I walked off again, turning back to say, "We've got to have a vote on this Vietnam issue, and don't you forget it, Carl."

The House convened at noon to debate the SST. My contribution: "There are a lot of arguments against the SST . . . but there is only one real argument for it: profits for a very few people. While we debate such false issues as the SST's effect on the balance of payments or the dangers of Russia or England or France producing the first 'White Elephants,' children in this country suffer from not having enough food to eat. . . . How long must the working people of this country watch their taxes spent, not for anything that might benefit them or their fellow human beings, but for useless pieces of metal that make some rich people richer?"

At lunch I went out for a bite with Ella Grasso, who's a new Congresswoman from Connecticut. Ella's a great gal who had served as Connecticut Secretary of State for twelve years before she was elected to Congress last year. We're both about the same age, and she has two kids too. Where we differ is that she, unlike me, is a real party regular. As a result, she has a very good relationship with the House leadership. Unlike some of the others in this situation, I like her because she stands where she stands, she's very straightforward and makes no pretense. If she votes with the leadership she's honest about it. She says she does it to preserve her good relationship with them. No phony moralizing. I often find I have a lot more in common with her than with people who *theoretically* agree with me on the issues, because she empathizes with me in a real human way. All through lunch she scolded me because I'm trying to do too much and because I'm not taking care of myself. Before the session convened, we considered living together down here, and in a way I'm sorry we didn't. We both lead lonely during-the-week lives, having to come back to our rooms alone after long, hard days. I mean, you should see my telephone bills from late night calls alone.

Ella was telling me an interesting story about a meeting she attended the other day with a representative from a huge airplane company in her state. A number of other Connecticut Congressmen were there with her, including a freshman moderate named Bill Cotter. When the guy from the corporation told Ella, "We hear you're friendly with Bella Abzug. We don't like that. She's against everything we need," Bill Cotter objected strongly.

"I know Mrs. Abzug too," he said, "and she's a very fine, sincere and charming woman. You have no right to say that about her."

March 18

I was in the office until past midnight last night, reading, writing, being interviewed and waiting desperately for my legislative assistant to bring me testimony she was preparing for my appearance today before the general labor subcommittee of the House Education and Labor Committee. Finally, at eleven o'clock she brought it in, and while two secretaries typed it up, somebody went out for some soul food. I didn't eat any because I'm trying to diet.

I woke up with a terrible sore throat. I testified at 9:30, suffering. My main point was that since women and minorities are still castoffs in the American economy, we should strengthen the enforcement authority of the Equal Employment Opportunity Commission, which can now only sweet-talk employers into obeying the Civil Rights Act of 1964. A press release and a transcript of my prepared remarks were available to the press, but I had to leave without answering questions since I had a subcommittee meeting of my own to go to.

I got to the Floor around 2:30 and the place was jammed. The SST debate was raging. I was disappointed that I had already made my remarks yesterday to an almost empty House, but I sat through the debate anyway, finding a chuckle here and there, such as when Gerry Ford got up clutching a photograph of the Russian SST. "If you vote against an American SST," he said, "you are ensuring that the Soviet Union, the British and the French will dominate the market in advanced aircraft over the next two decades." He was so funny, I booed out loud. After me, several other people booed too.

Several times I was called off the Floor by labor lobbyists. It was really pathetic to see unions fighting for the SST because jobs were involved. People's livelihoods should not be tied to war and pollution when there are so many things we really need in this country, such as hospitals and housing and schools. Finally, the vote got under way, and as it started to shape up, it looked like we might win. Hale Boggs walked by at this point and I heard him say, "We're losing by ten votes."

"What do you mean *we're* losing by ten votes?" I said. "*You're* losing, not *us*. And this is only the beginning, only the first defeat. From now on, it's going to be one after another. Next we're going to beat you on the war. We're going to beat you because we're where the people are, and you and your guys might as well face it."

I was ecstatic.

When the vote was officially announced, we won 216–204 and we were so happy that we violated the rules of decorum and applauded. A great event.

I didn't have much time to celebrate, unfortunately, because of my usual last-minute weekly rush to get my clothes and files together and catch the plane back to New York. I call this my clicking-off moment. Clicking off the problems of Washington and clicking on the problems of New York. It happens every Thursday. Anyway, I barely made the third section of the shuttle, arrived in New York at five o'clock, went home, made some calls, met Martin for dinner, spoke at the Village Independent Democratic Club, spoke at the Phoenix Democratic Club, went home, made some more phone calls, the last one to Ronnie Eldridge, my good friend who works as a special assistant to Mayor Lindsay. We talked about personal things, mixed in with some politics, and then I went to sleep, exhausted. I can't go on this way every day. I'm going to collapse.

Margaret Chase Smith and the Senate Fight against Joe McCarthy

by Frank Graham, Jr.

The early summer of 1950 has been described as Margaret Smith's finest hour. It was in June of that year that she delivered in the Senate her "Declaration of Con-

From Frank Graham, Jr., *Margaret Chase Smith: Woman of Courage* (New York: John Day, 1964), pp. 71–86.

science," a document treasured not so much for its eloquence as for its timeliness; not so much for its originality as for its common sense. It was a plea by the Senate's lone woman to her 95 male colleagues to return that institution to the state in which its traditions had flowered. It was, in short, a breath of fresh air, blown into an institution whose atmosphere had turned dishonorable.

There is no doubt now that atmosphere was dishonorable. It was not that the Senate abounded in dishonorable men, but that a few who were unscrupulous, sparked by a mediocre but curiously twisted man, had capitalized on the nation's fears in order to seize the initiative. Because of recent history, the Senate's decent members were paralyzed not so much by fear (though there was that, too) but by uncertainty. In the unique Cold War which blighted the postwar world, the judgment of honest men was shaken in the mass of revelations, in the confused discussion of "patriotism," with its charges and countercharges, that swirled around them.

While the better Senators were devoting themselves to the business of legislation, Wisconsin's Republican Senator Joseph R. McCarthy was manufacturing headlines with his frantic efforts to uncover a Communist in government. As in most such cases, there was a basis of fact underlying the national hysteria. Soviet Russia had increased its espionage activity in the United States after the war. When Alger Hiss, a government official under Presidents Franklin D. Roosevelt and Harry Truman, was accused of being a part of the Soviet spy apparatus, many prominent Democrats rushed to his defense. Hiss' subsequent conviction for perjury was a blow to his defenders. Afraid of being charged with Communist sympathies, and unsure now of their own judgment, many prominent men in government became reluctant to speak out in defense of others who had been accused of "treason." Given a free hand, unscrupulous or fanatical men competed for national publicity and the attendant votes of the gullible by accusing almost everybody in sight of being "a Communist."

George Santayana, the philosopher and poet, once defined a fanatic as a man who redoubles his effort after he has forgotten his aim. Such was Senator McCarthy. Cloaked in the immunity from libel granted to Senators when they speak on the floor, he rose time after time to blacken the names of defenseless people by accusing them of treason and subversion without the faintest shred of evidence. Shocked by the Hiss case (in which McCarthy had played no part), Democratic Senators lacked the courage or the confidence to speak out against McCarthy. Republican leaders, hoping that their colleague from Wisconsin would uncover "another Hiss" if he kept at it, failed to restrain him. This hardly admirable state of affairs had badly tarnished the Senate, and had damaged America's prestige in the eyes of the civilized world.

Margaret Smith, though a popular figure throughout the country, pulled little weight within the hierarchy of the Republican party. The Old Guard was not ready to accept a woman, especially one who did not fit into the mold of the traditional woman politician by being a "nice, pleasant soul anxious to please her betters." On the other hand, she shattered another popular picture of her sex: in an institution noted for its wordiness, she was distinguished by her ability to hold her tongue. She had yet to make a major speech in the Senate. And, when the Senate Republican Policy Committee (of which she was a member) met with the House Republican Policy Committee to draft a statement of their party's policy in the coming elections, she rebelled at the 2,500-word statement they produced. Upon her suggestion, and with the approval of the Republican National Committee, party leaders released a 99-word summary of their longer statement.

Now she was puzzled and disturbed by the unpleasant atmosphere around her in the Senate. Once, when asked by a reporter about McCarthyism, at a time when most Senators refused to discuss their colleague because of his attack on Senator Millard Tydings (who had displeased him), Margaret Smith did not evade the question.

"What is McCarthyism?" she repeated. "A lot of personal publicity for Senator McCarthy, I think."

Speaking of those days in later years, Margaret Smith has said: "Like everybody else I was hoping that Joe McCarthy would produce some solid evidence. Nobody wanted to cross him. You wondered when you were going to be called to task just because you'd said hello to the wrong person. It was so bad people were becoming almost deaf mutes."

Though, like most other Republicans, she believed the Democratic administration in Washington had been guilty of great carelessness in managing the country's security, she was appalled at the irresponsible attack McCarthy had made on so many earnest (if sometimes mistaken) Americans. She waited for her seniors in Congress to take action against McCarthy. Nothing happened.

"I've just about had it," she said one day to her administrative assistant, Bill Lewis.

Shortly afterward she boarded the little subway that shuttled back and forth between the Senate Office Building and the Capitol. Senator McCarthy took a seat beside her. One of McCarthy's assets was his agreeableness; many reporters and politicians had been won over to his side because he was "a nice guy." But Margaret Smith was not exchanging pleasantries that day.

"I'm going to make a speech, Joe," she told him. "And you're not going to like it."

"Be careful, Margaret," McCarthy replied, half seriously and half jokingly. "You know, you might lose Wisconsin's votes for Vice-President."

She did not rush hastily into battle. For six weeks, off and on, she thought about what she would say. She talked over her plans with men she trusted. Among them was Vermont's Republican Senator, George D. Aiken. Surprised at her determination, Aiken nevertheless encouraged her. She contacted five other Republicans who did not seem to her to be tied to the arch-conservatives who led the party. They were Charles Toby of New Hampshire, Irving Ives of New York, Edward Thye of Minnesota, Robert Hendrickson of New Jersey and Wayne Morse (who later became a Democrat) of Oregon. None of them disappointed her. Joined by Aiken, these five agreed to sign the "declaration" which she had prepared.

On June 1, she appeared in the green-carpeted, crescent-shaped Senate Chamber, her gray hair immaculately done, looking cool yet determined in her aquamarine silk suit; the fresh red rose, as always, sparkled on her lapel. Word had gotten around that she was to make her first important speech in the Senate, and a large crowd was on hand. She took her place at her desk, on the Republican side of the narrow center aisle. Just behind her sat the burly Senator from Wisconsin, Joe McCarthy.

When she rose to speak, other Senators on both sides of the aisle moved closer to hear her. Her voice wasn't loud, but it was clear and firm. As she spoke she occasionally looked down at the cards she held in her hands.

"I would like to speak briefly and simply about a serious national condition," she began. "It is a national feeling of fear and frustration that could result in national suicide and the end of everything that we Americans hold dear. It is a condition that comes from the lack of effective leadership in either the legislative branch or the executive branch of our government."

As McCarthy alternately scowled and placed his head in his hand, Margaret Smith lashed out at the tactics which had caused the Senate, once the most admired deliberative body in the world, to be "debased to the level of a forum of hate and character assassination sheltered by the shield of Congressional immunity."

Never mentioning McCarthy, or the party leaders who had privately encouraged him while publicly keeping their distance from his methods, Margaret Smith suggested that "it is high time for the United States Senate and its members to do some soul-searching. . . . It is high time that we remembered that the Constitution, as amended, speaks not only of freedom of speech but also of trial by jury instead of trial by accusation."

With simple force she pointed out that the very men who were shouting the loudest about their "Americanism" were those who were ignoring at the same time some of the basic principles of Americanism. She vigorously defended every American's right to criticize, to think independently and to hold unpopular beliefs.

"Who of us doesn't?" she asked the great hushed chamber. "Otherwise none of us could call our souls our own. Otherwise thought control would have set in. The American people are sick and tired of being afraid to speak their minds lest they be smeared as 'Communists' or 'Fascists' by their opponents. Freedom of speech is not what it used to be in America. It has been so abused by some that it is not exercised by others."

Shifting her attack to the Democratic administration, she said that the American people were not only sick of seeing innocent people smeared, but they were also sick of seeing the guilty whitewashed. She said that the administration's failure to vigorously combat internal subversion had caused the public to lose confidence in it, and led to "the confusion and suspicions that are bred in the United States Senate to spread like cancerous tentacles." She asserted her belief that the Truman administration was a burden on the country.

"Yet to displace it with a Republican regime embracing a philosophy that lacks political integrity or intellectual honesty would prove equally disastrous to this nation. The nation sorely needs a Republican victory. But I don't want to see the Republican party ride to political victory on the Four Horsemen of Calumny—Fear, Ignorance, Bigotry and Smear."

In closing, she said: "As an American, I want to see our nation recapture the strength and unity it once had when we fought the enemy instead of ourselves." She then read the brief "Declaration of Conscience," signed by the six Republicans she had spoken to earlier. They joined her in saying that it was time "we stopped being tools and victims of totalitarian techniques—techniques that, if continued here unchecked, will surely end what we have come to cherish as the American way of life."

When she sat down it was as if, with one ringing blow, she had cleared the atmosphere of the venerable chamber. Things happened that hadn't happened there in a long time. McCarthy, who had promised to "ask her some very pointed questions after the speech," got up and, his face grimly dark, left the Capitol without saying a word. Where, only a few short minutes before, the most powerful men in the country would have hesitated before consorting with those who had attacked McCarthy, her colleagues now came over to congratulate her. New York's Senator Herbert Lehman told reporters that "she said things which had to be said and should have been said a long time ago."

Maryland's Senator Millard Tydings called for a new word: "Stateswomanship." And Missouri's Democratic Senator Stuart Symington said: "Senator Smith represents just about all that is best today in American public life—even if she is a Republican."

"I didn't do it for approval or disapproval," Margaret Smith said. "I just thought it had to be done. It's one of the things I've felt strongly about."

Letters poured in from all over the country, running about eight to one in her favor. She answered them all, sending thanks to those who agreed with her, and politely acknowledging the others with an observation that "America is big enough and great enough to include people of various opinions." Editorial comment in the nation's newspapers was generally favorable. Margaret Smith had, in her country's hour of deep trouble, stepped in with a brave and independent gesture.

But she had not yet heard from Senator Joseph R. McCarthy.

It is difficult from this distance to appreciate the climate of fear which then prevailed in political, academic and scientific America. To speak out against Joseph McCarthy and his followers, or the views they held sacred, was to invite certain retaliation; the livelihood and reputations of many Americans were jeopardized or destroyed because of their insistence on what should have been their inviolate right to freedom of speech. Margaret Chase Smith was about to undergo her trial by fire.

McCarthy remained silent for less than twenty-four hours after her speech. Then he released a snarling, sarcastic statement in which he referred to Margaret Smith and the Senators who had signed her "Declaration of Conscience" as "Snow White and the Six Dwarfs." Names could not hurt Margaret Smith, but McCarthy's sticks and stones were still to come.

The Wisconsin Senator bided his time through the remainder of that session. Margaret Smith came under attack from his followers from time to time, but McCarthy first turned his attention to Maryland's Senator Millard Tydings, who had also affronted him, and who was especially vulnerable now because he was running for re-election. Moving into Maryland, McCarthy's followers waged such a vicious campaign while insuring Tydings' defeat that it became the subject of a later Senate investigation. With Tydings disposed of and the 1951 session of Congress now under way, McCarthy once more turned his attention to Margaret Smith.

After entering the Senate she had been appointed to the Senate Expenditures Committee (of which Harry Truman had been chairman when he was a Senator before World War Two); through this post she had become a member of that committee's key investigating subcommittee. Arkansas' Democratic Senator John McClellan was now the committee chairman because his party controlled the Senate, but Joe McCarthy was the committee's senior Republican member and so had the right to name the other Republicans to its subcommittees. When McCarthy passed around a memorandum designating the Republican assignments for the new session, Margaret Smith's name had been removed from the investigations subcommittee and placed on the less-important reorganization subcommittee. Her place on the investigations panel was filled by a freshman Senator from California named Richard M. Nixon.

The next morning eight members of the parent Expenditures Committee met in a closed session. Margaret Smith immediately stood up and challenged McCarthy's right to remove her from the subcommittee in favor of a Senator who was her junior. Senator McClellan evaded her demand for a ruling by claiming that it was McCarthy's right to assign his own members. She carried the battle to the Wisconsin Senator.

"Nobody here is fooling anybody else," she fumed. "I was bumped from that subcommittee."

McCarthy tried to calm the lady, explaining that he simply was anxious to have

Nixon, who had helped to destroy Alger Hiss, serve on the investigations subcommittee because of his experience. "He did a tremendous job on the House Un-American Activities Committee," McCarthy said.

Margaret Smith was ready for him. "Joe, I was making investigations in the House three years before you and Senator Nixon got to Washington!"

But the change had been made. Later McCarthy denied to reporters that her "Declaration of Conscience" in the previous session had had anything to do with the change of assignments. "I'm surprised there should be such a fuss over a routine matter," he said blandly. "Nixon, like everybody else, wanted to be on the investigations subcommittee, and a choice had to be made. But it's not right to say that Margaret was bumped. She was promoted to another highly important job."

Another blow fell almost immediately: she lost her place on the Republican Policy Committee to Senator Brewster, her old sparring partner from Maine. She was less bitter toward McCarthy, from whom she expected retaliation, than she was toward Senator Taft and the other Republican leaders; these changes could have been made only with their tacit consent. She had not always supported Taft's policies, of course; in a recent Republican statement which asked for the removal of Truman's Secretary of State, Dean Acheson, she had disassociated herself from the Republicans' savage attack and voted with the Democrats. But she had done several important favors for Taft, too, particularly on the proposed Lucas Amendment to the Taft-Hartley Labor Act. This amendment would have removed the injunction clause, which Taft had felt was vital to the bill's effectiveness. Had she voted for the amendment, it would have brought about a tie, and Vice-President Barkley (who was entitled to vote in the event of a tie in the Senate) would have ensured the amendment's passage. Instead, she bowed to Taft's plea and her vote defeated the amendment, 46–44. On another occasion she had deserted the other Republican liberals and cast her vote for Taft as chairman of the Senate Republican Policy Committee. Now she knew (and McCarthy had admitted it to her) that it was with the consent of Taft that she had been removed from this committee.

Again the press seemed solidly on Margaret Smith's side. "She could pursue a continuous crusade against McCarthyism only at the risk of party ostracism which would render it ineffective," *The Nation* said in an editorial. "So instead she has let the declaration ferment in the voters' consciences while she tries to be the best Senator and Republican she knows how to be."

Her colleagues in the Senate also said a good word for her in this dark moment. Democratic Senator Harry Byrd of Virginia made a public statement praising her economic views (implying that nobody who agreed with *his* orthodox economics could possibly be a Communist sympathizer), while that arch-conservative, Pat McCarran of Nevada, bestowed on her his own certificate of patriotism: "I would like very much to have her as a member of my committee investigating subversives."

The battle was to flare up at intervals for several years. There is no need here to go into all the sordid details of that period of the Senate's history, but a few of the highlights which marked one Senator's struggle against the "no-nothings" may prove instructive.

Though Margaret Smith did not carry on a personal vendetta against McCarthy (suggesting a more bipartisan policy by the administration, she asked President Truman to consult "such critical Republicans as Senators Joseph R. McCarthy and William F. Knowland before making decisions on affairs of state"), she remained alert for any outbreaks of "demagoguery." When McCarthy launched a vicious and unwarranted attack on General George C. Marshall, a respected soldier and statesman,

Margaret Smith had her "Declaration of Conscience" re-inserted in the *Congressional Record*, appending the remark that it was now more applicable than ever before. And, speaking in Houlton, Maine, that fall, she called for a return to the traditional initiative for which Americans used to be known.

"When we accept the statements and proposals of demagogues," she said, "because we are too lazy to think and test their statements we can blame no one but ourselves for subsequent events. . . . We are closer to surrendering our freedom than most of us are willing to recognize or admit."

By this time Margaret Smith was a member of a Senate committee which had been appointed to investigate the scandals connected with the defeat in Maryland of Senator Millard Tydings. McCarthy, of course, had ridiculed the investigation. But when Senator Taft agreed with him, Margaret Smith neatly turned the tables.

Taft had tried to brush off the Maryland election scandal with the comment that it was nothing compared to what had happened in Ohio, when he had run for reelection in 1950. Margaret Smith heard him through, then told the subcommittee:

"If this is so, perhaps we had better look into the Ohio elections too."

Taft was furious, especially because the investigation had not been cleared with him. Though his supporters later claimed that Taft had had nothing to do with the anti-Catholic whispering which had been a part of the campaign waged for him in Ohio (comparable to the fraudulent photographs which were supposed to link Tydings with Communists in the Maryland campaign) he was not anxious to have these charges investigated.

The investigation proved that Taft's bitter charges about the millions poured into his opponent's campaign were hogwash; Taft's own campaign had cost a great deal more. The most dramatic moment of the investigation came when Margaret Smith challenged Taft's campaign statement that linked the C.I.O. with Communism. In the presence of Willis B. Gradison, who had managed Taft's campaign, she read excerpts from a speech Taft had made at Cleveland. There the Ohio Senator had said that the C.I.O.'s Political Action Committee was conceived and nurtured by Communists.

"Wouldn't you say that this is a pretty extravagant statement you couldn't back up with facts?" she asked Gradison.

"I certainly couldn't back it up," Gradison said. "I have no doubt the Senator at least attempted to back it up."

Under questioning by Margaret Smith and the rest of the committee, Gradison admitted that he would not contend the C.I.O.–P.A.C. was controlled or dominated by Communists. It was, he said, only "infiltrated." He also softened his earlier testimony that Communist leader "Gus Hall blueprinted the campaign against Taft." He admitted that it would have been better to say simply that the Communists opposed Taft. Later Taft's treasurer claimed that he had kept no records of the money he gave in 1950 to such groups as the Advertising Committee for Taft and the Physicians' Committee for Taft. The investigations brought no charges against anybody.

The skirmishes went on. In 1952, when a move was brought by Connecticut's Senator William Benton to expel McCarthy from the Senate on the grounds that he had lied to that body, Margaret Smith and McCarthy clashed again. She was a member of a Senate subcommittee which had been given the task of investigating McCarthy. The Great Investigator was outraged at being investigated. He assailed the subcommittee and claimed that its members "were guilty of stealing just as clearly as though they engaged in picking the pockets of the taxpayers."

Margaret Smith, like the other Senators on the subcommittee, resented being called a thief. The entire Senate was asked to display its confidence in the subcommittee. Margaret Smith spoke to the Senate, quietly but firmly, tearing McCarthy's statement to shreds. As she continued her attack, a reporter in the press gallery could be heard to murmur: "She has guts!"

McCarthy, foreseeing that the Senate would vote its confidence in the subcommittee, tried to take the sting out of its action by announcing that if he were able to be there he too would give the subcommittee a vote of confidence; unfortunately, he had a pressing engagement elsewhere.

Though the very clannishness of the Senate prevented its various members from expelling one of their own, no matter how dangerous or obnoxious they found him to be (McCarthy was eventually "censured" in 1954, not for having committed outrages against the American public but for having obstructed the investigation of himself), the running battle continued. In 1953, when the Democratic members of McCarthy's investigating subcommittee resigned in disgust, McCarthy sought to issue reports in the entire subcommittee's name while the Senate was in recess. It was Margaret Smith who led the fight that prevented him from doing this.

The campaign against Margaret Smith reached its peak of absurdity in 1952 when a pair of reporters named Jack Lait and Lee Mortimer wrote a book called *U.S.A. Confidential*. Though dwelling on sin in its various sensational manifestations (chiefly sex) the book found time to link Margaret Smith to the Communist Conspiracy in the United States:

> Maine's other phenomenon is Margaret Chase Smith, sole female U.S. Senator. The last time we were in Washington she was making one of her boneheaded speeches. A Senate doorman couldn't stand it any longer. When she reached the high point of her peroration, he sniffed and remarked about the lone female, "There's too many women in the Senate!"
>
> She is a lesson in why women should not be in politics. When men argue matters of high policy they usually forget their grudges at the door. She takes every opposing speech as a personal affront and lies awake nights scheming how to "get even." She is sincere—but a dame—and she reacts to all situations as a woman scorned, not as a representative of the people. She is under the influence of the coterie of left-wing writers and reporters who dominate Washington and they praise her so assiduously she believes it.

Lait and Mortimer went on to claim that Margaret Smith was "pals" with a woman they described as a "security risk." They also claimed that she was a "left-wing apologist" and a "stunted visionary." Perhaps worst of all, as if they had intended to get under her skin, they referred to her as "Maggie." When the book was published and became a best seller, she sued the authors for one million dollars.

In her suit, which charged that they had brought her into "scandal as an associate of and sympathizer with Communists," her attorneys asked Lait and Mortimer to "specify the nights on which she lay awake scheming how to get even." They also asked the authors to specify the date on which they were in Washington to hear her speak, and to supply the name of the Senate doorman who remarked that there were too many women in the Senate. In reply, the authors' lawyer said that her questions were "specious," and he put her through an extensive pre-trial examination in which he attempted to find out where she deviated from McCarthy's beliefs. The suit lingered for four years, and was finally scheduled to come before Federal Judge Edward J. Dimmock in New York City. According to Richard H. Wels, Margaret Smith's attorney, both Estes Kefauver, Democratic Senator from Tennessee, and California's William F. Knowland, Republican leader in the Senate, were scheduled to testify in her behalf. Suddenly, Mortimer and his publisher (Lait had died) came to the conclusion that Margaret Smith was not a

"Communist sympathizer" after all. They agreed to pay her $15,000 in damages, and pay for advertisements which appeared in several Maine newspapers. The advertisements said, in part:

More thorough investigation since the publication of the book has convinced Lee Mortimer, the estate of Jack Lait and Crown Publishers, Inc., that the statements concerning Senator Margaret Chase Smith were mistaken and should not have been made.

Senator Smith enjoys an excellent and enviable reputation.

Nothing in the book was meant to reflect on the patriotism, honesty, morality or good citizenship of Senator Smith, nor was anything meant to say or imply that she was an apologist for or a sympathizer with Communists or Reds.

We regret very much these mistaken statements concerning Senator Smith. We are now convinced that they were untrue, although made unintentionally.

In fairness to Senator Smith we are happy to make these corrections.

25

THE PRESIDENCY

Before the end of the twentieth century, it seems safe to predict, the United States will have a woman president. Already India, Israel, and Great Britain, among others, have elected women their chief executives—and survived. In this country, more and more women are appearing higher and higher in government officialdom, including the cabinet and the Supreme Court as well as the elective offices. And the women in the general electorate—a majority of the citizenry—are probably organized more thoroughly today than ever before. That strength strengthens the odds for a woman president. The igniting spark will be a woman who leads like a president.

How will she rule? Probably she and her female successors will rule as variously as men have. A woman who came about as close to being a woman president as any we have seen so far is Eleanor Roosevelt. Overcoming a traumatic childhood, an uncertain marriage, crushing domination by her mother-in-law, her husband's infidelity, his crippling illness, and a host of other challenges, any of which would have sufficed to discourage another person into silence or self-indulgence, Eleanor Roosevelt instead threw herself into the mission of national rescue. She learned to make the ambiguity of her position not a weakness but a strength. Like some male presidents, she grew in office. And in the real world, she made a difference, not just a reputation.

Eleanor Roosevelt in Action

by Joseph P. Lash

By the beginning of Roosevelt's second term, his wife had become a virtuoso in making her views known and her influence felt throughout the vast reaches of the federal government. Of her husband it would later be written that "there never was a

---

From Joseph P. Lash, *Eleanor and Franklin* (New York: Norton, 1971), pp. 452–69, 472.

prominent leader who was more determined about his objectives and never one who was more flexible about his means." Something similar might be said about his wife's adeptness in the uses of government, except that in her case the flexibility related to the ways by which a woman exercises influence in a milieu where power was in the hands of the men. She had learned from experience that if women wanted to be effective in politics and government they needed "the wisdom of the serpent and the guileless appearance of the dove!"[1]

Since she held no office and possessed no authority except that which derived from her husband, she left it to official Washington to guess what she did at his request and what she did on her own, what she did with his knowledge and what she did in order to place a situation before him and thus prod him and his aides into action. Officials received invitations to lunch with her at the White House, and when she steered the conversation into some field of interest to her, everyone wondered if the president had put her up to it, and usually she did not enlighten them. Sometimes she invoked the president, as in the case of a conference on leisure and recreation, when she wrote that "the President thinks it would be a very good thing if we could have a meeting on leisure time activities. He does not want to have it a White House Conference, but he felt if it could be called he could give it his blessing." What the recipients of the letter did not know was that because of her interest in the problem she had gone to the president and suggested the national conference in the first place. How could they know, when the president himself liked to keep his associates guessing as to his wife's authority since it often served his purposes to have her test a plan's acceptability before he embraced it fully. . . .[2]

Eleanor refused to admit that she had any influence because of the power of her own personality, insisting that what she was able to accomplish had little to do with her as an individual. Rather, it had "a great deal to do with the circumstances in which I found myself."[3] She continually minimized her own importance. She advised a Texas woman whom she was encouraging to write and who decided an article about Eleanor Roosevelt was the way to break into the magazine market "not to tell only good things. . . . It will be more interesting if it is not too flattering. After all, you have only had the experience of helpful things whereas there are many people whom I have not been able to help and who probably feel that I could have done so if I had had the right understanding of their problem." When you know your own weaknesses, she said to a friend whose mother she had visited in her grocery shop, you know you are no better than other people, but because of your position you have a greater chance to do good. That is all. "You don't permit yourself false airs." She carried in her purse the prayer attributed to St. Francis in which the petitioner asks the Lord to grant "that I may not so much seek to be consoled as to console, to be understood as to understand, to be loved as to love . . ." We look at life as through a glass; the poet invests it with more poetry than it has in fact; the politicians see it as the struggle for power; Eleanor Roosevelt surrounded it with love. She profoundly influenced the thinking of some of her husband's aides, partly because she was the wife of the president but mostly by example. She insisted on being her natural self, and as Washington came to know her as a person rather than as a personage and began to sense her kindness, her genuine interest in people, her lack of egotism and boastfulness, it realized that here was no designing female Rasputin but a woman of mercy right out of First Corinthians. She ruled because she had learned to serve, and service became a form of control. She wanted people to feel that their government cared about them, and because she was in the White House she felt an added obligation to make people feel they knew her, had a right to tell her about themselves and to ask her for help.[4]

She showed compassion for all living things. "Can you suggest anything?" she asked Frances Perkins about a case that had come to her attention. "His legs are useless, his father is a drunkard, the home is very poor but he has put up a grand fight for an education." To Harry Hopkins at the Works Progress Administration, she wrote: "These poor gypsies seem to be having a difficult time. Is there any chance of their being put on a homestead in Florida or Arkansas, where they could be warm and where they might carry on their coppersmith work as well as farming? It seems to me the only solution for them." When Steve Vasilikos, the peanut vendor who stationed his cart near the White House, was driven away by the police, Eleanor wrote Steve Early from a sickbed at Hyde Park that he should take it up with the district authorities: "I would myself miss him on that corner. We had better let him stand at the White House gate." A protest against the manner in which Army mules were disposed of brought a memorandum to Steve Early: "Could the War Dept. either explain the reasons for doing so or make the whole situation clearer as I am quite sure they do not sell them without making sure they will have good homes."[5]

She transgressed against all the rules of tidy administration, though this, of course, was in the New Deal style. She asked help for supplicants whom officials often thought were malingerers and charlatans, and sometimes were. "Aside from the fact that I am disappointed in finding your story was made up entirely out of whole cloth," she wrote a woman in California, "I feel I must call your attention to the fact that when a letter is received which is as untrue as yours, it takes the time and energy of people here in Washington to follow it through which really should go toward trying to help someone who is really in difficulty."[6] She had not expected Governor Brann of Maine to help an applicant personally with a loan which she had referred to him, she wrote, slightly appalled, but since the governor and his aide had done so, Tommy informed them that "the money she [Mrs. Roosevelt] has is all pledged at the moment, but she does not want you and the Governor to suffer and she will take over the note and pay as she can."[7]

Officials often took her suggestions as commands when she had really meant them to use their own judgment, she said, but it was also true that she made her wishes known rather forcefully. Sometimes she was naïve and sometimes she asked for things that really meant a great deal of effort, yet only the most overweening in her husband's administration did not respond to the disinterested desire to be helpful that was back of her steady flow of communications to all the government departments. It might violate all the rules of political economy, but how was one to say no to a woman who felt the exhilaration of battling wind and snow on a wintry day and then immediately thought of what the foul weather meant to the poorly housed and poorly clothed?[8]

Her methods of getting the bureaucracy to respond varied with the degree of her outrage. Usually she sent a letter with a query—how should she answer? What was being done? Couldn't something be done? "Right in the mails she got a great many of these appeals," Will Alexander recalled. "She looked at the thing and decided whose business it was in the government to find out about it, and sent that letter with her own initials on it and wrote, 'Find out about this letter. You know what it's all about.' You'd better do it. She never forgot."[9] If she felt very strongly she invited the appropriate official to lunch and, since her right ear was slightly deaf, placed him on her left regardless of protocol. Or she asked him to tea. The day she received a delegation of sharecroppers in the Red Room she invited Henry Wallace and Dr. Alexander to be present. Sometimes she marched over to the offices of an agency in order to insure speedier action. On a letter she had from the National Federation of Federal Employees protesting the lack of housing for middle-income workers at a naval gun factory, she wrote,

> Take to Mr. Hillman and Mr. Knudsen. Make appointment for me on Tuesday at 12 with Mr. Hillman and Mr. Knudsen together if possible. Call Mr. Hillman and ask if it can be so arranged and I will go to their office. I want to talk about housing. If Tuesday not possible would Thursday at 11:30 do?[10]

If an administrator's response to a letter seemed inadequate, she took it up with the president. She sent Acting Secretary of War Louis Johnson complaints she had received from residents of Maroc, California, that the Air Force's use of Maroc Dry Lake as a bombing range was endangering life and property; she did not like the Army's reply. "Give whole thing to F. D. R. and say I think answer of Mr. Johnson a bit lame!"

Experience and intuition taught her to which officials she was obliged to use the formidable words, "The President has asked me . . ." The readiness to do her bidding did not follow ideological lines. With Wallace and Ickes she usually invoked the president's authority. Wallace steered clear of her. On the way over to the White House, Wallace warned Will Alexander, whom he had just appointed administrator of the Farm Security Administration, "Now, Will, I want to give you some advice. You want to let that woman alone. She's a very dangerous person. You don't want to get mixed up with her." Wallace did not trust her judgment, Alexander thought. "I, of course, trusted Mrs. Roosevelt almost more than anybody I ever saw."[11] Ickes was as distrustful of her judgment as Wallace. With Hopkins and Jim Farley it was quite the opposite. Hopkins' aides were under standing instructions to give her whatever help she required, and Farley did her bidding even when he did not quite understand what she was after. Although Chester C. Davis, who succeeded George Peek as administrator of the AAA, was the leader of the "agrarians" as opposed to Rex Tugwell's "liberals" in the Department of Agriculture, he was a relaxed, kindly man, and Eleanor found him open-minded. When she came back from a trip to upper New York State where farmers had complained to her about the operations of the Federal Loan Bank she got in touch with Davis about the matter. "Here is a concrete letter showing just what I mean," she followed up a few days after speaking to him about it. "Will you see that someone takes it up and looks into other conditions which I feel sure they will find throughout New York State?" No mention of the president. . . .[12]

[Eleanor and Franklin] were, in the White House years, consorts rather than bosom companions. Her relationship to him was less intimate than some wives had with their husbands after three decades of marriage but she was more influential. She had a point of view, a platform, a following, and he was a large and secure enough man to respect her for it.

Cabinet officers often grumbled, some of them used her, but generally they complied with her requests. Some, like Henry Morgenthau, Jr., did so because there were times when they wanted her to find out what the president's mood was before they went in to see him, sometimes even to intercede with him.

On one occasion Morgenthau, sensing presidential displeasure with his views on tax policy, wrote in his diary that he had gone to Eleanor Roosevelt. "I told her that if she would be willing to accept the responsibility I would like to place myself in her hands as I felt that Franklin and I were drawing further and further apart. She said she was going to talk to the President." A few days later the president seemed to have softened toward Morgenthau's views and remarked at the cabinet meeting that "he and his wife had a discussion on economics in the country. . . . When he got through he gave me a searching look," Morgenthau wrote in his diary. When Morgenthau and Hopkins were trying to get the president to approve a $250,000 special outlay for milk for needy children in Chicago and were getting no response, Morgenthau went to Eleanor. "I'll ask Franklin about it tonight," she told him, "not as though you said anything, but as though I were troubled." Her intercession worked, commented Morgenthau.[13]

The bristly Ickes occasionally sought her patronage for one of his projects. When she was in Knoxville, for example, he wanted her to drive through the newly opened Great Smoky Mountains National Park. She did and expressed her pleasure in a column. He even tried to enlist her in his empire building. The wife of the naval governor of Samoa complained to her about the sanitary conditions on that island after thirty-seven years of United States' ownership. She sent the letter to Ickes because Roosevelt had placed the Division of Territories and Island Possessions in the Interior Department. But in doing so, Ickes informed Eleanor, the president had excluded Samoa and Guam. "Needless to say, I would be happy if in the process of governmental reorganization Samoa and Guam should be transferred to the Division of Territories and Island Possessions." Eleanor, however, did not take up the hint.[14]

She was glad to agree to requests to receive the staffs of federal agencies at the White House, but she deftly put such visits to her own use. The assistant to the public printer, Jo Coffin, brought the women who worked in her office to tea at the White House. "The nicest thing of all," she informed Eleanor afterward, "was the little conference when you gathered the girls around you on the lawn. You spoke of the urgent need of raising the standard of living of the colored people." The Children's Bureau brought its child-welfare field staff to Washington. "The opportunity for informal discussion of problems with Mrs. Roosevelt following the delightful tea was the highlight of the conference," Katherine Lenroot, chief of the bureau, wrote Tommy.[15]

Eleanor was careful in dealing with the members of Congress, fully aware of how jealous that body was of its status and how quick to resent what it considered pressure from the president or his wife. Occasionally a flare-up of moral indignation caused Eleanor to depart from her rule not to comment publicly on what Congress was doing, but she did so circumspectly, almost always asking Franklin's permission beforehand. If she sent a letter to a senator or representative, the note that accompanied it was studiedly neutral; it was simply for the gentleman's information to do with as he saw fit and generally elicited a courtly letter of thanks. But even in this area, when she was confronted with injustice she was not to be contained, especially if there was some bond of fellowship, either political or social, to make a direct appeal for help to a congressman appear to be the most natural course. That was the case in the matter of the sharecroppers.

Sherwood Eddy, clergyman, reformer, and publicist, came to her with an agitated account of the reign of terror in Arkansas instigated by the landlords to keep their sharecroppers out of the Southern Tenant Farmers Union. Many had been evicted, and Eddy wanted to resettle them on a cooperative farm he had purchased at Hill House, Mississippi. He asked Eleanor if these sharecroppers could be placed on relief until the first crop was brought in. "Is there any way in which you could be helpful, if you feel he should be helped?" she in turn asked Hopkins. "I want to be sure, of course, that you think something should be done, but I was horrified at the things he told me." It was Tugwell's job, Hopkins told her, and Tugwell, with whom she promptly communicated, said the Resettlement Administration would be prepared to take over the farm but they must then have the management of it. Eddy refused, and Eleanor informed Clarence Pickett, who had brought Eddy to her, that "under the circumstances I do not know what more could be expected" of the government.[16]

She did, however, write Senate Majority Leader Joseph Robinson, an old acquaintance. Eleanor had been on the delegation in 1928 that had gone to Arkansas for Robinson's notification ceremonies as vice-presidential candidate, and she wrote him without invoking the president's name. She was troubled about what the leaders of the sharecroppers and Eddy had told her, she said; "I am very anxious about it and know you must feel the same way"—would it be possible to send someone down on a mission of reconciliation? Robinson proved to be wholly on the side of the planters; there was no trouble between landlords and tenants except that which was instigated by "a group of agitators from time to time," he replied, going on to say that the landlords were willing to provide houses for the tenants who had been evicted "but they were prevented from doing so by the agitators." Eleanor pressed no further. She had made her views known and done all she could, and there was no point in alienating a mainstay of Franklin's working majority in the Senate. "The situation is a difficult and complex one," she wrote Robinson mollifyingly. "The whole system is apparently wrong and will take patience and a desire on all sides to straighten things out ultimately."

Yet her desire not to irritate Robinson did not hold her back a few months later when the Emergency Committee for Strikers' Relief telegraphed her that there was "a new reign of terror against 5,000 tenant farmers in Arkansas. Wholesale arrests of striking farm workers. Thirty-five Negro and white men held in small jail at Earle . . . workers charged with vagrancy. . . ." She requested Hopkins to have someone investigate and let her know if this was true. Their man in Arkansas had confirmed the arrests, Hopkins informed her a few days later, and the Department of Justice had a man down there to see whether there had been any infringement of federal law. Her next request was for Hopkins to arrange relief for the sharecroppers.[17]

Eleanor's efforts to improve the social-welfare institutions of the District of Columbia usually involved Congress and usually meant getting the president's explicit approval. Jail Lodge #114 of the American Federation of Government Employees called her attention to the "unsatisfactory working conditions" in the District jail. "Take up after I've been there," she noted on their letter, meaning that she should take it up in her column, and in the meantime she had Tommy send the substance of the letter to District Commissioner George Allen. Allen readily acknowledged that the complaint had merit, but it all went back to getting more money from Congress. "Would it be proper for me unofficially to draw attention of Committee to this condition?" Eleanor queried her husband. "Yes—sure—!" was the economic reply. A two-page letter detailing the conditions she had found in the District jail went to all members of the Appropriations Subcommittee concerned with the District's budget. "We did a good job for the National Training School for Girls," Senator Copeland replied; "Let's help the jail!" Senator Capper went further than his colleague: "I spent a couple of hours at the jail and became convinced that you had not overstated matters. . . . I think it is wonderful that you are interested in a matter of this kind."[18]

The head of the League of Women Voters consulted Katherine Lenroot, the chief of the Children's Bureau, on how to persuade the Appropriations Committee to vote more money for improved children's services in the District. Miss Lenroot's advice was to ask Mrs. Roosevelt to convene a conference of citizen's groups and interested congressmen. Eleanor questioned whether such an approach might not stiffen congressional resistance, and the president, to whom she mentioned her doubts, agreed. "The President thinks the Congressional Committee might look upon it as an effort to coerce them," she wrote the league, but if they would get her a list of all the things the Social Service agencies wanted, she would ask the chairman "if he would get the Committee together and let me come up there and tell them that I realize I have more opportunity to see things first-hand than many of them," and they might like to know what she had learned. Congress did approve a budget for child welfare, but she was distressed, she wrote the chairmen of the House and Senate subcommittees a few weeks later, that no coordinator was named. "I know your deep interest in seeing that the children of the District are well cared for. This seems to me so vital that I am writing to you in the hope that you will immediately exert your influence to clear up that point." It was a moment when Roosevelt's influence with Congress was at its lowest point, and Eleanor's note ended, "I am sending this simply as a private citizen and I hope that you will not mention that I have sent it to you."[19]

Cautious as were her early approaches to Congress, by the end of the thirties they were increasingly unorthodox, occasionally even daring. In January, 1934, she told the Citizens Committee on Old-Age Security, "I could not possibly appear before a Congressional hearing on anything," but later she began to accept invitations to testify before congressional committees. She appeared before the Tolan Committee, which was investigating the problems of migratory workers, and was prepared to testify before a Senate subcommittee on discrimination against Negroes in defense industry. And in December, 1939, she created a sensation when she turned up uninvited at hearings of the House Un-American Activities Committee when it had subpoenaed her friends in the American Youth Congress.[20]

Often she used a report on what she had seen on one of her endless journeys around the country as a peg with which to begin an exchange either with her husband or with the director of a government agency. "I can't say what happens to these reports," she was quoted as saying. "Some of them may never be read at all. Some of them I know have been. But I made them because I have been trained that way." She usually made notes on the things she thought might interest the president, and local officials and the public generally took it for granted that what she saw went back to him. "No other President has had a trusted emissary going about the land talking to poor people, finding out what is good and what is bad about their condition, what is wrong and what is right in the treatment they receive," wrote Ruth Finney.[21]

Eleanor was as proficient as the president in the nonpolitical tour and inspection. Wherever she went she toured government projects, saw an endless stream of visitors, questioned reporters about local conditions—often as closely as they asked her about larger matters—and avoided public discussion of politics. Irrepressibly curious and a sympathetic questioner, she arrived in a community as her husband's inspector general, or so the local people thought, and came away its confidante.

"I would never presume to make recommendations," she insisted, speaking about the reports she submitted. But she defined "recommendations" in a Pickwickian sense, meaning they were not commands.

"I forgot to tell you the other day how much impressed I was by the hospital for tubercular Indians at Shawnee, Oklahoma," she wrote Ickes in one of those missives she insisted were not recommendations. "I did feel, however, that the occupational therapy work might be made of more value if they could develop some of the arts, in which some of the Indians must have skill and do a little better work than is being done at the present time." If less than a command, this was more than a suggestion. Ickes was in a benign mood; he thanked her for her letter: "It is gratifying that you found time during your busy trip to visit the Indian Sanitorium."[22]

Except for the homesteads, she was more deeply involved with the WPA than any other New Deal agency, and she did not hesitate to offer advice, often quite bluntly. She criticized the poor public-relations job the agency did, stating that some project officials seemed to avoid publicity "for fear of stirring up trouble. This is an age old attitude and never leads anywhere successfully." She admonished Aubrey Williams that the NYA representative in a discussion over which she had presided had been "rather dull. . . . Do you think a little coaching as to how to keep an audience on the *qui vive* would be advisable?" She returned from a visit to New York City and was immediately on the phone to Williams about the difficulties encountered there by the WPA-sponsored nursery school: "I think Dr. Andrus [the director of the nursery] is probably more interested in doing a good job than in government regulations. There ought to be a way by which both can be accomplished." Aubrey's follow-up report caused her to explode:

> The habit of having situations which arise investigated by the people about whom the complaint is made seems to me a most pernicious one and entirely futile. Exactly the same thing happened in the Illinois gravel pit situation. I do not see how you could expect a fair report from the people who are being accused of doing things which are not justifiable.

On the back of one of the letters in the series exchanged on this matter she wrote, "Give me these. Ask if he, Mrs. [Florence] Kerr & Harry [Hopkins] if he is in town would like to come & dine & talk NYA & WPA matters over. Will gladly have Mrs. Woodward also if they like." Her test of successful management was whether the job got done rather than whether a regulation was complied with. In Chicago she met at Hull House with the supervisors of Hilda Smith's Workers and Adult Education projects: "The main difficulty seems to be that Mr. Maurer because of the set-up has to contact so many people every time he does anything that most of the time is spent running around to the people above him rather than supervising the teachers." Couldn't Aubrey "dynamite" the WPA official in charge?[23]

Often she worked through the women in her husband's administration. She and Molly Dewson kept a watchful eye over all appointments on the distaff side to make sure that women were not overlooked. The right of women to be considered on the basis of merit for all jobs was still far from established. She protested Hull's plan to send a woman to succeed Mrs. Owen in Denmark; she and Molly would "far rather" see him "send a man to Denmark and put a woman in some other place." In 1937 Molly accepted an appointment as one of the three members of the Social Security Board, and Mrs. Emma Guffey Miller, sister of Senator Guffey and Democratic national committeewoman from Pennsylvania, maneuvered to succeed her. Eleanor and Molly considered Mrs. Miller too close to the old-line organization, too traditional in her political methods. "Molly has had a conception of work for the Women's Division which I consider very valuable," Eleanor wrote Mrs. Miller, who had mounted a considerable campaign against Molly;

"she has put education first and I think the women needed that more than anything else." Molly, backed by Eleanor, succeeded in having Jim Farley name Mrs. Dorothy McAllister of Michigan as director of the women's division. There was a weekly, sometimes daily, flow of memorandums from Mrs. McAllister asking for help, reporting on developments, building up regional meetings around her. Columnists spoke of the influence that Felix Frankfurter wielded in Washington through the many young lawyers, most of them graduates of Harvard Law School, whom he had spotted strategically throughout the New Deal. "Frankfurter's hot dogs," Hugh Johnson derisively named them. The women who looked to Eleanor for their marching orders and support were as numerous and perhaps more militant than Frankfurter's disciples.[24]

When women in the administration were attacked, as happened frequently, Eleanor defended them. There were periodic campaigns against Frances Perkins. "She has been quietly shoved in the wings," columnist Ray Tucker wrote in 1935, and her job was really being handled by the department's strong man, Edward McGrady. "FDR, this is being widely said. Is it part of the attack or has she not done well?" was Eleanor's query to her husband. "This is columnist's stuff and really silly," he assured her.[25]

Frances Perkins was one of the first targets of Representative Martin Dies, who accused her of malfeasance because she had not ordered the deportation of Harry Bridges, the radical leader of the Pacific Coast's longshoremen. When Dies threatened Miss Perkins with impeachment proceedings, her friend Ann (Mrs. Arthur Osgood) Choate sent an urgent call for assistance to Eleanor. She had talked with the president, Eleanor advised Mrs. Choate, who said he would appeal to the chairman of the House Judiciary Committee, Representative Hatton W. Sumners, on the basis of masculine chivalry to bring the matter to a vote—either to go ahead with impeachment proceedings or definitely turn them down. Then Eleanor offered some advice:

> I realize that Frances is under a strain and I wish she could take it more lightly because I think it is purely a political attack, and in public life women must accustom themselves to these things in the way that men have. She is alone and I wish that the women of this country, particularly in the organizations, could be induced to realize what the true story is on the whole Bridges question. Frances has it and, it seems to me, could give it to the heads of the different organizations if they would only request it. Then their backing could be made vocal. At present, many of the Federation of Women's Clubs members, who met down here, are down on Frances because they believe she is a Communist. When you get women started along those lines they are like sheep. They think Dies is doing a wonderful job and do not realize that he is doing something to make himself personally popular with the sole idea of being candidate for President, and Miss Perkins was the easiest victim.
>
> Frances does not know how to get on with newspaper people and neither has she a secretary who can do it. I did suggest that she try to get someone who would handle the press for her, but so far as I know she has never done it.[26]

Eleanor helped Frances, although she sensed a reserve in Frances's attitude toward her—perhaps it was Frances's fear that working too closely with Eleanor might make life more difficult for her in the man's world of the labor movement. The labor leaders had originally urged Roosevelt to appoint a man, and one of the stories current in Washington which, while not wholly accurate, was said to be in character so far as Eleanor was involved, described her as commiserating with her husband for the bad hour he must have put in with the labor leaders when he told them he had already made up his mind to appoint Miss Perkins.

"Oh, that's all right," Roosevelt was said to have replied. "I'd rather have trouble with them for an hour than have trouble with you for the rest of my life." But it was Molly, not Eleanor, who had organized the campaign for Frances in 1933, and when in 1939 Roosevelt asked his wife to tell Miss Perkins, if she got the chance, not to oppose a reorganization measure that took the Employment Service out of the Labor Department, Eleanor passed the job on to Molly: "I think if you speak to her, it will have more weight than if I were to do it?"[27]

As at Albany, civic organizations prospered under Eleanor's patronage. She brought the White House closer to the civic-minded through their organizations, and by getting them a hearing from the president enabled him to hear viewpoints that otherwise might not have reached him. Organizations like the League of Women Voters, the National Association for the Advancement of Colored People, the National Public Housing Conference, the National Consumers League, the National Sharecroppers Fund, and the Conference on the Cause and Cure of War as well as the more radical groups such as the Workers Alliance and the American Youth Congress suddenly felt themselves on the inside of government, holding their sessions at the White House, being briefed by the First Lady on the president's plans and difficulties, and, because of her sponsorship, getting a hearing from press and public. "What on earth would I do without you in the White House?" Lucy Randolph Mason, a key CIO official in the South, exclaimed after an expression of interest by Eleanor had finally brought intervention by the Department of Justice in the case of a union organizer who had been badly beaten in Georgia.[28]

Eleanor's assistance to the housing groups when they convened in Washington in January, 1937, to press for passage of the Wagner Housing Act made up for what they considered the president's lack of enthusiasm for the bill in the previous session of Congress. Eleanor addressed the conference, invited its leaders to the White House to fill them in on the president's thinking, and relayed messages from them to the president and from the president to them.[29]

This time, with an assist from the president, the Wagner-Steagall bill was approved, and in September the United States Housing Authority was created. Nathan Straus was appointed administrator, and he promptly wrote Eleanor, hailing her as "one of the first 'housers' in the country" and expressing the hope that he could discuss his problems with her. "We are all very much pleased that, when it is organized, you will be able to have the new housing group at the White House for one meeting at which you will preside. . . ." He regularly sent her the figures on the housing loans that he had approved and reports on the progress of the projects, and he even discussed the design of the apartments with her. To install closet doors, as she had suggested, would add approximately $225 to the cost of a dwelling unit, he advised her; every extra feature added to the costs and if he did not keep rehousing down to minimal standards he might endanger his hope to rehouse all slum dwellers. She did not protest, as she was more realistic now than she had been in 1934 about what Congress might be expected to sanction. "Surely closet doors are not worth $225 per house!" she agreed. "Come to lunch to talk it over."[30]. . .

As the thirties drew to a close, the jobless seemed to Eleanor to be a standing indictment of the American economy and an unredeemed claim on its conscience. She had grown close to Hopkins and the WPA because he and his top people were as ready as she to try unorthodox, even radical, methods to help the jobless. Franklin sensed political danger in the work projects started by the WPA for unemployed artists, musicians, writers, actors, and women, but Eleanor was all for them. There was "not the slightest doubt" in Aubrey Williams' mind "that had it not been for Harry Hopkins and Mrs. Roosevelt, for she was a powerful influence in support of width and variety in the work projects, the work program would have been much more limited in its variety and character."[31]

Eleanor wanted the well-off to visit the WPA projects because that would help them understand that "the unemployed are not a strange race. They are like we would be if we had not had a fortunate chance at life. . . . It is very hard for people who do not come face to face with suffering to realize how hard life can be." At Hyde Park Eleanor read aloud Martha Gellhorn's first story from *The Trouble I've Seen*, a series of WPA sketches, and some of her listeners wept. Then she was invited to the Colony Club to give a reading from the book. She trembled at the prospect, she said, but steeled herself to do it because it was important for the well-to-do to understand the situation of the unemployed.[32]

Because she felt the country had not as yet faced up in a fundamental way to the problem of the machine age, she was insistent that no plan, no point of view be rejected without someone giving it careful scrutiny. "There is a Mr. Albert Lytle Deane," she wrote Harry Hopkins, "who has submitted a plan to me. I, in turn, presented it to the President and he thinks it might be worthwhile to you to see Mr. Deane, and if, after talking to him, you think the plan has merit, the President will be glad to have you talk to him about it." Hopkins was a little annoyed: "Mr. Deane has discussed his plan with every official here in Washington at some time or other," he replied, and attached an analysis of the plan by Leon Henderson, who had found "very little of value" in it. Eleanor was not deterred. She wanted to be sure new ideas were not kept from the president. "This was sent me by a little man," Eleanor advised her son James, who was then acting as one of his father's secretaries, "and I just thought there might be something in it somewhere which would help you people who are working on the Supreme Court plan."[33]

A Tennessee farmer sent her a detailed proposal for establishing a silk industry in the United States. "He wants a silk industry. It was looked into but should we look further?" The president was sufficiently intrigued to send the proposal on to Wallace, inquiring, "Is there anything in this idea?" The labor costs were prohibitive, Wallace replied. "Did anyone go over this to find out if there is anything in it?" Eleanor asked her husband in regard to still another plan. "What can we say to Mrs. Roosevelt about this?" the president asked Lauchlin Currie, one of his administrative assistants. "A crank, and not worth bothering with," was Currie's summary judgment. But as long as someone looked into these matters Eleanor was satisfied. Usually they were wild goose chases, but one of the plans she passed on to Franklin was sent by Alexander Sachs, an economist with Lehman Brothers. In 1936 he had submitted a plan for agriculture, but in 1939 he came to the White House as the intermediary for Albert Einstein and other scientists who wanted to apprise the president about nuclear fission.[34]

In her search for a solution to the unemployment problem, Eleanor was as open to suggestions from the business community as from the labor movement and the left. It was through her* that John Maynard Keynes' letter on the 1937 recession dealing with the impasse between the business world and the New Deal reached the president. Keynes wrote:

> I think the President is playing with fire if he does not now do something to encourage the business world, or at any rate refrain from

---

* Leonard Elmhirst sent it to her, requesting that she pass it on to the president.

> frightening them further. If one is purporting to run a capitalist system, and not something quite different, there are concessions that have to be made. The worst of all conceivable systems is a capitalist one kept on purpose by authority in a state of panic and lack of confidence.[35]

Baruch—also through Eleanor—was another who advised the president to ease up on the business community. He sent her the statement he had made before the Special Senate Committee on Unemployment in which he had warned that it was wrong to rush from a "regulate nothing" position to a "regulate everything" position. She was not persuaded, Eleanor wrote Baruch later, but she was ready "to see us let business have some of the reforms which they think will solve their difficulties, not because I agree but because I think there is much in the psychological effect."[36] Her old friend Harry Hooker, now a Wall Street lawyer and counsel to Myron Taylor of U.S. Steel, was distressed to hear her say there was no solution known to her or to anyone else for full employment, and sent her a nine-page plan which called for repeal of the capital-gains tax, reduction in income taxes, and a ban on New Deal speeches attacking business. "Whether we like it or not, Capitalism is timid," Hooker summed up his recommendations.[37] Eleanor reported them to her husband, adding that she had also heard from a reputable economist that the way to bring about full employment was a large-scale housing program. She was for trying both. Fine, the president commented, but where was he going to get the money?

The First Lady was in advance of almost everyone in the administration in her emphasis on how much remained to be done despite New Deal achievements. At a Youth Congress dinner in February, 1939, a Republican speaker dismissed agencies such as the NYA and the CCC as ineffective and wasteful. "American youth does not want to be mollycoddled," the Republican official asserted; what it wanted was jobs. Eleanor was moved to make an impromptu answer. She agreed that WPA and NYA might not represent "fundamental" solutions; they were, she said quietly, stop-gap measures. But the NYA "gave people hope at a time when young people were desperate," and with the NYA and WPA we had "bought ourselves time to think." Although she believed in the measures enacted by the New Deal, she also noted that "they helped but they did not solve the fundamental problems. There is no use kidding ourselves. We have got to face this economic problem. And we have got to face it together. We have got to cooperate if we are going to solve it." Heywood Broun, who was in the audience, was so moved by her speech that he consulted his journalistic colleagues: "Am I just going into an impulsive handspring or is this one of the finest short speeches ever made in our times?"[38]. . .

She sought to hide her influence and effectiveness, and she held no office in government. Yet at the end of her husband's second term, Raymond Clapper included her among "The Ten Most Powerful People in Washington," saying that she was "a force on public opinion, on the President and on the government . . . a cabinet minister without portfolio . . . the most influential woman of our times." Grace Tully called her "a one-woman staff for the President," and Jesse Jones thought of her as "Assistant President." Without office she had developed an immense following throughout the country. It was never tested in a vote, but a poll on the subject published by Dr. Gallup at the beginning of 1939 showed that 67 per cent of those queried approved of the way she had conducted herself as First Lady, with women endorsing her activities by an even larger ratio than men.[39]

The philosopher Alfred North Whitehead, close to death in Cambridge, realized what she had accomplished during her husband's first two terms in office. Writing on behalf of Mrs. Whitehead and himself, he said, "We cannot exaggerate our appreciation of the wonderful work which you are doing in transforming the bleak social agencies of the past by the personal exercise of kindness, interest and directive knowledge." She was never able to forget, she told S. J. Woolf, "that this country or any other country is in the final analysis a collection of human beings striving to be happy, and it is the human element which is the most important consideration."[40]

Why does she bother him with such trivial matters, the president's aides sometimes complained and oftener thought. Life might have been more tranquil for Franklin if she had not done so, but the texture of the Roosevelt years would have been different, a human touch would have been missing, the people and their government would have been less intimately involved with each other.

NOTES

1. Rexford G. Tugwell, *The Democratic Roosevelt* (New York, 1957), p. 332; E. Roosevelt, *My Days*, p. 129.

2. Letter from Eleanor Roosevelt to Josephine Roche, March 6, 1939; letter from Eleanor Roosevelt to Sanford Bates, Feb. 17, 1939.

3. Eleanor Roosevelt, speech on receiving the *Churchman* Award, Nov. 29, 1939.

4. Letter from Eleanor Roosevelt to Mrs. Walker, May 17, 1939; Lash Diaries, May 10, 1940; Eleanor Roosevelt, *Churchman* Award speech.

5. Letter from Eleanor Roosevelt to Frances Perkins, Sept. 14, 1939; letter from Eleanor Roosevelt to Harry Hopkins, May 3, 1937; letters from Eleanor Roosevelt to Steve Early, Sept. 23, 1936, and Aug. 27, 1937.

6. Letter from Eleanor Roosevelt, May 4, 1935.

7. Letter from Eleanor Roosevelt to Helen Hanson, May 19, 1939; letter from Malvina Thompson Scheider to Helen Hanson, Aug. 13, 1939.

8. E. Roosevelt, *TIR*, p. 6; E. Roosevelt, *My Days*, p. 13.

9. Alexander, OHP.

10. *Ibid.*

11. *Ibid.*

12. Letter from Eleanor Roosevelt to Chester Davis, Aug. 31, 1936.

13. John Morton Blum, *Years of Urgency* (New York, 1964), pp. 27–28, 436.

14. Letter from Harold Ickes to Eleanor Roosevelt, July 19, 1937.

15. Letter from Jo Coffin to Eleanor Roosevelt, May, 1936; letter from Katherine Lenroot to Malvina Thompson Scheider, April 7, 1938.

16. Letter from Eleanor Roosevelt to Harry Hopkins, April 9, 1936; letter from Eleanor Roosevelt to Clarence Pickett, April 21, 1936.

17. Letter from Joseph Robinson to Eleanor Roosevelt, April 20, 1936; and Eleanor Roosevelt's reply, April 21, 1936; Emergency Committee telegram to Eleanor Roosevelt, May 21, 1936; letter from Harry Hopkins to Eleanor Roosevelt, June 4, 1936.

18. Letter from Sen. Capper to Eleanor Roosevelt, Feb. 12, 1937.

19. Letter from Mrs. Ottenburg to Eleanor Roosevelt, Feb. 1, 1939, and Eleanor Roosevelt's reply, Feb. 2, 1939; letter from Eleanor Roosevelt to Rep. Ross Collins and Sen. James O'Mahoney, May 19, 1938.

20. Letter from Eleanor Roosevelt to the Citizens Committee on Old-Age Security, Jan. 2, 1934; she appeared before the Tolan Committee Dec. 11, 1940.

21. Kathleen McLaughlin, in the *New York Times*, Jan. 21, 1940; Finney, series of articles.

22. Letter from Eleanor Roosevelt to Harold Ickes, April 18, 1937; letter from Harold Ickes to Eleanor Roosevelt, April 23, 1937.

23. Letter from Eleanor Roosevelt to Col. Harrington, April 15, 1939; letters from Eleanor Roosevelt to Aubrey Williams, March 7, 1936, Oct. 13, 1938, Dec. 12, 1938, and Oct. 21, 1938.

24. Letter from Eleanor Roosevelt to Franklin D. Roosevelt, Aug. 27, 1937; letter from Eleanor Roosevelt to Emma Guffey Miller, July 15, 1937.

25. Letter from Eleanor Roosevelt to Franklin D. Roosevelt, Nov. 18, 1935, and Franklin Roosevelt's reply, Nov. 22, 1935.

26. Letter from Eleanor Roosevelt to Ann Choate, Feb. 2, 1939.

27. H. H. Smith, "The First Lady," *McCall's*, Sept., 1935; letter from Eleanor Roosevelt to Molly Dewson, April 30, 1938.

28. Letter from Malvina Thompson Scheider to Frank Murphy, Jan. 13, 1940; letter from Lucy Mason to Eleanor Roosevelt, Jan. 23, 1940.

29. Letter from Eleanor Roosevelt to Mary Simkhovitch, Jan. 26, 1937; letter from Helen Alfred to Eleanor Roosevelt, Jan. 27, 1937.

30. Letters from Nathan Straus to Eleanor Roosevelt, Dec. 23, 1937, April 26, 1938, and May 23, 1938.

31. Aubrey Williams, *A Southern Rebel*, unfinished autobiography, in Williams papers, in FDRL.

32. Eleanor Roosevelt, speech to the Washington Conference of WPA Directors of Women's and Professional Projects.

33. Letter from Eleanor Roosevelt to Harry Hopkins, Jan. 29, 1937, and Hopkins' reply, Feb. 15, 1937; letter from Eleanor Roosevelt to James Roosevelt, June 16, 1937.

34. Letter from Robert Cohn to Eleanor Roosevelt, Aug. 10, 1939; letter from Franklin D. Roosevelt to Henry Wallace, Aug. 24, 1939; letter from Eleanor Roosevelt to Franklin D. Roosevelt, Oct. 19, 1939; letter from Alexander Sachs to Eleanor Roosevelt, Jan., 1936.

35. Letter from Leonard Elmhirst to Eleanor Roosevelt, Dec. 11, 1937.

36. Bernard Baruch, statement to the Special Senate Committee on Unemployment, Feb. 28, 1938; letter from Eleanor Roosevelt to Bernard Baruch, March 15, 1939.

37. Letter from Harry Hooker to Eleanor Roosevelt, April 14, 1939.

38. *New York Herald Tribune* and the *New York Times*, Feb. 22, 1939; Heywood Broun, "It Seems to Me," *New York World-Telegram*, Feb. 24, 1939.

39. Raymond Clapper, "The Ten Most Powerful People in Washington," *Look*, Jan. 28, 1941; Tully, p. 107; Jesse Jones, *Fifty Billion Dollars* (New York, 1951), p. 264; Gallup Poll files in Princeton, N.J.

40. Letter from Alfred North Whitehead to Eleanor Roosevelt, April, 1942; S. J. Woolf, in the *New York Times*, May 24, 1939.

26

CONGRESS VERSUS THE PRESIDENT

In its relations with the president, Congress guards two major powers, the power of the purse and the power of the sword. Both have been breached by presidents from time to time. Presidents have impounded (not spent) funds Congress voted to spend, and they have waged war and leapt into lesser military adventures without Congress's approval. Thus the balance of power between the two branches is not just a matter of cajolery and rhetoric; it is fundamental to the Constitution itself.

Standing even above money and warfare is Congress's power to make the laws. A president who usurps that power or, worse yet, breaks the law, puts himself in jeopardy of Congress's ultimate threat—impeachment. Congress can throw the president out. It has not yet happened (Andrew Johnson was spared by one vote), but President Richard Nixon came close. He is our only president who was sure to have been overwhelmingly impeached (charged) by the House of Representatives and overwhelmingly convicted by the Senate. He escaped that fate only by the unprecedented act of resigning the presidency.

Two women played major roles in that high drama: Elizabeth Holtzman and Barbara Jordan. Holtzman was a first-term member of the House who at age thirty-one had surprisingly defeated New York's eighty-four-year-old Emanuel Celler, a representative for no less than twenty-five consecutive terms. Serious and scholarly, Holtzman graduated from Radcliffe and Harvard Law School. Issues, especially the war in Vietnam, got her into politics.

Little did she—or anyone else—know what she was stepping into: the century's most serious test of the constitutional relationship between our two great elected forces of government.

Barbara Jordan, like Elizabeth Holtzman a new member of Congress and the House Judiciary Committee, reached that position by a very different route. She was a woman, to be sure, but also a black from Texas. She graduated from the Boston University law school and went back to Texas, where she kept rediscovering the one big factor in each of her initial opportunities: the law, especially laws meant to implement the true meaning of the Constitution of the United States. After losing twice in local politics, Jordan took over from the men who had planned her campaigns. She went on to campaign for a seat in the Texas Legislature, which had never had a black woman member. She won. Jubilantly she took her parents to Austin's True Level Lodge to celebrate.

Holtzman won as a woman who differed from the old-line clubhouse politicians. Jordan profited from a different approach. An experienced friend told her to get "to know the Kingpins, the people who are influential in the political arena. . . . You've got to get into the smoke-filled rooms in the back." After she was elected to Congress, she called on a Democratic big shot to get her on the right committee: ex-president Lyndon Johnson.

When she stepped into politics, Barbara Jordan quickly found that she had a talent for speechmaking. At first she would talk "to any group who wanted me, on any topic they requested." In the impeachment crisis of 1974, she spoke from her own life and thought to a nation in need of wisdom.

Elizabeth Holtzman and the Impeachment of Richard Nixon

by Peggy Lamson

There are those who contend that had it not been for Elizabeth Holtzman, Richard Nixon might have managed to finish out his second term as President. The scenario—to use a favorite Nixon White House term—goes this way: As long-time chairman of the House Judiciary Committee, Emanuel Celler had not been regarded as an adroit parliamentarian and certainly not a patient one. Thus he would never have adopted the painstakingly careful, thorough approach used by his successor, the comparatively unknown Peter Rodino, to conduct the impeachment hearings. And without the efforts of such a deliberate, even-handed chairman, the Republicans and Southern Democrats on the committee might never have voted for the articles of impeachment and Nixon might once again have slipped through the net.

As it happened, Holtzman played more than the role of Emanuel Celler's spoiler in the process, for when she arrived to take her place in the Ninety-third Congress, she found that she had been assigned to Celler's old place—although not of course to his rank—on the Judiciary Committee, a circumstance that should have delighted her. Most representatives who are lawyers—and a majority of them are—cherish a position on that prestigious committee. Holtzman, however, did not. In fact, she says, "I lobbied not to be on the Judiciary. I thought it was important to strike out in a new direction."

"Important for your district?"

"For my district, and for myself. I wanted very much to be on the Interstate and Foreign Commerce Committee because that dealt with a variety of things—health matters, narcotics, and transportation problems. It seemed to me that it had a broad jurisdiction that might be more relevant to the needs of my urban district. Of course nobody knew—I had no inkling at that time—that there was going to be

From Peggy Lamson, *In the Vanguard: Six American Women* (Boston: Houghton Mifflin, 1979), pp. 80–90.

an impeachment procedure and that the Judiciary Committee would be of crucial importance to be on. So, one of the great ironies is that I tried very hard not to be on that committee but, thank goodness, wiser heads than mine prevailed."

Meanwhile, with Watergate still a "third-rate burglary," the war in Vietnam was an overriding concern. Holtzman had won her seat as an outspoken critic of the war. The same was true of most of the Democrats elected with her. Although she says there were not enough young Turks in the new Congress to make a great splash, the mentality of the new freshman Democratic class was a "crusading" one (a word she says she hesitates to use).

Thus it was not surprising that one of Elizabeth Holtzman's first and most newsworthy acts was to bring a suit in Brooklyn's Federal District Court challenging the legality of President Nixon's bombing of Cambodia without the specific consent of Congress. Certainly an extraordinarily courageous step for a fledgling congresswoman—the youngest woman, incidentally, ever elected to Congress—to take in her first months in office, and one which her staff, almost to a man and woman, earnestly urged against. But Holtzman needed no more to proceed than her own conviction that what she was proposing to do was right and that the bombing was clearly unconstitutional. The American Civil Liberties Union represented her.

There is, in fact, little precedent for litigation by a member of Congress concerning the legality of war-making by the Executive. Prior to the presidency of Richard Nixon, according to the ACLU brief, the charge of unconstitutional power had been leveled only once, "by a then little known congressman from Illinois, Abraham Lincoln, against the initiation and conduct of the Mexican War." And although, during Nixon's term there had been other instances of senators and representatives bringing actions, it was still considered necessary to establish Holtzman's standing—that is, her right, as a member of Congress, to question the legality of the Cambodian bombing.

To this end, the ACLU brief said in part,

> The stake which Congresswoman Holtzman has in the outcome of this litigation is nothing less than her capacity to perform her constitutional obligations as a member of Congress. Perhaps the single greatest right and responsibility delegated to members of Congress by the Constitution is the casting of a meaningful vote on the issue of committing Americans to fight—and perhaps die in combat. Congresswoman Holtzman has been prevented from exercising that right and from fulfilling that responsibility by the action of the Executive in committing Americans to combat in Cambodia without consulting Congress and in opposition to the express will of Congress. Her battle to regain that critical right endows this litigation with classic "concrete adverseness."

Holtzman had been joined in her case by three air force officers, all members of a B-52 bomber crew engaged in combat air strikes over Cambodia. On July 25, 1973, Judge Orrin Judd of the United States District Court of New York, found in favor of Holtzman and the airmen: his ruling enjoined further bombing in Cambodia. However, as expected, the United States Court of Appeals for the Second Circuit promptly reversed the district court, found against Holtzman et al., and halted the injunction to cease the bombing. Their stay order was upheld by Supreme Court Justice Thurgood Marshall who has jurisdiction over the Second Circuit Court of Appeals, the thrust of his argument being the reluctance of the court to interfere with the Executive's right to conduct foreign policy.

The matter might have ended there and then, but Holtzman and the ACLU elected to seek one more recourse. If application for a stay is denied by one justice, it is permissible to make reapplication to another justice. Ordinarily the second application is made to the entire Court, but since this was summer the Court was not in session and the nine justices were scattered throughout the country. The petitioners therefore chose to apply to the one justice who they thought would be most sympathetic to their contention—Justice William O. Douglas.

Douglas, who was vacationing in Yakima, Washington, convened a hearing at the courthouse there on August 3, and the following day handed down his opinion vacating the stay of the appeals court (in other words, finding in favor of Holtzman and thus suspending the bombing) and reversing in the most courtly (in both senses of the word) manner his "brother" Marshall.

"He wrote a remarkable decision," says Holtzman. "What was remarkable about it was that aside from being beautifully written it forecast the future very well. What he said was that this had to be treated as if it were a capital case, because the lives of people were at stake—the lives of those who were bombing, American fliers—were in jeopardy because they might be shot down. And of course the lives of Cambodians were at stake.

"In a capital case, if there was any question of constitutionality or validity of the death sentence, there would be no execution until that validity was determined. And so this should be treated the same way."

Or as Justice Douglas concluded, "The merits of the present controversy are therefore, to say the least, substantial, since denial of the application before me would catapult our airmen as well as Cambodian peasants into the death zone. I do what I think any judge would do in a capital case . . ."

On that day, August 4, Justice Douglas' injunction against the bombing remained in effect for about three hours. Then Justice Marshall in what appears (to lawyers at least) to have been an extraordinary and unprecedented action, managed to avoid actually overruling Douglas' decision by first polling all of his other "brethren" on the Supreme Court, and then halting the *original* Second District Court's injunction against the bombing. Thus he simply bypassed the court of appeals ruling, which was the one that Justice Douglas had reversed.

To Holtzman the final irony was that one day after Douglas had been overruled, four planes mistakenly bombed a friendly Cambodian village and nearly a hundred friendly Cambodians were killed. "I was very shaken up by that," she says. "It was exactly what Justice Douglas had predicted and lives were lost needlessly and I think through unconstitutional actions on the part of our government."

If August 4 was a uniquely significant date for Elizabeth Holtzman, a date two and a half months later, October 20, 1973, was even more fateful for her and for the rest of the nation. On that day Richard Nixon fired Special Prosecutor Archibald Cox, thereby unleashing the Saturday Night Massacre, an action which set in motion the impeachment procedure against him.

"I remember the Saturday Night Massacre vividly," says Holtzman. "I had to make a television appearance virtually immediately after it was announced. And I was very, very upset and concerned as everybody was."

Especially concerned was "everybody" on the House Judiciary Committee, the thirty-six men and two women, the twenty-one Democrats and seventeen Republicans who suddenly came face to face with the fact that they were going to be called upon to act for the nation in determining whether or not the President of the United States should be impeached.

Elizabeth Drew, in her highly literate and perceptive *Washington Journal, The*

Events of 1973–1974, writes in her entry for October 24:

> A House Democrat, one in touch with many members, says that impeachment is now being moved along by an irresistible force. "The genie is out of the bottle," he says. "The unspeakable is being spoken . . . The shock of the past weekend changed everything. There had been the ordinary forbearance toward the President here, a great reluctance to move. I think the people were out ahead of us. They saw a frightening threat to the democratic process. What the President did over the weekend may not have been a high crime or misdemeanor, but it opened things up."

For Holtzman the period from late October to mid-December was terribly frustrating. The House Judiciary Committee had been specifically designated by the Democratic leaders in the House to take up the impeachment question. Yet for weeks nothing happened. Everyone read Raoul Berger's *Impeachment: The Constitutional Problems* and waited with growing impatience for forward movement, and above all for a chief counsel to be selected.

Many Republicans—mostly pro-Nixon hard-liners—believing that the sooner the impeachment process began the less likely it was to succeed, baited the Judiciary Committee and accused its chairman of stalling.

Meanwhile Spiro Agnew had resigned under fire and the Judiciary was also charged with conducting the hearing on the nomination of Gerald Ford for Vice President of the United States. Holtzman was one of only a few members who voted no on Mr. Ford. And when on December 6 his nomination came before the entire House, she was one of thirty-five to vote *Nay* as opposed to three hundred and eighty-seven *Ayes*. ("Yes, I'm very proud of that," Holtzman told me.)

Finally in February after John Doar, a Republican, had been chosen as chief counsel, the House, by a vote of 410–4 authorized the Judiciary Committee to conduct the impeachment inquiry. And the long winter months of amassing evidence and issuing subpoenas began. "As we went through the materials that were given to us, after a while you just began to feel that you'd fallen into quicksand," says Holtzman. "It was all around you: the misdeeds, the evil, the criminality of that Administration. Everything was linked together. It was a swamp that we were caught in. It wasn't one path here on Ellsberg and another path there on income tax and another on Watergate, it was all one big criminality, in a very overwhelming and a really horrifying sense. I never liked Nixon and I never made any bones about that. Before we started the impeachment inquiry I really had no way of knowing whether he had ordered the Watergate break-in, and had no real feeling as to whether or not he had. When I finished with the inquiry I was sure he had, if not in so many words, then through every action, every idea and every kind of plan he had authorized and supported and encouraged.

"And it was a very ugly thing for me—much as I disliked Nixon as President and the policies he espoused—to see a President of the United States so debase the trust that he had been given and behave in such a despicable manner."

Peter Rodino (D.–N.J.), an unknown quantity to most of the public when the impeachment procedure began, proved more and more adept as chairman, adroitly leading the Democratic members of the committee and quietly helping to persuade the Republicans.

In this latter effort, he says rather ruefully, he was sometimes not very much aided by Liz Holtzman, whom he describes warmly, nonetheless, as much respected and as "very impressive on a one-to-one basis." However, his problem with her was that when she felt strongly as she clearly did throughout the entire impeachment proceedings, her indignation created what he calls "an unhelpful climate." On several occasions he says he found her so uncompromising that he felt obliged to remonstrate with her, urging her to exercise a little more "forbearance" and to "develop a little keener understanding of what others were doing." Then he added quite explicitly that somehow he had not expected to have to use such persuasion with a woman.

Apparently Peter Rodino clings to the ideal of womanhood as soft and yielding; in Holtzman's case he also seems to have been somewhat thrown off stride by her implacable response to the degrading wrongdoings that permeated the White House, and perhaps even more by her complete lack of any good old boy we're-all-members-of-the-same-club mentality, so prevalent in the Congress.

Yet Holtzman, for her part, does have a keen appreciation of the "splendid job" she thinks Rodino did. She was well aware that the moderate Republicans were the key, that the narrow majority of Democrats on the committee could never have successfully referred the articles of impeachment to the entire House of Representatives.

Few of the millions who saw the formal Judiciary Committee hearings on television will ever forget the sight of and more particularly the feeling emanating from those thirty-eight legislators who were charged with voting, with the eyes of their fellow citizens upon them, whether or not to impeach the President of the United States.

The members sat on a two-tiered dais in Room 2141 of the Rayburn Building; the Democrats were on Chairman Rodino's right except for the three newest members, Elizabeth Holtzman and Wayne Owens and Edward Mezvinsky, who because of the larger number of Democrats had to spill over and sit on the Republican side. In the audience, using the two tickets allotted to each member of the committee, sat Holtzman's mother and her brother, Robbie.

Had he been nervous for her that night, I asked her brother. And he said no, that it all seemed too remote to him. After all, he pointed out, he and Elizabeth had been brought up not thinking about such a thing as being in Congress, but rather about going to Harvard. And when they had applied there, *then* they had been nervous for fear they would not be accepted, and thus greatly disappoint their parents. But this—"For me it was very matter of fact the way she had grown into that position. It seemed like the most natural thing in the world that she should be sitting up there."

At 7:45 on Wednesday, July 24, 1974, Rodino called the committee to order, the TV lights were turned on and the hearings were under way.

Prior to that moment and since April 4, the committee members had spent many hours together. "We'd meet in a briefing session at 7:30 or 8:00 in the morning," Holtzman recalls, "and then we'd go to the committee and meet often until 7:00 at night and then sometimes there would be another briefing session after that. It was a pretty rough schedule."

"Could you do anything else during those months?"

"Not really. It was just all-absorbing and there really wasn't time. There were a few things I had to pay attention to but more for purposes of distraction than substance."

"Did you have any trouble sleeping at night?"

"I never have any trouble sleeping. And I never had any doubt, when I finally came to a conclusion, about what was the correct thing to do."

After a moving opening statement by Chairman Rodino, each member of the committee was permitted fifteen minutes to make an initial statement giving his or her views on the grave constitutional crisis they were individually and collectively addressing. When it came to Holtzman's turn (she was the thirty-sixth of the thirty-eight members to speak, so it was Thursday night before they finally got to her), she noted that each of her thirty-seven colleagues on the committee had thoughtfully questioned what the Constitution of the United States meant and what duty their oath of office imposed upon them. President Nixon, in sharp contrast, had nowhere in the thousand pages of evidence presented to them, asked what the Constitution said, what were the limits of his power, what his oath of office required of him. "What we have seen," she said, "is a seamless web of misconduct so serious that it leaves me shaken."

Then for the benefit of those on the committee who continued to maintain that there was no hard evidence of high crimes and misdemeanors, she detailed from Nixon's own words a brief and horrifying rundown ranging from the Watergate break-in, to the CIA's order to limit the FBI's investigation, to Nixon's order to his staff to "screw things up" for the proposed investigation by the House Banking and Currency Committee (better known as the Patman Committee), and subsequently his effort to thwart fact-finding by the Ervin Committee. She pointed to the President's order to "stonewall it," to plead the Fifth Amendment; his approval of hush money for the Watergate burglars; his suggestion of executive clemency; and finally to his direct encouragement of witnesses to lie before the grand jury.

"Mr. Chairman," she concluded, "I feel very deeply that the President's impeachment and removal from office is the only remedy for the acts we have seen."

Her performance was slightly overshadowed, as were those of most of her fellow members on that Thursday evening (on prime time TV), by the stirring and unforgettable speech of Barbara Jordan (D.–Tex.) who had preceded her. (Millicent Fenwick who knows and admires both Holtzman and Jordan compares them thus: "Liz is bright-eyed, alert, sharp—more like a terrier. Barbara is quiet, monumental, impressive—like a lion.")

Nonetheless the thirty-three-year-old Holtzman had won her spurs in that first appearance as a forceful, clear-headed advocate of the people's constitutional rights.

It will be recalled by those who watched the impeachment hearings, or who heard one of dozens of replays, or who read accounts in the newspapers, that the word *specificity* was overworked, used repeatedly by the Nixon loyalists who were trying to stave off the President's impeachment on the grounds that the Articles did not include *specific* acts of criminality. On at least two occasions Holtzman spoke to beat back this ultimately losing but nonetheless potent tactic, used especially effectively by Charles Sandman (R.–N.J.), one of Nixon's most die-hard defenders.

Her one disappointment was that her own article—written by her but introduced by John Conyers (D.–Mich.), a prominent member of the black caucus—to impeach the President because of the secret bombing of Cambodia was never dealt with seriously by a majority of the committee members who seemed reluctant to inject the war issue into the debate. Article IV failed by a vote of 26–12. "I regret it," says Holtzman, "because I think the right to take people's lives unilaterally and secretly and with enormous power, and the perversion of that power, is certainly as serious as anything else the President did."

"Looking back," I asked her, "can you remember the dynamics that went on within the committee? There must have been a sort of flow toward the end."

She nodded. "I think all of a sudden it just fell together with this horrible sensation of this one big awful thing going on at the White House that had been going on for a long time. I could see that many people were reacting the same way I was. It was not glee, or elation, or excitement, vindictiveness, or vengeance. It was just very saddening. Saddening and exhausting."

Barbara Jordan on the Principles of Impeachment

by Barbara Jordan and Shelby Hearon

Before the Congress convened in January of 1973, I spent a month at what we called the Harvard Head Start. It was held in December for a few new members of Congress at the John F. Kennedy Institute of Politics. They paid us to go, and their theory was that freshman members needed help in making the transition to Congress. That they needed to know something about the agencies, the structure of the bureaus, how to select a staff, to know generally what a member of Congress does.

The Institute was directed by Mark Talisman, who was an administrative assistant to a relatively senior member of Congress, Charles Vanik of Ohio; Mark was considered the best administrative assistant on Capitol Hill.

Part of our orientation consisted of deciding what requests we would make for committee assignments once we got to Washington. Mark told us—Alan Steelman, Yvonne Burke, Bill Cohen, and me—that it was important to decide on our committee assignments and make those requests early. I talked to him about what I would like, and we mentioned the Judiciary Committee. In the meantime, the Congressional Black Caucus had decided that they would ask me to request the Armed Services Committee. The Caucus members had taken it upon themselves to look after me because Andy Young and I were the first blacks elected to Congress from the South since Reconstruction. So they were doing this. Now, members of Congress get one major committee and one minor committee assignment, and Judiciary and Armed Services are both major committees, which meant that I would have to decide between them. Mark and I chatted about that, and I told him that I bet LBJ would help me on the matter. So he said: "Well, why don't you see if he will?"

Which I did. I addressed a letter to Johnson and told him I was thinking about the Judiciary and Armed Services committees. It was a specific request that he help, primarily that he talk to Omar Burleson from Anson, Texas, who was a member of the Ways and Means Committee, which was the committee that made the other committee assignments. Also, that he talk to Wilbur Mills, who was the chairman of that committee.

Shortly after that I got a call at the faculty club where I was staying at Harvard, at the Institute. It was Johnson. He told me: "I got your letter and I've already acted on it. I talked to Omar. I talked to Wilbur. I had some trouble finding him because he was off fishing someplace in Arkansas, but I interrupted his fishing and told him he had to get on your committee assignment right away."

I said: "Well, thank you, Mr. President. Thank you for doing that." Then I started to discuss the assignment specifically. Had he asked Wilbur Mills to look out for me for Armed Services or for Judiciary? Johnson said: "You don't want to be on the Armed Services Committee. People will be cursing you from here to there, and the defense budget is always a sore spot and people don't want to spend the money. You don't want that. What you want is Judiciary.

From Barbara Jordan and Shelby Hearon, *Barbara Jordan: A Self-Portrait* (New York: Doubleday, 1979), pp. 177–193.

If you get the Judiciary Committee and one day someone beats hell out of you, you can be a judge."

So that made sense, and I thanked him.

One further order of business that Mark helped us with was the selection of a staff. One day I went to Washington from Cambridge because I had interviews scheduled in Charles Vanik's office with about a dozen prospects. These interviews went on all morning. One thing I knew for certain, that I wanted people with some Hill experience. I felt we didn't all need to get to the office and not know which way to the ladies' room. It did not make sense to bring anyone from my Houston office, as no one had any more experience than I had. So I talked with a number of people who knew the capitol scene, and I hired about five people. I hired Bud Myers, my assistant, at that time. My thinking was, if I had a black and a man, that would satisfy everyone. He had worked as administrative assistant to Andy Jacobs, and so was already knowledgeable.

Then we got our committee assignments, and I got the Judiciary Committee. I was told that when the Ways and Means Committee reached the matter of the Judiciary Committee on the agenda, Wilbur Mills said: "Now, after Barbara Jordan, who shall we put on here?" And being the first person named, I got seniority over any other freshman, which was important.

There were so many members of Congress. And I was coming from a 31-member state senate into that 435-member House of Representatives. It became obvious to me that it was going to be difficult to make any impact on anybody with all of these people also trying to make an impact, in order to create the impression back home among their constituents that they were outstanding.

The first thing was, I would have to get in good with my colleagues from Texas. I would be the unique new kid on the block to them, and I wanted to work comfortably with them. For instance, I knew that women had never been allowed to attend the Texas Democratic Delegation luncheon that had been meeting at twelve-thirty on Wednesdays since the early tenure of Sam Rayburn, and I intended to change that. Which I did.

Then we were officially sworn in. Before that session, one of my fellow Texans said that all the Texas delegation would stand around me for the swearing-in. And another said: "Well, now, but that might take away from Barbara Jordan. People might not be able to tell which one she is." I laughed and told him: "I think they'll be able to figure that out."

When that was over, I gave some thought to where I should sit on the floor of the House of Representatives. My conclusion was: You can hear better on the center aisle, and you can catch the eye of the presiding officer better on the center aisle, as you are in his direct line of vision. So I decided that is where I would always sit, leaving one seat next to me on the aisle vacant, for those people who might want to stop and visit from time to time.

I was accused of not wanting to sit with the liberals and the Congressional Black Caucus people, who sat to the far left, but that place near center aisle seemed the most advantageous location to me.

The evening of the swearing-in, Bob Eckhardt gave a reception for me, because he was so glad that we were both up there. The Texans in Washington gave a reception. And the Texas Southern University ex-students gave a reception. So we were thoroughly received.

Then almost immediately we got word that Lyndon Johnson had died. He had had a heart attack at the ranch. I was very saddened. I gave a statement on the floor of the House and I said: "The death of Lyndon Johnson diminishes the lives of every American involved with mankind. The depth of his concern for people cannot be quantified—it was big and all-encompassing." I said: "Old men straightened their stooped backs because Lyndon Johnson lived; little children dared look forward to intellectual achievement because he lived; black Americans became excited about a future of opportunity, hope, justice, and dignity." I said: "Lyndon Johnson was my political mentor and my friend. I loved him and I shall miss him."

I meant all of that. And at the bottom of my grief was the feeling that I was sitting up there all alone on that center aisle. Other people were always talking about what they had done for me. But Lyndon Johnson wasn't like that. He just did it and he didn't take credit for it.

My asking Barbara to be on the Judiciary Committee was quite a feather in her cap. It was against all odds, as she was a freshman member, and people vied for the position. But as she was a black, a woman, and a lawyer, and since I wanted to do whatever I could to enhance the committee, as I was coming new as chairman, I felt certain she would be a valuable addition.

As we began to get into impeachment she was articulate, balanced, not extremist. She began to display the ability to be concise and precise, but not aggressive. She was one who sat and listened; she followed my lead. I looked upon her as a protégé.

Peter Rodino
Chairman, Judiciary Committee

It was 1974 and the press and the people were rumbling about Watergate. Talk was heavy. But I was discounting all that, thinking: "Nothing like that is going to happen. You're talking about the presidency. You're not going to impeach the President."

Well, resolutions were introduced, and pressure was being placed on the Speaker, and on the Judiciary Committee, and on Peter Rodino to do something. The pressure built up in the Congress and among the people until we could not ignore it. We had to take some action. Which, I think rather reluctantly, we did.

Or, rather, Jaworski did. We were empowered to act, but we were never going to. We wouldn't have except that Jaworski got the matter into court, so that we had the United States of America versus Richard Nixon the President of the United States. And then we had the tapes. When the Court ordered the revelation of the tapes, when it told the President that he could no longer keep those sequestered, that made the impeachment of Richard Nixon possible. Without the tapes we would have just been spinning our wheels. Without Jaworski, we would never have got to the matter, not even to the beginnings of impeachment.

Rodino called the Judiciary Committee together and said: "We are going to go into the matter of the impeachment of Richard Nixon."

The first order of business then was to hire competent counsel, which took a while. The Democrats hired John Doar; the Republicans hired a lawyer from Chicago, Albert Jenner. And Doar and Jenner and the staff hired by them engaged in a lengthy in-depth investigation about what had been said and what had been done in terms of specific acts and whether they constituted a violation of the law. They compiled all of this into big black notebooks of reading material for us. And I gave credit for most of that to John Doar, who was an organizational genius.

So for weeks we met behind closed doors, going through these black notebooks. And the closed doors were legitimate, as the rules of the House said you did not have to have a public session if someone's character was to be discussed.

The big, major issue the committee had to deal with was how to define the charge. The Constitution said that the President shall be removed from office on impeachment for treason, bribery, or other high crimes and misdemeanors. So our job was to define "high crimes and misdemeanors," as that was the only reason that this

President could be impeached. Meanwhile, I was studying all that, and also reading everything I could find, from any source, which had ever been written, said, or uttered about impeachment.

It was a funny time. Every day when we would leave those closed-door sessions the media people would chase us down the hall asking: "Have you found the smoking gun?"

After we finished going through all of the black notebooks in the closed sessions, we went public with our information. We opened the doors and let the sunshine in. We invited the press. Rodino said: "This will be the format. Before we go into anything chargewise, offensewise, each person on the committee will have fifteen minutes to make an opening statement on television."

Now, there were thirty-five of us. And I recall that when Rodino said that, I thought: I don't think that's necessary. I said: "Let's deal with the issue and make a decision on the basis of the facts we have accumulated to this point. We don't need speechmaking." But I did not have much support for that position. The reaction from the other committee members was: "You must be out of your head." It seemed they all wanted that fifteen minutes on television.

The day we went public there were members who had been working on their opening statements for weeks, and I didn't have a word. I was still just reading my sources and trying to be sure that I understood the charge and the offenses. I was not going to vote to impeach Richard Nixon because I didn't like him. The knee-jerk thing. Because I figured that the easiest thing in the world would be for me to do just that, to say: "Yes, you ought to get out." So I was being extremely careful to review it all.

We arrived at the day for statements to begin, and the other people had prepared theirs, but I didn't have mine. I didn't intend to have an opening statement because I still didn't think that it was a good idea. All that speechmaking was a waste of the country's time, and the committee's time, and my time, was the way I felt about it then.

But of course it went right along as planned, with the committee members speaking all day and all night. It became apparent at some point that by the next evening they would get around to me, as we were proceeding by seniority. I was going to have to make a statement. Colleagues had come up to me all day to tell me: "I just can't wait to hear your opening statement. I want to hear what you have to say. I know you're going to let Nixon have it." I got this anticipation all day. One woman called up to say: "I have everything figured out. You're going to be on at nine o'clock and I'm having half a dozen people come over to my house so we can sit there and listen to you . . ."

So it was about five-thirty in the evening, and the Judiciary Committee was to reconvene at about eight-thirty. I went to my office and said to my assistant, Bud: "Would you believe the people who have come up to me today about my statement?" I was saying it in puzzlement; I knew there was nothing Bud could do about it. He asked: "Well, what are you going to say?" Now, Bud wanted to be perfectly clear that I really was coming out for impeachment. I told him: "Yes, I'm going to come out for impeachment. I have decided I am going to do that, and I am going to say why."

Then I told Marian Ricks, my secretary, "I know that you get off in fifteen minutes, but you're going to have to stay. I've got to write a statement, it seems." So while she was out there at her typewriter, I sat down at the desk in my office. It was now about six o'clock. I had all kinds of little disjointed notes that I'd written from all of my reading on impeachment. But I didn't have a statement. I had listened to statements for two days from other members. One thing that had struck me was how they had all started out by quoting the Preamble to the Constitution. Intoning about "We the People of the United States."

It occurred to me that not one of them had mentioned that back then the Preamble was not talking about *all* the people. So I said: "Well, I'll just start with that." I jotted down from this note and from that note and from this other note, and sent each page out to Marian when it was finished. I had already had my legislative assistant Bob Alcock parallel statements on impeachment—historical documents, Constitutions of the Confederacy, whenever impeachment had been talked about—against some of the offenses by Richard Nixon that we had talked about. So I also had that chart, that comparison about what had been said and what it was that Richard Nixon had done.

When I got in there, the Judiciary Committee was all seated and the camera was right there on us. We said what we had to say within our time span, and then we were through. The security was tight and no one applauded after you made a speech, so you didn't know how you had done.

[Biographer Shelby Hearon continues the account.]

On July 25, 1974, Barbara Jordan came before the television camera to present her position on the impeachment of the President of the United States. Solemn, tired, she hunched over four annotated amended pages of her own notes and four pages of historical impeachment criteria set against Nixon's actions.

Her black-rimmed glasses reflected the glare of the lights as she studied her notes. Then, improvising, she spoke to the unseen and unknown audience in living rooms across the country:

" 'We the people'—it is a very eloquent beginning. But when the Constitution of the United States was completed on the seventeenth of September in 1787, I was not included in that 'We the people.' I felt for many years that somehow George Washington and Alexander Hamilton just left me out by mistake. But through the process of amendment, interpretation, and court decision, I have finally been included in 'We the people.'

"Today I am an inquisitor. I believe hyperbole would not be fictional and would not overstate the solemnness that I feel right now. My faith in the Constitution is whole. It is complete. It is total. I am not going to sit here and be an idle spectator to the diminution, the subversion, the destruction of the Constitution.

" 'Who can so properly be the inquisitors for the nation as the representatives of the nation themselves?' (*The Federalist Papers*, No. 65). 'The subject of its jurisdiction are those offenses which proceed from the misconduct of public men.' In other words, the jurisdiction comes from the abuse or violation of some public trust.

"It is wrong, I suggest, it is a misreading of the Constitution for any member here to assert that for a member to vote for an Article of Impeachment means that the member must be convinced that the President should be removed from office. The Constitution doesn't say that. The powers relating to impeachment are an essential check in the hands of this body, the legislature, against and upon the encroachment of the Executive. In establishing the division between the two branches of the legislature, the House and the Senate, assigning to one the right to accuse and the other the right to judge, the framers of this Constitution were very astute. They did not make the accusers and the judges the same persons.

"We know the nature of impeachment. We have been talking about it for a while now. 'It is chiefly designed for the President and his high ministers' to somehow be called into account. It is designed to 'bridle' the Executive if he engages in excesses. It is designed as a method of national 'inquest into the conduct of public men' (*Federalist*, No. 65). The framers confined in the Congress the power, if need be, to remove the President in order to strike a delicate balance between a President swollen with power and grown tyrannical, and preservation of the independence of the Executive. The nature of impeachment is a narrowly channeled exception to the separation of powers maxim; the Federal Convention of 1787 said that. It limited impeachment to 'high crimes and misdemeanors' and discounted and opposed the term 'maladministration.' It is to be used only for great misdemeanors, so it was said in the North Carolina ratification convention. And in the Virginia ratification convention: 'We do not trust liberty to a particular branch. We need one branch to check the others.'

" 'No one need be afraid' it was said in the North Carolina ratification convention; 'No one need be afraid that officers who commit oppression will pass with immunity.'

" 'Prosecutions of impeachments will seldom fail to agitate the passions of the whole community,' said Hamilton in the *Federalist Papers*, No. 65, 'and to divide it into parties more or less friendly or inimical to the accused.' I do not mean political parties in that sense.

"The drawing of political lines goes to the motivation behind impeachment; but impeachment must proceed within the confines of the constitutional term 'high crimes and misdemeanors.'

"Of the impeachment process, it was Woodrow Wilson who said that 'nothing short of the grossest offenses against the plain law of the land will suffice to give them speed and effectiveness. Indignation so great as to overgrow party interest may secure a conviction; nothing else can.'

"Common sense would be revolted if we engaged upon this process for petty reasons. Congress has a lot to do: appropriations, tax reform, health insurance, campaign finance reform, housing, environmental protection, energy sufficiency, mass transportation. Pettiness cannot be allowed to stand in the face of such overwhelming problems. So today we are not being petty. We are trying to be big because the task we have before us is a big one.

"This morning, in a discussion of the evidence, we are told that the evidence which purports to support the allegations of misuse of the CIA by the President is thin. We are told that the evidence is insufficient. What that recital of the evidence this morning did not include is what the President did know on June 23, 1972. The President did know that it was Republican money, that it was money from the Committee for the Re-election of the President, which was found in the possession of one of the burglars arrested on June 17.

"What the President did know on the twenty-third of June was the prior activities of E. Howard Hunt, which included his participation in the break-in of Daniel Ellsberg's psychiatrist, which included Howard Hunt's participation in the Dita Beard ITT affair, which included Howard Hunt's fabrication of cables, designed to discredit the Kennedy administration.

"We were further cautioned today that perhaps these proceedings ought to be delayed because certainly there would be new evidence forthcoming from the President of the United States. There has not even been an obfuscated indication that this committee would receive any additional materials from the President. The committee subpoena is outstanding, and if the President wants to supply that material, the committee sits here.

"The fact is that yesterday, the American people waited with great anxiety for eight hours, not knowing whether their President would obey an order of the Supreme Court of the United States.

"At this point I would like to juxtapose a few of the impeachment criteria with some of the President's actions:

"James Madison said in the Virginia Ratification Convention: 'If the President be connected in any suspicious manner with any person and there be grounds to believe that he will shelter him, he may be impeached.'

"We have heard time and time again that the evidence reflects payment to the defendants of money. The President has knowledge that these funds were being paid and that these were funds collected for the 1972 presidential campaign.

"We know that the President met with [Assistant Attorney General] Henry Petersen twenty-seven times to discuss matters related to Watergate, and immediately thereafter met with the very persons who were implicated in the information Mr. Petersen was receiving and transmitting to the President. Madison's words again: 'If the President be connected in any suspicious manner with any person and there be grounds to believe that he will shelter that person, he may be impeached.'

"Justice Story: 'Impeachment is intended for occasional and extraordinary cases where a superior power acting for the whole people is put into operation to protect their rights and rescue their liberties from violation.'

"We know about the break-in at the psychiatrist's office. We know that there was absolute complete direction in August, 1971, when the President instructed Ehrlichman to 'do whatever is necessary.' This instruction led to a surreptitious entry into Dr. Fielding's office . . .

"The South Carolina Ratification Convention impeachment criteria: Those are impeachable 'who behave amiss or betray their public trust.'

"Beginning shortly after the Watergate break-in and continuing to the present time, the President has engaged in a series of public statements and actions designed to thwart the lawful investigation by government prosecutors. Moreover, the President has made public announcements and assertions bearing on the Watergate case which the evidence will show he knew to be false . . .

"James Madison said, again at the Constitutional Convention: 'A President is impeachable if he attempts to subvert the Constitution.'

"The Constitution charges that President with the task of taking care that the laws be faithfully executed, and yet the President has counseled his aides to commit perjury, willfully disregarded the secrecy of grand jury proceedings, concealed surreptitious entry, attempted to compromise a federal judge while publicly displaying his cooperation with the processes of criminal justice . . .

"If the impeachment provision in the Constitution of the United States will not reach the offenses charged here, then perhaps that eighteenth-century Constitution should be abandoned to a twentieth-century paper shredder. Has the President committed offenses and planned and directed and acquiesced in a course of conduct which the Constitution will not tolerate? That is the question. We know that. We know the question. We should now forthwith proceed to answer the question. It is reason and not passion which must guide our deliberations, guide our debate, and guide our decision."

Her audience sat stunned. It was the first time she had reached them with no one in between. The first time they had seen and heard her with their own eyes and ears. The first time she was a primary source to them. . . .

A man in Houston the next day went out and put up twenty-five billboards that said: THANK YOU, BARBARA JORDAN, FOR EXPLAINING THE CONSTITUTION TO US.

27

THE JUSTICE SYSTEM

A woman on the Supreme Court? That seemed about as likely as a female pope. Yet there she sits, a sister among "the brethren," Associate Justice Sandra Day O'Connor, sharing all the privileges and prestige—and power—of a full-fledged Supreme Court justice.

Whenever a new justice is appointed, speculation abounds as to how he or *she* will decide cases. That is hard to prophesy. Past predictions, especially that the new justice will cling to some ideology, have often failed to pan out. Perhaps when you remove someone from the turmoil of politics and/or the marketplace, and give him or her lifetime tenure, that person's perspective may change. Further, Supreme Court justices operate by legal reasoning, which is different from common sense and thus from the rationality of everyday life. It has to be. The whole idea of the law is decision by rules, fairly applied to all, so that much thought is devoted to which cases come under which rules. The answer is seldom simple or mechanical. It takes judgment. That is why you need judges. How a judge will judge when new cases are meshed with developing rules of law is hard to read in the tea leaves of the judge's past.

Here is how Sandra Day O'Connor looked to a predictor on the eve of her justiceship. You might try your hand at predicting how she would decide the case of one Joe Hogan, male, who thought he had the right to go to the all-female nursing school at the Mississippi University for Women.

Ceremony sets a judge apart: think of the robes, the bench, those in the courtroom standing up when the judge comes in, the title *Your Honor*, the ultimately decisive gavel. The law also sets a judge apart by requiring confirmation and by protecting the judge from dismissal except in extraordinary circumstances. This apartness is intentional, for through a long and difficult history, the need to protect the independence of the judiciary has grown from an idea to a principle. The whim of the day—even of the year—should not mold the administration of justice.

Still, there is a tension between judicial independence and the democracy's sense that the people should rule. So from time to time popular movements of the right or left have taken off after the courts, to bring them into line, the advocates say, with what the people want. The danger there is evident: a politicized judiciary, judges shaping their decisions for political advantage.

Recently a chief justice of the California Supreme Court, a woman with the unlikely name of Rose Bird, found herself at the center of just such a political storm.

Sandra Day O'Connor Joins the Supreme Court

by Lynn Hecht Schafran

First Monday in October: the day each year on which the United States Supreme Court convenes to begin its annual term and the title of a 1978 play, now a movie, about the first woman Supreme Court justice. When the play opened, much was made of what appeared to be the authors' wry notion of depicting the first woman justice as a conservative. But on Monday, October 5, 1981, when, if confirmation hearings proceed as expected, the first woman justice takes her seat, life will imitate art in the person of Sandra Day O'Connor, 51, a conservative state appellate court judge from Arizona. As Judge O'Connor's appointment breathes real life into *First Monday*'s fantasy, we may hope that as Justice O'Connor, she will breathe real life into the deliberations of the Supreme Court, whose ideas about women and the family are often as fanciful as anything on Broadway or the silver screen.

The appointment of the first woman justice is, of course, an event of momentous symbolic importance. The Supreme Court is the preeminent symbol of justice in our nation, and the 191-year exclusion of women from the ranks of "the brethren" speaks volumes about the history of women in our society. Though women still constitute less than 7 percent of the federal judiciary and tokenism is as much a danger on the Supreme Court as elsewhere, we may nonetheless take great pleasure in this historic and long overdue appointment.

As of this writing, Judge O'Connor is awaiting her September confirmation hearing. The far right, particularly the Moral Majority and Right-to-Life, has vowed to oppose her as being prochoice, pro–Equal Rights Amendment, "pro-pornography," and against state aid for private schools. But that opposition isn't shared by the more traditional conservatives. As Senator Barry Goldwater (R.–Ariz.) said of Reverend Jerry Falwell's opposition to Judge O'Connor: "Every good Christian ought to kick Falwell right in the ass." And leading conservative and liberal Senators of both parties, focusing on Judge O'Connor's ability, integrity, and judicial temperament (the criteria against which all judges are evaluated), have endorsed her, so it is expected that she will be confirmed.

Because the Supreme Court is the court of last resort, with the power to provide the ultimate interpretation of Constitutional rights and federal statutes and to nullify state and federal statutes that are unconstitutional, each new justice receives intense scrutiny from a variety of interest groups. Her reported decisions leave no doubt that Judge O'Connor is a judicial conservative: a judge who defers to the legislature, interprets statutes narrowly, upholds police against claims of technical violations of Constitutional rights, and is reluctant to read her own views into the law or substitute her judgment for that of the trial court.

During her six-and-a-half years as a judge (five years on the trial court, 18 months on the appellate bench), Judge O'Connor has not had to rule on cases involving sex discrimination, affirmative action, abortion, or the other controversial issues that will confront her as a member of the Supreme Court. Thus, those seeking

From Lynn Hecht Schafran, "Sandra O'Connor and the Supremes: Will the First Woman Make a Difference?" *Ms.*, October 1981, pp. 71ff.

clues as to what Judge O'Connor's appointment may mean for women's issues must examine her legislative record and her own life experience. As the great Justice Benjamin Cardozo said almost 50 years ago, "We are not to close our eyes as judges to what we must perceive as men." Or women.

The inferences drawn from the facts presented, the decision to hear a case or find some jurisdictional basis to refuse it, even the analysis of the applicable law, will be colored to some extent by a judge's personal history. The late Justice William O. Douglas's boyhood in the countryside of Washington State molded his lifelong concern for the environment. Justice Harry Blackmun was for many years counsel to the Mayo Clinic; his opinion in the 1973 abortion case, *Roe* v. *Wade*, was researched there, and its point of departure was not the rights of women but the rights of doctors to determine appropriate medical practice free of government interference. Justice Thurgood Marshall, the first black to serve on the high court and formerly lead litigator for many of the most crucial race discrimination cases of our times, brings a special sensitivity to cases bearing on race because of both his life and legal experience.

Sandra O'Connor's early career experiences parallel those of many women her age with similar talent and ambition. After graduating in the top 10 percent of her class at Stanford Law School in 1952, she could not get a job in a firm. "I interviewed with law firms in Los Angeles and San Francisco," she says, "but none had ever hired a woman before as a lawyer, and they were not prepared to do so." One San Francisco firm—ironically, that of William French Smith, now attorney general—offered her employment as a legal secretary.

Like most women lawyers in the 1950s and 1960s who were unwelcome at law firms, Judge O'Connor took a government job, becoming deputy county attorney of San Mateo County in California. She then followed her husband John O'Connor overseas during his military service, where she worked as a civilian lawyer with the Army, and on their return spent a brief period in private practice, followed by five years as a full-time homemaker, mother of three sons, and highly regarded volunteer. In 1965, Judge O'Connor again became a government lawyer, this time an assistant attorney general for the state of Arizona. In 1969, she was designated by the governor to fill a vacancy in the state senate, a seat to which she was later twice elected. In 1973, she was elected senate majority leader, the first woman in the country to hold that office.

A 1971 article in Arizona's *Phoenix* magazine reported: "What arouses Mrs. O'Connor's inner resentment—she never permits such feelings to surface—is the barefaced discrimination against women practiced in Arizona. 'A woman with four years of college earns typically $6,694 a year while her male counterpart earns $11,795 for the same job,' Senator O'Connor says. 'The more education a woman has, the wider the gap between men's and women's earnings for the same work.' "

Judge O'Connor's concern with gender discrimination and the problems of families at the poverty line expressed itself in many of her legislative initiatives. For instance: repeal of anachronistic "protective" labor laws for women; making Arizona's farm youth loans available to girls as well as boys; wide reform of the community property laws, including repeal of provisions that gave husbands sole management of community property and authority to sell the family homestead without the wife's permission; and liberalizing the state's penurious welfare laws. She also sought unsuccessfully to establish Medicaid, leaving Arizona the only state without it. And she supported a resolution calling on Congress to end forced busing for school integration and voted to reinstate Arizona's death penalty, which she later, as a judge, imposed.

Judge O'Connor supported the Equal Rights Amendment publicly in 1972 but backed off when she learned that Arizona's two Republican Senators opposed it. In 1974, she voted for a bill to have the amendment considered by the full senate and introduced a bill to put it up for a statewide referendum. Both failed.

The heated debate over Judge O'Connor's positions on abortion and family planning has all but obscured discussion of other issues. Her recorded votes show that she introduced a bill providing wide access to birth control; opposed an amendment cutting off abortion funds to the hospital at the University of Arizona; and supported legislation permitting medical personnel to refuse to provide abortions if abortion violated their religious or moral beliefs. According to news reports, Judge O'Connor told President Reagan that she finds abortion "personally repugnant," and told members of the Senate Judiciary Committee that she believes that "Supreme Court justices should follow existing high court rulings—including one that legalized abortion" and that abortion is "a subject that could be handled by Congress."

As a trial court judge, Sandra O'Connor had a reputation for being tough on law-and-order issues, but she was neither doctrinaire nor without compassion. One well-known story has it that after she jailed a woman convicted of passing bad checks, she wept in her chambers because the woman had two infants and had been abandoned by her husband. A less well-known episode involves her presiding at the trial of a battered wife who shot her husband and was found guilty by the jury despite her plea of self-defense. Judge O'Connor told the defense attorney that she thought the woman should not have been convicted, imposed the minimum sentence provided by law, and supported the woman's request for a commutation of her sentence.

It is also apparent that Judge O'Connor understands the need for women to join together to seek equality and recognition for their talents. She is a charter member of the National Association of Women Judges and of Arizona Women Lawyers, and serves on the Arizona panel for the American Council of Education's program to enhance opportunities for women college administrators.

Judge O'Connor is not without her blind spots. She and her husband are affiliated with two private clubs that have men-only grills. Friends say that she thinks women are foolish to fuss about not being able to join the boys for a hamburger and a beer, yet one assumes that if she visited an interracial club and found a whites-only section, she would not find the black members' objections foolish. Although such discrimination by private clubs is not illegal, at the urging of legal and civil rights groups, the United States Judicial Conference resolved in 1980 "that it is inappropriate for a judge to hold membership in an organization that practices invidious discrimination" ("invidious discrimination" being defined to include race, religion, sex, and national origin).

Although it would be totally erroneous to assume that Judge O'Connor's demonstrated sensitivity to discrimination against women would in any way guarantee her vote in a particular case, one can speculate about what difference her presence might have meant to recent Supreme Court deliberations. Last June, for example, the Court ruled in *McCarty* v. *McCarty* that the wife of a military man may not share in his pension upon divorce, even when (as was the case for Mrs. McCarty) she has been married for 19 years, raised three children, and moved seven times to accommodate her husband's assignments. Would the Court have dismissed Mrs. McCarty's contributions quite so easily with Judge O'Connor there to describe to her colleagues her own experiences as a woman who followed her husband overseas during his military duty, raised three sons, and worked for a time as a full-time homemaker? Last spring, in a pair of startling decisions, the Court held that a woman had no right to a lawyer in a case where she lost permanent custody of her child, but that a man in a paternity suit had a right to an expensive medical test to prove that he was not the father. Would the presence and experience of a woman have made a difference?

The Supreme Court's blindness to many aspects of real life has evoked widespread criticism both from some Court members and many commentators. Justice Marshall states frequently and with only the thinnest veneer of politeness that the majority of the Court is a bunch of rich, old, white men incapable of understanding what life is like for those who are black and/or poor and/or female. Decrying the impact on poor women of the Court's decision that states need not provide Medicaid funding for abortions, Justice Blackmun wrote: "There is another world out there, the existence of which the Court, I suspect, either chooses to ignore or fears to recognize." *New York Times* Supreme Court reporter Linda Greenhouse has exposed the fallacy of the Court's "rose-colored views of the family," and a *Times* editorial recently asked: "Do the justices really live among the rest of us?" Pulitzer prize-winning columnist Ellen Goodman said of the Court's last term: "In its judgments on women, sex, and sex discrimination, the justices behaved less and less like nine legal giants and more and more like the seven dwarfs."

Whatever her judicial philosophy, Sandra Day O'Connor will bring to the Supreme Court a solidly grounded understanding of the real lives of women in contemporary society. Judging from her professional style and her legislative record on women's issues, she also has the will and the ability to communicate the need for reform. I do not suggest that Judge O'Connor will either abandon her devotion to legal precedent or suddenly become a judicial activist on women's issues. I do suggest that she will bring to the Court's deliberations on these issues the touchstone of reality that has been so glaringly absent.

JUSTICE O'CONNOR'S DECISION FOR THE SUPREME COURT ON SEX DISCRIMINATION *(458 U.S. 718)*

. . . Mississippi has made no showing that women lacked opportunities to obtain training in the field of nursing or to attain positions of leadership in that field when the MUW School of Nursing opened its door or that women currently are deprived of such opportunities. In fact, in 1970, the year before the School of Nursing's first class enrolled, women earned 94 percent of the nursing baccalaureate degrees conferred in Mississippi and 98.6 percent of the degrees earned nationwide. United States Department of Health, Education, and Welfare, Earned Degrees Conferred: 1969–1970, 388 (1972). That year was not an aberration; one decade earlier, women had earned all the nursing degrees conferred in Mississippi and 98.9 percent of the degrees conferred nationwide. United States Department of Health, Education, and Welfare, Earned Degrees Conferred 1959–1960: Bachelor's and Higher Degrees 135 (1960). As one would expect, the labor force reflects the same predominance of women in nursing. When MUW's School of Nursing began operation, nearly 98 percent of all employed registered nurses were female. United States Bureau of the Census, 1981 Statistical Abstract of the United States 402 (1981).

[5, 6] Rather than compensate for discriminatory barriers faced by women, MUW's policy of excluding males from admission to the

---

Mississippi University for Women v. *Hogan* (458 U.S. 718).

School of Nursing tends to perpetuate the stereotyped view of nursing as an exclusively woman's job. By assuring that Mississippi allots more openings in its state-supported nursing schools to women than it does to men, MUW's admissions policy lends credibility to the old view that women, not men, should become nurses, and makes the assumption that nursing is a field for women a self-fulfilling prophecy. See *Stanton v. Stanton*, 421 U.S. 7, 95 S.Ct. 1373, 43 L.Ed.2d 688 (1975). Thus, we conclude that, although the State recited a "benign, compensatory purpose," it failed to establish that the alleged objective is the actual purpose underlying the discriminatory classification.

The policy is invalid also because it fails the second part of the equal protection test, for the State has made no showing that the gender-based classification is substantially and directly related to its proposed compensatory objective. To the contrary, MUW's policy of permitting men to attend classes as auditors fatally undermines its claim that women, at least those in the School of Nursing, are adversely affected by the presence of men.

MUW permits men who audit to participate fully in classes. Additionally, both men and women take part in continuing education courses offered by the School of Nursing, in which regular nursing students also can enroll. Deposition of Dr. James Strobel 56–60 and Deposition of Dean Annette K. Barrar 24–26. The uncontroverted record reveals that admitting men to nursing classes does not affect teaching style, Deposition of Nancy L. Herban 4, that the presence of men in the classroom would not affect the performance of the female nursing students, Tr. 61 and Deposition of Dean Annette K. Barrar 7–8, and that men in coeducational nursing schools do not dominate the classroom. Deposition of Nancy Herban 6. In sum, the record in this case is flatly inconsistent with the claim that excluding men from the School of Nursing is necessary to reach any of MUW's educational goals.

Thus, considering both the asserted interest and the relationship between the interest and the methods used by the State, we conclude that the State has fallen far short of establishing the "exceedingly persuasive justification" needed to sustain the gender-based classification. Accordingly, we hold that MUW's policy of denying males the right to enroll for credit in its School of Nursing violates the Equal Protection Clause of the Fourteenth Amendment.

B

[7] In an additional attempt to justify its exclusion of men from MUW's School of Nursing, the State contends that MUW is the direct beneficiary "of specific congressional legislation which, on its face, permits the institution to exist as it has in the past." Pet. Brief 19. The argument is based upon the language of § 901(a) in Title IX of the Education Amendments of 1972, 20 U.S.C. § 1681(a). Although § 901(a) prohibits gender discrimination in education programs that receive federal financial assistance, subsection 5 exempts the admissions policies of undergraduate institutions "that traditionally and continually from [their] establishment [have] had a policy of admitting only students of one sex" from the general prohibition. . . . Arguing that Congress enacted Title IX in furtherance of its power to enforce the Fourteenth Amendment, a power granted by § 5 of that Amendment, the State would have us conclude that § 1681(a)(5) is but "a congressional limitation upon the broad prohibitions of the Equal Protection Clause of the Fourteenth Amendment." Pet. Brief 20.

The argument requires little comment. Initially, it is far from clear that Congress intended, through § 1681(a)(5), to exempt MUW from any constitutional obligation. Rather, Congress apparently intended, at most, to exempt MUW from the requirements of Title IX.

Even if Congress envisioned a constitutional exemption, the State's argument would fail. Section 5 of the Fourteenth Amendment gives Congress broad power indeed to enforce the command of the Amendment and "to secure to all persons the enjoyment of perfect equality of civil rights and the equal protection of the laws against State denial or invasion. . . ." *Ex parte Virginia*, 100 U.S. (10 Otto) 339, 346, 25 L.Ed. 676 (1879). Congress' power under § 5, however, "is limited to adopting measures to enforce the guarantees of the Amendment; § 5 grants Congress no power to restrict, abrogate, or dilute these guarantees." *Katzenbach v. Morgan*, 384 U.S. 641, 651 n. 10, 86 S.Ct. 1717, 1724 n. 10, 16 L.Ed.2d 828 (1966). Although we give deference to congressional decisions and classifications, neither Congress nor a State can validate a law that denies the rights guaranteed by the Fourteenth Amendment. See, *e.g.*, *Califano v. Goldfarb*, 430 U.S. 199 at 210, 97 S.Ct. 1021 at 1028, 51 L.Ed.2d 270; *Williams v. Rhodes*, 393 U.S. 23, 29, 89 S.Ct. 5, 9, 21 L.Ed.2d 24 (1968).

The fact that the language of § 901(a)(5) applies to MUW provides the State no solace: "[A] statute apparently governing a dispute cannot be applied by judges, consistently with their obligations, when such an application of the statute would conflict with the Constitution. *Marbury v. Madison*, 1 Cranch 137 [2 L.Ed. 60] (1803)." *Younger v. Harris*, 401 U.S. 37, 52, 91 S.Ct. 746, 754, 27 L.Ed.2d 669 (1971).

IV

Because we conclude that the State's policy of excluding males from MUW's School of Nursing violates the Equal Protection Clause of the Fourteenth Amendment, we affirm the judgment of the Court of Appeals.

It is so ordered. . . .

Justice POWELL, with whom Justice REHNQUIST joins, dissenting.

The Court's opinion bows deeply to conformity. Left without honor—indeed, held unconstitutional—is an element of diversity that has characterized much of American education and enriched much of American life. The Court in effect holds today that no State now may provide even a single institution of higher learning open only to women students. It gives no heed to the efforts of the State of Mississippi to provide abundant opportunities for young men and young women to attend coeducational institutions, and none to the preferences of the more than 40,000 young women who over the years have evidenced their approval of an all-women's college by choosing Mississippi University for Women (MUW) over seven coeducational universities within the State. The Court decides today that the Equal Protection Clause makes it unlawful for the State to provide women with a traditionally popular and respected choice of educational environment. It does so in a case instituted by one man, who represents no class, and whose primary concern is personal convenience.

It is undisputed that women enjoy complete equality of opportunity in Mississippi's public system of higher education. Of the State's eight universities and 16 junior colleges, all except MUW are coeducational. At least two other Mississippi universities would have provided respondent with the nursing curriculum that he wishes to pursue. No other male has joined in his complaint. The only groups with any personal acquaintance with MUW to file *amicus* briefs are female students and alumnae of MUW. And they have emphatically rejected respondent's arguments, urging that the State of Mississippi be allowed to continue offering the choice from which they have benefited.

Nor is respondent significantly disadvantaged by MUW's all-female tradition. His constitutional complaint is based upon a single asserted harm: that he must *travel* to attend the state-supported nursing schools that concededly are available to him. The Court characterizes this injury as one of "inconvenience." *Ante*, at 3336 n.8. This description is fair and accurate, though somewhat embarrassed by the fact that there is, of course, no constitutional right to attend a state-supported university in one's home town. Thus the Court, to redress respondent's injury of inconvenience, must rest its invalidation of MUW's single-sex program on a mode of "sexual stereotype" reasoning that has no application whatever to the respondent or to the "wrong" of which he complains. At best this is anomalous. And ultimately the anomaly reveals legal error—that of applying a heightened equal protection standard, developed in cases of genuine sexual stereotyping, to a narrowly utilized state classification that provides an *additional* choice for women. Moreover, I believe that Mississippi's educational system should be upheld in this case even if this inappropriate method of analysis is applied.

I

Coeducation, historically, is a novel educational theory. From grade school through high school, college, and graduate and professional training, much of the nation's population during much of our history has been educated in sexually segregated classrooms. At the college level, for instance, until recently some of the most prestigious colleges and universities—including most of the Ivy League—had long histories of single-sex education. As Harvard, Yale, and Princeton remained all-male colleges well into the second half of this century, the "Seven Sister" institutions established a parallel standard of excellence for women's colleges. Of the Seven Sisters, Mount Holyoke opened as a female seminary in 1837 and was chartered as a college in 1888. Vassar was founded in 1865, Smith and Wellesley in 1875, Radcliffe in 1879, Bryn Mawr in 1885, and Barnard in 1889. Mount Holyoke, Smith, and Wellesley recently have made considered decisions to remain essentially single-sex institutions. See Carnegie Commission on Higher Education, Opportunities for Women in Higher Education ("Carnegie Report"), excerpted in B. Babcock, A. Freedman, E. Norton, & S. Ross, Sex Discrimination and the Law 1013, 1014 (1975). Barnard retains its independence from Columbia, its traditional coordinate institution. Harvard and Radcliffe maintained separate admissions policies as recently as 1975.

The sexual segregation of students has been a reflection of, rather than an imposition upon, the preference of those subject to the policy. It cannot be disputed, for example, that the highly qualified women attending the leading women's colleges could have earned admission to virtually any college of their choice. Women attending such colleges have chosen to be there, usually expressing a preference for the special benefits of single-sex institutions. Similar decisions were made by the colleges that elected to remain open to women only.

The arguable benefits of single-sex colleges also continue to be recognized by students of higher education. The Carnegie Commission on Higher Education has reported that it "favor[s] the continuation of colleges for women. They provide an element of diversity . . . and [an environment in which women] generally . . . speak up more in their classes, . . . hold more positions of leadership on campus, . . . and have more role models and mentors among women teachers and administrators." Carnegie Report, *supra*, quoted in K. Davidson, R. Ginsburg, & H. Kay, Sex-Based Discrimination 814 (1975 ed.). A 10-year empirical study by the Cooperative Institutional Research Program of the American Counsel of Education and the University of California, Los Angeles also has affirmed the distinctive benefits of single-sex colleges and universities. As summarized in A. Astin, Four Critical Years 232 (1977), the data established that

"[b]oth [male and female] single-sex colleges facilitate student involvement in several areas: academic, interaction with faculty, and verbal aggressiveness. . . . Men's and women's colleges also have a positive effect on intellectual self-esteem. Students at single-sex colleges are more satisfied than students at coeducational colleges with virtually all aspects of college life. . . . The only area where students are less satisfied is social life."

Despite the continuing expressions that single-sex institutions may offer singular advantages to their students, there is no doubt that coeducational institutions are far more numerous. But their numerical predominance does not establish—in any sense properly cognizable by a court—that individual preferences for single-sex education are misguided or illegitimate, or that a State may not provide its citizens with a choice.

II

The issue in this case is whether a State transgresses the Constitution when—within the context of a public system that offers a diverse range of campuses, curricula, and educational alternatives—it seeks to accommodate the legitimate personal preferences of those desiring the advantages of an all-women's college. In my view, the Court errs seriously by assuming—without argument or discussion—that the equal protection standard generally applicable to sex discrimination is appropriate here. That standard was designed to free women from "archaic and overbroad generalizations. . . ." *Schlesinger v. Ballard*, 419 U.S. 498, 508, 95 S.Ct. 572, 577, 42 L.Ed.2d 610 (1975). In no previous case have we applied it to invalidate state efforts to *expand* women's choices. Nor are there prior sex discrimination decisions by this Court in which a male plaintiff, as in this case, had the choice of an equal benefit.

The cases cited by the Court therefore do not control the issue now before us. In most of them women were given no opportunity for the same benefit as men. Cases involving male plaintiffs are equally inapplicable. In *Craig v. Boren*, 429 U.S. 190, 97 S.Ct. 451, 50 L.Ed.2d 397 (1976), a male under 21 was not permitted to buy beer anywhere in the State, and women were afforded no choice as to whether they would accept the "statistically measured but loose-fitting generalities concerning the drinking tendencies of aggregate groups." *Id.*, at 209, 97 S.Ct., at 463. A similar situation prevailed in *Orr v. Orr*, 440 U.S. 268, 279, 99 S.Ct. 1102, 1111, 59 L.Ed.2d 306 (1979), where men had no opportunity to seek alimony from their divorced wives, and women had no escape from the statute's stereotypical announcement of "the State's preference for an allocation of family responsibilities under which the wife plays a dependent role. . . ."

By applying heightened equal protection analysis to this case, the Court frustrates the liberating spirit of the Equal Protection Clause. It forbids the States from providing women with an opportunity to choose the type of university they prefer. And yet it is these women whom the Court regards as the *victims* of an illegal, stereotyped perception of the role of women in our society. The Court reasons this way in a case in which no woman has complained, and the only complainant is a man who advances no claims on behalf of anyone else. His claim, it should be recalled, is not that he is being denied a substantive educational opportunity, or even the right to attend an all-male or a coeducational college. See Brief for Respondent 24. It is *only* that the colleges open to him are located at inconvenient distances.

III

The Court views this case as presenting a serious equal protection claim of sex discrimination. I do not, and I would sustain Mississippi's right to continue MUW on a rational basis analysis. But I need not apply this "lowest tier" of scrutiny. I can accept for present purposes the standard applied by the Court: that there is a gender-based distinction that must serve an important governmental objective by means that are substantially related to its achievement. *E.g., Wengler v. Druggists Mutual Ins. Co.*, 446 U.S. 142, 150, 100 S.Ct. 1540, 1545, 64 L.Ed.2d 107 (1980). The record in this case reflects that MUW has a historic position in the State's educational system dating back to 1884. More than 2,000 women presently evidence their preference for MUW by having enrolled there. The choice is one that discriminates invidiously against no one. And the State's purpose in preserving that choice is legitimate and substantial. Generations of our finest minds, both among educators and students, have believed that single-sex, college-level institutions afford distinctive benefits. There are many persons, of course, who have different views. But simply because there are these differences is no reason—certainly none of constitutional dimension—to conclude that no substantial state interest is served when such a choice is made available.

In arguing to the contrary, the Court suggests that the MUW is so operated as to "perpetuate the stereotyped view of nursing as an exclusively women's job." *Ante*, at 3339. But as the Court itself acknowledges, *id.*, at 3334, MUW's School of Nursing was not created until 1971—about 90 years after the single-sex campus itself was founded. This hardly supports a link between nursing as a woman's profession and MUW's single-sex admission policy. Indeed, MUW's School of Nursing was not instituted until more than a decade *after* a separate School of Nursing was established at the coeducational University of Mississippi at Jackson. See University of Mississippi, 1982 Undergraduate Catalog 162. The School of Nursing makes up only one part—a relatively small part—of MUW's diverse modern university campus and curriculum. The other departments on the MUW campus offer a typical range of degrees and a typical range of subjects. There is no indication that women suffer fewer opportunities at other Mississippi state campuses because of MUW's admission policy.

In sum, the practice of voluntarily chosen single-sex education is an honored tradition in our country, even if it now rarely exists in state colleges and universities. Mississippi's accommodation of such student choices is legitimate because it is completely consensual and is important because it permits students to decide for themselves the type of college education they think will benefit them most. Finally, Mississippi's policy is substantially related to its long-respected objective.

IV

A distinctive feature of America's tradition has been respect for diversity. This has been characteristic of the peoples from numerous lands who have built our country. It is the essence of our democratic system. At stake in this case as I see it is the preservation of a small aspect of this diversity. But that aspect is by no means insignificant, given our heritage of available choice between single-sex and coeducational institutions of higher learning. The Court answers that there is discrimination—not just that which may be tolerable, as for example between those candidates for admission able to contribute most to an educational institution and those able to contribute less—but discrimination of constitutional dimension. But, having found "discrimination," the Court finds it difficult to identify the victims. It hardly can claim that women are discriminated against. A constitutional case is held to exist solely because one man found it inconvenient to travel to any of the other institutions made available to him by the State of Mississippi. In essence he insists that he has a right to attend a college in his home community. This simply is not a sex discrimination case. The Equal Protection Clause was never intended to be applied to this kind of case.

The Political Attack on California's Chief Justice Rose Bird

by Betty Medsger

In California, governors run against judges. At least in recent years, the judiciary there has been attacked by campaigning candidates for governor, Democratic and Republican. Most recently, the attacks have centered on a character named Rose Bird.

That's true despite the fact that Rose Bird has not been, and is not likely to ever be, a candidate for governor. She is the chief justice of the California Supreme Court. She is the first woman ever to serve on that court, let alone sit at its helm. As such, she is one among seven equal justices when it comes to judicial opinion-writing, but she is the administrator of the entire California judiciary, the largest judicial system in the world. She has been a major issue in numerous political races. Some candidates have spent more time running "against" her than they spent running against their real opponents.

The New Right in California has made Rose Bird what Earl Warren was for the Old Right of his day. Like Warren, she is attacked for her interpretation of the constitution. But she has a burden Warren never had: her gender. In different ways, both liberals and conservatives have used her gender against her.

The leaders of the coalition of right-wing groups that have tried to have her removed from the bench are quite open about the importance of her gender. The executive director of the Law and Order Campaign Committee, John Feliz, put it very succinctly: "We use her because it's easier to grasp a symbol. . . . *She is no different than the men on the court*. She is simply a convenient focus. She's a perfect symbol."

Since 1977, when Governor Edmund G. (Jerry) Brown, Jr., appointed her chief justice, Bird has been used by the right wing

---

Adapted from Betty Medsger, *Framed: The New Right Attack on Chief Justice Rose Bird and the Courts* (New York: Pilgrim Press, 1983), pp. 266–69. Revised especially for this book.

in California to symbolize that person who is supposed to be the nemesis of law-abiding citizens: the liberal judge. She is portrayed to the public as the symbol of the contention that judges are primarily the defenders of criminals, not of all citizens.

She is such a strong symbol that the successful Republican candidate for governor in 1982, then attorney general George Deukmejian, repeatedly told voters that one of the major faults of his opponent, Los Angeles Mayor Tom Bradley, was that Bradley was a "strong supporter" of Rose Bird. The Republican candidate for the U.S. Senate, San Diego mayor Pete Wilson, not only repeatedly drew attention to the fact that his opponent, Governor Brown, had appointed Bird as chief justice, but also took the unprecedented step of announcing as part of his Senate campaign that he favored her recall from the court unless she voted to uphold a controversial anti-crime measure then pending before the state's supreme court. During that campaign between Wilson and Brown, a prestigious statewide publication, *California Magazine*, claimed that Brown's appointment of Bird to the court was such a strong liability that it could cause his defeat. And it may have helped. The article was accompanied by a sketch that showed Bird pushing Brown underwater.

In that 1982 race Rose Bird was a major issue in the California governor's race, the U.S. Senate race for Sam Hayakawa's seat, and the race for state attorney general. Since Bird was appointed to the court, there have been repeated attempts to remove her from the bench, including five unsuccessful recall campaigns that never made it to the ballot stage. Not enough signatures have been gathered in any of these campaigns to get her recall on a ballot. If her recall ever does get to the ballot stage, it will be the first time in history Californians have been asked to vote on whether to recall a member of the California Supreme Court.

Recall is supposed to be an extreme act, used to remove officials who have engaged in malfeasance in office. It asks the voters to perform major political surgery on their own earlier decisions that approved these same people for public office. But in Bird's case, politicians seem to speak of this drastic political action as easily as they might vote to thank the senate chaplain for his prayers. They say Bird should be recalled because they disagree with her judicial opinions. Without blushing, they say they want to use recall in order to replace her with a judge of their ideological persuasion. Perhaps they do not blush because they feel confident that they have succeeded in recent years in inducing public amnesia about the fact that the United States and California constitutions both provide for an independent judiciary. It is an idea that many of the Californians involved learned at Ronald Reagan's knee when he was governor.

Who is this judge? How did she manage to become a more sensational election issue in 1982 than the highest unemployment rate in either the state or the country since World War II? How did she become more sensational in election rhetoric than a controversial statewide gun-control initiative? How did she, in 1977, the only time she has yet been before the voters for approval, achieve the lowest plurality, a mere 1.7 percent, that any appellate judge in the state's history has received?

She was a liberal appointed to head a court with a liberal reputation at a time when conservative rhetoric that made judges appear to be the real villains of our society was popular. But that's only part of the explanation of the peculiarly venomous and dishonest attack that has been waged against Bird since her appointment was first announced in 1977. That description could have been used against any of a number of appellate judges, including some others appointed to the supreme court by Brown. But few judges anywhere in the country have been attacked as Bird has been.

Bird has been attacked not only by the conservatives who oppose her for ideological reasons. She also has been attacked by a few liberal men who oppose her solely because they thought they or other men, not she, should have been appointed chief justice. Their reaction goes far beyond natural disappointment. It is difficult to imagine that their disappointment would have such enduring intensity if the person they had lost the appointment to had been another man instead of the first woman.

Bird did not know what these would-be chief justices felt until she took office. A widespread story is that one of them, supreme court justice Stanley Mosk, said to her on her first day at the court, "Somebody's sitting in *my* chair." But this Goldilocks, unlike the one in the children's story, did not run away. She did, however, discover that there were several bears in the woods, mostly Brown bears, judges who had been appointed to the state's superior (trial) courts or the court of appeals years earlier by Governor Edmund G. (Pat) Brown, Sr., Jerry's father, and who were confident now that Brown the son would give friends of Brown the father nice promotions when he became governor. More than one had expected not only to be elevated, but to become chief justice. One of these judges pounded Jerry Brown's desk furiously after he appointed Bird, cursing the governor for not appointing him chief justice.

For those who were looking for a better lightning rod for the attack on the courts, Rose Bird must have seemed like a dream come true. She already had an impressive list of enemies among the state's agricultural interests, which are of considerable importance to the state's law-and-order movement. In Brown's first cabinet, she had been secretary of agriculture and services, then the largest agency in the state government. Soon after taking over the agency she prohibited the use of the short hoe, a humane reform that agricultural interests and the Reagan administration had successfully blocked for the previous eight years despite considerable medical evidence that this tool, because it requires a perpetually bent back, is lethal to farm workers. Bird also was a key architect of the Agriculture Labor Relations Act, legislation that probably will be called Brown's most significant accomplishment in his eight years as governor. It guaranteed farm workers the right to organize and negotiate labor contracts. It also guaranteed Bird the permanent enmity of agribusiness, probably the most powerful lobby in California.

There were other factors that brought criticism. At age forty, she was young, as judges and popes go. She was an aggressive administrator, the cabinet member in the Brown administration responsible for the largest number of workers and the largest portion of the state budget. She also had been a public defender, not a frequent pool from which governors and presidents choose judges. Nearly her entire career before working in the Brown administration had been spent working as a public defender in Santa Clara County. She also had been a part-time instructor at Stanford University Law School.

The fact that she had never been a judge also was used against her. Others, of course, were quick to point out that a number of eminent judges had no experience on the bench before being appointed to high positions there. One of them was another Californian, Earl Warren, who had never served as a judge until President Eisenhower appointed him chief justice of the United States Supreme Court. Another such person was Potter Stewart, whom Eisenhower plucked from the obscurity of the Cincinnati City Council to serve on the federal court of appeals and then, two years later, on the U.S. Supreme Court.

When she graduated from law school in 1965, Bird applied at the public defender's office in Sacramento. The man who interviewed her said he would not hire a woman. He said he had never seen a good trial attorney who was a woman, "except one . . . and she ended up a terrible alcoholic." Bird smiles her ironic smile as she tells the story. She applied next at the Santa Clara County public defender's office and found a nonsexist public defender, Donald Chapman. She became that office's first woman attorney. When Chapman asked the staff of ten attorneys how they felt about having a woman on the staff, only two voted in favor.

Earlier, when she was a student at Boalt Hall, the law school of the University of California at Berkeley, her professors tried to discourage her from becoming a trial attorney. It was difficult, if not impossible, for women to get those jobs then, she said. But she was not deterred. By then Bird knew what she wanted to do. After graduating with honors from Long Island University, she had worked briefly as a secretary and then come to California to study political science in the graduate school at Berkeley. A year later she was one of ten students who won Ford Foundation scholarships to be interns for a year in the California legislature. Until then she had wanted to be a journalist. Her work in Sacramento focused her interest on law. While working on the staff of Assemblyman Gordon H. Winton, she wrote a report that led to Winton's important bill establishing statewide testing of elementary and secondary students.

Bird's lifelong tenacity has been shaped in part by a mother who saw education as a means of guaranteeing never having to do menial work and never having to be dependent on anyone. The three Bird children—Bird has two brothers—were taught to train their minds. "I knew that because I had no money if I were going to go to school, I had to make my own way, and I had to rely on scholarships," Bird recalls. "I'd lost my father when I was young, and I saw my mother, a very intelligent woman, have to work in a factory and slowly destroy her health. It was brought home to me very early that you are dependent on yourself, not on anyone else. She would say, 'You're not going to have somebody who's going to take care of you. The most important thing for you to do is to find work that you enjoy and not be stuck having to do manual labor.' "

It's unlikely that Ann Bird, who lives with her daughter in a small Palo Alto home, ever thought that an alternative to being a factory worker would be being chief justice of the California Supreme Court. But her early lessons and example undoubtedly helped shape the mind and talent that eventually convinced Jerry Brown to tap her daughter for this prestigious job.

When the state's Commission on Judicial Appointments met to vote on the appointment of Bird, it had more letters—pro *and* con—than it had ever received about a nominee. Many attacked the idea of a woman being appointed to the court. Others attacked her role as agriculture secretary. Some provided strong praise, like this one from an official of the Educational Employment Relations Board: "I have been impressed even startled by her acumen both in administrative efficiency and legal versatility. She possesses a unique combination of compassion and, for lack of a better word, toughness."

She needed that toughness. The clues were evident even before she arrived at her court chambers in San Francisco. At the same time Jerry Brown appointed Bird, he had appointed Wiley Manuel, a longtime state prosecutor and the first black person to be appointed to the state's highest court. Shortly before they were to begin their new jobs on the court, Manuel called Bird to ask if she would like to ride with him in a few days to the lunch the other justices were giving them. He was embarrassed and appalled when he discovered that the new chief justice had not been invited to the informal luncheon with all the members of the court. It was a men-only lunch.

The court had operated much like a family. It is a closed institution, with court employees protecting the confidential proceedings and writings as cases progress. It is like a small, protective village. Recent chief justices had been father figures, particularly Bird's predecessor, Chief Justice Donald Wright. Many members of the court staff also developed loyalties akin to family loyalties. When the new chief justice did not respond as they thought a warm mother should, they turned against her. She was treated like an intruder in their village.

Given the general respect for authority that some of them felt, their attitude toward her, their boss, was particularly remarkable. And often it was petty. They reacted to both substantial and insubstantial things. She bought a new desk. They called reporters, without pointing out that she paid for it herself. A small refrigerator arrived in her outer office. They called reporters and said she was wasting government funds. She hung plants in her office and placed on her desk a mug emblazoned with *Ms*. Some of them thought that meant she was inappropriately flaunting her feminism. She put the elegant artwork of Corita Kent in her outer office. They complained that it was gaudy. And, as always, they called reporters.

The press reaction to Bird is central to the impression of her, and the misinformation about her that people continued to believe long after the reaction to her inside the court staff had mellowed considerably.

On the outside people have continued to think of her as paranoid and inaccessible because they read of those qualities so often. Those two terms probably have been used about Bird more than they have been used about any recent public official except Richard Nixon. The proof of her paranoia stemmed from a story written and repeated many times. That story is a good example of press irresponsibility and unfairness.

Inside court sources told reporters that Bird had changed the locks on her chambers within her first year there and that this was another sign of her paranoia. Reporters wrote it as though it needed no explanation save that of the sources, known opponents of Bird. Routine journalistic diligence would have produced an even more interesting story—that she changed the locks because a court of appeals justice unlocked her door and entered her office late one Saturday evening. The surreptitious act would have gone unnoticed, perhaps, except for the fact that the chief justice and some members of her staff, to the surprise of the entering justice, were at work in her chambers. Had *San Francisco Examiner* reporter K. Connie Kang learned that information, a story she wrote entitled "The Locksmith Cometh" might have instead—and more accurately—been called "The Court of Appeals Judge Breaketh In."

Though it could not be known from a review of the many stories written about Bird during her first year on the court, not everyone on the court staff opposed her. Some were glad, for instance, that she was trying to prevent staff attorneys from conducting private law practices from their supreme court offices during work hours. A few were even glad that, as the administrator of the entire state court system, reportedly the largest judicial system in the world, she was trying to integrate the trial and appellate courts more. Many were appalled, for example, that instead of relying largely on retired judges to replace ailing appellate judges, she would appoint trial judges to sit temporarily on the appellate benches. After a few years, this innovation was widely recognized as an effective administrative change. It helped reduce error by trial-court judges, and it made appellate-court judges more aware of the special problems of the trial courts. But when she did it, she was accused of trying to make the trial-court judges loyal to her and of being "so stupid" that she wanted the company of "lower" judges on the appellate bench, including her own court. The levels of the hierarchy of the courts tend to be very sharply drawn. What right did this woman have, some of them complained angrily, to blur those lines?

It is natural for people to react negatively to change. It is particularly so when the institution is a powerful one and one that already is respected, as the California Supreme Court was. Though Rose Bird has introduced many changes that have improved judicial administration, she did not inherit a disaster area. It undoubtedly would have been more judicious for her to have moved more slowly.

But the reaction to her changes, both the significant and insignificant ones, was nearly irrational at times. Reporters often quoted unnamed sources, saying the sources wouldn't let their names be used in articles because they were afraid of retaliation from Bird. I talked to those people, too. Many of them were troubling sources. They made no distinction between mere gossip or assumptions, on the one hand, and evidence on the other hand.

Interestingly, some people on the staff who like or defend the chief justice told me they were afraid to let their names be used because they were afraid of retaliation from their colleagues. They also were afraid to initiate contact with the press, for they perceived the few reporters who wrote about the court regularly as being so biased against the chief justice the reporters either would not write their version of events or would reveal their identity to Bird opponents on the court staff. These people may have been at least partially accurate, for the stories written in Bird's first several years on the court appear to rely only on sources unfavorable to her.

One man who insisted on anonymity told me, "I was accused of being an informer—and just because I wasn't part of the hate campaign." He is both angry and sad as he describes the attitude toward Bird among some of his colleagues. "Sure," he says, "I was hoping someone on the court would get the job. After that was not the case, I felt she deserved my loyalty. But some said right away, 'Let's make it tough on her.' And they did."

Another member of the court staff told me of an extraordinarily unethical step taken by one supervisor. In one of the offices of the court where technical corrections on all justices' opinions are made, a supervisor gave at least one secretary specific orders not to correct any errors that appeared on opinions that came from Bird's office. The secretary told me the supervisor instructed her: "Don't correct any mistakes on Bird's papers. We don't want to do anything to help her. We want her to look foolish."

With the help of an unquestioning press, those who wanted to make Bird look foolish—or worse than foolish—succeeded. But none succeeded as well as those responsible for the story that appeared in *The Los Angeles Times* on election-day morning, November 7, 1978.

That day was important. Bird was on the ballot. In California, appellate justices are appointed by the governor. After a three-member Judicial Appointments Commission approves their nomination, their names appear on the ballot at the next statewide general election. They then serve out the remainder of their predecessor's term. At the end of that term, the justice is on the ballot for voter confirmation of a full twelve-year term, as Bird would be in 1986. But in November 1978 she was on the ballot for the first time. Probably no one—not even State Senator H. L. Richardson, the extreme-right-wing organizer of the Law and Order Campaign Committee and the person who first urged *The Los Angeles Times* to write the election day story—anticipated *how* unusual the events of that election day would be. Like Bird's appointment, they were historic.

As the 1978 election approached, Bird was threatened from within the court and from outside the court. The main forces organized against her outside the court were Richardson's Law and Order Campaign Committee, the most active and vehement, and No-on-Bird. The latter was an agriculture-based organization headed by Mary Nimmo, appointed later by President Reagan to be director of public relations for the United States Department of Commerce. Though the No-on-Bird group said it opposed Bird only because, it claimed, she was a poor administrator, in fact, the public statements of both anti-Bird organizations opposed her on ideological grounds.

From within the court, a few people based their opposition to her on ideological grounds. But most claimed it was simply because there had been too much change too fast. Many of the actions they complained about would have been applauded as good management practices in another branch of government or in corporate life. But not in the family of the court, where traditions change very slowly.

One of the most striking actions by someone inside the court came from a justice himself. In an action he probably realized would become public, a week before the election Justice Mosk, the most highly placed and most vocal of the would-be chief justices, informed the California Trial Lawyers Association that he would not receive the Appellate Justice of the Year Award from them because they had publicly endorsed Bird.

A few months earlier, in the summer of 1978, Senator Richardson said in an interview with national political columnist Richard Reeves, "We're not playing patty-cake. We're talking about the ideological direction of the court, and we've got to grab people's attention with tough talk."

A state senator since 1966, Richardson had been financing legislative races against liberal incumbents in the assembly for nearly a decade. Just a year earlier he had raised $600,000 to defeat Governor Brown's veto of the assembly's death-penalty bill. Richardson used the leftover money the next year to defeat those legislators who had voted against the override. Clearly, Richardson was a force to be reckoned with. To be a liberal and come within his campaign sights was more like playing hara-kiri than playing patty-cake.

Not until 1978 did Richardson venture into judicial elections. He was confident that Rose Bird, primarily because she was a woman, was vulnerable. He would try to do what no one had done: defeat an appellate court judge in a confirmation election. He was considered foolish. Not only was history against him. So were the polls. A mid-October *Los Angeles Times* story said a poll then showed that she had gained support since their late-September poll.

But on election-day morning anyone who had laughed at Richardson's audacity was eating crow for breakfast. Every newspaper, radio, and television was reporting that morning what was on the front page of *The Los Angeles Times*: a story claimed that the senior justice of the supreme court, Justice Matthew O. Tobriner, was holding back the announcement of a controversial court decision, even though the decision was completed and ready for release. The decision was to overturn a law requiring a term in prison for anyone using a gun during a violent crime. Chief Justice Bird had voted with the majority in favor of the overturn. Tobriner had been a strong Bird supporter, and the election-day story strongly implied what many later stories stated explicitly: that Tobriner, thinking the overturn decision would make Bird look soft on crime and thus cost her votes, delayed it until after the election. It was an extraordinary accusation. Delaying a case for political purposes is unethical and grounds for removal from the bench.

The effect was immediate. Bird almost lost, winning by less than two percentage points. There followed a year-long investigation by California's respected Commission on Judicial Performance. In a strange change of procedure, preliminary hearings were held in public, so the press reported all sorts of hearsay and innuendo. Still, the only public accuser was Bird's fellow supreme court justice William P. Clark, whom Governor Reagan had appointed to the court despite the facts that Clark had flunked out of both college and law school and was virtually unable to discuss the law. Another justice, Stanley Mosk, then sued to have the hearings closed; he won. At last the commission simply announced that the investigation was closed and no charges would be filed. As far as the public was concerned, the damage had been done, the charge of unethical behavior had gone unanswered. Only much later did the complex story of this affair finally emerge, a story that strongly indicated a plot by Clark and perhaps others to delay the case and thus discredit Rose Bird at the last minute before the election.

This ordeal was but part of a larger pattern. . . .

The attacks by strong law-and-order politicians are altering the courts of California in more than one way. Thanks primarily to Richardson and his allies, the idea has been successfully promoted that judges are politicians in the same sense that legislators are, and that "we" should throw "them" out when their philosophy is out of line with ours. In 1980 five out of seven incumbent trial judges who were challenged lost their seats. In all cases previous spending records for judicial races were broken. Five of the seven challengers were deputy district attorneys who ran law-and-order campaigns.

In 1980 the Law and Order Campaign Committee ran a full-page ad in the *Los Angeles Daily Journal* saying LOCC was "looking for a few good judges." It went on to announce that seventy-four superior court and forty-one municipal court seats could be contested at the June election. Then it listed the names of the incumbent judges, and the procedure for getting into the races. The *San Francisco Chronicle* condemned the ad, noting that "anyone running under the banner of 'law and order' or 'civil liberties' or any other fixed predilection becomes a captive of the slogan. And beholden to a special interest group is exactly what a judge should not be."

In 1981 the right-wing Political Advertising and Consulting (PAC) organization in Los Angeles sent a letter to prosecutors throughout the state. It began: "Dear Prosecutor: I'm sure you are aware that in 1982 over 300 judgeships will be on the ballot throughout the state of California. While many incumbent judges will be retiring or running for higher office, many lenient, soft-on-crime judges will be vulnerable to defeat. No longer are judges simply handpicked by the legal fraternity nor does the electorate merely rubberstamp appointees or Bar recommendations. Campaigns for judicial office have become just that—CAMPAIGNS!" The letter went on to say the faculty for the state would include John Feliz, executive director of Richardson's Law and Order Campaign Committee, and William Saracino, executive director of Richardson's Gunowners of California. The registration was so large that PAC could not accept all applications, despite the fact that the fee for the one-day seminars was $325 a person for each of the three regional seminars.

Some people accuse judges of not wanting to campaign because they want to be "above it all." Some judges are elitist and think they deserve a lifetime trust, no matter what their judicial behavior. But the truth is that campaigning as a judge presents some very real problems that cannot easily be overcome unless the ethics of the judiciary and the very concept of fair justices change significantly. If a legislator goes to a chamber of commerce or a labor-union banquet during his campaign, he or she can promise anything. They can say they will lower taxes, provide more community services, bring more industry to town, or outlaw smoking cabbage. But an incumbent judge who attends such a banquet can do little more than thank the group for dinner and kiss a baby. Judges cannot make pledges on how they will decide particular kinds of cases. They can't pledge to send more people to prison, can't pledge to reduce violence on the streets by making tougher sentences or instructing juries differently. About all they can say is that they have been a fair judge, will continue to be a fair judge. That isn't the kind of "rhetoric" that generates a lot of excitement, but judicial ethics require a sitting judge to say little more than that. In the meantime, an irresponsible opponent not on the bench and not bound by judicial ethics can promise to increase convictions and sentences.

There is the problem of campaign money. Raising campaign money, when opposed on the ballot, poses a special problem for judges. If not independently wealthy, where does a judge get it? Until war was declared on judges, they usually had only nominal campaign chests, perhaps $5,000 raised among friends, for a few posters and flyers. They seldom felt it was necessary to blanket their communities or to buy air time on radio and television, the lifeblood of other politicians. Now, full-fledged campaigns mean raising significant amounts of money from a much wider circle of people. A Los Angeles Superior Court judge who in his last campaign spent $5,000 has been told by his political consultant that he will need a minimum of $60,000 to win if he is opposed in the next election. Some judges think raising money for themselves puts them in a quasi-unethical position on the bench. "What would you think if you were a litigant in my court and you knew the opposing counsel had contributed to my campaign?" asks Judge Hollis Best, a superior court judge in Fresno County. "Wouldn't you wonder about the fairness of my decision if I had ruled in his favor? I don't think judges' decisions are being influenced by contributions. At least not yet, anyway. Nevertheless, the public thinks that money is contributed to campaigns because the contributor wants something."

Money is less of a problem for the incumbents' opposition, at least for those who were handpicked or approved by Richardson and have his treasures to draw from. In 1980 Feliz announced that the Law and Order Campaign Committee had chosen as that year's first target incumbent superior court judge Richard Calhoun of Contra Costa County. He said LOCC would support chief assistant district attorney Gary Strankman in the race. "We'll spend enough to remove the incumbent if it takes $1,000 or $100,000," said the LOCC's Feliz. Strankman won.

Then there are the campaign lies. Lies, of course, are not new to politics, and they weren't invented by the right wing. Lies and half-truths based on judicial records can be particularly clever and hard to rebut, especially if issued close to election day. A case in point is Pasadena Superior Court Judge Gil Allston. At the time of the June 1978 primary election he was an incumbent municipal court judge. A widely respected member of the community and a former deputy district attorney, he had a wide range of endorsements. He had a sedate campaign committee that had raised $5,000 and wanted to be very low-key. His opponent was new to the community, had not even given an interview to the local paper, seemed to be doing nothing. Allston's committee thought it would be almost tacky to even acknowledge that there was an opposition candidate. Allston and his committee were shocked out of their complacency the Wednesday before the Tuesday election. That day the district was blanketed with anti-Allston leaflets. One side had a photograph of a policeman looking in a store window with a flashlight. Under the photograph were these words: "The police are doing their job. The courts are not." On the other side, the voter was urged to vote for the opponent instead of Allston. What was most devastating was another message: the opponent claimed that during Allston's time on the bench he had never sent one person to state prison. Incredible. Yes—especially in view of the fact that as a municipal court judge he *could not* send anyone to state prison. Municipal court judges send people convicted in their courts to county jails, and Allston had sent many people to county jail. Allston and his sedate committee got to work fast and spent their $5,000 over the weekend distributing leaflets rebutting the challenger's deceptive claims. Allston won, but by the skin of his teeth. If the leafleting had been done against him on the eve of his election, as the accusations were made on the eve of Bird's election in 1978, Allston would not have had time to counter the false claims with the truth.

Another example of deception. In an evaluation of San Francisco judges, Richardson's LOCC rated one judge as follows: "weak . . . a public defender's mentality . . . a fondness for plea bargaining." The judge, assigned to civil cases, had not heard a criminal case in more than five years.

During the 1978 campaign against Rose Bird, Richardson said "We're not playing patty-cake." Truth or consequences is not his game either. . . .

Bird has been an unwilling and accidental decoy, in the sense of "one who leads another into danger, deception, or a trap." Bird is the decoy used maliciously to lead the public into thinking that the way to solve the crime problem is to blame the courts.

"It's headhunting time again" began one newspaper editorial in 1981 about a new recall attempt against Bird. The term *headhunting* was appropriate for its political symbolism. But it also is particularly chilling in Bird's case, for some former court staff members who continue to work actively against her—actually hope for Bird's death, failing a successful effort to remove her at the polls.

In the summer of 1981 three former employees of the court told me they had heard the chief justice had just started to wear a wig. They said they were sure she was having cobalt treatment for her cancer, thus the loss of hair and need for a wig. "That means she's in pretty bad shape," said a woman, not doing much to hide her joy. Bird, however, had merely changed to a more stylish hairdo. She has never had cobalt treatments and has never worn a wig for either cosmetic or medical purposes. In fact, by that time her cancer seemed to be in remission. But some were persisting in hoping otherwise. "Everybody says she's much sicker than we really know," a former member of the court staff told me rather happily. "We assume her illness will take care of the whole problem."

But in case it doesn't, and in case a recall campaign doesn't work, there's a contingency plan. Another former staff member, who left the court in great bitterness and who continues to work with people who want to remove Bird from the bench, sounded both ominous and hopeful as he told me, "We're watching her very, very closely. We are hoping that she will commit a major boo-boo to cause another investigation." His voice was fervent, his face intense, as he added: "And this time we will get her."

28

BUREAUCRACY

Despite their lack of titles, women have been managing large and significant enterprises for a long time. In the plantation South, for example, especially during the Civil War, many a "Southern Lady" took over the manor and made it produce. Today the titles are sometimes being bestowed along with the duties. The two cases to follow might start a long list.

In the first, ace bureaucrat Eleanor Holmes Norton illustrates what it takes to turn a government agency into an effective engine for making the law work. The law in question looked plain enough. Title VII of the Civil Rights Act of 1964 said:

> It shall be an unlawful employment practice for any employer to fail or refuse to hire or to discharge any individual or otherwise to discriminate against any individual with respect to his compensation, terms, conditions, or privileges of employment because of such individual's race, color, religion, sex, or national origin.

To put that into effect, an Equal Employment Opportunity Commission (EEOC) was created in 1965. But twelve years and seven directors later, the organization was widely rated a colossal mess. Thousands of complaints of discrimination had piled up—an enormous backlog of cases. EEOC could hardly initiate much action as long as it was not able even to keep up with the individual pleas for relief. A familiar enough problem in Washington and in every state capital: the bureaucratic logjam.

A tall, thin, black forty-year-old noted for her zeal and laughter, Norton took over. At her big welcoming party, she announced "I will control the backlog." And by the spring of 1978 she had done just that. Further, she did it not just by mounting an energetic frontal assault on the mound of cases itself, but also by redesigning EEOC machinery to prevent future pileups.

Eleanor Holmes Norton came up through the civil-rights movement—where her role was to try to put into practice the great principles of national equality. Born in Washington, D.C., to a middle-class family, she went to Antioch College and Yale Law School, and then plunged into the harrowing and dangerous work of agitating for racial justice in rural Mississippi. She arrived on the evening of June 12, 1963, and was met by Medgar Evers, NAACP regional director, who tried to get her to stay in Jackson, for her safety's sake. No, she would go out in the Delta country. He put her on the ten o'clock bus to Greenwood. Next morning she got word that Medgar Evers was dead—murdered. Soon she saw firsthand the typical cruelty and injustice in that region, such as Fannie Lou Hamer and Lawrence Guillot beaten by racist thugs. Still, she never lost either her laughter or her commitment. Or her principles: some found it hard to believe that Norton, as an American Civil Liberties Union attorney, represented Governor George Wallace (a notorious Alabama racist) when he sued to hold a political rally in New York's Shea Stadium. The suit brought her to the attention of New York's mayor, John Lindsay, who made her head of the city's Commission on Human Rights.

When Republicans speculate about who the first woman president will be, the name Elizabeth Hanford Dole pops up. In 1984, it was said, officials planning the Republican National Convention in Dallas drew back from making her the keynote speaker, thinking that might set off a Dole boom for vice-president. She good-humoredly welcomed the speculation, as she sidestepped any actual candidacy. Her husband, Senator Robert Dole of Kansas, after several hot pursuits of the presidential nomination, solemnly announced at a gathering that "Dole will not be a candidate for President in 1984"—at which his wife jumped up and shouted, "Speak for yourself, Sweetheart!"

North Carolinian Elizabeth Dole graduated from Duke University and Harvard Law School. From a place as President Reagan's White House assistant for public liaison, she was appointed secretary of the Department of Transportation, which employs 102,000 people. It includes the Coast Guard, which makes Dole the first woman to head a branch of the armed forces. Perhaps as important, "Liddy" Dole has earned the respect of a president who opposes the Equal Rights Amendment, on the one hand, and numerous leading feminists on the other. The first of the two selections on Dole that follow describes her background and illustrates her administrative work in the Department of Transportation. Then, in an interview, she sketches how the gender gap should be dealt with and how the principles of equal rights should be put into practice through effective reform of governmental regulations.

Eleanor Holmes Norton Reforms the Equal Employment Opportunity Commission

by Peggy Lamson

In 1971 the New York Commission on Human Rights received a grant from the federal EEOC to set up a systemic-pattern-and-practice sex-discrimination project. Charlotte Frank, who was brought to the commission as codirector of the pilot program (and who has since come to EEOC), believes that it was in large part due to Eleanor Norton's presence that the New York agency was one of five selected for this significant project; after her one year in the enforcement business, the EEOC already had great confidence in her management skills.

The phrase *systemic-pattern-and-practice cases* while perhaps sounding rather com-

From Peggy Lamson, *In the Vanguard: Six American Women* (Boston: Houghton Mifflin, 1979), pp. 169–76.

plex does in fact mean exactly what it says—cases against industries that practice a regular pattern of sex or minority discrimination. For the EEOC and related state and city enforcement agencies, however, it has a specific connotation because in pattern-and-practice cases it is the *agency* that initiates the action rather than an individual complainant.

The procedure is quite straightforward. All companies with fifty or more employees are required by law to fill out an EEO-1 survey form broken down into employment practices at various levels—professional, managerial, clerical, sales, and so forth. These surveys enable the enforcement agencies to study each category and, if there seem to be possibilities of discriminatory practices, to choose which company has the poorest record in employing women (in the upper categories) and minorities overall. Then the gross indicators and justifying data against the offending company are incorporated into a formal complaint stating that the New York Commission on Human Rights or the Massachusetts Commission against Discrimination or the Equal Employment Opportunity Commission itself charges the offender—let us say a mythical Universal Telecommunications Systems, Inc. (UTSI)—with discrimination. UTSI would be ordered to provide a work-force analysis, covering the entire array of personnel practices—from recruitment and selection standards to promotion policies—that affect employment in their company. Because pattern-and-practice cases do not have to wait for an individual to trigger a complaint, enforcement agencies can go farther afield to reach companies that might otherwise go untouched. They, therefore, have a far greater impact on the problems affecting millions of women and minorities who are trapped in the bottom levels of industries and corporations.

At the hearings held in Washington on May 24, 1977, before the Senate Human Resources Committee confirming Norton as chair of the EEOC, considerable attention was paid by both the designee and the senators who questioned her, to the systemic approach in discriminatory employment problems.

Norton described the outstanding success of the New York commission's pattern-and-practice work and pointed out that "We have a tough reputation in New York, but the fact is that when we issue a commission-initiated complaint a highly professional staff moves in with the company to help it totally redesign the personnel system that is keeping minorities and women from entering and going up in the company." She hoped, she said, to draw on that experience in Washington.

Asked by Committee Chairman Harrison A. Williams (D.–N.J.) how she would assign priorities between pattern-and-practice and individual cases in the EEOC, she replied that grievances from individuals were and always would be very important in the life of an antidiscriminatory agency. But she also believed that they could "process individual cases to the end of time without in fact substantially affecting the patterns and practices that bar minorities and women from the corporations and industries of America. After a while," she added, "we would begin to wonder why we had enacted antidiscrimination laws." Furthermore she said in response to a question by Senator Thomas F. Eagleton (D.–Mo.) she did not believe that "the forces that joined to struggle for the Civil Rights Act of 1964 and particularly for Title VII had in mind that the commission would be a sitting duck reacting only to the complaints that came before it."

Pursuing this line further and noting that at the moment the EEOC devoted 90 percent of its time to individual and only 10 percent to systemic cases, Eagleton suggested a possible legislative fiat that might help Norton achieve her own objective by compelling her in fiscal 1978 to spend at least one third of the EEOC's budget on systemic cases, 50 percent in 1979, and 75 percent in 1980.

Wisely Norton demurred knowing as she did that the backlog situation (which included many individual complaints) was an absolute priority which she, as entering chair, first had to conquer in order to restore public confidence in the beleaguered EEOC, which had been "bad-mouthed all across the country." And at that moment, she told Senator Eagleton she feared the backlog estimated at 130 thousand cases was so serious that she could not be certain it would be under control in time for her to meet the sort of mandatory target dates—much as she agreed with their objective—that Eagleton was proposing.

Eagleton had begun his questioning by extracting an agreement from the designee that, in view of the EEOC's history of six chairmen in twelve years, she would make an "unalterable, categorical pledge," to remain with the agency for the duration of her four-year term. When Senator Jacob Javits' (R.–N.Y.) turn to question her came, he commended her promise, but Chairman Williams interrupted to tell her, "That doesn't have to be written in stone. If some president demanded and drafted Ms. Norton for another position, we would release you from this." But not until they had looked over the other job, put in Senator Javits, to make sure that it was indeed a promotion.

On such an affable, sympathetic helpful note Norton was confirmed enthusiastically first by the committee and then by the entire Senate to become the seventh chair of the EEOC.

"Technical toil, bureaucratic innovation and system-changing . . ." The words were hers, written to describe the civil rights needs of the 70s. Now she had to put them into practice, quickly, surely, and skillfully.

First the backlog. What had caused it? What could eliminate it? What could reverse a further buildup? Fortunately numerous ailments were readily identifiable.

To begin with many of the complaints did not even belong in an antidiscrimination agency. For example, mythical Ruth Chandler, thirty-eight, white, comes to the EEOC to complain that she has been summarily fired without cause from the Universal Telecommunications Systems, Inc. A clerical worker at EEOC takes down the routine facts, gives Chandler's complaint a docket number and puts it at the bottom of the pile of other complaints to molder and become part of the backlog. But in fact a little skillful further investigation might soon have revealed that Ms. Chandler, who was fired by a woman and had been replaced by a woman, did not have a legitimate Title VII charge. Her grievance might indeed have been legitimate in terms of unfairness but not in terms of *discriminatory* unfairness.

Under Norton's new Rapid Case-Processing System the so-called intake procedure is now conducted by a trained professional prepared to take the time necessary to determine at the very first interview if the case violates Title VII and thus comes under EEOC jurisdiction. If it does not, the staff member makes a vigorous effort to refer the complainant to the proper channels, which may prove helpful.

Suppose, however, that Ms. Chandler is eligible by seniority and merit for a promotion and suppose there is an opening in the rank above hers and that instead of giving her the better position a man is brought in to fill the slot. Suppose furthermore that she is aware that there are no women holding positions in the higher echelon to which she rightfully aspires.

In this instance—pre-Norton—Ms. Chandler might have been called back after several months to supply information that was not elicited at her first interview. Then she would have been subjected to a staggering amount of paperwork with endless forms to fill out. Meanwhile—which often meant six months later—interrogatories would also have been sent to Universal Telecommunications Systems, Inc., in whose interest it was—especially if they had other complaints against them—to delay or to respond inadequately. Thus it would not have been unusual for several years to pass before the battle between Ms. Chandler and UTSI could even be joined, by which time Ms. Chandler may have married and moved away or UTSI mercifully gone out of business.

The Rapid Case-Processing System permits no such delays. Complainants and respondents are brought together for a face-to-face confrontation in an EEOC office within *three to four weeks* of filing the initial complaint in the hope that a negotiated settlement can be arrived at promptly.

The results of this procedure as tested in the three model offices promptly set up by Norton in Baltimore, Dallas, and Chicago to test the efficacy of the agency's reorganization were spectacularly good. Negotiated settlements resulting from the face-to-face meetings and satisfactory to both parties resolved 44 percent of the *new* cases in a four-month period of time as opposed to 6 percent the previous year.

If, however, a negotiated settlement cannot be arrived at in the fact-finding conference and if in post-conference actions continued settlement efforts fail, then the charging party may request and receive from the EEOC a Right to Sue letter. (Under Title VII no job discrimination litigation may be instituted without such permission from EEOC.) At this point, which under the Rapid Case-Processing System should now be arrived at within three or four months, a private attorney may enter the case and take it to federal court for settlement or, after further investigation, it may be referred to the commission's general counsel for litigation.

Backlogged cases must of necessity be handled separately because, of course, the intake procedure had long since taken place. Accordingly Norton instituted a separate Backlog Charging Process System and assigned a sizable staff to go through the entire inventory. Charges against a single respondent were grouped, individuals were contacted to see if they still wished to press charges, and, most important, older cases were set apart to receive the priority attention they obviously deserved. A management team set tight time-frames and kept close supervision of backlog case workers to see that the stepped-up schedules were met. Negotiated settlements were of course encouraged and facilitated here as in the new cases received.

At the model offices the results again were encouraging. Dallas, for example, closed 83 percent more backlogged cases than it received new cases over a four-month period and 21 percent of these were by negotiated settlement as opposed to 9 percent in the equivalent amount of time the year before.

The model offices also successfully tested a new Systemic Case Processing System in which, instead of the previous hit-or-miss method of expanding individual cases into vehicles for class actions and pattern-and-practice suits, the cases were chosen more rationally, partially on the basis of the importance of a culpable company to the district in which it is located.

A new field service structure was designed to make EEOC more accessible to the public everywhere in the country. Norton completely changed the setup of thirty-two district offices and five litigation centers she had inherited. Her feeling was that the lawyers should actually be *in* the field offices rather than isolated as a separate unit. She abolished the litigation center altogether, and spread the lawyers out among twenty-two *new* district offices, each of which is fully staffed to handle all three new charge-processing systems, rapid charge, backlog charge, and systemic charge. Thirty-seven smaller area offices feed cases into the parent units.

The headquarters office in Washington also underwent an extensive reorganization with a view to providing better support for the field offices, preventing overlapping, implementing management accountability, and initiating policy through guidelines, interpretations, and hearings.

Of sheer necessity this stem-to-stern reorganization was pushed through with great speed (the field offices were, however, phased in gradually) and with great attendant disruption of personnel, particularly in the Washington office. No one, of course, was fired; as everyone knows it is almost impossible to fire a civil-service worker (or was until Carter's reorganization), but some EEOC employees claimed, doubtless with justification, that they were being pushed around.

Partially the rebellion stemmed from the fact that old-line EEOC people, many of whom had fallen into rather sloppy work habits, were put off by a bunch of city slickers from New York moving in and telling them they all had to shape up in a hurry.

As Brooke Trente, one of the "city slickers," describes it, "Eleanor is tough—we're all tough—and those of us who came from New York [Preston David, Brooke Trente, and Charlotte Frank in the top echelon] were also considered arrogant. And do you know something? We were. But my view was that this was the time for arrogance and for knowing what we were doing in this agency."

It was true of course that the reorganization plan had been successfully tested out in New York and that the new brooms did indeed know what they were doing. But the employees in the Washington office were made uneasy by the mere fact of change, and even more so by the fact that change was being hurled at them with such speed that they were not able to absorb it. ("You are going to see speed some might view as unfair," Norton had warned them all that first day.) Furthermore they were angry because they felt their opinions were not sought out—they who had been so long at the agency were simply being told what to do. "Efficiency" was the bugaboo word. Norton was accused of elevating efficiency over the interests of minority staffers. "Are you telling us that an agency that is minority dominated cannot be efficient," was the underlying inference.

Ultimately because the EEOC workers were after all experts in litigation and complaint filing—suing the employer being the focus of most of their jobs—they turned on their own boss. EEOC headquarters in Washington and fourteen district offices were picketed by the American Federation of Government Employees (AFGE); one sign read EEOC WORKERS CARE ABOUT CIVIL RIGHTS—EVEN OURS!

Norton accepted this internal strife, according to Trente, "about as calmly as she accepts anything," quiescence not being one of her outstanding characteristics. Eventually she and the president of AFGE signed an agreement fully protecting employees' rights during reorganization. Meanwhile Norton continued to insist that the majority of the staff was in fact very supportive and understood that she had to ram through her reforms—which were indeed showing startlingly good results. Overall, 28 percent more discrimination cases were resolved each month than had been in the past. "But," she said, "I could not inspire confidence in the new system if I did not move fast."

Speed and substance paid off. On February 23, 1978, the headline of the lead story in the *New York Times* read: PRESIDENT PROPOSES MERGER OF PROGRAMS TO FIGHT JOB BIAS. EEOC ASSIGNED MOST POWER.

Secretary of Transportation Elizabeth Dole: First Madame President?

SENATOR AND SECRETARY DOLE: BALANCE OF POWER

by Douglas B. Feaver

When Transportation Secretary Elizabeth Hanford Dole proposed last summer to cut traffic at every congressman's favorite airport, Washington National, the $28 billion appropriations bill for the entire Transportation Department became a hostage on Capitol Hill.

"I figured she'd strike out," said Sen. Robert J. Dole (R–Kan.), her husband and chairman of the Senate Finance Committee. He volunteered that assessment at dinner. She took umbrage.

"It was just an offhand comment by one Bob Dole," she said. "It was kind of like a challenge. . . . I've got a little note pad and pencil by my bed, and I scribble all these things down. So my strategy evolved while he was sleeping away next to me. 'I'll do this and this. I'll show him.' "

The troops were marshalled; the appropriation saved. The plan to reduce traffic at National Airport is alive if unresolved.

A strikeout?

"No. She got about a single on it," the senator said.

"That shows who's the smarter politician," said Sen. Mark Andrews (R–N.D.), a Dole family friend who is also chairman of the Senate Appropriations subcommittee on transportation.

Elizabeth Dole may or may not be the smarter politician, but there is no question that she is half of one of the more fascinating acts in town: the powerful senator and the able Cabinet secretary, the successful two-career marriage. It is an aggregation of public power under one roof, one that creates ambiguous situations not often seen here.

The senator is politically committed to modifying the tax on heavy trucks. The transportation secretary testifies in favor of an administration position that can be compromised to fit the senator's.

The transportation secretary makes a political appearance for Sen. Ted Stevens (R–Alaska). Campaign America, the senator's political action committee (PAC), contributes to Stevens' campaign, as it does to the campaigns of many Republicans.

A number of transportation interests contribute to the senator's PAC, a normal thing for the chairman of the Senate's tax-writing body. Do their contributions reflect their knowledge that he also happens to be married to the transportation secretary?

There is no way to tell, and no evidence of anything improper. But Federal Election Commission records show that 18 firms or persons readily identifiable with transportation companies contributed a total of $22,300 to Sen. Dole's PAC in 1983, a pittance for a PAC that took in $846,700.

Together and apart, the Doles are building an impressive list of political IOUs; there is nothing more entertaining than the Bob and Elizabeth show.

"She gets two to three times as many invitations to speak as [former transportation secretary] Drew Lewis did, because she

---

From Douglas B. Feaver, "Senator and Secretary Dole: Balance of Power," *Washington Post*, March 18, 1984, p. A1, col. 2.

gets them not only from the transportation groups but also the women's groups and people who think it would be nice to get Bob and Elizabeth together," said Ralph Stanley, who is head of the Urban Mass Transportation Administration after working for both Lewis and Dole at the Transportation Department.

Both Doles are clearly aware of the potential for conflicts of interest. Both say they pay little attention to the other's activities.

"Right now," Elizabeth Dole said, "he's got a couple of major things up there [in the Senate] and I'm learning more about it from your newspaper than I am from him. . . . He doesn't know what I'm doing on Conrail; I don't know what he's doing on some of the intricacies of his issues. . . ."

"It is a legitimate question," Sen. Dole said. "I would say we just don't discuss a lot of that. She'll take some work home with her and get tied up on it; if you get home at 8 o'clock, 8:30, the last thing I want to do is get right into business. Get that Lean Cuisine out and eat it."

Of the two Doles, she appears to have the more difficult balancing act. At one time or another in the same day, she is:

- The eighth U.S. secretary of transportation.
- An effective Reagan administration fire extinguisher for smoldering gender-gap issues.
- The helpful spouse of the politically ambitious senior senator from Kansas.
- A potential political candidate in her own right.

There have been a few joint appearances with Sen. Dole, including a tour of Topeka, Atchison and Wichita on Kansas Day last summer. She accompanied Sen. Dole in February to a Los Angeles fund-raiser for Campaign America and several Republican incumbents and candidates. But she did not speak and was not introduced.

The secretary of transportation is not subject to the Hatch Act's prohibition on government employees participating in partisan politics. The department's ethics officer, Rosalind Knapp, said Secretary Dole was briefed on ethics questions, as all incoming secretaries are briefed.

"She is subject to the same conflict rules with respect to what Sen. Dole does as she is with respect to anybody else," Knapp said. "She should avoid fund-raising events that are focused on [transportation] interests with which she would have a conflict, but that does not preclude events" attended by a few transportation personalities.

Last June, she made a political swing through the Northwest that included appearances on behalf of Sen. Mark O. Hatfield (R–Ore.) in Portland and Sen. Slade Gorton (R–Wash.) in Seattle. Then she was joined by Sen. Dole for a visit and vacation with Sen. Stevens that included a tour of the federally owned Alaska Railroad, which DOT is selling to the state. Her Christmas card is a picturesque photograph of the smiling Doles waving from the back of an Alaskan railroad passenger car bearing the DOT seal.

About the same time, Sen. Dole's Campaign America PAC handed out contributions to a number of Republicans seeking election, including $5,000 for Stevens. "I give money to all my potential opponents," Dole said, referring to the fact that he and Stevens are among those seeking to replace Sen. Howard H. Baker Jr. (R–Tenn.) as majority leader.

The Doles and Baker showed up in New Hampshire recently to campaign for President Reagan. Secretary Dole attacked Democratic presidential candidate Walter F. Mondale. Sens. Dole and Baker—both presidential prospects for 1988—defended Republicanism. Bob Dole dropped one-liners, such as: "Howard and I came along to keep an eye on Elizabeth and see if she's running for president."

She has been seriously suggested as a

future vice presidential nominee. "What do you think of a Bush-Dole ticket?" Sen. Dole tells crowds he was asked by a reporter. "I said I just don't think I'd have any interest," Dole says he replied. "That's a good thing," said the reporter, according to Dole. "We didn't have you in mind."

Do you see a situation, Dole was asked, where you and she might have conflicting political ambitions? "I think that's a possibility," he said. "I think she's hotter property than I am right now."

The Senate Finance Committee has direct responsibility for only a few transportation-related matters, including "user fee" taxes to support federal trust funds for highways and airport development. "I'm in charge of loopholes; she's in charge of potholes," Sen. Dole said.

There is only one occasion when the Doles seem to have joined forces to attack a problem. The Transportation Department has made no secret of its desire to eliminate the United States Railway Association, a small federal agency set up to oversee Conrail. The USRA's mission is almost complete now that Conrail makes money, all bankruptcy questions have been settled and the railroad is ready for sale to the private sector.

But Congress, especially the House, wants to keep the USRA's experts around to monitor the sale. Last July, during debate on the Transportation Department's appropriations bill, Sen. Dole rose on the floor to call the USRA "a quasi-governmental body whose useful life has long expired, in my opinion."

Asked about that, Secretary Dole said, "You're never going to believe me, but it was independent. It really was. We didn't talk about it."

She was sworn in as transportation secretary Feb. 7, 1983, after serving as Reagan's assistant for public liaison, where she was often isolated from decision-making. People who know her give two reasons for that: she was a woman in a male-dominated White House and she was Sen. Dole's wife, which made some staffers nervous when it came time to talk about strategy in dealing with the Senate Finance Committee on tax issues, for example.

For a variety of reasons, it took months for Dole to get her key sub-Cabinet positions filled after she became transportation secretary. Her strongest aide, Deputy Secretary James H. Burnley IV, was widely perceived within the transportation community as the one really running things.

Burnley, a North Carolinian like Secretary Dole, has taken great pains to shoot down that notion, which serves neither his nor her interests. "We have a very clear understanding about who's in charge around here," he said. "She is."

Those early reviews are being revised, because it is clear that Dole has made the Transportation Department her own and redefined its issues along lines that interest her, such as careful policy development and safety in transportation.

There is no shortage of issues: whether to mandate automobile airbags; how to guarantee consumer protection for airline passengers when the Civil Aeronautics Board dies next Jan. 1; how to manage burgeoning air traffic without constraining the deregulated airlines; how to allocate scarce federal funds among many competing new mass transit systems, and how to denationalize Conrail and keep Congress smiling.

There are also major and minor controversies about further deregulation of trains, planes, boats and busses; management of the mammoth highway and bridge project fund; port development; truck and waterway taxes; what to do about drunken railroad engineers; airline safety; Coast Guard drug interdiction; even the commercialization of outer space.

It takes time to master those subjects, particularly for someone who wants to know all the details before she opens her mouth. "We send in paper, it comes out with questions; we send in more paper, it comes out with more questions," one member of her staff explained.

"I've said that I consider myself a perfectionist," Dole said. "So if there's something driving me, it's that kind of thing. It's the fact that my family members are all perfectionists, too. . . . It's something from within that says give it your best. I don't think it's any more complex than that."

There has been some grumbling, always not for attribution, among congressional aides that the Transportation Department runs on automatic pilot while Secretary Dole studies details. As for members of Congress, nobody is going to fire at her, on or off the record.

Sen. John C. Danforth (R–Mo.), a member of the Finance Committee and chairman of the Commerce Committee's surface transportation subcommittee, has worked hard over the last two years to move a truck safety bill. Safety is Secretary Dole's first priority, she says over and over. The day Danforth held hearings on truck safety, he had to settle for Burnley as the Transportation Department witness.

Secretary Dole was busy later that day testifying on truck taxes in front of Sen. Dole, over at the Finance Committee, in a hearing that was widely covered by the media and watched closely by the trucking lobby.

"Elizabeth Dole is such a strong person and such an effective person herself, I really don't think of her as Mrs. Bob Dole," Danforth said. "She is very able. Also Bob has his own agenda. It's not a problem."

House Democrats also praise her performance. Rep. William Lehman (D–Fla.), chairman of the House Appropriations subcommittee on transportation, called Secretary Dole "a voice of reason and moderation in an administration that can often become extreme."

The two major Senate panels that handle transportation issues—the Commerce, Science and Transportation Committee and the Environment and Public Works Committee—have nine members who also are members of Sen. Dole's Finance Committee. Three of them are chairmen of significant transportation committees or subcommittees. Sen. Nancy Landon Kassebaum (R–Kan.), a friend of both Doles, is chairman of the Commerce Committee's aviation subcommittee.

The Transportation Department's new federal railroad administrator, John Riley, was chief legislative assistant to Sen. David F. Durenberger (R–Minn.). Its new assistant secretary for governmental affairs is Charles G. Hardin, who was the chief transportation staffer for Andrews' transportation appropriations subcommittee. One of Secretary Dole's new special assistants is Rebecca C. Gernhardt, who was Sen. Stevens' chief of staff.

Secretary Dole is a member of the club. "She's a Senate wife; I'm a Cabinet spouse," Sen. Dole said.

The Transportation Department's proposed fiscal 1985 budget was clearly a victory for Dole. Mass transit and aviation expenditures rose, and the number of safety inspectors, cut earlier in the Reagan administration, was increased.

Before Dole arrived, Drew Lewis had managed the air traffic controllers' strike with skill, had turned the administration around on the need for new gasoline and trucking taxes to support highway and transit improvements and had won a number of lesser skirmishes. But Lewis ignored automobile safety issues, which are subject to regulation by the department's National Highway Traffic Safety Administration (NHTSA).

Under Lewis, NHTSA abandoned a Carter administration rule requiring the installation of airbags or other so-called passive restraints in new automobiles. The Supreme Court subsequently ruled that NHTSA had given insufficient grounds for abandoning the airbag rule and remanded it to NHTSA. Dole reopened the case, promising a decision by April 12. That date will slip into late April, she said, but not by much.

Whatever she proposes will have to pass White House muster. "I will make a recommendation to the president based on what the record shows," she said. Her personal view is that airbags are effective; she has had one installed in her DOT car.

Consumer advocate Ralph Nader attaches cataclysmic importance to the airbag question. That decision, he said, "will either confirm the impression that Elizabeth Dole is not willing to stand up for victims against power or it will make Elizabeth Dole the most courageous Cabinet secretary in the Reagan administration."

Neither Dole nor the White House supports federal laws raising the drinking age to 21. They believe that the states should do it themselves. She said on NBC's "Meet the Press" recently that if states pass a law, "I think there's more of an effort for enforcement, and it's more effective."

When Dole is asked what she is doing about auto safety, she talks about new regulations and about using "the bully pulpit" to support getting drunk drivers off the street or to advocate seat-belt use, an effort started during Lewis' tenure as a substitute for requiring airbags.

She persuaded the Office of Management and Budget to approve a requirement that new autos have brake lights mounted on the top center of the trunk—a proven reducer of rear-end collisions. That idea had been kicking around NHTSA for at least seven years. She approved the use of anti-lacerative windshields.

The NHTSA under Dole has been more active in pursuing defects in new cars than it was under Lewis, although there is a belief on Capitol Hill that more needs to be done. Rep. Timothy E. Wirth (D–Colo.), chairman of the House Energy and Commerce subcommittee on telecommunications, consumer protection and finance, wrote Dole recently that NHTSA's "track record over the last three years is extremely disappointing and poses grave dangers for the driving public."

Dole responded that "the number of defect investigative actions is up significantly over the last six months. Moreover, NHTSA influenced the recall of 70 percent of the vehicles recalled in 1983—the highest level since 1971." She also noted that the Justice Department, at her department's urging, sued General Motors for X-car defects and that Transportation has budgeted more highway money for safety improvements.

"Part of the good statistics we've had on safety have to be due to this kind of thing," Dole said, referring to the fact that the highway death toll of 43,028 in 1983 was the lowest in 20 years and that there were fewer highway fatalities over the Christmas holiday than at any time since 1946.

Dole has shaken up the Federal Aviation Administration after a flurry of disturbing air safety incidents indicated that FAA inspectors were overworked or underdirected. In addition to authorizing more inspectors, Dole ordered a system-wide investigation of airline safety.

She and Sen. Dole have worked at avoiding obvious conflicts. When several small Kansas cities were interested in being selected as the site for a new, centralized FAA flight service station, Wichita got it. The others will lose existing stations.

Normally, the senior senator from Kansas would just pick up the phone and call the transportation secretary and tell her of his great concern. In this case, he could mention it at dinner.

"I didn't lobby her on the flight service station," Sen. Dole said. Pause. "I lobbied Burnley. I just called him and said, 'Now Jim, are you sure you made the right choice?' "

THE GENDER GAP FROM THE REAGAN CAMP

by Judy Mann

Judy Mann: Is the gender gap real?

Elizabeth Dole: Yes. The gender gap does exist. There has been in my view a revolution in this country, what I call the quiet revolution. I experienced it myself, which makes it very real to me, because at the time I entered law school back in 1962 I was on the cutting edge of a social revolution and didn't realize it. I was one of 25 women in a class of 550. Today that same class in law school is almost 40 percent women. That is just representative of the kind of change that has gone on all across the country, and I think a lot of ramifications of that tidal wave of women coming into the work force are not fully felt yet, but it's changed our society tremendously. And I do feel that any President sitting in the Oval Office today would be faced with a number of problems that need to be addressed, very real needs of women in the work force.

You combine all this change with a period of recession, where you have women the last hired, first fired, and those kinds of problems—the median income for women is $11,000—it's not surprising that there is a sense of uncertainty on the part of women about whether institutions, whether government can really solve their problems. They're concerned about their future, their children's future.

Over the years, there has been a divergence between men and women with regard to the use of force. Not just war and peace, but gun control, capital punishment. That goes back over other presidencies, too.

But economic equity to me is where the real needs are; if those problems are properly handled, I believe the gender gap can be closed. The last six months I was at the White House, the President asked me to chair a coordinating council on women. This was the first time we'd had a lot of assistants to the President working on women's issues—child care, dependent care, issues like enforcement of child-support laws. You have women who may be raising a couple of children alone because of divorce; they've got real needs; they need help. You've got women who are older, who, maybe because of divorce or for other reasons later in life, find themselves alone. Pension reform is very helpful there. To me those are the real needs.

What the President asked the coordinating council to do was first of all to try to surface across the Administration issues of concern to women and be sure they were focused on. And second to look at this phenomenon that's taken place in our society, this quiet revolution, this tidal wave of women coming into the work force, and then suggest areas where action should be taken.

As a result of that council, the State of the Union message last year contained a number of phrases on economic equity, pension reform, child care, dependent care, child-support enforcement, and we have been fleshing out those issues this year.

What I'm trying to say is basically that number one, you address the needs of real people. Number two, a by-product of that is help with the gender gap.

You can also bring in dropping the rate of inflation and how that impacts on women because, heaven knows, the woman on an $11,000 median income is going to have $1,050 more in her pocket because inflation has been brought down. She's also going to have an extra $284 from the tax-rate cuts if she's a woman raising two children.

J. M.: How did the gender gap happen in an Administration headed by the Great Communicator?

E. D.: (Laughter) I don't think we are communicating our message as well as we should. And part of that must be that we are dealing with some very complex issues. When you talk about enforcement of child-support laws, this is an area where there's about $4 billion that the court has awarded and that women are not receiving.

The key to that, in my view, and this is what

From Judy Mann, "The Gender Gap From the Reagan Camp," *Ms.*, March 1984, pp. 74 ff.

the Administration ultimately did in their legislation by shifting incentives, was to provide child-support enforcement for women, period, not just for the women on welfare, but it's a very complex thing. I think that's also true on pension reform. So maybe that's part of it: there are more complex issues to articulate, but I don't think we've done a good enough job of getting that message out.

Also, this is the first time there have been three women in the Cabinet. You have the first woman on the Supreme Court, which is a real breakthrough. Helene von Damm was the first woman to head Presidential personnel, and I never heard anything about that at the time Helene was serving in that job, but she was in charge of personnel for the entire Administration.

J. M.: There are a lot of firsts and yet there still is a very real perception that this is not an Administration that is particularly favorable toward women.

E. D.: You take, for example, the difference between the Equal Rights Amendment and trying to change laws and regulations. The President was criticized early on for not supporting the Equal Rights Amendment, but I talked with women's groups about the fact that he did want to move forward immediately to change laws and regulations that were sex-biased, where there were vestiges of discrimination. I said this is in no way inconsistent with the goal of the Equal Rights Amendment. Every one of them agreed: while they're working for the Equal Rights Amendment, there's nothing to stop them from working with us to change those laws and regulations now. All of these efforts are very important for women. One example is the pension laws the President is supporting—this is one my husband introduced in the Senate—to change the age when you're eligible to participate from 25 to 21 because so many women come into the work force earlier. Or legislation to change the situation as it is now concerning survivor's benefits, where a husband can sign away his wife's rights without the wife ever even seeing the form. And then legislation to provide a pro-rata share of pensions for the divorced wife. Also with regard to pregnancy, time-out without changing your eligibility.

Estate taxes are a major initiative for women. The average woman outlives her husband by eight years. I can remember when my husband was running for office and the farm women telling me that they often have to sell the farm to pay the estate taxes. The same thing with small businesses. The child-care tax credit was almost doubled in the 1981 tax law. Recently the incentives were shifted, so it's more geared to low income. Then there's providing for homemakers to utilize IRAs and increasing the IRAs from $2,250 to $4,000. Those are the kinds of things that somehow don't make the best copy, but they are significant steps for women. We are going to continue to come out with those kinds of initiatives.

So the President is moving to make those kinds of changes, but I think that just to say he doesn't support the Equal Rights Amendment doesn't tell the story about what he does support.

We worked so hard on child-support enforcement because that just means so much to so many people. These are the kinds of issues you can put your heart into. You know it's going to matter.

J. M.: Is there something that's going to be a showcase accomplishment that the Administration is going to be able to say to women voters, "Look, this is what we've done"?

E. D.: I think it's going to be more a compilation of the record. We say on the one hand that ERA provides a shorthand, but let's not lose sight of the fact that at least in all the polls I've seen it's not ERA and abortion that cause the gender gap. There's not a divergence between men and women there. I just use ERA as an example because it says something that's a little harder to say with these more complex laws. And yet a lot of this is going to the same goal, of changing laws, changing regulations, in order to provide equality and equity for women. So it's reaching the same goal by a different path.

J. M.: Do you think the gender gap can be closed?

E. D.: I really do. A lot of it is getting out there and really working with women around the country. Because I know this is something that is not finished, there are going to be more initiatives. I've asked the women's organizations to continue talking to me over here, because I want to hear what their concerns are and where we ought to be moving.

J. M.: What are you going to do during the campaign?

E. D.: I'm going to be out on the campaign trail. I'll be doing transportation forums, but I'll also probably have an opportunity to speak to a number of women's organizations. I think I can help to carry the message of what has been done, both on issues of economic equity and appointments as well as on the general economy.

J. M.: What is the President going to be doing to get this across?

E. D.: I think all of us will be going forward to articulate the initiatives and I think there's a sensitivity to considering women and their concerns throughout the issues that are being developed—for example, talking about crime that certainly impacts on elderly women. I see that aspect being considered in issues that may not seem to be women's issues.

I'll probably talk about the kinds of things we do here at Transportation, too, to be of assistance to women, because I think our women's program is working. When you've got 102,000 people working for the Department of Transportation—it's traditionally a male area, heavy construction and that kind of thing—to move up our percentage even one percentage point is a lot of people, a lot of women. I'll be talking to business groups also, to get them to realize that, in a postindustrial society, it's really the management of people, not so much the management of machinery and materials as you have in the industrial era, and those are the kinds of skills that women have traditionally been thought to be very good at. It's a matter of making male managers in business realize that the times and the talents should be brought together—that women should have unusual opportunities right now to advance.

J. M.: Assuming the GOP wants to go after the women's vote, what will be the strategy?

E. D.: To me it's not so much a strategy as it is a continuing desire to address the real needs of women. That's the way I'm proceeding on it because that's what I heard the President tell me to do. And I know that he wants to bring more women in at all levels of government, so I think it's going to be a continuing emphasis on women's concerns. But I do think we have to do a better job of talking about what we have done. The campaign will present an opportunity to be out there on the platform talking about a lot of these issues.

J. M.: Some progressive Republicans have put together an interesting scenario in which Vice-President George Bush bows out around May or June. And you bow in.

E. D.: (Laughter) No, I think right now I'm absolutely confident the President's going to run and George Bush is going to be running with him. It's a winning ticket. So why change a winning ticket?

29

FOREIGN POLICY

Foreign policy seems a man's domain. Militarily, it evokes soldiers; economically, the businessman; diplomatically, the striped-pants ambassador. But here as elsewhere, important women leaders are emerging, not only as quiet executors of policies male leaders issue, but also as major contributors to foreign policy in their own right.

Two contemporary examples are Patricia Derian and Jeane Kirkpatrick—two individuals who could hardly disagree more. Their controversy has been public and vigorous. And it has clearly played a significant part in shaping changes in United States foreign policy on a question of life-and-death significance for thousands: human rights. Both would claim to be compassionate yet realistic. Their strong differences attest to the variety behind the label *woman*.

Derian, a longtime activist in civil- and human-rights work and in the Democratic party, became assistant secretary of state for human rights and humanitarian affairs in the Carter administration. Kirkpatrick, a professor of government at Georgetown University and resident scholar at Washington's American Enterprise Institute, became ambassador to the United Nations in the Reagan administration.

In the selections below, Derian looks back at the Carter human-rights effort, Kirkpatrick analyzes what she sees as Carter's failure and the different approach Reagan should take, and Derian responds in a speech at American University.

Patricia Derian Versus Jeane Kirkpatrick on Human Rights in Latin America

PATRICIA DERIAN ON HUMAN RIGHTS IN LATIN AMERICA

by Patricia Derian

I am glad that you have chosen to discuss human rights in the Latin American context. It is both relevant and important. A popular theme we often hear in these first few months of 1980 is how some objective, product, or issue relates to the decade of the 1980s. This theme is particularly appropriate to describe concern for human rights, which I can firmly state has come of age and will continue to be a priority issue as we move through this period, not only in our country but worldwide.

Concern for the individual's right to enjoy civil, political, and economic freedoms are fundamental principles which we hold in common with many governments in this hemisphere. More importantly, they are principles with which the peoples of the Americas identify.

President Carter reaffirmed this government's deep commitment to human rights and to meeting human needs in his State of the Union address on January 23 when he stated that it ". . . is in our own national interest as well as part of our own national character." Secretary Vance, in a statement to the Senate Committee on Foreign Relations on March 27, noted that ". . . we pursue our human rights objectives not only because they are right but because we have a stake in the stability that comes when people can express their hopes and find their futures freely. Our ideals and our interests coincide."

Is it compatible with national security interests? Of course. It has always been understood that human rights policy operates in tandem with our pursuit of other interests. Secretary Vance addressed this point in the same statement mentioned earlier. He said that:

> We must constantly weigh how best to encourage the advancement of human rights while maintaining our ability to conduct essential business with governments—even unpopular ones—in countries where we have important security interests.
>
> But the fact remains that over the longer term, our pursuit of human rights is not only generally compatible with our national security, it contributes to that security.

There is much evidence to support the emergence of human rights as a major priority in our hemisphere. We have seen substantial progress regarding both personal and political rights, significant actions by both governments and international bodies, and more precise attention given to serious problems which still need alleviating.

In 1979 Ecuador and Bolivia installed civilian governments; Bolivia averted renewed efforts to install a military govern-

From Patricia M. Derian, "Review of Human Rights in Latin America," *Department of State Bulletin*, 80 (October 1980), pp. 51–55. Address prepared for presentation to the Center for Inter-American Relations in New York on April 24, 1980.

ment. Peru adopted a new Constitution. Brazil maintained a steady course of liberalization. There was a decline in violations of the integrity of the person in countries where abuses have been most serious. Fewer disappearances occurred in Argentina. Cases of prolonged arbitrary detention were down in Chile. The Uruguayan Armed Forces adopted apparently effective internal measures to stop the use of torture. Cuba released about 3,900 political prisoners. But, as we have recently seen in the sad situation of thousands of Cubans seeking asylum in the Peruvian Embassy in Havana, people are still voting with their feet to flee from the Cuban model of life. Honduras has just held its first national election in almost a decade.

The American Convention on Human Rights, which entered into force in 1978, established an Inter-American Court on Human Rights. The Court has begun to meet at its permanent site in San Jose, Costa Rica. The American convention strengthened the role of the Inter-American Human Rights Commission (IAHRC), and the General Assembly of the Organization of American States (OAS) in its October 1979 meeting approved new statutes for both bodies. The IAHRC has undertaken five on-site investigations during the past 2 years, including a landmark visit to Argentina in 1979. The IAHRC has just released a report on human rights in Argentina, based, in part, on its on-site observations. The report confirms the findings of many human rights organizations that systematic and massive violations of human rights have occurred during the past 5 years, notes that the scale of abuses has declined in recent months, and makes numerous constructive recommendations to the Argentine Government for needed improvements.

The October 1979 OAS General Assembly devoted much attention to human rights issues. It approved resolutions urging reforms in Paraguay, Uruguay, and Chile and emphasized the need to deal with the problem of disappearances.

The U.N. Human Rights Commission (UNHRC), which met for 6 weeks in Geneva in February and March, achieved very positive results, which we hope will have lasting beneficial impact. The United States strongly supported efforts to insure that the United Nations acts evenhandedly in applying human rights criteria to all countries. Among the actions taken by the UNHRC were the following:

- Condemned the U.S.S.R. invasion of Afghanistan;
- Condemned the Vietnamese invasion of Kampuchea as well as human rights abuses within that country;
- Extensively debated the suppression of dissidents in the Soviet Union and maintained the Andrei Sakharov case on the agenda as a priority item;
- Took public action on South Africa, Equatorial Guinea, Malawi, Israeli-occupied territories, Chile, and Guatemala; and
- Discussed in detail specific abuses in 11 countries in Africa, Asia, and Latin America in closed sessions.

Perhaps the most far-reaching achievement of the UNHRC was the establishment of a five-member working group to investigate reports of disappearances. The group, composed of independent experts acting in their own capacity, will deal worldwide with the thousands of cases of missing persons. The group is empowered to seek and receive information from governments, intergovernmental organizations, humanitarian organizations, and other reliable sources. This is the first time in its history that the UNHRC has adopted a procedure for possible immediate action on human rights cases. The need for this type of action is particularly appropriate to the situation in Argentina, where thousands of persons have been abducted by security forces in recent years.

There should be little doubt that concern for human rights has now become universal. Our representative to the U.N. Human Rights Commission, Jerry Shestack, wrote eloquently that "human rights is far from a passing fad; on the contrary it has an increasingly wide appeal." He reported that the significance of the recent overthrow of repressive rulers in Uganda, the former Central African Empire, Equatorial Guinea, Nicaragua, and, I might add, El Salvador was not lost on the nations represented at the commission.

The positive accomplishments are encouraging. Government officials and oppositionists alike in this hemisphere have acknowledged that the steady application of U.S. human rights policies has been an important stimulant in maintaining an improving trend. This is good news, but we cannot take credit; no improvement in human rights can be sustained unless it emanates from the will of the people and their governments. Our objective is to encourage governments to take necessary action to fulfill their obligation to their own people, to their international commitments, for the sake of improving their relations with us and achieving respect in the international community.

It is our hope that the gathering momentum of human rights awareness can be brought to bear on the many serious problems that remain. In this connection I will focus my remarks on Argentina, Chile, Guatemala, Nicaragua, Panama, Grenada, Haiti, Cuba, and El Salvador.

Argentina

A distinguished recent resident of Argentina has said:

> . . . it is up to the Argentine military government to prove that it does, as it claims, wish to return to a "stable pluralistic democracy" by ending all violations of law and by accounting for those who have disappeared. The military has long argued that their aims are respectable and that the methods employed were forced upon them by a ruthless enemy. . . . It is time that the so-called moderates in the Argentine Government showed the resolution needed to account for the past and to ensure that the atrocities committed by extremists on the left and the right are not allowed to happen again. . . . It is important to get the truth out into the open and demand that if the Argentine Government wishes to have a respectable place in the estimation of the democratic world, it must act swiftly and promptly to return to the rule of law.

The message that we are getting from groups in Argentina is an expression of hope that the U.S. Government and private sectors will not ease the human rights pressure on the Argentine Government because of geopolitical contingencies. I can tell you today that we have not. One of the objectives of recent visits by U.S. Ambassador at Large Gerard Smith and Gen. Andrew Goodpaster to Argentina was to exchange views and achieve a better understanding of our respective positions regarding human rights.

Some areas of our continuing concern are the following.

Disappearances. As we noted in our report to Congress, the most carefully recorded and documented list of unexplained disappearances in Argentina, compiled by the Permanent Assembly for Human Rights in Buenos Aires, contains about 6,500 cases for the period 1976–79. Some estimates run considerably higher. Our records contain 44 cases of disappearances for 1979, compared to over 500 in 1978 and many more in earlier years. We are aware of three cases thus far in 1980. The Argentine Government has taken no meaningful action to provide to families or other interested parties an accounting of the many thousands who have disappeared during the past 4 years.

Executive Detention Prisoners. There are approximately 1,300 persons being held in this category. Most have never been charged with any offense. I should note, however, that there has been a gradual reduction in the number of executive prisoners. There has also been some improvement in prison conditions.

Torture. There are credible allegations that torture of new detainees during interrogation continues. We are aware of no measures taken by authorities to halt this practice.

"Right of Option" Program. Although the Government of Argentina reactivated a constitutional provision permitting executive detainees to choose self-exile, and the U.S. Government established a special parole program to accept qualified applicants, almost two-thirds of our requests for interviews have been denied and the Government of Argentina has refused a large number of option requests submitted by detainees to whom we have issued certificates of eligibility.

With respect to bilateral relations, U.S. military assistance and sales remain prohibited by law. At the multinational level, since January 1977 and through January 31, 1980, the U.S. Government has opposed 18 and supported 2 out of a total of 20 loan applications submitted by Argentina to the International Development Bank. At the same time, since September 1978, we have been approving financing of U.S. exports to Argentina through the Export-Import Bank in large amounts.

Chile

Serious problems remain although there have been some improvements in the human rights situation in Chile during the past 2 years. Our bilateral relations continue to be affected by that government's disposition of the Orlando Letelier and Ronni Moffitt assassination case. The Chilean Government has failed to fully investigate or prosecute three former security officers indicted in the United States for complicity in the 1976 assassinations.

In October 1979, the Chilean Supreme Court denied a U.S. Government extradition request for the three officers. A domestic investigation of the same case in Chile has dragged on for nearly 2 years without a full and diligent effort. Following the October 1979 decision of the Chilean Supreme Court, President Carter took a number of actions:

- Reduced the size of our mission in Santiago;
- Terminated the foreign military sales (FMS) pipeline of military equipment;
- Removed the U.S. military group;
- Suspended all Eximbank financing in Chile; and
- Terminated new Overseas Private Investment Corporation (OPIC) business.

Despite the Letelier case, there are some encouraging signs in Chile. There have been no disappearances since 1977. There is relative freedom to speak out and to criticize the government. Although institutionalized or legal guarantees against violations of the integrity of the person are weak, there are some indications that the courts and the press are taking more interest in defending human rights.

We continue to have concern in some areas.

- The IAHRC reported in October 1979 that the rights to a fair trial and to due process were subject to significant limitations, principally because of the active role of the military courts in judicial proceedings and the reluctance of the civil courts actively to investigate human rights violations.
- While fewer than in past years, in 1979 there were one dozen allegations of torture by credible sources.
- Political parties remain formally dissolved.
- While having pledged eventual restoration of an elected government, the Pinochet regime has not set a timetable for relinquishing control.

- On March 7, 1980, the Chilean Supreme Court upheld internal banishment for those who participated in the proscribed women's day activities. A total of 17 have been affected.
- The Chilean courts continue to side with the government in prohibiting the return of exiles the Government of Chile doesn't want.

The status of bilateral relations, in addition to the actions taken in the Letelier case, is that all new military assistance and sales remain terminated since 1976. New economic development assistance is also terminated. In the multinational development banks, the U.S. Government has voted "no" on all loans since 1977. At the United Nations and the OAS, we have supported resolutions criticizing Chilean human rights abuses and those establishing international procedures to work toward improvements. In recent U.N. meetings on this subject, we have issued statements taking note of the improvements mentioned earlier.

Guatemala

Guatemala is a country where human rights are in jeopardy and where the government is doing little or nothing to bring violence under control. Many human rights groups have focused concern on the level of violence. Amnesty International began a worldwide campaign in September 1979 and estimated in December that more than 2,000 persons had been killed for political reasons in the last 18 months. The International Commission of Jurists in a September 1979 report stated that the Lucas government had "embarked on a systematic campaign to suppress dissent which has, in fact, generated a widespread climate of fear, demoralization, and the growth of clandestine opposition."

Numerous other groups have spoken out against the violence, and two international unions have organized boycotts to protest specific violations. Our own estimation of political and death squad murders for 1979 is between 800 and 900. Since our report was written, violence has increased both from the right and left. Perhaps the most graphic incident was the burning of the Spanish Embassy, when government security forces broke into it in an attempt to dislodge a group of occupiers. Thirty-nine persons, the majority of whom were Guatemalan *campesinos*, died in the fire. The Spanish Embassy broke diplomatic relations as a result, and the U.S. Government expressed shock and called it deplorable because it could have been avoided.

The Guatemalan Government has invited the IAHRC to make an inspection visit, which should take place later this year. The UNHRC, in a resolution approved March 11, 1980, concerning the assassination of Dr. Alberto Fuentes Mohr, expressed profound concern at the situation of human rights and fundamental freedoms in Guatemala.

In our bilateral relations, Guatemala has not received security assistance since FY 1978. We have continued to give economic development assistance for projects which meet basic human needs criteria. In the multinational development banks, the United States abstained on a tourism and industrial development loan in 1979, the only application to be considered.

We recognize the instability of Central America and the threat of terrorism which exists. Nevertheless, ways must be found to strengthen the democratic processes; vital reforms are essential and acknowledged to be necessary by influential sectors of the Guatemalan society. Violence must be investigated and the instigators brought under control in order to avoid a serious radicalization of that country.

Nicaragua

There can be no doubt that the overthrow of the Somoza government in July 1979 reflected the will of the majority of the people of Nicaragua. The victory of the Sandinista forces ended a repressive family dynasty of more than 40 years' duration. The civil war that resulted in the violent change of government cost an estimated 30,000–50,000 lives and left the country in economic shambles. Nine months after the event, there is still little discernible evidence of significant economic recovery. Another legacy of the war was over 7,500 political prisoners held by the Sandinistas for association with the former Somoza National Guard or for some other relationship with that government.

The U.S. Government is making a sincere effort to have good relations and assist the revolutionary government. We worked hard to obtain a $75 million supplemental appropriation from the Congress to assist the economic recovery efforts.

The Nicaraguan revolution did not, however, bring an end to human rights concerns. A number of summary executions have occurred. Allegations of torture continue, particularly with respect to political prisoners. The Nicaraguan Permanent Commission on Human Rights, a private organization which has courageously documented abuses both under this government and under Somoza, on March 27 presented a specific case of torture to the Nicaraguan Supreme Court. Other disturbing developments include efforts to intimidate the free press, the resignations this week of the two prominent moderate members of the ruling junta and the moderate Central Bank president, the slow pace of the special tribunals conducting the trials of the political prisoners, and concern that proper judicial safeguards are not being applied. This latter concern motivated a mission of the International Commission of Jurists to visit Nicaragua to observe the trial process.

These and other developments portend a consolidation of control by the Sandinistas and lead to serious speculation about the future of pluralism in that society. Thus, we believe the scheduled visit of the IAHRC to Nicaragua this summer, at the invitation of that government, is of particular importance, and we look forward to its findings.

Panama

Panama is another country in the hemisphere where important segments of the public are not satisfied with the pace of the transition to free elections. In September 1979, there was a major teachers strike dedicated to the repeal of a controversial educational reform plan. On October 9 there was an extraordinary series of protest marches throughout Panama wherein the teachers attracted widespread support for their opposition to the reform plan.

Within human rights and opposition circles in the country and elsewhere, there is criticism of the lack of independent judicial and legislative branches of government, certain penal and judicial practices, such as interrogation techniques, the "night courts," limitations on freedom of expression, and restrictions on political party formation.

Our annual report commented on the lack of freedom of expression, noting that the Panama Government's point of view dominates the media. It cited a law implemented in 1979, requiring the licensing of journalists, which was subject to criticism by many newsmen as a threat to freedom of expression and as a guarantee of self-censorship. This concern was well founded. On March 3, 1980, the licenses of four radio commentators were canceled. They were charged with distorting facts with the intention of disrupting public order and jeopardizing security and attacking the reputation of President Royo.

Opposition and human rights groups in Panama have called these sanctions a violation of human rights. I would mention that one of those sanctioned, Julio Ortega, is currently in the United States on a travel grant under our USICA [U.S. International Communication Agency] education and cultural exchange program. I understand that a suit has been filed with Panamanian courts on behalf of all four commentators asking for immediate suspension of the cancellation orders.

Grenada

The government of Prime Minister Gairy was overthrown by a coup d'etat in March 1979 by leaders of a former opposition party, the New JEWEL Movement. Our annual report documents human rights violations by the former Gairy government. There were also charges of corruption, rigging of the 1976 elections, and intimidation of the opposition by violent means. The new People's Revolutionary Government, which came into being, had the advantage of replacing a dictatorial and unpopular regime. It has maintained a reputation for honesty and begun some necessary economic programs, particularly in the agricultural field.

However, the revolutionary nature of the coup has led to the replacement of one set of human rights concerns by others equally serious. The constitution has been suspended, opponents have been detained indefinitely and without legal representation, freedom of assembly and private enterprise have been limited or abridged, and the independent press has been abolished. The Church has been a target for pressure. A publication called the *Catholic Focus* published only its initial issue before it was suspended, allegedly at the instigation of the new government. On a positive note, some 13 prisoners were released on March 25. We believe there are in excess of 50 persons still detained.

Grenada continues to send mixed signals in the international arena concerning its human rights stance. It has participated actively in human rights issues in the OAS forum but voted against the U.N. General Assembly resolution condemning Soviet aggression in Afghanistan.

Haiti

Haiti continues to be the poorest country in the Western Hemisphere, and it continues to function under authoritarian rule. In 1979 the first independent political parties in recent history emerged, but negative developments outweighed the positive. A restrictive new press law was enacted; the political opposition was further intimidated by the militia and the executive. Objective observers characterized our report on the 1979 human rights situation in Haiti as accurate representation.

Last week the IAHRC issued a report on its August 1978 inspection visit to Haiti. Prior to its release, the report was updated to December 1979. The report concluded, among other things, that the right to life was violated, particularly in the mid-1970s, by means of summary executions, prison terms, and lack of medical care, but there has been improvement in this regard since. However, numerous persons continue to be detained without benefit of legal procedure or access to an attorney.

Freedom of inquiry, speech, and dissemination of thought do not exist, though freedom of religion does. Freedom of association is extremely limited. There have been violations of the right to residence, movement, and nationality. Numerous civil and political rights and certain prerogatives of the judiciary have been suspended. The OAS report makes a series of specific recommendations for amelioration of its findings and makes a special appeal to international organizations to give Haiti aid to improve living conditions in order that the country can establish respect for the rights currently being violated. In one development, we understand that the Haitian Government has modified the 1979 press law in response to criticism, but details are lacking.

The case of Haitian "boat people" is a topic of serious concern. The plight of these people involves disputed matters of human rights as well as issues of refugee policy. Since 1972 thousands have arrived illegally in Florida, in small boats and, therefore, at considerable risk. Many request political asylum. There are over 9,000 such cases pending in Florida. The U.S. Government is committed to the careful case-by-case evaluation of all claims for political asylum, according to our law which relates to the U.N. Protocol on Refugees. Last week President-for-Life Duvalier issued a statement on the "boat people," reiterating that Haitians deported from Florida "have not been and will not be harassed."

The Administration is urgently reassessing the situation of the Haitian "boat people." Meanwhile, none are being deported.

Cuba

Returning to the question of Cuba, I noted earlier that 3,900 prisoners had been released in 1979. According to Huber Matos, the prominent political prisoner released last October, there are about 1,100 still being held. We do not know if this number has been increased in the last 2 weeks. This situation is now complicated by the immediate problem of the 10,000 Cubans who sought refuge in the Peruvian Embassy in Havana. The Cuban Government does not permit free emigration and arbitrarily determines who may leave the country through issuance of exit permits. It has, furthermore, not held to its earlier agreement to permit those who were in the Peruvian Embassy to proceed to any country willing to receive them.

We are lending our efforts to break the impasse by cooperating with governments in this hemisphere and elsewhere to facilitate their departure. The United States has agreed to take 3,500 who meet our immigration, refugee, or asylum criteria. We believe that the boat owners and captains from the country who are taking people out of Cuba and trying to land them in the United States are playing into the hands of the Cuban authorities.

El Salvador

Those who subscribe to the domino theory in Central America view what is happening in El Salvador as the next target of international marxism after Nicaragua. Those who study El Salvador know that the problem is home grown and has been building to the present crisis level for many years. Solutions to the problems of that beleaguered country are not handy, and the current U.S. Government policy is highly controversial, particularly with U.S. religious groups. What is incontrovertible is that urgent reforms are absolutely essential to the survival of the revolutionary junta now governing the country.

In early March 1980, the Salvadoran Government bit the bullet and instituted both agrarian and financial reforms, after the original junta, installed by the military coup in October 1979, failed to act before it expired at the beginning of 1980. The junta's reforms have been violently opposed by both extremes of the right and the left. It is clear that reforms must be made. The agrarian reform, if fully implemented, could be one of the most profound and far-reaching social experiments in the modern history of Central America.

I know that the U.S. Government's decision to provide security assistance to the junta is controversial. The volume of mail on this subject received in Washington in recent weeks is near the level of correspondence regarding the Iranian question. One widespread misconception that I wish to clarify is that this security assistance consists of arms; it does not. It is restricted to credits to enable the Salvadoran Armed Forces to purchase communications and transportation equipment to improve its ability to control the violence. We remain deeply concerned at the level of violence now prevalent in El Salvador, some of it the responsibility of undisciplined security forces in the countryside. Most of it, we believe, comes from rightist groups opposed to all reforms who are engaging in indiscriminate assassinations.

Before his tragic death, Archbishop Oscar Romero was given written assurance by Secretary Vance that "the advancement of human rights . . . underlies every aspect of U.S. policy toward El Salvador."

There is much that has been written about the brutal assassination of Archbishop Romero, and much that I could say. Perhaps I should merely conclude my remarks by saying that his death is a noble symbol of the human rights struggle we all are facing and that many have given their lives defending.

I returned to the United States from a month-long visit to the Near East and South Asia the day before the beautiful Requiem Mass given for Archbishop Romero at Georgetown University on March 29. I would like to quote from the eulogy given by Reverend Timothy Healy, which I profoundly believe best expresses what human rights is all about.

His message was the simplest teaching of modern theology and he couched it in the words of the Second Vatican Council. Again and again he raised his voice, in his Cathedral, in his radio station (until it was bombed out from under him), and with everyone he met, to remind his countrymen, oppressors and oppressed, the hunters and the hunted, that no man can reach his full religious being unless he enjoys some dignity, some freedom, some self-determination in his daily life; unless he has some hope of something better for his children.

JEANE KIRKPATRICK ON HUMAN RIGHTS IN LATIN AMERICA

by Jeane Kirkpatrick

While American attention in the past year has been focused on other matters, developments of great potential importance in Central America and the Caribbean have passed almost unnoticed. The deterioration of the U.S. position in the hemisphere has already created serious vulnerabilities where none previously existed, and threatens now to confront this country with the unprecedented need to defend itself against a ring of Soviet bases on and around our southern and eastern borders.

In the past four years, the Soviet Union has become a major military power within the Western hemisphere. In Cuba, the Soviets have full access to the naval facilities at Cienfuegos, nuclear submarines, airstrips that can accommodate Backfire bombers. From these, Soviet naval reconnaissance planes have on several occasions flown missions off the east coast of North America. They also have electronic-surveillance facilities that monitor American telephone and cable traffic and a network of intelligence activities under direct Soviet control. And, of course, a Soviet combat brigade.

During the same four-year period the Soviets have continued to finance, train, and staff a Cuban military establishment which has by now become a significant instrument of Soviet expansion in Africa, the Middle East, and South Asia as well as throughout the Caribbean and Central and South America. Today Cuba possesses a small navy; a sizable number of supersonic aircraft—including Il-14's and MIG 21's and 23's—that can be quickly armed with nuclear weapons; modern transport planes capable of airlifting Cuban troops anywhere in the area; a huge army; and an estimated 144 SAM-2 anti-aircraft missile sites. The presence of more than 50,000 Cuban troops and military advisers in Af-

---

From Jeane Kirkpatrick, "U.S. Security and Latin America," *Commentary*, January 1981, pp. 29ff.

rica and the Middle East provides one measure of the size and utility of Cuba's armed forces. The Cuban role in training, supplying, and advising revolutionary groups throughout the Caribbean and Central America illustrates the hemispheric implications of this build-up.

The first fruits of these efforts are the new governments of Grenada and Nicaragua, whose commitment to Marxist-Leninist principles and solidarity with Soviet/Cuban policies led Castro to brag on returning from Managua, "Now there are three of us." There may soon be four. El Salvador, having arrived now at the edge of anarchy, is threatened by progressively well-armed guerrillas whose fanaticism and violence remind some observers of Pol Pot. Meanwhile, the terrorism relied on by contemporary Leninists (and Castroites) to create a "revolutionary situation" has reappeared in Guatemala. . . .

If commitment to "change" was the rock on which Carter's Latin American policy was built, his human-rights policy was the lever to get change started. Two aspects of the Carter approach to human rights are noteworthy. First, concern was limited to violations of human rights by governments. By definition, activities of terrorists and guerrillas could not qualify as violations of human rights, whereas a government's efforts to repress terrorism would quickly run afoul of Carter human-rights standards.

Secondly, human rights were defined not in terms of personal and legal rights—freedom from torture, arbitrary imprisonment, and arrest, as in the usage of Amnesty International and the U.S. Foreign Assistance Acts of 1961 and 1975—but in accordance with a much broader conception which included the political "rights" available only in democracies and the economic "rights" promised by socialism (shelter, food, health, education). It may be that no country in the world meets these standards; certainly no country in the Third World does. The very broadness of the definition invited an arbitrary and capricious policy of implementation. Panama, for instance, was rather mysteriously exempt from meeting the expansive criteria of the State Department's human-rights office, while at the same time the other major nations of Central America were being censored (and undermined) for violations.

Why Panama, a dictatorship with a higher per-capita income than Nicaragua, El Salvador, or Guatemala, did not qualify as a gross violator of human rights while the latter countries did; why and how an administration committed to nonintervention in the internal affairs of nations could try to replace an unacceptable government in Nicaragua with one more palatable to it; why such an administration should attempt not only to "normalize" relations with Cuba but also to destabilize the governments of El Salvador and Guatemala—to answer these questions required on the part of policy-makers an intuitive understanding of which governments were outmoded and which reflected the wave of the future. What was *not* required was an ability to distinguish between which were Communist and which non-Communist. The President and other members of his administration apparently believed with Brzezinski that in most of the world ideological thinking had already given way to pragmatism and problem-solving, and that a concern with Communist ideology was therefore just another artifact of a past epoch, "the era of the cold war."

Ignoring the role of ideology had powerful effects on the administration's perception of conflicts and on its ability to make accurate predictions. Although Fidel Castro has loudly and repeatedly proclaimed his revolutionary mission, and backed his stated intentions by training insurgents and providing weapons and advisers, Carter's Assistant Secretary for Inter-American Affairs, William Bowdler, described Cuba as "an inefficient and shabby dictatorship"—a description more appropriate to, say, Paraguay, than to an expansionist Soviet client state with troops scattered throughout the world. The refusal to take seriously, or even to take into account, the commitment of Fidel Castro or Nicaragua's Sandinista leadership to Marxist-Leninist goals and expansionist policies made it impossible to distinguish them either from traditional authoritarians or from democratic reformers, impossible to predict their likely attitudes toward the United States and the Soviet Union, impossible to understand why in their view Costa Rica and Mexico as well as Guatemala and Honduras constituted inviting targets. Ignoring the force of ideology—and its powerful contemporary embodiments—fatally distorted the Carter administration's view of politics in Central America and elsewhere.

The policies which grew out of these expectations have had a large impact on U.S. relations with most nations of South America. In Central America in particular, the direction of administration policy interacted with the presence there of weak regimes and Cuban-supported insurgents to transform the region into a battleground in an ideological war that the administration did not understand and could not acknowledge.

Except for Mexico, the nations of Central America are quite small, and, by North American standards, quite poor. There are significant social and economic differences among them. Guatemala's large traditionalist Indian population and multiple linguistic groups are unique in the region, and bring with them special problems of economic, social, and political integration. El Salvador's overcrowding places especially heavy strains on its institutions. Revenues from the Canal and the Canal Zone give Panama a higher per-capita income than any of its neighbors except Costa Rica and about twice that of the sparse, scattered people of Honduras.

Despite their differences, these countries also share a good many social and economic characteristics. All are "modernizing" nations in the sense that in each, urban, industrial, mobile, "modern" sectors coexist with traditional patterns of life. In each, a large portion of the population is still engaged in agriculture—most often employed as landless laborers on large estates and plantations that have long since made the transition to commercial agriculture. Economic growth rates in Central America have been above the Latin American average and per-capita income is high enough to rank these nations among the "middle-income" countries of the world. But in all of them wealth is heavily concentrated in a small upper class and a thin but growing middle class, and large numbers live as they have always lived—in deep poverty, ill-nourished, ill-housed, illiterate.

Things have been getting better for the people of Central America—infant mortality rates have dropped, years in school have increased—but they have been getting better slowly. It has been easier to break down the myths justifying the old distribution of values in society than to improve access to education, medical care, decent housing, good food, respect, and political power.

There are also *political* differences among the small nations of Central America. Costa Rica has managed to develop and maintain (since 1948) a genuine democracy. Honduran politics have been especially violent, while Nicaragua (under the Somozas) was the most stable political regime. But again despite differences, Guatemala, Honduras, El Salvador, Nicaragua, and Panama (like Costa Rica before 1948) share several characteristics with one another and with most of the nations of Latin America. These include a continuing disagreement about the legitimate ends and means of government, a pervasive distrust of authority, a broad ideological spectrum, a low level of participation in voluntary associations, a preference for hierarchical modes of association (church, bureaucracy, army), a history of military participation in politics, and a tradition of *personalismo*.

The boundaries between the political system, the economy, the military establishment, and the Church are often unclear and unreliable. Weak governments confront strong social groups, and no institution is able to establish its authority over the whole. Economic, ecclesiastical, and social groups influence but do not control the government; the government influences but does not control the economy, the military, the Church, and so on.

A democratic façade—elections, political parties, and fairly broad participation—is a feature of these systems. But the impact of democratic forms is modified by varying degrees of fraud, intimidation, and restrictions on who may participate. Corruption (the appropriation of public resources for private use) is endemic. Political institutions are not strong enough to channel and contain the claims of various groups to use public power to enforce preferred policies. No procedure is recognized as *the* legitimate route to power. Competition for influence proceeds by whatever means are at hand: the Church manipulates symbols of rectitude; workers resort to strikes; businessmen use bribery; political parties use campaigns and votes; politicians employ persuasion, organization, and demagoguery; military officers use force. Lack of consensus permits political competition of various kinds in various arenas, and gives the last word to those who dispose of the greatest force. That usually turns out to be the leaders of the armed forces; most rulers in the area are generals.

Violence or the threat of violence is an integral, regular, predictable part of these political systems—a fact which is obscured by our way of describing military "interventions" in Latin political systems as if the system were normally peaceable. Coups, demonstrations, political strikes, plots, and counterplots are, in fact, the norm.

Traditionally, however, actual violence has been limited by the need to draw support from diverse sectors of the society and by the fact that politics has not been viewed as involving ultimate stakes. The various competitors for power have sought control of government to increase their wealth and prestige, not for the "higher" and more dangerous purpose of restructuring society. In traditional Latin politics, competitors do not normally destroy each other. They suffer limited defeats and win limited victories. The habit of permitting opponents to survive to fight another day is reflected in the tendency of Latin regimes to instability. In such a system a government normally lasts as long as it is able to prevent a coalition from forming among its opponents. Because there is no consensus on what makes government itself legitimate, successive regimes remain vulnerable to attacks on their legitimacy. They are also especially vulnerable to attacks on public order, which tends to be tenuous and to lack a firm base in tradition, habit, and affection.

To these patterns of political interaction there has been added in recent years the unfamiliar guerrilla violence of revolutionaries linked to Cuba by ideology, training, and the need for support, and through Cuba to the Soviet Union. Such groups rely on terrorism to destroy public order, to disrupt the economy and make normal life impossible, to demoralize the police, and mortally wound the government by demonstrating its inability to protect personal security and maintain public authority. As Robert Chapman has emphasized, with the advent of terrorism as a *form* of revolution, a revolutionary situation can be created in any country whose government is weak or whose economy is vulnerable or dependent, with or without the participation of the masses.[1]

The nations of Central America (including Mexico) and the Caribbean suffer from some form of institutional weakness—because significant portions of the population have not been incorporated into the political system, and/or because political action is not fully institutionalized, and/or because the legitimacy of the government is in doubt, and/or because there is no consensus concerning legitimacy within the political elite, and/or because the economy is vulnerable to shifts in the international market, and/or because regular infusions of aid are required, and/or because rising expectations have outstripped capacities. All are vulnerable to disruption, and must rely on force to put down challenges to authority.

It is at this point that the roles of Cuba on the one hand, and the U.S. on the other hand, become crucial. Cuba stands ready to succor, bolster, train, equip, and advise revolutionaries produced within these societies and to supply weapons for a general insurgency when that is created. The U.S. is important as a source of economic aid and moral and military support. Traditionally it has also exercised a veto power over governments in the area and reinforced acceptable governments with its tacit approval. Thus, to the objective economic and political dependency of nations in the area has been added a widespread sense of psychological dependency. When aid and comfort from the U.S. in the form of money, arms, logistical support, and the services of counterinsurgency experts are no longer available, governments like those of Nicaragua, El Salvador, and Guatemala are weakened. And when it finally sinks in that the U.S. desires their elimination and prefers insurgents to incumbents, the blow to the morale and confidence of such weak traditional regimes is devastating.

The case of Nicaragua illustrates to perfection what happens when "affirmative pressures for change" on the part of the U.S. interact with Cuban-backed insurgency and a government especially vulnerable to shifts in U.S. policy.

The Nicaraguan political tradition combined participatory and autocratic elements in a characteristic Latin mix. *Personalismo*, popular sovereignty, and brute force were present in the politics of Nicaragua from its founding as a separate nation in 1938 to the Sandinista triumph in July 1979. Throughout the 19th century and the first three decades of the 20th, geographically-based political factions representing a single, small ruling class competed under a symbolic two-party system in elections in which neither contender was willing to accept an unfavorable outcome. Frequently victory was obtained by enlisting the help of foreign governments and/or financial interests.

The United States was repeatedly called on by incumbent governments for assistance in maintaining peace. In 1910 it was the Conservatives who requested financial assistance and advice, and in 1912, again at their request, the U.S. posted a 100-man legation guard to Nicaragua. From then until 1933 an American military presence was a regular feature of the Nicaraguan political system. These U.S. troops (who at their height numbered about 2,700) supervised presidential elections and organized a National Guard which was conceived as a professional national police force that would remain aloof from politics. In 1936, less than three years after American military forces had withdrawn, the leader of this "non-political army," Colonel Anastasio Somoza García, ousted the Liberal president, Juan B. Sacasa. In this manner began the more than four decades of Nicaraguan politics dominated by the Somoza family.

Somocismo was based in the first instance on the military power of the National Guard. Its durability, however, also owed much to the political skills of the successive Somozas who ruled the country and headed its armed forces. These skills were reflected in the construction of an organizational base to support their personal power, long-standing success in exploiting divisions among their opponents, and the ability to retain U.S. support. The organizational basis of the Somozas' power is the most interesting factor because, like that of Juan Perón, it was largely created rather than captured.

The Somoza organization rested on four pillars: a hierarchically structured national party forged on the base of the traditional Liberal party; an expanded bureaucracy whose members also served as party workers; a national federation of trade unions created by the Somozas; and the National Guard. The whole operated rather like an efficient urban political machine, oiled by jobs, pensions, profits, and status, and perquisites of various kinds. Most urban machines, however, do not have a private army. The loyalty of the National Guard is the most powerful testimony to the Somozas' political skill, for in Latin America armed forces are more easily won than retained. Nicaragua's National Guard remained loyal until after the last Somoza had fled.

Nicaraguan politics in the Somoza period featured limited repression and limited opposition. Criticism was permitted and, in fact, carried on day after day in the pages of *La Prensa* (whose editor was an opposition leader). Although the Somozas had large landholdings, the government enjoyed no monopoly of economic power, and made no serious effort to absorb or control the Church, education, or the culture. The government was moderately competent in encouraging economic development, moderately oppressive, and moderately corrupt. It was also an utter failure at delivering those social services American and Europeans have come since the Depression to regard as the responsibility of government.

Anastasio Somoza Debayle, a West Point graduate with an American wife and an expansive appetite for women and alcohol, had accommodated successive American administrations and received aid from successive Congresses. He had every reason to suppose that his regime would continue to enjoy U.S. favor, and no reason to suppose that his power could be brought down by the small group of Cuban-backed terrorists who periodically disturbed the peace with their violence.

Three things seem to have disturbed these calculations. One was the progressive alienation of certain members of the country's *oligarchia* and business class when, after the earthquake of 1973, *Somocistas* raked off too large a share of the international relief; a second factor was Somoza's heart attack; the third and most important factor was the election of Jimmy Carter and the adoption of an all-new Latin American policy.

At the time the Carter administration was inaugurated in January 1977, three groups of unequal strength competed for power in Nicaragua: the President and his loyal lieutenants—who enjoyed the advantages of incumbency, a degree of legitimacy, a nationwide organization, and the unwavering support of the National Guard; the legal opposition parties which had been gathered into a loose coalition headed by Joaquin Chamorro, editor of *La Prensa*; and several small revolutionary groups whose Cuban-trained leaders had finally forged a loose alliance, the FSLN (Sandinist National Liberation Front).

From the moment the FSLN adopted the tactics of a broad alliance, the offensive against Somoza was carried out on a variety of fronts. There was violence in the form of assassinations and assaults on army barracks. When the government reacted, the U.S. condemned it for violations of human rights. The legal opposition put forward demands for greater democracy which had the endorsement of the FSLN, thus making it appear that democracy was the goal of the insurgency.

Violence and counterviolence weakened the regime by demonstrating that it could not maintain order. The combination of impotence and repression in turn emboldened opponents in and out of the country, provoking more reprisals and more hostility in a vicious circle that culminated finally in the departure of Somoza and the collapse of the National Guard.

What did the Carter administration do in Nicaragua? *It brought down the Somoza regime.* The Carter administration did not "lose" Nicaragua in the sense in which it was once charged Harry Truman had "lost" China, or Eisenhower Cuba, by failing to prevent a given outcome. In the case of Nicaragua, the State Department *acted* repeatedly and at critical junctures to weaken the government of Anastasio Somoza and to strengthen his opponents.

First, it declared "open season" on the Somoza regime. When in the spring of 1977 the State Department announced that shipments of U.S. arms would be halted for human-rights violations, and followed this with announcements in June and October that economic aid would be withheld, it not only deprived the Somoza regime of needed economic and military support but served notice that the regime no longer enjoyed the approval of the United States and could no longer count on its protection. This impression was strongly reinforced when after February 1978 Jimmy Carter treated the two sides in the conflict as more or less equally legitimate contenders—offering repeatedly to help "both sides" find a "peaceful solution."

Second, the Carter administration's policies inhibited the Somoza regime in dealing with its opponents while they were weak enough to be dealt with. Fearful of U.S. reproaches and reprisals, Somoza fluctuated between repression and indulgence in his response to FSLN violence. The rules of the Carter human-rights policy made it impossible for Somoza to resist his opponents effectively. As Viron Vaky remarked about the breakdown in negotiations between Somoza and the armed opposition: ". . . when the mediation was suspended we announced that the failure of the mediation had created a situation in which it was clear violence was going to continue, that it would result in repressive measures and therefore our relationships could not continue on the same basis as in the past." When the National Palace was attacked and hostages were taken, Somoza's capitulation to FSLN demands enhanced the impression that he could not control the situation and almost certainly stimulated the spread of resistance.

Third, by its "mediation" efforts and its initiatives in the Organization of American States (OAS), the Carter administration encouraged the internationalization of the opposition. Further, it demoralized Somoza and his supporters by insisting that Somoza's continuation in power was the principal obstacle to a viable, centrist, democratic government. Finally, the State Department deprived the Somoza regime of legitimacy not only by repeated condemnations for human-rights violations but also by publishing a demand for Somoza's resignation and by negotiating with the opposition.

Without these "affirmative pressures," William Bundy concluded in *Foreign Affairs*:

> It seems a safe bet that Tacho Somoza would still be in charge in Nicaragua and his amiable brother-in-law still extending abrazzos to all and sundry in Washington as dean of the diplomatic corps.

Why did the Carter administration do these things? Because it thought the fall of Somoza would bring progress to Nicaragua. Viron Vaky put it this way:

> Nicaragua's tragedy stems from dynastic rule. Times have changed. Nicaragua has changed, but the government of Nicaragua has not.

History was against Somoza. He was an obstacle to progress. He should relinquish power to make room for "change." When he declined to do so, the Carter administration accused him of "polarizing" the situation. When the National Guard responded to FSLN violence with violence, the State Department said that the National Guard had "radicalized the opposition."

On the other hand, the fact that Cubans were supplying arms to the FSLN was not regarded as being of much importance. Brandon Grove, Jr., Deputy Assistant Secretary for Inter-American Affairs, explained to the Committee of the House (June 7, 1979):

> The flow of such supplies is a symptom of the deeper problem in Nicaragua: polarization and its attendant violence that day by day are contributing to the growing alienation of the Nicaraguan government from its people. . . .
>
> The real cause for concern today should be the breakdown . . . of trust between government and people essential for the democratic process to function.

Since the "real" problem was not Cuban arms but Somoza, obviously the U.S. should not act to reinforce the regime that had proved its political and moral failure by becoming the object of attack. Because the State Department desired not to "add to the partisan factionalism," it declined to supply arms to the regime. "The supplying of arms in a war situation we feel only adds to the suffering. We have urged others not to do that."

In the event, the Carter administration did a good deal more than "urge." In June 1979, after the U.S. and the OAS had called for Somoza's resignation, and U.S. representatives William Bowdler and Lawrence Pezzulo had met with the FSLN, the State Department undertook to apply the final squeeze to the Somoza regime—putting pressure on Israel to end arms sales, and working out an oil embargo to speed the capitulation of Somoza's forces. They were so successful that for the second time in a decade an American ally ran out of gas and ammunition while confronting an opponent well armed by the Soviet bloc.

The FSLN were not the State Department's preferred replacement for Somoza. Nevertheless, from spring 1977, when the State Department announced that it was halting a promised arms shipment to Somoza's government, through the summer of 1980, when the administration secured congressional approval of a $75-million aid package for Nicaragua, U.S. policy under Jimmy Carter was vastly more supportive of the Sandinistas than it was of the Somoza regime, despite the fact that Somoza and his government were as doggedly friendly and responsive to U.S. interests and desires as the Sandinistas have been hostile and non-responsive.

The Carter administration expected that democracy would emerge in Nicaragua. Their scenario prescribed that the winds of change should blow the outmoded dictator out of office and replace him with a popular government. Even after it had become clear that the FSLN, which was known to harbor powerful anti-democratic tendencies, was the dominant force in the new regime, U.S. spokesmen continued to speak of the events in Nicaragua as a democratic revolution. In December 1979, for example, Warren Christopher attempted to reassure doubting members of the Senate Foreign Relations Committee that "the driving consensus among Nicaraguans" was "to build a new Nicaragua through popular participation that is capable of meeting basic human needs."

The expectation that change would produce progress and that socialism equaled social justice made it difficult for Carter policy-makers to assess Nicaragua's new rulers realistically, even though grounds for concern about their intentions, already numerous before the triumph, continued to multiply in its aftermath.

Revolution begins with destruction. The first fruit of the destabilization of Somoza and the reinforcement of his opponents was a civil war in which some 40,000 Nicaraguans lost their most basic human right (life), another 100,000 were left homeless, and some $2 billion worth of destruction was wrought. Nicaragua was left in a shambles.

Where did the expectations, the hopes, the intentions of the Carter administration then lead us, and the Nicaraguans who took the consequences? Although the FSLN had solemnly committed itself to hold free elections, its leaders have shown no disposition to share the power they seized in July 1979. To the contrary, the consolidation and centralization of power have moved steadily forward. Despite the strenuous opposition of the two non-FSLN junta members, the Sandinista directorate which has effectively ruled Nicaragua since the fall of Somoza moved in the spring of 1980 to institutionalize its control of Nicaragua's Council of State by expanding and "restructuring" it to insure the Sandinistas a permanent majority. (Under the reform they would be assured of 24 of 47 seats where previously they had been entitled to only 13 of 33.)

Meanwhile, the election to which the FSLN had committed itself has been pushed further and further into a receding future, even though the new rulers, who need all the help they can get, have been under heavy pressure from the governments of Venezuela, Costa Rica, and the United States to set a date. Sandinista leaders have made no secret of their opinion that competitive elections are an unsatisfactory and unnecessary mechanism for choosing rulers. Junta members have asserted that the people spoke through the revolution—"with their blood and with the guns in their hands the people have cast their votes" (as a junta member told *The Economist*)—and that anyway, having been brainwashed by forty years of Somoza rule, they are not capable of choosing among candidates—at least not until they have been "reeducated."

In the last days of August 1980, the restructured Council of State announced that elections will not be held before 1985. And those elections, declared Humberto Ortega Saavedra (Minister of Defense), "will serve to reinforce and improve the revolution and not to give just anyone more power, which belongs to the people." Meanwhile, no "proselytizing activities" on behalf of any candidate will be permitted before candidates are officially designated by an electoral agency which itself will be created in 1984 (and violations will be punished by terms of three months to three years in jail).

Decrees accompanying these decisions have underscored the junta's distaste for criticism. Henceforth, dissemination of news concerning scarcities of food and other consumer goods is prohibited on pain of imprisonment (from two months to two years), as is "unconfirmed" information concerning armed encounters or attacks on government personnel.

These restrictions constitute one more significant step in the Sandinistas' gradual campaign to control the climate of opinion. The television and radios had already been brought under control. Among opposition newspapers, only *La Prensa* remains; it has already come under pressures more harsh than those applied to the media during the Somoza era, and its continuation as an independent critical voice is at best uncertain. The requirement that all professional journalists join a new government-sponsored union as a condition of employment represents yet another move to bring the press under control. The literacy campaign has extended the junta's reach further into the minds of Nicaragua's people as well as into the countryside. Every lesson in the literacy textbooks instructs students (and teachers) in the prescribed interpretation of Nicaragua's past, present, and future.

Parallel efforts to organize and coordinate other traditionally non-governmental associations reflect the characteristic totalitarian desire to absorb the society into the state, to transform social groups into agencies and instruments of the government. This has required taking over some existing institutions (banking, industries, television and radio, trade unions), coopting and/or intimidating others (the private sector, trade unions, the educational establishment, portions of the press), and forcibly eliminating still others—such as the National Guard, whose members have either fled into exile or remain in prison with little prospect of ever being tried, much less released.

When, in early November 1980, representatives of the private sector (COSEP) and the labor federation (CUS) withdrew from the State Council to protest the Sandinistas' ever-tightening grip on all aspects of the economy, no concessions were forthcoming. Instead, the offices of the leading opposition party, the social-democratic MND, were sacked, and an unarmed leader of the private sector, Jorge Salazar, was gunned down by Sandinista police.

Among the traditional pillars of Nicaraguan society only the Church remains relatively intact. While the presence of priests in prominent roles in the Sandinista directorate has facilitated communications between the two groups, this has not been translated into political domination of the Church hierarchy.

But the Sandinistas do not rely on control of these agencies or rules to preserve their power. To accomplish that task new institutions have been forged, the most important of which are an enormous, all-new revolutionary army whose training (military and political) and equipment have been provided by Cubans, and a new internal police force which is already more extensive and effective than Somoza's.

Other institutions developed to support the new government include the "block" committees which were found to be so useful in Cuba (and in Nazi Germany), and the revolutionary brigades initially assigned to the literacy campaign.

The most telling indicator of Sandinista intentions and commitments is their unambiguous identification of Nicaragua with the foreign policy and perspectives of the Soviet Union. The first step was somewhat tentative: Nicaragua only "abstained" on the UN resolution condemning the Soviet invasion of Afghanistan. Subsequent moves have left less room for doubt. At the Havana conference for the nonaligned nations, Nicaragua became one of the few countries in the world to recognize Kampuchea (the regime imposed by North Vietnam on Cambodia), an act which Foreign Minister Miguel d'Escoto explained as "a consequence of our revolutionary responsibility as Sandinistas to recognize the right of the peoples of Kampuchea to be free." In Pyongyang, another Sandinista leader, Tomás Borge, assured the North Koreans of Nicaraguan solidarity, and promised, "The Nicaraguan Revolution will not be content until the imperialists have been overthrown in all parts of the world."

In March 1980 the Sandinista directorate offered a public demonstration that its ties extended beyond Cuba to the Socialist Fatherland itself when four top leaders—Moises Morales Hassan, Tomás Borge, Henry Hernandez Ruiz, and Humberto Ortega Saavedra—paid an official visit to the Soviet Union. A joint comminiqué formalized the attachment of Nicaragua to Soviet global policy. In addition to signing multiple agreements concerning trade and cooperation, condemning South Africa and Chile, applauding Zimbabwe, Khomeini's Iran, and the "legitimate national rights of the Arab people of Palestine," the "two sides" strongly attacked the NATO decision to deploy medium-range nuclear missile weapons and condemned the "mounting international tension in connection with the events in Afghanistan, which has been launched by the imperialist and reactionary forces aimed at subverting the inalienable rights of the people of the Democratic Republic of Afghanistan and of other peoples . . . to follow a path of progressive transformation."

Since "Zionism's loss of a bastion in Nicaragua" (Moises Hassan), the ties with the "Palestinian people" have become not closer, but more public. The PLO and the Sandinistas have long enjoyed a relationship of mutual support, we are now told. Sandinistas trained in Palestinian camps, and participated in PLO raids; the PLO reciprocated by ferrying arms to the Sandinistas in their hour of need. Yasir Arafat received high honors when in July 1980 he opened a PLO embassy in Managua where he assured the "workers" that "the triumph of the Nicaraguans is the PLO's triumph."

"We have emerged from one dictatorship and entered another," asserted MND leader Alfonso Robelo recently. "Nicaragua has become a satellite of a satellite of the Soviet Union."

Nothing that happened in Nicaragua seemed able to dampen the Carter people's enthusiasm for "change" in Central America. In El Salvador, Guatemala, Bolivia, and wherever else the opportunity presented itself, the administration aligned the United States with the "forces of change." "The fundamental problem we share with our neighbors," Deputy Secretary of State Warren Christopher explained, "is not that of defending stability in the face of revolution. Rather, it is to build a more stable, equitable, and pluralistic order. That is the challenge of Nicaragua in the present day and that is the challenge of the whole region."

To meet the challenge the administration welcomed with enthusiasm a military coup in El Salvador which, in October 1979, overthrew President Carlos Humberto Romero, an event the State Department described as a "watershed date" on which "young officers broke with the old repressive order" and along with "progressive civilians" formed a government committed to "profound social and economic reforms, respect for human rights and democracy."

Until the violent events of November-December 1980, which also saw the suspension of U.S. aid, the Carter administration backed the new Salvadoran junta in the only way it knew how: by helping it to bring about "profound social and economic reforms." In the effort to preempt the revolution and expedite the achievements of "social justice," the administration supplied experts who have planned the most thoroughgoing land reform in the Western hemisphere. To encourage and finance these and related reforms, the U.S. embassy provided nearly $20 million in long-term loans at very low interest. Under the direction of the American Institute for Free Labor Development, an AFL-CIO-sponsored group, a plan was drafted to transfer to some 250,000 of El Salvador's 300,000 peasants ownership of the land they work.

So far, not all the land has been transferred, and titles have not been delivered for much of what has been transferred. Few of the former owners have yet received any significant compensation. In theory, the reforms will vaccinate the masses against Communism by giving them a stake in the society. In practice, as was made dramatically clear by the murder of three American nuns and a social worker in early December, continuing violence from Communists, anti-Communists, and simple criminals has brought death and destruction to El Salvador. Under the pressure of that violence, the society has begun to come apart. "There is no name for what exists in my country," commented a Salvadoran, describing the almost random murder, intimidation, and looting. But there is a name; it is anarchy.

The U.S. under Carter was more eager to impose land reform than elections in El Salvador. Although claims and counter-claims have been exchanged, there is no way of knowing whether the junta (in any of its manifestations) has enjoyed much popular support. It combines Christian Democrats, committed to finding a middle way of "true democracy" between capitalism and Communism, with representatives of various tendencies within the armed forces. It is chronically threatened with schism from within and coup from without. Though its civilian members and their State Department supporters have consistently emphasized the danger from the Right—that is, from authoritarian, intensely anti-Communist defenders of the status quo—El Salvador is more likely in the long run to fall to a coalition of revolutionaries trained, armed, and advised by Cuba and others. The cycle of escalating terror and repression is already far advanced. By failing to offer the junta the arms and advice required to turn back the well-equipped insurgency, the Carter administration undermined the junta's ability to survive and encouraged the insurgents in their conviction of ultimate victory. . . .

Because it failed to take account of basic characteristics of Latin political systems, the Carter administration underestimated the fragility of order in these societies and overestimated the ease with which authority, once undermined, can be restored. Because it regarded revolutionaries as beneficent agents of change, it mistook their goals and motives and could not grasp the problem of governments which become the object of revolutionary violence. Because it misunderstood the relations between economics and politics, it wrongly assumed (as in El Salvador) that economic reforms would necessarily and promptly produce positive political results. Because it misunderstood the relations between "social justice" and authority, it assumed that only "just" governments can survive. Finally, because it misunderstood the relations between justice and violence, the Carter administration fell (and pushed its allies) into an effort to fight howitzers with land reform and urban guerrillas with improved fertilizers.

Above all, the Carter administration failed to understand *politics*. Politics is conducted by persons who by various means, including propaganda and violence, seek to realize some vision of the public good. Those visions may be beneficent or diabolic. But they constitute the real motives of real political actors. When men are treated like "forces" (or the agents of forces), their intentions, values, and world view tend to be ignored. But in Nicaragua the intentions and ideology of the Sandinistas have *already* shaped the outcome of the revolution, as in El Salvador the intentions and ideology of the leading revolutionaries create intransigence where there might have been willingness to cooperate and compromise, nihilism where there might have been reform.

The first step in the reconstruction of U.S. policy for Latin America is intellectual. It requires thinking more realistically about the politics of Latin America, about the alternatives to existing governments, and about the amounts and kinds of aid and time that would be required to improve the lives and expand the liberties of the people of the area. The choices are frequently unattractive.

The second step toward a more adequate policy is to assess realistically the impact of various alternatives on the security of the United States and on the safety and autonomy of the other nations of the hemisphere.

The third step is to abandon the globalist approach which denies the realities of culture, character, geography, economics, and history in favor of a vague, abstract, universalism "stripped," in Edmund Burke's words, "of every relation," standing "in all the nakedness and solitude of metaphysical abstraction." What must replace it is a foreign policy that builds (again Burke) on the "concrete circumstances" which "give . . . to every political principle its distinguishing color and discriminating effect."

Once the intellectual debris has been cleared away, it should become possible to construct a Latin American policy that will protect U.S. security interests and make the actual lives of actual people in Latin America somewhat better and somewhat freer.

CRITIQUE OF REAGAN ADMINISTRATION HUMAN RIGHTS POLICY

By Patricia Derian

We are here tonight to consider the stance that the new administration suggests, and has so far demonstrated, that it will take in the world. Are we to dance with dictators again? Would it matter if we did? I believe the answer to both questions is yes.

Before discussing the current direction of American foreign policy, its tone and symbols and themes, I might take a moment to supply a frame of reference.

During the four years of the Carter administration the laws enacted by Congress in the area of foreign policy and human rights were obeyed, there was an active and vigorous policy supported by word and deed from the President down through the administration.

It was not perfect. And if the November election had gone to the Democrats, I'd probably be standing here tonight suggesting ways that the policy might be improved.

In his inaugural address, President Carter said, "Because we are free, we can never be indifferent to that fate of freedom elsewhere." A year later the Deputy Secretary of State, Warren Christopher, said, "Our strength as a nation and our magnetism to the world at large are predicated on our commitment to human rights. It is only proper that the human rights considerations so important to our national life be reflected in our international life as well. This means they must be fully integrated into our diplomacy. . . . The pursuit of this cause is not an ideological luxury cruise with no practical port of call. Our idealism and our self-interest coincide. Widening the circle of countries which share our human rights values is at the very core of our security interests. Such nations make strong allies. Their commitment to human rights gives them an inner strength and stability which causes them to stand steadfastly with us on the most difficult issues of our time."

And there you have the heart of the Carter policy; we have an active human rights policy because it is right and because it is in our interest.

It is also our obligation.

Articles 1, 55, and 56 of the UN charter signed in 1945 outline the three basic categories of rights which are fully expanded in the Universal Declaration of Human Rights (December 10, 1948). Article 56 provides: "All members pledge themselves to take joint and separate action in cooperation with the (organization/UN) for the achievement of the purposes set forth in Article 55." In addition the United States is a party to or has signed 22 treaties and agreements pertaining to international human rights. They do not define our right to pursue a human rights policy, they outline our duty. The argument that such a policy interferes in "the internal affairs"

From Patricia Derian, address at American University, 1981.

of other nations ignores international law as well as the American tradition and is without merit.

Of course, implementing the policy was difficult and, as I said earlier, [the policy was] imperfect in its execution. But what stands is sound and honorable because for the first time, in a formal structured way our human rights obligations and objectives were given consideration when decisions on American policy were taken. They did not overshadow all other interests, but they did have a voice on nearly the same par with military and commercial/economic issues.

The policy was pursued globally, largely in private diplomatic discourse as part of the official agenda. U.S. law on security and economic assistance was applied. Both allow exceptions (security in instances where the national security was involved; economic to meet the basic human needs of the poorest of the poor) and the exceptions were often exercised, but the policy was followed in the bilateral and multilateral aspects of our diplomacy. In the case of South Korea we continued to supply military men, material, and dollars to protect against North Korean invasion while we pursued a vigorous human rights dialogue. South Korea is a particularly sad situation in that for a brief interlude it seemed that a democratic government had a chance to come into being. That chance was abruptly terminated by the seizure of power by the general who is now called President Chun.

In 1977 Vice President Mondale said, "I know every American is proud that in the councils of the world today our nation stands for human dignity. We stand for human liberty, and we stand for human rights."

From Thomas Jefferson who declared the rights "unalienable" to Woodrow Wilson who said, "I would rather belong to a poor nation that was free than a rich nation that had ceased to be in love with liberty," to Franklin Roosevelt who outlined "Four Essential Human Freedoms" through our own generation, our leaders have firmly proclaimed that the rights of humankind cannot be ignored. We cannot ignore them here at home, and we cannot ignore them in our conduct of international affairs.

With that as a brief and sketchy base, let us attempt to discover the direction we're headed in the 1980's.

During his confirmation hearings (Jan. 9–15) Secretary Haig said, in answer to a question, "In general I support this provision of the Foreign Assistance Act. I do not believe we should, other than in the most exceptional circumstances, provide aid to any country which consistently and in the harshest manner violates the rights of its citizens."

In his first press conference on January 28, in answer to questions, Secretary Haig offered two curious and confusing responses in which there seems to be a blurring of the difference between human rights and terrorism.

> International terrorism will take the place of human rights [in] our concern, because it is the ultimate abuse of human rights. It is time that it be addressed with added clarity and greater effectiveness by western nations and the U.S. as well.

He was then asked how that might be accomplished and replied:

> I'm talking about . . . functional, priority areas. It's been my view that human rights is an essential and fundamental aspect of American foreign policy and domestic policy and as such when you remove it from the mainstream of fundamental policymaking and give it an extraordinary role in organizational terms you frequently result in distortions that probably put in jeopardy the well-meaning objectives you seek to achieve. So, I would like to see some organizational change in the period ahead, no de-emphasis, a change in priorities. The greatest problem to me in the human rights area today is the area of rampant international terrorism on

both sides of the Iron Curtain and as one looks at the menu [*sic*] of those who have been most disturbed by it, it's surprising that the Soviet Union itself has been victimized by it. But be that as it may, they today are involved in conscious policies and programs, if you will, which foster support and expand this activity which is hemorrhaging in many respects throughout the world today. . . . I would anticipate that each and every regional policy director in this department will have human rights high on his agenda in his across the board assimilation and assessment of what is in the vital interest of the American people and this country.

What is one to make of all of that?

In Senate testimony he affirmed his support of the Foreign Assistance Act's provision prohibiting aid to gross violators of human rights.

At month's end he says that international terrorism will take the place of human rights. Moments later he says that human rights is an essential and fundamental aspect of American foreign policy. And that is followed by a phrase which could mean that he thinks having a Human Rights Bureau and a decision making mechanism "frequently result in distortions." He wanders afield to raise the curious problem of terrorism in the Soviet Union and then caps it all by saying that he's expecting that [each regional director] will "have human rights high on his agenda in his assimilation and assessment of U.S. interests."

The best I can make of it is that he personally has a high regard for human rights and thinks it's fundamental and essential to U.S. policy but that he doesn't want to do anything to factor human rights into foreign policy and that he's going to change priorities and restructure the bureaucracy. Perhaps it's a riddle.

And since the maker of the riddle is not here to tell us the answer, it is probably reasonable to move away from those spoken words to others and to actions.

The person appointed to head the Bureau of Human Rights and Humanitarian Affairs, the person who is working in that capacity now, is on the record, in congressional testimony, favoring the repeal of foreign policy human rights legislation. This is the same legislation which Secretary Haig said that he supported, "in general."

President Reagan in an interview says he thinks South Africa is making a good faith effort to improve. There is talk that the South African Prime Minister might pay the President a state visit. The chief of military intelligence in South Africa and three of his colleagues travel to the United States on official diplomatic passports, requested by the South African foreign minister, and we are told that the matter was handled by a young foreign service officer who didn't recognize the names. And told, too, that two of the names are as common as Smith in the phone book. I don't believe it. I don't believe it in the same way I didn't believe that these high level South African intelligence officers were not received by U.S. officials. The State Department said they were not received.

Days later, the statement was corrected to say that indeed they were received by a cabinet officer, ironically our UN Ambassador, and also in a "just pals" visit, by an officer in our military intelligence. When the State Department issued the first denial, why didn't either of these people come forward at once to correct the record? It was suggested that our UN Ambassador didn't know who they were. I can assure you, the UN Ambassador and her office know who is being received. Administration officials have laid down clear markers that they will turn their backs on the international community, turn their backs on the black citizens of South Africa and try to snuggle right up to the government of apartheid if they can get away with it. As Bernard Aronson wrote, "To live in liberty and dignity without fear is not a privilege granted by an arm of the state, but a birthright from the hand of God." We've got no business supporting the arm of any state which practices and believes otherwise.

The strong man who snuffed out hope for democracy in the foreseeable future for the citizens of South Korea was warmly received and praised by our President for continuing 3000 years of democratic tradition in his country. Should we laugh or weep? If you were a South Korean and you heard the flattery and you saw the pictures of your current dictator with the President of the United States, and you can be sure that South Koreans saw and heard, if you were one of them, what is the message you got from America? What does it tell you about our fidelity to liberty, to human rights, to democracy?

When a group of right wing fascists tried to seize the government of Spain, it took the Department of State several hours to affirm that the administration supported the democratically elected government. Does this indicate that our administration wished the coup leaders success? No. It does indicate that the administration isn't clear on its support for democracy and freedom. It doesn't know what to say about them.

As General Zia of Pakistan, the reluctant military aid non-recipient, rounds up the political opposition in his country, we rush to press arms on him. I was in Pakistan about this time last year. I met a lot of people who believed that they had fought, and many had died, for freedom and justice and democracy. What they got after all was another dictator, one we rush to embrace. Let me anticipate the question. Do I think the people of Pakistan would be better off if the Soviets extended their illegal occupation to Pakistan? Of course not. But I do think that if Pakistan wants our military assistance, and our assessment is that they need it, we ought to be sure while "saving" Pakistan that we have some idea of what they're being saved for. For a continued dictatorship? Of course not. Can we, then, exact some conditions? Can we make sure that our supplies, our bullets, our tanks and missiles and airplanes aren't used to help General Zia control the citizens of Pakistan? Can't we exact some conditions that don't escalate the capacity of the government for oppression? We can and we should. I don't think we are.

We didn't in El Salvador. We're sending military supplies that the President of El Salvador kept saying he didn't need until we convinced him that he did need it. He kept proclaiming that his army was licking the guerrillas all by itself. And what are we to make of the Secretary of State's sly allusion to the possibility that the 3 nuns and the social worker murdered in that pathetic land were maybe somehow at fault? I know that the Secretary and the department claimed that his statement was misunderstood and didn't mean anything of the kind. It *doesn't* mean anything in terms of what happened or why it happened because there is not one shred of evidence that even hints at such a possibility. Then what made those words pop from the mouth of the Secretary of State of the United States of America? It read like one of those talking points government officials study and learn before they testify. It was irresponsible, recklessly and dangerously irresponsible. And a retraction later isn't likely to wash it all away.

The administration has asked the Congress to repeal legislation barring security assistance and military relations with Argentina. They say that human rights conditions are better. There are fewer disappearances, but there are disappearances. There is unwarranted detention. There is torture, there are thousands of disappeared, and there is no accounting. Argentina, our great ally and friend say the administration officials, will probably improve more if we're friendly. They've steadfastly refused to sign the nuclear non-proliferation treaty, they refused to join the grain boycott of the Soviet Union. I can't think when they've been there as great friends and allies. Not unless you count the just ended meeting of the UN Human Rights Commission. We palled with them, and with Brazil and Uruguay, to make a minority of four on the commission opposing the resolution calling on Chile to improve its human rights performance. This year we changed our vote.

The same Chile is also feeling the warm sun of the new administration. The annual South American naval exercise is going to resume with the Chilean Navy participating this year. And the ban on Export-Import Bank loans for Chile is being lifted. The ban was imposed when the Chilean Supreme Court refused to honor either of its two extradition treaties with the United States. The United States was trying to extradite men it believes participated, with Chilean government approval, in the execution of Orlando Letelier and American citizen Ronni Moffitt. The administration is considering the sale of police equipment to the People's Republic of China and Yugoslavia. Yes, they are communist governments. Yes, they are totalitarian states. But they are not the Soviet Union.

And that seems to be the one and only string in the foreign policy bow of the United States today. All issues must be played on it, even if they must be distorted for the purpose. The music sounds, the U.S. invites the wallflower dictator to the floor and the dance begins.

But to what end? Why?

Ambassador Kirkpatrick says the policy was a failure. How did it fail? It didn't solve all the human rights problems of the world in four years. That isn't failure, that's the real world we hear so much about. Dictators don't like it. That isn't failure. Who expected them to like it? She said that if you understood Central America, you'd know that it had always been a rough and tumble place; she indicated that the people wouldn't know what to do with democracy if they had it. What arrogance—is it only Americans who value freedom, who wish to live without the possibility of summary execution or torture?

And what of Costa Rica and its long experience with democracy or its relative immunity to subversion and civil war? Is there nothing to be noted as one looks at Costa Rica and its neighboring dictatorships? It is the dictator that must maintain tighter and tighter repression, not that nation of Central American democrats, the Costa Ricans. Is there nothing to be learned from that reality?

In sum then, I find the picture bleak. A simplistic American policy focused on one enemy, unable to articulate its goals beyond sabre rattling, rife with retractions and denials, laced with bizarre assertions as in the four point formulation which in point one ceded Nicaragua to Communism and was the next day denied.

I see no commitment to universal standards, to our own ideals. More than lip service is required for ideals and less than lip service is what we've seen so far.

To see the land of the free and the home of the brave deliberately turn its back on freedom and justice is a shocking thing. Consider now the plight of the dissident voice, the prisoner confined for wishing to live in another country or writing of freedom, consider the victims of torture, the victims of racism. Who will care when the most authoritative voice no longer speaks for liberty and justice? Many will care, other governments, international organizations, non-governmental organizations and millions of individuals. But it is a disgrace for the voice and actions of this nation to be stilled.

So many of the world's people believe as Archibald MacLeish wrote: "There are those who will say that the liberation of humanity, the freedom of man and mind, is nothing but a dream. They are right. It is the American dream."

Thank you.

NOTES

1. Other new participants in the traditional pattern of political competition include the Socialist International and the Catholic Left. A number of socialist leaders (Willy Brandt, Olof Palme, François Mitterrand, Michael Manley), unable to win popular support for peaceful revolution in their own countries, have grown progressively enthusiastic about revolution elsewhere and less fastidious about the company they keep and the methods utilized. As for the Catholic Left, its interest in revolution on this earth has waxed as its concern with salvation in heaven has waned. Both the Socialist International and the radical Catholics conceive themselves as specialists in political rectitude, and their participation in Central American politics has enhanced its moralistic content at the same time that Cuban/Soviet participation has enhanced its violence.

30

THE FUTURE OF AMERICAN POLITICS

Actually, various groups have run women for Vice-President and even President in the past. But none of them had a real chance to win. Geraldine Ferraro was different. As the Democratic Party's nominee for Vice-President in 1984, she might well have wound up a winner and, given the historical odds of succession, she might well have progressed to the Presidency itself.

Ferraro lost, but in the running she demonstrated that a woman can get herself taken very seriously at the highest level of American politics. Her campaign had its ups and downs, but she set a precedent in insisting on addressing hard issues directly and forcefully—a mode of campaigning many had thought had gone out of style. Along the way, she was subjected to attentions no other major candidate had encountered.

Ferraro's candidacy affirms once again that American democracy is, at its foundation, a political culture. That is, government as an instrument for securing the rights to life, liberty, and the pursuit of happiness will work only if we the people want it to and are willing to make it happen.

Our history clearly shows that laws and systems and structures of government can be crucial to the operation of democracy, for they set the channels for political action. It was a political fool who said, "For forms of government, let fools contest; that which is best administered is best." Forms count. Ask the outsider. Ask the insider. Forms shape politics, which shapes life.

But it is culture that fires politics. The spirit of a people, in a given time and place, enlivens and directs the machinery of government. In a government by consent of the governed, what the people find self-evident—their bedrock political beliefs—will eventually rule, however temporarily blocked or distorted. In the end, ideas rule the world. Wrong ideas in a democracy can rule with great cruelty and injustice; right ideas, ideas that bridge old divisions with new understandings of common humanity, have healed and will again heal and advance the democratic enterprise.

In the years to come, should we survive them, women and men in the American culture will struggle in the political arena. The immediate stakes will be laws and systems and structures. But if that struggle is to end, not in victory for one side and defeat of the other, but in a new birth of freedom for both, people need to change their minds. Men do. Women also. Let that bridging begin—as it has for noble and peasant, free and slave, rich and poor, black and white, North and South, faithful and secular—and there will be no stopping it short of genuine equality.

In the final essay, we confront a baseline belief about politics: that it belongs to men because it belongs to aggression. By outlining the logic and evidence for that deduction, Gloria Steinem once again takes up the cause.

Thus, from the courage of Anne Hutchinson to the insight of Gloria Steinem, the voices of successive futures call the present to the march. The goal is nothing less than the fulfillment of democracy itself. The achievement is in the hands of each new generation of inheritors.

A Woman Runs for Vice-President

by Gloria Steinem

Monday

It's 6:45 on a warm, fall morning, and I am waiting with two reporters for the rented jet that will carry Geraldine Ferraro, her traveling staff, and the inevitable press corps from a small New York airport to campaign stops in Ohio and North Carolina. For me, it is a sense memory of all my trips as a reporter on Presidential races in the late '60s and '70s.

But this is different.

A first sign of change comes from these two reporters' questions about the politics of women's groups and their efforts to register voters. A second comes when one confesses that he had thought George McGovern might win in 1972.

I try to remember male journalists on past Presidential planes who showed even a passing interest in women's votes, or who cheerfully admitted they had been wrong. I can't. All I can conjure up are memories of guys swapping stories about how right they had been in some risky prediction, or how clear it was that women would vote for the most sexually attractive male. Of course, those same journalists are now national experts, too important to travel the campaign trail. But perhaps there is a new wave of male pundits coming up.

Once on the plane, the visual change is enormous. At least a third of the press corps are women. Not all the faces, male and female, are white. There are women producers representing all three major networks, two have women as on-camera correspondents, and ABC has a black camerawoman. Though most of the two dozen or so "pencil press" are white men, there are two black women representing major newspapers. There is also one black cameraman from CBS, who, as a member of that network's "combat crew," a television team often reserved for Beirut and other high-risk assignments, had covered the primary campaign of Jesse Jackson. Now he is no longer wearing a bulletproof vest. Among those who send death threats, a "first" like Ferraro is still not as threatening as the first black man believed to hold real, electoral power.

Nonetheless, as a result of the 1968 assassination of Robert Kennedy, the Secret Service provides protection to Presidential and Vice Presidential candidates from the primaries onward. A handful of Secret Service men are conspicuous in this crowd finding seats on the plane. If two-way radios plugged in their ears aren't enough, their jackets occasionally flap open to reveal guns. There's even one Secret Service woman, "in case the candidate has to go to the ladies' room," a woman reporter says sardonically. Since 1971 when women's pressure for jobs combined with the possibility of women important enough to protect, the Secret Service has acquired about 80 women among its force of 1,800 or so. The number is a reminder of both the slowness of equality and its ripple effect.

On this plane, one female Secret Service agent is a tall, ample, young woman in a blazer. When she takes her jacket off, her holster straps over her white, schoolgirl blouse look oddly like a baby carrier from the back. Irrational or not, I find myself feeling more comfortable with this armed

From Gloria Steinem, "Election Roundup," *Ms*., December 1984, pp. 53ff.

woman than I do with her short-haired, burly male colleague. At least she won't have masculinity to prove.

There are a cluster of accomplished women on this plane: Ellen Goodman, the Pulitzer-prize winning columnist; Lynn Sherr, correspondent for ABC-TV; Madeleine Albright, a Georgetown University professor who was Mondale's foreign policy adviser and is now Ferraro's; Barbara Roberts Mason, a black educator who is also a senior adviser; Patricia O'Brien, correspondent for the Knight-Ridder Newspapers chain; Maureen Dowd of the New York *Times*; Marilyn Milloy, a *Newsday* reporter who covered the Jackson campaign; and Marlene Cimons, a Washington correspondent for the Los Angeles *Times*. There would be fewer women journalists, well-known or otherwise, if this were a Presidential plane and thus more important (I'm told the mix on Vice President George Bush's plane is about the same), but Ellen Goodman and others who can influence their own assignments are here out of choice—and that is new. Just a few years ago, a woman's journalistic success was measured by writing about (and exactly like) important men.

"Finally," explains Marlene Cimons, "women's issues aren't only a sidebar. They can be the main event." As *Time* writer Jane O'Reilly noted just after Ferraro's nomination: "The same guys who breezed past a bunch of women colleagues without a word yesterday are now slowing down. You can practically see them thinking: 'Maybe something important is going on.' "

Right now, Ferraro's Kennedyesque mane of hair is visible above her seat toward the front of the plane, nodding animatedly beside a reporter. Unlike most campaign planes, this one has no separation from first class. Her dozen or so staff people wander the aisles giving briefings, answering questions, or ushering a reporter up for a short but much-coveted interview. Ferraro herself often holds the tape recorder that helps reporters to capture her fast, New York-accented speech.

We get off the plane in Akron—candidate and staff by the front door and into a waiting crowd, press by the back door and into buses—to discover that it's raining. The planned outdoor rally at a community economic development site has had to be moved on two-hours' notice to the University of Akron.

Nonetheless, the Student Union is jammed by the time we get there: students, senior citizens, union members, and NOW women are among the identifiable groups. News spreads that the candidate's motorcade has arrived. Banners declaring "Gerry Means Jobs" and "This Land Is Your Land" bob excitedly. Right-to-life signs denouncing Ferraro as a murderer remain ominously still in the back. I wonder if this meeting will be disrupted by antiabortion, pro-Reagan hecklers as so many Ferraro rallies have been.

"I'm betting against it," says a reporter who has covered Ferraro's campaign from the beginning. "Ever since NBC ran a story connecting the Reagan campaign to the demonstrators in California, they've cooled down. For my money, nothing is better evidence that they're centrally directed."

The crowd chants "*GerrEE, GerrEE*." She enters with John Seiberling, the local Democratic Congressman, and Dagmar Celeste, the feminist activist. She is also the wife of Ohio governor Richard Celeste whose election was largely a tribute to women's votes.

Seiberling introduces Ferraro enthusiastically as "a woman, but one of intellect. . . ." Would he say "a black, but one of intellect"? "a Jew, but one of generosity"? Clearly, we're not at the same consciousness, but just as clearly, Seiberling is full of goodwill. Ferraro congratulates the crowd warmly for having elected this Congressional colleague who votes for equality. After all, a verbal slip must seem like nothing compared to being quizzed by a Mississippi Democrat on whether she can bake blueberry muffins, and monitored by the press for her hairstyle and clothes.

Ferraro gets into her stump speech: a short, punchy, compassionate listing of issues that dramatizes the gulf between Mondale and Reagan. Though she has been nursing a cold for days, she visibly gains strength from the enthusiasm of the crowd:

"You deserve a leader who calls for peace talks on his first day in office, not on the first day of his reelection campaign."

"You deserve a President who takes polluters to court, not to lunch."

"When I take the oath to support the Constitution in our *second* Administration," she pauses for cheers as the audience realizes what she's saying, "I want to support a Constitution with the Equal Rights Amendment in it." The crowd is clearly hers.

I notice that even the reporters, who are not supposed to betray partisanship, are smiling and nodding as we stand together, scribbling notes. The only unsmiling island of silence is the cluster of antiabortion picketers who stand grimly toward the back of the hall. Last week in St. Paul, a network soundman was punched by an antiabortion demonstrator and returned to the plane complete with bruises. Ferraro greeted him as "my hero," and supplied an ice pack. . . .

In Greensboro, we arrive at a pleasant plaza amid government buildings. About 3,000 people are waiting to hear Ferraro and Governor Jim Hunt, whose race for the U.S. Senate against right-wing, former television personality Jesse Helms, is the hottest contest in North Carolina, and one of the most expensive and symbolically important in the country.

Hunt speaks briefly, explaining the budget deficit in a way that Ferraro—and especially Mondale, who tends to use confusing detail—would do well to imitate. He contrasts "tax-and-spend" with a Reaganesque "borrow-and-spend," and suddenly the danger of a mortgaged future—and a big chunk of the budget going for interest—becomes clear. "Now I get it," says a woman standing near me. "Reagan put the country on a credit card so he could buy more guns."

Ferraro makes a direct, emotional appeal to the audience, this time more on foreign policy. "You don't fight Communism by helping people who repress peasants and murder nuns." And later: "The Genocide Treaty is opposed by the right wing because they think it will make the United States subject to the World Court. They're right. It will. And I think every country should be accountable when it comes to genocide."

But the audience, including a substantial sprinkling of black listeners, cheers the loudest for the ERA line from the last speech and three new domestic points:

"We don't want Jerry Falwell choosing the next Justices of the Supreme Court."

"Reagan tells the unemployed to check the want ads. The problem is that the unemployed don't get the foreign press where their jobs are being advertised."

"The people of North Carolina don't want someone who smears the name of Martin Luther King," a clear reference to Jesse Helms's campaign against making King's birthday a national holiday by questioning King's loyalty. In fact, Ferraro's own mostly white Congressional district in Queens had opposed that holiday, too, but she voted for it nonetheless.

Ferraro has changed since she started out this campaign only a few weeks ago with a reluctance to speak at big rallies. The only remnant of nervousness is a tendency to look surprised when the audience cheers and she can't start the next sentence. Unlike Bella Abzug or Barbara Jordan, who know how to slow their cadence and build enthusiasm, Ferraro sometimes steps on her own applause.

Still, that surprise adds to her sincerity. As for her mental toughness and ability to think on her feet, reporters have had little doubt about that since her televised press conference to answer charges about her past campaign finances, her own tax returns, and those of her husband. Such accusations cost valuable time and tarnished her newly-minted image with some, but the crisis did allow the country to see Ferraro under pressure.

Now, the crowd almost blocks Ferraro's exit. One would never guess that the opinion polls in North Carolina favor the Reagan-Bush ticket by almost 20 percent; so big a margin that Hunt supporters fear the governor's neck-and-neck race with Helms will be lost on Reagan's coattails.

The rush also separates me from the press buses. I am rescued by a "stragglers' car" driven by an elegant, gray-haired woman, a local campaign worker. "It's lack of leadership," she says, explaining Reagan's lead. "My neighborhood isn't different from any other, but eight or nine of us have worked hard to explain the issues to young people and to show what Reagan's policies really do—so my precinct is for Mondale. Mostly you only have religious and business groups explaining."

The widow of a postal worker, she tells me that she couldn't be politically active while he was alive because "in those days, wives of government workers were supposed to be nonpartisan, too." Though she looks like a Southern club lady, she is a former dancer who misses both show business conventions in New York and her late husband's liberal heart. "If he could see me working for what we both cared about, he would be so proud of me."

In Raleigh's Fayetteville Street Mall, about 5,000 people have gathered to hear Ferraro and an array of white and black leaders that includes former governor Terry Sanford, who was one of the few pro-equality Presidential contenders in 1972, and is now president of Duke University. His introduction of Ferraro is the most forceful and well-thought-out so far (". . . captured the imagination of the nation and is capable of the toughest job in the nation . . ."), and so are the friendly signs:

"Baby women for Ferraro"
"Baptists for Gerry and Fritz"
"Ayatollah Helms"

There is also a bouncy, irresistible band. Hundreds of office workers lean out of their windows to cheer. Green-and-white NOW balloons float above the crowd. Clearly inspired by all this, Ferraro gives her best speech, attacking Jesse Helms as "extreme right-wing, out of step with the mainstream"; slamming Reagan's Latin American policy for not opposing "both Communism of the left and death squads of the right"; urging a new leadership "that doesn't tell people what you think they want to hear, but what they need to know."

As we leave, people seem especially kind to each other.

A middle-aged black woman wearing both Mondale and Jackson buttons says, "Why can't the world be like this crowd?"

Tuesday

In Detroit, off the campaign and on my way to a speech of my own, I find a very different mood. Since television news gives equal time to both sides regardless of merit—except for paid Mondale-Ferraro commercials that rarely capture real people or real emotion—there is little sense of momentum. For most people, there is no Mondale-Ferraro campaign at all.

In this city, Edith Van Horn, an active feminist from the United Auto Workers, Erma Henderson, first black woman president of the city council, and councilmember Maryann Mahaffey have formed the Detroit Women's Register and Vote Project. They've captured the imagination of both the press and women by using ironing boards as tables to register voters in shopping centers. They've also encouraged senior citizens to volunteer by turning work sessions into communal gatherings with a free lunch, and are planning to send letters home with school kids that tell parents, "Vote for me. I can't vote."

But Mayor Coleman Young, who has the major Democratic Party voter registration money, is waiting until the last week before the deadline to move into full gear, and seems too worried about Henderson as a future mayoralty rival to support an effort in which she is involved. The women are disheartened by the Mondale-Ferraro appearance in a Detroit suburb instead of the inner city where they believe the votes to be. An alarming number of UAW men are voting for Reagan in spite of their union's endorsement of Mondale-Ferraro. ("We're the victims of our own success," says Edie. "They're making money, inflation is down, and they can't see beyond that.")

In the feminist community itself, there are a few purists who want to work only for Ferraro—which would be fine, were not some of them also tearing down Mondale without explaining his differences from Reagan. Again, this is partly lack of exposure. Mondale can be inspirational, strong, funny, charismatic, and even an understanding feminist in his speeches, but it takes him 20 minutes to warm up—not fast enough for television. Some of it is also women's mistrust of an electoral system that hasn't represented us, combined with leftover, sixties' arguments that no one "inside" the system can be trusted.

I try to cheer up my friends by explaining that I haven't found this "Down with Mondale, Up with Ferraro" impossibility anywhere else. Most feminist groups regard the electoral system realistically as one way—but only one—of unifying a sex-divided world.

Yesterday, these hard-working women mounted a demonstration of 500 against Reagan's appearance at the Economic Club of Detroit, plus his use of the Presidency to personally swear in new U.S. citizens. Today, the Detroit *Free Press* reported on Reagan—but not one line about his opposition.

My own speech is in Grand Rapids, a city that feels dominated by the national headquarters of Amway, the door-to-door selling empire whose top executives often provide leadership for right-wing, pro-Reagan groups. Nonetheless, the Professional Women's Network, the sponsor of this public speech, is delighted and surprised to discover the hall is packed as only Eleanor Roosevelt and Robert Frost have filled it before; in fact, 1,000 people were unable to get tickets. As always, the majority support for equality is there. It just doesn't have the same organization as does the right wing—from chambers of commerce to the thousands of churches claimed by the Moral Majority.

For instance: many women here got in touch with the Mondale-Ferraro campaign and then waited to be given tasks. Their frequent question is, "Can Mondale beat Reagan?" Meanwhile, pro-Reagan forces have organized on their own. Their motto is, "*We* can beat Mondale." The difference is lethal.

Wednesday

In Atlanta, with the campaign again, reporters fill me in. Ferraro has impressed them by signing to a group of deaf children outside her hotel in North Carolina, and carrying on an impromptu meeting with pro-Reagan UAW workers in Illinois.

"She's more of a natural with crowds than anyone since the Kennedys," says one veteran. "Probably more so. Jack was rhetorical, Bobby was shy—but she explains issues in the way people experience them. She likes people—so they like her back."

Twenty thousand people gather downtown at a noon rally to see the candidate plus Mayor Andrew Young and Coretta Scott King. It is a bigger crowd than

Reagan drew when he appeared, but the question is: Do these crowds translate into votes? Are people coming to see a historic "first"—but still voting for a temporarily better economy and Reagan?

Signs wave in the sunshine:

"Strong Women Make America Strong"

"A Woman's Woman, a Man's Choice, the Nation's Need"

"Nuclear Freeze—the True Pro-life Movement."

Ferraro's upbeat speech has cycled in some new points:

"This Administration thinks that two thousand dollars for a coffee machine is okay, but thirty-five dollars a month for a mother trying to feed a baby is too much."

"It has a calculator where its heart should be."

"To citizens, it says, 'Sue me,' and then cuts legal services so you can't do that."

The crowd is enthusiastic. But if you don't happen to be where Ferraro is at some time in the campaign, will you know who she is?

There are audible voices telling us what Reagan's Supreme Court appointments could mean to our lives. (Indeed, even Sandra Day O'Connor would have been screened out by the antiabortion test espoused in this year's Republican platform.) There are few leaders explaining Reagan's support for the issues of the Family Protection Act, which includes a prohibition of federal funding for battered women's shelters and child-abuse centers. There are few articles about his weakening of equality guarantees in everything from military service to a college education.

In Memphis, Ferraro and Jesse Jackson are to speak on the same platform for the first time. Given the behind-the-scenes tension between some of their supporters, I feel apprehensive. For one thing, Ferraro's nomination has played into fears that black activists bring the pressure, but white women get the benefit; all the more so because Mondale interviewed two black male politicians, but no black women in his Vice Presidential search. Press reports that the National Organization for Women was only supporting a woman Vice Presidential nominee—when the NOW resolution clearly stated "a woman or a minority"—didn't help either. For another, Jackson himself is being pressured by supporters who feel he didn't get enough in return for his strong primary showing; that he should have won all four of the minority planks he backed, instead of a compromise version of only one.

On the other hand, some white women delegates felt wrongly blamed for the failure of minority planks that many non-Jackson black delegates didn't vote for either (and that Gary Hart traded away in return for Mondale's acceptance of *his* plank). There are also some experienced women politicians, white and black, who blame Jackson's tactic of hanging tough until the very end—or his just not knowing that successful floor fights must be organized even before a convention begins—for the defeat of minority planks that feminist groups had fought for in the platform committee, too.

There is also pressure on Mondale and Ferraro from some Jewish leaders; pleas to distance the campaign from Jackson because of his belief in negotiating with the PLO, or his delay in disavowing black Muslim leader Louis Farrakhan after he directed violent invectives at Judaism.

Nonetheless, Jackson has been campaigning for the Democratic ticket. And Mondale and Ferraro have been praiseful of Jackson, and included two black political experts in Ferraro's newly assembled staff.

In this campus field house, so jammed that the band has to leave to make room for the press, an audience that is at least one third black, plus a surprising sprinkling of young Orthodox Jews in yarmulkes, cheers and applauds Jackson from the moment he rises to the podium. "In a nation where seventy percent of poor children live in households headed by a woman," he says, "if you don't support ERA, you don't understand ERA. . . . I want a leader who says to my daughter and wife and mother and aunt, 'You are not diminished because you are female.' " He also raises a danger of the Reagan Administration's position on Title IX: "This weakening of the Civil Rights Act of 1964 means that . . . blacks can be used to fill up the basketball stadiums—and then discriminated against in the classroom."

When he finishes, the question is how Ferraro can follow him. If the comic's dictum is, "Never follow a music act," a politician's should be, "Never follow Jesse Jackson."

Ferraro doesn't try to match his emotional style. Instead, she praises him gracefully: "Every now and then, a person comes along who makes us better, not by winning but by trying, not by incumbency but by decency, not by ordering but by inspiring." She stakes out the common ground of legal equality for the civil rights and the feminist movements, just as legal identity was the common ground of abolitionists and suffragists: "Jesse Jackson and I share a dream. We hope that, after our candidacies, no American will ever again be disqualified from the highest office in the land because of race, religion, or sex."

Though most of the crowd may have had no knowledge of tensions, there is a shared sense of resolution. Outside, there are pickets—antiabortion signs, and Young Americans for Freedom chanting "four more years"—but inside, there are two speakers who have brought a very disparate crowd together.

As we leave, Jim East, a writer and campaign official in Tennessee, brings back reality. Mondale is so far behind in state polls that Victor Ashe, Republican candidate for the U.S. Senate, has offered to give $5 to any charity if his Democratic opponent, Albert Gore, Jr., will mention Mondale's name just once. Gore has refused to do it. . . .

In the lobby while we wait for luggage, a newsweekly reporter says he has never seen a "candidate who is more of a natural campaigner, or one the press likes better."

It occurs to me that only a male reporter would say this about Ferraro. Many women journalists are still sensitive to accusations that they won't be objective. In fact, the danger is more that they hold Ferraro to a higher standard, precisely because there is a sense of identification; a fear that an error of hers would reflect on all of us.

But when women do praise Ferraro, that shared identity gives even restrained statements more power. Patricia O'Brien, a respected reporter who deserves a national medal, as do so many single mothers, for supporting four children mostly on her own, explains: "No matter what happens, women will never have to be ashamed of the first woman to represent us."

Thursday

On the misty morning of a rural Dayton suburb, dozens of reporters troop across a field to a long table set up on the grass. Ferraro is holding a hearing of residents from the area near this Powell Road landfill and four other such sites. There are at least 27 similar locations in Ohio alone. They are all hazardous waste dumps.

The peaceful setting seems to belie any danger. Ferraro, who has a gift for saying what people are thinking, takes a risk: "This doesn't look so bad."

Residents tell Ferraro what even local reporters seem not to know. Since this hearing was announced several days before, the fields have been mysteriously covered with straw and the gullies filled with dirt.

The local residents' stories continue: a man who paid $150,000 for property he now can't sell; a widow who paid $7,800 to dig a well that, she says, turned out to be polluted; the older woman who followed trucks dripping chemicals which she reports were dumped at night; and the conviction of all these families that they are living "on top of a toxic time bomb."

As Ferraro questions, she also draws national lessons. State governments estimate that more than 7,000 such sites need cleaning up by the Environmental Protection Agency's Superfund, yet only six sites have been taken off the target list during this Administration. More than 264 million metric tons of hazardous waste are generated each year—more than one ton for every American man, woman, and child. Seventy-eight percent of all active hazardous waste sites are in violation of the law; yet this Administration scuttles the budget for cleanup, and opposes laws to restrict companies doing the dumping.

"Could someone tell me about any site in the state of Ohio that has been cleaned up?" Ferraro asks. Silence.

Because Ferraro has spent more time listening than lecturing, the local press now has leads for investigative reports, and residents have shared experiences. She hasn't neglected political points—including her own experience on a Congressional committee looking into the Superfund—but she has taken the risk of questioning people she doesn't know, and letting them take the lead.

She herself seems moved by the result. Walking back to the motorcade, she tells an aide to "write down a promise" on the list she has been keeping throughout the campaign. "I don't make many promises," she explains grimly. "But I promise to come back to this place."

In Harrisburg, Pennsylvania, she conducts a similar town meeting in a civic arena with 3,500 people. After an introduction by Speaker of the House K. Leroy Irvis, an older black politician who is clearly much-loved ("This country was founded on a dream," he says to cheers, "a dream that working-class women and men could govern themselves . . ."), Ferraro is left sitting on a stool in the middle of a vast old-fashioned stage.

This is the kind of community meeting she has always conducted in her Queens Congressional district—only bigger. First, she says, she wants to be a "one-woman truth squad." A Reagan TV commercial has accused Mondale of proposing a tax increase of $1,800 a year for the average family. "Yeah, that's right," says Ferraro in her slightly slangy, down-to-earth style, "providing you think the average family earns $90,000 a year. Maybe that's what Reagan's friends earn—but I want to see a show of hands: How many people here earn $90,000 a year?" There is laughter—and no hands.

She answers questions from the audience, always bringing the point back to the Reagan Administration.

On Reagan's support for equal pay: "He should support it—that's the law."

On foreign policy: "Reagan says we're 'standing tall'—but fifty-two American hostages came home safe from Iran. Two hundred and sixty-eight American boys have been killed in Beirut."

On American women's victories in the Olympics: "Reagan takes credit for these women's triumphs—and then opposes Title IX and the very programs that got them there."

At the end, people crowd around the stage. A woman hands Ferraro her baby for a photograph. This is the first time, several reporters comment, they've ever seen a candidate who looks comfortable holding a baby. "Someone held up a baby to Gary Hart," says one of them, "and he shook the baby's hand."

At a press conference in a Harrisburg hotel, Ferraro fields questions about the U.S. steel industry and the war in Northern Ireland. As foreign policy adviser Madeleine Albright has noted, some reporters seem to take special pleasure in trying to quiz Ferraro on supposedly unfeminine subjects, and so ask more detailed questions than they might of a man. She explains well, and is also tough enough to say, "I've already answered that," when a reporter rephrases a question she has just answered at length. In fact, her service in Congress gives her as much foreign policy experience as Nixon had when he became Vice President, and more than Carter or Reagan—who had been governors—when they became President. Nonetheless, doubts about her qualifications go on.

Unlike national reporters, however, these local journalists don't ask about the Ferraro/Zaccaro finances. I realize that I have heard no such questions during this entire time on the road. Most ordinary voters just seem relieved to hear that the family paid 40 percent of its income in taxes ("I always thought rich people paid *less* than the rest of us," as one woman put it), and impressed with her performance during a nearly two-hour television grilling.

The inevitable challenge about abortion gets her stock answer: she accepts the teachings of her church for herself, but if she became pregnant as the result of rape, "I'm not sure I would be so self-righteous." In any case, she supports the law and thinks the question should be up to the individual woman, even if she is poor and on Medicaid. When tired, as she is now, she also just abbreviates this to: "I believe my position is right."

I find it frustrating that she never quotes opinion polls. After all, over 70 percent of Americans, women and men, oppose the criminalization of abortion. It's an issue that almost everyone can understand, and thus is one of the most popular in the country, with more support in public opinion polls than either the Reagan Administration *or* the ERA. In spite of forceful opponents, majority support for safe and legal abortion crosses party lines.

Still, her pro-choice position is steadfast—and Ferraro, as a woman and a Catholic, seems to have been singled out for more harassment than either men or non-Catholics with the same position. Even Mondale, whose position is legally the same as Ferraro's and rhetorically stronger, attracts less anti-choice venom. After all, who could better symbolize the potential strength of women's rebellion—a fear among religious patriarchies—than Ferraro?

Looking at her as she closes this press conference, I realize that she is one of the few women with "masculine" power who has not sacrificed her sensuality. In everything from dress (she has rejected male-invented "dress-for-success" suits) to values (she is quite comfortable speaking about her experience as a woman and a mother), Ferraro is a remarkably whole person.

This wholeness comforts many women. It says we do not have to be "like men" to succeed. But it may threaten some men who try to separate sex from power when they're dealing with women. After all, if a Vice President is a woman they might want to go to bed with, then the woman in their bed might want to be a Vice President.

Back at the New York airport where we leave the campaign, a staff member expresses worry about a new poll showing an increase in Ferraro's disapproval rating. Do I think she is seen as "too aggressive"?

No one can be sure, but I think the problem is more that Ferraro herself is not being seen. Period. In the absence of the particular, the general dominates. A poll question like "Would you work for a woman boss?" may get fewer "yes" answers than a question about working for a *particular* woman boss. Similarly, Ferraro will remain subject to all the mythology about "women in politics" until she emerges as an individual.

This weekend, Ferraro begins preparation for her debate with George Bush. From all that I have seen, the public responds well to her combination of strength and compassion, populism and style, humor and hard facts. I hope she is not pressured into changing.

I ask if Ferraro's impressive encounters with UAW workers or toxic waste hearings or deaf children have been filmed for television commercials. Certainly, Reagan or Bush might envy those spontaneous moments of street smarts and emotional response from crowds.

But the answer is no. Those moments are lost. Apparently, a beleaguered Mondale/Ferraro campaign suffers from both lack of money and coordination. It's the latter that advertising experts find especially frustrating. It's notoriously tough to get media decisions out of this Mondale staff. . . .

Saturday

I know just how important the outcome of this election is to me when I'm with people to whom it doesn't really matter. New York dinner parties are full of them.

The more kindly try to save me from futile effort by quoting inevitabilities. For instance: Reagan's 20-point lead means we might as well stop trying. Or this banker's law: No incumbent President has ever been defeated in a year that saw a growth in real disposable personal income of more than 3.8 percent—and this year's growth is 5.9 percent.

The more optimistic try to make a sow's ear into a silk purse. For instance: because Reagan's deficit is so large (close to the combined deficits of all Presidents from Roosevelt through Carter), Mondale would head into sure economic disaster, be defeated in 1988, and discredit liberals for decades to come.

The most insulated from damage by Reagan's policies try to convince me that strength, no matter what the content, is better than weakness. For instance: Reagan's ability to win big and get economic policy, *any* policy, through Congress, is better than Mondale's narrow victory and ambivalent policy.

I am left angry, arguing, trying to be rational in spite of a lump in my throat.

What about the majority of Americans—minorities, women, working labor, unemployed, environmentalists, peace people—who will feel specifically rejected and voted *against* by a Reagan victory?

What about all the people—religious fundamentalists, supply-side economists, military advocates, corporate conservatives, people who think women who have abortions should be convicted of murder—who will feel specifically empowered and voted *for* if Reagan wins?

Given the comfortable economics of those dinner parties, what about the unfairness with which this supposed recovery is distributed? After all, the depression brought people together precisely because enlightened leadership tried to distribute the burden equally; while the prosperous fifties divided us precisely because minorities were left out and women were left home. Isn't it in the long-term self-interest, even of the prosperous few, to keep the country from feeling polarized? Isn't a sense of fairness the most important single mainstay of democracy?

I try to limit my arguments at dinner parties to fund raising. I try not to get angry. I try.

Thursday

One week later, a large hall in Philadelphia has sprouted all the paraphernalia of a national debate. The audience of Bush and Ferraro supporters are divided by television platforms into what is soon dubbed "the groom's side" and "the bride's side."

Given Reagan's shaky performance in the first Presidential debate, a new sense of viability has focused attention on this Vice Presidential event. I try to imagine what Ferraro must be feeling, much as I once tried to imagine what Billie Jean King must have felt before her match with Bobby Riggs. Both must survive the pressure of international attention, plus the knowledge that a certain number of people are hoping they will make damn fools of themselves.

The two candidates are introduced by Dorothy Ridings, the president of the League of Women Voters. They shake hands and begin.

Bush seems to adopt a shrill, forced style that in a woman would be called hysterical. On the other hand, Ferraro seems low-key, Presidential, and calm. She is not as feisty as usual. She misses some opportunities to challenge Bush on facts. (For example, his insistence that welfare payments and food stamps have increased under Reagan isn't nailed for the truth: the payments have increased because there are more poor people, not because individual payments are higher.)

But she does break his stride when she objects to his condescending tone and his offer to "teach" her about foreign policy. She has dared to name the game—and thus to change it. On a big margin of character and a small margin of debating skill, she seems to have won.

Yet when we listen to Tom Brokaw on NBC, and other national commentators, many seem to have witnessed a different event. They found her uncertain, too tied to her notes, not in eye contact with her audience, and not strong enough on foreign policy. They ignore Bush's shrillness and condescension—for instance, his refusal to call her "Congresswoman," as she had requested, and his use of "Mrs." instead—and they also perceive his bombast as strength.

Many commentators feel the debate was a draw at best. Post-debate polls cite Bush as the winner.

But I wonder: How much opinion was already in the minds of viewers? Sociological experiments have found that the very same article will be judged more authoritative when its byline is "John Jones" than when its author is "Jane Jones." That phenomenon has diminished, especially among women, but it hasn't disappeared.

Nonetheless, two things are clear. First, Ferraro's learning curve is like a rocket. This woman who was a part-time lawyer and full-time homemaker only 10 years ago is now an equal contestant in the nation's most important political event.

Second, she has given women the chance to feel proud. . . .

Sunday

It is 48 hours until Election Day. Back on the Ferraro campaign, I'm struck again by the difference between this reality of huge, cheering crowds touched by Ferraro's magic, and the rest of the world that barely knows who she is. If the outcome of the election is as definitive as the pro-Reagan polls now say, one lesson may be this: for national office, we should nominate women who have had a chance to build a national image *before* the campaign.

As Maureen Dowd, the perceptive reporter for the New York *Times* puts it, "Her appeal certainly hadn't come across to me before I began covering her. She would have benefited greatly from more of a getting-to-know-you phase coming out of the initial San Francisco rush—a phase she was robbed of by the Bert Lance appointment mess and then by the financial flap."

Now, I wonder how she has survived the pressures of campaigning while the accusations about her husband's real estate dealings continue, at least from some journalistic and political quarters. The New York *Post* has even gone back 40 years or more to find some gambling accusations against her parents. Though many voters sympathize and find such reporting unfair, she still must get up with this Sword of Damocles hanging over her head: What will the story be today?

Sitting next to her for a half hour or so between last-ditch rallies in Michigan and Rhode Island, I ask how she manages to function so well on days when her family has been attacked publicly, or when she has just learned privately that some new investigation is under way.

"First, because John is such an honest man," she says. "I know he's done nothing wrong. He's taken care of people all his life. Do you know what we used to get from older people who couldn't pay their rent? At Eastertime, they would give us baskets of food.

"Second, I know how to concentrate. I have to do that if I'm to do the job right. I spend my time doing interviews, writing speeches—I haven't even had time to keep a daily diary, and I regret that.

"But there were points when I worried that John might break under the pressure. One day, he said, 'I'm so embarrassed by all this.' He's a strong man, but I worried about him."

When asked about the worst surprise of this campaign, she cites the gambling accusations against her parents as especially "unfair and irrelevant." ("No one even questions what it meant that Reagan's father was an alcoholic. It's just not relevant," she adds.) When asked about the peak of personal pressure just before her debate with Bush, she thinks for a moment, searching for the right sense memory. "It was like getting in the car to go to the hospital when I was pregnant with John. I remember thinking, 'How did I ever get myself into a spot like this?' " she says, laughing. "But you know you've got to go through with it. You've got to get it over with."

As the best surprise, she puts first, "the response of people to me. I didn't expect such emotion." The second is her family's support and their grace under pressure. "Some mothers wait until their deathbed to hear, 'I've wanted to tell you all my life how wonderful you are.' I got to hear and see it when it mattered."

What about the women who won't support her? Will gender ever make women as smart about their own self-interest as race often does for both women and men? After all, 85 percent of black voters supported Jesse Jackson in the primaries, and at least that proportion is expected to support Mondale-Ferraro over an anti-equality Reagan Administration; yet a voting majority of women are supporting Reagan, regardless of his policies toward them.

"The other half of women's lives is probably a man, but the other half of a black individual's life is another black person," she says thoughtfully. "Besides, it's a generational thing. A lot of women have been told all their lives that they have to be dependent on a man. They vote his interest, not their own.

"I've often said that if my father hadn't died, I might not have done anything. But I saw my mother left suddenly with kids and no money. I saw what happened to her, how hard she had to work and how generous she still was to the rest of the family. In a way, I became the 'husband' in the house. I would come home from school and try to keep her from giving her whole self away.

"That's why I always wanted to have my own life, to have options. I didn't want to be dependent on my husband to support my mother, for instance, or to have to ask him if I wanted to buy something. If he died or walked out—I love my husband very much, but I wanted to be able to take care of myself and not miss a beat.

"I suppose the remarkable thing is that so many women, even being told all their lives that they must be dependent and do what is good for men, still support me. We get contributions in cash from Republican women who say, 'I can't send a check, I don't want my husband to know that I'm contributing.' Women have raised more than $4 million for the Democratic National Committee. We get thousands of volunteers.

"Pollsters think there is a hidden women's vote of about two percent—those who say one thing to the world, but do something else in the polling booth."

Has she given any thought to what we do if the polls are right and Reagan wins?

"I haven't had a chance to think ahead. We can pray daily that those four Supreme Court Justices last. My mother makes novenas for a lot of things, including them.

"The first thing I'm going to do is rest for ten days on an island, and go on a diet.

"But we will have to focus in on what's most important. We'll have to get together and plan. And we will."

The plane bumps down in Providence, and Ferraro is off to another mammoth rally. I am struck again by her strength and authenticity; her ability to remain herself, in private and in public.

Robert Squier, a Democratic strategist and NBC political expert, noted: "The thing you hope for in politics is literally communication. Other politicians are asked questions and the answers come right out of the briefing book. With her, you feel her brain at work, you can track the process of her development from week to week. She's not trying to be somebody else."

But how many people beyond political consultants, journalists, and rallies got to know this woman?

If there are errors in retrospect, they may be these: first, not being entirely herself in the Vice Presidential debate, the major chance most people had to know her; second, not seizing control of her own television commercials. (As she told Maureen Dowd: "I'm not running the commercials. I'm not a media expert. All I know about are voters and people.")

Still, she is a crucial advance over many political candidates. They suffer not from lack of exposure, but from knowing them too well.

Tuesday

It's eleven o'clock on election night. Ferraro is surrounded by family, staff, supporters, and three television sets in a New York hotel suite. The ticket's loss has been clear since early evening.

She has talked to Fritz Mondale in Minnesota, who is about to give his concession speech. It is not sure yet that even his home state will give him a majority. She smiles at his joking about it: the polls are not too bad, he thinks there may be a trend.

"At least when I see him now, I can give him a kiss and thank this wonderful man," she says. "We can finally forget all this stuff about how the first male-female team has to behave in public."

She has just congratulated George Bush, whom she quotes as thanking her and saying, "We must have lunch sometime." He put his wife, Barbara, on the phone, the woman who had referred to Ferraro as something that "rhymes with rich," and she congratulated Barbara, too.

What troubles her and angers others in the room is the networks' interpretation of exit polls: 16 percent of all voters said they were more likely to vote for the Democratic ticket because of her presence, 26 percent less likely, and 55 percent said it didn't matter. Because the negative outweighs the positive—and because 47 percent of those negatives were women—NBC calls her influence a net loss, and dismisses the gender gap.

In fact, it was always clear that a quarter to a third of voters opposed a woman on the ticket; that's the nature of prejudice. But those were likely to be Reagan voters who wouldn't have supported Mondale-Ferraro under any circumstances. The question is whether or not Ferraro served to bring out more voters, enthusiasm, volunteers, and money among Mondale's natural constituency. There is evidence that her presence was a net plus.

For instance: a CBS-New York *Times* poll showed that 10 percent of voters cited a Vice President as one of the top two reasons for voting. Of that group, a whopping two thirds were female, and 63 percent of them chose the Mondale-Ferraro ticket. (Among the one third who were men, 59 percent chose Reagan.)

For instance: when asked in a CBS-New York *Times* poll to choose directly between Ferraro and U.S. Senator Alfonse D'Amato, whose seat she may challenge in 1986, New York State voters found that men favored D'Amato by 42 percent to 32 percent while women favored Ferraro by 40 percent to 28 percent.

Because there has been a loss, there will be more than enough blame to go around. There is a sense in the room not only of this disappointment, but of all the struggles to come.

But we will be there. After all, 23 percent of all adult women said that Ferraro's candidacy had made them more interested in politics. That translates to 21 million women.

I try to concentrate on an even bigger number, the 41 percent of voting Americans who supported equality in general and the first woman Vice President in particular, but I feel anger and disappointment and even some sense of having no country, now that the right wing can claim its leadership. It's a familiar feeling that began in 1968 with Robert Kennedy's assassination and the rise of Richard Nixon; indeed, with the assassination of John Kennedy and Martin Luther King as well. I wrote in an article then: "It wasn't the victory of one man or the death of another. It was the death of the future . . . because we might be rather old before the conservers left and compassionate men came back."

But there is also a sense of peace in the room. It comes from knowing that Ferraro made history by doing her best, and how very good that was.

In 1984, there are compassionate women. In 1968, I had never seen them as elected leaders.

Ferraro has helped teach the country that intelligence and heart and strength reside in a Queens homemaker. If the future includes even a million like her, there is nothing we cannot do.

Moving Beyond Sexism

by Gloria Steinem

It has been culturally assumed that men are by nature more aggressive and more violent than women, and are therefore better suited to politics. This assumption of man's nature was based on no evidence at all in the beginning—only on an observation of the status quo, which, of course, was thought to be sacred.

Later, scientists discovered some isolated facts they thought justified this status quo, and the socially impotent position of women. The most provable of them had to do with hormones. When given large doses of the male hormone, individuals tended to become more aggressive or irritable. When given the female hormone, they became more calm.

Thus, men and women, the leaders and

From Gloria Steinem, "The Myth of Masculine Mystique," *International Education*, 1 (1972), pp. 134–39.

the led, were said to be locked into their roles by nature.

In fact, if hormones really were the chief dictators of behavior, women could now turn that bit of science to our own advantage. In the atomic era, after all, it would be equally logical to insist on women as chiefs-of-state precisely because we are supposed to be innately more calm, less aggressive.

But women are not trying to prove the innate superiority of one sex to another. That would only be repeating a masculine mistake.

The truth is that hormonal difference between the sexes is much less great than our similarities as human beings. A recent study by the World Health Organization could find no marked differences between men and women in intellectual or emotional capacity. More surprising, the study found that the much touted difference in physical strength was marginal and transitory; that it was evident in child-bearing years but tended to disappear thereafter. The forces locking us into so-called masculine and feminine roles turn out to be cultural, not biological. The brainwashing comes from all sides—parents, peer groups, art, education, television—and it is very effective. So much so that a boy and a girl may live in almost separate cultures, though they go to the same school and even come from the same family.

According to the California Gender Identity Center, for instance, it is easier to surgically change the sex of a young male wrongly brought up as a female, than it is to change his cultural conditioning.

The first tragedy of this role-playing is personal. Men are made to feel they must earn their manhood by suppressing emotion, perpetuating their superiority over women (and, in racist societies, over non-white men as well), and imposing their will on others whether by violence or by economic means.

Women are made to feel they must earn their femininity by suppressing their intellect, accepting their second-class position, and restricting all normal ambitions to the domination of their children—so the cycle of conditioning can start all over again.

The second tragedy is political. That half of the population not brainwashed into aggressiveness is kept out of the political process, and expected to throw away socially valuable talents besides. The other half is left with the compulsion to prove manhood, and no more wilderness frontiers or natural enemies to prove it on.

There is no doubt that we pay a price in domestic policy. The National Commission on the Causes and Prevention of Violence noted that this country "is the clear leader among modern, stable, democratic nations in its rates of homicide, assault, rape and robbery, and at least among the highest in incidence of group violence and assassination."

Why? Well, the Commission adds that most of these violent crimes are committed by men between the ages of 15 and 24. "Proving masculinity," the report explains, "may require frequent rehearsal of toughness, the exploitation of women, and quick, aggressive responses."

For American leaders, however, domestic problems have traditionally been less of a proving ground for masculinity than have foreign relations. True, there is the constant Masculine Mystique pressure to be tough on law-breakers and youthful demonstrators, to "support your local police" and push for law and order. But domestic affairs are characterized by a short term political feedback which tends to restrain the transformation of psychological needs into policy.

Foreign affairs, on the other hand, are characterized by little feedback, and greatly increased opportunity to portray the adversary as different, and therefore evil; less than human.

Moreover, a leader afflicted by the Masculine Mystique need never confront the human cost to any of his victims—as he occasionally must if those victims are American minorities, or students, or unemployed.

Since World War II and the sanctifying of our overseas interventions, foreign policy has provided the ideal arena for politicians and intellectuals who feel the cultural need to play tough. Those few who buck the masculine ethic fare poorly.

Political reporter Richard Barnet provides this inside view of policy-making:

> One of the first lessons a National Security Manager learns after a day in the bureaucratic climate of the Pentagon, State Department, White House or CIA is that toughness is the most highly prized virtue. Some of the National Security Managers of the Kennedy-Johnson era . . . talk about the "hairy-chest syndrome." The man who is ready to recommend using violence against foreigners, even where he is overruled, does not damage his reputation for prudence, soundness, or imagination, but the man who recommends putting an issue to the UN, seeking negotiations, or—horror of horrors—"doing nothing" quickly becomes known as "soft." To be "soft"—that is, unbelligerent, compassionate, willing to settle for less—or simply to be repelled by homicide, is to be "irresponsible." It means walking out of the club.
>
> To demonstrate toughness, a National Security Manager must accept the use of violence as routine . . . Even the language of the bureaucracy—the diminutive "nucs" for instruments that kill and mutilate . . . "surgical strike" for chasing and mowing down peasants from the air—[are part of] the socialization process . . . designed to accustom bankers, lawyers and military technocrats . . . to the idea of killing in the national interest, much as at lower levels recruits are trained to grunt and shout "kill!" as they thrust their bayonets into sawdust bags.

Mr. Barnet's term for this behavior is "bureaucratic machismo." Even winning the Presidency doesn't seem to put an end to it.

Bill Moyers recalls being "deeply troubled by the problems of ego and pride" that afflicted the Johnson era. "It was as if there had been a transfer of personal interest and prestige to the war, and to our fortunes there," explains Mr. Moyers. "It was almost like a frontier test, as if he were saying, 'By God, I'm not going to let those little puny brown people push me around.' "

Aside from identifying one's notions of manhood with America's nationhood, there is the additional problem of comparing masculinity with other Presidents.

After a National Security Council meeting with McNamara and other ex-Kennedy men, Moyers recalls President Johnson's fear that they would think him "less of a man" than President Kennedy if Johnson did not carry through with Vietnam. He even mentioned his concern that the ex-Kennedy advisors would call up Joseph Alsop, tell Alsop that Johnson was "less of a man" than Kennedy and that Alsop would publicize that. Excesses of violence don't seem to worry our foreign policy makers nearly as much as peaceful and therefore unmanly behavior. It was Senator Charles Goodell whom Vice-President Agnew attacked for being a "Christine Jorgensen," not a Ku Klux Klan leader, or even a Vietcong chief.

President Nixon has accused those to the left of our Vietnam policy of being "appeasers," "compromisers," or "bums." Lt. Calley on the other hand, convicted of battlefield atrocities by a military court, was spared such reflections on his masculine character, and transferred from the stockade to the comfort of his own apartment by Presidential command.

Nixon's statements are full of concern that the United States may become a "pitiful, helpless giant," "a second rate power": that the country may be "defeated" or "humiliated."

He seems to identify strongly with wartime leaders, particularly Winston Churchill, and states often that he doesn't want to be the President "to see this nation accept the first defeat in its proud 190-year history." Two years ago in Saigon, he spoke of the Vietnam War as "one of America's finest hours."

After the Republican convention in 1968, Nixon was quoted as saying that he chose Agnew as Vice-President because, among other things, he had been a "tough guy" with Black leaders as Governor of Maryland. Nixon also admired his "forcefulness" and "strong-looking chin." At the same time, Agnew was not likely to be a "superstar," in Nixon's phrase, who would outshine him as a man.

In his book, *Six Crises*, Nixon describes his life experience in battlefield or sports terms, speaking often of "victory" or "defeat."

Unfortunately, foreign affairs rarely afford an opportunity for a clear victory or defeat, as required by the masculine ethic. Certainly, the war in Indochina does not.

So an obsession with winning becomes an even greater obsession with *not losing*, in appearances at least, an obsession with not losing face.

No single theme emerges more obviously from the Pentagon Papers than this conviction that any retreat would mean unbearable humiliation. It is the underlying premise of nearly every document.

John McNaughton, Assistant Secretary of Defense under McNamara, believes that this face-saving was the single most important goal of our policy in Vietnam—more than keeping territory from the Communists, and much more than permitting the South Vietnamese to enjoy a better, freer way of life.

Peace at any price is humiliation, but victory at any price—even genocide in Indochina and chaos at home—is quite all right. So goes the Masculine Mystique.

It's this kind of thinking that has caused us to consistently overestimate the domestic sacrifices Russia was willing to make for the arms race.

It's this kind of thinking that makes an SST crucial to our prestige, though it may be a disaster from every other point of view; that makes us add MIRVs to our existing capacity for overkill; that sees being Number One as an end in itself.

It's this kind of thinking that denies the courage in admitting mistakes, in forfeiting false positions, and so locks us into the unnecessary, inhuman gamesmanship of global showdowns in the O.K. Corral.

Increasingly, there are male leaders, not all of them young, with the courage to question the Masculine Mystique. Some of them work for the Government—though they are not faring very well, as we have seen. Some of them are even in Congress.

But women are the only large group not usually conditioned to believe their identity depends upon violence and aggression. Again, the difference is cultural, not biological. No one is preaching the superiority of women: in 50 years or so, after the sex roles have been humanized, it may turn out that men and women are aggressive in similar degrees.

But until then, it will be vital to have women in positions of power, particularly in the area of foreign policy. And not just one or two tokens, who may have to conform in order to survive. Enough of us so that we can challenge and change "bureaucratic machismo."

Challenge and change from women may be exactly what some men are afraid of, but that's their problem. (I do not believe, for instance, that women are spared military service because men want to protect us from being killed; if that were true, anti-abortion laws would be repealed so that American women would not be dying from butchered abortions at about the same rate American men are dying in Indochina. I believe men are afraid that women would not play the hierarchical game of the army, and would not be cruel enough. Which is, of course, exactly why we should be there.)

There are other men—Daniel Ellsberg, for instance—who are giving speeches about women's political power as a way of turning foreign policy around.

"Women don't respond to the issue of humiliation, prestige, and Number Oneism so important to Nixon's Imperial policy," Ellsberg explains. "Polls show that they are more against the war by any measure. I believe the sex differences in political opinion are much larger than we have been led to believe, and much more independent of social class and education."

One more point for those who still doubt the potential depth of this social revolution:

Geoffrey Gorer, an anthropologist who set out to study the few nonwarring tribes, discovered that the less militaristic the society, the less polarized the sex roles—and vice versa, as we can see in the church-kitchen-children role of women in Hitler's Germany.

"What seems to me the most significant common traits in peaceful societies," concluded Gorer, "are that they manifest enormous gusto for concrete physical pleasures—eating, drinking, sex, laughter—and that they make very little distinction between the ideal character of men and women, particularly that they have no ideal of brave aggressive masculinity."

We may survive the Atomic Age, and get to humanism yet. But only if we are willing seriously to question the Masculine Mystique.

BIBLIOGRAPHY

1. Selma R. Williams, *Divine Rebel: The Life of Anne Marbury Hutchinson* (New York: Holt, Rinehart & Winston, 1981).
2. Linda Kerber, *Women of the Republic: Intellect and Ideology in Revolutionary America* (Chapel Hill: University of North Carolina Press, 1980).
3. Lester J. Cappon, ed., *The Adams-Jefferson Letters* (Chapel Hill: University of North Carolina Press, 1959).
4. Janet K. Boles, "Building Support for the ERA: A Case of 'Too Much, Too Late,' " *PS*, Fall 1982.
   Mark R. Daniels, Robert Darcy, and Joseph W. Westphal, "The ERA Won—At Least in the Opinion Polls," *PS*, Fall 1982.
5. Susan Bysiewicz, *Ella: A Biography* (Old Saybrook, Conn.: Peregrine Press, 1984).
6. Eugene Kennedy, "Hard Times in Chicago," *New York Times Magazine*, March 9, 1980.
7. Margaret Sanger, *Margaret Sanger* (New York: W. W. Norton, 1938).
8. Angela Davis, *Angela Davis: An Autobiography* (New York: Random House, 1974).
9. John Anthony Scott, *Women Against Slavery: The Story of Harriet Beecher Stowe* (New York: Thomas Y. Crowell, 1978). Copyright © 1978 by John Anthony Scott, reprinted by permission of Harper & Row, Publishers, Inc.
10. Hertha Pauli, *Her Name Was Sojourner Truth* (New York: Avon, 1976). Reprinted with permission of the author's agent, Knox Burger Associates, Ltd.
11. Ellen Cantarow and Susan Gushee O'Malley, "Ella Baker: Organizing for Civil Rights," in *Moving the Mountain: Women Working for Social Change*, ed. Ellen Cantarow (Old Westbury, Conn.: Feminist Press, 1980).

12. Mitchell Pacelle, "The Joyce Davenport of Dade County," *American Lawyer*, May 1984.
Robin Reisig, "The Improbable Rise of Pamela Chepiga," *American Lawyer*, May 1984.
13. Betty Friedan, *The Feminine Mystique* (New York: W. W. Norton, 1983, 1974, 1973, 1963).
Phyllis Schlafly, *The Power of the Positive Woman* (New Rochelle, NY: Arlington House, 1977).
14. Gloria Steinem, *Outrageous Acts and Everyday Rebellions* (New York: Holt, Rinehart & Winston, 1983).
15. Letty Cottin Pogrebin, *Growing Up Free: Raising Your Child in the 80's* (New York: McGraw-Hill, 1980).
16. Barbara Matusow, *The Evening Stars: The Making of the Network News Anchor* (Boston: Houghton Mifflin, 1983).
17. Elizabeth Cady Stanton, Susan B. Anthony, and Matilda Josephine Gage, eds., *History of Woman Suffrage* (New York: Arno; *New York Times*, 1969).
18. Florence Howe Hall, *Julia Ward Howe and the Woman Suffrage Movement* (New York: Arno; *New York Times*, 1969).
19. Doris Stevens, *Jailed for Freedom* (New York: Boni & Liveright, 1920, copyright renewed 1949 by Liveright Publishing Corporation).
20. William Henry Chafe, *The American Woman* (London: Oxford University Press, 1972).
21. Jo Freeman, "The Women's Movement and the 1984 Democratic and Republican Conventions." Written especially for this book.
22. Bella Abzug with Mimi Kelber, *Gender Gap* (Boston: Houghton Mifflin, 1984).
23. Ruth B. Mandel, *In the Running: The New Woman Candidate* (New Haven and New York: Ticknor & Fields, a Houghton Mifflin Company, 1981).
24. Bella S. Abzug, *Bella! Ms. Abzug Goes to Washington*, ed. Mel Ziegler (New York: Saturday Review Press, 1972). Reprinted by permission of E. P. Dutton, Inc.
Frank Graham, Jr., *Margaret Chase Smith: Woman of Courage* (New York: John Day, 1964). Reprinted by permission of Harper & Row, Publishers, Inc.
25. Joseph P. Lash, *Eleanor and Franklin* (New York: Norton, 1971).
26. Peggy Lamson, *In the Vanguard: Six American Women* (Boston: Houghton Mifflin, 1979).
Barbara Jordan and Shelby Hearon, *Barbara Jordan: A Self-Portrait* (New York: Doubleday, 1979).
27. Lynn Hecht Schafran, "Sandra O'Connor and the Supremes: Will the First Woman Make a Difference?" *Ms.*, October 1981.
Mississippi University for Women v. *Hogan* (458 U.S. 718).
Betty Medsger, *Framed: The New Right Attack on Chief Justice Rose Bird and the Courts* (New York: Pilgrim Press, 1983). Revised especially for this book.
28. Peggy Lamson, *In the Vanguard: Six American Women* (Boston: Houghton Mifflin, 1979).
Douglas B. Feaver, "Senator and Secretary Dole: Balance of Power," *Washington Post*, March 18, 1984.
Judy Mann, "The Gender Gap From the Reagan Camp," *Ms.*, March 1984.

29. Patricia M. Derian, "Review of Human Rights in Latin America," *Department of State Bulletin,* 80 (October 1980).
Jeane Kirkpatrick, "U.S. Security and Latin America," *Commentary*, January 1981.
Patricia Derian, address at American University, 1981.

30. Gloria Steinem, "Election Roundup," *Ms.*, December 1984.
Gloria Steinem, "The Myth of Masculine Mystique," *International Education*, 1 (1972).